THE BOOK OF MAGICAL PSALMS

Part 2

THE BOOK OF MAGICAL PSALMS

Part 2

Shadow Tree Series
Volume 5

Jacobus G. Swart

THE SANGREAL SODALITY PRESS
Johannesburg, Gauteng, South Africa

First edition, 2022
First printing, 2022

Published by The Sangreal Sodality Press
74 Twelfth Street
Parkmore 2196
Gauteng
South Africa
Email: jacobsang@gmail.com

Copyright © Jacobus G. Swart

All rights reserved. No part of this publication may be reproduced or transmitted in any form or by any means, electronic or mechanical, including photocopy, without permission in writing from the publisher. Reviewers who wish to quote brief passages in connection with a review written for inclusion in a magazine, newspaper or broadcast need not request permission.

ISBN 978-0-6397-0958-1

Dedicated to Dirk Cloete

"Unbreakable are links of love which faith and friendship forge among all souls discerning one another by the Light within them. Welcome indeed are they that enter with entitlement our closest circles of companionship."

—William G. Gray (*The Sangreal Sacrament*)

Shadow Tree Series

Volume 1: The Book of Self Creation
Volume 2: The Book of Sacred Names
Volume 3: The Book of Seals & Amulets
Volume 4: The Book of Immediate Magic – Part 1 & 2
Volume 5: The Book of Magical Psalms – Part 1, 2 & 3

Contents

Introduction i

3. *Ma'alah* — **Psalms & Sefirot** 1
   A. *ha-Tikun ha-K'lali*: Comprehensive Rectification 4
   B. Seven *Sefirot* & the *Menorah Psalm* 13
   C. Psalms, *Sefirot* & Holy Days 21
      1. Introduction 21
      2. *Psalm 29* 26
      3. *Psalm 150* 33

4. *Darom* — **The Psalms of David — Book II** 43
   Psalm 42 43
   Psalm 43 52
   Psalm 44 56
   Psalm 45 62
   Psalm 46 72
   Psalm 47 83
   Psalm 48 90
   Psalm 49 94
   Psalm 50 100
   Psalm 51 106
   Psalm 52 117
   Psalm 53 121
   Psalm 54 125
   Psalm 55 130
   Psalm 56 140
   Psalm 57 145
   Psalm 58 151
   Psalm 59 155
   Psalm 60 162
   Psalm 61 168
   Psalm 62 175
   Psalm 63 180
   Psalm 64 184
   Psalm 65 187
   Psalm 66 192
   Psalm 67 197
   Psalm 68 206
   Psalm 69 218
   Psalm 70 230

Psalm 71.. 233
Psalm 72.. 239

5. *Tzafon* — The Psalms of David — Book III.......... 247
Psalm 73.. 247
Psalm 74.. 253
Psalm 75.. 259
Psalm 76.. 262
Psalm 77.. 266
Psalm 78.. 271
Psalm 79.. 287
Psalm 80.. 292
Psalm 81.. 299
Psalm 82.. 305
Psalm 83.. 309
Psalm 84.. 315
Psalm 85.. 321
Psalm 86.. 326
Psalm 87.. 332
Psalm 88.. 337
Psalm 89.. 342

Index of Magical Applications..................... 353
   1. General.. 353
   2. Health, Healing & General Physical Well-being...... 354
   3. Mental & Emotional Well-being................... 356
   4. Sleep & Dreams................................... 359
   5. Intelligence, Study, Memory, Speech
      & Secret Sciences............................... 360
   6. Journeys & Travel 360
   7. Success.. 361
   8. Career, Trade, Transactions, Business Success, Livelihood
      Good Fortune & Charity 362
   9. Food, Agriculture, Plant Growth, Fisheries, Animal
      Husbandry & Nature 364
  10. Human Interaction, Friendship, Brotherhood
      & Reconciliation 366
  11. Relationships, Love, Marriage, Family & Homes.... 367
  12. Pregnancy, Childbirth & Children................. 369
  13. Dying, Death, Orphans, Old Age & Life Extension .. 370
  14. Religion & Spirituality.......................... 371
  15. Malevolent Spirit Forces, Ghosts & Evil Spells 373
  16. Hatred, Jealousy, Evil Eye, Enemies, Adversity
      & Animosity................................... 375
  17. Slander, Falsehood & Wrongdoing 377
  18. Robbery, Theft & Common Criminality 378
  19. Justice, Legal Matters, Law Suits & Judgment 378
  20. Punishment, Vengeance & Imprisonment 379

21. Anger, Rage, Belligerence, Violence, War & Peace 379

References & Bibliography..................... **383**

Illustrations

Cover Illustration... *Shiviti* lithograph constructed by Moshe ben Yitschak Mizrachi, Jerusalem 1902.
Page 13... *ha-Tikun ha-K'lali*: *Tehilim/El Elohim* Conjunction
Page 15............................. *Menorah Psalm*
Page 41................... *Psalm 150* Musical Notation
Page 49... *Psalm 42:5*—Divine Name construct for protection against danger in fire storms at sea or on land.
Page 67... *Psalm 45:5*—Amulet to expedite financial success
Page 68... *Psalm 45:5*—Divine Name construct for financial success: *Sefer Raziel ha-Malach*.
Page 69... *Psalm 45:5*—Divine Name construct for financial success: *Shorshei ha-Shemot*.
Page 70.... *Psalm 45:5*—Divine Name construct for success in business.
Page 71... *Psalm 45:11*—Divine Name construct for finding long lasting love.
Page 77.......... *Psalm 46:8*—The "Seven Sacred Names"
Page 78–79.................. The "Seven Mystical Seals"
Page 82............ שעטנ"ז ג"ץ (*ShATNeZ GaTz*) *Tagin*.
Page 128............... *Psalm 54*—*Menorah* arrangement
Page 135–136..... *Psalm 55:23*—Divine Name constructs to encourage a good livelihood.
Page 201..... *Psalm 67*—Divine Name construct employed as a call for help, to ward off trouble, against diseases of the head, and to alleviate fever.
Page 202.... Amulet against miscarriage and other afflictions which might beset the unborn.
Page 214........ Divine Name construct against subterfuge, sabotage and corruption.
Page 228.......... *Psalm 69:7*—Divine Name construct for healing purposes.
Page 243.......... *Psalm 72:1*—Divine Name construct for petitionary prayers.
Page 270......... *Psalm 77:15*—Divine Name construct to disclouse the identity of a thief.
Page 285............. *Psalm 78:9*—Divine Name construct "to transform a hater into a lover."
Page 296......... *Psalm 80:4, 8 & 20*—"Name of the *Seraf*"
Page 319............ *Psalm 84:12*—Divine Name construct to bring success.
Page 328.............. *Psalm 86:11*—Walking meditation

Hebrew Transliteration

There are transliterations of Hebrew words and phrases throughout this work. In this regard I have employed the following method. The Hebrew vowels are pronounced:

>"a" — like "a" in "father";
>"e" — like the "e" in "let" or the way the English pronounce the word "Air" without enunciating the "r";
>"i" — like the "ee" in "seek";
>"o" — like the "o" in "not" or the longer "au" in "naught"; or again like the sound of the word "Awe";
>"u" — like the "oo" in "mood";
>"ai" — like the letter "y" in "my" or "igh" in "high" or like the sound of the word "eye"; and
>"ei" — like the "ay" in "hay."

The remaining consonants are as written, except for:

>"ch" which is pronounced like the guttural "ch" in the Scottish "Loch" or the equivalent in the German "Ich," or letter "j" in Spanish, and
>"tz" which sounds like the "tz" in "Ritz" or like the "ts" in "hearts."

In most cases an apostrophe (') indicates a glottal stop which sounds like the "i" in "bit" or the concluding "er" in "father," otherwise it is a small break to separate sections of a word or create a double syllable. For example, I often hear people speak of Daat (Knowledge), sounding one long "ah" between the "D" and the concluding "T." The correct pronunciation is however Da'at, the apostrophe indicating that the term comprises actually two syllables, "dah" and "aht." In this word a quick glottal stop separates the one syllable from the other. As a vowel it is the same sound made when one struggles to find the right word, and say something like "er.....er......er......"

One further rule is that the accent in Hebrew is, more often than not, placed on the last syllable of the word. Of course there are numerous instances which disprove this rule, but it applies almost throughout Hebrew incantations, e.g. those found in Merkavistic literature, etc.

"Suddenly, the Golem sprang up on his feet. Then we dressed him in the clothes we had brought with us.... We also put shoes on him. In short, he looked like the rest of us: he saw, heard, and understood, but he did not have the capacity for speech... ... .

Introduction

Kabbalah, whether of the theoretical or the practical kind, is all about language. In this regard, we are informed that "the core of kabbalistic teaching" is that "language penetrates to the heart of reality," and thus "Kabbalah is quintessentially a mysticism of language."[1] As I noted elsewhere, Kabbalistic teaching maintains the entirety of existence to have come into being by means of the Hebrew alphabet, of which each component glyph is understood to comprise a specific power.[2] In this regard, Rabbi Avraham Azulai wrote "know that there is no body, vital soul (*nefesh*), spirit (*ruach*) or higher soul (*neshamah*) that has not been created through the twenty-two letters of the Torah."[3] Thus it is maintained that "language is at the heart of creation and retains its power in the human world."[4] In fact, from a Jewish perspective, it is understood that "language penetrates to the very core of the divine mystery," and that "language is the key to everything: it is the agency of God's creativity and it defines the workings of the human mind."[5] It is the belief that "language is the key to everything" which underpins not only the Kabbalistic use of "language to engage consciously with God,"[6] but equally the magical applications of Divine and Angelic Names in "Practical Kabbalah."

In Jewish mysticism the twenty-two glyphs of the Hebrew alphabet are understood to embody powerful spiritual forces, and thus we are told that as "vessels and chambers of God, and by means of the kavanah (focussed intention), man draws down within them the emanation of the supernal light"[7] In this regard it was maintained that "the highest domain of study, which transcends even the study of the *Zohar*, the most important text of Kabbalah, is knowledge of the 'spiritual force of the letters and their existence and their combination with each other,' for this knowledge enables the Kabbalist 'to create worlds'."[8] It is this "knowledge" which inspires "Practical Kabbalah," and renders it so attractive as a tool for greater wellbeing on this planet. After all, simple reason tells the practitioner of Jewish Magic that if the "Whole" is created by means of the twenty-two letters of the Hebrew Alphabet, then by extension everything within that "Whole" could be manipulated, so to speak, in some or other manner by means of the said twenty-two glyphs. This is the basis of "Jewish Magic," but the term "magic" unfortunately conjures up images of loathsome personalities whose sole intention is to do evil to their fellow humankind.

Of course, we are all aware that language can kill or cure, and this is not the exclusive domain of "conjurers," since numerous actions which impacted humankind for better or worse, commenced with "words." Many battles have been, and will be fought over "words." Yet, I find it particularly curious that in mainstream religion a prayer-request commencing with the standard request יְהִי רָצוֹן מִלְּפָנֶיךָ (*Y'hi ratzon mil'fanecha*—"May it be your will") directed at the Eternal One, and which results in an outcome termed a "miracle," is considered to be quite different from the prayer-incantation of "Practical Kabbalah," which commences with the exact same phrase which is equally addressed at the Divine One, and results in an outcome termed "magical." As mentioned elsewhere, it appears to me "the term 'miracle' was substituted for the word 'magical,' and the first is said to be a manifestation from the 'realms of glory,' whilst anything associated with the latter is construed a regurgitation of the 'infernal diabolical'."[9] Again, as noted before, "mainstream religion knew....that a lot of money can be made from those 'miracles,' which turn out to be a thinly veneered super-brand of plain 'ritual magic'," and thus I concluded that "in my estimation, both 'Religious Worship' (passive 'exoteric magic') and '*Practical Kabbalah*' (active 'esoteric magic') are valid and extremely powerful in the process of our eternal 'Self Creation'!"[10] Thus I pray that "The Book of Magical Psalms" will benefit both religionists and esotericists, all in fact, who are attempting to

Introduction / iii

arrange their lives in harmony with the "Divine Intention" within themselves.

✳✳✳

To those who are studying and practising the material shared in this tome, I again recommend that you consider commencing any study of Kabbalistic material by sitting in a restful, peaceful manner, and then, with eyes shut for a minute or so, to meditate on these words:

> "Open my eyes so that I may perceive the wonders of Your teaching."

Whisper the phrase repeatedly and allow yourself to "feel" the meaning of the words you are uttering within the depths of your Self. It is again important not to attempt any mental deliberation on the meaning of the actual words, but to simply repeat them a number of times. As stated previously,[6] it is a good idea to read a section in its entirety, without trying to perceive any specific meaning, then to pause for a few seconds, and afterwards attempt to understand within yourself the general meaning of what was being said. In this way you begin to fulfil an important teaching of *Kabbalah*, which tells you to unite two "worlds"—the inner and the outer within your own Being. By allowing yourself to "feel" the meaning of what you are reading, you learn to surrender to the words. You open yourself, again fulfilling one of the requirements of Kabbalistic study, which is to surrender the "me," the ego, and to remove arrogance and bias. You simply attempt to sense with your being what is being portrayed in the section you are perusing. This act is a serious step on the path of perfecting one's personality, because it stops the expansion of the ego, and increases the chance of obtaining "True Knowledge."

✳✳✳

As noted before, none of the volumes comprising this "Shadow Tree Series" of texts on "Practical Kabbalah" (Jewish Magic) would have been written without the wonderful inspiration and support of my dear friends, my Companions in the Sangreal Sodality, and all my acquaintances whose incisive questioning inspired the expansion of my consciousness, enriched my life in numerous ways, and who are yet fetching the very best out of me. In this regard, I again express my most profound gratitude to Dirk Cloete for not only proofreading this text, but for being the greatest and most caring friend anyone could wish for. He is a veritable "Fountain of Magical Knowledge," and, as noted previously, a true visionary with formidable research skills. Again I humbly acknowledge that this volume would not have been written without his enormous input, encouragement, and incredible support.

To my wife Gloria, the love of my life, who uplifts my body, mind, soul and spirit, sometimes in the most difficult circumstances, I offer my most profound gratitude for her unwavering love, for her total support in all my endeavours, and for being the joy and laughter in my heart. I again acknowledge my late mentor, William G. Gray, who led me along the "Inner Ways of Truth and Goodness," who taught me what "the straight and narrow" is really all about, and how to leave fresh toeholds for future generations who might desire to climb the "magic mountain" the Kabbalistic way.

I again offer my most heartfelt appreciation to my South African friends and Companions: in Johannesburg Norma Cosani, Gidon Fainman, Geraldine Talbot, Francois le Roux, Gerhardus Muller, Ryan Kay, Simon O'Regan; in Pretoria Carlien Steyn, Norman Mans, Helene Vogel and Gerrit Viljoen; in Durban Marq and Penny Smith; and Dirk Cloete and Sean Smith in the fairest of Capes.

I also wish to acknowledge my Sangreal Sodality Companions and friends residing beyond the borders of South Africa: Marcus Claridge and Elizabeth Bennet in England; Hamish Gilbert in Poland; Bence Bodnar, Lukács Gábor, and Dániel Szeretõ in Hungary; Roberto Siqueira Rodrigues in Brazil; Roger Caliste in Trinidad; Taron Plaza in Japan; Yuriy Fyedin in China; and all those intimates "whose identities are known unto Omniscience alone."

I again offer my most profound gratitude to my dear friend Jonti Mayer for his enormous support in reading and checking the transliterations of the prayers and incantations shared in this tome.

I further extend my heartfelt thanks to Rabbi Yosef Cohen who alerted me to a remarkable set of six "love psalms" listed in a manuscript titled *"Kabbalah Ma'asit uS'gulot"* (The National Library of Israel Ms. Heb. 4°601).

In conclusion I wish to pay tribute to John Jones, my beloved friend and dear Companion in the Sangreal Sodality. May his memory be a blessing!!! With that I leave Part 2 of *"The Book of Magical Psalms"* in your care, and once again pray that it will serve you in a most meaningful manner.

Happy Reading!

Jacobus Swart
Johannesburg
July 2022

. ...At six in the morning, before the break of dawn, four men returned home. As we walked back, the Maharal told the golem: 'Know that we created you out of the dust of the earth to guard the Jews from all harm and from all the ills and troubles they suffer at the hands of their enemies and oppressors. Your name will be Yosef. You will live with me, sleep in a room in my court, and serve as the shamesh of the court. No matter where I send you, you will obey each one of my commands....'... ... .

Chapter 3
Ma'alah — Above
Psalms & *Sefirot*

עלי עשור....
שמחתני יהוה בפעלך....
מה גדלו מעשיך יהוה
מאד עמקו מחשבתיך

(*alei ashor....*
simach'tani YHVH b'fa'alecha....
mah gad'lu ma'asecha YHVH
m'od am'ku mach'sh'votecha—
"On an instrument of ten strings....
Thou, *YHVH*, hast made me glad through Thy work;
How great are Thy works *YHVH!*
Thy thoughts are very deep.")
—*Psalms 92:4–6*

הללו יה הללו אל בקדשו
הללוהו ברקיע עזו

(*hal'lu Yah hal'lu el b'kad'shu*
hal'luhu bir'ki'a uzo—
"*Hallelujah.* Praise God in His sanctuary;
praise Him in the firmament of His power.")
—*Psalms 150:1*

Jewish spiritual systems are generally truly "magical"! Developed over many centuries from a great variety of sources, the order of prayers in the various Hebrew liturgies are filled with spiritual, mystical, and, I dare say, "magical" meaning intended to direct the body, mind, soul, and spirit of the worshipper into a profound understanding of the ways of Universal Truth and Divine Goodness. It has been said that "Judaism is not a creed."[1] I concur "*Judaism is not a creed,*" because "*Judaism is a conduct.*"

It pertains to the *conduct* of the one who is prepared to plunge into the infinite depths of even the simplest prayer uttered at home or in the synagogue, an action which necessitates total commitment of the one who is seeking spiritual transformation in the "Jewish way." In this regard, it is worth noting that the mystical doctrines of *Kabbalah*, with special reference to the yearning for a sacred union with the feminine Divine Presence (*Shechinah*), which I have addressed in detail in the earlier volumes,[2] greatly impacted normative Jewish worship. Furthermore, the chapters and verses of the sacred texts comprising the Hebrew Bible were, and still are, interpreted in a variety of mystical and magical ways.

Regarding the "Book of Psalms," we are informed that this biblical text is primarily composed of ten types of song and praise. Thus we are told in the *Talmud* that "Rabbi Yehoshua ben Levi said: the Book of Psalms is said by ten expressions of praise: by ניצוח (*Nitzu'ach*—'conducting'), נגון (*Nigun*—'melody'), משכיל (*Mas'kil*—'giving wisdom'), מזמור (*Miz'mor*—'tune'), שיר (*Shir*—'song'), אשרי (*Ash'rei*—'fortunate'), תהלה (*Tehilah*—'praise'), תפלה (*Tefilah*—'prayer'), הודאה (*Hoda'ah*—'thanksgiving'), and הללויה (*Haleluyah*—'Praise God'). He continues: The greatest of them all is *Haleluyah*, as it includes God's name and praise at one time." [*TB Pesachim 117a*] This statement is reiterated with some variation in the order and slight changes in nomenclature in Rashi's commentary on the Book of Psalms,[4] as well as in the *Zohar*.[3] In this regard, Rashi's presentation reads *Nitzu'ach, Nigun, Miz'mor, Shir, Halel, T'filah, B'rachah* ('blessing'), *Hoda'ah, Ashrei, Haleluyah*, whilst the *Zohar* lists *Nitzu'ach, Nigun, Mas'kil, Mich'tam* ('golden song'), *Miz'mor, Shir, Ash'rei, Tefilah, Hoda'ah*, and *Haleluyah*.

In terms of the Hebrew word הללויה (*Haleluyah*) being understood to be "the greatest of them all, we are informed this is because it includes the name of the Divine One (יה—*Yah*), as well as "praise" (הלל—*halel*) "in a single word."[5] It is also worth noting that *Psalm 150*, which could be termed the "*Haleluyah* Psalm," includes ten successive phrases which commence with the term (*Halelu/Haleluhu*—"praise/praise Him"). However, we are told that "Rav called the entire Book [of Psalms] *halleluyah*."[6] Be that as it may, it should come as no surprise that the figure ten, which features prominently in the Hebrew Bible, is considered of great significance in kabbalistic thought. In this regard, it was noted that "in the Tikunei Zohar ('the garments of the Zohar')....it is said that there are ten kinds of songs, and that the emotions they express correspond to the Sefirot on the Tree of Life," and that "together these ten emotional qualities are a template of our spiritual anatomy."[7]

Whilst there are variants in the order, and, in some instances, also in the appellatives of the "ten types of song," their respective sefirotic associations have been delineated in the following manner as a "soul path" in the process of "divine revelation and union with the Holy Spirit (*Ruach HaKodesh*, רוח הקדוש) and the Divine Immanence (*Shechinah*, שכינה)":[8]

1. אשרי (*Ash'rei* —"praise") Sublime insight: *Keter*
2. שיר (*Shir*—"song") Jubilant song: *Chochmah*
3. ברכה (*B'racha*—"blessing") Drawing down blessings: *Binah*
4. ניגון (*Nigun*—"melody") Soaring melody: *Chesed*
5. זמר (*Zemer*—"singing") Breaking through: *Gevurah*
6. הלל (*Haleil*—"praise") Radiating praise and joy: *Tiferet*
7. ניצוח (*Netzu'ach*—"orchestration") Song of victory: *Netzach*
8. הודאה (*Hodu'ah*—"thanksgiving" [also "confession"]) Majestic humility: *Hod*
9. רננו צדיקים (*Ran'nu Tzadikim*—"rejoice righteous ones") Song of devotion: *Yesod*
10. תהלה (*T'filah*—"Prayer") Self-reflection: *Malchut* [9]

This brief delineation references a most meaningful process in the journey to spiritual enlightenment. However, in the current instance we are focussing specifically on the "ten types of song" in terms of the Book of Psalms, as elucidated by the remarkable Rabbi Nachman of Bratslav. In this regard, he shared the remarkable spiritual procedure termed התיקון הכללי (*ha-Tikun ha-K'lali*—"Comprehensive Rectification").

A. התיקון הכללי—*ha-Tikun ha-K'lali*: Comprehensive Rectification

Rabbi Nachman of Bratslav was a teller of kabbalistic tales which are filled with infinite meaning for those who are able to lift "allegory" from the written page, and able to apply it in a practical manner in their daily lives. In this regard, in his wondrous saga of the "the Seven Beggars," a tale replete with references to the number ten, the "sixth Beggar" tells of a group of men who boasted about the incredible power each held in his hands. One of these men maintained that "he had such great power in his hands that even after an arrow had been shot, he could return it and bring it back to him."[10] A respondent queried "'What kind of arrow can you retrieve? There are ten types of arrows.' This is because there are ten types of poisons."[11] It was further noted that "when one coats the arrow with the first type of poison, it does a certain degree of harm. If the arrow is coated with the second type of poison, it does worse harm. Thus, there are ten types of poison, each one more harmful than the other."[12] The story continues that a Princess was wounded by the ten arrows having been fired at her, and that she can be healed only by the one, i.e. the "sixth beggar" who "has the ability to shoot all these arrows and retrieve them."[13]

We are told the "Princess" is the שכינה (*Shechinah*), the "Mother Principle," whom I noted elsewhere is "the Divine Presence as a 'Feminine Force',"[14] i.e. the one through whom all life comes into existence, and who is, as it were, manifested as the "*Neshamah*," i.e. the "Divine Self" within each one of us. I believe this is the primary meaning of the statement נר יהוה נשמת אדם (*Ner YHVH nish'mat adam*—"The spirit of man is the lamp of YHVH") (Proverbs 20:27). Be that as it may, we are informed "the ten types of arrows denote the ten types of spiritual damage caused by sin."[15] We are also reminded that there are "ten unclean Crowns" [*Tikunei Zohar 69*], which are said to be "the root forces of all evil," and these have been noted to reference the ten poisons in our saga.[16] As readers of Kabbalistic literature know well enough, the term "Crown" references the highest of the *sefirot*, i.e. כתר (*Keter*—"Crown"), which is said "includes everything, even evil." Furthermore, since it "contains all ten levels of holiness, it can rectify all ten levels of evil."[17] This is the "power" in the hands of the earlier mentioned individual "who heals the Princess" since he "has the power both to shoot the arrows and to retrieve them."[18] In this regard, it is said that the "remedy for the arrows is through repentance," and that "*Keter* is the root of repentance,"[19] i.e. תקון (*Tikun*—"restoration").

Readers are probably wondering as to the exact make-up of the "ten arrows," i.e. what are the relevant associated "sins," and how are they rectified? These have not been defined exactly, but it has been said that they pertain mainly to "sadness and sexual temptation,"[20] which are claimed to be the domains of the demoness לילית (*Lilit*). Some readers may query why *Lilit*, termed "the mother of all demons,"[21] should still be "demonised" when "she" was supposedly "liberated," or "rehabilitated," in "our times." In this regard, it appears a lot of disinformation led to many being poorly informed as to what *Lilit* actually represents. The fundamental issue is factually literalness on the part of those who see a maligned woman, i.e. the belief that the prudish, sexist patriarchal Jews reviled an actual, as it were, "personage" by that name, a "person" who just wanted to have some fun, who is in fact squeaky clean, and in whom there is no malice. As noted elsewhere, *Lilit* derives from Babylonian demonology, with some Sumerian antecedents.[22] It is worth noting that in ancient near-eastern demonology, the equivalents of this demoness fulfill a variety of nefarious functions. In this regard, I mentioned an incantation in an Assyrian ritual against an *Ardat-Lili* who preys on males,[23] and others of the same ilk would strangle infants, and threaten pregnant women.[24]

Jewish lore similarly maintains that לילית (*Lilit*), whose name is associated with the Hebrew word לילה (*Lailah*—"night"), and equally with ילל (*y'leil*—"wailing"/"howling"), is understood to be a "night demon"[25] who is a sexual predator preying on men, and endangering the life of infants.[26] In fact, besides sadness and sexual wantonness, *Lilit*, who is understood to be "the root of all despondence,"[27] and entailing blindness,[28] represents melancholy, depression, despair, and maliciousness.[29] Simply then, those who seek to "liberate" *Lilit*, would need to defeat and transcend the qualities "she" represents within themselves, and certainly not legitimise misery. It should be clearly understood that the reference to "sexuality" here is not intended to deprecate sex, but rather to approach it as a sacred act. I certainly do not intend dragging God down to sex, but to let sex raise us up to the Divine One. In other words, we should go up with sex instead of down. In this regard, sex is in my estimation one of the highest forms of worship, i.e. if it is approached from the perspective of, for example, the Kabbalistic doctrine in which it is understood "that when a loving human couple are conjoined in a sexual union, they are not only imitating the Divine One in the creative act, but are causing a 'Supernal Coupling' within Divinity."[30] I have discussed this in an earlier volume of this series of texts on Practical Kabbalah, and the subject is addressed in several serious studies.[31]

Be that as it may, it has been said that "sexual sin includes all sins."[32] In this regard, it is worth noting that sex is often the, as it were, outlet for psychological difficulties, and, as we know well enough, sex, violence, and all manner of criminal activity often go hand in hand. In fact, the subject matter is considered of such importance, that numerous works have been penned on this topic throughout the centuries, and especially in modern times in which the predominant "wailing of the age" revolves around *"my freedom of choice,"* and *"my personal rights,"* whatever the cost may be to everyone and everything else, even to our planet itself. In fact, the fundamental attitude accompanying these "rights" is disrespectful and thoughtless entitlement, which have turned human existence into an undisciplined, chaotic, and narcissistic "free-for-all."[33]

Thus it was that, with sexual transgressions in mind, and with specific reference to nocturnal emissions, that Rabbi Nachman developed his הכללי התיקון (*ha-Tikun ha-K'lali*—"The Comprehensive Rectification") to purify both the body and soul of the practitioner. In this regard, we need to look again at the earlier mentioned "ten types of song" in the Book of Psalms, which we noted are aligned with the "Ten *Sefirot*." In this regard, Breslov

Hasidism equally acknowledges the correspondence between the "ten types of song" and the *"Ten Sefirot,"* the latter being understood to be "the mystical attributes through which the Creator brought the universe into being."[34] We are told that the "Ten Sefirot are called 'Direct Light,' shining from the Creator to the world," whilst "human song is viewed as a kind of 'Reflected Light,'" which is employed to reflect the Direct Light back by fulfilling Divine Will."[35] We are taught that, written under "Divine Inspiration" (*Ru'ach haKodesh*), the biblical Psalms "are most effective in mirroring back the Direct Light, bearing extra spiritual power,"[36] an action which "can facilitate the process of selecting good from evil, merging left with right, sweetening Judgement with supernal Mercy."[37] In this regard, we are reminded that joy is a mighty power which overcomes melancholy, and, as we know well enough, Chasidic tradition places "a high value on joy, song, and dance."[38] To this Bratslav Chasidism appears to have added a further value, i.e. "joy emerging from despair,"[39] which, expressed in song and dance, will counteract the traumatic melancholy and "howls" of *Lilit*.[40]

In terms of "magical instruments" which could be employed to evoke joy, the biblical psalms, comprising the "ten types of sacred song," truly stand supreme. In fact, it is intimated that the psalms balance the powers of "mercy" (*Chesed*) and "might" (*Gevurah*). In this regard, Rabbi Nachman noted that the *gematria* of the word תהלים (*Tehilim*) is equal to the numerical value of the expanded spelling of the letters comprising the Divine Names אל אלהים (*El Elohim*),[41] and, as is well known, these Sacred Names are aligned respectively with חסד (*Chesed*—"Loving-kindness") and גבורה (*Gevurah*—"Might").[42] Keeping these details in mind, Rabbi Nachman of Bratslav formulated התיקון הכללי (*ha-Tikun ha-K'lali*—"Comprehensive Rectification") by selecting ten of the hundred and fifty psalms comprising the Book of Psalms. He maintained the said ten psalms to be "healing psalms," which incorporated all of the mentioned "ten types of song."[43] It has been said these ten psalms "embody the concentrated power of the entire Book of Psalms,"[44] and we are told that Rabbi Nachman maintained "that these ten varieties of song correspond to ten parallel types of song found in the *kelippa*, the cosmic evil force according to Kabbalah."[45] In fact, Rabbi Nachman informed us that "there are places that are so fine and narrow that no remedy has the power to penetrate them except through the General Remedy, which injects healing into even the narrowest, finest places," and in this regard it is said that "first it is necessary to apply the General Remedy, and through this all the individual flaws will automatically be rectified."[46]

Hence, whilst the initial intention behind the formulation of התיקון הכללי (*ha-Tikun ha-K'lali*) was the healing of sexual transgressions, the reading of the ten psalms "became an antidote for all sorts of spiritual and physical offences, big and small."[47] It should be noted that the English word "sin" offers many difficulties. The Hebrew word, as well as the Greek equivalent, derive from roots which pertain to "missing the mark." Thus I noted elsewhere, "'sin' has *nothing* to do with trespasses against 'a touchy, ill-tempered God raging away at the antics of Man because those 'offended' His ideas of propriety,' but *everything* with 'wrongful behaviour which damages us by the doing in such a way, that we fail to achieve anything like the 'Intention of God' in ourselves for our period of incarnation. Therefore, in 'falling short' of the mark by so far, we hinder our progression towards 'Perfection' by that much. In sinning against ourselves, we sin against the 'God-in-us'."[48]

Rabbi Nachman's ten "healing psalms" comprise *Psalms 16, 32, 41, 42, 59, 77, 90, 105, 137* and *150*.[49] As indicated, these psalms are understood to have "a unique therapeutic quality"[50] when they are recited in Hebrew in the exact order. In this regard, we are told that "viewed together, the Ten Psalms reflect an unfolding of many emotions and reactions common to those dealing with illness."[51] Furthermore, whilst we are told that everyone "should approach the Ten Psalms from his/her own individual experience and vantage point—and may thus arrive at a different understanding and personal interpretation,"[52] it is worth keeping in mind that התיקון הכללי (*ha-Tikun ha-K'lali*) "covers an array of themes prevalent in the Book of Psalms: Joy (Ps. 16), forgiveness (Ps. 32), suffering (41), longing (Ps. 42), deliverance (Ps. 59), affliction (Ps. 77), human finitude (Ps. 90), thanksgiving (Ps. 105), redemption (Ps. 137) and praise (Ps. 150)."[53]

As far as the actual procedure is concerned, the format of *ha-Tikkun ha-K'lali* ("The Comprehensive Rectification") varies somewhat amongst different communities. In this regard, the simplest way of working it, is to:

1. Commence by fixing your *Kavvanah*, i.e. your fully focused intention and attention, on the task at hand, and enunciate the following statement:

    הריני מזמן את פי להודות ולהלל ולשבח את
    בוראי לשם יחוד קדשא בריך הוא ושכינתה
    בדחילו ורחימו על ידי ההוא טמיר ונעלם
    בשם כל ישראל

    Transliteration:
    > hareini m'zamein et fi l'hodot ul'haleil ul'shabei'ach et bor'i l'shem yichud kud'sha b'rich hu ush'chin'teih bid'chilu ur'chimu al y'dei hahu matir v'ne'elam b'shem kol yis'ra'eil

    Translation:
    > I am preparing my mouth to thank, and praise, and honour my Creator, for the sake of unifying the Holy One, blessed be He, and the *Shechinah*, in awe and reverence, through that which is hidden and concealed, in the name of all of Israel.

2. Continue by reciting *Psalm 95:1–3*, these verses being traditionally enunciated prior to reciting psalms:

    [1] לכו נרננה ליהוה‭‬אדני‭‬יאהדונהי נריעה
    לצור ישענו
    [2] נקדמה פניו בתודה בזמרות נריע לו
    [3] כי אל גדול יהוה‭‬אדני‭‬יאהדונהי ומלך גדול
    על כל אלהים

Transliteration:

[1] *l'chu n'ran'nah laYHVH nari'ah l'tzur yish'einu*
[2] *n'kad'mah fanav b'todah biz'mirot nari'a lo*
[3] *ki el gadol YHVH umelech gadol al kol elohim*

Translation:

[1] O come, let us sing unto *YHVH*; let us shout for joy to the Rock of our salvation.
[2] Let us come before His presence with thanksgiving, let us shout for joy unto Him with psalms.
[3] For *YHVH* is a great God, and a great King above all gods;

3. Religious Jews traditionally bind themselves to the *Tzadikim*, the Righteous Saints past and present, by uttering the following statement prior to narrating the ten psalms:

הריני מקשר עצמי באמירת העשרה מזמורים
אלו לכל הצדיקים האמתיים שבדורנו ולכל
הצדיקים האמתיים שוכני עפר קדושים אשר
בארץ המה ובפרט לרבנו הקדוש צדיק יסוד
עולם נחל נבע מקור חכמה (*Proverbs 18:4*)
רבנו נחמן בן פיגא אשר גלה ותקן לומר אלו
העשרה מזמורי תהלים משביל תקון הברית
זכותם יגן עלינו ועל כל ישראל אמן

Transliteration:

hareini m'kasheir atz'mi ba'amirat ha'asarah miz'morim eilu l'chol hatzadikim ha'amitiyim sheb'doreinu ul'chol hatzadikim ha'amitiyim shoch'nei afar k'doshim asher ba'aretz heimah uvif'rat l'rabeinu hakadosh tzadik y'sod olam nachal novei'a m'kor choch'mah (Proverbs 18:4) rabeinu nach'man ben feige asher gilah v'tikein lomar eilu ha'asarah miz'morei t'hilim bish'vil tikun hab'rit z'chutam yagein aleinu v'al kol yis'ra'el Omein.

Psalms & Sefirot / 11

Translation:
> I am binding myself in reciting these ten chapters to all the true Righteous Ones (*Tzadikim*) in our generation, and to all the true Righteous Ones who are departed, Holy Ones who are buried in the earth, and especially to our Holy Rabbi, the Righteous One, Foundation of the World, "Flowing Brook, a Fountain of Wisdom" (*Proverbs 18:4*), our Rabbi Nachman the son of Feige who revealed and commenced the recital of these ten psalms as a rectification for damaging the covenant. May their merit protect us and all Israel. *Amen*.

4. Recite *Psalms 16, 32, 41, 42, 59, 77, 90, 105, 137* and *150* in exact order, and conclude with the following three verses:

> (*Psalm 14:7*) מִי יִתֵּן מִצִּיּוֹן יְשׁוּעַת יִשְׂרָאֵל בְּשׁוּב
> יְהוָֹהאדנ"יאהדונהי שְׁבוּת עַמּוֹ יָגֵל יַעֲקֹב יִשְׂמַח יִשְׂרָאֵל
> (*Psalm 37:39*) וּתְשׁוּעַת צַדִּיקִים מֵיְהוָֹהאדנ"יאהדונהי
> מָעוּזָּם בְּעֵת צָרָה
> (*Psalm 37:40*) וַיַּעְזְרֵם יְהוָֹהאדנ"יאהדונהי וַיְפַלְּטֵם
> יְפַלְּטֵם מֵרְשָׁעִים וְיוֹשִׁיעֵם כִּי חָסוּ בוֹ

Transliteration:
> (*Psalm 14:7*) mi yitein mitziyon y'shu'at yis'ra'eil b'shuv YHVH sh'vot amo yageil ya'akov yis'mach yis'ra'eil
> (*Psalm 37:39*) ut'shu'at tzadikim meiYHVH ma'uzam b'eit tzarah
> (*Psalm 37:40*) vaya'z'reim YHVH vay'fal'teim y'fal'teim meir'sha'im v'yoshi'im ki chasu vo

Translation:
> (*Psalm 14:7*) If only the salvation of Israel would come from Zion! When *YHVH* returns the captivity of His people, Jacob will rejoice, Israel will be glad.
> (*Psalm 37:39*) But the salvation of the righteous is of *YHVH*; He is their stronghold in the time of trouble.

(*Psalm 37:40*) And *YHVH* helpeth them, and delivereth them; He delivereth them from the wicked, and saveth them, because they have taken refuge in Him.

Kabbalists, and others who are more mystically minded, and are seeking a greater, as it were, spiritual intensity in their spiritual activities, would work a special meditation prior to enunciating the ten psalms, or any other psalm for that matter. Thus, regarding the narration of psalms in general, Rabbi Nachman informed an individual that the vital factor is "to find oneself inside each and every psalm."[54] As a case in point, the great Rabbi stated that "all of the battles, for which King David, peace be upon him, sought that God would save him from them, need to be interpreted about oneself, about the battle with one's evil inclination and its forces. Similarly with other psalms." Following this statement, the said individual queried "how one can interpret some of the verses as referring to oneself," when King David, the author of the Psalms, in fact made reference to his own person in certain verses, e.g. *Psalm 86:2* reading "Guard my soul for I am pious," or in the official English translation "Keep my soul, for I am godly." To this question, Rabbi Nachman responded "that one needs also to interpret this about oneself. For one needs to judge oneself in the scale of merit, to find in oneself some merit and some good point, and through the aspect of this good point one is indeed pious."[55]

As far as psalms are concerned, I noted earlier that the entire biblical Book of Psalms is understood to balance the powers of "mercy" (*Chesed*) and "might" (*Gevurah*). I also referenced the *gematria* of the word תהלים (*Tehilim* [ת = 400 + ה = 5 + ל = 30 + י = 10 + ם = 40 = 485]) being equal to that of the fully spelled out letters comprising the Divine Names אל אלהים (*El Elohim* [א = 1 + ל = 30 + פ = 80 + ל = 30 ם = 40 + ד = 4 + א = 1 + ל = 30 + פ = 80 + ל = 30 + ם = 40 + ד = 4 + ה = 5 + י = 10 + י = 10 + ו = 6 + ד = 4 + ם = 40 + ם = 40 = 485]), further noting that the latter Divine Name combination is traditionally aligned with both חסד (*Chesed*—"Loving-kindness") and גבורה (*Gevurah*—"Might"). In this regard, Rabbi Nachman stated that a "person must have this in mind when he recites the [ten] psalms."⁵⁶ It is thus customary amongst those practitioners who believe that the rectification of transgressions are achieved by conjoining the powers of *Chesed* ("Loving-kindness") and *Gevurah* ("Might") within themselves, to contemplate the conjunction of the word תהלים (*Tehilim*) with אל אלהים (*El Elohim*), as well as to mentally recount the spelling of the letters comprising this Divine Name combination, doing so prior to reciting the ten psalms of *ha-Tikun ha-K'lali* (the Comprehensive Rectification):

$$תהלים = אל\ אלהים$$
$$אלף\ למד\quad אלף\ למד\ הי\ יוד\ מם$$

The basic premise here is that a thought is as good as a deed, and the fully focussed mental act of contemplation/meditation is believed to be powerful enough to work the conjunction of the said *sefirot*, as well as to release the "Divine Sparks" trapped in the realm of the קליפות (*K'lipot*—Demonic Shards), and to redirect them into the realm of קדושה (*K'dushah*—"Holiness"),⁵⁷ i.e. the realm of "Wholeness," "Oneness," or "Divine Unification."

Some practitioners conclude the התיקון הכללי (*ha-Tikun ha-K'lali*) procedure with an extensive prayer penned by Rabbi Noson of Bratzlav, the acclaimed disciple of Rabbi Nachman, and it is worth noting that some Breslaver Chasidim recite the "The Comprehensive Rectification" every day.

B. Seven *Sefirot* & the *Menorah Psalm*

Kabbalah teaches that the Divine One interrelates with the universe by means of the "Ten *Sefirot*," the latter being said to be "the most basic modes" of the creative power of Divinity.⁵⁸ We are told "the Sefirot are reflected in man, and in this way, man partakes of the Divine."⁵⁹ Kabbalistic tradition further maintains "that the most basic qualities of human emotionality are love and fear," and that "together they enable man to interact meaningfully with the world around him."⁶⁰ In this regard, Kabbalists emphasize that we are interacting with our world by means of the lower seven *Sefirot*, these having been referenced in exact order in the biblical verse reading "Thine, *YHVH*, is the greatness (*Gedulah*), and the power (*Gevurah*), and the beauty (*Tiferet*), and the victory (*Netzach*), and the majesty (*Hod*); for all (*Yesod*) that is in the heaven and in the earth is Thine; Thine is the kingdom, *YHVH* (*Malchut*)" (*1 Chronicles 29:11*). The seven lower *Sefirot* are also said to be the so-called "seven pillars" referenced in the biblical verse reading חכמות בנתה ביתה חצבה עמודיה שבעה (*choch'mot ban'tah veitah chaz'vah amudeha shiv'ah*—"Wisdom hath built her house, she hath hewn out her seven pillars") (*Proverbs 9:1*).[61]

Viewed in terms of practical considerations, the seven lower *Sefirot* are delineated חסד (*Chesed*—"Kindness/Care/Love"); גבורה (*Gevurah*—"Might/Discipline/Restraint"); תפארת (*Tiferet*—"Beauty/Balance/Harmony/Empathy"); נצח (*Netzach*—"Victory/Dominance/Endurance"); הוד (*Hod*—"Mindfulness/Humility/Gratitude"); יסוד (*Yesod*—"Foundation/Friendship/Bonding"); and מלכות (*Malchut*—"Sovereignty/Rulership/Nurturance").[62] These attributions of the seven lower *sefirot* to human "emotional/behavioural attributes," resulted in the largest practical application of the *sefirot* in existence, i.e. the annual "Counting of the *Omer*" comprising forty-nine days of profound personal introspection, which I have addressed in a previous volume of this series of texts on "Practical Kabbalah."[63]

Be that as it may, it should be noted that *Psalm 67*, which was termed "A Sanctuary Song about God's Universal Blessings,"[64] features particularly prominently over this period, and it is the association of this psalm with the numbers 7 and 49 which determines its extensive application in mainstream Judaism. In this regard, it has been noted that *Psalm 67*, without the superscription verse, comprises seven verses and forty-nine words, whilst the fifth verse is equally composed of exactly forty-nine letters, as indicated below. These figures led to the psalm being directly aligned with the מנורה (*Menorah*—"seven-branched candelabrum") in the Holy Temple, and to it being employed over the seven weeks (7 x 7 = 49 days) of the "Counting of the *Omer*."[65]

Referencing the sacred practices of the Kabbalists in 16th century Safed, it was reported in the name of Rabbi Abraham Galante, who was one of the main disciples of Rabbi Moses Cordovero, that "every night during the period of the *'Omer*, they concentrate upon a different word of the Psalm 'The Lord will forgive us' [Ps. 67], which is composed of forty-nine words, as well as upon one letter from the verse 'Let the nations be glad and sing for joy....' [Ps. 67:5]. Each night on which they recite this Psalm following the counting of the *'Omer*, they raise their voices when they come to the particular letter designated for that night. There is a tradition among them that an individual who contemplates in this fashion will never spend a single night in prison, even if he should commit some capital offence."[66] Besides the prominence of the sixty-seventh Psalm in the *"Counting of the Omer,"* the primary importance of this psalm in Jewish worship is further emphasised by the fact that it is often included in the stylized *Menorah* format for contemplation purposes in סידורים (*Sidurim*—"Prayer Books").[67] It is likewise included in most *Shiviti* plaques and amulets. In this regard *Psalm 67* has enormous value as an object of daily spiritual contemplation and meditation. I have addressed one such *Shiviti* construct in great detail in a previous volume of this series of texts on "Practical Kabbalah."[68] Hence it is only necessary to stress that the seven verses comprising the *Menorah Psalm*, align with the seven phrases of the *"Ana B'cho'ach Prayer," senza* the concluding blessing, as well as the seven portions of the "Forty-two Letter Name of God"; the seven Planets; the seven Days of the Week; the seven lower *Sefirot*; as well as the earlier mentioned seven Weeks of counting the *Omer*.[69]

Regarding the unique, as it were, affinity between *Psalm 67* and the *Menorah*, tradition has it that Moses found it difficult to visualise the golden *Menorah* when it was first revealed it to him. Hence the Divine One sent him a second vision of a *"Menorah of fire,"* with verses 2 to 8 of the current psalm inscribed on its seven branches, and the glyphs comprising the first verse arranged as the seven flames of the candelabrum.[70] However, whilst considering the saga of the origins of the *Menorah* psalm, it has been conjectured that King David did not compose the sixty-seventh Psalm, but that "it was revealed to him on a golden plate which was in the same form of the *menorah* shown to Moses."[71] As I have noted elsewhere, Isaac Arama, the 15th century Kabbalist, maintained in *"Akedat Yitzchak"* that *Psalm 67* was engraved in the image of the *Menorah* on the shield of the King,[72] and it was further claimed that the *Menorah* Psalm, rather than the hexagram, comprised the original *"Magen David."*[73] Thus we read in a 16th century tractate titled *"The Golden Menorah,"* that "this psalm together with the *menorah* alludes to great things....When King David went out to war, he used to carry on his shield this psalm in the form of a *menorah* engraved on a golden tablet and he used to meditate on its secret. Thus he was victorious."[74] Amongst the "secrets" of *Psalm 67*, we are told that:

1. The psalm comprises 216 letters, which are the exact number of Hebrew glyphs in the "Name of Seventy-two Names."[75]
2. The *gematria* of the initials of the seven verses comprising the branches of the *Menorah* totals 72 [א = 1 + ל = 30 + י = 10 + י 10 = + י 10 = + א = 1 + י = 10 = 72], which we are told aligns with the "Seventy-two Letter Name of God,"[76] this Divine Name being quite different from the "Name of Seventy-two Names." The said Divine Name comprise the four letters of the Ineffable Name expanded by means of their full spelling. As I noted elsewhere, there are four such spellings of the tetragrammaton, which relate to the "Four Worlds" of Kabbalah. In the current instance, the expansion of the four letters is by means of what is termed *Milui de-Yodin* (*Yod* filling), or the ע"ב (*AV*) expansion said to pertain to העולם האצילות (*ha-Olam ha-Atzilut*—"The World of Emanation"), i.e. the highest realm of Spirit, and to חכמה (*Choch'mah*—"Wisdom") on the sefirotic Tree.[77] As indicated below, the numerical value of this expansion of the Ineffable Name equals 72:

   י — י (*Yod*) = 10 + ו (*Vav*) = 6 + ד (*Dalet*) = 4   = 20

   ה — ה (*Heh*) = 5 + י (*Yod*) = 10   = 15

   ו — ו (*Vav*) = 6 + י (*Yod*) = 10 + ו (*Vav*) = 6   = 22

   ה — ה (*Heh*) = 5 + י (*Yod*) = 10   = 15

   Total 72

3. The central verse, which we are told "contains in miniature the entire psalm,"[78] commences with the letter י (*Yod*) and concludes with the letter ה (*Heh*), thus spelling יה (*Yah*), the Divine Name which is said to reference "the union of the *sefirot* of *Chokhmah*/Wisdom and *Binah*/Understanding." It is further noted that "archetypally, *yod* represents the masculine principle and *heh* represents the feminine principle."[79] It is thus understood that the Divine Name יה (*Yah*) "expresses the essential harmony of the universe in its supernal root."[80]

4. Regarding the figure 216, which we noted is the number of letters comprising the sixty-seventh Psalm, we are further told that this is the sum of the *gematria* of the concluding letters "of the six branches to the right and left of the Menorah (201), plus the *yod-hey* (15) of the central shaft." This is again understood to reference the 216 glyphs of the "*Shem Vayisa Vayet*," i.e. "Name of Seventy-two Names."[81] However, we are reminded that the *gematria* of גבורה (*Gevurah*—"Might") [ג = 3 + ב = 2 + ו = 6 + ר = 200 + ה = 5] is equally 216.[82]

5. As stated, the acrostic formed by the initial letters of the seven verses bear the *gematria* of 72. This is equally the numerical value of the word חסד (*Chesed*—Mercy/Lovingkindness) [ח = 8 + ס = 60 + ד = 4 = 72], and thus we are informed that the *Menorah/Menorah Psalm* "reflects the balance of the two opposite forces,"[83] i.e. those of "Mercy" and of "Might."

There are several additional somewhat complex details which I elected not to include here. As it is, many readers may well wonder why the shared particulars are of any importance to Kabbalists, and herein lies one of the great, as it were, "secrets" of Kabbalah. Actions pertaining to the "revelation" of greater meaning in Hebrew words, phrases, biblical verses, and even in a complete psalm, such as the current one, are considered to be very special כונות (*Kavanot*),[84] i.e. unique "intentions" which are believed to "open up" or "bind" the practitioner to the spiritual power inherent in the psalm. Whilst many would consider these details to hold special significance only to Kabbalists, it should be noted that those less esoterically minded individuals who wish to use the *Menorah* Psalm for spiritual growth, only need to keep in mind that the seven branches of the *Menorah* "represent the seven orifices of the face (eyes, ears, nostrils, and mouth), and the seven major parts of the body (arms, legs, head, torso, and reproductive organ)."[85] In this regard, it is said that "our task is to purify all of these aspects of ourselves, so that our bodies become holy and our souls shine forth like the radiant light of the Menorah."[86]

However, there are those amongst my fellow religionists and Kabbalists who do find the revelation of "hidden meanings" within the *Menorah Psalm* to not only expand their consciousness to embrace a greater whole, but to "open up" their inner beings to an influx of "sacred power." In this regard, we are informed that contemplating the *Menorah Psalm* in the manner delineated above, is firstly "meant to put one into the proper frame of mind for prayer,"[87] as well as to preclude oneself from mental distractions, and also to purify "the mind of all evil thoughts."[88] Secondly, the image of the *Menorah*, indicating, as it were, a "singularity in diversity," i.e. the conjunction of the seven branches of the sacred candelabrum into a harmonious whole, will facilitate a profound understanding of "Divine Oneness." In this regard, we are taught that despite the multiplicity of human existence, we are "One" and all part of the selfsameness of one great consciousness called "I Am." In the ultimate reality of the whole of existence, there is in effect no separateness whatsoever. Therefore it is clear that whatever we do unto others, we do unto ourselves. It has thus been said that this "Divine Oneness" can be sensed by meditating on the *Menorah Psalm*,[89] and that whilst "we go about the business of everyday life," we come to realise that the uniqueness of the diversity we are experiencing around us, is simultaneously an expression of the Divine Oneness.[90] Thus, in my estimation, the primary power of the *Menorah Psalm*, lies in the statement that "together, the seven verses represent the perception of 'oneness in multiplicity' that the Menorah in the Holy Temple radiated to the world."[91] I believe this is the reason why we are told that reciting the verses of *Psalm 67*, whilst focusing on their respective alignments to the shape of the *Menorah*, "has a spiritual effect similar to lighting the Menorah in the Holy Temple."[92]

The method of reciting the *Menorah Psalm* is fairly straightforward:

1. Focus on the conjoined image of the *Menorah* and *Psalm 67*, "gaze upon the form as a whole, to see how the words of the Menorah make up one unit,"[93] which is then followed by contemplating the inner meanings and power of the *Menorah Psalm*.
2. Whilst scanning the Hebrew texts on the *Menorah*, recite the psalm slowly in a thoughtful manner. After tracing the

letters of the first verse comprising the seven flames of the sacred candelabrum, enunciate the seven succeeding verses whilst focussing mentally on their respective sefirotic associations, i.e. commencing with the leftmost branch, read downwards verse 2 aligned with חסד (*Chesed*), followed by verse 3 associated with גבורה (*Gevurah*), verse 4 with תפארת (*Tiferet*), etc. To be truly effective in performing the task of scanning each verse, it would be necessary to align with seven essential מידות (*midot*), i.e. emotional qualities, respectively associated with the seven lower *Sefirot*. This is relatively easily accomplished by engendering inside yourself a "feeling appreciation" for these seven Divine qualities, and, as it were, invoking them one by one as you enunciate their respectively associated verses in *Psalm 67*. Thus when you focus on the left-most branch of the *Menorah Psalm*, you would commence by focussing on *Chesed* ("Loving-kindness"). With your attention fixed on your upper chest, ask yourself what "loving-kindness" feels like. Use the word "love" to trigger a response inside your chest, and increase it as you mentally repeat the word "love," "loving-kindness," or "*Chesed*" if you prefer, feeling it grow in strength inside your chest, and flood your being. Then you may proceed to tracing and reading the first branch of the *Menorah Psalm*. Repeat this action prior to reading each of the successive verses, each time calling up inside your chest the relevant emotional quality prior to tracing the relevant branch of the *Menorah*. I have discussed a similar, if somewhat more intense, technique titled "*Opening the Gates*" in previous volumes.[94]

3. You could further intensify the current procedure by imagining "Divine Light" entering your inner being. In this regard, it has been noted that whilst reciting the *Menorah Psalm*, "it is fitting to silently pray that this light be revealed anew, driving away all spiritual darkness."[95] This action is understood to both engender a full recognition of "Divine Oneness" inside oneself, as well as to banish inner darkness and mitigate "all harsh judgments." Practitioners might further envisage the "Divine Light" extending to all of humankind.

C. Psalms, *Sefirot* & Holy Days

1. INTRODUCTION

In the previous part of *"The Book of Magical Psalms"* I have made several references to psalms associated with the *Sefirot*. In this regard, I noted certain instances in which individual verses from the Book of Psalms are aligned with *Sefirot*. I referenced seven verses, five from psalms, which are recited during הושענא רבא (*Hoshana Raba*—"Great Supplication") on the seventh day of *Sukkot* ("Festival of Booths"). As indicated these verses represent "seven 'Divine Qualities' related to the seven lower *sefirot* on the kabbalistic Tree of Life, i.e. חסד (*Chesed*—'Mercy'): *Psalm 89:3*; גבורה (*Gevurah*—'Might'): *Psalm 89:14*; תפארת (*Tif'eret*—'beauty'): *Micah 7:20*; נצח (*Netzach*—'Victory'): *Psalm 16:11*; הוד (*Hod*—'Glory'): *Psalm 8:2*; יסוד (*Yesod*—'Foundation'): *Psalm 145:17*, and מלכות (*Malchut*—'Kingdom'/'Kingship'): *Zechariah 14:9*."[96] I further noted the single statement in *Psalm 33:6* reading בדבר יהוה שמים נעשו וברוח פיו כל צבאם (*bid'var YHVH shamayim na'asu uv'ru'ach piv kol tz'va'am*—"By the word of *YHVH* were the heavens made; and all the host of them by the breath of His mouth"), to be related to the ten "*Ma'amarot*" ("Sayings") with which "the heavens and the earth and all creatures in them" were created.[97] As mentioned elsewhere, "the notion of the ten *Ma'amarot* and ten creative potencies ultimately found their way into the primary texts of the early Kabbalists, in the form of the doctrine of the ten *Sefirot*."[98]

Be that as it may, I equally addressed *Psalm 30* in terms of sefirotic attributions. In this regard, I indicated two Divine Names which feature prominently in this psalm, i.e. יהוה (*YHVH*) nine times, and אדני (*Adonai*) once, and noted that "these ten appearances of the Name of the Eternal One are said to align with the Ten Commandments, and equally with the ten *Sefirot*."[99] As mentioned elsewhere, these two Divine Names are respectively aligned with תפארת (*Tiferet*—"Beauty") and מלכות (*Malchut*—

"Kingdom") on the sefirotic Tree,[100] and, as indicated, their conjunction is of special importance in the recitation of the biblical psalms.[101] Curiously enough, the conjoint *Gematria* of יהוה (*YHVH* [י = 10 + ה = 5 + ו = 6 + ה = 5 = 26]) and אדני (*Adonai* [א = 1 + ד = 4 + נ = 50 + י = 10 = 65]) is 91. This figure is also said to equate with the number of words comprising the following set of special biblical verses, of which all bar one have been derived from the Book of Psalms: *Psalm 42:9, Psalm 69:14, Psalm 34:5, Psalm 31:3, Psalm 70:2, Psalm 109:21, Psalm 77:15, Psalm 106:8, Isaiah 12:2,* and *Psalm 71:12.*[102]

Rabbi Ariel bar Tzadok noted these verses to be constituting 365 letters, these being "the number of days in the Solar year, as well as the number of portions in the Incense Offering."[103] Furthermore, the said verses are attributed to the ten *Sefirot*, and the capitals of the verses, when read in exact order, spell the יוד הא ואו הא (*Yod-Vav-Dalet Heh-Alef Vav-Alef-Vav Heh-Alef*) expansion of the *Tetragrammaton*. The *gematria* of this expansion is 45, and for this reason it is termed מה (*Mah* [מ = 40 + ה = 45]), or the "Forty-Five Letter Name of God."[104] As mentioned earlier, I have addressed the four expansions of the Ineffable Name in great detail elsewhere in this series of texts on Practical Kabbalah.[105] Thus, in terms of the current study, it would be necessary to only briefly clarify the said מה (*Mah* [מ = 40 + ה = 45]) expansion. In this regard, I previously noted "that the important 'Sacred Marriage' of the 'higher' and the 'lower' as expressed in the Divine Name יאהדונהי (*Yahadonahi*)," the aforementioned conjunction of יהוה (*YHVH*) and אדני (*Adonai*), "is also fundamental to the four expansions of *YHVH*."[106] I further noted the "*Mah*" expansion to be motivating the union between *Tiferet* (Beauty/Male [King]) and *Malchut* (Kingdom/Female [Queen]).[107]

Be that as it may, the said ten verses are aligned with the ten *Sefirot* in the following manner. Keep in mind that in this instance the upper three sefirot are listed as חכמה (*Chochmah*), בינה (*Binah*), and דעת (*Da'at*):

יוד (Yod)

1. י (Yod)—חכמה (Chochmah)—Psalm 42:9

    יומם יצוה יהוה חסדו ובלילה שירה עמי תפלה לאל חיי

    Transliteration:
    > Yomam y'tsaveh YHVH chas'do uvalailah shiroh imi t'filah l'eil chayai

    Translation:
    > By day *YHVH* will command His lovingkindness, and in the night His song shall be with me, even a prayer unto the God of my life.

2. ו (Vav)—בינה (Binah)—Psalm 69:14

    ואני תפלתי לך יהוה עת רצון אלהים ברב חסדך ענני באמת ישעך

    Transliteration:
    > Va'ani t'filati l'cha YHVH eit ratzon elohim b'rov chas'decha aneini be'emet yish'echa

    Translation:
    > But as for me, let my prayer be unto Thee *YHVH*, in an acceptable time; *Elohim*, in the abundance of Thy mercy, answer me with the truth of Thy salvation.

3. ד (Dalet)—דעת (Da'at)—Psalm 34:5

    דרשתי את יהוה וענני ומכל מגורותי הצילני

    Transliteration:
    > Darash'ti et YHVH v'anani umikol m'gurotai hitzilani

    Translation:
    > I sought *YHVH*, and He answered me, and delivered me from all my fears.

הא (Heh)

4. ה (Heh)—חסד (Chesed)—Psalm 31:3

    הטה אלי אזנך מהרה הצילני היה לי לצור מעוז לבית מצודות להושיעני

Transliteration:
> *Hateih eilai oz'necha m'heirah hatzileini heyeih li l'tzur ma'oz l'veit m'tzudot l'hoshi'eini*

Translation:
> Incline Thine ear unto me, deliver me speedily; be Thou to me a rock of refuge, even a fortress of defence, to save me.

5. א (*Alef*)—גבורה (*Gevurah*)—Psalm 70:2

אלהים להצילני יהוה לעזרתי חושה

Transliteration:
> *Elohim l'hatzileini YHVH l'ez'rati chushah*

Translation:
> *Elohim* to deliver me, *YHVH* to help me, make haste.

ואו (*Vav*)

6. ו (*Vav*)—תפארת (*Tiferet*)—Psalm 109:21

ואתה יהוה אדני עשה אתי למען שמך כי טוב חסדך הצילני

Transliteration:
> *V'atah YHVH Adonai aseih iti l'ma'an sh'mecha ki tov chas'd'cha hatzileini*

Translation:
> But Thou, *YHVH Adonai*, deal with me for Thy name's sake; because Thy mercy is good, deliver Thou me.

7. א (*Alef*)—נצח (*Netzach*)—Psalm 77:15

אתה האל עשה פלא הודעת בעמים עזך

Transliteration:
> *Atah ha'el oseih feleh hoda'ta va'amim uzecha*

Translation:
> Thou art the God that doest wonders; Thou hast made known Thy strength among the peoples.

8. ו (*Vav*)—הוד (*Hod*)—Psalm 106:8

וישיעם למען שמו להודיע את גבורתו

Transliteration:
> *Vayoshi'eim l'ma'an sh'mo l'hodi'a et g'vurato*

Translation:
> Nevertheless He saved them for His name's sake, that He might make His mighty power to be known.

הא (*Heh*)

9. ה (*Heh*)—יסוד (*Yesod*)—Isaiah 12:2

הנה אל ישועתי אבטח ולא אפחד כי עזי וזמרת
יה יהוה ויהי לי לישועה

Transliteration:
> *Hineih el y'shu'ati ev'tach v'lo ef'chad ki ozi v'zim'rat Yah Adonai vay'hi li lishu'ah*

Translation:
> Behold, God is my salvation; I will trust, and will not be afraid; for *Yah Adonai* is my strength and song; and He is become my salvation.

10. א (*Alef*)—מלכות (*Malchut*)—Psalm 71:12

אלהים אל תרחק ממני אלהי לעזרתי חושה

Transliteration:
> *Elohim al tir'chak mimeni elohai l'ez'rati chushah*

Translation:
> *Elohim* be not far from me; O my God, make haste to help me.

Regarding the enunciation of these verses, Rabbi Ariel bar Tzadok, who is one of the greatest living exponents of "Practical Kabbalah," stated that this action is said "to create a strong spiritual surge of kedusha (holiness) that will serve to protect one against harm and mishap."[108] He further noted that "whoever recited these verses every day will receive Divine protection and find grace and prosperity."[109] In this regard, Rabbi Tzadok maintained these verses "should be recited daily, all year round,"[110] and mentioned that the great thirteenth century Rabbi Moshe ben Nachman (*Ramban*), who is indicated to be the originator of this prayer-incantation, "was amazed at the results of reciting these ten verses, or to write them in an amulet."[111]

As might be expected, there is a lot more to be said about "Psalms & *Sefirot*." However, it should be kept in mind that a comprehensive investigation of this topic is far too extensive to include in full in this tome. Hence I am obliged to scale this study down to psalms which were directly affiliated with the *Sefirot*, and especially to those psalms which I believe will be most meaningful to both the casual reader, and the serious practitioner of Jewish Magic. Some may well wonder why I excluded the alphabetic acrostic *Psalm 145*, which is not only very important in Jewish worship, but has been associated with the sefirotic Tree. In this regard, it is should be noted that this psalm is viewed more in terms of the twenty-two צנורות (*Tzinorot*), i.e. "Conduits" or "Channels" often termed "Paths," on the sefirotic Tree, rather than the *Sefirot* per se. As it is, I address this psalm in great detail in the third and concluding part of this tome. Thus, from a practical perspective, I wish to focus specifically on the following two psalms:

2. PSALM 29

As noted in the first part of "*The Book of Magical Psalms*," the twenty-ninth Psalm is recited on *Shabbat*, and during the morning service (*Shacharit*) on festivals.[112] In fact, it was Rabbi Isaac Luria, the great 16th century Kabbalist who lived and taught in Safed, Israel, who maintained that the Friday night service should commence with the recitation of this psalm. In this regard, it is reported that he would say *Psalm 29* when he went out into the open fields to watch the setting sun, and welcome the arrival of *Shabbat*.[113] We are further told that he would walk around the table in his home "in commemoration of the *Mizbayah* ('altar'),"[114] and would recite the current psalm "slowly, with much concentration and joy."[115] In this regard, it should be noted that "Shabbat celebrates the union of male and female," and that this is sometimes "seen as uniting two aspects of God," i.e. the Divine One and the שכינה (*Shechinah*), and at "other times as uniting God and Israel."[116] It is further said, "this union involves a reciprocal exchange of potency," hence the statement "ascribe unto

YHVH glory and strength" in verse 1 is, as it were, reciprocated in verse 11 reading "*YHVH* will give strength unto His people."[117]

As noted in the previous part, the figure seven is considered particularly important here, since the word קוֹל (*kol*—"voice") is listed seven times in the twenty-ninth Psalm. Whilst it has been suggested that this pertains to seven different kinds of voices related to seven *Middot* (Divine "Emotive Qualities" or "Measures"), we are further informed that the seventh day, Shabbat, is "a wedding anniversary," and hence "seven also evokes the seven-blessing wedding ceremony, which in turn evokes the seven-blessing Shabbat Amidah, which in turn evokes the seven-fold mention of Adonai [*YHVH*] in 'the musical psalm for the Sabbath day'."[118] Furthermore, as mentioned previously, "the seven appearances of the 'voice of *YHVH*,' which King David enunciated over the waters, align with the seven-blessing *Shabbat Amidah*, and equally with the seven *hakafot*, i.e. the circumambulations around the *Bimah* (central reading desk) on הושענא רבא (*Hoshanah Rabah*—'Great Supplication'), and on שמחת תורה (*Simchat Torah*—'Rejoicing with the *Torah*'). This was cited to be the reason why some recite the twenty-ninth Psalm after the seven circuits on *Hoshana Raba* ('Great Supplication')."[119]

However, we are also reminded that as far as mainstream Judaism is concerned, "the seven repetitions remind us of the seven days of creation, the seven rounds that we envelop in the phylacteries, the seventy times of the siege and conquest of Joshua surrounding Jericho, the seven circles around one's spouse before entering the pact of marriage, the seven steps of the *mikvah* (Jewish ritual bath), the seven stops that we do before a burial, the seven rounds of Torah (*Hakafot*) when we finish its reading and start again, the seven days of cleaning and purification before entering again into the sacredness of intimacy and sexuality, and the seven stages and levels between earth and heavens."[120] We are further informed that "seven is about cycles, about renewing ourselves, about preparations to a higher purpose, and about conquering a supreme level. Seven allows us to grow in our spiritual life and emotional balance."[121]

As with *Psalm 67*, great mystical meaning was found in the "seven voices," as well as in the eighteen appearances of the

Ineffable Name in the current psalm. In this regard, the 19th century Rabbi Ze'ev Wolf of Zhitomir suggested that the seven appearances of the word "voice" in the Psalm, are referencing seven different kinds of voices.[122] In classical rabbinic sources these were equated with "seven voices" which the Israelites are said to have encountered during the Divine Revelation at Mount Sinai as referenced in *Exodus 19*.[123] Whilst there is no specific reference to more than one divine "voice" in the biblical saga of the Israelites at the foot of Mount Sinai, tradition has it that "the one Voice went on and divided into seven voices."[124] Thus we read in the *Sefer ha-Bahir* regarding the "seven voices" in *Psalm 29*, that "this teaches us that the Torah was given with seven voices. In each of them the Master of the universe revealed Himself to them, and they saw Him. It is thus written, 'And all the people saw the voices' (*Exodus 20:15*)."[125] We are informed that there is great power in this Divine Revelation. In this regard, I noted that it is said "the remarkable qualities embodied in the twenty-ninth Psalm, results in תקונים (*Tikunim*—'corrections'/'restorations') of cosmic proportions being enacted in the celestial realms through the enunciation of the twenty-ninth Psalm on the arrival of *Shabbat*."[126] In this regard, Rabbi Alexander Susskind of Grodno maintained that the recitation of the expression הבו ליהוה (*havu la'YHVH* —"Give [Ascribe] unto *YHVH* [enunciated "*Adonai*"]), results in "a special *tikkun* is performed in the worlds on high," and that another is achieved through the seven enunciations of the word קול (*kol*—"voice") in this psalm.[127]

However, this is not the entirety of the search for greater meaning in the current psalm. Kabbalists noted that the numerical value of the four letters of Ineffable Name (יהוה) multiplied by the eighteen times they appear in the current psalm is 72. This is again understood to indicate the "Name of Seventy-two Names," as well as the *sefirah* חסד (*Chesed*—"Loving-kindness"), the *gematria* of which, as indicated earlier, is also 72.[128] Thus it is written that the Divine One gave the Sabbath to Israel "as an act of chesed."[129] Other than that, it has been said that the eleven verses of *Psalm 29* align with וה (*VH* [ו = 6 + ה = 5 = 11]), the concluding glyphs of the *Tetragrammaton*.[130] We are further informed that the ninety-one words comprising *Psalm 29*, equate with the collective numerical value of the Divine Names יהוה (*YHVH* [י = 10 + ה = 5 + ו = 6 + ה = 5 = 26]) and אדני (*Adonai* [א = 1 + ד = 4 + נ = 50 + י = 10 = 65]). In this regard, it was stated that "praying the psalm with the proper intention integrates the two names, a process known as *yichud*. This process corresponds to the union of 'The Holy one, blessed be He' (*Tiferet*) and his bride, the *Shekhinah*,"[131] i.e. *Malchut*. I have addressed the said two Divine Names extensively in previous volumes,[132] and the union of the Ineffable Name and *Adonai* features prominently throughout "*The Book of Magical Psalms*."

Paraphrasing statements found in the *Zohar* regarding the "seven voices," the acclaimed 16th century Kabbalist Meir ben Ezekiel ibn Gabbai, noted that "there are seven Palaces of Light below, corresponding to the seven voices in [Ps. 29]: 'Ascribe unto the Lord.' There are eighteen citations of the divine Name therein, by means of which the Holy One courses through 18,000 worlds: 'The Chariots of God, etc'."[133] I have previously noted that the eighteen enunciations of the Ineffable Name in the twenty-ninth Psalm, is believed to result in the enactment of a special celestial *Tikkun* ("restoration"),[134] and the figure 18 is associated with חי (*Chai*—"Live" [ח = 8 + י = 10 = 18]), a word which is popularly carried as a Hebrew amulet. Be that as it may, we have also seen that the eighteen enunciations are aligned with the eighteen-blessings of the *Amidah* prayer, and that with each vocalisation of the Ineffable Name (*Adonai*) in the Psalm, it is said "we advance one more blessing in the *Amidah*."[135] Thus we are told that "as *Psalm 29* ends with 'May *Adonai* bless his people with shalom,' so the final blessing of the *Amidah* ends with '*Adonai* who blesses his people with *shalom*'."[136]

However, what is of particular importance to us here, is again the alignment of the "seven voices" with the lower seven *Sefirot*, these being understood to represent unique מידות (*midot*), certain "Emotive Qualities" or "Measures," i.e. Kindness, Severity, Harmony, Endurance, Humility, Foundation, and Royalty, and which were delineated "character traits that correspond to aspects of the divine in the kabbalistic system explaining the modes of divine manifestation."[137] The "primary magical factor" here is "voice," which has been said "is more spiritual than speech,"[138] the latter having been aligned with מלכות (*Malchut*), whilst voice is said to pertain "to the six sefiroth of *Zer Anpin*,"[139] i.e. the "revealed aspect" of the Divine One comprising the sefirot from חסד (*Chesed*) to יסוד (*Yesod*). One might say that in this instance "speech," is perceived to be the physical expression of "voice," whilst the latter is more subtle or "spiritual," i.e. it is in your head, heart, everywhere in fact. Spiritually/mystically/magically speaking the "voice" can be perceived even in the silence. As we know well enough, "speech" is really audial, i.e. heard through our ears, whatever imagery it may invoke in the listener, whilst the concept of "voice" mentioned here is universal and often more visual, whatever the sound of it may be within ourselves. It is in this regard that Rabbi Kalonymus Kalman Shapira noted "Even now the voice of the Torah can be heard emerging everywhere, from within one's own body as well as from the entire outside world."[140]

We are told "*Psalm 29* is a reaffirmation that God's voice is manifested in our cosmic life."[141] This is one of the many reasons why the recitation of this magnificent psalm is of great importance in my personal spiritual/magical life. In this regard, I heed the words of the earlier mentioned Rabbi Alexander Susskind of Grodno, who maintained that one should recite the twenty-ninth Psalm "with great deliberation and with a most powerful joy. He should have in mind that his intention in reciting this Psalm is in order to perform great *tikkunim* in the worlds on high and to give satisfaction to the Creator, blessed and exalted be He for ever. Then it will undoubtedly be accounted to him as if he had had all the intentions in mind."[142] These "intentions" are qualified with the statement that "the All-Merciful desires the heart,"[143] an as noted in the first part of this tome, "reciting the twenty-ninth Psalm in this manner, is as if one is fulfilling the sacred obligation of Kabbalah expressed in the statement:

לשם יחוד קודשא בריך הוא ושכינתיה בדחילו
ורחימו ליחד שם י"ה ב"ה ביחודא שלים

Transliteration:
> *l'shem yichud kud'sha b'rich hu ush'chinteih bid'chilu ur'chimu l'yacheid shem Y"H b'V"H b'yichuda sh'lim*

Translation:
> For the sake of unifying the Holy One, blessed be He and the *Shechinah*, in awe and reverence, to unify *YH* and *VH* in complete unity."[144]

When it comes to reciting the current psalm, I acknowledged the way the Holy Ari did so in welcoming the "Divine Bride" every *Shabbat*, as well as the stated guidelines of Rabbi Alexander Susskind of Grodno. However, in constantly seeking greater meaning, as well as spiritual intensity in listening and hearing, I chanced upon a paraphrase of the prayerful expressions on the "seven voices," said to have been penned by Rabbi Yaakov Koppel Lipschitz of Mezritch. It reads:

> 1. The voice of God opens the gates of compassion and love.
> 2. The voice of God opens the gates of courage.
> 3. The voice of God opens the gates of shining truth.
> 4. The voice of God opens the gates of endurance and patience.
> 5. The voice of God opens the gates of splendorous beauty.
> 6. The voice of God opens the gates of deep connection.
> 7. The voice of God opens the gates of presence.[145]

I conjoined the seven "voice" verses of the *Psalm 29*, with these seven phrases, and in this manner greatly enhanced the intensity and power of the psalm within myself in both the outward verbal recitation/hearing, as well as in the inward enunciation/listening. In this regard, I commenced by mindfully enunciating the first two verses of the psalm aloud in the standard Hebrew manner. This is succeeded by conjoining the third verse with the first of the seven English phrases, the fourth with the second phrase, etc. Each time I would slowly exclaim and hear the biblical verse, then pause, think, and listen to the relevant English expression mentally. For example, I would commence by exclaiming aloud *Psalm 29:3*

קול יחוה על המים אל הכבוד הרעים יחוה על מים רבים

(*kol YHVH al hamayim el hakavod hir'im YHVH al mayim rabim*—"The voice of *YHVH* is upon the waters; the God of glory thundereth, even *YHVH* upon many waters"). This is followed by a pause, during which I mentally recite and listen to the phrase "The voice of God opens the gates of compassion and love." This *modus operandi* is repeated with the remaining six "the voice of *YHVH*" verses, and the action is concluded with the aural recitation of the final two verses of the psalm.

In my estimation the value of procedures such as these, is dependent on how much "feeling appreciation" the practitioner can summon from the words. Since the twenty-ninth Psalm is often associated with water, especially in its magical applications, some might want to recite it in "living water," i.e. in a *Mik'veh* (Jewish Ritual Bath), or in a running brook, or a river. I am reminded of a fascinating report by Rabbi Eleazer of Worms, the acclaimed 13th century Jewish Mystic, who chronicled a fascinating "ritual of sanctification" in which a master transmits a Divine Name to disciples, doing so after they have submerged themselves in "flowing water." In this regard, the great Rabbi wrote:

> "The name is transmitted only to the *senu'im* [the initiates], who are not prone to anger, who are humble and God-fearing, and carry out the commandments of their Creator. And it is transmitted only over water. Before the master teaches it to his pupil, they must both immerse themselves and bathe in forty measures of flowing water, then put on white garments and fast on the day of instruction. Then both must stand up to their ankles in the water, and the master must say a prayer ending with the words: "The voice of God is over the waters!" [Ps. 29:2] Praised be Thou, O Lord, who revealest Thy secret to those who fear Thee, He who knoweth the mysteries." Then both must turn their eyes toward the water and recite verses from the Psalms, praising God over the waters....[At this time, the master transmits one of the secret names of God that the adept is permitted to hear, whereupon] they return to the synagogue or schoolhouse, holding water in a pure vessel and the rabbi says: "Blessed art thou, the Lord, our God, King of the Universe, who has sanctified us by His commandments and has distinguished us from all the nations and revealed to us His mysteries."[146]

3. PSALM 150

As noted earlier, this psalm, termed "a paean and musical symphony of praises,"[147] concludes Rabbi Nachman of Bratslav's הַתִיקוּן הַכְּלָלִי (*ha-Tikun ha-K'lali*) procedure. However, considering the importance of *Psalm 150*, I commenced this chapter with a quote from this remarkable psalm, my intention having been to focus attention on a word(s) which would, as it were, automatically impact the mind of the reader — *Hallelujah!* As I am sure most readers know well enough, this Hebrew expression is quite universal, since it is employed in virtually every language on earth. Whether written as two words הַלְלוּ יָהּ (*Hal'lu Yah*) in Hebrew, or transcribed *Hallelujah, Halelujah, Allelouia, Alleluia, Aleluya,* etc., every Jew, Christian, and others of different faiths and spiritualities, whether they be Hindu, Buddhist, or Muslim; whether they are believers in Folk Magic, such as those espoused by modern-day followers of purportedly "ancient Pagan traditions"; whether they express the doctrines of the religions derived from the African diaspora, such as Voodoo, Macumba, Santeria, etc.; whether consciously or unconsciously; whether in speech or in mind; whether they approve, or vociferously proclaim their distaste, of "Abrahamic religions," the latter including Judaism, Christianity, Islam, as well as the Samaritan, Druse, Yezidi, Bahá'í, and the Rastafari faiths for that matter.... *ALL* would have given praise to the "One God" if they sang along with Handel's acclaimed "*Hallelujah Chorus*," or more likely, with Leonard Cohen's famous "*Hallelujah*." I have even observed a group of self-styled "Jew baiters," who made no bones about their hatred for me and my kind, and who, under the intense fervour of the phrase "He is trampling out the vintage where the grapes of wrath are stored" from "*The Battle Hymn of the Republic*," hollered with great gusto "Glory, glory, Hallelujah."

The expression "*Hallelujah*" appears twenty-four times in the Hebrew Bible, in fact, solely in the Book of Psalms. The Hebrew term הַלְלוּ (*halelu*—"praise ye") features likewise almost exclusively in the Book of Psalms, and it is with regards to this term that I wish to address the association of the *sefirot* with *Psalm 150*, the last of the five "*Hallelujah Psalms*" which conclude the biblical "Book of Psalms." This very brief psalm comprises exactly six verses reading:

[1] הללו יה הללו אל בקדשו הללוהו ברקיע עזו
[2] הללוהו בגבורתיו הללוהו כרב גדלו
[3] הללוהו בתקע שופר הללוהו בנבל וכנור
[4] הללוהו בתף ומחול הללוהו במנים ועוגב
[5] הללוהו בצלצלי שמע הללוהו בצלצלי תרועה
[6] כל הנשמה תהלל יה הללו יה

Transliteration:
[1] *hal'lu Yah hal'lu El b'kod'sho hal'luhu bir'ki'a ozo*
[2] *hal'luhu vig'vurotav hal'luhu k'rov gud'lo*
[3] *hal'luhu b'teika shofar hal'luhu b'neivel v'chinor*
[4] *hal'luhu b'tof umachol hal'luhu b'minim v'ugav*
[5] *hal'luhu v'tzil'tz'lei shama hal'luhu b'tzil'tz'lei t'ru'ah*
[6] *kol han'shamah t'haleil Yah hal'lu Yah*

Translation:
[1] *Hallelujah*. Praise *El* in His sanctuary; praise Him in the firmament of His power.
[2] Praise Him for His mighty acts; praise Him according to His abundant greatness.
[3] Praise Him with the blast of the horn; praise Him with the psaltery and harp.
[4] Praise Him with the timbrel and dance; praise Him with stringed instruments and the pipe.
[5] Praise Him with the loud-sounding cymbals; praise Him with the clanging cymbals.
[6] Let every thing that hath breath praise *Yah. Hallelujah*.

In the hundred-and-fiftieth Psalm the Divine One is glorified a number of times with the word הללו (*halelu*—"praise ye"). We are informed that as far back as the 13th century, the Provençal Kabbalist Rabbi Yitzhak Saggi Nehor (Isaac the Blind), maintained in his famous epistle to Gerona, that, commencing at the phrase הללו אל בקדשו (*hal'lu El b'kod'sho* —"praise *El* in His sanctuary," (verse 1) and reading to הללוהו בצלצלי תרועה

(*hal'luhu b'tzil'tz'lei t'ru'ah*— "praise Him with the clanging cymbals" (verse 5), the ten appearances of the term הללו (*hal'lu*—"praise ye") align with the ten *sefirot*.[148] In this regard, it is said "he noted that the ten *Halelu's* in verses 1–5 chart a progressive descent from *Hokhmah* to *Shekhinah*, whereas the last two phrases (in verse 6) describe an ascent back to *Binah* and *Hokhmah*."[149] Whilst Kabbalists maintained the attribution of the said ten *Hal'lu*'s to the ten Divine Emanations, it was noted that the term *Halel* appears a total of thirteen times in the current psalm, and this number is said to correspond "to the Thirteen Attributes of Mercy manifested by God's loving-kindness."[150] Others commented that the exact term *Hal'lu* "appears in the psalm twelve times, corresponding to the twelve months of the year,"[151] and that "the last verse is repeated to make it thirteen in order that it corresponds to a leap year having thirteen months."[152]

However, it should be noted that the standard inquisitive mindset of Kabbalists would detect further, as it were, "hidden details" regarding the association of *Psalm 150* with the *sefirot*, and these pertain to the musical aspects of the psalm. In my estimation the "magic" of this psalm, and, for that matter, of the whole of the biblical "Book of Psalms," lies in the word הללו יה (*Hal'lu Yah*—"*Hallelujah*"). After all, the Hebrew appellative for "Psalms," i.e. תהלים (*Tehilim*), correctly translates "Praises," hence a good translation of the "Book of Psalms" would be "Songs of Praise." In this regard, the sole purpose of *Psalm 150* is for religionists to extoll the "abundant greatness" of the Divine One in ecstatic "Song and Dance." That is equally its "magical purpose," and whilst we are informed in one recension of the *Shimmush Tehillim* ("Magical Use of Psalms") that "this psalm is good for answering prayer before your Creator," the primary intention is "to praise Him for the abundance of His miracles, and His mighty deeds which He does every day."[153]

Rabbi Matityahu Glazerson, whom I had the good fortune to listen to during his stay and subsequent visits to South Africa, reminded us that "music, melody, and harmonic sounds have the ability to move and uplift human emotions. They are invaluable tools in man's never-ending quest to praise and laud his Maker. King David himself played seventy musical instruments, and his

Psalm 150 (קן) mentions nine of them, each representing a division in a system of classification relating to the kabbalistic spheres, as well as a category of those human emotions used by man to stir and free his soul to extol God, and help him to fulfill his spiritual potential and purpose."[154] In this regard, the Eternal Living Spirit is acclaimed in *Psalm 150* with the following musical instruments, which are said to align with the *sefirot*.[155] They are listed in exact order of their appearance in the psalm:

1. כתר (*Keter*)—שופר (*Shofar*—"Horn", correctly a "ram's horn").
2. חכמה (*Wisdom*)—נבל (*Neivel*—"Lute" [translated "Psaltry"])
3. בינה (*Binah*)—כנור (*Kinor*—"Harp")
4. חסד (*Chesed*)—תף (*Tof*—"Drum" [translated "Timbrel"])
5. גבורה (*Gevurah*)—מחול (*Machol*—"Dance")
6. תפארת (*Tiferet*)—מנים (*Minim*—"Organ" [translated "String Instruments"])
7. נצח (*Netzach*)—עוגב (*Ugav*—"Flute" [translated "Pipe"])
8. הוד (*Hod*)—צלצלי שמע (*Tzil'tz'lei shama*—"Clanging Cymbals" [translated "Loud-sounding Cymbals"])
9. יסוד (*Yesod*)—צלצלי תרועה (*Tzil'tz'lei t'ruah*—"Sounding Trumpets" [translated "Clanging Cymbals"])

That leaves מלכות (*Malchut*) with no apparent affiliated "instrument." However, further reasoning has it that the word כל (*Kol*—"All"/"Everything") in the last verse of the psalm reading "Let every thing that hath breath [all souls] praise *Yah*. Hallelujah," is referencing the "Voice." In this regard, it was noted that the word כל (*Kol*—"All") "hints to the word 'voice' (קול—*Kol*), since the כ of כל (all) and the ק of קול (voice) are interchangeable."[156] Thus we have:

10. מלכות (*Malchut*)—קול (*Kol*—"Voice")

In Rabbi Glazerson's estimation, "the voice, beyond a means of expressing praises musically, is the most harmonic and versatile instrument of all."[157] Yet it should be kept in mind that the most primary factor underlying not only the voice, but the existence of every living entity, is breath. All life is dependent on breathing in and breathing out. It is in acknowledgement of this reality, that we are reminded in the biblical saga of creation, that humankind "was created as a synthesis of body and spirit, a combination of the 'Divine breath' and the dust of the earth'."[158] In this regard, we are told that "the link between the spiritual soul — the Divine Breath — and the physical breathing that signifies life was noted by the Sages."[159]

Every human who is truly mindful of his or her ability to breathe, would be conscious of the fragility of life. With an inhalation we are born and with an exhalation we die. In this regard, it has been said that the concluding phrase of *Psalm 150* "brings us to an awareness of the breath, rooting our being in the present moment, its reality and blessing. Fully present and mindful, we recognize that at all times, sick or well, we 'have only moments to live'."[160] Translated in a literal manner the mentioned phrase reads "Let every soul praise *Yah*," but in virtually every English translation the expression כל הנשמה (*kol neshamah*—"all souls") is interpreted "every thing that has breath." Some may wonder why this should be, yet the translation is in fair alignment with the teaching in which we find an interplay between the words נשמה (*n'shamah*—"soul") and נשימה (*n'shimah*—breath).[161] We are informed that "the Sages taught: 'For every single breath (*neshima*) that a person takes, he must praise his Creator' (*Gen. Rabbah 14:11*). Underlying this homily—which may be construed as simply a play on words—is the idea of the intimate bond between soul and breath, a bond that was forged at the time of Creation, but lasts for all eternity. In light of this bond, man must give thanks to the Creator of his soul and the Creator of his breath."[162] It was further said that the association of "the word *neshamah* with *neshimah*—breath," means that individuals "should learn to praise God with every breath of life,"[163] and in this regard it has been noted that "the most breathy name of God is used here: *Yah*."[164]

Rabbi Avi Baumol asked "Why would universal praise be considered one of the ultimate acts of mankind?" He responded, "if we were to view it as merely a verbal exercise, then we would agree that God is in no need of, nor does He desire acknowledgment, accolades and commendations. Instead, we realize that praising God is an expression of our desire to acknowledge Him. *God, I know You exist, I recognize You in my life, I am aware of what You have done for me and for all humankind throughout history. I thank You, I praise You. I encourage all those around me to do the same. Let everything and everyone praise You for eternity.*"[165] Whilst I am perfectly aware that the Divine One is eternally the same with or without praise, I am equally aware that I am extolling the infinite goodness of the Creator for my own sake. Like a bird raising its voice at daybreak in exuberant, uncontrolled song, I sense the necessity to raise my voice in joyous praise of the "Infinite Creative Intelligence" behind all existence, doing so whenever I am filled with wonder as I contemplate the magnificence of "Creation." As noted elsewhere, "the English words 'feel,' 'Psalm' and 'palpitate' derive from the same basic root meaning 'to experience' and 'to have sensation of'." In this regard, "I know that I touch and caress the Divine One every time I sing a Psalm," and that "on close reflection I realised that I was doing so inside my own being."[166] Referencing *Psalm 81:10* reading לא יהיה בך אל זר (*lo yih'yeh v'cha eil zar*—"There shall no strange God be in thee"), I mentioned that in my estimation "mystical union" or דבקות (*D'veikut*—"Divine Adhesion"), "is a union in which the Divine One is no stranger, since He is to be found *within* oneself."[167] I further noted that "praise is to value and to commend highly." Thus, "if you love your God and your Tradition, you extol them as a matter of course. This pertains to what Moshe Idel termed 'the theurgy of augmentation,' meaning that in this world you increase the value of your God and your Tradition through הלל (*Haleil*—'Praise')."[168]

Be that as it may, it has been said that the expression הנשמה (*han'shamah*— "the soul") in *Psalm 150:6* "refers to all the powers of the soul,"[169] and we are informed that "there are ten spiritual layers of the soul and the power of song is to awaken each level, slowly reaching the climax of spiritual ecstasy."[170] In this regard, Rabbi Baumol appropriately asked "What's in a song?....What is so great about singing a song to God?....What are the unique gifts of song?"[171] In response he noted:

> "1. Song includes emotions and feelings unbounded by letters and words.
> 2. Song is timeless.
> 3. Song is an equalizer: all can participate, all can enjoy.
> 4. Song draws on many faculties at once: auditory, intellectual, emotional, spiritual.
> 5. Song resonates within people.
> 6. Prophets used song in order to raise their spiritual levels.
> 7. A song is inspirational, infinite and universal.
> 8. Finally, a song can unite disparate instruments or voices into a harmonious symphony of sound, melding unique individuality into an enhanced, sublime collective."[172]

The "song" referenced here is a joyous one, and the basic idea is to praise the Divine One "with each and every breath (*neshima*), so you can say at every moment and continually....*B'rich Rachmana, Malka d'Alma, Marai d'hai Riga* (Blessed is the Merciful One, Sovereign of the Universe, Master of this Moment and Wholly Present),"[173] However, nobody is ever in a state of permanent bliss, and all of us are met with times of great sadness. In this regard, it has been said that "it may require a psycho-spiritual tour de force to praise God with joy and gladness in the midst of illness.... Psalm 150 is nothing short of ecstatic, a glorious symphony which rises to a dazzling crescendo: Shofar blasts, harp and lyre, timbrel, dance, lute and pipe, cymbals crashing loudly, furiously. Perhaps the music one makes is loud and furious to drown out one's own complaint. Perhaps the wildness expresses something crazed. Or perhaps, in a rare moment of grace, one might play the music without fury, in touch with happiness, miraculously connected to

God with praise in one's heart, *lamrot hakol*: Despite everything."[174]

As far as the actual recitation or chanting of this unique psalm is concerned, Jewish worshippers are informed "that the high point in the moment of liturgy connects worshippers to eternal time, to the time beyond time. But as Psalm 150 shows, the liturgy that occurs in the space of the sanctuary is also connected to the space beyond space, the space in which the earthly and heavenly Jerusalem merge.... This is the 'fulness of space' that is filled with dancing, singing, resounding and clanging sounds....Sacred space in Jewish liturgy moves back and forth from profane space outside of Jerusalem carefully through the gates of Jerusalem to the Temple to a process of purification and transformation whereby humans become 'little less than angels.' From this point the transformed ones look out on the world with a new perception in which all space is God's creation and therefore all space is sacred space. God's glory then can be recognized not only in the synagogue, Jerusalem, and the Temple, but everywhere."[175]

Of course, it is perfectly clear that just as not every reader of this book is a religious Jew, neither is every practitioner of the "Magical Use of Psalms" specifically Jewish, with his or her "Sacred Space/Time" focussed "in the synagogue, Jerusalem, and the Temple." Thus, whether you are a Jew or not, the keywords are "all space is God's creation and therefore all space is sacred space."[176] In fact, "sacred space" is within you as well, and in this regard I noted the Divine Name מקום (*Makom*—the "Omnipresent" or "Place") to be referencing "the heart and the sphere of *Tiferet* on the sefirotic Tree."[177] All are One in the "Sacred Space" of your heart. Keeping this in mind, chanting *Psalm 150* in a "magical manner" is simply a matter of focusing on the "Sacred Space" inside your heart, and with great love and joy "sing a new song" unto the Eternal One who resides in the Eternal Now inside your heart.

For readers interested in a beautiful musical rendition of *Psalm 150*, I included the following musical notation referencing a traditional chant, with abeyance to its interpretation by the Israeli singer Eyal Golan:[178]

. ...'I called the golem Yosef,' the Maharal told us, 'because I drew into him the spirit of Yosef Sheyda who is mentioned in the Talmud, a creature half man and half demon, who also served the sages of the Talmud and saved them a number of times from great calamities'... ... ...
.

Chapter 4
Darom — South
The Psalms of David — Book II

PSALM 42

[1] למנצח משכיל לבני קרח
[2] כאיל תערג על אפיקי מים כן נפשי תערג אליך אלהים
[3] צמאה נפשי לאלהים לאל חי מתי אבוא ואראה פני אלהים
[4] היתה לי דמעתי לחם יומם ולילה באמר אלי כל היום איה אלהיך
[5] אלה אזכרה ואשפכה עלי נפשי כי אעבר בסך אדדם עד בית אלהים בקול רנה ותודה המון חוגג
[6] מה תשתוחחי נפשי ותהמי עלי הוחלי לאלהים כי עוד אודנו ישועות פניו
[7] אלהי עלי נפשי תשתוחח על כן אזכרך מארץ ירדן וחרמונים מהר מצער
[8] תהום אל תהום קורא לקול צנוריך כל משבריך וגליך עלי עברו
[9] יומם יצוה יהוה‎אהדונהי חסדו ובלילה שירה עמי תפלה לאל חיי
[10] אומרה לאל סלעי למה שכחתני למה קדר אלך בלחץ אויב
[11] ברצח בעצמותי חרפוני צוררי באמרם אלי כל היום איה אלהיך
[12] מה תשתוחחי נפשי ומה תהמי עלי הוחילי לאלהים כי עוד אודני ישועת פני ואלהי

Transliteration:
[1] *lam'natzei'ach mas'kil liv'nei korach*
[2] *k'ayal ta'arog al afikei mayim kein naf'shi ta'arog eilecha elohim*

[3] *tzam'ah naf'shi leilohim l'el chai matai avo v'eira'eh p'nei elohim*
[4] *haitah li dim'ati lechem yomam valailah be'emor eilai kol hayom ayeih elohecha*
[5] *eileh ez'k'rah v'esh'p'chah alai naf'shi ki e'evor basach edadeim ad beit elohim b'kol rinah v'todah hamon chogeig*
[6] *mah tish'tochachi naf'shi vatehemi alai hochili leilohim ki od odenu y'shu'ot panav*
[7] *elohai alai naf'shi tish'tochach al kein ez'kor'cha mei'eretz yar'dein v'cher'monim meihar mitz'ar*
[8] *t'hom el t'hom korei l'kol tzinorecha kol mish'barecha v'galecha alai avaru*
[9] *yomam y'tsaveh YHVH chas'do uvalailah shiroh imi t'filah l'eil chayai*
[10] *om'rah l'eil sal'i lamah sh'chach'tani lamah kodeir eileich b'lachatz oyeiv*
[11] *b'retzach b'atz'motai cheir'funi tzor'rai b'om'ram eilai kol hayom ayeih elohecha*
[12] *mah tish'tochachi naf'shi umah tehemi alai hochili leilohim ki od odenu y'shu'ot panai veilohai*

Translation:
[1] For the Leader; *Maschil* of the sons of Korah.
[2] As the hart panteth after the water brooks, so panteth my soul after Thee *Elohim*.
[3] My soul thirsteth for *Elohim*, for the living God: 'When shall I come and appear before *Elohim*?'
[4] My tears have been my food day and night, while they say unto me all the day: 'Where is Thy God?'
[5] These things I remember, and pour out my soul within me, how I passed on with the throng, and led them to the house of *Elohim*, with the voice of joy and praise, a multitude keeping holyday.
[6] Why art thou cast down, O my soul? and why moanest thou within me? Hope thou in *Elohim*; for I shall yet praise Him for the salvation of His countenance.
[7] O my God, my soul is cast down within me; therefore do I remember Thee from the land of Jordan, and the Hermons, from the hill Mizar.
[8] Deep calleth unto deep at the voice of Thy cataracts; all Thy waves and Thy billows are gone over me.

[9] By day *YHVH* will command His lovingkindness, and in the night His song shall be with me, even a prayer unto the God of my life.

[10] I will say unto God my Rock: 'Why hast Thou forgotten me? Why go I mourning under the oppression of the enemy?'

[11] As with a crushing in my bones, mine adversaries taunt me; while they say unto me all the day: 'Where is Thy God?'

[12] Why art thou cast down, O my soul? and why moanest thou within me? Hope thou in *Elohim*; for I shall yet praise Him, the salvation of my countenance, and my God.

Psalm 42 is one of a number of psalms recited to express gratitude.[1] It is enunciated in the Sefardi liturgy prior to מעריב (*Ma'ariv*—evening prayer service) on the first two nights of סוכות (*Sukkot*—Festival of Booths),[2] and includes the first of two verses which express the profound yearning of the soul for "Divine Union." The first reads "As the hart panteth after the water brooks, so panteth my soul after Thee *Elohim*" [*Psalm 42:2*], and the second is the phrase "O God, Thou art my God, earnestly will I seek Thee; my soul thirsteth for Thee" [*Psalm 63:2*]. These sublime verses have inspired me over the past fifty years in the endless haunting of the, as it were, "gates" of the *Shechinah*. As noted elsewhere, the *Shechinah-Matronit* is the "Feminine Presence" of the Divine One in manifestation, who comprises the true "Selves" of everyone in creation; the very "Soul" of all manifestation, and is represented by every woman alive.[3]

In Jewish Magic we find the forty-second Psalm is recommended for recitation in conjunction with *Psalms 41* and *43* prior to building a house,[4] or, according to Rabbi Chaim Yosef David Azulai, to build the בית המקדש (*Beit haMikdash*—"Holy Temple").[5] However, the current psalm is listed in the *Shimmush Tehillim* as useful for a variety of purposes. In this regard, as in the case of the previous psalm, *Psalm 42* is recommended for an individual who was dismissed from his place of work, or whose position was given to someone else. The said individual is instructed to recite the current psalm three times a day conjointly with *Psalms 40 and 43*.[6] However, the most important use of the current psalm in "Practical Kabbalah" (Jewish Magic), is for the purposes of dream questioning,[7] which the "Jewish Encyclopedia" note is all about the "interpretation of dreams,"[8] and which others maintain is about finding "help in understanding a dream."[9]

Whatever the manner in which the Hebrew text of the popular published version of the *Shimmush Tehillim* is interpreted and translated into English, we are informed that the forty-second Psalm is good, tried and tested for dream questioning, and in this regard the simplest procedure is to recite the psalm seven times whilst fasting.[10] One recension noted that on the day of working this procedure, the practitioner should rise at the time of his or her morning meal, and then to fast the remainder of the day. Following this action the psalm is recited seven times prior to falling asleep at night.[11] Other recensions of the *Shimmush Tehillim* maintain the Psalm should be recited three times during the day, at a time when you are not speaking to anybody, then again three times in the evening, and once more after having retired to bed.[12]

Godfrey Selig's usual verbose German/English versions of the *Shimmush Tehillim*, aligns here in the main with the standard Hebrew version with minor additions. In this regard he noted that "the 42nd Psalm possesses this peculiar characteristic. If you wish to be sure in regard to a certain cause, and desire to obtain information through a dream, you must fast one day, and shortly before retiring to rest you must pray this Psalm and the holy name, *Zawa*, (which means the Lord of Hosts), belonging to the Psalm, seven times, making known your desires, each time, in an appropriate prayer, in which your wishes should be plainly named."[13] The "holy name" he referenced is the Hebrew word צבא (*Tz'va*—"host") which is said to be the Divine Name associated with the current psalm, and which, as stated in the first part of the current tome, is to be focused on whilst reciting the psalm. In the current instance it is maintained that this Name was derived: צ (*Tzade*) from *Kaf* (כ) in (*k'ayal*—"as the hart"): verse 2, the letter having been converted by means of the אח"ס בט"ע (*Achas Beta*) cipher; ב (*Bet*) from מ (*Mem*) in מה תשתוחחי (*mah tish'tochachi* —"Why art thou cast down"): verse 12, the second letter having been transposed by means of the א"ל ב"ם (*Albam*) cipher; and א (*Alef*) said to have been derived from אלהי (*Elohai*—"my God): verse 7.[14]

It is worth noting that there is no reference in the standard version of the *Shimmush Tehillim* to any "appropriate prayer" to be recited with the associated Divine Name construct. Whilst this is the standard version of the magical use of the current Psalm for the purpose of "Dream Questioning," a different recension of this work maintains the psalm should not only be recited seven times at night after you have retired to bed, but that each recitation should be succeeded with the enunciation of the following prayer-incantation. The latter includes the Divine Name מלך שר צבא (*Melech Sar Tz'va*—"King Ruler of the Host"), and reads:

אל מלך יושב על כסא רחמים תשב בשעה זאת
על כסא רחמים אשר איוותה נפשי לבקש מלפניך
שתעניני ותודעני בלילה הזה דבר [....insert query....]
שאני שואל בדברים אמתיים ונכונים ורצויים על
הלב ומפורשים בלי ספק בהם כלל בשם מלך שר
צבא אמן אמן אמן סלה סלה סלה

Transliteration:
> *El melech yosheiv al kisei rachamim tasheiv b'sha'ah zot al kisei rachamim asher iv'tah naf'shi l'vakesh mil'fanecha sheta'aneini v'todi'eini b'lailah hazeh davar* [....insert query....] *she'ani sho'el b'd'varim amitiyim v'n'chonim ur'tzuyim al haleiv um'furoshim b'li safeik bahem k'lal b'shem Melech Sar Tz'va Omein Omein Omein Selah Selah Selah*

Translation:
> God, King, who sits on a throne of mercy, you shall sit on the throne of mercy in this hour, for my soul desires to inquire before you that you answer me and let me know the matter of [....insert query....] this night, which I ask with true, correct, heartfelt, and explicit words in which there is no doubt whatsoever. In the Name *Melech Sar Tz'va* ["King Ruler of the Host"] *Amen Amen Amen Selah Selah Selah.*[15]

The same recension maintains *Psalm 42* to be equally good for "the answering of prayer." In this regard, the instruction is to recite this psalm three times, each time concluding by enunciating the three Divine/Angelic Names שמועאל מטטרון יהואל (*Shemu'el Metatron Yeho'el*), as well as the Divine Name יֶאֱהֳוֵהְיֶה (*Y'eih'hoveih'yeh*). We are informed that this will ensure that your prayer is answered forthwith.[16] The very potent *Shemu'el Metatron Yeho'el* angelic combination features elsewhere in "Jewish Magic," and is also employed in conjunction with a unique Divine Name construct formed from *Psalm 119:105*,[17] of which more anon. The great "Spirit Intelligences" (angels) bearing these appellatives are said to be covered respectively in the first three divisions of the primordial "Light of Wisdom" which streams from the infinite "hiddenness" of the Eternal One.[18] In this regard, we are informed that the capitals of the names of these three mighty angelic princes spell the word שמי (*sheimi*—"my name"), meaning they bear the "Name" of the Divine One, and thus direct and control the most primary powers of creation.[19]

Be that as it may, the last mentioned recension of the *Shimmush Tehillim* further notes that the forty-second Psalm is good for the purpose of being saved from every need. In this regard, you would need to follow the recitation of the psalm with the following brief supplication:[20]

אנא השם שמע תפילתי והצילני מכל צרה וצוקה ומכל רע

Transliteration:
> *Ana Hashem sh'ma t'filati v'hatzileini m'chol tzarah v'tzukah um'chol ra*

Translation:
> Please *Hashem* hear my prayer and deliver me from every trouble, and anguish, and from all evil.

As readers might expect, there are again individual verses from the current psalm which are employed for magical purposes quite separate from those pertaining to the psalm as a whole. In this regard, the letters comprising *Psalm 42:5* is arranged in the following Divine Name construct:[21]

אֶאֱעָלְרָג לְיִבוֹנְגֶ הֶבְּרְקֹהוּ
אִיבַּבְוֹחַ וְשִׂסְמַח בְּפִכְיוּ
רְנָאהְךָ הְיַדלְהָ וְלַדֵאָה
אֶעְמְתָם שֶׁהָעֵיוּ פְּכַדְבֵּן

This very powerful Divine Name construct is said to be good for protection against danger in a conflagration, i.e. a fire storm, at sea or on land. It necessitates recitation mentally with כוונה (*Kavvanah*), i.e. strongly focused attention and intention. In this regard, the mouth is kept firmly shut, which means that the letters would be formulated in, as it were, a "physical" sense whilst uttering them exclusively in the mind. In this manner you would employ what could be termed "think-speak" to formulate the Divine Name construct, as you would when using your mouth, tongue, and throat. In other words, you focus your attention on sensing each letter being enunciated in the relevant physical locales employed in its standard vocalisation, without moving a single muscle of your face, mouth and throat. This internal enunciation without any audible sound is particularly potent and effective, and is one of my favourite ways of vocalising Divine Names.

 Be that as it may, we are warned not to use this powerful Divine Name construct, except in a condition of holiness and purity in times of great need. We are further informed that it is best to perform this procedure alone in a very clean and special locale, where the practitioner will work unobtrusively, and without being disturbed by anyone.[22] An important point which should be kept in mind by all practitioners of this art, is that it is more important to perform your "magical practices" in private, without seeking acknowledgement or self-aggrandisement. The best work is done when nobody but you and the Eternal Living Spirit are aware of your sacred actions, and perhaps sharing such actions, when it appears necessary to do so, only with those intimates in whom you have absolute trust. In the current instance the Divine Name construct is included in the following prayer-incantation which is uttered audibly, whilst the Divine Name construct is enunciated in the manner delineated:

יהי רצון מלפניך יהוה אלהינו ואלהי אבותינו צוה
אלי למלאכיך הקדושים והטהורים שתשקע אש
הזה ולא ישרף עוד מאומה בשם אָאֶעְלרִג׳ לֵיבוֹנַגֵ
הֱכִרְקֹהָו אֱיַבַּבְוֹחַ זְשַׂסָמְת כְּפִכְיוֹ רָנַאֱהְדָ
הַיַדַלֹהָ וְלַדֵאֱהָ אֱעָמְתָם שְׁהָעַיוֹ פְּכָדְבֵּן ברוך
שם כבוד מלכותו לעולם ועד

Transliteration:

Y'hi ratzon mil'fanecha YHVH eloheinu veilohei avoteinu tzaveih eilai l'mal'achecha hak'doshim v'hat'horim shetish'ka esh hazeh v'lo yisareif od m'umah b'shem Ei'e'el'rig' Leyivonagei Hekir'kohavo Eyibab'v'cho Z'shisam'to K'f'ch'yivo Rana'ehida Hayadaloha V'ladei'eha E'am't'mo Sh'ha'ayeivo P'chad'bein baruch shem k'vod malchuto l'olam va'ed

Translation:

May it be your will *YHVH* our God and God of our fathers, to command to me your holy and pure angels that this fire will abate and burn no more, in the name *Ei'e'el'rig' Leyivonagei Hekir'kohavo Eyibab'v'cho Z'shisam'to K'f'ch'yivo Rana'ehida Hayadaloha V'ladei'eha E'am't'mo Sh'ha'ayeivo P'chad'bein*, blessed be the Name of His glorious Kingdom throughout eternity.[23]

Besides the listed magical applications, I have seen the forty-second Psalm recited against illness in general and for healing. It is equally employed against enemies who cause loss; for protection in all perilous situations, and in times of trouble; to counteract depression, sadness, despair, and especially sorrow resulting from the dissolution of relationships. It is further recited to find favour, and to express gratitude, especially gratitude for good fortune. It is also uttered by Jewish religionists to end the exile.

In contrast to the use in Jewish Magic of *Psalm 42* when losing your employment, in Christian Magic the current psalm is listed in the Byzantine magical manuscripts for the detestable purpose of ousting someone whose office you are coveting.[24] An equally abhorrent use is listed elsewhere in the same manuscripts, in which the forty-second Psalm is employed for the purpose of "compelling the love of a woman by ritual means."[25] Elsewhere we find a modified version of *Psalm 42:2* to stir passionate love in a woman.[26] Thankfully there is also a more benevolent use of the current psalm in Christian magic, in which it is written and carried as an amulet to facilitate the healing of "someone who has been bewitched." In this regard, the instruction is to write the psalm and carry it on the arm.[27] We are further informed that the current psalm is recited to send enemies fleeing.[28] In a similar vein, "*Le Livre d'Or*" maintains that reciting *Psalm 42* three times during "Vespers," i.e. the Roman Catholic evening prayer service, will cause enemies to be dispersed, and result in them having no power over you.[29] Lastly, this psalm is listed in the "*Key of Solomon*" as one of seven psalms, i.e. *Psalms 3, 9, 31 42, 60, 51* and *130,* which are employed in the consecration of "the needle and other iron instruments."[30]

PSALM 43

[1] שפטני אלהים וריבה ריבי מגוי לא חסיד מאיש מרמה ועולה תפלטני

[2] כי אתה אלהי מעוזי למה זנחתני למה קדר אתהלך בלחץ אויב

[3] שלח אורך ואמתך המה ינחוני יביאוני אל הר קדשך ואל משכנותיך

[4] ואבואה אל מזבח אלהים אל אל שמחת גילי ואודך בכנור אלהים אלהי

[5] מה תשתוחחי נפשי ומה תהמי עלי הוחילי לאלהים כי עוד אודנו ישועת פני ואלהי

Transliteration:

[1] *shof'teini elohim v'rivah rivi migoi lo chasid mei'ish mir'mah v'av'lah t'fal'teini*

[2] *ki atah elohei ma'uzi lamah z'nach'tani lamah kodeir et'haleich b'lachatz oyeiv*

[3] *shelach or'cha va'amit'cha heimah yan'chuni y'vi'uni el har kod'sh'cha v'el mish'k'notecha*

[4] *v'avo'ah el miz'bach elohim el el sim'chat gili v'od'cha v'chinor elohim elohai*

[5] *mah tish'tochachi naf'shi umah tehemi alai hochili leilohim ki od odenu y'shu'ot panai veilohai*

Translation:

[1] Be Thou my judge *Elohim*, and plead my cause against an ungodly nation; O deliver me from the deceitful and unjust man.

[2] For Thou art the God of my strength; why hast Thou cast me off? Why go I mourning under the oppression of the enemy?

[3] O send out Thy light and Thy truth; let them lead me; let them bring me unto Thy holy mountain, and to Thy dwelling-places.

[4] Then will I go unto the altar of *Elohim*, unto God, my exceeding joy; and praise Thee upon the harp *Elohim*, my God.

[5] Why art thou cast down, O my soul? and why moanest thou within me? Hope thou in *Elohim*; for I shall yet praise Him, the salvation of my countenance, and my God.

As in the case of the previous psalm, *Psalm 43* is likewise recited in the Sefardi rite prior to *Ma'ariv*, i.e. the evening prayer service, on the first two evenings of *Sukkot* (Festival of Booths). We are informed that the sentiments expressed in the third verse reading " send out Thy light and Thy truth; let them lead me; let them bring me unto Thy holy mountain, and to Thy dwelling-places," are understood to be "the contributing factors for reciting this psalm on the festival of *Sukkot*."[1] In this regard, it is said that the term "light" references the משיח (*M'shi'ach*—"Messiah"), as is written in the concluding phrase of *Psalm 132:17* reading נר למשיחי ערכתי (*arach'ti neir lim'shichi*—"I have prepared a lamp for My anointed"). It is further maintained that the word "truth" in *Psalm 43:3* "indicates Elijah, who is the true and trustworthy prophet," and the concluding phrase "let them bring me unto Thy holy mountain, and to Thy dwelling-places," is said to refer to the Holy Temple.[2] The latter phrase would seem to be the inspiration for the current psalm to be recited in Jewish Magic in conjunction with *Psalms 41* and *42* before building a house,[3] or again, prior to the construction of the "Holy Temple."[4] The current psalm is likewise recited three times a day in conjunction with the previous two psalms, when an individual was dismissed from his profession, the latter having been passed on to someone else.[5] In this regard, I have shared Godfrey Selig's version of this procedure when I addressed the same material in the forty-first Psalm.[6]

Whilst the forty-third is not the most popular psalm in "Practical Kabbalah," it is listed as useful for those who find themselves in a storm at sea.[7] Furthermore, one recension of the *Shimmush Tehillim* maintains that it is good to recite the current psalm, as well as its associated Divine Name שר צבא (*Sar Tz'va*—"Ruler of the Host") included in the following prayer, when an individual has to appear before a judge:

אלהים עניני מהר קדשו (Psalm 3:5) וישמור משפטי
בל יטוחו רשעי ארץ ובל יבעתוחו בשם שר צבא
אמן אמן אמן סלה סלה סלה

Transliteration:
>*Elohim aneini meihar kod'sho (Psalm 3:5) v'yish'mor mish'pati bal yituvu rishei eretz ubal yiv'atuvu b'shem Sar Tz'va Omein Omein Omein Selah Selah Selah.*

Translation:
>May *Elohim answer me from his holy mountain (Psalm 3:5)*, and preserve my legal rights, lest they be bent and overthrown by the wicked of the land, in the name *Sar Tz'va. Amen Amen Amen Selah Selah Selah.*[8]

As in the case of the previous psalm, I have seen the forty-third Psalm employed against enemies who cause loss, and to counteract depression and sadness. It is further recommended to those who have been dismissed from their place of work; to alleviate anxiety caused by enemies; to halt wars, and free prisoners of war. In this regard, it is enunciated by Jewish religionists to end the sorrows of the Jewish people, to protect the fatherland, and also for the building of the Holy Temple. Alternatively the current psalm is equally employed against epidemics; for energy; and for honest love.

It would seem *Psalm 43* is used for a greater variety of purposes in Christian Magic, including the healing of certain physical ailments. In this regard, the Byzantine magical manuscripts instruct an individual with an eye infection to recite this psalm over rose oil, or grape-leaf oil in the absence thereof, and to pour this substance into the eye.[9] Elsewhere in the *De Sigillis*, the pseudo-Arnaldus medical treatise attributed to Arnaldus de Villanova, and which deals with the preparation of twelve astrological amulets, the forty-third Psalm is recited during the preparation of the golden "*sigillum leonis*." In this regard, we are informed that "combining scripture with the astral power of the constellation Leo, the seal offered general protection against kidney and stomach ailments, abscesses, severe fevers, and other afflictions."[10]

On the other hand, the Byzantine magical manuscripts maintain *Psalm 43* to be good when you are faced with the accusations of enemies, and when encountering contempt.[11] Also, on a more positive note, we are informed in "*Le Livre d'Or*" that anyone who wishes to meet with a King, Prince, and presumably any higher authority, should write the forty-third Psalm, following which it is to be attached to the right arm in order to ensure that the said individual will be well received.[12]

PSALM 44

[1] למנצח לבני קרח משכיל
[2] אלהים באזנינו שמענו אבותינו ספרו לנו פעל פעלת בימיהם בימי קדם
[3] אתה ידך גוים הורשת ותטעם תרע לאמים ותשלחם
[4] כי לא בחרבם ירשו ארץ וזרועם לא הושיעה למו כי ימינך וזרועך ואור פניך כי רציתם
[5] אתה הוא מלכי אלהים צוה ישועות יעקב
[6] בך צרינו ננגח בשמך נבוס קמינו
[7] כי לא בקשתי אבטח וחרבי לא תושיעני
[8] כי הושעתנו מצרינו ומשנאינו הבישות
[9] באלהים הללנו כל היום ושמך לעולם נודה סלה
[10] אף זנחת ותכלימנו ולא תצא בצבאותינו
[11] תשיבנו אחור מני צר ומשנאינו שסו למו
[12] תתננו כצאן מאכל ובגוים זריתנו
[13] תמכר עמך בלא הון ולא רבות במחיריהם
[14] תשימנו חרפה לשכנינו לעג וקלס לסביבותינו
[15] תשימנו משל בגוים מנוד ראש בלאמים
[16] כל היום כלמתי נגדי ובשת פני כסתני
[17] מקול מחרף ומגדף מפני אויב ומתנקם
[18] כל זאת באתנו ולא שכחנוך ולא שקרנו בבריתך
[19] לא נסוג אחור לבנו ותט אשרינו מני ארחך
[20] כי דכיתנו במקום תנים ותכס עלינו בצלמות
[21] אם שכחנו שם אלהינו ונפרש כפינו לאל זר
[22] הלא אלהים יחקר זאת כי הוא ידע תעלמות לב
[23] כי עליך הרגנו כל היום נחשבנו כצאן טבחה
[24] עורה למה תישן אדני הקיצה אל תזנח לנצח
[25] למה פניך תסתיר תשכח ענינו ולחצנו
[26] כי שחה לעפר נפשנו דבקה לארץ בטננו
[27] קומה עזרתה לנו ופדנו למען חסדך

Transliteration:
[1] lam'natzei'ach liv'nei korach mas'kil
[2] elohim b'oz'neinu shamanu avoteinu sip'ru lanu po'al pa'al'ta vimeihem bimei kedem
[3] atah yad'cha goyim horash'ta vatita'eim tara l'umim vat'shal'cheim
[4] ki lo v'char'bam yar'shu aretz uz'ro'am lo hoshi'ah lamo ki y'min'cha uz'ro'acha v'or panecha ki r'tzitam
[5] atah hu mal'ki elohim tzaveih y'shu'ot ya'akov
[6] b'cha tzareinu n'nage'ach b'shim'cha navus kameinu
[7] ki lo v'kash'ti ev'tach v'char'bi lo toshi'eini
[8] ki hosha'tanu mitzareinu um'san'einu hevishota
[9] beilohim hilal'nu chol hayom v'shim'cha l'olam nodeh selah
[10] af zanach'ta vatach'limeinu v'lo teitzei b'tziv'oteinu
[11] t'shiveinu achor mini tzar um'san'einu shasu lamo
[12] tit'neinu k'tzon ma'achal uvagoyim zeiritanu
[13] tim'kor am'cha v'lo hon v'lo ribita bim'chireihem
[14] t'simeinu cher'pah lish'cheineinu la'ag vakeles lis'vivoteinu
[15] t'simeinu mashal bagoyim m'nod rosh bal'umim
[16] kol hayom k'limati neg'di uvoshet panai kisat'ni
[17] mikol m'chareif um'gadeif mip'nei oyeiv umit'nakem
[18] kol zot ba'at'nu v'lo sh'chachanucha v'lo shikar'nu biv'ritecha
[19] lo nasog achor libeinu vateit ashureinu mini or'checha
[20] ki dikitanu bim'kom tanim vat'chas aleinu v'tzal'mavet
[21] im shachach'nu shem eloheinu vanif'ros kapeinu l'eil zar
[22] halo elohim yachakor zot ki hu yodei'a ta'alumot lev
[23] ki aleicha horag'nu chol hayom nech'shav'nu k'tzon tiv'chah
[24] urah lamah tishan adonai hakitzah al tiz'nach lanetzach
[25] lamah fanecha tas'tir tish'kach on'yeinu v'lachatzeinu
[26] ki shachah le'afar naf'sheinu dav'ka la'aretz bit'neinu
[27] kumah ez'ratah lanu uf'deinu l'ma'an chas'decha

Translation:
[1] For the Leader; a Psalm of the sons of Korah. *Maschil*.
[2] *Elohim*, we have heard with our ears, our fathers have told us; a work Thou didst in their days, in the days of old.
[3] Thou with Thy hand didst drive out the nations, and didst plant them in; Thou didst break the peoples, and didst spread them abroad.
[4] For not by their own sword did they get the land in possession, neither did their own arm save them; but Thy right hand, and Thine arm, and the light of Thy countenance, because Thou wast favourable unto them.
[5] Thou art my King *Elohim*; command the salvation of Jacob.
[6] Through Thee do we push down our adversaries; through Thy name do we tread them under that rise up against us.
[7] For I trust not in my bow, neither can my sword save me.
[8] But Thou hast saved us from our adversaries, and hast put them to shame that hate us.
[9] In *Elohim* have we gloried all the day, and we will give thanks unto Thy name for ever. *Selah*
[10] Yet Thou hast cast off, and brought us to confusion; and goest not forth with our hosts.
[11] Thou makest us to turn back from the adversary; and they that hate us spoil at their will.
[12] Thou hast given us like sheep to be eaten; and hast scattered us among the nations.
[13] Thou sellest Thy people for small gain, and hast not set their prices high.
[14] Thou makest us a taunt to our neighbours, a scorn and a derision to them that are round about us.
[15] Thou makest us a byword among the nations, a shaking of the head among the peoples.
[16] All the day is my confusion before me, and the shame of my face hath covered me,
[17] For the voice of him that taunteth and blasphemeth; by reason of the enemy and the revengeful.
[18] All this is come upon us; yet have we not forgotten Thee, neither have we been false to Thy covenant.

[19] Our heart is not turned back, neither have our steps declined from Thy path;
[20] Though Thou hast crushed us into a place of jackals, and covered us with the shadow of death.
[21] If we had forgotten the name of our God, or spread forth our hands to a strange god;
[22] Would not *Elohim* search this out? For He knoweth the secrets of the heart.
[23] Nay, but for Thy sake are we killed all the day; we are accounted as sheep for the slaughter
[24] Awake, why sleepest Thou *Adonai*? Arouse Thyself, cast not off for ever.
[25] Wherefore hidest Thou Thy face, and forgettest our affliction and our oppression?
[26] For our soul is bowed down to the dust; our belly cleaveth unto the earth.
[27] Arise for our help, and redeem us for Thy mercy's sake.

The uses of *Psalm 44* in Jewish Magic is somewhat sparse. However, it is listed in "Practical Kabbalah" as a protection against, and to be saved from, enemies.[1] Selig echoes this in his German-English version of the *Shimmush Tehillim*, noting that "if you wish to be safe from your enemies the frequent praying of this Psalm will, it is said, answer your expectations."[2] In this regard, it is maintained that the current psalm should be recited with an unmentioned associated "Name."[3] This psalm is also referenced to be good "for sinners,"[4] and in one manuscript in which we find it noted in terms of being saved from enemies, there is also a reference to it being good for sinners when recited with "its Name."[5] Elsewhere we are told that the "sin" of these "sinners" is that of "nocturnal emission," and in this regard the associated Divine Name is said to be חי (*Chai*—"life"). This is claimed to be a Divine Name construct which was derived: ח (*Chet*) from ה (*Heh*) in קומה (*kumah*—"arise"): verse 27, the letter having been interchanged by means of the א"ל ב"כ (*Albach*) cipher, and י (*Yod*) from אלהים (*Elohim*): verse 2, the glyph having been transposed by means of the א"יק בכ"ר (*Ayak Bachar*) cipher.

In a different recension of the *Shimmush Tehillim* we find *Psalm 44* recommended for someone who suffers a heart condition, i.e. who has "pain in the heart."[7] In this regard, the sufferer is instructed to enunciate the psalm eleven times, each time completing the recitation with the following prayer-incantation:

אלהי הרוחות יהוה שתרפאני רפואה שלימה
ככתוב רפיני יהוה וארפא הושיעני ואושעה כי
תהלתי **אתה** (Jeremiah 17:14) והסר ממני החולי
הרע הזה והכאב הזה כי לא יניחני לעשות מצוה
ולא שום דבר אחר על כן יכמרו רחמיך עלי אלהי
עולם ורפאיני רפואה שלימה במהרה בעגלא ובזמן
קריב אמן אמן סלה סלה

Transliteration:
Elohei haruchot YHVH shetar'peini r'fu'ah sh'leimah kakatuv r'fa'eini YHVH v'eirafei hoshi'eini v'ivashei'ah ki t'hilati atah (Jeremiah 17:14) v'haseir mimeni hacholi hara hazeh v'haka'eiv hazeh ki lo yanicheini l'asot mitz'vah v'lo shum davar acher al kein yich'm'ru rachamecha alai Elohei olam ur'fa'eini r'fu'ah sh'leimah bim'heirah b'agala uviz'man kariv Omein Omein Selah Selah

Translation:
God of souls, *YHVH*, who will completely heal me, as it is written *Heal me YHVH and I shall be healed; save me, and I shall be saved; for Thou art my praise* (*Jeremiah 17:14*) remove from me this bad ailment and this pain, for it does not allow me to fulfill any *Mitz'vah* [sacred religious ordinance] or anything else. Therefore, let your mercy rest upon me God of the Universe, and heal me completely, quickly, suddenly, and soon. *Amen Amen Selah Selah*.[8]

Regarding "matters of the heart" of the more emotional kind, I have seen *Psalm 44* recommended as a remedy to heal misunderstanding between a couple, and to encourage marital love.

It would seem there are not many uses of single verses from the current psalm employed on their own in Jewish Magic. However it should be noted that *Psalm 44:5* is indirectly associated with נלך (*Nelach*), the twenty-first portion of the "*Shem Vayisa Vayet*." In this regard, we are informed that the *gematria* of נלך [נ = 50 + ל = 30 + ך = 20 = 100] equates with that of the word ימלך (*yimloch*—"He shall reign" [י = 10 + מ = 40 + ל = 30 + ך = 20 = 100]), and that a permutation of ימלך (*yim'loch*) is מלכי (*mal'ki*—"my king"). We are informed that the latter term pertains to אתה הוא מלכי אלהים צוה ישועות יעקב (*Atah hu mal'ki elohim tzaveih y'shu'ot ya'akov*—Thou art my King, *Elohim*; command the salvation of Jacob) (*Psalm 44:5*).[9] We are reminded that this pertains to the *mitzvah*, i.e. the sacred duty or good deed, "which is both light unto and nourishment for the soul," this being the מאה ברכות (*mei'ah b'rachot*), "the hundred blessings we need to utter every day [*TB Menachot 43b*], which will aid the raising of the 'fallen sparks'."[10] We might also note that there is an amulet from the Cairo Geniza in which *Psalm 44:7* is "employed as a prayer, before a direct petitionary formula," the latter being about the achievement of success in business.[11]

The use of the forty-fourth Psalm is equally sparse in Christian Magic. It does not appear to feature in the Byzantine magical manuscripts, but it is referenced in "*Le Livre d'Or*" in a procedure designed to destroy enemies.[12]

PSALM 45

[1] למנצח על ששנים לבני קרח משכיל שיר ידידת

[2] רחש לבי דבר טוב אמר אני מעשי למלך לשוני עט סופר מהיר

[3] יפיפית מבני אדם הוצק חן בשפתותיך על כן ברכך אלהים לעולם

[4] חגור חרבך על ירך גבור הודך והדרך

[5] והדרך צלח רכב על דבר אמת וענוה צדק ותורך נוראות ימינך

[6] חציך שנונים עמים תחתיך יפלו בלב אויבי המלך

[7] כסאך אלהים עולם ועד שבט מישר שבט מלכותך

[8] אהבת צדק ותשנא רשע על כן משחך אלהים אלהיך שמן ששון מחברך

[9] מר ואהלות קציעות כל בגדתיך מן היכלי שן מני שמחוך

[10] בנות מלכים ביקרותיך נצבה שגל לימינך בכתם אופיר

[11] שמעי בת וראי והטי אזנך ושכחי עמך ובית אביך

[12] ויתאו המלך יפיך כי הוא אדניך והשתחוי לו

[13] ובת צר במנחה פניך יחלו עשירי עם

[14] כל כבודה בת מלך פנימה ממשבצות זהב לבושה

[15] לרקמות תובל למלך בתולות אחריה רעותיה מובאות לך

[16] תובלנה בשמחת וגיל תבאינה בהיכל מלך

[17] תחת אבתיך יהיו בניך תשיתמו לשרים בכל הארץ

[18] אזכירה שמך בכל דר ודר על כן עמים יהודוך לעלם ועד

Transliteration:
> [1] *lam'natzei'ach al shoshanim liv'nei korach maskil shir yedidot*
> [2] *rachash libi davar tov omer ani ma'asai l'melech l'shoni et sofeir mahir*
> [3] *yof'yafita mib'nei adam hutzak chein b'sif'totecha al kein beirach'cha elohim l'olam*
> [4] *chagor char'b'cha al yareich gibor hod'cha vahadarecha*
> [5] *vahadar'cha tz'lach r'chav al d'var emet v'an'vah tzedek v'tor'cha nora'ot y'minecha*
> [6] *chitzecha sh'nunim amim tach'techa yip'lu b'lev oy'vei hamelech*
> [7] *kis'acha elohim olam va'ed sheivet mishor sheivet mal'chutecha*
> [8] *ahav'ta tzedek vatis'na resha al kein m'shachacha elohim elohecha shemen sason meichaveirecha*
> [9] *mor va'ahalot k'tsi'ot kol big'dotecha min heich'lei shein mini sim'chucha*
> [10] *b'not m'lachim b'yik'rotecha nitz'vah sheigal limin'cha b'chetem ofir*
> [11] *shim'i vat ur'i v'hati oz'neich v'shich'chi ameich uveit avich*
> [12] *v'yit'av hamelech yof'yeich ki hu adonayich v'hish'tachavi lo*
> [13] *uvat tzor b'min'chah panayich y'chalu ashirei am*
> [14] *kol k'vudah vat melech p'nimah mimish'b'tzot zahav l'vushah*
> [15] *lir'kamot tuval lamelech b'tulot achareha rei'oteha muva'ot lach*
> [16] *tuval'nah bis'machot vagil t'vo'enah b'heichal melech*
> [17] *tachat avotecha yih'yu vanecha t'shiteimo l'sarim b'chol ha'aretz*
> [18] *az'kirah shim'cha b'chol dor vador al kein amim y'hoducha l'olam va'ed*

Translation:
> [1] For the Leader; upon *Shoshannim*; a Psalm of the sons of Korah. *Maschil*. A Song of loves.

[2] My heart overfloweth with a goodly matter; I say: 'My work is concerning a king'; my tongue is the pen of a ready writer.
[3] Thou art fairer than the children of men; grace is poured upon thy lips; therefore *Elohim* hath blessed thee for ever.
[4] Gird thy sword upon thy thigh, O mighty one, thy glory and thy majesty.
[5] And in thy majesty prosper, ride on, in behalf of truth and meekness and righteousness; and let thy right hand teach thee tremendous things.
[6] Thine arrows are sharp—the peoples fall under thee—they sink into the heart of the king's enemies.
[7] Thy throne given of *Elohim* is for ever and ever; a sceptre of equity is the sceptre of thy kingdom.
[8] Thou hast loved righteousness, and hated wickedness; therefore *Elohim*, thy God, hath anointed thee with the oil of gladness above thy fellows.
[9] Myrrh, and aloes, and cassia are all thy garments; out of ivory palaces stringed instruments have made thee glad.
[10] Kings' daughters are among thy favourites; at thy right hand doth stand the queen in gold of Ophir.
[11] 'Hearken, O daughter, and consider, and incline thine ear; forget also thine own people, and thy father's house;
[12] So shall the king desire thy beauty; for he is thy lord; and do homage unto him.
[13] And, O daughter of Tyre, the richest of the people shall entreat thy favour with a gift.'
[14] All glorious is the king's daughter within the palace; her raiment is of chequer work inwrought with gold.
[15] She shall be led unto the king on richly woven stuff; the virgins her companions in her train being brought unto thee.
[16] They shall be led with gladness and rejoicing; they shall enter into the king's palace.
[17] Instead of thy fathers shall be thy sons, whom thou shalt make princes in all the land.
[18] I will make thy name to be remembered in all generations; therefore shall the peoples praise thee for ever and ever.

Psalm 45 is said to be good for one who has a nasty, wicked, or evil wife,[1] and presumably equally for an evil husband. Not every published version of the *Shimmush Tehillim* includes the forty-fifth Psalm, but in those in which it is listed, the standard version advises an individual who has an evil wife, to recite the current psalm over olive oil, and then rub his body therewith,[2] or his face according to some recensions.[3]

Addressing *Psalms 45* and *46* conjointly, Godfrey Selig noted "these two Psalms are said to possess the virtue of making peace between man and wife, and, especially, to tame cross wives." In this regard, he likewise stated that "whoever has a scolding wife, let him pronounce the 45th Psalm over pure olive oil, and anoint his body with it, when his wife, in the future, will be more lovable and friendly."[4] However, besides this simple procedure, which I noted is shared in the standard published version of the *Shimmush Tehillim*, we find in another recension of this text a somewhat more expanded procedure of the forty-fifth Psalm being employed against an angry woman.[5] In this instance the instruction is to take olive oil in a new glass vessel, and then to recite the current psalm twenty times over it. Each recitation is succeeded by the following prayer-incantation:

יהי רצון מלפני **אלהי אמן** שתרחם עלי כי ידעתי
כי אתה אל רחום וחנון על כן אני מחלה פניך
שתסיר ממני הרעה הזאת ותטה לב אשתי אחרי
אני [.... personal name ....] לאהבתי ולעשות כל חפצי
ולהטיב אתי בעניין שלא תדיע לי ולא תלך עוד
כנגדי ולא תאמר דבר כנגד דברי כי גלוי וידוע
לפניך מלך רחמן שבטלה אותי מכמה מצוות כי
אני משלשה בני אדם שאמר חכמים זכרונם לברכה
עליהם שחייהם אינם חיים על כן **אלהי אמן** תשיב
אהבתה לאהבתי ותעשה לי כל חפצי בקירוב זמן
אמן אמן סלה סלה

Transliteration:
>*Y'hi ratzon milif'nei Elohei Omein shet'rachem alai ki yada'ti ki atah el rachum v'chanun al kein ani machaleh panecha shetasir mimeni hara'ah hazot v'tateh lev ish'ti*

> *acharai ani* [....personal name ....] *l'ahavati v'la'asot kol chef'tzi ulaheitiv iti b'in'yan shelo tedi'a li v'lo teilech od k'neg'di v'lo tomar davar k'neged d'varai ki galui v'yado l'fanecha melech rachaman shebat'lah oti mikamah mitz'vot ki ani mish'loshah b'nei adam she'amar chachamim zich'ronam liv'rachah aleihem shechayeihem einam chayim al kein Elohei Omein tashiv ahavatah l'ahavati v'ta'aseh li kol chef'tzi b'kiruv z'man Omein Omein Selah Selah*

Translation:

> May it be your will, *Elohei Amen*, for you to have mercy on me, for I know that you are a merciful and gracious God. Therefore, I appease your face, that you may remove this calamity from me and incline the heart of my wife towards me [....personal name....], so that she may love me and fulfill all my desire. Turn the matter of her not sleeping with me to good, no longer opposing me, and speaking no word against my words. For it is evident and known to you, King, Merciful, that she has kept me away from some *Mitzvot*, for I am of the three people about whom the sages, of blessed memory, said that their lives were no life. Therefore, *Elohei Amen*, you should return her affections to love for me, and soon fulfill all my desires. *Amen Amen. Selah Selah.*[6]

The statement in the prayer-incantation regarding "the three people" whose lives are said to be "no life," is derived from the statement in the *Talmud* that "there are three whose lives are not lives, and they are: the one who looks to the table of others for his sustenance; the one whose wife rules over him; and the one whose body is ruled by suffering" [*TB Beitzah 32b*]. Elsewhere in the Talmud the "three types of people whose lives are not lives, due to their suffering," are said to be "the compassionate, the hot tempered (quick tempered/irascible), and the delicate (sensitive)" [*TB Pesachim 113b*].

Be that as it may, *Psalm 45* has been recommended to alleviate certain physical ailments, specifically ailments of the heart, diseases of the kidneys, and pain in the jaws. This psalm is equally employed to reestablish peace between a husband and a wife, but it was also recommended against all manner of troubles and tribulations, as well as to mitigate public disasters. It has been suggested to Jewish religionists as a prayer for the arrival of the Messiah, and it is highly recommended to empower the establishment of universal brotherhood and peace.

The magical application of individual verses of the current psalm is a lot more diverse and interesting. In this regard, it should be noted that *Psalm 45:5* is indirectly affiliated with דני (*Dani*), the fiftieth portion of the "*Shem Vayisa Vayet*." This pertains to the *gematria* of דני [ד = 4 + נ = 50 + י = 10 = 64] which is equal to that of נוגה (*nogah*—a "glowing light" [נ = 50 + ו = 6 + ג = 3 + ה = 5 = 64]). Doubling the *gematria* of דני totals the numerical value of the word צלח (*tzalach*—"to prosper" or "to be successful" [צ = 90 + ל = 30 + ח = 8 = 128]). Since this is said to pertain to the phrase והדרך צלח רכב (*v'hadarcha tz'lach r'chav*— "And in thy majesty prosper, ride on") (*Psalm 45:5*), we are informed that the Name דני is employed to good effect in the generation of prosperity.[7] However, it is the mentioned word צלח (*tzalach*— "prosper") in the fifth verse, which holds the prime position in the following amulet from the acclaimed *Sefer Raziel ha-Malach*,[8] and which was designed to expedite financial success, i.e. to improve financial earnings, and for "furthering business enterprises."[9]

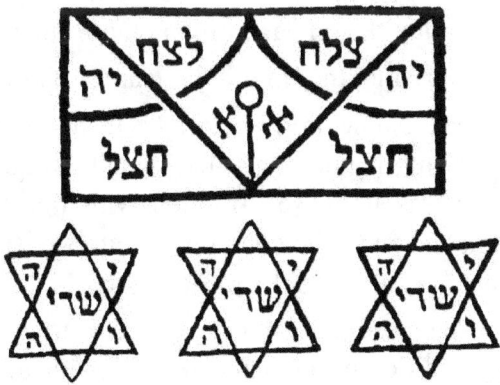

As noted elsewhere, the vital word in the amulet is צלח (*Tzelach*) which is translated "prosper" in the English Bible, but could also be rendered "succeed," the latter being the primary intention of the amulet. As indicated, the *Kamea* is mainly comprised of צלח

(*Tzelach*) and two of its permutations, i.e. לצח top left and twice חצל located bottom right and left. As mentioned before, in Jewish Magic it is fairly common to write "permutations of words representing vital components of the basic intention of the individual requiring an amulet."[10]

Beside the term *Tzelach* and its permutations, we note the combination יה (*Yah*) which is an abbreviation of the Ineffable Name, and itself an acknowledged Divine Name. The double *YH* appearing in the amulet could be read conjointly, i.e. *Yiyeh* meaning "will be." There are also two adjacent letters א (*Alef*) located centrally, these being separated by a short vertical line with a circle on top. Regarding these glyphs, I was told that they are abbreviations of Hebrew terms. In this regard, depending on the context, this letter combination could be read *Amen Amen*; *Adonai Elohecha* (Lord your God); *Ani Omer* (I say); etc. Whilst the current abbreviation could well mean א אמן (*Amen Amen*), I was informed that respectively these letters, when read in conjunction with the first two letters of the Ineffable Name repeated in the amulet, are hidden references to the Divine Name אהיה (*Eh'yeh*).[11]

The bottom portion of the Amulet comprises three images of the "Shield of David," on each of which are superimposed the four letters comprising the Ineffable Name, as well as שדי (*Shadai*), the great "Name of Protection."[12] It should be noted that the following Divine Name construct, which is equally derived from *Psalm 45:5*, is likewise affiliated with this "Amulet for Success." In this instance, the component letters of the said verse were transposed in exact order by means of the א"יק בכ"ר (*Ayak Bachar*) cipher. The resultant Divine Name construct shared in the standard printed edition of the *Sefer Raziel* is indicated to be:[13]

סנמכד טנף כרכ זג מכב יתם עזך
סג טמי סמסברך הכיסס קתקדר

As I noted elsewhere, a very different version appears in the *Sefer Rafael ha-Malach*, and I am informed that there are also variations to be found in the various recensions of the *Sefer Razi'el*. However, Moses Zacutto, who examined all sources of this amulet, maintained in the *Sefer Shorshei ha-Shemot* the correct Names to be:

סַנָמָבְךָ טְגַף בְּרַר זַג מְכַב יֶדֶד סְזַהְסַן
טֵתֵא סְדֹסְבְךָ הֹסְבָקֹסְךָ אִדִיהֵבָ

Keeping in mind the vowel points employed in the said verse, Moses Zacutto noted that this Divine Name construct should be vocalised *Sanamav'ra t'gaf b'rar zag m'chav yeded s'zah'san tete s'dos'v'ra hos'vakos'd' idi'heva*.[14] The amulet also includes the following prayer-incantation reading:

יהי רצון מלפניך יהוה אלהי ישראל שתצוה
למלאכיך אלו לבא אל בית [....name of recipient....]
וללכת עמו ויצליחו אותו בסחורתו ובכל מעשה
ידיו בהצלחה ובהרווחה גדולה בין ביום בין
בלילה בין בבית בין בחוץ לבית בין בעיר בין
בחוץ לעיר ושמך וחותמך הקדוש ירחיבו במעשיו
ובביתו והצליחו ל׳[....name of recipient....] אמן סלה

Transliteration:
    Y'hi ratzon milfanecha YHVH Elohei Yis'ra'eil shet'tzaveh l'mal'achecha elu lavo el beit [....name of recipient....] *v'lalechet imo v'yatz'lichu oto bis'chorato uv'chol ma'aseh yadav b'hatz'lachah uv'har'vachah g'dolah bein bayom bein balailah bein babayit bein b'chutz labayit bein ba'ir bein b'chutz la'ir v'shim'cha v'chotam'cha hakadosh yar'chivu b'ma'asav uv'veito v'hatz'lichu l'*[....name of recipient....] *Omein Selah*

Translation:
    May it be your will *YHVH*, God of the God-wrestler, to command your angels to visit the house of [....name of recipient....], to accompany him, to make him successful with all his endeavours, and bring success in all his actions [works of his hands], and great expansion, whether in the

day, whether in the night; whether at home, whether outside the house; whether in the city, whether outside the city; and in Your Name and with Your Holy Seal, magnify his actions, and expand his house, and bring success to [....name of recipient....] *Amen Selah.*

I was informed to write the amulet, i.e. the associated biblical verse, the set of Divine Names, the magical seals, as well as the incantation, on a "kosher parchment," which is traditionally deerskin. However, as I noted elsewhere, "it works equally well when written on a clean sheet of good quality white paper."[15] Thereafter the completed *Kamea* is carried on the left side of the individual for whom the amulet was written.[16]

It is worth noting that the glyphs comprising *Psalm 45:5* were also reconstituted into a set of ten Divine Name constructs employed to enhance or expand, as it were, the "powers of success" in amulets formulated for financial purposes, or as an additional support in furthering success in business.[17] The said Divine Name construct is as follows:

וועמי התנינ דמותך ראהו דרצא
צבדר לדקו חלונ רעתך כבור

Again as noted elsewhere, the first letters of these ten Divine Names comprise the first ten glyphs of the verse read in the standard manner, these being the first two words of the verse and the first two letters of the third word. Reversing as it were the flow, i.e. commencing with the second letter of the tenth Name, and reading the second letters of the verse in reverse to the first Name, will reveal the concluding letter of the third word, the fourth, fifth and sixth words, as well as the first letter of the seventh word of the current verse. Continuing the flow by reversing direction again and reading the third letter of each Name back to the tenth Name, will indicate the remainder of the seventh word, the eighth word, and the first three letters of the ninth. In conclusion, reversing the flow once more and reading the fourth letters of the ten Divine Names again in reverse, we trace the last two letters of the ninth verse as well as the concluding two words of *Psalm 45:5*.[18]

Whilst the current psalm is employed in its entirety to placate an abusive spouse, the letters comprising *Psalm 45:11* reading שמעי בת וראי והטי אזנך ושכחי עמך ובית אביך (*shim'i vat ur'i v'hati oz'neich v'shich'chi ameich uveit avich*—"Hearken, O daughter, and consider, and incline thine ear; forget also thine own people, and thy father's house"), were arranged into the following Divine Name construct which is employed to find long lasting love, one which is said will endure in both good and bad times:[19]

שְׁחִי מְבַע עְשַׁם יוֹכ
בְכוּתְנֶ וְזִי רְאָת אִיאָ
יִטְב וְהַיְכ

In terms of its application to find love which endures, this Divine Name construct can presumably be both mentally recited and carried as an amulet on the person of the one needing this support.

Be that as it may, it would seem there has been some spillover between Jewish Magic and the Christian variety when it comes to the forty-fifth Psalm, which is listed in the Byzantine magical manuscripts as useful "when one has a quarrel with his wife and is distressed."[20] In this regard, the instruction to the husband is to write the psalm, take some of the hair on his head and to fold this into the centre of the written page, which is afterwards buried at the entrance of a bathhouse. Following this action, the psalm is recited over water at sunrise, and the wife made to wash her face with it."[21] It is curious that there is no consideration by the husband as to why his wife should be behaving in a specific manner.

Curiously enough, similarly to the earlier use of the eleventh verse of the current psalm in Jewish Magic to find enduring love, "*Le Livre d'Or*" advises a man to write the psalm with the name of the woman he desires during the waxing moon. Following the item having been perfumed with certain aromatic herbs and gums, the item is afterwards buried at the entrance of her home, which is said will cause her to love him.[22] *Psalm 45* is additionally listed in the said text as being "good against those who seek to ensnare you under the pretext of offering favours."[23]

PSALM 46

[1] למנצח לבני קרח על עלמות שיר
[2] אלהים לנו מחסה ועז עזרה בצרות נמצא מאד
[3] על כן לא נירא בהמיר ארץ ובמוט הרים בלב ימים
[4] יהמו יחמרו מימיו ירעשו הרים בגאותו סלה
[5] נהר פלגיו ישמחו עיר אלהים קדש משכני עליון
[6] אלהים בקרבה בל תמוט יעזרה אלהים לפנות בקר
[7] המו גוים מטו ממלכות נתן בקולו תמוג ארץ
[8] יהוה‎אדני‎אהדונהי צבאות עמנו משגב לנו אלהי יעקב סלה
[9] לכו חזו מפעלות יהוה‎אדני‎אהדונהי אשר שמות בארץ
[10] משבית מלחמות עד קצה הארץ קשת ישבר וקצץ חנית עגלות ישרף באש
[11] הרפו ודעו כי אנכי אלהים ארום בגוים ארום בארץ
[12] יהוה‎אדני‎אהדונהי צבאות עמנו משגב לני אלהי יעקב סלה

Transliteration:
   [1] *lam'natzei'ach liv'nei korach al alamot shir*
   [2] *elohim lanu machaseh va'oz ez'rah v'tzarot nim'tza m'od*
   [3] *al kein lo nira b'hamir aretz uv'mot harim b'leiv yamim*
   [4] *yehemu yech'm'ru meimav yir'ashu harim b'ga'avato selah*
   [5] *nahar p'lagav y'sam'chu ir elohim k'dosh mish'k'nei el'yon*
   [6] *elohim b'kir'bah bal timot ya'z'reha elohim lif'not boker*
   [7] *hamu goyim matu mam'lachot natan b'kolo tamug aretz*
   [8] *YHVH tz'va'ot imanu mis'gav lanu elohei ya'akov selah*
   [9] *l'chu chazu mif'alot YHVH asher sam shamot ba'aretz*

[10] *mash'bit mil'chamot ad k'tzeih ha'aretz keshet y'shabeir v'kitzeitz chanit agalot yis'rof ba'esh*
[11] *har'pu ud'u ki anochi elohim arum bagoyim arum ba'aretz*
[12] *YHVH tz'va'ot imanu mis'gav lanu elohei ya'akov selah*

Translation:

[1] For the Leader; a Psalm of the sons of Korah; upon Alamoth. A Song.
[2] *Elohim* is our refuge and strength, a very present help in trouble.
[3] Therefore will we not fear, though the earth do change, and though the mountains be moved into the heart of the seas;
[4] Though the waters thereof roar and foam, though the mountains shake at the swelling thereof. *Selah*
[5] There is a river, the streams whereof make glad the city of *Elohim*, the holiest dwelling-place of the Most High.
[6] *Elohim* is in the midst of her, she shall not be moved; *Elohim* shall help her, at the approach of morning.
[7] Nations were in tumult, kingdoms were moved; He uttered His voice, the earth melted.
[8] *YHVH* of hosts is with us; the God of Jacob is our high tower. *Selah*
[9] Come, behold the works of *YHVH*, who hath made desolations in the earth.
[10] He maketh wars to cease unto the end of the earth; He breaketh the bow, and cutteth the spear in sunder; He burneth the chariots in the fire.
[11] 'Let be, and know that I am *Elohim*; I will be exalted among the nations, I will be exalted in the earth.'
[12] *YHVH* of hosts is with us; the God of Jacob is our high tower. *Selah*

Whereas the previous psalm is indicated to be beneficial for an individual who has an angry or vicious wife, *Psalm 46* is said to be useful in the case of a man who hates his wife,[1] or, who "tires of his wife."[2] Yet there are a couple of English versions of the *Shimmush Tehillim*, in which it is maintained that the current psalm is equally "for one whose wife hates him."³ In this regard, I noted earlier that Godfrey Selig addressed *Psalms 45* and *46* conjointly in terms of their virtue "to tame cross wives."⁴ However, as far as the current psalm is concerned, he further noted that "if a man has innocently incurred the enmity of his wife, and desires a proper return of conjugal love and peace, let him pray the 46ᵗʰ Psalm over olive oil, and anoint his wife thoroughly with it, and, it is said, married love will again return."⁵

Be that as it may, all the complete published Hebrew versions of the *Shimmush Tehillim* which I have consulted, maintain *Psalm 46* should be employed by an individual who hates his wife.⁶ In this regard, the simplest instruction to the "hater" is to recite the forty-sixth Psalm over olive oil, following which the woman should anoint her body with it.⁷ However, one recension of the *Shimmush Tehillim* insists that the man should first take some hair from the head of his wife, locate it under the door-hinges of their residence, and then recite the current psalm "with its Name" over olive oil, or rose oil according to some recensions, with which the woman is anointed afterwards.⁸ Other recensions reference only the face of the individual to be anointed.⁹

It should be noted that in all the mentioned instances there is a Divine Name construct associated with *Psalm 46*, which is mostly indicated to be אדי״ה, the origins of which is said to be: א (*Alef*) from אלהים לנו (*elohim lanu*—"God is our [refuge and strength]"): verse 2, and ד (*Dalet*) from נמצא מאד (*nim'tza m'od*—"very present") in the same verse.¹⁰ One recension of the *Shimmush Tehillim* maintained the second glyph to have been derived from ד״ה (*Dalet Heh*), i.e. in accordance with the א״ח ב״ז (*Achbaz*) cipher. This peculiarity might be due to the fact that in one recension the associated Divine Name is said to be אהי״ה (*Eh'yeh*), and the same recension maintains that the ה (*Heh*) was derived from ד (*Dalet*).¹¹ Be that as it may, the concluding two letters of the אדי״ה Divine Name construct is maintained to have been derived: י (*Yod*) from יהוה צבאות (*YHVH tz'va'ot*—"YHVH of hosts"): verse 12; and ה (*Heh*) from סלה (*selah*)¹² or, according to one recension, סלה יעקב (*ya'akov selah*—"Jacob Selah"):

verse 12.[13] Godfrey Selig, who noted that "the holy name is Adojah (this name is composed of the first syllables of the two most holy names of God. Adonai and Jehovah)," generally agrees with the listed origins of the said Divine Name construct, except for the letter י (*Yod*) which he maintains was derived from the Ineffable Name in verse 8.[14]

In another variant of the *Shimmush Tehillim* the Divine Name of the current psalm is said to be אהיה אשר אהיה (*Eh'yeh asher Eh'yeh*—"I am that I am"), which is equally employed "for a person who hates his wife."[15] Curiously enough, we find the latter Divine Name listed for the very same purpose in a Hebrew magical manuscript titled קבלה מעשית וסגולות (*Kabbalah Ma'asit uSegulot*—"Practical Kabbalah & Magical Virtues").[16] Be that as it may, in this instance the magical procedure shared in the said version of the *Shimmush Tehillim* is very different indeed. In this instance the man is instructed to take one of his hairs, and locate it "under the sign of his nakedness," the latter being a euphemism for the sexual organ. I presume that, in the light of the previous instructions, the hair should be taken from his head. Whatever the case may be, following this action, the said individual should then recite the forty-sixth Psalm with its associated Divine Name, and then place the hair in rose oil. The poorly treated woman is afterwards expected to anoint her face with this oil, and it is said love will be established between them by means of this substance.[17] The procedure is concluded with the recitation of the following prayer-incantation:

יהי רצון מלפניך אהיה אשר אהיה שתתן אהבה
[....name of the male....] ואחוה שלום ורעות בין
ו[....name of the female....] בשם אהיה אשר אהיה אל
רחום וחנון ארך אפים ורב חסד ואמת (*Exodus 34:6*)
(*Psalm 86:15*;) יהיה הדבר הזה לאהבה גדולה
ל[....name of the male....] מ[....name of the female....] אמן
אמן אמן סלה סלה סלה

Transliteration:
> *Y'hi ratzon mil'fanecha Eh'yeh asher Eh'yeh shetitein ahavah v'ach'vah shalom v'rei'ut bein* [....name of the male...] *u'* [....name of the female...] *b'shem Eh'yeh asher Eh'yeh el rachum v'chanun erech apayim v'rav chesed v'emet* [*Exodus 34:6; Psalm 86:15*] *yih'yeh hadavar hazeh l'ahavah g'dolah l'* [....name of the male....] *mi* [....name of the female....] *Omein Omein Omein Selah Selah Selah*

Translation:
> May it be your will *Eh'yeh asher Eh'yeh*, that you grant love and brotherhood, peace and companionship between [....name of the male....] and [....name of the female....]. With the name *Eh'yeh asher Eh'yeh, God, merciful and gracious, long-suffering, and abundant in goodness and truth* [*Exodus 34:6; Psalm 86:15*]. This will be the (magic) word for great love from [....name of the male....] to [....name of the female....] *Amen Amen Amen Selah Selah Selah*.[18]

Before considering the magical uses of individual verses of the current psalm, I should mention that besides being recited to revitalise love and companionship between a husband and wife, and equally to reestablish peace in a marriage, *Psalm 46* has been recommended for recitation when an individual is getting married. It is equally employed to strengthen faith, to invoke peace generally,[19] and was recommended for recitation conjointly with *Psalm 47* to halt a war.

As far as the application of individual verses for magical purposes is concerned, it should be noted that *Psalm 46:2* is directly associated with מום (*Mum*), the concluding tri-letter portion of the *Shem Vayisa Vayet* ("Name of Seventy-two Names"). In this regard, we are informed that the *gematria* of מום [מ = 40 + ו = 6 + מ = 40 = 86] is equal to that of the Divine Name אלהים [א = 1 + ל = 30 + ה = 5 + י = 10 + מ = 40 = 86], and this is said to relate to the said verse, as well as to *Psalm 67:2*.[20]

Apart from this, it is worth noting that the capitals of the first three or five words comprising *Psalm 46:8* are respectively combined into the Divine Name constructs יצע and יעמעל,

which are employed in amulets as a call for help.[21] However, it should be noted that *Psalm 46:12* is the exact repeat of the eighth verse, and thus could be equally applicable for the same purpose. Be that as it may, *Psalm 46:8* is also said to be the source of the following important Divine Name construct in Jewish Magic.[22] Beyond the fact that the thirty-one letters comprising the seven "Sacred Names" of this Divine Name construct, are equal in number to that of the Hebrew glyphs in the said verse, I have been unable to ascertain exactly how these Names were derived from the said verse. Whatever the case may be, the "Seven Sacred Names" are listed as:[23]

יְמַת מַת סְטִיט סְטִיטְיָה
אַגְרֶפְטִי מֵרוּם שַׁמְרִיאֵל

Vocalised *Y'tat Tat S'tit S'tit'yah Agrap'ti Meirum Sham'ri'eil*,[24] or alternatively *Yitat [Yatat] Tat Satit Satit'ya Agrep'ti Marom [M'rom] Sham'ri'el*,[25] it should be noted that six of the seven Names comprising this Divine Name construct, are said to be acronyms.[26] In studying these, I relied mainly on the details shared in *Shoshan Yesod ha-Olam*,[27] since these appear to me to be the most reliable. Thus, in terms of their acronym status, the mentioned six Divine Names are indicated to represent:

ימת	יה טוב תחיה	(*Yah tov tich'yeh*—"*Yah* to live good")
מת	טוב המותה	(*tov t'mutah*—"good death [mortality]")
סטיט	סוד טוב יד טוב	(*sod tov yad tov*—"a good secret, a good hand")
סטיטיה	סוד טהור יעלה טובו יעלה הוויתו	(*sod tahor ya'aleh tovo ya'aleh haviyato*—"the pure secret will raise his goodness, will elevate his existence [being]")
אגרפטי	אדיר גדולתו רבע פאתי טובו יהוה	(*Adir*—"mighty is his greatness, a quarter of the goodness of *YHVH*")

שדי מביט רואה יתגלו אליו לבבות   שמריאל

(*Shadai mabit ro'ah yit'galo eilav l'vavot*—"*Shadai* [Almighty] looks to see that hearts will turn to him")

The seven Divine Names are also aligned with what is termed שבע רזי חותמת (*Sh'va razi chotamet*—"Seven Mystical Seals"), and these mysterious "Seals" have been depicted in several ways, with four variances to be found in a single manuscript (trace right to left):

1a. [28]
1b. [28]
1c. [28]
1d. [28]
2a. [29]
2b. [29]
3. [30]
4. [31]

Dating back to around the thirteenth century, these seals have been attributed to, amongst others, "the great Rabbi Moshe bar Nachman," i.e. Nachmanides, whom we are told "would use it when necessary."³² In case you are wondering which of the listed sets of enigmatic symbols should be considered "correct," so to speak, only the first of the two sets (2a) attributed to the *Ramban*, and published in the *Toldot Adam*, has been designated "wrong."³³ Whichever of the listed illustrations of the "Seven Mystical Seals" may pique your interest, it should be noted that in delineating the meaning of each of the seven symbols, the seals were respectively assigned a specific designation which I believe will aid you in ascertaining the "correct" set. In this regard versions 3 and 4 fit the bill. They were included in the writings of Rabbi Aryeh Kaplan, and are most popularly employed today.³⁴ Whilst the size of this tome precludes the inclusion of the complete explication of the seven seals, this is not of any specific value in terms of the magical applications of psalms addressed in this tome. Hence for interest sake I am sharing below only the seven simple descriptions included in the primary manuscripts, which was translated by Rabbi Aryeh Kaplan in his acclaimed *Sefer Yetzirah* in the following manner:³⁵

1.	◯	*Yitat*	"Ring"
2.	⫘	*Tat*	"Spear over three lines"
3.	⌒	*S'tit*	"Curved line"
4.	H	*S'tit'yah*	"Ladder with two steps"
5.	‖‖‖‖	*Agrapti*	"Spear over four lines"
6.	◯	*Marom*	"Ring"
7.	↙	*Sham'ri'eil*	"Crooked *Mem*"

There are further correspondences of the "seven kind" aligned with the "Seven Mystical Seals," e.g. seven planets, seven days, seven angels, etc.³⁶ In this regard, we are informed that the "*Malachim* (Angels) express their energy in the Seven Mystical Seals."³⁷

However, whilst the days of the week feature prominently in the manufacture of a unique amulet to aid a woman who suffers difficulties during childbirth,[38] and who finds herself in grave danger, the mentioned "magical correspondences" are equally not of any specific value in terms of this magical application of the seven Divine Names and "Seven Mystical Seals" addressed here. As far as the said amulet is concerned, this item is constructed from pure new lead, i.e. it should be free from any admixture of other metals, and it should not have been employed previously for any other purpose whatsoever.[39] However, the construction of the amulet necessitates special purification and preparation of the practitioner beforehand. Thus the said individual is expected to be prepared "in all manner of holiness and purity," and have a ritual submersion in a *Mikveh* every day during the manufacture of the amulet. In this regard, the practitioner is instructed to cut the nails of his hands and his feet before the first submersion, to remove all dirt from his body, comb his hair, to wear a clean white shirt and white trousers while engraving the Seals and Divine Names. The said individual is further expected to put on new footwear which has not stepped in mud or muck of any kind.[40]

When properly prepared in this manner, and whilst focussing firmly on the intention to create this specific amulet, the procedure commences by shaping the lead into a square tablet, and writing the name of the woman on the amulet. This is usually done by indicating her identity as "so-and-so born of so-and-so."[41] As noted previously, it is often difficult to follow this format today when, other than Jews, the identities of most individuals cannot be ascertained in this manner. In this regard, I have observed amulets constructed in the standard name and surname of the one requiring the item, and this worked perfectly well. Be that as it may, the said action is succeeded by engraving the "Seven Mystical Seals" one per day with a new knife, and ensuring that all the seals are in a single format (style). Thus having concluded engraving the lead tablet with the seals on the seventh day, the associated seven Divine Names are similarly etched into the lead one per day, and all located directly underneath their respective seals. The amulet is thus completed in fourteen or fifteen days.[42]

Naturally this amulet should be prepared in advance of the woman going into labour. In the case of difficulties being encountered during the birth process, the amulet is placed on her left thigh, and it is said she will give birth forthwith.[43] In this

The Psalms of David — Book II : 81

regard, everybody around her is instructed to stand back from her when she gives birth, for the fact that she has been sorely tried, and lest she is being endangered.[44] The amulet is indicated to be of further benefit for the woman. In this regard, it is recommended to the woman to carry the item in a bag suspended around her neck, so as to aid her in returning to her original strength.[45]

Aside from the mentioned support for a woman who suffers distress during labour, the current amulet is said to be "of great benefit," and most useful in saving an individual from every evil, bad incidents, and wicked plots, and similar matters. In this regard, the amulet is prepared in exactly the same manner as delineated earlier, ensuring that the Seals and Names are clearly illustrated and that each of the Names is precisely located under a relevant seal.[46] A further instruction, is that in the current instance the practitioner is not allowed to eat or drink anything prior to the daily inscription of the lead tablet with a Seal and Divine Name. Likewise the individual employing the amulet for any of the said purposes, is required to fast every day until that matter is settled.[47]

A curiosity about this amulet is that it is referenced in the *Toldot Adam* as having been employed as a kind of "magical GPS." It is said that in the case of a murder having been committed, if the tablet is hung on the mast of a ship the vessel will be guided directly to "the killer without any impediment and delay at all."[48] However, there is again the proviso that this action requires great sanctity, purification, and a ritual submersion of the user. Some might well wonder whether this should work with our modern motorised vehicles.

Whatever the case may be, the amulet is as indicated mainly employed for difficulties during childbirth. In this regard, it should be noted that the seven Divine Names are equally employed without the "Seven Mystical Seals" for the same purpose. In this instance, the Divine Name construct is written on a kosher deerskin parchment, but, as noted earlier, a clean white sheet of good paper will suffice. The practitioner is again exhorted to dress in white garments (shirt and pants), and to have a ritual submersion prior to writing the amulet.[49] The Divine Name construct חוֹק חֹזָק חָדָשׁ חֲזִיר יְבוּשׁ אוּפִילָה (*Chok Chovak Chadash Ch'zir Y'vush Ufilah*) is included in the amulet, and the practitioner is further exhorted to ensure that this Divine

Name is not written adjacent to the first set of seven Divine Names, but is located in a separate space on the parchment. A further proviso is that this Divine Name construct should be written in *Ashurit* (Biblical script) with the threefold שעטנ"ז ג"ץ (*ShATNeZ GaTz*) *Tagin* (crownlets), as indicated below:[50]

When required the properly prepared amulet is placed under the navel of the pregnant woman who is believed will be alleviated from the travails of a difficult confinement, and caused to give birth right away.[51]

The forty-sixth Psalm is employed in Christian magic for a very different reason to those listed in "Practical Kabbalah." Thus we read in "*Le Livre d'Or*" that *Psalm 46:1–10* is recited seven times to render one invincible in armed combat.[52] Aside from this application, *Psalm 46* is one of nineteen psalms in the "Key of Solomon," which are recited over the wax from which ritual candles are constructed, the full compliment of psalms being *Psalms 8, 15, 22, 46, 47, 49, 51, 53, 68, 72, 84, 102, 110, 113, 126, 130, 131, 133,* and *139*.[53]

PSALM 47

[1] למנצח לבני קרח מזמור
[2] כל העמים תקעו כף הריעו לאלהים בקול רנה
[3] כי יהוה‎ אדני‎ עליון נורא מלך גדול על כל הארץ
[4] ידבר עמים תחתינו ולאמים תחת רגלינו
[5] יבחר לנו את נחלתנו את גאון יעקב אשר אהב סלה
[6] עלה אלהים בתרועה יהוה‎ אדני‎ בקול שופר
[7] זמרו אלהים זמרו זמרו למלכנו זמרו
[8] כי מלך כל הארץ אלהים זמרו משכיל
[9] מלך אלהים על גוים אלהים ישב על כסא קדשו
[10] נדיבי עמים נאספו עם אלהי אברהם כי לאלהים מגני ארץ מאד נעלה

Transliteration:
   [1] lam'natzei'ach liv'nei korach miz'mor
   [2] kol ha'amim tik'u chaf hari'u leilohim b'kol rinah
   [3] ki YHVH el'yon nora melech gadol al kol ha'aretz
   [4] yad'beir amim tach'teinu ul'umim tachat rag'leinu
   [5] yiv'char lanu et nachalateinu et g'on ya'akov asher aheiv selah
   [6] alah elohim bit'ru'ah YHVH b'kol shofar
   [7] zam'ru elohim zameiru zam'ru l'mal'keinu zameiru
   [8] ki melech kol ha'aretz elohim zam'ru mas'kil
   [9] malach elohim al goyim elohim yashav al kisei kod'sho
   [10] n'divei amim ne'esafu am elohei av'raham ki leilohim maginei eretz m'od na'alah

Translation:
   [1] For the Leader; a Psalm for the sons of Korah.
   [2] O clap your hands, all ye peoples; shout unto *Elohim* with the voice of triumph.
   [3] For *YHVH* is most high, awful; a great King over all the earth.
   [4] He subdueth peoples under us, and nations under our feet.

[5] He chooseth our inheritance for us, the pride of Jacob whom He loveth. *Selah*
[6] *Elohim* is gone up amidst shouting, *YHVH* amidst the sound of the horn.
[7] Sing praises to *Elohim*, sing praises; sing praises unto our King, sing praises.
[8] For *Elohim* is the King of all the earth; sing ye praises in a skilful song.
[9] *Elohim* reigneth over the nations; *Elohim* sitteth upon His holy throne.
[10] The princes of the peoples are gathered together, the people of the God of Abraham; for unto *Elohim* belong the shields of the earth; He is greatly exalted.

Psalm 47 celebrates Divine Kingship, and is recited seven times in most Jews communities on *Rosh Hashanah* (Jewish New Year) directly prior to the sounding of the *Shofar* (Ram's Horn).[1] Reckoned amongst the oldest musical instruments which is still being in use today, the *Shofar* is much older than Judaism.[2] Its pre-biblical use was mainly for magical purposes, since it was believed that its sound banished demons. The same application is referenced in the *Talmud* in which it is maintained that the *Shofar* can banish evil spirits.[3] Hence, as far as its use on *Rosh Hashanah* is concerned, we are informed that the "the sounding of the shofar on Rosh Hashana is accompanied by the same religious-magical awe, the same faith in the shofar's power to subdue the mightiest forces of nature and overcome the greatest evil."[4] For Jewish religionists the most terrifying "Spiritual Force" which they would like to avoid at the, as it were, "great reckoning" on *Rosh Hashanah*, is what has been termed the "'prosecuting attorney,' the angel who seeks to convict people when they are on trial for their lives,"[5] and which is equally said is blasted away by the *Shofar* on this High Holy Day.[6] None of these details feature in the Hebrew Bible, in fact, we are reminded that there is no reason listed in the *Torah* for blowing the *Shofar* on *Rosh Hashanah*.[7] However, it should be noted that *Psalm 47:6* informs us that the Divine One ascends "amidst the sound of the *Shofar*." In this regard, it has been noted that since this statement "alludes to God arising to the Throne of Judgment and ascending to the Throne of Mercy," it is "most fitting to recite the psalm on Rosh Hashanah."[8] Yet we are also reminded that "the sounding of the Shofar" is "the most ancient rite in the Rosh Hashanah observances," and "has been interpreted as a summons to the soul to present itself before God's judgment seat."[9] However, the blast of the *Shofar* on this High Holy Day is not only to acknowledge "Divine Judgment," but equally "to inspire mankind and to arouse God's mercy."[10] Thus the sounding of the *Shofar* on *Rosh Hashanah* "symbolizes the individual soul's redemption from its sins."[11]

It is highly likely that many modern readers of magical literature, who perhaps have adopted a most judgmental stance on the so-called "Abrahamic religions," will find this talk of "Divine Sovereignty," "Throne of Judgment," "arousing Divine Mercy," and "redemption from sins" to be archaic, uncomfortable, and unacceptable. Yet I should make it plain that such views show a lack of understanding of what these concepts are all about. As I noted elsewhere, in my estimation "we are punished *by* our sins, not *for* them. Hence when I pray for 'mercy' from the Eternal Living Spirit, I am attempting to rectify my position of imbalance whilst aligning with the, as it were, natural 'Forces of Correction' within the vast ocean of Collective Consciousness which we all share, and in which the 'laws of cause and effect,' or, perhaps better, the 'process of rectification' functions automatically."[12] As said before, "'sin' is obviously wrongful behaviour which damages us by the doing in such a way, that we fail to achieve anything like the 'Intention of God' in ourselves for our period of incarnation. Therefore, in 'falling short' of the mark by so far, we hinder our progression towards 'Perfection' by that much. In sinning against ourselves, we sin against the 'God-in-us'."[13] It has been said that the Divine One "exercises His sovereignty through us,"[14] and thus to assign to others the responsibility of our personal ethical behaviour is to deny the establishment of Divine Kingship within ourselves.

Furthermore, in the same manner as the "Kingdom of God" is within you, so is your "salvation" in your own hands. Therefore it has been said regarding the blast of the *Shofar* on *Rosh Hashanah*, that תרועת מלך (*t'ru'at melech*—"saluting the King") is for Jewish worshippers a "salute to the Sovereign, with all its implications of fealty and allegiance," as well as an invitation to renew our "oath of unqualified allegiance and loyalty to those ideals."[15] Thus the onus is really on you to live mindfully and to constantly improve your behaviour whilst incarnated in the flesh. In this regard, it has been said that the phrase in *Psalm 81:4* reading תִּקְעוּ בַחֹדֶשׁ שׁוֹפָר (*tik'u bachodesh shofar*—"blow the horn at the new moon"), the word חדש (*Chodesh*—"new moon") infers שפרו מעשיכם (*shaf'ru ma'aseichem*—"improve your deeds").[16] We are told it is as if "the Holy One, blessed be He, said: 'My children, if you will improve your deeds, I will act unto you as the Shofar. Just as you blow into one end of the Shofar and the sound comes out at the other end, so will I rise from the throne of law and sit on the throne of mercy, changing my attribute of law to that of mercy'."[17]

Thus we have come full circle, and arrived back at *Psalm 47:6* informing us that "*Elohim* is gone up amidst shouting, *YHVH* amidst the sound of the horn." These two Divine Names are respectively the "Measure of Justice" and the "Measure of Mercy,"[18] i.e. the *sefirot* of גבורה (*Gevurah*—"Might") and חסד (*Chesed*—"Lovingkindness") on the sefirotic Tree, depicted as the "Throne of Justice" and the "Throne of Mercy." However, it is said there is a single "Throne of Glory" with two sides of which "one side is high and one side is low."[19] In this regard we are told:

> "When the Holy One blessed be He sits on the chair in the measure of justice, then he is elevated, sitting and ascending on the high side, as it is said: God has risen in the voice of the shofar (Psalm 47:6). Elohim is the measure of justice, and then he arises, when he hears the cry of Israel, Lord is the measure of mercy, the voice of shofar [means] that when they pray loudly they improve their deeds, and then it is transformed to the measure of mercy, it is as if the glory descends to the lower side of the throne. And then it is called YHVH, because [El] YHVH in etbash is MTzPTz [מצפץ], which is, in gematria, 'with mercy' [ברחמים— *b'rachamim*] This is the name of his holiness without a form or image, only voice and wind and speech, and he is like the lights in the west, and this is 'for I am holy, I the Lord' (*Leviticus 20:26*)."[20]

In the current instance the most significant Divine Name is אלהים (*Elohim*), which we are told "refers to God's manifestation as the Dispenser of Strict Justice."²¹ This Divine Name appears seven times in the forty-seventh Psalm, which, as noted, is recited seven times on *Rosh Hashanah*. This figure is said to pertain to the "seven firmaments,"²² i.e. the "seven heavens through which prayers must penetrate to reach the throne of God";²³ the "seven circuits around Jericho before the walls fell";²⁴ and probably several other "sevens" addressed in Jewish Mysticism, i.e. the "Seven Planets"; "Seven Days of the Week"; "Seven Lower *Sefirot*"; etc. There is certainly much meaning to be found in the sevenfold recitation of the current psalm. We are informed that by repeating the psalm the said number of times, the Divine Name אלהים (*Elohim*) is uttered forty-nine times. In this regard, we are told "the Sages teach that there are forty-nine levels of spiritual impurity before the lowest depth from which no redemption is possible. Correspondingly, there are forty-nine ascending levels of sanctity which man can attain. The forty-nine times which the Name is recited allude to the power of these verses to transform the forty-nine possible levels of spiritual uncleanliness into forty-nine corresponding levels of sanctity and purity. When Israel is inspired to purify and perfect itself with such intensity, surely God's strict justice will be changed to His Attribute of Mercy.²⁵ Thus we concentrate on the Divine Name אלהים (*Elohim*) as we recite *Psalm 47* seven times in recognition of the sovereignty of the Divine One, and to enthrone Him in our hearts, as we escort the Divine Glory, i.e. the *Shechinah*, "down to the Throne of Mercy."²⁶

The, as it were, "Power of Seven" associated with the current psalm, appeared to have spilled over into the magical application of the forty-seventh Psalm. Whilst some works references *Psalm 47* to be enunciated for repentance (*Teshuvah*),²⁷ "to do penance,"²⁸ and "to win favour,"²⁹ without any indications of repeated recitations, the standard published recension of the *Shimmush Tehillim* maintains that the psalm should be recited seven times each day in order to be received kindly by all people.³⁰ Godfrey Selig's version of this text is in agreement, adding "do you wish to be beloved, respected and well received by all your fellow-men, pray this Psalm seven times daily."³¹ However, differences do appear in some recensions of the *Shimmush Tehillim* regarding the magical applications of the forty-seventh Psalm. In this regard, we are told that *Psalm 47* is good to pray for Divine support when enemies besiege and attack a city. In this regard, it is said that, in order to strengthen his troops and to protect himself, a troop commander should recite the current psalm nineteen times over olive oil, and anoint his troops therewith every day. Here the recitation of the psalm is concluded with the following prayer-incantation:

רחמנא דבשמיא חוסנא ורחם ופרוק ושיזיב יתי מכל
בר איש וית כל חילותי ואתחזק ואתגבר לבל יהיו נא
נחלשים ונהרגים במלחמה אף כל אשר יפגעו יפילו
חללים מושלכים ארצה בשם אדון יהיה זה הדבר
אמן אמן אמן סלה סלה סלה

Transliteration:
> Rach'mana d'bish'maya chusana v'racheim up'rok v'siziv yati mikol bar ish v'yat kol cheiloti v'it'chazeik v'it'gaber l'bal yih'yu na nech'lashim v'neheragim bamil'chamah af kol asher yif'g'u yapilu chalalim mush'lachim ar'tzah b'shem Adon yih'yeh zeh hadavar Omein Omein Omein Selah Selah Selah

Translation:
> Merciful One who is in heaven, strengthen, and have mercy, and redeem, and save me before everyone and all my troops. I will strengthen and fortify myself so that, please, they will not be weakened and slain in war. Also all that they hurt and overthrow, the slain thrown to the earth. In the name *Adon* it will be the so. *Amen Amen Amen Selah Selah Selah*.[32]

Besides the listed applications, I have seen *Psalm 47* recommended to those who seek to be uplifted; to find work; to be loved and respected by their fellow humans; and is also enunciated during childbirth. As noted earlier, the current psalm is recited conjointly with *Psalm 46* to halt a war, and, interestingly enough, it is employed in haunted houses.

In Christian Magic *Psalm 47:1–9* is listed in the Byzantine manuscripts in conjunction with a set of magical symbols as useful in support of "a woman who miscarries."[33] In this regard, the practitioner is advised to fast for three days, consuming only bread and water, and to recite the psalm seven times over olive oil. Following this action, the lower back and thighs of the woman in question is anointed with the oil. The said individual is then required to carry the magical symbols on her person.[34] The forty-seventh Psalm is otherwise referenced in "*Le Livre d'Or*" as useful for individuals who want to be fortunate in everything. In this regard, they are instructed to copy the psalm, carry it on their persons, and recite it seven times per day. In this way what "you desire will come to you in all goodness, and your enemies will not be able to harm you."[35] A similar use is listed in a Solomonic grimoire in which an individual desiring "to be lucky in all things," is advised to recite the current psalm before sunrise and prior to eating anything.[36]

Elsewhere we find the *Psalm 47* employed for purposes which are similar to the Jewish magical applications. In this regard, verses 3 and 4 of the current psalm are employed "to be pleasing to all men and to obtain their favours," and verses 3 and 5 "to be lucky in all affairs."[37] *Psalm 47:4* is equally employed on its own for the purpose of finding favour with authorities, but in this instance the primary intention is to enforce the "supreme and undying love of a king, prelate, lord or, in general, any man you wish," by means of an elaborate ritual.[38]

In conclusion it should be noted that *Psalm 47* is one of six listed in the *Key of Solomon* to be recited before or during the creation of the magic circle, the others being *Psalms 2, 54, 67, 68* and *113*.[39] It is likewise one of nineteen psalm enunciated over the wax from which ritual candles are constructed, the full compliment being *Psalms 8, 15, 22, 46, 47, 49, 51, 53, 68, 72, 84, 102, 110, 113, 126, 130, 131, 133,* and *139*.[40]

PSALM 48

[1] שיר מזמור לבני קרח
[2] גדול יהוה‎אדני‎יאהדונהי ומהלל מאד בעית אלהונו הר קדשו
[3] יפה נוף משוש כל הארץ הר ציון ירכתי צפון קרית מלך רב
[4] אלהים בארמנותיה נודע למשגב
[5] כי הנה המלכים נועדו עברו יחדו
[6] המה ראו כן תמהו נבהלו נחפזו
[7] רעדה אחזתם שם חיל כיולדה
[8] ברוח קדים תשבר אניות תרשיש
[9] כאשר שמענו כן ראינו בעיר יהוה‎אדני‎יאהדונהי צבאות בעיר אלהינו אלהים יכוננה עד עולם סלה
[10] דמינו אלהים חסדך בקרב היכלך
[11] כשמך אלהים כן תהלתך על קצוי ארץ צדק מלאה ימינך
[12] ישמח הר ציון תגלנה בנות יהודה למען משפטיך
[13] סבו ציון והקיפוה ספרו מגדליה
[14] שיתו לבכם לחילה פסגו ארמנותיה למען תספרו לדור אחרון
[15] כי זה אלהים אלהינו עולם ועד הוא ינהגנו על מות

Transliteration:
    [1] *shir miz'mor liv'nei korach*
    [2] *gadol YHVH um'hulal mei'od b'ir eloheinu har kod'sho*
    [3] *yefeih nof m'sos kol ha'aretz har tziyon yar'k'tei tzafon kir'yat melech rav*
    [4] *elohim b'ar'menoteiha noda l'mis'gav*
    [5] *ki hineih ham'lachim no'adu av'ru yach'dav*
    [6] *heimah ra'u kein tamahu niv'halu nech'pazu*
    [7] *r'adah achazatam sham chil kayoleidah*

[8] *b'ru'ach kadim t'shabeir oniyot tar'shish*
[9] *ka'asher shamanu kein ra'inu b'ir YHVH tz'va'ot b'ir eloheinu elohim y'chon'nenah ad olam selah*
[10] *diminu elohim chas'decha b'kerev heichalecha*
[11] *k'shim'cha elohim kein t'hilat'cha al katz'vei eretz tzedek mal'ah y'minecha*
[12] *yis'mach har tziyon tagel'nah b'not y'hudah l'ma'an mish'patecha*
[13] *sobu tziyon v'hakifuhah sif'ru mig'daleha*
[14] *shitu lib'chem l'cheilah pas'gu ar'm'noteha l'ma'an t'sap'ru l'dor acharon*
[15] *ki zeh elohim eloheinu olam va'ed hu y'nahageinu al mut*

Translation:
[1] A Song; a Psalm of the sons of Korah.
[2] Great is *YHVH*, and highly to be praised, in the city of our God, His holy mountain,
[3] Fair in situation, the joy of the whole earth; even mount Zion, the uttermost parts of the north, the city of the great King.
[4] *Elohim* in her palaces hath made Himself known for a stronghold.
[5] For, lo, the kings assembled themselves, they came onward together.
[6] They saw, straightway they were amazed; they were affrighted, they hasted away.
[7] Trembling took hold of them there, pangs, as of a woman in travail.
[8] With the east wind Thou breakest the ships of Tarshish.
[9] As we have heard, so have we seen in the city of *YHVH* of hosts, in the city of our God—*Elohim* establish it for ever. *Selah*
[10] We have thought on Thy lovingkindness *Elohim*, in the midst of Thy temple.
[11] As is Thy name *Elohim*, so is Thy praise unto the ends of the earth; Thy right hand is full of righteousness.
[12] Let mount Zion be glad, let the daughters of Judah rejoice, because of Thy judgments.

[13] Walk about Zion, and go round about her; count the towers thereof.

[14] Mark ye well her ramparts, traverse her palaces; that ye may tell it to the generation following.

[15] For such is *Elohim*, our God, for ever and ever; He will guide us eternally.

Psalm 48 is the שיר של יום (*shir shel yom*—"Psalm of the Day") for the second day of the week, i.e. Monday.[1] In this regard the *Talmud* informs us that "this is because on the second day of Creation" the Divine One "separated His works, dividing between the upper waters and the lower waters, and ruled over them as King." [*TB Rosh Hashanah 31a*]

Whilst the forty-eighth Psalm is listed amongst those psalms which are recited for protection,[2] it is mainly employed in Jewish Magic to scare enemies.[3] In this regard we are informed in the *Shimmush Tehillim* that you could cause your "haters to fear you," by reciting the forty-eighth Psalm regularly with its associated Divine Name. The latter is indicated to be a Divine Name construct זך, which is said to have been derived: ז (*Zayin*) from רעדה אחזתם (*r'adah achazatam*—"Trembling took hold of them"): verse 7; and כ (*Kaf*) from כי זה (*ki zeh*—"for this [such]"): verse 15.[4] Godfrey Selig's German/English translations of the *Shimmush Tehillim* is in agreement with the details shared, but with his standard verbosity he wrote "if you have many enemies without cause, who hate you out of pure envy, pray this Psalm often, and with it think of the holy name Sach, which means Pure, Clear and Transparent, and your enemies will be seized with fear, terror and anxiety, and in future they will no more attempt to injure you."[5]

As you might expect by now, variant uses are found of the psalms in different recensions of the *Shimmush Tehillim*, and this is also the case with the current psalm. Whereas the previous psalm is employed to safeguard a besieged city, and strengthen the defending troops in conditions of war, *Psalm 48* is referenced in one recension of the *Shimmush Tehillim* for the opposite and very belligerent intention of conquering and pillaging a city.[6] It would seem that whilst one would not welcome this to happen to oneself and one's kin, it does not matter an inch if you met others with the same nastiness! Thus, in alignment with my stance regarding such abhorrent practices, the relevant procedure is not included in this tome. However, what should be noted is that the current psalm was recommended for recitation to alleviate disaster; preclude harm being inflicted by enemies; halt gangs of criminals; counteract all manner of disruptive changes in life, and to remove the fear of death. On a more positive level, the forty-eighth Psalm is employed to support spiritual science, aid those who seek to be uplifted, and to counteract apathy.

Psalm 48 is used in Christian magic mainly for the purpose of detecting the identities of thieves. In this regard, the Byzantine magical manuscripts recommend the psalm to be written "on skin taken from an unborn animal," this being done in the house where the theft occurred. Following this action, the item is placed on the head of the one working this procedure, and it is said the thief will be seen clearly.[7] Two Latin manuscripts equally list the current psalm as good for detecting a thief. In one the practitioner has to copy the psalm in conjunction with a set of magical signs, which is afterwards located under his or head. It is said that "night or day, you will see the thief."[8] In the second Latin manuscript the forty-eighth Psalm is again written down, and located under the pillow when the practitioner retires to sleep. It is said this action will lead to the thief appearing in dream.[9] The same application appears in *"Le Livre d'Or"* with one difference. The psalm is again copied with a set of magical characters, but it is located above the head of the user when in bed, who is said will then see the thief.[10] Other than this specific application, it is worth noting that in a Byzantine *Hippiatrikon Psalm 48:1–7* is recommended to ease the birth process for a mare.[11]

PSALM 49

[1] למנצח לבני קרח מזמור
[2] שמעו זאת כל העמים האזינו כל ישבי חלד
[3] גם בני אדם גם בני איש יחד עשיר ואביון
[4] פי ידבר חכמות והגות לבי תבונות
[5] אטה למשל אזני אפתח בכנור חידתי
[6] למה אירא בימי רע עון עקבי יסובני
[7] הבטחים על חילם וברב עשרם יתהללו
[8] אח לא פדה יפדה איש לא יתן לאלהים כפרו
[9] ויקר פדיון נפשם וחדל לעולם
[10] ויחי עוד לנצח לא יראה השחת
[11] כי יראה חכמים ימותו יחד כסיל ובער יאבדו ועזבו לאחרים חילם
[12] קרבם בתימו לעולם משכנתם לדור ודר קראו בשמותם עלי אדמות
[13] ואדם ביקר בל ילין נמשל כבהמות נדמו
[14] זה דרכם כסל למו ואחריהם בפיהם ירצו סלה
[15] כצאן לשאול שתו מות ירעם וירדו בם ישרים לבקר וצורם לבלות שאול מזבל לו
[16] אך אלהים יפדה נפשי מיד שאול כי יקחני סלה
[17] אל תירא כי יעשר איש כי ירבה כבוד ביתו
[18] כי לא במותו יקח הכל לא ירד אחריו כבודו
[19] כי נפשו בחייו יברך ויודך כי תיטיב לך
[20] תבוא עד דור אבותיו עד נצח לא יראו אור
[21] אדם ביקר ולא יבין נמשל כבהמות נדמו

Transliteration:
 [1] *lam'natzei'ach liv'nei korach miz'mor*
 [2] *shim'u zot kol ha'amim ha'azinu kol yosh'vei chaled*
 [3] *gam b'nei adam gam b'nei ish yachad ashir v'ev'yon*
 [4] *pi y'dabeir choch'mot v'hagut libi t'vunot*
 [5] *ateh l'mashal oz'ni ef'tach b'chinor chidati*
 [6] *lamah ira bimei ra avon akeivai y'subeini*
 [7] *habot'chim al cheilam uv'rov osh'ram yit'halalu*
 [8] *ach lo fadoh yif'deh ish lo yitein leilohim kof'ro*
 [9] *v'yeikar pid'yon naf'sham v'chadal l'olam*
 [10] *vichi od la'netzach lo yir'eh hashachat*

[11] *ki yir'eh chachamim yamutu yachad k'sil vava'ar yoveidu v'az'vu la'acheirim cheilam*
[12] *kir'bam bateimo l'olam mish'k'notam l'dor vador kar'u vish'motam alei adamot*
[13] *v'adam bikar bal yalin nim'shal kab'heimot nid'mu*
[14] *zeh dar'kam keisel lamo v'achareihem b'fihem yir'tzu selah*
[15] *katzon lish'ol shatu mavet yir'eim vayir'du vam y'sharim laboker v'tzuram l'valot sh'ol miz'vul lo*
[16] *ach elohim yif'deh naf'shi miyad sh'ol ki yikacheini selah*
[17] *al tira ki ya'ashir ish ki yir'beh k'vod beito*
[18] *ki lo v'moto yikach hakol lo yeireid acharav k'vodo*
[19] *ki naf'sho b'chayav y'vareich v'yoducha ki teitiv lach*
[20] *tavo ad dor avotav ad netzach lo yir'u or*
[21] *adam bikar v'lo yavin nim'shal kab'heimot nid'mu*

Translation:

[1] For the Leader; a Psalm of the sons of Korah.
[2] Hear this, all ye peoples; give ear, all ye inhabitants of the world,
[3] Both low and high, rich and poor together.
[4] My mouth shall speak wisdom, and the meditation of my heart shall be understanding.
[5] I will incline mine ear to a parable; I will open my dark saying upon the harp.
[6] Wherefore should I fear in the days of evil, when the iniquity of my supplanters compasseth me about,
[7] Of them that trust in their wealth, and boast themselves in the multitude of their riches?
[8] No man can by any means redeem his brother, nor give to *Elohim* a ransom for him—
[9] For too costly is the redemption of their soul, and must be let alone for ever—
[10] That he should still live alway, that he should not see the pit.
[11] For he seeth that wise men die, the fool and the brutish together perish, and leave their wealth to others.
[12] Their inward thought is, that their houses shall continue for ever, and their dwelling-places to all generations; they call their lands after their own names.

[13] But man abideth not in honour; he is like the beasts that perish.
[14] This is the way of them that are foolish, and of those who after them approve their sayings. *Selah*
[15] Like sheep they are appointed for the nether-world; death shall be their shepherd; and the upright shall have dominion over them in the morning; and their form shall be for the nether-world to wear away, that there be no habitation for it.
[16] But *Elohim* will redeem my soul from the power of the nether-world; for He shall receive me. *Selah*
[17] Be not thou afraid when one waxeth rich, when the wealth of his house is increased;
[18] For when he dieth he shall carry nothing away; his wealth shall not descend after him.
[19] Though while he lived he blessed his soul: 'Men will praise thee, when thou shalt do well to thyself';
[20] It shall go to the generation of his fathers; they shall never see the light.
[21] Man that is in honour understandeth not; he is like the beasts that perish.

Considering the theme of this psalm, it should come as no suprise that it is customary to recite *Psalm 49* during the *Shiva Minyan* (prayers for the dead) at the "House of Mourning," i.e. the residence of a mourner.[1] It may be uncomfortable for anyone to accept the sentiment expressed in the concluding verse reading "Man that is in honour understandeth not; he is like the beasts that perish." Yet, whilst it is true that there are many ways in which each of us ends our incarnations in the flesh, the fact of the matter is that every living thing on this planet dies, and indeed we are all "like the beasts that perish." The quicker we understand and accept that fact, the greater will be our respect for all life.

The forty-ninth Psalm is employed in "Practical Kabbalah" against fever.[2] The "fever" referenced in this instance is קדחת (*Kedachat*) which reads both "fever" and "malaria," hence it is said that the current psalm be written down and "worn as an amulet" by one who has fever or malaria.[3] However, in terms of aiding someone who is suffering a fever, the *Shimmush Tehillim* instructs that the forty-ninth Psalm should be written down with its associated Divine Name, and it further states that it is equally good to include the first six verses of *Psalm 50*. The entire inscription is afterwards worn on the person of the afflicted individual.[4] The affiliated Divine Name is said to be שד"י (*Shadai*), which is indicated to be a Divine Name construct formed: ש (*Shin*) from שמעו (*shim'u*—"hear"): verse 2; ד (*Dalet*) from אדם (*Adam*—"man"): verse 21; and י (*Yod*) from ק (*Kof*) in עקבי (*akeivai*—"supplanters"): verse 6, the letter having been transposed by means of the א"יק בכ"ר (*Ayak Bachar*) cipher.[5] One commentator suggests the concluding letter י (*Yod*) is from ק (*Kof*) in קרבם (*kir'bam*—"their inward"): verse 12,[6] and Selig's German/English translations claims it was derived from ק (*Kof*) in ויקר (*v'yeikar*—"and costly"): verse 9,[7] both of the latter again having been transposed by means of the said cipher. As expected, Selig embroidered heavily on the simple and concise statement in the *Shimmush Tehillim*, saying "is one of your family burdened with a fever and perhaps incurable fever, then take a new pen and ink prepared for this purpose, and write the 49th Psalm and the first six verses of the 50th Psalm, together with the appropriate holy name *Schaddi*, which signifies Almighty, and which belongs to these Psalms, upon pure parchment prepared for this particular case, and hang it around the patient's neck with a silken string."[8] However, the forty-ninth Psalm was not only employed against severe, and, for that matter, incurable fever, but is also enunciated for illness and healing in general.

One recension of the *Shimmush Tehillim* recommends the current psalm to individuals who travel or go out alone at night. In this regard, we are informed that the psalm should be recited many times in conjunction with the following prayer-incantation:

יהי רצון מלפניך שדי מלא רחמים וחסדים למען
רחמיך וחסדיך ולמען שמך הגדול והנורא תנחיני
ותנהליני והצילני נא מיד כל אויב ואורב בדרך
למען שמך יהוה וסלחת לעוני כי רב הוא (*Psalm 25:11*)

אל אל בך חסיתי (Psalm 7:2) אל יעלצו אויבי לי (Psalm 25:2) אל אבושה (Psalm 25:2) ותצעידני לשלום ותוליכני בדרך שלום אל מקום חפצי בשם הקדוש אל שדי

Transliteration:
> Y'hi ratzon mil'fanecha Shadai malei rachamim v'chasadim l'ma'an rachamecha v'chasadecha ul'ma'an shim'cha hagadol v'hanora tan'cheini ut'nahaleini v'hatzileini na miyad kol oyeiv v'oreiv baderech l'ma'an shim'cha YHVH v'salach'ta la avoni ki rav hu (Psalm 25:11) el el b'cha chasiti (Psalm 7:2) al ya'al'tzu oy'vai li (Psalm 25:2) al evoshah (Psalm 25:2) v'tatz'ideini l'shalom utolicheini baderech shalom el makom chef'tzi b'shem hakadosh El Shadai.

Translation:
> May it be your will *Shadai* full of mercy and kindness, for the sake of your mercy and your grace, and for the sake of your great and awesome Name, you shall calm me, guide me, and rescue me from the hand of every enemy and highwayman. *For Thy name's sake YHVH, pardon mine iniquity, for it is great (Psalm 25:11). El El, in Thee have I taken refuge (Psalm 7:2). Let not mine enemies triumph over me (Psalm 25:2), let me not be ashamed (Psalm 25:2).* And advance me in peace, and guide me on a peaceful path to the place of my desire, in the Holy Name *El Shadai*.[9]

Practitioners who are farmers, horticulturists or gardeners, should note that the current psalm is recited against storms in general, and is employed for the protection of gardens, fields, as well as of vines and vineyards. This psalm is further employed in the caring for birds, ensuring the health of horses, and in the raising of cattle and livestock. *Psalm 49* is also employed for protection in performing dangerous work, in perilous situations and in times of trouble, and it is enunciated during a time of mourning. It should be further noted that this psalm was also recommended against envy of the rich, and to deal with any confusion which may result from witnessing the success of the wicked.

As far as the use of individual verses for magical purposes are concerned, it is worth noting that the capitals of the seven words comprising *Psalm 49:6*, are conjoined in the Divine Name construct לאב רעעי, which is included in a multi-purpose amulet, i.e. it counteracts fear, protects against danger, and infections.[10]

It would seem that in Christian Magic the application of the forty-ninth Psalm is somewhat sparse. In this regard, we are informed in *"Le Livre d'Or"* that a man who loves someone, and wishes "to be honoured by her," should write the psalm and carry it on his person, which will ensure that he "will be loved and cherished."[11] Elsewhere there is a reference to the current psalm being employed in conjunction with other psalms, as well as a set of magical symbols, for the purpose of detecting the identity of a thief.[12] However, *Psalm 49* is listed in the *"Key of Solomon"* as one of nineteen psalms which are recited over the wax from which ritual candles are constructed, the complete set being *Psalms 8, 15, 22, 46, 47, 49, 51, 53, 68, 72, 84, 102, 110, 113, 126, 130, 131, 133,* and *139*.[13]

PSALM 50

[1] מזמור לאסף אל אלהים יהוה‎אדני‎אהדונהי דבר ויקרא ארץ ממזרח שמש עד מבאו

[2] מציון מכלל יפי אלהים הופיע

[3] יבא אלהינו ואל יחרש אש לפניו תאכל וסביביו נשערה מאד

[4] יקרא אל השמים מעל ואל הארץ לדין עמו

[5] אספו לי חסידי כרתי בריתי עלי זבח

[6] ויגידו שמים צדקו כי אלהים שפט הוא סלה

[7] שמעה עמי ואדברה ישראל ואעידה בך אלהים אלהיך אנכי

[8] לא על זבחיך אוכיחך ועולתיך לנגדי תמיד

[9] לא אקח מביתך פר ממכלאתיך עתודים

[10] כי לי כל חיתו יער בהמות בהררי אלף

[11] ידעתי כל עוף הרים וזיז שדי עמדי

[12] אם ארעב לא אמר לך כי לי תבל ומלאה

[13] האוכל בשר אבירים ודם עתודים אשתה

[14] זבח לאלהים תודה ושלם לעליון נדריך

[15] וקראני ביום צרה אחלצך ותכבדני

[16] ולרשע אמר אלהים מה לך לספר חקי ותשא בריתי עלי פיך

[17] ואתה שנאת מוסר ותשלך דברי אחריך

[18] אם ראית גנב ותרץ עמו ועם מנאפים חלקך

[19] פיך שלחת ברעה ולשונך תצמיד מרמה

[20] תשב באחיך תדבר בבן אמך תתן דפי

[21] אלה עשית והחרשתי דמית היות אהיה כמוך אוכיחך ואערכה לעיניך

[22] בינו נא זאת שכחי אלוה פן אטרף ואין מציל

[23] זבח תודה יכבדנני ושם דרך אראנו בישע אלהים

Transliteration:

[1] *miz'mor l'asaf el elohim YHVH diber vayik'ra aretz mimiz'rach shemesh ad m'vo'o*

[2] *mitzi'on mich'lal yofi elohim hofi'a*

[3] *yavo eloheinu v'al yecherash esh l'fanav tocheil us'vivav nis'arah m'od*
[4] *yik'ra el hashamayim mei'al v'el ha'aretz ladin amo*
[5] *is'fu li chasidai kor'tei v'riti alei zavach*
[6] *vayagidu shamayim tzid'ko ki elohim shofeit hu selah*
[7] *shim'ah ami va'adabeirah yis'ra'eil v'a'idah bach elohim elohecha anochi*
[8] *lo al z'vachecha ochichecha v'olotecha l'neg'di tamid*
[9] *lo ekach mibeit'cha far mimich'l'otecha atudim*
[10] *ki li chol chaito ya'ar b'heimot b'har'rei alef*
[11] *yada'ti kol of harim v'ziz sadai imadi*
[12] *im er'av lo omar lach ki li teiveil um'lo'ah*
[13] *ha'ochal b'sar abirim v'dam atudim esh'teh*
[14] *z'vach leilohim todah v'shaleim l'elyon n'darecha*
[15] *uk'ra'eini b'yom tzarah achaletz'cha ut'chab'deini*
[16] *v'larasha amar elohim mah l'cha l'sapeir chukai vatisa v'riti alei ficha*
[17] *v'atah saneita musar vatash'leich d'varai acharecha*
[18] *im ra'ita ganav vatiretz imo v'im m'na'afim chel'kecha*
[19] *picha shalach'ta v'ra'ah ul'shon'cha tatz'mid mir'mah*
[20] *teisheiv b'achicha t'dabeir b'ven im'cha titen dofi*
[21] *eileh asita v'hecherash'ti dimita heyot eh'yeh chamocha ochichacha v'e'er'chah l'eineicha*
[22] *binu na zot shoch'chei eloha pen et'rof v'ein matzil*
[23] *zovei'ach todah y'chab'dan'ni v'sam derech ar'enu b'yeisha elohim*

Translation:

[1] A Psalm of Asaph. God, *Elohim YHVH*, hath spoken, and called the earth from the rising of the sun unto the going down thereof.

[2] Out of Zion, the perfection of beauty, *Elohim* hath shined forth.

[3] Our God cometh, and doth not keep silence; a fire devoureth before Him, and round about Him it stormeth mightily.

[4] He calleth to the heavens above, and to the earth, that He may judge His people:

[5] 'Gather My saints together unto Me; those that have made a covenant with Me by sacrifice.'
[6] And the heavens declare His righteousness; for *Elohim*, He is judge. *Selah*
[7] 'Hear, O My people, and I will speak; O Israel, and I will testify against thee: *Elohim*, thy God, am I.
[8] I will not reprove thee for thy sacrifices; and thy burnt-offerings are continually before Me.
[9] I will take no bullock out of thy house, nor he-goats out of thy folds.
[10] For every beast of the forest is Mine, and the cattle upon a thousand hills.
[11] I know all the fowls of the mountains; and the wild beasts of the field are Mine.
[12] If I were hungry, I would not tell thee; for the world is Mine, and the fulness thereof.
[13] Do I eat the flesh of bulls, or drink the blood of goats?
[14] Offer unto *Elohim* the sacrifice of thanksgiving; and pay thy vows unto the Most High;
[15] And call upon Me in the day of trouble; I will deliver thee, and thou shalt honour Me.'
[16] But unto the wicked *Elohim* saith: 'What hast thou to do to declare My statutes, and that thou hast taken My covenant in thy mouth?
[17] Seeing thou hatest instruction, and castest My words behind thee.
[18] When thou sawest a thief, thou hadst company with him, and with adulterers was thy portion.
[19] Thou hast let loose thy mouth for evil, and thy tongue frameth deceit.
[20] Thou sittest and speakest against thy brother; thou slanderest thine own mother's son.
[21] These things hast thou done, and should I have kept silence? Thou hadst thought that I was altogether such a one as thyself; but I will reprove thee, and set the cause before thine eyes.
[22] Now consider this, ye that forget God, lest I tear in pieces, and there be none to deliver.

[23] Whoso offereth the sacrifice of thanksgiving honoureth Me; and to him that ordereth his way aright will I show the salvation of *Elohim*.'

Psalm 50 is employed in Jewish Magic for the purpose of escaping enemies, robbers, and brigands.[1] To this the *Shimmush Tehillim* adds that it is good to carry the psalm in case of danger.[2] The Divine Name associated with the current psalm, and which should be concentrated on whilst reciting the psalm, is said to be חי (*Chai*—"Living").[3] Godfrey Selig, who wrote in his version of the *Shimmush Tehillim* that the fiftieth Psalm should be written and worn on the person of the one seeking to "be safe from all danger, and escape from all the machinations of robbers,"[4] maintains the associated Divine Name was derived: ח (*Chet*) from זבח (*zavach*—"sacrifice"): verse 5, and י (*Yod*) from אנכי (*anochi*—"am I"): verse 7.[5] I have seen no references anywhere else to the said Divine Name being derived from the listed verses in the current psalm.

However, as far as the amuletic uses are concerned, *Psalm 50* is listed in one recension of the *Shimmush Tehillim* as "good to carry with its Name,"[6] as a protection against all sorrow, ghosts, and harmful spirits. In this regard, the psalm is written in conjunction with the following prayer-incantation:

יהי רצון מלפניך מלך אמיץ הרם הנשגב והנכבד
המתנשא לכל לראש בך יהוה חסיתי (*Psalm 31:2; 71:1*)
ובצל כנפיך אחסה (*Psalm 57:2*) תסתירני ועליך מחסי
שתנהליני על מי מנוחות ותסור ממני כל אנחות וכל
רוחין ומזיקין שבעולם לבל יכשילוני ולבל יגעו
ממאתיים וארבעים ושמונה איברים בשם רחום רחום
צבי צבי יהוה צבאות אמן אמן אמן סלה סלה סלה

Transliteration:

Y'hi ratzon mil'fanecha melech amitz haram hanis'gav v'hanich'bad hamit'nasei l'chol l'rosh b'cha YHVH chasiti (Psalm 31:2; 71:1) uv'tzeil k'nafecha ech'seh (Psalm 57:2) tas'tireini v'aleicha mach'si shet'nahaleini al mei m'nuchot v'tasir mimenu kol anachot v'chol ruchin

> umazikin sheba'olam l'val yach'shiluni ul'val yig'u mimatayim v'ar'ba'im ush'monah eivarim b'shem Rachum Rachum Tz'vi Tz'vi YHVH Tz'va'ot Omein Omein Omein Selah Selah Selah.

Translation:
> May it be your will valiant King, the exalted and honoured venerable One, who towers over all. *In Thee YHVH, have I taken refuge (Psalm 31:2; 71:1), and in the shadow of Thy wings will I take refuge (Psalm 57:2).* You shall conceal me, and with you is my refuge, so that you may lead me over calm waters, and remove from me all sighing, all ghosts and harmful spirits that are in the world, so that they may not make me stumble, nor injure my 248 limbs. In the Name *Rachum Rachum Tz'vi Tz'vi YHVH Tz'va'ot* ("Merciful Merciful Glorified Glorified *YHVH* of Hosts"). Amen Amen Amen Selah Selah Selah.[7]

As indicated, the current psalm is enunciated in order to be saved from bandits, but it was equally recommended for protection against all theft, thieves, and robbers, and it is further recited for protection against enemies. Earlier I mentioned that the first six verses of *Psalm 50* is employed in conjunction with *Psalm 49* to alleviate a fever, whether it be of the severe or incurable kind. In this regard the current psalm is recited in its entirety for the same purpose, and it was also recommended against paralysis. It should be noted that the fiftieth Psalm supports honesty and honest people, and in this regard it is uttered for personal willpower, and against, as well as for relief from, temptation. If an individual succumbed to the latter, it was said the current psalm should be recited for the forgiveness of errors and transgressions, and for penitence. Conversely the current psalm was recommended for comprehension of the "Occult Sciences," and to acquire the gift of speech.

It has also been noted that the *Psalm 50* is recited "against noxious animals,"[8] and the capitals of the phrase in *Psalm 50:21* reading אהיה דמית היות והחרשתי (*v'hecherash'ti dimita heyot eh'yeh*—"and should I have kept silence?") is arranged into the Divine Name construct וְהִדְאָ אָהִדְוָ for the purpose of driving out an Evil Spirit. In forming the Divine Name construct, the first four-letter combination comprises the capital of the first word conjoined with that of the third, and the second with the fourth. In the second four letter combination, the four letters are written in their exact order in reverse.[9]

Aside from the suggestion in *"Le Livre d'Or"* that individuals "who wish to kill a sheep and distribute it amongst the poor," should recite *Psalm 50:1–8* seven times,[10] I have not seen much use made of the current psalm in Christian Magic.

PSALM 51

[1] למנצח מזמור לדוד
[2] בבוא אליו נתן הנביא כאשר בא אל בת שבע
[3] חנני אלהים כחסדך כרב רחמיך מחה פשעי
[4] הרב כבסני מעוני ומחטאת טהרני
[5] כי פשעי אני אדע וחטאתי נגדי תמיד
[6] לך לבדך חטאתי והרע בעיניך עשיתי למען תצדק בדברך תזכה בשפטך
[7] הן בעוון חוללתי ובחטא יחמתני אמי
[8] הן אמת חפצת בטחות ובסתם חכמה תודיעני
[9] תחטאני באזוב ואטהר תכבסני ומשלג אלבין
[10] תשמיעני ששון ושמחה תגלנה עצמות דכית
[11] הסתר פניך מחטאי וכל עונתי מחה
[12] לב טהור ברא לי אלהים ורוח נכין חדש בקרבי
[13] אל תשליכני מלפניך ורוח קדשך אל תקח ממני
[14] השיבה לי ששון ישעך ורוח נדיבה תסמכני
[15] אלמדה פשעים דרכיך וחטאים אליך ישובו
[16] הצילני מדמים אלהים אלהי תשועתי תרנן לשוני צדקתך
[17] אדני שפתי תפתח ופי יגיד תהלתך
[18] כי לא תחפץ זבח ואתנה עולה לא תרצה
[19] זבחי אלהים רוח נשברה לב נשבר ונדכה אלהים לא תבזה
[20] היטיבה ברצונך את ציון תבנה חומות ירושלם
[21] אז תחפץ זבחי צדק עולה וכליל אז יעלו על מזבחך פרים

Transliteration:

[1] lam'natzei'ach miz'mor l'david
[2] b'vo eilav natan hanavi ka'asher ba el bat shava
[3] choneini elohim k'chas'decha k'rov rachamecha m'cheh f'sha'ai

[4] *herev kab'seini mei'avoni u'meichatati tahareini*
[5] *ki f'sha'ai ani eida v'chatati neg'di tamid*
[6] *l'cha l'vad'cha chatati v'hara b'einecha asiti l'ma'an titz'dak b'dov'recha tiz'keh v'shof'techa*
[7] *hein b'avon cholal'ti uv'chet yechemat'ni imi*
[8] *hein emet chafatz'ta vatuchot uv'satum choch'mah todi'eini*
[9] *t'chat'eini v'eizov v'et'har t'chab'seini umisheleg al'bin*
[10] *tash'mi'eini sason v'sim'chah tagel'nah atzamot dikita*
[11] *has'teir panecha meichata'ai v'chol avonotai m'cheih*
[12] *lev tahor b'ra li elohim v'ru'ach nachon chadeish b'kir'bi*
[13] *al tash'licheini mil'fanecha v'ru'ach kod'sh'cha al tikach mimeni*
[14] *ha'shivah li s'son yish'echa v'ru'ach n'divah tis'm'cheini*
[15] *alam'dah fo'sh'im d'rachecha v'chata'im eilecha yashuvu*
[16] *hatzileini midamim elohim elohei t'shu'ati t'ranein l'shoni tzid'katecha*
[17] *adonai s'fatai tif'tach ufi yagid t'hilatecha*
[18] *ki lo tach'potz zevach v'eteinah olah lo tir'tzeh*
[19] *ziv'chei elohim ru'ach nish'barah lev nish'bar v'nid'keh elohim lo tiv'zeh*
[20] *heitivah vir'tzon'cha et tziyon tiv'neh chomot yerushalam*
[21] *az tach'potz ziv'chei tzedek olah v'chalil az ya'alu al miz'bachacha farim*

Translation:
[1] For the Leader. A Psalm of David;
[2] When Nathan the prophet came unto him, after he had gone in to Bath-sheba.
[3] Be gracious unto me *Elohim*, according to Thy mercy; according to the multitude of Thy compassions blot out my transgressions.

[4] Wash me thoroughly from mine iniquity, and cleanse me from my sin.
[5] For I know my transgressions; and my sin is ever before me.
[6] Against Thee, Thee only, have I sinned, and done that which is evil in Thy sight; that Thou mayest be justified when Thou speakest, and be in the right when Thou judgest.
[7] Behold, I was brought forth in iniquity, and in sin did my mother conceive me.
[8] Behold, Thou desirest truth in the inward parts; make me, therefore, to know wisdom in mine inmost heart.
[9] Purge me with hyssop, and I shall be clean; wash me, and I shall be whiter than snow.
[10] Make me to hear joy and gladness; that the bones which Thou hast crushed may rejoice.
[11] Hide Thy face from my sins, and blot out all mine iniquities.
[12] Create me a clean heart *Elohim*; and renew a steadfast spirit within me.
[13] Cast me not away from Thy presence; and take not Thy holy spirit from me.
[14] Restore unto me the joy of Thy salvation; and let a willing spirit uphold me.
[15] Then will I teach transgressors Thy ways; and sinners shall return unto Thee.
[16] Deliver me from bloodguiltiness *Elohim*, Thou God of my salvation; so shall my tongue sing aloud of Thy righteousness.
[17] *Adonai*, open Thou my lips; and my mouth shall declare Thy praise.
[18] For Thou delightest not in sacrifice, else would I give it; Thou hast no pleasure in burnt-offering.
[19] The sacrifices of *Elohim* are a broken spirit; a broken and a contrite heart *Elohim*, Thou wilt not despise.
[20] Do good in Thy favour unto Zion; build Thou the walls of Jerusalem.
[21] Then wilt Thou delight in the sacrifices of righteousness, in burnt-offering and whole offering; then will they offer bullocks upon Thine altar.

Psalm 51, listed amongst the set of additional psalms enunciated on *Yom Kippur* ("Day of Atonement") in the Sefardi liturgy, has been called "The Chapter of Repentance," which we are told is "because its contents are the foundations of the principles of atonement." In this regard, it has been suggested that "if one wishes to repent for his sins, its words are a fitting **prayer**."[1] This psalm is the singular one which was recommended to me decades ago in my remote youth, to purify myself psychologically and spiritually, prior to performing any serious magical working. In this regard, it should be noted that repentance finds expression also in the magical applications of the current psalm, since it is recommended to anyone defiled with the sins of זנות (*z'nut*—fornication),[2] debauchery, or when an individual is feeling guilty.[3]

Whilst it has been suggested that the fifty-first Psalm should be recited "three times a day: evening, morning and afternoon," by "one who sinned,"[4] there are further details to consider as delineated in the *Shimmush Tehillim*. The popular published version of this text maintains the psalm should be enunciated over sesame oil, whilst focusing on the Name דם (*dam*—"blood"), following which the body is anointed with the oil.[5] Some recensions add that practitioners should commence by purifying themselves, and then pray the psalm seven times in the morning, the same number of times at noon, in the afternoon, and in the evening, following which the entire body is brushed with the oil.[6] As mentioned, the associated word here is דם (*dam*—"blood") which is indicated to be a Divine Name construct derived: ד (*Dalet*) from מ (*Mem*) in פרים (*parim*—"bullocks"): verse 21, the said glyph having been transposed by means of the א"יק בכ"ר (*Ayak Bachar*) cipher; and מ (*Mem*) from the second ב (*Bet*) in בבא (*b'vo*—"came"): verse 2, this letter having been likewise transposed, in this instance by means of the א"ל ב"ם (*Albam*) cipher.[7]

Once again Godfrey Selig embellished the quite simple instructions in the standard version of the *Shimmush Tehillim*, and maintains the oil should be "poppy oil." Thus he wrote "is any one troubled with an anxious and restless conscience on account of the commission of a heavy sin, then let him pronounce this Psalm with the word *Dam* connected with it in the mind, three times a day, namely, early at noon and in the evening over poppy-oil, and at the same time utter a prayer suitable to the occassion in which the evil deed must be mentioned in deep humility and sorrow, which must be obtained from the just yet merciful Judge of all men through a contrite heart, then let him anoint himself with the consecrated oil over the body, and he will find in a few days that he has found grace and that the heavy burden has been **removed**."[8] However, the current procedure is even further expanded in one recension of the *Shimmush Tehillim*, in which it is noted that individuals who wish to confess their sins, transgressions they have committed, or who have indulged in fornication, should clean their bodies twice a day, and say *Psalm 51* as well as the following fairly long prayer-incantation three times a day, in this instance over olive oil, at the times of the morning, afternoon, and evening synagogal prayers. The prayer-incantation reads:

יהי רצון מלפניך רם על כל רמים נשא על כל נשאים
גלוי וידוע לפניך כי יצר הרע שמת בנו ואמת הדבר
כי לטובה עשית ולצורך העולם הזה ועתה מה **אעשה**
כי גבר עלי יצר הרע ועתה יהוה חסד ואמת יקדמו
פניך (Psalm 89:15) על כן באתי לבקש כפרה וסליחה
מלפניך ותשוב מחרון **אפיך** ותמחול ותסלח לבל
עונותי ופשעי וזדוני אשר עשיתי כזאת וכזאת ועתה
יהוה אלהי יכבשו רחמיך את כעסיך ויתגוללו רחמיך
עלי וקבל תעניתי אשר אני מתענה לפניך וסלח לי
העון הגדול הזה אשר עשיתי כאשר סלחת למשיח
צדקך עון בת שבע כן תמחול לי ואל תשחיתני מן
העולם ברוב עונותי ומעללי הרעים כאמור והוא
רחום יכפר עון ולא ישחית והרבה להשיב אפו ולא
יעיר כל חמתו (Psalm 78:38) **אמן אמן אמן סלה סלה**
סלה

Transliteration:

Y'hi ratzon mil'fanecha ram al kol ramim naso al kol n'si'im galui v'yadu'a l'fanecha ki yetzer hara sam'ta bano v'emet hadavar ki l'tovah asita ul'tzorech ha'olam hazeh v'atah mah e'eseh ki gavar alai yetzer hara v'atah YHVH chesed v'emet y'kad'mu fanecha (Psalm 89:15) al

> *kein ba'ati l'vakeish kaparah v'slichah mil'fanecha v'tashuv meicharon apecha v'tim'chol v'tis'lach l'chol avonotai up'sha'ai uz'donai asher asiti k'zot v'k'zot v'atah YHVH elohai yich'b'shu rachamecha et ka'asecha v'yit'gol'lu rachamecha alai v'kabel ta'aniti asher ani mit'aneh l'fanecha v's'lach li ha'avon hagadol hazeh asher asiti k'asher salach'ta l'mashi'ach tzid'kecha avon bat sh'va kein tim'chol li v'al tash'chiteinu min ha'olam b'rov avonotai umei'alalai hara'im k'amur v'hu rachum y'chaper avon v'lo yash'chit v'hir'bah l'hashiv apo v'lo ya'ir kol chamato (Psalm 78:38) Omein Omein Omein Selah Selah Selah.*

Translation:
> May it be your will, loftiest above all the lofty, exalted above all the exalted, it is evident and known to you that you have put the evil impulse in us, and it is true that you made (this) for the good and the needs of this world. And now, what should I do, since the evil impulse has prevailed over me? Now *YHVH, mercy and truth go before Thee (Psalm 89:15)*, therefore I have come to ask for atonement and forgiveness before you. You shall turn from your divine wrath and excuse and pardon all my transgressions, iniquity and wickednesses which I have done so and so. Now, *YHVH* my God, let your mercy control your anger, and let your compassion flow over me. Receive my fast that I keep before you, and forgive me this great offense that I have committed. As you have forgiven the anointed one of your righteousness the offense of Bathsheba, so shall you forgive me. You shall not destroy me from the world because of my many transgressions and evil deeds, as it is said *But He, being full of compassion, forgiveth iniquity, and destroyeth not; yea, many a time doth He turn His anger away, and doth not stir up all His wrath (Psalm 78:38)*. Amen Amen Amen Selah Selah Selah.

Following this action, the oil is smeared over the body of the practitioner, and the psalm said a further thirty times whilst concentrating on its associated Divine Name, which in the current instance is indicated to be the word רם (*Ram*—"high [lofty]").[9] As an aside, the "the anointed one of your righteousness the offense of Bathsheba" reference in the prayer-incantation, pertains to the biblical saga of King David's adulterous relationship with a married woman whom he later married, and who became the mother of King Solomon.

Regarding the term דם (*dam*— "blood"), which we noted is a Divine Name construct associated with the current psalm, it is interesting that the capitals of the words comprising *Psalm 51:3* are conjoined in the Divine Name construct חאב כרמפ, which is included in amulets employed against haemorrhage and loss of blood.[10] Interestingly enough, the initials of the phrase in *Psalm 51:12*, reading לב טהור ברא לי אלהים (*lev tahor b'ra li elohim*— "Create me a clean heart *Elohim*"), are combined in the Divine Name construct לטבלא, which is employed in amulets for heart ailments.[11] This is understandable since, besides the heart being referenced directly in the said verse, this is the organ which pumps the blood distributed throughout our bodies. Be that as it may, the capitals of the nine words comprising this verse was conjoined in the Divine Name construct לְטָב לְאֵו נָחָב (*Leitab' Li'ev' Nachab'*), which is a personal favourite, since it is good for thought and contemplation.[12] It should be noted, that the two succeeding verses are also employed for magical purposes. In this regard, the capitals of the first three words of *Psalm 51:13* are combined in the Divine Name construct אהמ which is employed in amulets by individuals who are having problems with dreams.[13] As far as *Psalm 51:14* is concerned, it is employed to find grace and kindness in the eyes of anybody. This must assuredly be the quickest way to achieve this aim, since all that is required is to place the back of the right hand on the forehead with the thumb pointing down, the little finger up, and the middle three fingers bent inwards, and then to recite the said verse three times.[14]

Special attention should be given to *Psalm 51:8*, the magical application of which is particularly effective. In this regard, the initials of the seven words comprising this verse were arranged into the Divine Name construct הֵאֶחֲבַוְחֹת, which, in accordance with the sounding of these glyphs in the said verse, is enunciated *Hei'echava'uchoto*. It is employed for שאלה בהקיץ

(*She'elah b'Hakitz*), i.e. seeking answers to life questions from "Divine Sources" in a "magical manner" whilst fully awake.[15] It could be viewed as a manner of receiving answers by means of a controlled "daydream." However, this Divine Name is further employed in a procedure to ascertain answers by means of the ever popular pendulum. In this regard, you are instructed to take a gold signet ring with no stone affixed to the square, and tie a linen thread to the ring so that the face of the ring seal faces downwards.[16] I personally use a simple signet ring with a hexagram engraved on the seal. In this instance, the opposite end of the said string is tied to the right index finger, and the ring-pendulum suspended just inside the rim of a relatively small empty copper vessel. Following this you should think the question to which you seek an answer in your heart, and then address the ring-pendulum saying "if such-and-such applies to the question you will swing (run) from North to South, and if not you will swing from East to West." Do this whilst thinking the question in your heart, and then recite *Psalm 51:8* three or seven times. The ring will then start beating on the sides of the copper vessel. However, if you wish to receive answers in the opposite manner, you should say to the pendulum "if you agree you will move from East to West, and if you do not, you will move from North to South."[17]

We are informed that if the ring-pendulum fails to move, you should tell it to swing, and if it still does not swing strongly, you should firmly focus on the ring-pendulum and say to it:

יהוה גוער בים ויבשהו (*Nahum 1:4*) המרגיז ארץ
ממקומה ועמודיה יתפלצון (*Job 9:6*) יושב הכרובים
אלהי ישראל שמו שתרוץ בחוזק וירוץ מיד

Transliteration:
> YHVH go'eir bayam vayab'sheihu (*Nahum 1:4*) hamar'giz eretz mim'komah v'amodeha yit'falatzon (*Job 9:6*) yosheiv hak'ruvim elohei yis'ra'eil sh'mo shetarutz b'chozek v'yarutz miyad.

Translation:
> YHVH He rebuketh the sea, and maketh it dry (*Nahum 1:4*), who shaketh the earth out of her place, and the pillars

thereof tremble (*Job 9:6*), the One sitting on the *Cherubim*, the God of Israel is His Name, swing powerfully and swing immediately.

We are also told that it is good to recite *Psalm 51:8* multiple times until you have received the complete answer, following which you are required to keep still, and to allow the ring-pendulum to move at random until it becomes completely still, and recite the Divine Name construct formed from this verse with wisdom and knowledge.[18]

Besides the use of the current psalm against blood-loss and for heart conditions, it was also recommended against epidemics, and illness, and for healing in general. Regarding it being employed to confess and rectify personal transgressions, the fifty-first Psalm is recommended to individuals who are being burdened with sins, and who wish to pray for forgiveness. It is further recommended to those who desire to pray or recite psalms, or, for that matter, simply wish to speak to the Divine One. This psalm was further suggested for recitation against jealousy and resentment; witchcraft and bewitchment; against and to be saved from defamation, slander and gossip; against wrongful judgement; for protection in perilous situations; in times of trouble; and also for the abhorrent practice of working vengeance in secret.

Psalm 51 is listed in Christian Magic for the purposes of countering a physical attack,[19] recovering stolen property, affecting invisibility, and stopping blood loss.[20] As far as becoming "invisible and insensible to all beings" is concerned, one fifteenth century magical handbook instructs the practitioner to be "chaste for three days beforehand, and cut hair and beard, and dressed in white, in a secret place outside of town, under a clear sky, on level ground, trace a circle....with a magnificent sword," then to write a set of name of Spirit Intelligences, etc., and utter *Psalm 51:9* whilst sprinkling himself and the circle with holy water.[21] Elsewhere in the same source we find the fifty-first Psalm employed to summon a "flying throne," to obtain knowledge from a mirror, and it is recited on a Sunday during the waxing moon whilst "gazing constantly" at a crucifix, for the purpose of finding "hidden treasure."[22] A similar use is mentioned elsewhere in which a simple ring is tied to a string and suspended in a glass of water whilst reciting *Psalm 51:8* for the purpose of finding a hidden object.[23]

However, amongst all of these magical applications, halting a haemorrhage appears to be the most important use of the current psalm. In this regard, we find *Psalm 51:16* "against Nose Bleeds and Haemorrhages in all other parts of the body."[24] We also read in the Byzantine Christian magical manuscripts that when a woman is hemorrhaging "from her posterior," hot water should be boiled with laurel, myrtle, rosemary, and garlic leaves whilst reciting the fifty-first Psalm three times over the mixture. Following this action, the woman is to wash herself with the concoction.[25] *Psalm 51:3* is recommended elsewhere to inhibit the eruption of a flow of blood from the womb of a woman, or to control an excessive effusion of blood during her menstrual period. In this regard, the instruction is to write and recite the said verse on a Saturday prior to sunrise, following which the writing is tied to the right arm of the said woman, and kept there for the duration of the bloodflow.[26] Another source advises the practitioner to recite the current psalm seven times over the individual who is suffering blood loss, as well as over a glass of wine which the said individual should consume afterwards.[27] It is further maintained that bleeding could also be stopped by copying the fifty-first Psalm as well as a set of magical signs "on a piece of virgin parchment," which is afterwards tied to the navel of the sufferer.[28] Similar instructions are found in *"Le Livre d'Or,"* though in this instance *Psalm 51:1–16* is written directly on the person of the individual who is bleeding or suffering from haemophilia.[29] In addition to halting blood loss, the current psalm is employed in Christian Magic "to recover stolen property," and, as indicated, "to make oneself invisible."[30]

In conclusion it should be noted that the fifty-first Psalm is of particular importance in the *"Key of Solomon,"* since it is listed amongst the psalms recited during the construction of the "pentacles," the rest being *Psalms 8, 21, 27, 32, 29, 72,* and *134*. It is also one of the group of eight psalms, i.e. *Psalms 4, 30, 51, 102, 114, 119:97, 126* and *139*, which is recited whilst robing after taking a ritual bath, and it is also the seventh amongst the nineteen psalms recited over the wax from which ritual candles are manufactured, the full set being *Psalms 8, 15, 22, 46, 47, 49, 51,*

53, *68*, *72*, *84*, *102*, *110*, *113*, *126*, *130*, *131*, *133*, and *139*. Lastly, it is one of the seven psalms, i.e. *Psalms 3*, *9*, *31*, *42*, *60*, *51*, and *130*, employed in the consecration of "the needle and other iron instruments."[31]

PSALM 52

[1] למנצח משכיל לדוד
[2] בבוא דואג האדמי ויגד לאשאול ויאמר לו
בא דוד אל בית אחימלך
[3] מה תתהלל ברעה הגבור חסד אל כל היום
[4] הוות תחשב לשונך כתער מלטש עשה רמיה
[5] אהבת רע מטוב שקר מדבר צדק סלה
[6] אהבת כל דברי בלע לשון מרמה
[7] גם אל יתצך לנצח יחתך ויסחך מאהל ושרשך
מארץ חיים סלה
[8] ויראו צדיקים וייראו ועליו ישחקו
[9] הנה הגבר לא ישים אלהום מעוזו ויבטח ברב
עשרו יעז בהותו
[10] ואני כזית רענן בבית אלהים בטחתי בחסד
אלהים עולם ועד
[11] אודך לעולם כי עשית ואקוה שמך כי טוב
נגד חסידיך

Transliteration:
[1] lam'natzei'ach maskil l'david
[2] b'vo do'eig ha'adomi va'yageid l'sha'ul vayomer lo ba david el beit achimelech
[3] mah tit'haleil b'ra'ah hagibor chesed el kol ha'yom
[4] havot tach'shov l'shonecha k'ta'ar m'lutash oseih remiyah
[5] ahav'ta ra mitov sheker midabeir tzedek selah
[6] ahav'ta chol div'rei vala l'shon mir'mah
[7] gam el yitotz'cha lanetzach yach't'cha v'yisachacha mei'ohel v'sheiresh'cha mei'eretz chayim selah
[8] v'yir'u tzadikim v'yira'u v'alav yis'chaku
[9] hineih hagever lo yasim elohim ma'uzo vayiv'tach b'rov osh'ro ya'oz b'havato
[10] va'ani k'zayit ra'anan b'veit elohim batach'ti v'chesed elohim olam va'ed
[11] od'cha l'olam ki asita va'akaveh shim'cha chi tov neged chasidecha

Translation:
> [1] For the Leader. *Maschil* of David;
> [2] when Doeg the Edomite came and told Saul, and said unto him: 'David is come to the house of Ahimelech.'
> [3] Why boastest thou thyself of evil, O mighty man? The mercy of God endureth continually.
> [4] Thy tongue deviseth destruction; like a sharp razor, working deceitfully.
> [5] Thou lovest evil more than good; falsehood rather than speaking righteousness. *Selah*
> [6] Thou lovest all devouring words, the deceitful tongue.
> [7] God will likewise break thee for ever, He will take thee up, and pluck thee out of thy tent, and root thee out of the land of the living. *Selah*
> [8] The righteous also shall see, and fear, and shall laugh at him:
> [9] 'Lo, this is the man that made not *Elohim* his stronghold; but trusted in the abundance of his riches, and strengthened himself in his wickedness.'
> [10] But as for me, I am like a leafy olive-tree in the house of *Elohim*; I trust in the mercy of *Elohim* for ever and ever.
> [11] I will give Thee thanks for ever, because Thou hast done it; and I will wait for Thy name, for it is good, in the presence of Thy saints.

Psalm 52 is not extensively employed in "Practical Kabbalah," but it is used to prevent one from speaking לשון הרע (*lashon hara*—"evil tongue"),[1] i.e. to keep off slander,[2] or simply to halt the temptation of meddling in the affairs of others.[3] This is indeed a very useful magical tool, considering the human predilection for stirring trouble with tongues spreading falsehoods. Whilst the current psalm is not listed in every published version of the *Shimmush Tehillim*, those in which it is mentioned, it is noted that it should be copied to be worn as an amulet on the person of the one who is accustomed to spreading slander.[4] According to Selig the one "who is so unfortunate as to be disturbed through frequent slanders is advised to utter this Psalm daily in the morning, and no special prayer or holy name is needed to obtain the benefit of the

Psalm."[5] There is no reference in his version of the *Shimmush Tehillim* to the fifty-second Psalm being worn as an amulet, but in a different recension of the said text we find the current Psalm recited every day in conjunction with a prayer-incantation, so that people "do not speak lies about you."[6] The prayer-incantation reads:

ברוך אתה יהוה אלהינו ואלהי ישראל מן העולם
ועד העולם לפניך באתי שתשמרני מאיש רכיל
ומאיש חמס תפלטני ומאיש נרגן תושיעני יהי רצון
מלפניך אלהים חיים שתצילני היום ובכל יום ויום
מלשון הרע שלא אומר על שום אדם דבר דופי
ושקר ולא אחרים עלי לאמר דברים שלא כהוגן
לא היום ולא לעולם ולא שאר ימים בשם אלהים
חיים אמן אמן אמן סלה סלה סלה

Transliteration:

Baruch atah YHVH Eloheinu v'elohei Yis'ra'eil min ha'olam v'ad ha'olam l'fanecha ba'ati shetish'm'reini m'ish rachil um'ish chamas t'fal'teini um'ish nir'gan toshi'eini y'hi ratzon mil'fanecha elohim chayim sh'tatzileini hayom ub'chol yom vayom milashon hara shelo omer al shum adam davar dofi v'sheker v'lo acheirim alai leimor d'varim sh'lo k'hogen lo hayom v'lo l'olam v'lo sha'ar yamim b'shem elohim chayim Omein Omein Omein Selah Selah Selah.

Translation:

Blessed are you, Lord our God and God of Israel, from eternity to eternity. I have come before you so that you might keep me from the slanderer. You shall save me from the perpetrator of violence, deliver me from the heckler. May it be your will living God, that you keep me from slander today and every day, that I do not speak a harmful word or a lie about anyone, and that others do not speak words about me that are not proper, neither today nor forever, nor in the days to come. In the name of the living God *Amen Amen Amen Selah Selah Selah.*[7]

Whilst there is not much to be found in official literature regarding the magical applications of the current psalm, the fifty-second Psalm is recommended in folk customs not only against defamation, slander, and gossip, but also against malice and hard-hearted employers, and equally against any torment inflicted by employers and superiors. It is further employed to counter disbelief, i.e. incredulity, and to aid individuals who are frustrated with the wickedness of their fellow humankind.

Psalm 52 is equally not extensively referenced in Christian magic, and the listed uses are somewhat obscure. In this regard, we are told that writing the fifty-second Psalm with certain magical signs will inspire "the dread of all."[8] Elsewhere, in "*Le Livre d'Or*," it is maintained that "if a pregnant woman corrupts her fruit," she will be healed if the current psalm is written and attached to her arm.[9]

PSALM 53

[1] למנצח על מחלת משכיל לדוד
[2] אמר נבל בלבו אין אלהים השחיתו והתעיבו עול אין עשה טוב
[3] אלהים משמים השקיף על בני אדם לראות היש משכיל דרש את אלהים
[4] כלו סג יחדו נאלחו אין עשה טוב אין גם אחד
[5] הלא ידעו פעלי און אכלו עמו אכלו לחם אלהים לא קראו
[6] שם פחדו פחד לא היה פחד כי אלהים פזר עצמות חנך הבשתה כי אלהים מאסם
[7] מי יתן מציון ישעות ישראל בשוב אלהים שבות עמו יגל יעקב ישמח ישראל

Transliteration:
[1] *lam'natzei'ach al machalat mas'kil l'david*
[2] *amar naval b'libo ein elohim hish'chitu v'hit'ivu avel ein oseih tov*
[3] *elohim mishamayim hish'kif al b'nei adam lir'ot hayeish mas'kil doreish et elohim*
[4] *kulo sag yach'dav ne'elachu ein oseih tov ein gam echad*
[5] *halo yad'u po'alei aven och'lei ami ach'lu lechem elohim lo kara'u*
[6] *sham pachadu fachad lo hayah fachad ki elohim pizar atz'mot chonach heivishotah ki elohim m'asam*
[7] *mi yitein mitziyon yishu'ot yis'ra'eil b'shuv elohim sh'vut amo yageil ya'akov yis'mach yis'ra'eil*

Translation:
[1] For the Leader; upon *Mahalath. Maschil* of David.
[2] The fool hath said in his heart: 'There is no *Elohim*'; they have dealt corruptly, and have done abominable iniquity; there is none that doeth good.
[3] *Elohim* looked forth from heaven upon the children of men, to see if there were any man of understanding, that did seek after *Elohim*.
[4] Every one of them is unclean, they are together become impure; there is none that doeth good, no, not one.

[5] 'Shall not the workers of iniquity know it, who eat up My people as they eat bread, and call not upon *Elohim*?'

[6] There are they in great fear, where no fear was; for *Elohim* hath scattered the bones of him that encampeth against thee; Thou hast put them to shame, because *Elohim* hath rejected them.

[7] Oh that the salvation of Israel were come out of Zion! When *Elohim* turneth the captivity of His people, let Jacob rejoice, let Israel be glad.

Psalm 53 is said to be good "to frighten your haters," i.e. to scare your foes.[1] Whilst this psalm is wrongly numbered in one of the published editions of the *Shimmush Tehillim*,[2] we are told in other publications of the said text that anyone wishing to instil fear in their enemies, should recite the psalm every day with its associated Divine Name, the latter indicated to be a Divine Construct אי, א (*Alef*) from אמר (*amar*—"said"): verse 2; and י (*Yod*) from ישמח (*yis'mach*—"be glad"): verse 7.[3] Godfrey Selig addresses *Psalms 53* to *55* conjointly, maintaining that "these three Psalms are ordained to be uttered by him who is persecuted without cause by open and secret enemies."[4] Regarding the current psalm, his version, with minor embellishments, aligns with the sentiments expressed in the standard editions of the *Shimmush Tehillim*. In this regard, he noted that if someone "desires only to quiet his enemies, or fill them with fear," he should enunciate the psalm every day "with the holy name *Ai*," the latter Divine Name having been derived from the earlier listed sources with, in his opinion, a specific reference to the capitals of the Divine Names אדני (*Adonai*) and יהוה, the Ineffable **Name**.[5]

There is once again a variant application of the current psalm shared in a different recension of the *Shimmush Tehillim*, in which it is said *Psalm 53* is good to say by those who have been captured by non-Jews, specifically those who "have their faith in the corpse,"[6] the latter expression being a reference to the Christian saviour. In this regard, the prisoner is instructed to recite the psalm in conjunction with a prayer-incantation reading:

כח רחמים מאת השם יהיו לי אני [....personal name....]
אשר נשביתי לבין הגוים בדתיהם לבר מנן וישמרני

The Psalms of David — Book II : 123

אלהי ארך אפים לבל אחטא ובל אלמוד מעשיהם
ויבא איש מקרובי ויפדני ויוליכני קוממיות למקומי
הראשון ואל אהיה עוד לבז ולמשסה בשם אלהי
ארך אפים אמן אמן אמן אמן סלה סלה סלה

Transliteration:
> Ko'ach rachamim mei'eit hashem yih'yu li ani [....personal name....] asher nish'veiti l'bein hagoyim b'dateihem l'bar minan v'yish'm'reini Elohei Erech Apayim l'val ech'te ubal el'mod ma'aseihem v'yavo ish mik'rovai v'yaf'deini v'yolicheini kom'miyut lim'komi harishon v'al eh'yeh od lavuz v'lamishasah b'shem Elohei Erech Apayim Omein Omein Omein Selah Selah Selah

Translation:
> By the power of mercy from *Hashem* [God], be with me [....personal name....], the one who was captured by gentiles with their faith in the corpse. And it will guard me *Elohei Erech Apayim* [the long-suffering God], so that I do not sin and do not learn their ways. And may someone from my relatives come and ransom me, and lead me upright to my home ground. And I will no longer be spoil and prey. In the Name of *Elohei Erech Apayim* [the long-suffering God] *Amen Amen Amen Selah Selah Selah*.[7]

Psalm 53 is employed by the common folk against frightening experiences, and when they are feeling afraid. In this regard, a most fearful experience for the Jewish people, is to be captured by non-Jews. In fact, whether readers consider this a valid fear or not, everyone knows the horrors Jews have endured over the last two millennia of intense anti-semitism. It should thus come as no surprise that the current psalm is employed in the said manner, and it is recited for the Jewish people and Judaism. As noted, anyone can speak the fifty-third Psalm to scare and subdue enemies, whether the latter be known or hidden. It is further recited against threats, abuse, and oppression, and, as in the case of the previous psalm, it is likewise uttered when an individual is frustrated with the wickedness of others. By contrast, it is worth noting that the fifty-third Psalm was also recommended to fishermen who are seeking to fill their nets.

Psalm 53 is employed in Christian Magic for virtually the same purpose as in Jewish Magic, with some procedural variations. In this regard the practitioner is instructed in *"Le Livre d'Or"* to take some powder, and read the psalm over it seven times with devotion. Following this action the said substance is cast in the faces of enemies, who are said will flee forthwith.[8] Readers may well wonder at the patience of "enemies," who would have to patiently stand around whilst waiting for the "defender" to recite the current psalm seven times! Be that as it may, *Psalm 53* is listed in the *"Key of Solomon"* as one of nineteen recited over the wax from which ritual candles are made, i.e. *Psalms 8, 15, 22, 46, 47, 49, 51, 53, 68, 72, 84, 102, 110, 113, 126, 130, 131, 133,* and *139.*[9] It is listed amongst a set, i.e. *Psalms 14, 53, 27, 54, 81* and *105,* any of which is recommended for recitation whilst the practitioner is disrobing in preparation for taking a ritual bath.[10]

PSALM 54

[1] למנצח בנגינת משכיל לדוד
[2] בבא הזיפים ויאמרו לשאול הלא דוד מסתתר עמנו
[3] אלהים בשמך הושיעני ובגבורתך תדינני
[4] אלהים שמע תפלתי האזינה לאמרי פי
[5] כי זרים קמו עלי ועריצים בקשו נפשי לא שמו אלהים לנגדם סלה
[6] הנה אלהים עזר לי אדני בסמכי נפשי
[7] ישיב הרע לשררי באמתך הצמיתם
[8] בנדבה אזבחה לך אודה שמך יהוה‎אדני/אהדונהי כי טוב
[9] כי מכל צרה הצילני ובאיבי ראתה עיני

Transliteration:
[1] *lam'natzei'ach bin'ginot mas'kil l'david*
[2] *b'vo hazifim vayom'ru l'sha'ul halo david mis'tateir imanu*
[3] *elohim b'shim'cha hoshi'eini uvig'vurat'cha t'dineini*
[4] *elohim sh'ma t'filati ha'azinah l'im'rei fi*
[5] *ki zarim kamu alai v'aritzim bik'shu naf'shi lo samu elohim l'neg'dam selah*
[6] *hineih elohim ozeir li adonai b'som'chei naf'shi*
[7] *yashiv ha'ra l'shor'rai ba'amit'cha hatz'miteim*
[8] *bin'davah ez'b'chah lach odeh shim'cha YHVH ki tov*
[9] *ki mikol tzarah hitzilani uv'oy'vai ra'atah eini*

Translation:
[1] For the Leader; with string-music. *Maschil* of David:
[2] when the Ziphites came and said to Saul: 'Doth not David hide himself with us?'
[3] *Elohim* save me by Thy name, and right me by Thy might.
[4] *Elohim* hear my prayer; give ear to the words of my mouth.
[5] For strangers are risen up against me, and violent men have sought after my soul; they have not set *Elohim* before them. *Selah*

[6] Behold, *Elohim* is my helper; *Adonai* is for me as the upholder of my soul.
[7] He will requite the evil unto them that lie in wait for me; destroy Thou them in Thy truth.
[8] With a freewill-offering will I sacrifice unto Thee; I will give thanks unto Thy name *YHVH*, for it is good.
[9] For He hath delivered me out of all trouble; and mine eye hath gazed upon mine enemies.

Psalm 54 is recited in times of trouble.[1] It is employed for protection against,[2] as well as to take revenge on, enemies.[3] In this regard, we are instructed in the popular published Hebrew version of the *Shimmush Tehillim*, in which the psalm is correctly listed, that reciting the current psalm will affect this aim. It was further noted that the Divine Name י״ה (*Yah*) is associated here, the latter said to have been derived: י (*Yod*) from ראתה עיני (*ra'atah eini*—"mine eye hath gazed"): verse 9, and ה (*Heh*) from ו (*Vav*) in מסתתר עמנו (*mis'tateir imanu*—"hide himself with us"): verse 2, the glyph having been transposed in accordance with the numerical value of ה״א (*Heh–Alef*) [ה = 5 + א = 1 = 6], the *Gematria* of this letter combination being equal to that of the letter ו [6].[4] It is mentioned elsewhere that the letter ה (*Heh*) was derived from ו (*Vav*) by means of the cipher ה״ו,[5] i.e. in accordance with the very obscure and rarely, if ever, used א״י ב״ט (*Ayabat*) cipher. Be that as it may, another recension of the *Shimmush Tehillim* lists the psalm to be good for someone who hides him or herself in a shelter, for fear of being found by enemies or robbers. In this regard the said individual is instructed to recite the fifty-fourth Psalm fifteen times in conjunction with the following prayer-incantation:

יהי רצון מלפניך מלך רב העיצה שתצפניני נא
ותמלטיני נא ואמלט הפעם הזאת לבל ימצאוני אויבי
ושונאי בשם רב העיצה ושם הגדול עלם אגלא
אמן אמן אמן סלה סלה סלה

Transliteration:
    Y'hi ratzon mil'fanecha melech Rav Ha'eitza shetatz'pineini na v'tam'liteini na v'amaleit hapa'am hazot

> l'bal im'tza'uni oy'vai v'son'ai b'shem Rav Ha'eitza
> v'shem hagadol Elem Agala'a Omein Omein Omein Selah
> Selah Selah

Translation:
> May it be your will King, *Rav Ha'eitza* (the Great Council), that you hide me and let me escape, and I shall escape this time so that my enemy and hater will not find me. In the Name *Rav Ha'eitza* (the Great Council) and the great Name *Elem Agala'a, Amen Amen Amen Selah Selah Selah*.[6]

The Divine Name עלם (*Elem*) is the fourth tri-letter portion of the "Name of Seventy-two Names." We have already encountered this tri-letter combination in connection with a magical application of *Psalm 32* in which it is conjoined with והו (*Vehu*), the first portion of the "*Shem Vayisa Vayet*," both Divine Name combinations being concentrated on in "a plea for mercy from the Name of God."[7] It has been said that the simple *Gematria* of עלם [ע = 70 + ל = 30 + ם = 40; 7 + 3 + 4 = 14] is equal to that of the word יד (*Yad*—"hand" [י = 10 + ד = 4 = 14]), the latter said to refer to the hand of the Almighty. We are informed that this aligns with the "Fourteen Letter Name of God," כוזו במוכסז כוזו (*Kuzu B'mochsaz Kuzu*), which pertains to *Gevurah* (Severity/Might) on the sefirotic Tree, and is a transposition of the biblical phrase יהוה אלהינו יהוה (*YHVH Eloheinu YHVH*) [*Deuteronomy 6:4*].[8] Interestingly, the second listed Divine Name construct אגלא (*Agala'a*), which is composed of the initials of the phrase in the *Amidah* prayer reading אתה גיבור לעולם אדני (*Atah Gibor l'Olam Adonai*—"You are mighty throughout eternity *Adonai*"), is likewise associated with *Gevurah* (Severity/Might) on the sefirotic Tree. In this regard, both names commands protective powers.[9]

Whilst the applications of the current psalm are somewhat sparse in official Jewish magical literature, informal sources recommend *Psalm 54* for a greater variety of purposes. Thus it is not only employed for protection against, or taking revenge, on enemies, but, as in the case of the previous as well as the succeeding psalm, it is recited to subdue enemies both known or secret, and equally to alleviate anxiety caused by enemies. The fifty-fourth Psalm is one of a number of psalms recommended for protection in perilous situations, and to be recited in times of trouble. In this regard, we are informed that the fifty-fourth Psalm is good to enunciate against theft, thieves and robbers; hostility and quarreling; malice; fierce persecution; and, for that matter, against assassins. It is also said to offer safety from fear; counteract despair; minimise fear of death; reveal false friendships; protect against loan sharks (userers); and to free slaves. On the other hand, this psalm is employed against earthquakes, and is particularly useful in sharpening and increasing intelligence.

As far as individual verses from the current psalm being employed for magical purposes are concerned, it should be noted that the capitals of the first four words of *Psalm 54:6* are conjoined in the Divine Name construct האעל, which is employed in amulets "to subdue an enemy."[10] Likewise the initials of the opening four words of *Psalm 54:9* are combined in the Divine Name construct כמצה or מצה, and included in an amulet meant to save and rescue the bearer from trouble.[11] Furthermore, as indicated below, *Psalm 54* is also one of the psalms which were arranged in the format of the *Menorah* (seven-branched candelabrum) for inclusion in *Shiviti* plaques and amulets:[12]

Psalm 54 is employed in Christian Magic for the purpose of counteracting slander. In this regard we are informed in *"Le Livre d'Or"* that if an individual has been slandered, and due to this was brought before an authority, that individual should recite the current psalm seven times "in his supplication and he will be delivered."[13] Other than that, we find the fifty-fourth Psalm as well as the succeeding one listed in the Byzantine magical manuscripts "for thoughts of lethargy,"[14] which I presume pertains to laziness. Whatever the case may be, we find elsewhere *Psalm 54:3* recited whilst carrying a cryptic spell written against epilepsy.[15]

In conclusion, it is worth noting that in the *"Key of Solomon" Psalms 2, 47, 54, 67, 68* and *113* are listed as the psalms recited either before or during the construction of the "magic circle," and the current psalm is also one of the psalms, i.e. *Psalms 14, 53, 27, 54, 81* and *105*, any of which is recommended for recitation whilst the practitioner is disrobing in preparation for taking a ritual bath.[16] It is equally listed in conjunction with *Psalms 102, 6* and *67* for recitation whilst adding salt during the consecration of water to be employed in ritual work.[17]

PSALM 55

[1] למנצח בנגינת משכיל לדוד
[2] האזינה אלהים תפלתי ואל תתעלם מתחנתי
[3] הקשיבה לי וענני אריד בשיחי ואהימה
[4] מקול אויב מפני עקת רשע כי ימיטו עלי און ובאף ישטמוני
[5] לבי יחיל בקרבי ואימות מות נפלו עלי
[6] יראה ורעד יבא בי ותכסני פלצות
[7] ואמר מי יתן לי אבר כיונה אעופה ואשכנה
[8] הנה ארחיק נדד אלין במדבר סלה
[9] אחישה מפלט לי מרוח סעה מסער
[10] בלע אדני פלג לשונם כי ראיתי חמס וריב בעיר
[11] יומם ולילה יסובבה על חומתיה ואון ועמל בקרבה
[12] הוות בקרבה ולא ימיש מרחבה תך ומרמה
[13] כי לא אויב יחרפני ואשא לא משנאי עלי הגדיל ואסתר ממני
[14] ואתה אנוש כערכי אלופי ומידעי
[15] אשר יחדו נמתיק סוד בבית אלהים נהלך ברגש
[16] ישי מות עלימו ירדו שאול חיים כי רעות במגורם בקרבם
[17] אני אל אלהים אקרא ויהו‏**אדני**‏ה יאהדונהי יושיעני
[18] ערב ובקר וצהרים אשיחה ואהמה וישמע קולי
[19] פדה בשלום נפשי מקרב לי כי ברבים היו עמדי
[20] ישמע אל ויענם וישב קדם סלה אשר אין חליפות למו ולא יראו אלהים
[21] שלח ידיו בשלמיו חלל בריתו

[22] חלקו מחמאת פיו וקרב לבו רכו דבריו משמן והמה פתחות
[23] השלך על יהוה‎/אדוני יהבך והוא יכלכלך לא יתן לעולם מוט לצדיק
[24] ואתה אלהים תורדם לבאר שחת אנשי דמים ומרמה לא יחצו ימיהם ואני אבטח בך

Transliteration:

[1] lam'natzei'ach bin'ginot mas'kil l'david
[2] ha'azinah elohim t'filati v'al tit'alam mit'chinati
[3] hak'shivah li va'aneini arid b'sichi v'ahimah
[4] mikol oyeiv mip'nei akat rasha ki yamitu alai aven uv'af yis't'muni
[5] libi yachil b'kir'bi v'eimot mavet naf'lu alai
[6] yir'ah vara'ad yavo vi vat'chaseini palatzut
[7] va'omar mi yiten li eiver kayonah a'ufah v'esh'konah
[8] hinei ar'chik n'dod alin bamid'bar selah
[9] achishah mif'lat li meiru'ach so'ah misa'ar
[10] bala adonai palag l'shonam ki ra'iti chamas v'riv ba'ir
[11] yomam valailah y'sov'vuha al chomoteha v'aven v'amal b'kir'bah
[12] havot b'kir'bah v'lo yamish meir'chovah toch umir'mah
[13] ki lo oyeiv y'char'feini v'esa lo m'san'i alai hig'dil v'esateir mimenu
[14] v'atah enosh k'er'ki alufi um'yuda'i
[15] asher yach'dav nam'tik sod b'veit elohim n'haleich b'ragesh
[16] yashi mavet aleimo yeir'du sh'ol chayim ki ra'ot bim'guram b'kir'bam
[17] ani el elohim ek'ra va'YHVH yoshi'eini
[18] erev vavoker v'tzohorayim asichah v'ehemeh vayish'ma koli
[19] padah b'shalom naf'shi mik'rav li ki v'rabim hayu imadi
[20] yish'ma el v'ya'aneim v'yosheiv kedem selah asher ein chalifot lamo v'lo yar'u elohim
[21] shalach yadav bish'lomav chileil b'rito

[22] *chal'ku mach'ma'ot piv uk'rav libo raku d'varav mishemen v'heimah f'tichot*
[23] *hash'leich al YHVH y'hav'cha v'hu y'chal'k'lecha lo yitein l'olam mot latzadik*
[24] *v'atah elohim torideim liv'eir shachat an'shei damim umir'mah lo yechetzu y'meihem va'ani ev'tach bach*

Translation:

[1] For the Leader; with string-music. *Maschil* of David.

[2] Give ear *Elohim*, to my prayer; and hide not Thyself from my supplication.

[3] Attend unto me, and hear me; I am distraught in my complaint, and will moan;

[4] Because of the voice of the enemy, because of the oppression of the wicked; for they cast mischief upon me, and in anger they persecute me.

[5] My heart doth writhe within me; and the terrors of death are fallen upon me.

[6] Fear and trembling come upon me, and horror hath overwhelmed me.

[7] And I said: 'Oh that I had wings like a dove! then would I fly away, and be at rest.

[8] Lo, then would I wander far off, I would lodge in the wilderness. *Selah*

[9] I would haste me to a shelter from the stormy wind and tempest.

[10] Destroy *Adonai*, and divide their tongue; for I have seen violence and strife in the city.

[11] Day and night they go about it upon the walls thereof; iniquity also and mischief are in the midst of it.

[12] Wickedness is in the midst thereof; oppression and guile depart not from her broad place.

[13] For it was not an enemy that taunted me, then I could have borne it; neither was it mine adversary that did magnify himself against me, then I would have hid myself from him.

[14] But it was thou, a man mine equal, my companion, and my familiar friend;

[15] We took sweet counsel together, in the house of *Elohim* we walked with the throng.

[16] May He incite death against them, let them go down alive into the nether-world; for evil is in their dwelling, and within them.
[17] As for me, I will call upon *Elohim*; and *YHVH* shall save me.
[18] Evening, and morning, and at noon, will I complain, and moan; and He hath heard my voice.
[19] He hath redeemed my soul in peace so that none came nigh me; for they were many that strove with me.
[20] God shall hear, and humble them, even He that is enthroned of old, *Selah*, such as have no changes, and fear not *Elohim*.
[21] He hath put forth his hands against them that were at peace with him; he hath profaned his covenant.
[22] Smoother than cream were the speeches of his mouth, but his heart was war; his words were softer than oil, yet were they keen-edged swords.
[23] Cast thy burden upon *YHVH*, and He will sustain thee; He will never suffer the righteous to be moved.
[24] But Thou *Elohim*, wilt bring them down into the nethermost pit; men of blood and deceit shall not live out half their days; but as for me, I will trust in Thee.

Psalm 55 is recommended for protection against harm.[1] Whilst it is said to be effective against all evil, and any bad thing,[2] it is, as in the case of the previous psalm, more popularly employed in Jewish Magic "to be avenged on one's foes."[3] In this regard, we are informed in the *Shimmush Tehillim* that to retaliate or take vengeance on your enemies, the current psalm should be recited whilst focussing on its associated Divine Name construct, the latter indicated to be וה, which is said to have been derived: ו (*Vav*) from ואתה (*v'atah*—and thou): verse 24, and ה (*Heh*) from the initial of האזינה (*ha'azinah*—"give ear"): verse 2.[4] As one might expect, the term "vengeance" means different things to different people, and it is certainly not part of my personal vocabulary, since I believe what you do unto others you do unto yourself. However, there is nothing ambiguous about the intention behind the said term in Godfrey Selig's version of the *Shimmush Tehillim*, in which he recommended **the psalm to an individual who seeks "to render his enemies evil for evil."**[5]

As is the case with most of the psalms, we find the current one employed for a very different magical purpose in a variant recension of the *Shimmush Tehillim*. In this regard, the fifty-fifth Psalm is recommended to someone whose opponents are conspiring to have their personal verdict passed in a court of law.[6] In this regard the said individual is instructed to recite the psalm thirteen times, each time with the following prayer-incantation:

את אשר במשפט הכחת ארץ תעמידני על משפטי
ותצילני לבל יטו אלה האנשים דיני וידונוני במשפט
ואל יעותוני ואל יאמרו במשפטי דבר שלא במשפט
בשם מלך המשפט אמן אמן אמן סלה סלה סלה

Transliteration:

Et asher b'mish'pat hochach'ta eretz ta'amideini al mish'pati v'tatzileini l'bal yatu eileh ha'anashim dini viyadununi b'mish'pat v'al ya'av'tuni v'al yom'ru b'mish'pati d'var shelo b'mish'pat b'shem Melech Hamish'pat Omein Omein Omein Selah Selah Selah.

Translation:

You who judge the earth with a decree, you shall affirm my right, and save me so that these people do not decide my verdict, and condemn me according to (their) ruling. And they should not twist me, and state anything in my legal case which is not lawful. In the Name *Melech Hamish'pat* ("King of the Law") *Amen Amen Amen Selah Selah Selah*.[7]

Selected verses from the current psalm are extensively employed in "Practical Kabbalah." In this regard, the capitals of the six words comprising *Psalm 55:9* are combined into the Divine Name construct אמלמסם, which is employed in an amulet "to subdue an enemy."[8] Elsewhere the same verse is employed in conjunction with *Genesis 21:1*, reading ויהוה פקד את שרה כאשר אמר [*v'YHVH pakad et Sarah ka'asher amar*—"And *YHVH* remembered Sarah as He had said"], as well as the following prayer-incantation, all of which are written on deerskin parchment, or a sheet of clean good quality paper, to be carried on the arm of a woman who suffered a miscarriage:[9]

בְּשֵׁם שַׁדַּי תְּהֵא קְמִיעַ זוּ לְ[....name of the sufferer....]
שֶׁלֹּא תַּפִּיל יְלָדֶיהָ וְלֹא מְטַפֵּת דַּם הַמַּפֶּלֶת לֹא יִהְיֶה
מַשְׁכֵּל וּמְשַׁכֵּלָה בְּשֵׁם אֶהְיֶה אֲשֶׁר אֶהְיֶה יָהּ יהוה
וּבְשֵׁם מִיכָאֵל גַּבְרִיאֵל רְפָאֵל דָּנִיאֵל כְּתוּתִיאֵל
פָּנִיאֵל סנוֹי סנסנוֹי סמנגלוֹף אָמֵן נֶצַח סֶלָה וָעֶד

Transliteration:

B'shem Shadai tehe kamei'a zu l'[....name of the sufferer....] *shelo tapil yeladei'ah v'lo mitipat dam hamapelet lo yiyeh mis'kal v'mis'kalah b'shem Eh'yeh asher Eh'yeh Yah YHVH ub'shem Micha'el Gavri'el Rafa'el Dani'el Katuti'el Pani'el Sanoi Sansanoi Semangelof Omein Netzach Selah Va'ed*

Translation:

In the Name *Shadai* this amulet will be for [....name of the sufferer....] that she will not abort her children, and not emit any blood of a miscarriage, and will not loose boys or girls. In the Name *Ehyeh asher Ehyeh Yah YHVH*, and in the name *Micha'el, Gavri'el, Rafa'el, Dani'el, Katuti'el, Pani'el, Sanoi Sansanoi Semangelof,* **Amen** Enduring [Victory] **Selah** Forever.[10]

It should be further noted that the opening phrase of *Psalm 55:23*, reading הַשְׁלֵךְ עַל יהוה יְהָבְךָ וְהוּא יְכַלְכְּלֶךָ (*hash'leich al YHVH y'hav'cha v'hu y'chal'k'lecha*—"Cast thy burden upon *YHVH*, and He will sustain thee"), was arranged in the following Divine Name construct, which is carried as an amulet to encourage a good livelihood:[11]

הַבְ שְׁבָ לֵו כָה עֻו לָא
יְיָ הֹבַ וַל הְבִ יַל הָבָ

This Divine Name construct was formulated by means of the ever popular *Serugin* (trellis) method of constructing Divine Names. In the current instance the first twelve letters of the said phrase were intertwined directly with the second twelve. If the Divine Name was meant to be vocalised, which thankfully it is not, it would sound *Hav' Sh'cha Leiv' Ch'ho A'u L' Y'y' Hocha Val' H'ch' Y'la*

Haka. The vowel punctuations align more or less with the enunciation of the letters in the verse. Be that as it may, the Divine Name construct is presented in the following three formats, which are included in the exact order in the said amulet:[12]

הבשכלו   כהעולא
ייהכול   הכילהך

הוו שתא ליי כהכ
עבל לכב יול ההך

היבי שהכב לוול
ייהכול   הכילהך

We are informed that this amulet for livelihood should be written on kosher deerskin parchment, but, as noted earlier, a clean sheet of good quality white paper will suffice. Furthermore, the individual preparing the amulet is required to fast beforehand, and to act in purity and holiness.[13] Interestingly, we also find the said portion of *Psalm 55:23* enlisted in conjunction with three biblical verses for the purpose of encouraging a better livelihood.[14] Those who are seeking such support are instructed to recite the opening phrase of *Proverbs 3:25* reading אל תירא מפחד פתאם (*al tira mipachad pit'om*—"Be not afraid of sudden terror"); the mentioned opening phrase of *Psalm 55:23*; three times the first three words of *Genesis 49:19* גד גדוד יגודנו (*gad g'dud y'gudenu*—"Gad, a troop shall troop upon him"), and conclude with *1 Samuel 18:14* reading דוד לכל דרכו משביל ויהוה עמו ויהי (*vay'hi david l'chol d'rachav mas'kil va'YHVH imo*—"And David had great success in all his ways; and *YHVH* was with him"). It was suggested this procedure should be done after the עלינו לשבח (*Aleinu L'shabei'ach* ["It is our duty (to praise God)"]) prayer,[15] which is enunciated at the conclusion of each of the three daily Jewish religious services. Since it is highly unlikely that non-Jewish readers would be familiar with this prayer, I suggest they perform this procedure either before or after their daily prayers.

Be that as it may, *Psalm 55:23* is also recited in its entirety in conjunction with a related prayer-incantation for livelihood, and to encourage good business negotiations.[16] In terms of the latter, we are told that individuals who wish to strengthen their position in any negotiation, should make the following statement, followed by the said prayer-incantation:

אני הולך לשא ולתן באמונה לשם יחוד קדשא בריך
הוא על ידי ההוא טמיר ונעלם

Translation:
> *Ani holeich lisa v'litein b'emunah l'sheim yichud kud'sha b'rich hu al y'dei hahu t'mir v'ne'lam*

Transliteration:
> I am going to negotiate in confidence (faith) for the sake of the unity of the Holy One, Blessed be He, by means of that which is disguised and concealed.

The associated prayer-incantation reads:

יהוה אלהים אמת תן לי ברכה והצלחה בכל מעשי
ידי ואני בוטח בך שעל ידי עסק זה תשלח לי ברכה
ויקים בי מקרא שכתוב השלך על יהוה יהבך
[....brief pause....] והוא יכלכלך לא יתן לעולם מוט
לצדיק (*Psalm 55:23*) אנא רחום וחנון רחם נא עלי
והצילנו מאסור גזל וגנבה אונאה ושקר ותזמין
פרנסתי שתהיה בהתר ולא באסור יהיו לרצון
אמרי פי והגיון לבי לפניך יהוה צורי וגאלי
(*Psalm 19:15*)

Transliteration:
> *YHVH elohim emet tein li b'rachah v'hatz'lachah b'chol ma'asei yadai va'ani votei'ach b'cha she'al y'dei eisek zeh tish'lach li b'rachah viy'kuyam bi mik'ra shekatuv hash'leich al YHVH yahav'cha* [....brief pause....] *v'hu y'chal'k'lecha lo yitein l'olam mot latzadik* (*Psalm 55:23*) *ana rachum v'chanun racheim na alai v'hatzileinu mei'isur gazeil v'g'neivah ona'ah v'sheker v'taz'min par'nasati shetih'yeh b'heteir v'lo b'isur yih'yu l'ratzon im'rei fi v'heg'yon libi l'fanecha YHVH tzuri v'go'ali* (*Psalm 19:15*)

Translation:
> *YHVH, Elohim* of truth, grant me blessing and success in all my deeds, and my trust is in you regarding this business, send me a blessings, and may be fulfilled in me that which is written *cast thy burden upon YHVH* [....brief pause....] *and He will sustain thee, He will never suffer the righteous to be moved.* (*Psalm 55:23*) Please be merciful and gracious. Have mercy on me, and save me from plunder and theft, deception and falsehood. And arrange my livelihood to be permissible and not forbidden. *Let the words of my mouth and the meditation of my heart be acceptable before Thee YHVH, my Rock, and my Redeemer.* (*Psalm 19:15*)[17]

Psalm 55 is also recommended for a variety of purposes not listed in generally published sources. In this regard, we have seen the psalm recommended for recitation against enemies, and, as in the case of the previous psalm, to be freed from anxiety caused by enemies. However, this psalm is equally enunciated against all manner of trouble and distress, and, as in the case of the previous psalm, for protection in perilous situations, and in times of trouble. As indicated earlier, *Psalm 55:9* is included in an amulet meant to subdue an enemy, but it should be noted that the entire psalm is recited for the same purpose. In fact, *Psalms 53, 54* and *55* are all recommended to subdue enemies, both known and unknown. It is equally employed against betrayal (treachery); and uttered to restore the honour of a family following an unjust accusation, as well as to invoke Divine retribution against enemies. In conclusion, it should be noted that the fifty-fifth Psalm is enunciated against being hurt, and for illness and healing in general.

In Christian Magic *Psalm 55* is dealt with mainly from personal protection perspectives. Thus, in harmony with the sentiments expressed in an earlier mentioned recension of the *Shimmush Tehillim*, it is listed in the Byzantine Christian manuscripts against injustice.[18] The same sources recommend reciting the current and the next psalm "when meeting your adversary face to face."[19] It was further noted that writing *Psalm 55*, and then carrying it on your right side, will ensure that you do not fear enemies.[20] As far as dealing with enemies is concerned, a much more billigerent intention is listed in *"Le Livre d'Or,"* in which it is noted that you could make it impossible for an enemy to build a house by reciting the current psalm over the foundations of the would-be residence.[21] Otherwise, as in the case of the previous psalm, the current psalm is also listed "for thoughts of lethargy."[22]

PSALM 56

[1] לַמְנַצֵּחַ עַל יוֹנַת אֵלֶם רְחֹקִים לְדָוִד מִכְתָּם בֶּאֱחֹז אוֹתוֹ פְלִשְׁתִּים בְּגַת
[2] חָנֵּנִי אֱלֹהִים כִּי שְׁאָפַנִי אֱנוֹשׁ כָּל הַיּוֹם לֹחֵם יִלְחָצֵנִי
[3] שָׁאֲפוּ שׁוֹרְרַי כָּל הַיּוֹם כִּי רַבִּים לֹחֲמִים לִי מָרוֹם
[4] יוֹם אִירָא אֲנִי אֵלֶיךָ אֶבְטָח
[5] בֵּאלֹהִים אֲהַלֵּל דְּבָרוֹ בֵּאלֹהִים בָּטַחְתִּי לֹא אִירָא מַה יַּעֲשֶׂה בָשָׂר לִי
[6] כָּל הַיּוֹם דְּבָרַי יְעַצֵּבוּ עָלַי כָּל מַחְשְׁבֹתָם לָרָע
[7] יָגוּרוּ יִצְפּוֹנוּ הֵמָּה עֲקֵבַי יִשְׁמֹרוּ כַּאֲשֶׁר קִוּוּ נַפְשִׁי
[8] עַל אָוֶן פַּלֶּט לָמוֹ בְּאַף עַמִּים הוֹרֵד אֱלֹהִים
[9] נֹדִי סָפַרְתָּה אָתָּה שִׂימָה דִמְעָתִי בְנֹאדֶךָ הֲלֹא בְּסִפְרָתֶךָ
[10] אָז יָשׁוּבוּ אוֹיְבַי אָחוֹר בְּיוֹם אֶקְרָא זֶה יָדַעְתִּי כִּי אֱלֹהִים לִי
[11] בֵּאלֹהִים אֲהַלֵּל דָּבָר בַּיהֹוָ‎ה‎אֲדֹנָי‎אֲהַלֵּל דָּבָר
[12] בֵּאלֹהִים בָּטַחְתִּי לֹא אִירָא מַה יַּעֲשֶׂה אָדָם לִי
[13] עָלַי אֱלֹהִים נְדָרֶיךָ אֲשַׁלֵּם תּוֹדֹת לָךְ
[14] כִּי הִצַּלְתָּ נַפְשִׁי מִמָּוֶת הֲלֹא רַגְלַי מִדֶּחִי לְהִתְהַלֵּךְ לִפְנֵי אֱלֹהִים בְּאוֹר הַחַיִּים

Transliteration:
[1] *lam'natzei'ach al yonat eilem r'chokim l'david mich'tam b'echoz oto f'lish'tim b'gat*
[2] *choneini elohim ki sh'afani enosh kol hayom locheim yil'chatzeini*
[3] *sha'afu shor'rai kol hayom ki rabim lochamim li marom*
[4] *yom ira ani eilecha ev'tach*
[5] *beilohim ahaleil d'varo beilohim batach'ti lo ira mah ya'aseh vasar li*
[6] *kol hayom d'varai y'atzeivu alai kol mach'sh'votam lara*
[7] *yaguru yitz'ponu heimah akeivai yish'moru ka'asher kivu naf'shi*
[8] *al aven palet lamo b'af amim horeid elohim*
[9] *nodi safar'tah atah simah dim'ati v'nodecha halo b'sif'ratecha*

[10] *az yashuvu oy'vai achor b'yom ek'ra zeh yada'ti ki elohim li*
[11] *beilohim ahaleil davar ba'YHVH ahaleil davar*
[12] *beilohim batach'ti lo ira mah ya'aseh adam li*
[13] *alai elohim n'darecha ashaleim todot lach*
[14] *ki hitzal'ta naf'shi mimavet halo rag'lai midechi l'hit'haleich lif'nei elohim b'or hachayim*

Translation:

[1] For the Leader; upon *Jonath-elem-rehokim*. A Psalm of David; *Michtam*; when the Philistines took him in Gath.
[2] Be gracious unto me *Elohim*, for man would swallow me up; all the day he fighting oppresseth me.
[3] They that lie in wait for me would swallow me up all the day; for they are many that fight against me, O Most High,
[4] In the day that I am afraid, I will put my trust in Thee.
[5] In *Elohim*—I will praise His word—in *Elohim* do I trust, I will not be afraid; what can flesh do unto me?
[6] All the day they trouble mine affairs; all their thoughts are against me for evil.
[7] They gather themselves together, they hide themselves, they mark my steps; according as they have waited for my soul.
[8] Because of iniquity cast them out; in anger bring down the peoples *Elohim*.
[9] Thou has counted my wanderings; put Thou my tears into Thy bottle; are they not in Thy book?
[10] Then shall mine enemies turn back in the day that I call; this I know, that *Elohim* is for me.
[11] In *Elohim*—I will praise His word—in *YHVH*—I will praise His word—
[12] In *Elohim* do I trust, I will not be afraid; what can man do unto me?
[13] Thy vows are upon me *Elohim*; I will render thank-offerings unto Thee.
[14] For thou hast delivered my soul from death; hast Thou not delivered my feet from stumbling? that I may walk before *Elohim* in the light of the living.

Psalm 56 is recommended to inmates who find themselves shackled in irons.[1] However in the *Shimmush Tehillim* this psalm is not only recommended for a prisoner in chains, but equally for anyone to be saved from יצר הרע (*yetzer ha-ra*—"evil inclination").[2] Focusing exclusively on the "personal passions" matter, Godfrey Selig noted in his German/English translations of the *Shimmush Tehillim* that "this Psalm is recommended to him, who is desirous of freeing himself from the bonds of passion and of sense, and who is anxious to be delivered from the so-called *Jeser Horra*, which means, the evil lusts or the desire to commit sin."[3] Actually, the "evil inclination" could be defined simply as the "desire to receive." However, there is an additional prayer-incantation listed in one of the recensions of the *Shimmush Tehillim*, for those who find themselves imprisoned, whether by the authorities or by their passions. Thus following the recitation of the current psalm, they should say:

חי וקיים אלהי ואלהי אבותי שמע והקשיבה אלי
והוציאני והתירני מהרה מן המצר הזה ואל נא
יעכבוני עונותי בזו התפיסה ואל אכשל במעללי
הרעים אך עונותי יושלכו במצולות ים במקום
שלא ימצאו עוד ולא יזכרו ולא יפקדו ולא יעלו על
לב לעולם כי אתה יהוה מתיר אסורים (Psalm 146:7)
תפול לפניך אנקת אסיר כגודל זרועך הותר בני
תמותה (Psalm 79:11) אנא בשם שוכן שחקים תולה
ארץ על בלימה חי וקיים מרום וקדוש אמן אמן
אמן סלה סלה סלה

Transliteration:
> *Chai v'Kayam elohai veilohei avotai sh'ma v'hag'shivah eilai v'hotzi'eini v'hatireini m'heirah min hameitzar hazeh v'al na y'ak'vuni avonotai b'zo hat'fisah v'al ekashel b'ma'alalai hara'im ach avonotai yush'l'chu bim'tzolot yam b'makom sh'lo yimatzu od v'lo yizach'ru v'lo yipak'du v'lo ya'alu al leiv l'olam ki atah YHVH matir asurim (Psalm 146:7) tipol l'fanecha en'kat asir k'godel z'ro'acha hoteir b'nei t'mutah (Psalm 79:11) ana b'shem shochein*

> *shechakim toleh eretz al b'limah Chai v'Kayam Marom v'Kadosh Omein Omein Omein Selah Selah Selah*

Translation:

> *Chai v'Kayam* ("Alive and Well [Enduring]"), my God and God of my fathers, hear and answer me, bring me out and deliver me speedily from this tribulation. Let not my transgressions detain me in this confinement. I shall not stumble because of my evil deeds, but my offenses will be cast into the depths of the sea, into a place which can no longer be found, which cannot be recalled, which will not be sought out, and will forever not be remembered. For you are *YHVH* who *looseth the prisoners (Psalm 146:7)*. Discard *the groaning of the prisoner come before Thee; according to the greatness of Thy power set free those that are appointed to death (Psalm 79:11)*. Please, in the Name of the one who lives in the clouds, who suspends the earth above the void, *Chai v'Kayam Marom v'Kadosh* ["Alive and Well, Lofty and Holy"], *Amen Amen Amen Selah Selah Selah*.[4]

Besides being suggested to those who suffer imprisonment in chains, the fifty-sixth Psalm has been recommended against imprisonment in general, and, as in the case of the previous two psalms, it is recited for protection in perilous situations and in times of trouble. It is further employed against, and to be saved from, defamation, slander and gossip. Furthermore, like the previous two psalms, it is also enunciated to alleviate apprehension caused by enemies, and against anxiety in general. This psalm is also employed to find safety from fear; against sadness and despair; and to increase trust in the Divine One. In conclusion, it is worth noting that the current psalm is equally used against slavery to base and sinful passions.

As noted earlier, *Psalm 56* is recited in Christian Magic in conjunction with the previous psalm when meeting adversaries in person.[5] It is further listed in the Byzantine Magical Manuscripts as good "for a multitude of thoughts,"[6] and "to put evil to flight."[7] It is further maintained that writing the psalm on a sword or a spear, to be carried on your right side, will render you fearless,[8]

The same source informs us that the fifty-sixth Psalm should be recited over a cup of wine, which is to be given to halt a patient from haemorrhaging.[9] Interestingly enough, in "*Le Livre d'Or*" we are told that "if a woman is bleeding," the psalm should be recited seven times over a glass of wine. Afterwards she is to consume the liquid, and it is said "she will be delivered."[10] Elsewhere we are told that enunciating *Psalm 56:5* will facilitate the very same result.[11]

In conclusion it is worth noting that *Psalm 56:12* features in the "*Key of Solomon*" in the outer border of the "*Second Pentacle of Moon*," which is said to serve "against all perils and dangers by water." Thus "if it should chance that the Spirits of the Moon should excite and cause great rain and exceeding tempests about the Circle," all you need to do is to show them the pentacle, and the tempests "will all speedily cease."[12]

PSALM 57

[1] לַמְנַצֵּחַ אַל תַּשְׁחֵת לְדָוִד מִכְתָּם בְּבָרְחוֹ מִפְּנֵי שָׁאוּל בַּמְּעָרָה
[2] חָנֵּנִי אֱלֹהִים חָנֵּנִי כִּי בְךָ חָסָיָה נַפְשִׁי וּבְצֵל כְּנָפֶיךָ אֶחְסֶה עַד יַעֲבֹר הַוּוֹת
[3] אֶקְרָא לֵאלֹהִים עֶלְיוֹן לָאֵל גֹּמֵר עָלָי
[4] יִשְׁלַח מִשָּׁמַיִם וְיוֹשִׁיעֵנִי חֵרֵף שֹׁאֲפִי סֶלָה יִשְׁלַח אֱלֹהִים חַסְדּוֹ וַאֲמִתּוֹ
[5] נַפְשִׁי בְּתוֹךְ לְבָאִם אֶשְׁכְּבָה לֹהֲטִים בְּנֵי אָדָם שִׁנֵּיהֶם חֲנִית וְחִצִּים וּלְשׁוֹנָם חֶרֶב חַדָּה
[6] רוּמָה עַל הַשָּׁמַיִם אֱלֹהִים עַל כָּל הָאָרֶץ כְּבוֹדֶךָ
[7] רֶשֶׁת הֵכִינוּ לִפְעָמַי כָּפַף נַפְשִׁי כָּרוּ לְפָנַי שִׁיחָה נָפְלוּ בְתוֹכָהּ סֶלָה
[8] נָכוֹן לִבִּי אֱלֹהִים נָכוֹן לִבִּי אָשִׁירָה וַאֲזַמֵּרָה
[9] עוּרָה כְבוֹדִי עוּרָה הַנֵּבֶל וְכִנּוֹר אָעִירָה שָּׁחַר
[10] אוֹדְךָ בָעַמִּים אֲדֹנָי אֲזַמֶּרְךָ בַּלְאֻמִּים
[11] כִּי גָדֹל עַד שָׁמַיִם חַסְדֶּךָ וְעַד שְׁחָקִים אֲמִתֶּךָ
[12] רוּמָה עַל שָׁמַיִם אֱלֹהִים עַל כָּל הָאָרֶץ כְּבוֹדֶךָ

Transliteration:
    [1] *lam'natzei'ach al tash'cheit l'david mich'tam b'vor'cho mip'nei sha'ul bam'arah*
    [2] *choneini elohim choneini ki v'cha chasayah naf'shi uv'tzeil k'nafecha ech'seh ad ya'avor havot*
    [3] *ek'ra leilohim el'yon la'el gomeir alai*
    [4] *yish'lach mishamayim v'yoshi'eini cheireif sho'afi selah yish'lach elohim chas'do va'amito*
    [5] *naf'shi b'toch l'va'im esh'k'vah lohatim b'nei adam shineihem chanit v'chitzim ul'shonam cherev chadah*
    [6] *rumah al hashamayim elohim al kol ha'aretz k'vodecha*
    [7] *reshet heichinu lif'amai kafaf naf'shi karu l'fanai shichah naf'lu v'tochah selah*
    [8] *nachon libi elohim nachon libi ashirah va'azam'rah*
    [9] *urah ch'vodi urah haneivel v'chinor a'irah shachar*
    [10] *od'chah va'amim adonai azamer'cha bal umim*

[11] *ki gadol ad shamayim chas'decha v'ad sh'chakim amitecha*

[12] *rumah al shamayim elohim al kol ha'aretz k'vodecha*

Translation:

[1] For the Leader; *Al-tash'heth*. A Psalm of David; *Michtam*; when he fled from Saul, in the cave.

[2] Be gracious unto me *Elohim*, be gracious unto me, for in Thee hath my soul taken refuge; yea, in the shadow of Thy wings will I take refuge, until calamities be overpast.

[3] I will cry unto *Elohim* Most high; unto God that accomplisheth it for me.

[4] He will send from heaven, and save me, when he that would swallow me up taunteth; *Selah*; *Elohim* shall send forth His mercy and His truth.

[5] My soul is among lions, I do lie down among them that are aflame; even the sons of men, whose teeth are spears and arrows, and their tongue a sharp sword.

[6] Be Thou exalted *Elohim*, above the heavens; Thy glory be above all the earth.

[7] They have prepared a net for my steps, my soul is bowed down; they have digged a pit before me, they are fallen into the midst thereof themselves. *Selah*

[8] My heart is steadfast *Elohim*, my heart is steadfast; I will sing, yea, I will sing praises.

[9] Awake, my glory; awake, psaltery and harp; I will awake the dawn.

[10] I will give thanks unto Thee *Adonai*, among the peoples; I will sing praises unto Thee among the nations.

[11] For Thy mercy is great unto the heavens, and Thy truth unto the skies.

[12] Be Thou exalted *Elohim*, above the heavens; Thy glory be above all the earth.

Psalm 57 is recited for success and "good fortune,"[1] and it is equally recited to express gratitude.[2] In terms of achieving success, we are informed in the *Shimmush Tehillim* that the current psalm should be recited with its associated Divine Name in a synagogue,[3] "in secret" according to one recension of the said text.[4] Godfrey Selig maintains in his German/English translations of the *Shimmush Tehillim*, that the psalm should be recited "after the morning prayer in a church."[5] Whatever the case may be, it is noted in some recensions of this text that this psalm should be recited by those who wish to have success acquiring some or other commodity, making a deal, or in doing business.[6] The associated Divine Name is said to be חַי (*Chai*— "living"), which we are told was derived: ח (*Chet*) from חנני אלהים (*choneini elohim*—"Be gracious [merciful] unto me *Elohim*"): verse 2; and י (*Yod*) from על [כל] הארץ כבודך (*al [kol] ha'aretz k'vodecha*— "Thy glory be above [all] the earth"): verse 12.[7] It has been noted that the stated derivation of the second letter "is obviously corrupt."[8] In one recension of the *Shimmush Tehillim* the said letter is said to have been derived from ר (*Resh*) in (*rumah*): verse 12, the glyph having been transposed by means of the ר"י (*Resh–Yod*) interchange,[9] i.e. the very obscure א"ב ז"ו (*Azbav*) cipher. Godfrey Selig maintains the second letter of the Divine Name construct was derived from אלהים (*Elohim*): verse 6.[10]

In one recension of the *Shimmush Tehillim* we find the current psalm listed for a very different application. We are told that it is good for a fugitive who flees from place to place due to the affliction of enemies, or because of some other matter. In this regard, the said individual is instructed to recite the psalm, as well as the following prayer-incantation along the way:

נוטה כדוק שמים (*Isaiah 40:22*) לך אני מודה ומתודה
על עונותי וחטואתי ופשעי שתצילני לבל אהיה לשמה
ולא אכשל בבריחה זו ולבל ירדפוני אויבי מבקשי
רעתי בשם יָהּ ייה יהוי אמן אמן אמן סלה סלה סלה

Translation:
> *Noteh chadok shamayim* (Isaiah 40:22) *l'cha ani modeh umit'vadeh al avonotai v'chatotai up'sha'ai sh'tatzileini l'bal eh'yeh l'shamah v'lo ikashel bib'richa zu ul'bal yir'd'funi oy'vai m'vak'shei r'ati b'shem Yahi Y'yahi Yih'vi Omein Omein Omein Selah Selah Selah.*

Transliteration:
> He that stretcheth out the heavens as a curtain (*Isaiah 40:22*), to you I confess and divulge my transgressions, sins and iniquities, so that you will deliver me, that I may not become a horror, that I may not stumble upon this flight, and that the enemies who wish me evil may not pursue me. In the name *Yahi Y'yahi Yih'vi, Amen Amen Amen Selah Selah Selah.*[11]

I noted that *Psalm 57* is employed for success and good fortune, however, it is worth noting that it is recited for success in general and in all endeavours, and for good fortune in all undertakings. When this is achieved, the current psalm is narrated to proclaim gratitude for the good fortune, as it is to express gratitude in general. It is further said that the fifty-seventh Psalm is good to recite against all manner of disaster; disruptive changes in life; and for protection against wild, dangerous and savage beasts. We are further informed that the current psalm is enunciated against tyranny; lies; witchcraft and bewitchment; to invoke Divine justice and equality; to relieve headaches brought on by stress, and, as in the case of the previous psalms, to alleviate anxiety caused by enemies. It is worth noting that the current psalm is recited regularly to ensure a safe pregnancy.

As far as the magical use of individual verses are concerned, it should be noted that a single verse from the fifty-seventh Psalm is employed for quite a unique purpose, i.e. a "magical alarm clock." In this regard, there are two procedures, the first of which incorporates the Divine Name construct עדה ישר which is said to have been derived from *Psalm 57:9*. In this regard, we are told that if you want to go to sleep, and wish to wake at a specific time, you should recite the said verse seven times in the standard straight manner, whilst focusing on the Divine Name עדה ישר. This action is understood to prepare you "in the measure (counting) of the day."[12] Next the verse is recited seven times in reverse, i.e. you start with the last word and read the entire phrase backwards, whilst concentrating on the reverse of the two tri-letter combinations, i.e. ישר עדה.[13] Thus you have prepared yourself also "in the measure (counting) of the night." The action is concluded by uttering the following prayer-incantation:

יהי רצון מלפניך יהוה אלהינו ואלהי אבותינו שתשלח
לי [....personal name....] המלך הממונה על הקיצה ויקיצני
בשעה פלוני כדי שאקום ואתעסק בתורתך

Transliteration:
> Y'hi ratzon mil'fanecha YHVH eloheinu veilohei avoteinu shetish'lach li [....personal name....] hamalach ham'muneh al hakitzah v'yakitzeini b'sha'ah p'loni k'dei she'akum v'et'aseik b'toratecha.

Translation:
> May it be your will *YHVH*, our God and God of our fathers, to send me [....personal name....] the angel in charge of waking, to wake me up at a certain time, so that I may rise and deal with [engage in] your *Torah* teachings.[14]

The second procedure, which is a lot easier, and works like clockwork, is another personal favourite, since I regularly need to wake at specific times when I do not wish to disturb the sleep of my partner. In this instance the instruction reads that whoever needs to rise at a specific time in the early hours of the morning, should recite *Psalm 57:9* seven times prior to going to sleep at night, then mentally set the time at which he/she wishes to wake up. The latter action is done whilst reciting *Proverbs 6:22* seven times. The said verse reads:

בהתהלכך תנחה אתך בשכבך תשמר עליך
והקיצות היא תשיחך

Transliteration:
> b'hit'halech'cha tan'cheh otach b'shoch'b'cha tish'mor alecha vahakitzota hi t'shichecha

Translation:
> When thou walkest, it shall lead thee, when thou liest down, it shall watch over thee; and when thou awakest, it shall talk with thee.[15]

In Christian Magic the Byzantine magical manuscripts list the fifty-seventh Psalm "for a blessing." The practitioner has to collect "unspoken water" from "a pure spring," i.e. water over which no word has been spoken. The psalm is pronounced seven times a day for three days over this substance whilst making the Christian "sign of the cross," following which the water is consumed "for a blessing."[16] The same source recommends that individuals needing to leave their homes, should recite *Psalm 57*, concluding with "Have mercy on me, God, have mercy on me, for in you my soul has trusted."[17] This psalm is also recited "to bind the tongues of enemies,"[18] and again to halt "thoughts of lethargy."[19] Elsewhere we find the current psalm recommended for a very different purpose, i.e. ridding oneself of fear of animals.[20] In this regard, "*Le Livre d'Or*" instructs individuals who find themselves in a desert, and afraid of being attacked by "ferocious beasts" to recite *Psalm 57* seven times. This is said to ensure that the practitioner "will have naught to fear with the aid of God."[21]

PSALM 58

[1] למנצח אל תשחת לדוד מכתם
[2] האמנם אלם צדק תדברון מישרים תשפטו בני אדם
[3] אף בלב עולת תפעלון בארץ חמס ידיכם תפלסון
[4] זרו רשעים מרחם תעו מבטן דברי כזב
[5] חמת למו כדמות חמת נחש כמו פתן חרש יאטם אזנו
[6] אשר לא ישמע לקול מלחשים חובר חברים מחכם
[7] אלהים הרס שנימו בפימו מלתעות כפירים נתץ יהוה‎
[8] ימאסו כמו מים יתהלכו למו ידרך חציו כמו יתמללו
[9] כמו שבלול תמס יהלך נפל אשת בל חזו שמש
[10] בטרם יבינו סירתכם אטד כמו חי כמו חרון ישערנו
[11] ישמח צדיק כי חזה נקם פעמיו ירחץ בדם הרשע
[12] ויאמר אדם אך פרי לצדיק אך יש אלהים שפטים בארץ

Transliteration:

[1] *lam'natze'ach al tash'cheit l'david mich'tam*
[2] *ha'um'nam eilem tzedek t'dabeirun meisharim tish'p'tu b'nei adam*
[3] *af b'leiv olot tif'alun ba'aretz chamas y'deichem t'faleisun*
[4] *zoru r'sha'im meirachem ta'u mibeten dov'rei chazav*
[5] *chamat lamo kid'mut chamat nachash k'mo feten cheireish ya'teim oz'no*
[6] *asher lo yish'ma l'kol m'lachashim chover chavarim m'chukam*
[7] *elohim haras shineimo b'fimo mal't'ot kefirim netotz YHVH*
[8] *yima'asu chemo mayim yit'hal'chu lamo yid'roch chitzav k'mo yit'molalu*

[9] *k'mo shab'lul temes yahaloch neifel eishet bal chazu shamesh*
[10] *b'terem yavinu siroteichem atad k'mo chai k'mo charon yis'arenu*
[11] *yis'mach tzadik ki chazah nakam p'amav yir'chatz b'dam harasha*
[12] *v'yomar adam ach p'ri la tzadik ach yeish elohim shof'tim ba'aretz*

Translation:

[1] For the Leader; *Al-tash'heth*. A Psalm of David; *Michtam*.
[2] Do ye indeed speak as a righteous company? Do ye judge with equity the sons of men?
[3] Yea, in heart ye work wickedness; ye weigh out in the earth the violence of your hands.
[4] The wicked are estranged from the womb; the speakers of lies go astray as soon as they are born.
[5] Their venom is like the venom of a serpent; they are like the deaf asp that stoppeth her ear;
[6] Which hearkeneth not to the voice of charmers, or of the most cunning binder of spells.
[7] Break their teeth *Elohim*, in their mouth; break out the cheek-teeth of the young lions *YHVH*.
[8] Let them melt away as water that runneth apace; when he aimeth his arrows, let them be as though they were cut off.
[9] Let them be as a snail which melteth and passeth away; like the untimely births of a woman, that have not seen the sun.
[10] Before your pots can feel the thorns, He will sweep it away with a whirlwind, the raw and the burning alike.
[11] The righteous shall rejoice when he seeth the vengeance; he shall wash his feet in the blood of the wicked.
[12] And men shall say: 'Verily there is a reward for the righteous; verily there is *Elohim* that judgeth in the earth.'

Psalm 58 is recommended in the *Shimmush Tehillim* for protection against vicious dogs.[1] Whilst there is no indication of any Divine Name connected to the current psalm in any of the popular published versions of the said text, one recension maintains the associated Divine Name construct to be וה (*Vav–Heh*), said to have been derived: ה (*Heh*) from (*ha'um'nam*—"Do ye indeed"): verse 2, and ו (*Vav*) from (*v'yomar adam*—"And men shall say"): verse 12.² In a different recension of the *Shimmush Tehillim* the psalm is employed in conjunction with the following prayer-incantation for the same purpose, the latter reading:

עליך יהוה השלכתי (*Psalm 22:11*) אל תשיבני ריקם
מלפניך והושיעני מן הכלב הזה לבל ישכני ולבל יזיקני
בשם אל חי גבור כח אמן אמן אמן סלה

Translation:
> *Alecha YHVH hash'lach'ti (Psalm 22:11) al t'shiveini reikam mil'fanecha v'hoshi'eini min hakelev hazeh l'val yish'cheini ul'val yazikeini b'shem El Chai Gibor Ko'ach Omein Omein Omein Selah*

Transliteration:
> *Upon thee YHVH I have been cast (Psalm 22:11),* send me not away from you empty-handed, and deliver me from this dog, that he may not bite me nor hurt me. In the name *El Chai Gibor Ko'ach* [Living God, mighty Hero] *Amen Amen Amen Selah.*³

Whilst that is more or less the extent of the use of *Psalm 58* in official literature on Jewish Magic, the current psalm is recommended in folk customs against oppressors, and, as in the case of *Psalm 57*, against tyranny. It is further employed for the protection of diligent workers against crooked people, and perverse actions, and it is likewise enunciated when an individual is frustrated with the wickedness of others.

In Christian magic the magical application of the fifty-eighth Psalm is again more varied. In this regard, we are informed in the Byzantine magical manuscripts that the psalm should be turned into an amulet and carried on your person. However, no reason is given for this action.⁴ Elsewhere in the same manuscripts *Psalm 58* is written down to alleviate fear of robbers and "an untrustworthy person."⁵ This psalm is also recommended "for banishing enchantments."⁶ A similar application is listed in "*Le*

Livre d'Or," in which it is said that reciting the current psalm seven times will "destroy the effects of enchantment." We are told it will ensure that "no one will be able to harm you," and is equally "good against treacheries."[7] We also find *Psalm 58:11—12* listed against judges who abuse the poor.[8]

PSALM 59

[1] למנצח אל תשחת לדוד מכתם בשלח שאול וישמרו את הבית להמיתו
[2] הצילני מאיבי אלהי ממתקוממי תשגבני
[3] הצילני מפעלי און ומאנשי דמים הושיעני
[4] כי הנה ארבו לנפשי יגורו עלי עזים לא פשעי ולא חטאתי יהוה‎אהדונהי
[5] בלי עון ירצון ויכוננו עורה לקראתי וראה
[6] ואתה יהוה‎אהדונהי אלהים צבאות אלהי ישראל הקיצה לפקד כל הגוים אל תחן כל בגדי און סלה
[7] ישובו לערב יהמו ככלב ויסובבו עיר
[8] הנה יביעון בפיהם חרבות בשפתותיהם כי מי שמע
[9] ואתה יהוה‎אהדונהי תשחק למו תלעג לכל גוים
[10] עזו אליך אשמרה כי אלהים משגבי
[11] אלהי חסדי יקדמני אלהים יראני בשררי
[12] אל תהרגם פן ישכחו עמי הניעמו בחילך והורידמו מגננו אדני
[13] חטאת פימו דבר שפתימו וילכדו בגאונם ומאלה ומכחש יספרו
[14] כלה בחמה כלה ואינמו וידעו כי אלהים משל ביעקב לאפסי הארץ סלה
[15] וישבו לערב יהמו ככלב ויסובבו עיר
[16] המה יניעון לאכל אם לא ישבעו וילינו
[17] ואני אשיר עזך וארנן לבקר חסדך כי היית משגב לי ומנוס ביום צר לי
[18] עזי אליך אזמרה כי אלהים משגבי אלהי חסדי

Transliteration:
[1] *lam'natzei'ach al tash'cheit l'david mich'tam bish'lo'ach sha'ul vayish'm'ru et habayit lahamito*
[2] *hatzileini mei'oy'vai elohai mimit'kom'mai t'sag'veini*

[3] *hatzileini mipo'alei aven umei'an'shei damim hoshi'eini*
[4] *Ki hinei ar'vu l'naf'shi yaguru alai azim lo fish'i v'lo chatati YHVH*
[5] *b'li avon y'rutzun v'yikonanu urah lik'rati ur'eih*
[6] *v'atah YHVH elohim tz'va'ot elohei yis'ra'eil hakitzah lif'kod kol hagoyim al tachon kol bog'dei aven selah*
[7] *yashuvu la'erev yehemu chakalev visov'vu ir*
[8] *hinei yabi'un b'fihem charavot b'sif'toteihem ki mi shomei'a*
[9] *v'atah YHVH tish'chak lamo til'ag l'chol goyim*
[10] *uzo eilecha esh'morah ki elohim mis'gabi*
[11] *elohei chas'di y'kad'meini elohim yar'eini v'shor'rai*
[12] *al tahar'geim pen yish'k'chu ami ha hani'eimo v'cheil'cha v'horideimo magineinu adonai*
[13] *chatat pimo d'var s'fateimo v'yilach'du vig'onam umei'alah umikachash y'sapeiru*
[14] *kaleih v'cheimah kaleih v'eineimo v'yeid'u ki elohim mosheil b'ya'akov l'af'sei ha'aretz selah*
[15] *v'yashuvu la'erev yehemu chakalev visov'vu ir*
[16] *heimah y'ni'un le'echol im lo yis'b'u vayalinu*
[17] *va'ani ashir uzechah va'aranein laboker chas'decha ki hayita mis'gav li umanos b'yom tzar li*
[18] *uzi eilecha azameirah ki elohim mis'gabi elohei chas'di*

Translation:

[1] For the Leader; *Al-tash'heth*. A Psalm of David; *Michtam*; when Saul sent, and they watched the house to kill him.

[2] Deliver me from mine enemies, O my God; set me on high from them that rise up against me.

[3] Deliver me from the workers of iniquity, and save me from the men of blood.

[4] For, lo, they lie in wait for my soul; the impudent gather themselves together against me; not for my transgression, nor for my sin, *YHVH*.

[5] Without my fault, they run and prepare themselves; awake Thou to help me, and behold.

[6] Thou therefore, *YHVH Elohim* of hosts, the God of Israel, arouse Thyself to punish all the nations; show no mercy to any iniquitous traitors. *Selah*

[7] They return at evening, they howl like a dog, and go round about the city.

[8] Behold, they belch out with their mouth; swords are in their lips: 'For who doth hear?'

[9] But Thou, *YHVH*, shalt laugh at them; Thou shalt have all the nations in derision.

[10] Because of his strength, I will wait for Thee; for *Elohim* is my high tower.

[11] The God of my mercy will come to meet me; *Elohim* will let me gaze upon mine adversaries.

[12] Slay them not, lest my people forget, make them wander to and fro by Thy power, and bring them down, *Adonai* our shield.

[13] For the sin of their mouth, and the words of their lips, let them even be taken in their pride, and for cursing and lying which they speak.

[14] Consume them in wrath, consume them, that they be no more; and let them know that *Elohim* ruleth in Jacob, unto the ends of the earth. *Selah*

[15] And they return at evening, they howl like a dog, and go round about the city;

[16] They wander up and down to devour, and tarry all night if they have not their fill.

[17] But as for me, I will sing of Thy strength; yea, I will sing aloud of Thy mercy in the morning; for Thou hast been my high tower, and a refuge in the day of my distress.

[18] O my strength, unto Thee will I sing praises; for *Elohim* is my high tower, the God of my mercy.

Psalm 59 is included in Jewish Magic amongst the list of psalms employed for protection against harm.[1] It is recommended against יצר הרע (*yetzer hara*—"evil inclination"),[2] which I noted earlier could be defined the "desire to receive," and which an associate defined as "always acting in your personal interest at any cost." Whilst all of us do have the inclination to act in our "personal interests," this should not be the overriding quality in our lives, the latter being prevalent mainly in the lives of those who suffer narcissistic personality disorders,[3] with special reference to those who would see the entire world destroyed provided they get their own way. Be that as it may, we are informed in the *Shimmush Tehillim* that *Psalm 59:2—12* should be recited three times a day for three days by those who wish to conquer the evil impulse,[4] or who wish to counteract an evil spell according to one recension,[5] each recitation concluding with the following prayer-incantation:

יהי רצון מלפניך יהוה אלהי השם הגדול והקדוש
היוצא מן המזמור הזה שתצילנו מיצר הרע ומכל
דבר רע וממחשבה רעה כמו שהצלת למי שהתפלל
לפניך זה המזמור אמן אמן אמן סלה סלה סלה

Transliteration:
> *Y'hi ratzon mil'fanecha YHVH elohai hashem hagadol v'hakadosh hayotzei min hamiz'mor hazeh shetatzileinu miyetzer hara umikol davar ra umimach'shavah ra'ah k'mo shehitzal'ta l'mi shehit'paleil l'fanecha zeh hamiz'mor Omein Omein Omein Selah Selah Selah.*

Translation:
> May it be your will, Lord my God, the great and holy Name that comes forth from this psalm, that you save me from the evil inclination, from every evil word (spell), and from evil thoughts, as you saved the one who prayed this psalm before you *Amen Amen Amen Selah Selah Selah.*[6]

The statement "the one who prayed this psalm before you," is a reference to King David, the author of the psalm. Be that as it may, in his verbose German/English versions of the *Shimmush Tehillim*, Godfrey Selig queries "would you be entirely free from the *Jezor Horra*, that is, from the inclination which all men possess to do evil, and the sinful appetites and passions which often overcome them." Should your thoughts be in the affirmative, it is recommended to pray the fifty-ninth Psalm "from the second verse to the end, for three days in succession, at early noon and in the evening, and the holy name belonging thereto, namely, *Paltioel*, which signifies Strong God, My Rescuer and Saviour."[7] Selig noted this Divine Name "may be found in the words *Pischii*, verse

3; *Elohim* verse 5; *Chattati*, verse 3; *Jehovah*, verse 8; *Aschir*, verse 15, and *Maschel*, verse 14.[8] However, beyond the expression "*Yetzer Harah*," and the fact that the psalm should be recited over a period of three days, none of Selig's remarks relate to anything mentioned, either in the popular Hebrew edition, or in any of the existent recensions of the *Shimmush Tehillim*. At least some portions of his "prescribed prayer" accompanying the current psalm, which he noted will make you "aware of the most wonderful changes within yourself," can be found in the mentioned Hebrew versions. Thus the English translation of his prayer-incantation reads "Lord, my Father and the Father of mine, mighty God! May it please thee for the sake of thy great, holy and adorable name, *Paltioel*, to release me from the *Jezer Harra* (from my evil desires and passions and from all evil thoughts and acts), as thou didst the author of this Psalm when he prayed to thee. Amen Selah!"[9]

In one recension of the *Shimmush Tehillim* we find the fifty-ninth Psalm employed against murderers who are coming to the residence of an individual to slaughter him or her.[10] In this instance the said individual is informed to recite the psalm eleven times, each time adding:

מלך מלכי המלכים לפניך אני מפיל תחנתי וכורע
ומשתחוה שתשמע ותאזין את צעקתי ותצילני מן
האויבים האלו המבקשים נפשי לקחתה על לא חמס
מכפי (Job 16:17) יהי רצון מלפניך שלא יוכלו
להמיתני ולא להזיקני והפוך כל רעתם ורצונם שלא
יוכלו לעשות לי רעה מרוב אהבתם בי כי בשמך
הגדול במטחתי יְהֹוָה יְהֹוָה יַהֲוָה שמרני אל כי חסיתי
בך (Psalm 16:1) שמרני כאישון בת עין בצל כנפיך
תסתירני (Psalm 17:8) אמן אמן אמן סלה סלה סלה

Transliteration:
> *Melech mal'chei ham'lachim l'fanecha ani mapil t'chinati v'korei'a umish'tachaveh sh'tish'ma v'ta'azin et tza'akati v'tatzileini min ha'oy'vim ha'eilu ham'vak'shim naf'shi l'kach'tah al lo chamas mikapai (Job 16:17) y'hi ratzon mil'fanecha shelo yoch'lu l'hamiteini v'lo l'hazikeini*

> *v'hafoch kol ra'atam ur'tzonam shelo yoch'lu la'asot li ra'ah meirov ahavatam bi ki b'shim'cha hagadol batach'ti YuHuVuHa YiH'Vah YaHaV'Ha shom'reini el ki chasiti vach (Psalm 16:1) shom'reini k'ishon bat ayin b'tzeil k'nafecha tas'tireini (Psalm 17:8) Omein Omein Omein Selah Selah Selah.*

Translation:

> King, King of kings, I cast my supplication before you, and I kneel and prostrate myself, that you may hear and answer my cry. You will deliver me from these enemies who desire to take my soul, *although there is no violence in my hands.(Job 16:17)* May it be your will that they cannot kill me nor harm me. And turn away all their mischief and their will, so that they can do me no evil, because of the abundance of their love for me. For in your great name I am secure, *YuHuVuHa YiH'Vah YaHaV'Ha. Keep me, O God; for I have taken refuge in Thee. (Psalm 16:1) Keep me as the apple of the eye, hide me in the shadow of Thy wings. (Psalm 17:8)* Amen Amen Amen Selah Selah Selah.[11]

It has been said that *Psalm 59* should be recited for those who are unable to speak, i.e. mutes. It is further enunciated to ease the anxiety caused by enemies, and to mitigate slavery to sinful passions, e.g. lust, gluttony, etc. We are told the current psalm is good against infidelity of both the personal and "national" kind, and it is said to empower personal fidelity to religion, justice and righteousness, and to alleviate spiritual troubles.

In the Christian Byzantine magical manuscripts the *Psalm 59* is recommended against blasphemy,[12] and is recommended to men who are impotent. The current psalm is also suggested to those who seek to overcome impotence,[13] and especially to a man who is suffering "binding," i.e. he has been rendered impotent by magical means. In terms of the latter condition, the current psalm is written down with a set of magical signs, which the afflicted individual needs to carry "on his right thigh, and he will be released."[14] Curiously enough, we find the fifty-ninth Psalm employed for the same purpose in "*Le Livre d'Or*," in which it is likewise written down with a set of magical characters, over which the psalm is recited seven times. This item is afterwards bound to the thigh of the afflicted individual, who is said "will be delivered from the charm."[15] The current psalm was equally written down with magical characters on "virgin parchment," to be "worn around the neck night and day for protection."[16]

PSALM 60

[1] למנצח על שושן עדות מכתם לדוד ללמד
[2] בהצותו את ארם נהרים ואת ארם צובה וישב יואב ויך את אדום בגיא מלח שנים עשר אלף
[3] אלהים זנחתנו פרצתנו אנפת תשובב לנו
[4] הרעשתה ארץ פצמתה רפה שבריה כי מטה
[5] הראית עמך קשה השקיתנו יין תרעלה
[6] נתתה ליראיך נס להתנוסס מפני קשט סלה
[7] למען יחלצון ידידיך הושיעה ימינך וענני
[8] אלהים דבר בקדשו אעלזה אחלקה שכם ועמק סכות אמדד
[9] לי גלעד ולי מנשה ואפרים מעוז ראשי יהודה מחקקי
[10] מואב סיר רחצי על אדום אשליך נעלי עלי פלשת התרועעי
[11] מי יבלני עיר מצור מי נחני עד אדום
[12] הלא אתה אלהים זנחתנו ולא תצא אלהים בצבאותינו
[13] הבה לנו עזרת מצר ושוא תשועת אדם
[14] באלהים נעשה חיל והוא יבוס צרינו

Transliteration:

[1] *lam'natzei'ach al shushan eidut mich'tam l'david l'lameid*

[2] *b'hatzoto et aram naharayim v'et aram tzovah vayashav yo'av vayach et edom b'gei melach sh'neim asar alef*

[3] *elohim z'nach'tanu f'ratz'tanu anaf'ta t'shoveiv lanu*

[4] *hir'ash'tah eretz p'tzam'tah r'fah sh'vareha chi matah*

[5] *hir'itah am'cha kashah hish'kitanu yayin tar'eilah*

[6] *natatah lirei'echa neis l'hit'noseis mip'nei koshet selah*

[7] *l'ma'an yeichal'tzun y'didecha hoshi'ah y'min'cha va'aneini*

[8] *elohim diber b'kad'sho e'lozah achal'kah shechem v'eimek sukot amadeid*

[9] *li gil'ad v'li m'nasheh v'ef'rayim ma'oz roshi y'hudah m'chok'ki*
[10] *mo'av sir rach'tzi al edom ash'lich na'ali alai p'leshet hit'ro'a'i*
[11] *mi yovileini ir matzor mi nachani ad edom*
[12] *halo atah elohim z'nach'tanu v'lo teitzei elohim b'tziv'oteinu*
[13] *havah lanu ez'rat mitzar v'shav t'shu'at adam*
[14] *beilohim na'aseh chayil v'hu yavus tzareinu*

Translation:

[1] For the Leader; upon *Shushan Eduth*; *Michtam* of David, to teach;

[2] when he strove with Aram-naharaim and with Aram-zobah, and Joab returned, and smote of Edom in the Valley of Salt twelve thousand.

[3] *Elohim*, Thou hast cast us off, Thou hast broken us down; Thou hast been angry; O restore us.

[4] Thou hast made the land to shake, Thou hast cleft it; heal the breaches thereof; for it tottereth.

[5] Thou hast made Thy people to see hard things; Thou hast made us to drink the wine of staggering.

[6] Thou hast given a banner to them that fear Thee, that it may be displayed because of the truth. *Selah*

[7] That Thy beloved may be delivered, save with Thy right hand, and answer me.

[8] *Elohim* spoke in His holiness, that I would exult; that I would divide Shechem, and mete out the valley of Succoth.

[9] Gilead is mine, and Manasseh is mine; Ephraim also is the defence of my head; Judah is my sceptre.

[10] Moab is my washpot; upon Edom do I cast my shoe; Philistia, cry aloud because of me!

[11] Who will bring me into the fortified city? Who will lead me unto Edom?

[12] Hast not Thou *Elohim*, cast us off? And Thou goest not forth *Elohim* with our hosts.

[13] Give us help against the adversary; for vain is the help of man.

[14] Through *Elohim* we shall do valiantly; for He it is that will tread down our adversaries.

Psalm 60 is recommended for victory in a war.¹ In this regard, the *Shimmush Tehillim* maintains that those who want to be victorious in battle, should recite the current psalm seven times before going off to war.² In the general printed version of this text יה (*Yod–Heh*) is indicated to be the Divine Name construct associated with the psalm: י (*Yod*) from צרינו (*tzareinu*—"enemies"): verse 14, and ה (*Heh*) from ד (*Dalet*) in ללמד (*l'lamed*—"to teach"), the said glyphs appearing to have been exchanged by means of the obscure א"ח ב"ז (*Achbaz*) cipher.³ In other recensions of the *Shimmush Tehillim* the Divine Name construct is listed as וה (*Vav–Heh*), these letters having being derived from the same two listed verses.⁴ Godfrey Selig's oft mentioned version of the *Shimmush Tehillim* aligns with the views expressed in the popular Hebrew editions, though he expanded on the "war theme" noting "if you are a soldier in an army, and are about marching into the field, repeat this Psalm, keeping in mind the holy name of *Jah*, and at the conclusion of each repetition of the Psalm, utter a suitable prayer in full reliance upon the endless omnipotence of Him, who can give the victory where he will, and you will be enabled to return to your home uninjured."⁵

Yet Selig's is not the largest expansion on the mentioned magical use of the current psalm. In one of the recensions of the *Shimmush Tehillim* the sixtieth Psalm is recommended to citizens who fear enemy troops will attack and plunder their city.⁶ To avert such carnage the inhabitants are enjoined to recite the current psalm thirty times, each time adding the following prayer-incantation:

אנא יהוה הושיעה נא (*Psalm 118:25*) אלהינו ואלהי
אבותינו בך יהוה חסינו אל נבושה ואל נשוב ריקים
מלפניך הושיענו אלהי ישענו למען שמך יהוה תחנינו
ותפלטינו ותצילנו מן החיל הזה אשר באעלינו
להשפילנו ולהשמידנו ולהכניענו ואתה יהוה צבאות
אל גבור ונורא בעל מלחמות הלחם עמהם בעבורינו
כאשר נלחמת עם פרעה מלך מצרים כדבר שנאמר
יהוה ילחם לכם ואתם תחרישון (*Exodus 14:14*) כן

The Psalms of David — Book II : 165

הלחם בעבורינו עם זה החיל תרדוף ב**אף** ותשמידם
מתחת שמי יהוה והשב גמולם בראשם ותוליכם מעלינו
בבושה ובחרפה ואל יבואו עוד לעולם בשם מהש
ללה **אפה** עזרינו בשם יהוה עושה שמים וארץ אמן
אמן אמן סלה סלה סלה

Transliteration:

Ana YHVH hoshi'ah na (Psalm 118:25) eloheinu v'eilohei avoteinu b'cha YHVH chasinu al n'vosha v'al nashuv reikam mil'fanecha hoshi'einu elohei yish'einu l'ma'an shim'cha YHVH t'chaneinu ut'fal'teinu v'tatzileinu min hachayil hazeh asher ba'aleinu l'hash'pileinu ul'hash'mideinu ul'hach'ni'einu v'atah YHVH tz'va'ot el gibor v'nora ba'al mil'chamot hilacheim imahem b'avoreinu k'asher nil'cham'ta im par'oh melech mitz'rayim k'davar shen'emar YHVH yilacheim lachem v'atem tacharishun (Exodus 14:14) kein hilacheim b'avoreinu im zeh hachayil tir'dof b'af v'tash'mideim mitachat sh'mei YHVH v'hasheiv g'mulam b'rosham v'tolicheim mei'aleinu b'bushah ub'cher'pah v'al yavo'u od l'olam b'shem Mahash Lelah Apah az'reinu b'shem YHVH oseh shamayim va'aretz Omein Omein Omein Selah Selah Selah.

Translation:

We beseech Thee, YHVH, save now! (*Psalm 118:25*), our God and God of our fathers. In you *YHVH*, we have taken refuge, let us not be put to shame nor return dishonored before you. Deliver us, God of our salvation, for your name's sake *YHVH*, have mercy on us. You shall save us and deliver us from this army, which has come upon us to humiliate, destroy, and subdue us, and you are the Lord of hosts, heroic and fearful God. Lord of wars, fight against them for us, as you fought with Pharaoh, king of Egypt. Like the word in which it is said *YHVH will fight for you, and ye shall hold your peace* (*Exodus 14:14*), so he fought for us with this army. You shall pursue them with anger and destroy them under the heavens of the Lord. Return their deeds upon their heads, and lead them away from us in shame and disgrace, and they shall never again return. In the name *Mahash Lelah Apah*, help us with the Name of the Lord who makes the heavens and the earth. *Amen Amen Amen Selah Selah Selah.*[7]

Considering this, as it were, "military application" of *Psalm 60*, it is most curious that the *Yismach Moshe*, the Hungarian *tzaddik* Rabbi Moshe Teitelbaum (1759–1841), whom I noted elsewhere "was highly esteemed as 'the Light of all of Hungary',"[8] once blessed a very young Lajos Kossuth, who would later become the Governor General of Hungary, and leader of the Hungarian Revolution. It is said the *Yismach* blessed the child Kossuth by placing his hands on the head of the infant, and reciting *Psalm 60:6* reading נתתה ליראיך נס להתנוסס מפני קשט סלה (*natata lirei'echa neis l'hitnoseis mip'nei koshet selah*—"Thou hast given a banner to them that fear Thee, that it may be displayed because of the truth. *Selah*"). We are told that the remarkable "Wonder Worker" was punning on the term *"Koshet"* ("truth") in reference to the surname of the boy, i.e. "Kossuth," and we are further informed that Rabbi Teitelbaum did not only bless the child, but also prophesied his future greatness.[9] It should be noted that the sixtieth Psalm is also recited to invoke safety for soldiers, and to support exiles and refugees. It has been further recommended to recover heritage, clear groups of people who are accused unjustly, and for Divine justice and equality.

As far as the individual verses from the current psalm are concerned, it is interesting that the "Name of Seventy-two Names," is said to be associated with *Psalm 60:7*. In this regard, I mentioned elsewhere that the tri-letter Divine Name construct והו (*Vehu*), the first tri-letter name combination of this very important Divine Name construct, is said to be directly affiliated with the Ineffable Name (*YHVH*), and hence "it is fitting that it is located at the 'head,' at the very beginning of the '*Shem Vayisa Vayet*,' being in a position of control over the entire 'Name of Seventy-two Names'."[10] I also noted that והו (*Vehu*) governs the first thirty-six tri-letter combinations, i.e. the "male" half of the seventy-two Names, whilst אני (*Ani*), the thirty-seventh tri-letter combination, heads the second or "female" half. Combining the two tri-letter combinations into אני והו (*Ani Vaho*). Thus commencing with the term אני (*Ani*—"I" ["Self"]) and concluding with והו (*Vehu*), the

"Divine One," we recite the words אני והו הושיעה נא (*Ani Vaho Hoshi'ah Na*—"I and It please save"), a phrase considered a *Segulah* ("magical treasure"), which is used in times of great trouble, distress and oppression,[11] and hence very relevant to the magical use of the current psalm. It is this phrase which is said to be directly affiliated with the concluding portion of *Psalm 60:7* reading הושיעה ימינך וענני (*Hoshi'ah yemin'cha va'aneini*—"Save with Thy right hand, and answer me") (*Psalm 60:7*).[12]

Psalm 60 is referenced in the Christian Byzantine magical manuscripts for protection against wind, hail, and lightning. In this regard, the psalm is written down with a set of magical symbols, fumigated with saffron and musk, and carried as an amulet.[13] The same sources maintain that the psalm written on crystal "is useful also for divine anger."[14] Aside from this, it is said that reciting the psalm is good for someone who is "afraid of anyone."[15] Elsewhere we are informed in "*Le Livre d'Or*" that the sixtieth Psalm should be written with the blood of a billy goat in conjunction with a set of magical characters, by one who is "in bondage" because of his or her "affairs." Afterwards, whilst reciting the psalm, the object is buried "under the hinge of the door," which is said will ensure good fortune.[16]

In conclusion, *Psalm 60* is listed in the "*Key of Solomon*" as one of seven psalms, i.e. *Psalms 3, 9, 31, 42, 60, 51*, and *130*, employed in the consecration of "the needle and other iron instruments."[17]

PSALM 61

[1] למנצח על נגינת לדוד
[2] שמעה אלהים רנתי הקשיבה תפלתי
[3] מקצה הארץ אליך אקרא בעטף לבי בצור ירום ממני תנחני
[4] כי היית מחסה לי מגדל עז מפני אויב
[5] אגורה באהלך עולמים אחסה בסתר כנפיך סלה
[6] כי אתה אלהים שמעת לנדרי נתת ירשת יראי שמך
[7] ימים על ימי מלך תוסיף שנותיו כמו דר ודר
[8] ישב עולם לפני אלהים חסד ואמת מן ינצרהו
[9] כן אזמרה שמך לעד לשלמי נדרי יום יום

Transliteration:

[1] *lam'natzei'ach al n'ginat l'david*
[2] *shim'ah elohim rinati hak'shivah t'filati*
[3] *mik'tzeih ha'aretz eilecha ek'ra ba'atof libi b'tzur yarum mimeni tan'cheini*
[4] *ki hayita mach'seh li mig'dal oz mip'nei oyeiv*
[5] *agurah v'ahol'cha olamim echeseh v'seiter k'nafecha selah*
[6] *ki atah elohim shama'ta lin'darai natata y'rushat yir'ei sh'mecha*
[7] *yamim al y'mei melech tosif sh'notav k'mo dor vador*
[8] *yeisheiv olam lif'nei elohim chesed ve'emet man yin'tz'ruhu*
[9] *kein azam'rah shim'cha la'ad l'shal'mi n'darai yom yom*

Translation:

[1] For the Leader; with string-music. A Psalm of David.
[2] Hear my cry *Elohim*; attend unto my prayer.
[3] From the end of the earth will I call unto Thee, when my heart fainteth; lead me to a rock that is too high for me.
[4] For Thou hast been a refuge for me, a tower of strength in the face of the enemy.
[5] I will dwell in Thy Tent for ever; I will take refuge in the covert of Thy wings. *Selah*

[6] For Thou *Elohim* hast heard my vows; Thou hast granted the heritage of those that fear Thy name.
[7] Mayest Thou add days unto the king's days! May his years be as many generations!
[8] May he be enthroned before *Elohim* for ever! Appoint mercy and truth, that they may preserve him.
[9] So will I sing praise unto Thy name for ever, that I may daily perform my vows.

Psalm 61 is recommended in Jewish Magic to those who are afraid to stay at home,[1] i.e. those for whom entering their residence is a "cause for apprehension,"[2] or who are "apprehensive about going home."[3] In this regard, the *Shimmush Tehillim* informs us that success is ensured when the psalm is recited upon entering the house.[4] The associated Divine Name construct is שד״י (*Shadai*), the component glyphs of which is said to have been derived: ש (*Shin*) from שמעה (*shim'ah*—"hear"): verse 2; ד (*Dalet*) from כ (*Kaf*) in כן אזמרה (*kein azamrah*—"so will I sing praise"): verse 9, the glyph having been exchanged by means of the אח״ס בט״ע (*Achas Beta*) cipher; and י (*Yod*) from the second מ (*Mem*) in יום יום (*yom yom*—"daily"): verse 9, the concluding letter of the psalm having been transposed by means of the א״ת ב״ש (*Atbash*) cipher.[5] Godfrey Selig incorrectly claims the second and third glyphs were converted by means of the א״יק בכ״ר (*Ayak Bachar*) cipher.[6]

It should be kept in mind that focussing on the Divine Name שד״י (*Shadai*) during the recitation of the psalm on entering a residence, is not a random recommendation. This Divine Name is affiliated with every מזוזה (*Mezuzah*) affixed to the entrances of Jewish homes. In this regard, I noted elsewhere that the striking feature of *Mezuzot*, "is a little hole or a little window on the front of the container, through which one can observe the Divine Name *Shadai*, or the Hebrew letter *Shin* (which represents the name). Thus, to this day the Divine Name invoking protection is placed on the doors of every Jewish home who takes the practice seriously, and the power of *Shadai* is being invoked every moment of the day somewhere in the world....even as you are reading this."[7]

Be that as it may, elsewhere it is said the sixty-first Psalm should be recited by those who wish to succeed in a new residence or apartment.[8] Curiously enough, "a new residence" is also referenced in Selig's German/English translations of the *Shimmush Tehillim*, in which he wrote "when you are about taking possession of a new dwelling, repeat this Psalm just before moving in, with a suitable prayer, trusting in the name of *Schaddei*, and you will experience blessing and good fortune."[9] Besides living unafraid and with great success in a residence, *Psalm 61* is recommended in one recension of the *Shimmush Tehillim* for a long life.[10] In this regard, the instruction comprises the recitation of the psalm seven times, each time in conjunction with the following very lengthy prayer-incantation:

אדיר ואמיץ וחזק בך חסיתי (*Psalm 7:2*) ובשמך
שמתי סברי ותקותי ומשגבי ומנוסי אל נא תשיבני
ריקם מלפניך ואל תמיתני ברוב עונותי וחטאי אכן
ברוב חסדיך ורחמיך חייני כאמור רחמיך רבים יהוה
כמשפטיך חייני (*Psalm 119:156*) ותאריך ימי ושנותי
בעת אעשה ואקיים מצותיך ואלמוד תורתיך כאמור
אורך ימים בימינה בשמאלה עושר וכבוד (*Proverbs 3:16*)
ונאמור כי אורך ימים ושנות חיים ושלום יוסיפו לך
(*Proverbs 3:2*) ואומר כי מוצאי מצא חיים ויפק רצון
מיהוה (*Proverbs 8:35*) ואומר עץ חיים היא למחזיקים
בה ותומכיה מאושר (*Proverbs 3:18*) ונאמור כי בי ירבו
ימיך ויוסיפו לך שנות חיים (*Proverbs 9:11*) ונאמור
ואתם הדבקים ביהוה אלהיכם חיים כולכם היום
(*Deuteronomy 4:4*) על כן יהוה אלהי אל תעליני בחצי
ימי ברוב פשעי ואל תשחיתני ואל תאבדני מן העולם
אך רחמיך יקדמו רגזיך ותרחמני ותאריך ימי ושנותי
בטובה ואשוב בתשובה שלימה לפניך כאשר אמרו
רבותינו זכרונם לברכה ושוב יום אחד לפני מיתתך
כי לא תעזוב נפשי לשאול לא תתן חסידך לראות שחת
תודיעני אורה חיים שובע שמחות את פניך נעימות
בימינך נצה (*Psalm 16:10—11*) כי יהוה אלהיך מלך

חפץ בחיים ואמרת על יד נביאך כי לא אחפוץ במות
הרשע כי אם בשוב רשע מדרכו והיה (Ezekiel 33:11)
כי לא אחפוץ במות המתי כי אם בשובו מדרכיו והיה
ונאמר שובו שובו מדרכיכם הרעים ולמה תמותו בית
ישראל (Ezekiel 33:11) ואתה חפץ בתשובה שנאמר שובה
ישראל עד יהוה אלהיך כי כשלת בעוניך קחו עמכם
דברים ושובו אל יהוה (3—Hosea 14:2) אמרו רבותינו
זכרונו לברכה בכמה מקומות כח התשובה עולה עד
כסא הכבוד על כן תשובתי ותפלתי תעלה עד כסא
כבודך ותקבליני בתשובה שלימה לפניך בשם **אדיר
ואמיץ וחזק** אמן אמן אמן אמן סלה

Transliteration:

Adir v'Amitz v'Chazak b'cha chasiti uv'shim'cha sam'ti s'vari v'tik'vati umis'gavi umanosi al na t'shiveini reikam mil'fanecha v'al t'miteini b'rov avonotai v'chata'ai achein b'rov chas'decha v'rachamecha chayeini ka'amur rachamecha rabim YHVH k'mish'patecha chayeini (Psalm 119:156) v'ta'arich yamai ush'notai b'eit e'eseh v'ekayeim mitz'votecha v'el'mod toratecha k'amur orech yamim biminah bis'molah osher v'chavod (Proverbs 3:16) v'ne'emar ki orech yamim ush'not chayim v'shalom yosifu lach (Proverbs 3:2) v'omar ki motz'i matza chayim vayafek ratzon mei'YHVH (Proverbs 8:35) v'omar etz chayim hi lamachazikim bah v'tom'cheyah m'ushar. (Proverbs 3:18) v'ne'emar ki vi yir'bu yamecha v'yosifu l'cha sh'not chayim. (Proverbs 9:11) v'ne'emar v'atem had'veikim ba'YHVH eloheichem chayim kul'chem hayom (Deuteronomy 4:4) al kein YHVH elohai al ta'aleini b'chatzi yamai b'rov p'sha'ai v'al tash'chiteini v'al t'av'deini min ha'olam ach rachamecha yikad'mu rog'zecha ut'rachameini v'ta'arich yamai ush'notai b'tovah v'ashuv b't'shuvah sh'leimah l'fanecha k'asher am'ru raboteinu zich'ronam liv'rachah v'shuv yom echad lif'nei mitat'cha ki lo ta'azov naf'shi lish'ol lo titein chasid'cha lir'ot shachat todi'eini orach chayim sova s'machot et panecha n'imot bimin'cha netzach (Psalm 16:10—11) ki YHVH elohecha melech chapeitz bachayim v'amar'ta al yad n'vi'echa ki lo ech'potz b'mot harasha ki im b'shuv rasha midar'ko v'chayah (Ezekiel 33:11) *v'ne'emar shuvu shuvu midar'cheichem hara'im v'lamah tamutu beit yis'ra'eil.* (Ezekiel 33:11) *v'atah chafeitz b't'shuvah shen'emar shuvah yis'ra'eil ad YHVH elohecha ki chashal'ta ba'avonecha k'chu imachem d'varim v'shuvu el YHVH* (Hosea 14:2—3) *am'ru raboteinu zich'ronam liv'rachah b'kamah m'komot ko'ach hat'shuvah oleh ad kisei hakavod al kein t'shuvati ut'filati t'aleh ad kisei k'vodecha v'tikab'leini b't'shuvah sh'leimah l'fanecha b'shem Adir v'Amitz v'Chazak Omein Omein Omein Selah.*

Translation:

Adir v'Amitz v'Chazak (Mighty and Brave and Strong), *in Thee have I taken refuge (Psalm 7:2)*, and in your name I have placed my verity, my hope, my refuge, and my way out. You shall not, I pray thee, turn me away from you empty-handed, nor slay me for the multitude of my offences and my transgressions, but by the multitude of your grace and your mercy enliven me, as it is said, *Great are Thy compassions YHVH; quicken me as Thou art wont. (Psalm 119:156)* You shall prolong my days and my years, as I do and keep your commandments. And I will learn your Torah, as it is said, *Length of days is in her right hand; in her left hand are riches and honour. (Proverbs 3:16)* And as it is said *For length of days, and years of life, and peace, will they add to thee. (Proverbs 3:2)* And it is said, *For whoso findeth me findeth life, and obtaineth favour of YHVH. (Proverbs 8:35)* And it is said, *She is a tree of life to them that lay hold upon her, and happy is every one that holdest her fast. (Proverbs 3:18)* And it is said, *For by me thy days shall be multiplied, and the years of thy life shall be increased. (Proverbs 9:11)* And it is said, *But ye that did cleave unto YHVH your God are alive every one of you this day. (Deuteronomy 4:4)* Wherefore, YHVH my God, you shall not take me away in the half of my days because of the multitude of my iniquities. You shall not destroy me nor make me disappear from the world. Rather, your mercy shall forestall your anger. You shall have mercy on me and prolong my days and years for good. I will return to thee in complete repentance, as our rabbis, of blessed memory, have said, *Return one day before your death!* (*TB Shabbat 153a*) *For Thou wilt not abandon my soul to the nether-world; neither wilt Thou suffer Thy godly one to see the pit. Thou makest me to know the path of life; in Thy presence is fulness of joy, in Thy right hand bliss for evermore.* (*Psalm 16:10–11*) For YHVH your God is a king who delights in life. And you said through your prophet, For I will not delight *in the death of the wicked, but that the wicked turn from his way and live.* (*Ezekiel 33:11*) And it is said, *turn ye, turn ye from your evil ways; for why will ye die, O house of Israel?* (*Ezekiel 33:11*) You delight in repentance, as it is said, *Return, O Israel, unto YHVH thy God; for thou hast stumbled in thine iniquity. Take with you words, and return unto YHVH.* (*Hosea 14:2–3*) Our rabbis, of blessed memory, said in some places, *The power of repentance ascends to the throne of glory* (paraphrased from *TB Yoma 86a*). So shall my repentance and my prayer also ascend up to the throne of thy glory. You will accept me in complete repentance before you. In the Name *Adir Amitz v'Chazak. Amen Amen Amen Selah.*[11]

We are informed in "unofficial" sources that *Psalm 61* is good against all manner of trouble and tribulations, and is enunciated for the safety and well-being of places. It is further recited against assassins, unmerited malediction, and against theft, thieves and robbers. It is also employed for protection of the fatherland, and for perseverance.

In Christian Magic *Psalm 61* is recited to have love reciprocated.[12] In the Byzantine magical manuscripts the psalm is similarly listed to engender "honour and love." In this regard, practitioners are encouraged to write the sixty-first Psalm with certain magical characters "on white paper with white pigment or with saffron and musk," and doing so "at an eclipse of the moon on Saturday or Tuesday."[13] Elsewhere in the same sources the current psalm is employed to halt dissension between a husband and wife, the quarrel having been engendered by magical means. The details include the psalm and some magical symbols being written with the blood of a white rooster, and the psalm recited on five Sundays three times a day over the heads of the couple, etc.[14] The very same magical application is listed in "*Le Livre d'Or*," though somewhat simplified. In the latter instance, the current psalm and some magical signs is also written with the blood of a white **cockerel**, following which the psalm is recited over it, and the amuletic construct tied to the arm of the woman, who is said "will return."[15]

PSALM 62

[1] לַמְנַצֵּחַ עַל יְדוּתוּן מִזְמוֹר לְדָוִד
[2] אַךְ אֶל אֱלֹהִים דּוּמִיָּה נַפְשִׁי מִמֶּנּוּ יְשׁוּעָתִי
[3] אַךְ הוּא צוּרִי וִישׁוּעָתִי מִשְׂגַּבִּי לֹא אֶמּוֹט רַבָּה
[4] עַד אָנָה תְּהוֹתְתוּ עַל אִישׁ תְּרָצְּחוּ כֻלְּכֶם כְּקִיר נָטוּי גָּדֵר הַדְּחוּיָה
[5] אַךְ מִשְּׂאֵתוֹ יָעֲצוּ לְהַדִּיחַ יִרְצוּ כָזָב בְּפִיו יְבָרֵכוּ וּבְקִרְבָּם יְקַלְלוּ סֶלָה
[6] אַךְ לֵאלֹהִים דּוֹמִּי נַפְשִׁי כִּי מִמֶּנּוּ תִּקְוָתִי
[7] אַךְ הוּא צוּרִי וִישׁוּעָתִי מִשְׂגַּבִּי לֹא אֶמּוֹט
[8] עַל אֱלֹהִים יִשְׁעִי וּכְבוֹדִי צוּר עֻזִּי מַחְסִי בֵּאלֹהִים
[9] בִּטְחוּ בוֹ בְכָל עֵת עָם שִׁפְכוּ לְפָנָיו לְבַבְכֶם אֱלֹהִים מַחֲסֶה לָּנוּ סֶלָה
[10] אַךְ הֶבֶל בְּנֵי אָדָם כָּזָב בְּנֵי אִישׁ בְּמֹאזְנַיִם לַעֲלוֹת הֵמָּה מֵהֶבֶל יָחַד
[11] אַל תִּבְטְחוּ בְעֹשֶׁק וּבְגָזֵל אַל תֶּהְבָּלוּ חַיִל כִּי יָנוּב אַל תָּשִׁיתוּ לֵב
[12] אַחַת דִּבֶּר אֱלֹהִים שְׁתַּיִם זוּ שָׁמָעְתִּי כִּי עֹז לֵאלֹהִים
[13] וּלְךָ אֲדֹנָי חָסֶד כִּי אַתָּה תְשַׁלֵּם לְאִישׁ כְּמַעֲשֵׂהוּ

Transliteration:
[1] *lam'natzei'ach al yedutun miz'mor l'david*
[2] *ach el elohim dumiyah naf'shi mimenu y'shu'ati*
[3] *ach hu tzuri vishu'ati mis'gabi lo emot rabah*
[4] *ad anah t'hot'tu al ish t'ratz'chu chul'chem k'kir natui gadeir had'chuyah*
[5] *ach mis'eito ya'atzu l'hadi'ach yir'tzu chazav b'fiv y'vareichu uv'kir'bam y'kal'lu selah*
[6] *ach leilohim domi naf'shi ki mimenu tik'vati*
[7] *ach hu tzuri vishu'ati mis'gabi lo emot*
[8] *al elohim yish'i uch'vodi tzur uzi mach'si beilohim*
[9] *bit'chu vo v'chol eit am shif'chu l'fanav l'vav'chem elohim machaseh lanu selah*
[10] *ach hevel b'nei adam kazav b'nei ish b'moz'nayim la'alot heimah meihevel yachad*
[11] *al tiv't'chu v'oshek uv'gazeil al teh'balu chayil ki nanuv al tashitu leiv*

[12] *achat diber elohim sh'tayim zu shama'ti ki oz leilohim*
[13] *ul'cha adonai chased ki atah t'shaleim l'ish k'ma'aseihu*

Translation:

[1] For the Leader; for *Jeduthun*. A Psalm of David.
[2] Only for *Elohim* doth my soul wait in stillness; from Him cometh my salvation.
[3] He only is my rock and my salvation, my high tower, I shall not be greatly moved.
[4] How long will ye set upon a man, that ye may slay him, all of you, as a leaning wall, a tottering fence?
[5] They only devise to thrust him down from his height, delighting in lies; they bless with their mouth, but they curse inwardly. *Selah*
[6] Only for *Elohim* wait thou in stillness, my soul; for from Him cometh my hope.
[7] He only is my rock and my salvation, my high tower, I shall not be moved.
[8] Upon *Elohim* resteth my salvation and my glory; the rock of my strength, and my refuge, is in *Elohim*.
[9] Trust in Him at all times, ye people; pour out your heart before Him; *Elohim* is a refuge for us. *Selah*
[10] Men of low degree are vanity, and men of high degree are a lie; if they be laid in the balances, they are together lighter than vanity.
[11] Trust not in oppression, and put not vain hope in robbery; if riches increase, set not your heart thereon.
[12] *Elohim* hath spoken once, twice have I heard this: that strength belongeth unto *Elohim*;
[13] Also unto Thee *Adonai* belongeth mercy; for Thou renderest to every man according to his work.

Several texts incorporating abbreviated quotes from the *Shimmush Tehillim*, simply lists *Psalm 62* "to be said after מנחה (*Min'chah* —the afternoon prayer service) and after מעריב (*Ma'ariv [Arvit]* —evening prayer service)," without any indication as to the reason for this action,[1] the latter being the "forgiveness of sins."[2] The full statement in the popular Hebrew editions of the *Shimmush Tehillim* maintains the current psalm should be recited on a Sunday night after the evening prayer, and on a Monday after the afternoon prayer,³ to which one recension of the said text added "and likewise on a Thursday."⁴ The associated Divine Name construct is indicated in the standard version of the *Shimmush Tehillim* to be איטמי, and which Godfrey Selig maintains is pronounced "*Ittami*,"⁵ was derived: א (*Alef*) from אך אל אלהים (*ach el elohim*—"only for *Elohim*"): verse 2; י (*Yod*) from the first letter of ישועתי (*y'shu'ati*—"my salvation"): verse 2; ט (*Tet*) from לא אמוט (*lo emot*—"shall not be moved"): verse 3; מ (*Mem*) from עז לאלהים (*oz leilohim*—"strength belongeth unto *Elohim*"): verse 12; and י (*Yod*) from לאיש כמעשהו (*l'ish k'ma'aseihu*—"to every man according to his work"): verse 13.⁶ Another recension of the *Shimmush Tehillim* maintains the Divine Name construct to be איטעו, the concluding two letters of which are said to have been derived: ע (*Ayin*) likewise from עז לאלהים (*oz leilohim*— "strength belongeth unto *Elohim*"): verse 12; and ו (*Vav*) from כמעשהו (*k'ma'aseihu*—"according to his work"): verse 13.⁷

Be that as it may, the recitation of the current psalm is succeeded by the following prayer-incantation:

יהי רצון מלפניך אל אחד שתמחול ותסלח ותכפר
עוני כמו שסלחת ומחלת וכפרת למי שהתפלל לפניך
המזמור הזה

Transliteration:
> *Y'hi ratzon mil'fanecha El Echad shetim'chol v'tis'lach ut'chaper avoni k'mo shesalach'ta umachal'ta v'chafar'ta l'mi shehit'paleil l'fanecha hamiz'mor hazeh.*

Translation:
> May it be your will, *El Echad* ("the one God"), that you forgive, pardon, and atone for my transgressions, as you forgave, pardoned, and absolved the one who prayed this psalm before you.⁸

Godfrey Selig once again embellished these details in his German/English version of the *Shimmush Tehillim*, noting that the sixty-second Psalm should be spoken "with proper reverence on Sunday immediately after the evening prayer, and on Monday after vespers, and at the same time think of the holy name *Ittami*, which means 'concealed, hidden, or invisible' (which most probably refers to the Invisible God, who covers the transgressions of penitent sinners), and utter the following prayer: Great, mighty and merciful God, may it be thy holy will to pardon me all my sins, transgressions and offences; wilt thou cover them, and blot them out as thou didst the sins and transgressions of him who uttered this Psalm in thy presence, wilt thou do this for the sake of the adorable name of *Ittami*. Amen *Selah*!"[9]

In a variant recension of the *Shimmush Tehillim* we find *Psalm 62* recommended "for one whom wicked men incite with injustice and violence."[10] The said individual is enjoined to recite the psalm in conjunction with the following prayer-incantation:

יהי רצון מלפניך דגול מרבבה (*Song of Songs 5:10*)
לפניך באתי בבכי ובתחנונים שתרחם עלי והושיעני
והצילני מן האנשים האלה אשר מתגרים בי על לא
חמס בכפי (*Job 16:17*) על כן יהוה אלהי ברחמיך
הצילני מידם והשב גמולם בראשם והפר עצתם
בשמך הקדוש דגול מרבבה אמן אמן אמן סלה
סלה סלה

Transliteration:
> Y'hi ratzon mil'fanecha Dagul Meir'vavah (*Song of Songs 5:10*) l'fanecha bati babechi ub'tachanonim shet'rachem alai v'hoshi'eini v'hatzi'leini min ha'anashim ha'eileh asher mit'garim bi al lo chamas b'chapai (*Job 16:17*) al kein YHVH elohai b'rachamecha hatzileini miyadam v'hasheiv g'mulam b'rosham v'hafer atzatam b'shim'cha hakadosh Dagul Meir'vavah Omein Omein Omein Selah Selah Selah

Translation:
> May it be your will *Dagul Meir'vavah* [pre-eminent above ten thousand] (*Song of Songs 5:10*). I have come before you with weeping and supplication, that you may have mercy on me. Deliver me and save me from these people who incite me, *although there is no violence in my hands*

(*Job 16:17*). Therefore *YHVH* my God, deliver me from their hand with your mercy, and return their deeds upon their heads. Destroy their plans with your holy name *Dagul Meir'vavah*. *Amen Amen Amen Selah Selah Selah*.[11]

Whilst the sixty-second Psalm is mainly employed by those who are, as it were, pouring out their hearts in seeking forgiveness for their transgressions, the Divine Name construct שלל, being the initials of the phrase in *Psalm 62:9*, reading שפכו לפניו לבבכם (*shif'chu l'fanav l'vav'chem*—"pour out your heart before Him") [*Psalm 62:9*], is included in an amulet for heart ailments.[12] As far as "pouring your heart out" is concerned, it should be noted that the current psalm is not only recited as a prayer for forgiveness, and for atonement [תשובה— *teshuvah* (spiritual return)], but equally to increase trust in the Divine One. Considering the sentiments expressed in this psalm, it should come as no surprise that it is further employed against and to be saved from defamation, slander and gossip, and generally against malice and perjury. On a more positive level, *Psalm 62* is enunciated for good crops; to get rain; for financial prosperity; and is recited by those who are anxiously concerned about personal livelihood. Aside from this, the current psalm is recommended to those who suffer from insomnia.

The sixty-second Psalm is recommended in the Christian Byzantine manuscripts to those who are suffering slander,[13] and elsewhere it is employed to scatter enemies.[14] Whilst these applications may be fairly innocuous, the use of the current psalm listed in "*Le Livre d'Or*" is sinister in the extreme. Instead of "scattering enemies," the intention here is to collect ashes from underneath the altar of a church immediately after a mass has been said, utter the current psalm a number of times over it, and scatter this substance at the residence of an enemy, the intention being to "cut him down" and destroy his house.[15] Elsewhere we find the much more useful employment of *Psalm 62:11* and *13*, these verses being recited for the purpose of "obtaining things necessary for living."[16]

PSALM 63

[1] מזמור לדוד בהיותו במדבר יהודה
[2] אלהים אלי אתה אשחרך צמאה לך נפשי כמה לך בשרי בארץ ציה ועיף בלי מים
[3] כן בקדש חזיתך לראות עזך וכבודך
[4] כי טוב חסדך מחיים שפתי ישבחונך
[5] כן אברכך בחיי בשמך אשא כפי
[6] כמו חלב ודשן תשבע נפשי ושפתי רננות יהלל פי
[7] אם זכרתיך על יצועי באשמרות אהגה בך
[8] כי היית עזרתה לי ובצל כנפיך ארנן
[9] דבקה נפשי אחריך בי תמכה ימינך
[10] והמה לשואה יבקשו נפשי יבאו בתחתיות הארץ
[11] יגירהו על ידי חרב מנת שעלים יהיו
[12] והמלך ישמח באלהים יתהלל כל הנשבע בו כי יסכר פי דוברי שקר

Transliteration:

[1] *miz'mor l'david bih'yoto b'mid'bar y'hudah*
[2] *elohim eili atah ashachareka tzam'ah l'cha naf'shi kamah l'cha v'sari b'eretz tziyah v'ayeif b'li mayim*
[3] *ken bakodesh chaziticha lir'ot uz'cha uch'vodecha*
[4] *ki tov chas'd'cha m'chayim s'fatai y'shab'chun'cha*
[5] *ken avarech'cha v'chayai b'shim'cha esa chapai*
[6] *k'mo cheilev vadeshen tis'ba naf'shi v'sif'tei r'nanot y'halel pi*
[7] *im z'char'ticha al y'tzu'ai b'ash'murot eh'geh bach*
[8] *ki hayita ez'ratah li uv'tzeil k'nafecha aranein*
[9] *dav'kah naf'shi acharecha bi tam'chah y'minecha*
[10] *v'heimah l'sho'ah y'vak'shu naf'shi yavo'u b'tach'tiyot ha'aretz*
[11] *yagiruhu al y'dei charev m'nat shu'alim yih'yu*
[12] *v'hamelech yis'mach beilohim yit'haleil kol hanish'ba bo ki yisacheir pi dov'rei shaker*

Translation:
> [1] A Psalm of David, when he was in the wilderness of Judah.
> [2] *Elohim*, Thou art my God, earnestly will I seek Thee; my soul thirsteth for Thee, my flesh longeth for Thee, in a dry and weary land, where no water is.
> [3] So have I looked for Thee in the sanctuary, to see Thy power and Thy glory.
> [4] For Thy lovingkindness is better than life; my lips shall praise Thee.
> [5] So will I bless Thee as long as I live; in Thy name will I lift up my hands.
> [6] My soul is satisfied as with marrow and fatness; and my mouth doth praise Thee with joyful lips;
> [7] When I remember Thee upon my couch, and meditate on Thee in the night-watches.
> [8] For Thou hast been my help, and in the shadow of Thy wings do I rejoice.
> [9] My soul cleaveth unto Thee; Thy right hand holdeth me fast.
> [10] But those that seek my soul, to destroy it, shall go into the nethermost parts of the earth.
> [11] They shall be hurled to the power of the sword; they shall be a portion for foxes.
> [12] But the king shall rejoice in *Elohim*; every one that sweareth by Him shall glory; for the mouth of them that speak lies shall be stopped.

Psalm 63 is again one of the psalms recommended for recitation to express gratitude.[1] It is recommended to those who seek success in business,[2] or "good fortune in trade."[3] In the *Sefer Rafa'el ha-Malach* doing "business" is termed a "store,"[4] thus the sixty-third Psalm is understood to be good for encouraging success in all manner of commerce. However, we are informed the current psalm is also employed to receive "a good portion when dissolving a partnership"[5] In this regard, we are told in the standard Hebrew version of the *Shimmush Tehillim* that the current psalm is good for success in commerce, and that reciting it will ensure the better portion of the share profits.[6] As expected, a greater expansion of this theme appears in Godfrey Selig's version of the *Shimmush Tehillim*, reading "if you have reason to believe that your business-partners are about to take unfair advantage of you, and that you will suffer loss through them, and if you desire, on this account, to withdraw from the firm, repeat this Psalm, and with it think of the holy name *Jach*, and you will not only be able to withdraw without loss, but you will obtain further good fortune and blessings."[7] In actual fact, the associated Divine Name is י־ה (*Yah*): י (*Yod*) from והמלך ישמח באלהים (*v'hamelech yis'mach beilohim*—"But the king shall rejoice in God"): verse 12; and ה from במדבר יהודה (*b'mid'bar y'hudah*—"in the wilderness of Judah"): verse 1.[8] Selig derived his version of the said Divine Name from the same sources, though he misspelled the relevant Hebrew terms, e.g. the name יהודה (*Y'hudah*) was rendered יחודה (*Y'chudah*).[9] It should be noted that in another recension of the *Shimmush Tehillim* the affiliated Divine Name construct is said to be וה, which was equally listed as having been derived from the same verses.[10]

In yet another recension of the *Shimmush Tehillim*, the sixty-third Psalm is recommended to individuals who are seeking a partnership with associates.[11] With this objective in mind, the practitioner is instructed to recite the current psalm conjointly with the following prayer-incantation:

יהי רצון מלפניך יהוה אלהי ואלהי אבותי שתהיה שותפותי עם [....name of partner....] במזל טוב ונצליח היום ובכל יום ויום בשותפותינו וישלח השם ברחמיו רוח והצלחה וברכה שלימה וחיים ושלום בכל עסקינו ובכל מעשה ידינו בשם יה יה יה ודי ונהיה בשלום ובנחת ולא יהיה שום עול ולא שום מרמה בידינו בשם אלהים יהוה מלך עולם ועד אמן אמן אמן סלה סלה סלה

Transliteration:

Y'hi ratzon mil'fanecha YHVH elohai veilohei avotai shetihiyeh shutafuti im [....name of partner....] b'mazal tov v'natz'li'ach hayom ub'chol yom vayom b'shut'futeinu v'yis'lach hashem b'rachamav ru'ach v'hatz'lachah

> ub'rachah sh'leimah v'chayim v'shalom b'chol as'keinu ub'chol ma'aseh yadeinu b'shem Yah Yah Yah Vahei v'nih'yeh b'shalom uv'nachat v'lo yih'yeh shum avel v'lo shum mir'mah b'yadeinu b'shem Elohim YHVH melech olam va'ed Omein Omein Omein Selah Selah Selah.

Translation:
> May it be your will, *YHVH* my God and God of my fathers, that my partnership with [....name of partner....] is under a good planet, and that today and every day we have success with our partnership, and may *Hashem* [the Divine One] in His mercy send me prosperity, success, complete blessing, life, and peace in all our endeavours, and in all the deeds of our hands. In the Name *Yah Yah Yah Vahei*, we will be in peace and in comfort. There will be neither injustice nor fraud in our hands. In the Name of *Elohim YHVH*, the eternal and everlasting King, *Amen Amen Amen Selah Selah Selah*.[12]

Once again we find the current psalm employed for purposes not generally listed in published sources. In terms of the aforementioned application, the seventy-third Psalm is also recommended against unfair business partners, and to express gratitude for good fortune. Aside from these applications, the sixty-third Psalm is recommended for recitation in the synagogue, to counter bad language, and is also enunciated for the fertility of fields during a water scarcity.

In Christian Magic *Psalm 63* is recommended in the Byzantine manuscripts to an individual who wishes to determine whether an expected visitor "is coming or is sitting idle."[13] In this regard, the said individual is advised to recite the current psalm over wine, and consume it afterwards. It is said "if you get drunk, he is coming in haste, but if not, he is sitting idle."[14] Elsewhere in the same sources the sixty-third Psalm is recited for the abominable purpose of destroying those who were defined "evil."[15] To my mind much better use is made of the current psalm in "*Le Livre d'Or*," in which the psalm is written down and bound to the arm of an infant, in order to stop him or her from crying incessantly.[16] Elsewhere *Psalm 63:5* and *6* is suggested "for a man to be rewarded with good things in his family."[17]

PSALM 64

[1] למנצח מזמור לדוד
[2] שמע אלהים קולי בשיחי מפחד אויב תצר חיי
[3] תסתירני מסוד מרעים מרגשת פעלי און
[4] אשר שננו כחרב לשונם דרכו חצם דבר מר
[5] לירות במסתרים תם פתאם ירהו ולא ייראו
[6] יחזקו למו דבר רע יספרו לטמון מוקשים אמרו מי יראה למו
[7] יחפשו עולת תמנו חפש מחפש וקרב איש ולב עמק
[8] וירם אלהים חץ פתאום היו מכותם
[9] ויכשילוהו עלימו לשונם יתנדדו כל ראה בם
[10] וייראו כל אדם ויגידו פעל אלהים ומעשהו השכילו
[11] ישמח צדיק ביהוֹ‏אהדונהיּ‏הוה וחסה בו ויתהללו כל ישרו לב

Transliteration:

[1] *lam'natzei'ach miz'mor l'david*
[2] *sh'ma elohim koli v'sichi mipachad oyeiv titzor chayai*
[3] *tas'tireini misod m'rei'im meirig'shat po'alei aven*
[4] *asher shan'nu chacherev l'shonam dar'chu chitzam davar mar*
[5] *lirot bamis'tarim tam pit'om yoruhu v'lo yira'u*
[6] *y'chaz'ku lamo davar ra y'sap'ru lit'mon mok'shim am'ru mi yir'eh lamo*
[7] *yach'p'su olot tam'nu cheifes m'chupas v'kerev ish v'leiv amok*
[8] *vayoreim elohim cheitz pit'om hayu makotam*
[9] *vayach'shiluhu aleimo l'shonam yit'nod'du kol ro'eih vam*
[10] *vayir'u kol adam vayagidu po'al elohim uma'aseihu his'kilu*
[11] *yis'mach tzadik ba'YHVH v'chasah vo v'yit'hal'lu kol yish'rei leiv*

Translation:
>   [1] For the Leader. A Psalm of David.
>   [2] Hear my voice *Elohim*, in my complaint; preserve my life from the terror of the enemy.
>   [3] Hide me from the council of evil-doers; from the tumult of the workers of iniquity;
>   [4] Who have whet their tongue like a sword, and have aimed their arrow, a poisoned word;
>   [5] That they may shoot in secret places at the blameless; suddenly do they shoot at him, and fear not.
>   [6] They encourage one another in an evil matter; they converse of laying snares secretly; they ask, who would see them.
>   [7] They search out iniquities, they have accomplished a diligent search; even in the inward thought of every one, and the deep heart.
>   [8] But *Elohim* doth shoot at them with an arrow suddenly; thence are their wounds.
>   [9] So they make their own tongue a stumbling unto themselves; all that see them shake the head.
>   [10] And all men fear; and they declare the work of *Elohim*, and understand His doing.
>   [11] The righteous shall be glad in *YHVH*, and shall take refuge in Him; and all the upright in heart shall glory.

Psalm 64 is recited in Jewish Magic for the purpose of fording a watercourse, i.e. crossing a river in safety.[1] As one has come to expect, an instruction comprising a single sentence such as this in the *Shimmush Tehillim*, would not sit well with Godfrey Selig who, in his German/English translations of the said text, explained that "in reference to this Psalm it is only necessary to say, that seafarers who daily pray it with devotion will complete their voyage without accident, and reach their place of destination in good health. As for the rest, neither holy name nor especial prayer have been considered necessary."[2] Be that as it may, in a variant recension of the *Shimmush Tehillim* the current psalm is pronounced to ensure that enemies do not lie to an individual because of a personal sin, and thereby entice the said individual into further **transgressions**.[3] Obvious examples would be alcohol addiction, substance abuse, gambling, etc. In this regard, the psalm is enunciated in conjunction with the following prayer-incantation:

יהי רצון מלפניך וה וה וה והו אלהי עולם
הצילני מחטא ובל יחטיאוני אויבי אלה אני
[....personal name....] בשמך הטהור והנקי וה וה
וה והו אמן אמן אמן סלה סלה סלה

Transliteration:
> Y'hi ratzon mil'fanecha Vah Vah Vah Vaho elohei olam hatzileini meicheit ubal yach'ti'uni oy'vai eileh ani [....personal name....] b'shim'ka hatahor v'hanaki Vah Vah Vah Vaho Omein Omein Omein Selah Selah Selah.

Translation:
> May it be your will *Vah Vah Vah Vaho*, eternal God. Save me from sin, lest these mine enemies tempt me to sin, me, [....personal name....], in your pure and refined Name *Vah Vah Vaho*. Amen Amen Amen Selah Selah Selah.[4]

Besides its use to safely cross a river, *Psalm 64* is recited to complete a voyage in good health. Aside from this, I have seen the current psalm enunciated against verbal abuse, defamation, slander and gossip. It was further suggested to victims of wrongdoing, and, curiously enough, it was also recommended to one who was bitten by a rabid animal.

As in Jewish Magic, the application of *Psalm 64* is equally sparse in Christian Magic where we are likewise informed that the current psalm is enunciated to defeat an enemy.[5] In this regard, it is said in *"Le Livre d'Or"* that reciting the current psalm as well as *"Jubilate Deo,"* i.e. *Psalm 100*, over a set of magical characters to be attached to the arm of the practitioner, will aid him or her in overcoming personal enemies.[6] A very different use is made of the sixty-fourth Psalm in the *"Key of Solomon,"* where it is listed with *Psalms 72*, *82*, and *134*, for recitation during the "perfuming" of the silk cloth in which "the instruments of art" are wrapped when not in use.[7]

PSALM 65

[1] למנצח מזמור לדוד שיר
[2] לך דמיה תהלה אלהים בציון ולך ישלם נדר
[3] שמע תפלה עדיך כל בשר יבאו
[4] דברי עונת גברו מני פשעינו אתה תכפרם
[5] אשרי תבחר ותקרב ישכן חצריך נשבעה בטוב ביתך קדש היכלך
[6] נוראות בצדק תעננו אלהי ישענו מבטח כל קצוי ארץ וים רחקים
[7] מכין הרים בכחו נאזר בגבורה
[8] משביח אשון ימים שאון גליהם והמון לאמים
[9] וייראו ישבי קצות מאותתיך מוצאי בקר וערב תרנין
[10] פקדת הארץ ותשקקה רבת תעשרנה פלג אלהים מלא מים תכין דגנם כי כן תכינה
[11] תלמיה רוה נחת גדודה ברביבים תמגגנה צמחה תברך
[12] עטרת שנת טובתך ומעגליך ירעפון דשן
[13] ירעפו נאות מדבר וגיל גבעות תחגרנה
[14] לבשו כרים הצאן ועמקים יעטפו בר יתרועעו אף ישירו

Transliteration:
[1] lam'natzei'ach miz'mor l'david shir
[2] l'cha dumiyah t'hilah elohim b'tziyon ul'cha y'shulam neder
[3] shomei'a t'filah adecha kol basar yavo'u
[4] div'rei avonot gav'ru meni p'sha'einu atah t'chap'reim
[5] ash'rei tiv'char ut'kareiv yish'kon chatzeirecha nis'b'ah b'tuv beitecha k'dosh heichalecha
[6] nora'ot b'tzedek ta'aneinu elohei yish'einu miv'tach kol katz'vei eretz v'yam r'chokim
[7] meichin harim b'chocho ne'zar big'vurah
[8] mash'bi'ach sh'on yamim sh'on galeihem vahamon l'umim
[9] vayir'u yosh'vei k'tzavot mei'ototecha motza'ei voker va'erev tar'nin

[10] *pakad'ta ha'aretz vat'shok'keha rabat ta'sh'renah peleg elohim malei mayim tachin d'ganam ki chein t'chineha*
[11] *t'lameha raveih nacheit g'dudeha bir'vivim t'mog'genah tzim'chah t'vareich*
[12] *itar'ta sh'nat tovatecha uma'galecha yir'afun dashen*
[13] *yir'afu n'ot mid'bar v'gil g'va'ot tach'gor'nah*
[14] *lav'shu charim hatzon va'amakim ya'at'fu var yit'ro'a'u af yashiru*

Translation:

[1] For the Leader. A Psalm. A Song of David.
[2] Praise waiteth for Thee, *Elohim*, in Zion; and unto Thee the vow is performed.
[3] O Thou that hearest prayer, unto Thee doth all flesh come.
[4] The tale of iniquities is too heavy for me; as for our transgressions, Thou wilt pardon them.
[5] Happy is the man whom Thou choosest, and bringest near, that he may dwell in Thy courts; may we be satisfied with the goodness of Thy house, the holy place of Thy temple!
[6] With wondrous works dost Thou answer us in righteousness, O God of our salvation; Thou the confidence of all the ends of the earth, and of the far distant seas;
[7] Who by Thy strength settest fast the mountains, who art girded about with might;
[8] Who stillest the roaring of the seas, the roaring of their waves, and the tumult of the peoples;
[9] So that they that dwell in the uttermost parts stand in awe of Thy signs; Thou makest the outgoings of the morning and evening to rejoice.
[10] Thou hast remembered the earth, and watered her, greatly enriching her, with the river of *Elohim* that is full of water; Thou preparest them corn, for so preparest Thou her.
[11] Watering her ridges abundantly, settling down the furrows thereof, Thou makest her soft with showers; Thou blessest the growth thereof.
[12] Thou crownest the year with Thy goodness; and Thy paths drop fatness.

[13] The pastures of the wilderness do drop; and the hills are girded with joy.
[14] The meadows are clothed with flocks; the valleys also are covered over with corn; they shout for joy, yea, they sing.

Psalm 65 is one of the additional psalms recited in the Sefardi liturgy on *Yom Kippur* ("Day of Atonement"), and the phrase from the fifth verse reading "may we be satisfied with the goodness of Thy house, the holy place of Thy temple," is especially recited in both the Ashkenazi and Sefardi rites during circumcisions.[1] This psalm is also listed amongst those enunciated to express gratitude.[2]

As far as its use in Jewish Magic is concerned, *Psalm 65* is said to be useful "for exerting influence,"[3] or to ensure a request to anyone is successfully granted.[4] In this regard, we are informed in the standard version of the *Shimmush Tehillim* that the psalm should be recited with the associated Divine Name construct יָהּ (*Yah*): י (*Yod*) from יָשִׁירוּ (*yashiru*—"they sing"): verse 14, and ה (*Heh*) from דֻמִיָּה (*dumiyah*—"waiteth"): verse 2.[5] Curiously enough, the capitals of the opening two words of *Psalm 65:3* reading שֹׁמֵעַ תְּפִלָּה (*shome'a t'filah*—"Thou that hearest prayer"), are conjoined in the Divine Name construct שת, which is likewise employed for the purpose of having a wish fulfilled.[6] Thus it should come as no surprise that the sixty-fifth Psalm is further recommended for success in general.[7] It is with this purpose in mind that Godfrey Selig noted, in his version of the *Shimmush Tehillim*, that "whosoever utters this Psalm with its appropriate name *Jah*, persistently, will be fortunate in all his undertakings, and everything he attempts will result to his best advantage.[8]

The current psalm is recommended in a different recension of the *Shimmush Tehillim* against storms at sea, and "for the answer to the prayer of the one who seeks to return in penance."[9] In this regard, *Psalm 65* is recited whilst focusing on the associated Divine Name ייה (*YYH*), and in conjunction with the following prayer-incantation:

יהי רצון מלפניך השם הגדול שתשמע תפילתי
ותקבלני בתשובה שלימה ותושיעני משאון ימים
ותרחם עלי ברוך **אתה** יהוה שומע תפילה

Transliteration:
> Y'hi ratzon mil'fanecha hashem hagadol sh'tish'ma t'filati ut'kab'leinu b't'shuvah sh'leimah v'toshi'eini misha'on yamim ut'rachem alai baruch atah YHVH shomei'a t'filah

Translation:
> May it be your will, the great Name, that you hear my prayer and accept me with complete repentance. You shall deliver me from the noise of the days, and have mercy on me. Blessed be you *YHVH*, Hearer of Prayer.[10]

The sixty-fifth Psalm has been recommended for a variety of purposes which have been passed on by word of mouth amongst generations past and present. As mentioned earlier, it is recited to have "a wish fulfilled," but it is also employed to have good fortune in all undertakings, as well as to express gratitude to the Divine One. In this regard, it is one of several psalms enunciated to express gratitude for good fortune, success and prosperity, and to give praise. It is therefore understandable why we are told to recite this psalm in the synagogue. It is further said that this psalm is particularly good in aiding convalescence. However, on the flip side, it should be noted that *Psalm 65* is recited against torment by employers, dishonest merchants, and against all manner of trouble and tribulations.

Psalm 65 is employed for virtually the same purposes in Christian Magic, as those listed in the Jewish variety. In this regard, we are informed in the Byzantine magical manuscripts that reciting the current psalm in a residence at the beginning of the year, will ensure a prosperous year for the occupants.[11] Elsewhere, in *"Le Livre d'Or,"* it is noted that if an individual has fallen into bad times, the current psalm should be read seven times every day, which will secure the recovery of the said individual.[12] In terms of ensuring abundance, it is said that reciting *Psalm 56:10 and 11* will cause rain to fall "at the appropriate time," and it is claimed that enunciating verses twelve and thirteen will result in a plentitude of "the fruits of the Earth."[13]

Again, as in the case of Jewish Magic, the sixty-fifth Psalm is likewise enunciated to control storms at sea. In this regard, the practitioner is instructed in the Byzantine magical manuscripts to recite the psalm to calm the rough seas, and if there is no success, to write and carry it with a magical sign, "then take olive oil and go to the stern or prow of the boat," from which seven drops are poured into the sea whilst making the Christian "sign of the cross" with the liquid, and saying some accompanying words.[14] Elsewhere, with specific reference to bad weather and fishing-boats, the same source suggests writing the psalm with a magical seal comprising additional words, doing so on a Friday during the first hour of the day, in order to ensure divine protection."[15] *Psalm 65* is also recommended in the Byzantine magical manuscripts to an individual who wishes to have sexual relations with his wife for the first time. In this regard, he is instructed to read the psalm three times, and carry it on his person prior to the said sexual union.[16] In conclusion, the current psalm is enunciated "to bind the tongues of enemies."[17]

PSALM 66

[1] למנצח שיר מזמור הריעו לאלהים כל הארץ
[2] זמרו בכוד שמו שימו כבוד תהלתו
[3] אמרו לאלהים מה נורא מעשיך ברב עזך יכחשו לך איביך
[4] כל הארץ ישתחוו לך ויזמרו לך יזמרו שמך סלה
[5] לכו וראו מפעלות אלהים נורא עלילה על בני אדם
[6] הפך ים ליבשה בנהר יעברו ברגל שם נשמחה בו
[7] משל בגבורתו עולם עיניו בגוים תצפינה הסוררים אל ירומו למו סלה
[8] ברכו עמים אלהינו והשמיעו קול תהלתו
[9] השם נפשנו בחיים ולא נתן למוט רגלנו
[10] כי בחנתנו אלהים צרפתנו כצרף כסף
[11] הבאתנו במצודה שמת מועקה במתנינו
[12] הרכבת אנוש לראשנו באנו באש ובמים ותוציאנו לרויה
[13] אבוא ביתך בעולות אשלם לך נדרי
[14] אשר פצו שפתי ודבר פי בצר לי
[15] עלות מיחים אעלה לך עם קטרת אילים אעשה בקר עם עתודים סלה
[16] לכו שמעו ואספרה כל יראי אלהים אשר עשה לנפשי
[17] אליו פי קראתי ורומם תחת לשוני
[18] און אם ראיתי בלבי לא ישמע אדני
[19] אכן שמע אלהים הקשיב בקול תפלתי
[20] ברוך אלהים אשר לא הסיר תפלתי וחסדו מאתי

Transliteration:

[1] lam'natzei'ach shir miz'mor hari'u leilohim kol ha'aretz

[2] zam'ru ch'vod shemo simu chavod t'hilato

[3] im'ru leilohim mah nora ma'asecha b'rov uz'cha y'chachashu l'cha oy'vecha

[4] *kol ha'aretz yish'tachavu l'cha vizam'ru lach y'zam'ru shim'cha selah*
[5] *l'chu ur'u mif'alot elohim nora alilah al b'nei adam*
[6] *hafach yam l'yabashah banahar ya'av'ru v'ragel sham nis'm'chah bo*
[7] *mosheil big'vurato olam einav bagoyim titz'penah hasor'rim al yarumu lamo selah*
[8] *bar'chu amim eloheinu v'hash'mi'u kol t'hilato*
[9] *hasam naf'sheinu bachayim v'lo natan lamot rag'leinu*
[10] *ki v'chan'tanu elohim tz'raf'tanu kitz'rof kasef*
[11] *haveitanu vam'tzudah sam'ta mu'akah v'mot'neinu*
[12] *hir'kav'ta enosh l'rosheinu banu va'esh uvamayim vatotzi'einu lar'vayah*
[13] *avo veit'cha v'olot ashaleim l'cha n'darai*
[14] *asher patzu s'fatai v'diber pi batzar li*
[15] *olot meichim a'aleh lach im k'toret eilim e'eseh vakar im atudim selah*
[16] *l'chu shim'u va'asap'rah kol yir'ei elohim asher asah l'naf'shi*
[17] *eilav pi karati v'romam tachat l'shoni*
[18] *aven im ra'iti v'libi lo yish'ma adonai*
[19] *achein shama elohim hik'shiv b'kol t'filati*
[20] *baruch elohim asher lo heisir t'filati v'chas'do mei'iti*

Translation:

[1] For the Leader. A Song, a Psalm. Shout unto *Elohim*, all the earth;

[2] Sing praises unto the glory of His name; make His praise glorious.

[3] Say unto *Elohim*: 'How tremendous is Thy work! Through the greatness of Thy power shall Thine enemies dwindle away before Thee.

[4] All the earth shall worship Thee, and shall sing praises unto Thee; they shall sing praises to Thy name.' *Selah*

[5] Come, and see the works of *Elohim*; He is terrible in His doing toward the children of men.

[6] He turned the sea into dry land; they went through the river on foot; there let us rejoice in Him!

[7] Who ruleth by His might for ever; His eyes keep watch upon the nations; let not the rebellious exalt themselves. *Selah*

[8] Bless our God, ye peoples, and make the voice of His praise to be heard;
[9] Who hath set our soul in life, and suffered not our foot to be moved,
[10] For Thou, *Elohim*, hast tried us; Thou hast refined us, as silver is refined.
[11] Thou didst bring us into the hold; Thou didst lay constraint upon our loins.
[12] Thou hast caused men to ride over our heads; we went through fire and through water; but Thou didst bring us out unto abundance.
[13] I will come into Thy house with burnt-offerings, I will perform unto Thee my vows,
[14] Which my lips have uttered, and my mouth hath spoken, when I was in distress.
[15] I will offer unto Thee burnt-offerings of fatlings, with the sweet smoke of rams; I will offer bullocks with goats. *Selah*
[16] Come, and hearken, all ye that fear *Elohim*, and I will declare what He hath done for my soul.
[17] I cried unto Him with my mouth, and He was extolled with my tongue.
[18] If I had regarded iniquity in my heart, *Adonai* would not hear;
[19] But verily *Elohim* hath heard; He hath attended to the voice of my prayer.
[20] Blessed be *Elohim*, who hath not turned away my prayer, nor His mercy from me.

Psalm 66 is employed in Jewish Magic "against evil spirits,"[1] i.e. to alleviate the plight of one who is demon possessed.[2] I have seen the simple statement that the current psalm is for an individual "who has a spirit (רוח—*ruach*),"[3] interpreted as a reference to anyone who suffers a "black mood" or depression. I have also interacted with an individual who maintained that she managed to overcome manic depression by reciting the current psalm three times every day. However, whilst it might be assumed that what was termed "demon possession" in times gone by is purely a reference to some or other "dark" mental condition, and whilst the sixty-sixth Psalm may indeed be useful in offering relief to individuals who are severely bi-polar, the use of this psalm in "Practical Kabbalah" pertains to supporting an individual who is overshadowed by a spirit, the latter being generally understood to be of the "evil" or "demonic" kind. In this regard, to alleviate the plight of the demoniac, we are informed in the *Shimmush Tehillim* to write and suspend the psalm on his or her person, whilst simultaneously whispering *Psalm 69:2* over the afflicted individual,[4] saying:

הושיעני אלהים כי באו מים עד נפש

Transliteration:
hoshi'eini elohim ki va'u mayim ad nefesh
Translation:
Save me *Elohim*; for the waters are come in even unto the soul.

According to Godfrey Selig the psalm should be written on parchment, and the concluding pronouncement made whilst stretching the hands over the sufferer.[5] Elsewhere, in a variant recension of the *Shimmush Tehillim* the current psalm is employed for the very different purpose of coaxing those who cannot fulfil their vows, to keep their promises.[6] In this regard, *Psalm 66* is recited in the morning in the synagogue, doing so in conjunction with the following brief prayer-incantation, whilst focussing on the Divine Name צבי צבי צבי (*Tz'vi Tz'vi Tz'vi* — "Glorified Glorified Glorified") which is said to be associated with the current psalm:

שמע יהוה קולי הסכת מלי ותן לי יבולת לשלם
נדרי ככתוב נדרי ליהוה אשלם נגדה נא לכל
עמו (*Psalms 116:18*) והשם מזה המזמור צבי צבי
צבי אמן סלה

Transliteration:
Sh'ma YHVH koli his'kata mili v'tein li y'cholet l'shaleim n'darai kakatuv n'darai la'YHVH ashaleim neg'dah na

> *l'chol amo (Psalms 116:18) v'hashem mizeh hamiz'mor Tz'vi Tz'vi Tzvi Omein Selah*

Translation:
> Hear *YHVH* my voice, listen to my words, and grant me the ability to fulfill my vows, as it is written "I will pay my vows unto *YHVH*, yea, in the presence of all His people." (*Psalms 116:18*), and the Name of this psalm is *Tz'vi Tz'vi Tzvi. Amen Selah.*[7]

Apart from these applications, the current psalm is also employed against sorrow resulting from domestic obstacles, and, as in the case of the previous psalm, for praise of the Divine One.

Psalm 66 is said in the Byzantine Christian magical manuscripts to be "useful for judgments at court." In this regard, they instruct the psalm to be written with certain magical characters "on Sunday in the first hour," and the object carried on the person of the one requiring this support.[8] However, as in the case of the previous psalm, the current one appears to be equally employed to benefit those in need. Thus we are informed in "*Le Livre d'Or*" that those who are "poor and needy," should read the sixty-sixth Psalm "seven times in the morning and seven times in the evening."[9] It is believed that with Divine support, this action would change the fortunes of those who are impoverished.[10] On the other hand, it is said that those who are benefiting greatly from the "goods of the Earth," could increase abundance by reciting *Psalm 66:4* and *5* in praise of the Divine One for their prosperity.[11]

PSALM 67

[1] לַמְנַצֵּחַ בִּנְגִינֹת מִזְמוֹר שִׁיר
[2] אֱלֹהִים יְחָנֵּנוּ וִיבָרְכֵנוּ יָאֵר פָּנָיו אִתָּנוּ סֶלָה
[3] לָדַעַת בָּאָרֶץ דַּרְכֶּךָ בְּכָל גּוֹיִם יְשׁוּעָתֶךָ
[4] יוֹדוּךָ עַמִּים אֱלֹהִים יוֹדוּךָ עַמִּים כֻּלָּם
[5] יִשְׂמְחוּ וִירַנְּנוּ לְאֻמִּים כִּי תִשְׁפֹּט עַמִּים מִישֹׁר וּלְאֻמִּים בָּאָרֶץ תַּנְחֵם סֶלָה
[6] יוֹדוּךָ עַמִּים אֱלֹהִים יוֹדוּךָ עַמִּים כֻּלָּם
[7] אֶרֶץ נָתְנָה יְבוּלָהּ יְבָרְכֵנוּ אֱלֹהִים אֱלֹהֵינוּ
[8] יְבָרְכֵנוּ אֱלֹהִים וְיִירְאוּ אוֹתוֹ כָּל אַפְסֵי אָרֶץ

Transliteration:
[1] *lam'natzei'ach bin'ginot miz'mor shir*
[2] *elohim y'choneinu vivar'cheinu ya'eir panav itanu selah*
[3] *lada'at ba'aretz dar'kecha b'chol goyim y'shu'atecha*
[4] *yoducha amim elohim yoducha amim kulam*
[5] *yish'm'chu viran'nu l'umim ki tish'pot amim mishor ul'umim ba'aretz tan'cheim selah*
[6] *yoducha amim elohim yoducha amim kulam*
[7] *eretz nat'na y'vulah y'var'cheinu elohim eloheinu*
[8] *y'var'cheinu elohim v'yir'u oto kol af'sei aretz*

Translation:
[1] For the Leader; with string-music. A Psalm, a Song.
[2] *Elohim* be gracious unto us, and bless us; may He cause His face to shine toward us; *Selah*
[3] That Thy way may be known upon earth, Thy salvation among all nations.
[4] Let the peoples give thanks unto Thee *Elohim*; let the peoples give thanks unto Thee, all of them.
[5] O let the nations be glad and sing for joy; for Thou wilt judge the peoples with equity, and lead the nations upon earth. *Selah*
[6] Let the peoples give thanks unto Thee *Elohim*; let the peoples give thanks unto Thee, all of them.
[7] The earth hath yielded her increase; may *Elohim*, our own God, bless us.
[8] May *Elohim* bless us; and let all the ends of the earth fear Him.

Psalm 67, whilst relatively small in size, holds a position of enormous stature in Judaism. It is recited at a number of different times, these being always in accordance with variances in the liturgies of the three daily prayer services within the once far-flung and greatly dispersed Jewish communities of previous centuries. Thus the current psalm is enunciated in the weekday *Shacharit* (Morning Prayer Service) of Sefardi and Syrian communities, as well as in the נוסח האר״י (*Nusach ha'Ari*), i.e. the order of prayers based on the kabbalistic doctrines of Rabbi Isaac Luria, and which is employed by the East European Chasidim.[1] It is also recited after the weekday *Arvit* (Evening Prayer Service) of the Sefardim and Kabbalists, and prior to *Arvit* on a Saturday by both Ashkenazi and Sefardi Jewry.[2] Spanish and Portuguese Jews speak the sixty-seventh Psalm during the weekday *Min'chah* (Afternoon Prayer Service),[3] and the current psalm is further enunciated prior to ברכת המזון (*Bir'kat Hamazon*—"Blessing after a Meal") by the *Sefardim* as well as by those who follow the mentioned "*Nusach ha'Ari*" order of prayers, this action being said to be "an encouraging message summoning all peoples of the earth to pay homage to God."[4] It is equally recited at ברכת הלבנה (*Bir'kat Halevanah*—"Blessing of the Moon");[5] read and enunciated, as noted in the previous chapter, in the pattern of a *Menorah* (seven-branched candelabrum) during ספירת העומר (*Sefirat ha-Omer* — "Counting of the Sheaves [of wheat]");[6] and pronounced during the ritual circumambulations (הקפות—*Hakafot*) on שמחת תורה (*Sim'chat Torah*—"Rejoicing with the Torah").[7]

However, it is the utterance of the sixty-seventh Psalm at מוצאי שבת (*Motza'ei Shabat*), i.e. the exiting of the Sabbath at dusk on a Saturday, when we escort the ceremonial departure of שבת המלכה (*Shabat Hamal'kah*—"the Sabbath Queen") in the same joyful manner as we celebrated the arrival of the "Divine Bride" at the advent of שבת (*Shabbat*),[8] which is of greatest significance to me personally. Be that as it may, the immense popularity of the sixty-seventh Psalm pertains to several unique factors. Defined "a Sanctuary Song about God's Universal Blessings,"[9] the acclaimed "Priestly Blessing" (*Numbers 6:24-26*) is referenced in this wondrous psalm in terms of all nations, and the quality of goodness and well-being invoked in terms of the "fruitfulness of all the earth."[10] Yet, as noted earlier, it is the association of the current psalm with the numbers 7 and 49 which determines its most intensive application in mainstream Judaism, i.e. over the forty-nine days "Counting of the *Omer*."[11]

Psalm 67 is recommended in Jewish Magic against persistent קַדַּחַת (*Kedachat*), which, as noted earlier, is a chronic fever or malaria,[12] and it is also recommended to those who are arrested or imprisoned.[13] In this regard, as noted earlier, it has been reported in the name of Abraham Galante, that "done with proper *Kavvanah*," i.e. strongly focussed attention and intention, the current psalm "protects against imprisonment."[14] These applications of the sixty-seventh Psalms are also listed in the *Shimmush Tehillim*, in this instance in conjunction with an associated Divine Name construct יָהּ (*Yah*), the component glyphs of which are said to have been derived: י (*Yod*) from יְחָנֵּנוּ (*y'choneinu*—"be gracious unto us"): verse 2; and ה (*Heh*) from סֶלָה (*Selah*): verse 2 or 5.[15] In the said text the latter term is indicated to be "at the end of the psalm,"[16] but, as indicated, it appears twice in the current psalm, i.e. at the end of the second and fifth verses, and is not indicated at the conclusion of the psalm. It should be noted that the sixty-seventh Psalm is also said to be beneficial as a protection against harm in all perilous situations.[17] Furthermore, to find grace in the eyes of God and man, we are told it is a magical virtue to read *Psalm 67* every day in the form of the *Menorah* (seven-branched candelabra),[18] which I have addressed in great detail elsewhere,[19] as well as in the previous chapter of this tome. In this regard, it has been said that the one doing so will not suffer injury, and will be pleasing equally to both humans and the Divine One.[20] In a similar vein, we are informed in a different recension of the *Shimmush Tehillim* that it is good to pray this psalm on every one of the 49 days of the earlier mentioned "Counting of the *Omer*,"[21] and, as noted earlier, the current psalm is likewise perused and read in the shape of a *Menorah* over the said period. Furthermore, the same version of the *Shimmush Tehillim* maintains that anyone who seeks grace and favour, to be saved from an evil word, i.e. an evil spell, and also to be protected against thieves, should pray the current psalm every night in conjunction with the following prayer-incantation which includes an associated Divine Name combination:

רחמנא מן שמיא רחם עלי והושיעני מכל אויב
ואורב בלילה הזה ובכל לילה ולא יוכל שום גנב
ליכנס בביתי ולא ליטול ממוני שממנו אתפרנס אני
ובני וביתי בשם צבא צבא רם רם אל כל רמים
יהיה דבר זה אלי לישועתך קויתי יהוה (Genesis 49:18)
אמן סלה

Transliteration:
> *Rach'mana min shamaya racheim alai v'hoshi'eini mikol oyeiv v'oreiv balailah hazeh uv'chol lailah v'lo yuchal shum ganav likanes b'beiti v'lo litol mamuni shemimenu et'par'neis ani ubanai ubeiti b'shem Tzava Tzava Ram Ram al chol ramim yih'yeh davar zeh elai lishu'at'cha kiviti YHVH (Genesis 49:18) Omein Selah*

Translation:
> Merciful One from heaven, have mercy on me and deliver me from every enemy and highwayman this night and every night. And no thief shall be able to enter my home and take my property by means of which I support myself, my children, and my household. In the name *Tzava Tzava Ram Ram* (Host Host [Army Army] Lofty Lofty) over all the lofty, this shall be the (magic) word for me. *I wait for Thy salvation YHVH* (Genesis 49:18) Amen Selah.[22]

In yet another recension of the *Shimmush Tehillim* we find the sixty-seventh Psalm referenced in conjunction with *Psalm 61*, noting that if an individual wishes to request something from someone, that success is guaranteed when these two psalms are recited whilst "on the go."[23]

As one has come to expect by now, the entire psalm as well as single verses therefrom are employed for magical purposes, often in abbreviated format in amulets. In this regard, I stated elsewhere that such condensations are considered equally effective, and noted that abbreviations of *Psalm 67* were arranged into the "*Menorah*" format to be engraved on the surface of relatively small metal amulets,[24] for protection of "women in childbirth against the 'evil eye' and the demoness *Lilit*."[25] It should be noted that the current psalm is also abbreviated and employed on Hebrew amulets for the purpose of "protection against troublesome situations, and as a call for help by individuals who find themselves in grievous circumstances."[26] In terms of this purpose, the capitals of the words comprising the entire sixty-seventh Psalm are conjoined into the following Divine Name construct, which is employed in amulets either as a call for help,²⁷ or to ward off trouble,²⁸ and it is equally employed against diseases of the head, as well as to alleviate all kinds of fevers:²⁹

לבמ שאי ויפ אסל בדב גיי עאי עבי ולב
תעמ ובת סיע איע כאנ ייא איא ואב אא

I have seen the complete psalm, as well as this abbreviation, engraved on *Hamsot* for protection, as well as to banish misfortune. Furthermore, the initials of the words of single verses are equally formulated into Divine Name constructs serving as a "call for spiritual help" when in dire need. In this regard, the initials of the words comprising *Psalm 67:1–2* and the second verse on its own, are respectively formulated into the Divine Name constructs לבמשאי ויפאס and איויפאס, both of which are employed in amulets as a "call for help."³⁰ The initials of the concluding five words of the second verse, conjoined with the first word of the third verse, are likewise combined in the Divine Name construct ויפאסל which is included in amulets for the same purpose.³¹ In fact, any of these reductions could be successfully applied for the very same purpose assigned to the abbreviation of the entire Psalm.

The capitals of the first word of *Psalm 67:5–8*, i.e. ישמחו (*yishm'chu*—"be glad"), יודוך (*yoducha*—"thanks unto Thee"), ארץ (*aretz*—"earth"), and יברכנו (*y'var'cheinu*—"bless us"), were conjoined into the Divine Name construct ייאי. This Divine Name is the concluding portion of a larger Divine Name construct אלייאי³² incorporating the initials of the first words of *Psalm 67:2—8*, hence the tri-letter prefix comprising the initials of the words אלהים (*Elohim*); לדעת (*lada'at*—"to know"); and יודוך (*yoducha*—"thanks unto Thee"). In fact, the complete Divine Name construct pertains to the very apexes of the seven branches of the "*Menorah*," with which, as mentioned earlier, the current psalm is fully aligned. This Divine Name construct is said to pertain to the wonders of the sacred incense (*k'toret*),³³ which plays a significant role in mainstream Jewish worship, as well as in Jewish magic. Be that as it may, the Divine Name construct יאי׳ was further intertwined with יהוה (*YHVH*), אדני (*Adonai*), and אהיה (*Eh'yeh*), in order to formulate what is termed "the great and awesome Name" יאיא הדיה ונאי הייה. In this instance the first letters of these four-letter combinations spell the Ineffable Name; the second four the Divine Name *Adonai*; the third trace the Divine Name construct formed from the current psalm; and the concluding four spell the Name *Eh'yeh*. We are informed that the power of this Divine Name combination "is brought to bear by means of prayer and fasting."[34] It was incorporated in the following amulet in conjunction with other Divine and Angelic Names, which I addressed in some detail in previous volumes,[35] as well as with an *Eh'yeh/Ineffable Name* letter square, for the purpose of protecting women "against miscarriage and other afflictions which might beset the unborn":[36]

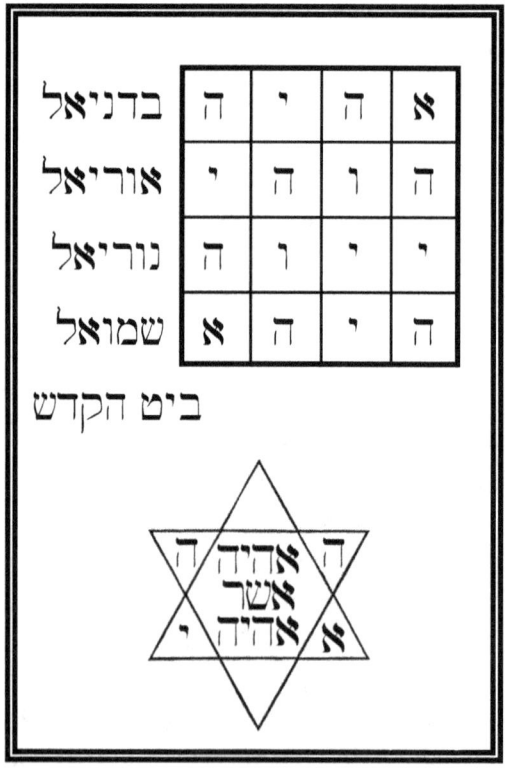

This amuletic construct is inscribed on a metal disk conjointly with the following written prayer-incantation, the latter including the Divine Name combination under discussion:

צורטק בשם רחמים וחסד בזחות המלאכים הקדושים
והטהורים יאיא הדיה ונאי היה יהא רעוא מן כדמך
שם יהוה שישמרו אלו השמות ל [....name of recipient....]
למלאת חדשי עיבורה ולקיים את העובר בבטנה
ויוציאנו חי ויהיה ולד של קיימא בכח אתניק צורת
חותמך שבו נחתמו שמים וארץ בכח השם הגדול
כוזו במוכסז כוזו

Transliteration:
> *Tzurtak b'shem rachamim v'chesed biz'chut hamalachim hak'doshim v'hat'horim YAYA HDYH VNAY HYYH y'hei ra'ava min kadamach shem YHVH sheyish'meru eilu hashemot l'*[....name of recipient....] *lem'le'at chod'shei iburah v'l'kayeim et ha'ubar b'bit'nah vayotzi'einu chai v'yiyeh valad shel kayama b'ko'ach Atneik tzurat chotam'cha shebo nech't'mu shamayim v'aretz b'ko'ach hashem hagadol Kuzu B'moch'saz Kuzu.*

Translation:
> *Tzurtak* in the Name of mercy and loving-kindness, in the merit of the holy and pure angels, *YAYA HDYH VNAY HYYH*, may your will extend from your name *YHVH*, with these names to protect [....name of recipient....] for the months of pregnancy, keeping the foetus in her stomach and to bring it forth alive, and to be brought into existence by the power of *Atneik*, the pattern of the magical seal signed in heaven and earth in the power of the great name *Kuzu B'moch'saz Kuzu.*

The entire magical construct is afterwards suspended around the neck of the pregnant woman.[37]

As an aside, it should be noted that *Psalms 42* to *83* are collectively termed "Elohistic Psalms," due to אלהים (*Elohim*) being the most prominent Divine Name in these Psalms.[38] Whilst the Ineffable Name do appear in these psalms, אלהים (*Elohim*) is the exclusive Divine Name of the sixty-seventh Psalm. In this regard, we are informed that the *gematria* of מום [מ = 40 + ו = 6 + ם = 40 = 86], the concluding tri-letter portion of the "*Name of Seventy-two Names*," is equal to that of the Divine Name אלהים [א = 1 + ל = 30 + ה = 5 + י = 10 + ם = 40 = 86]. This is said to be directly related to the biblical phrase אלהים יחננו ויברכנו (*Elohim y'choneinu vi'var'cheinu*—"God be gracious unto us, and bless us") [*Psalm 67:2*], as well as to אלהים לנו מחסה ועז (*Elohim lanu machaseh va'oz*—"God is our refuge and strength") [*Psalm 46:2*].[39]

Tremendous powers of healing and protection are attributed to *Psalm 67*. In this regard, we noted that the current psalm is employed against imprisonment, and is likewise recited for liberation from imprisonment, i.e. the release of prisoners. It has also been recommended for protection against, and to avert, attacks from evil spirits. It has been reported that enunciating this psalm seven times prior to undertaking a journey, will ensure "safety and prosperity."[40] The sixty-seventh Psalm is further recited in support of orphans, widows and widowers, against despair, as well as to diminish poverty. It is equally enunciated to halt the diminishing of morality, and is spoken by Jewish religionists as a "prayer to end the exile." Aside from these applications, the sixty-seventh Psalm is said when undertaking journeys, and if such journey should be by boat, it is utilised to avoid shipwreck. In conclusion, the current psalm has been recommended to farmers for the well-being of their flocks and hen-houses, and it is employed against storms in general.

We are informed that *Psalm 67* was employed in Christian Magic in "aggressive procedures" delineated "in anonymous recipes in manuscripts of the fourteenth century and later," e.g. in rituals "to bind the tongues of enemies."[41] On the other hand, the previously mentioned Byzantine Christian magical manuscripts suggest any magic of the harmful kind can be countered by writing the current psalm on four pieces of paper to be located in the four corners of the residence of the afflicted.[42] Elsewhere in the same literature, we find this psalm employed against enemies. In this regard, the sixty-seventh Psalm is recited over water, which is afterwards poured out at the door of the enemy. Further instructions suggests the psalm to be copied with a set of letters and signs to be carried on the person of the one who is acting against enemies.[43] The Byzantine manuscripts also recommend *Psalm 67* for recitation at the beginning of the year,[44] I presume for well-being throughout the coming year. Another very benign application of the current psalm is listed in "*Le Livre d'Or,*" in which we are informed that illness will be healed by enunciating this psalm over "pure water" which is afterwards imbibed by the sufferer. Additionally, the said text also includes a set of magical characters to be written and carried by the individual requiring healing.[45] Elsewhere *Psalm 67:7—8* is appropriately recited to thank the Divine One "for the abundance of the fruits of the earth."[46]

In conclusion, it should be noted that the "*Key of Solomon*" lists *Psalms 2, 47, 54, 67, 68* and *113* for recitation either before or during the construction of the "magic circle."[47] It is equally, amongst a set of seven psalms, i.e. *Psalms 15, 131, 137, 117, 67, 68,* and *127*, which is recited whilst donning the ritual garments.[48] It is further listed in conjunction with *Psalms 54, 102* and *6* for enunciation whilst adding salt during the consecration of water to be employed in ritual work,[49] and it is enunciated conjointly with *Psalm 83* over a feather of a swallow or a crow, which is to be fashioned into a writing pen.[50]

PSALM 68

[1] לַמְנַצֵּחַ לְדָוִד מִזְמוֹר שִׁיר
[2] יָקוּם אֱלֹהִים יָפוּצוּ אוֹיְבָיו וְיָנוּסוּ מְשַׂנְאָיו מִפָּנָיו
[3] כְּהִנְדֹּף עָשָׁן תִּנְדֹּף כְּהִמֵּס דּוֹנַג מִפְּנֵי אֵשׁ יֹאבְדוּ רְשָׁעִים מִפְּנֵי אֱלֹהִים
[4] וְצַדִּיקִים יִשְׂמְחוּ יַעַלְצוּ לִפְנֵי אֱלֹהִים וְיָשִׂישׂוּ בְשִׂמְחָה
[5] שִׁירוּ לֵאלֹהִים זַמְּרוּ שְׁמוֹ סֹלּוּ לָרֹכֵב בָּעֲרָבוֹת בְּיָהּ שְׁמוֹ וְעִלְזוּ לְפָנָיו
[6] אֲבִי יְתוֹמִים וְדַיַּן אַלְמָנוֹת אֱלֹהִים בִּמְעוֹן קָדְשׁוֹ
[7] אֱלֹהִים מוֹשִׁיב יְחִידִים בַּיְתָה מוֹצִיא אֲסִירִים בַּכּוֹשָׁרוֹת אַךְ סוֹרְרִים שָׁכְנוּ צְחִיחָה
[8] אֱלֹהִים בְּצֵאתְךָ לִפְנֵי עַמֶּךָ בְּצַעְדְּךָ בִישִׁימוֹן סֶלָה
[9] אֶרֶץ רָעָשָׁה אַף שָׁמַיִם נָטְפוּ מִפְּנֵי אֱלֹהִים זֶה סִינַי מִפְּנֵי אֱלֹהִים אֱלֹהֵי יִשְׂרָאֵל
[10] גֶּשֶׁם נְדָבוֹת תָּנִיף אֱלֹהִים נַחֲלָתְךָ וְנִלְאָה אַתָּה כוֹנַנְתָּהּ
[11] חַיָּתְךָ יָשְׁבוּ בָהּ תָּכִין בְּטוֹבָתְךָ לֶעָנִי אֱלֹהִים
[12] אֲדֹנָי יִתֶּן אֹמֶר הַמְבַשְּׂרוֹת צָבָא רָב
[13] מַלְכֵי צְבָאוֹת יִדֹּדוּן יִדֹּדוּן וּנְוַת בַּיִת תְּחַלֵּק שָׁלָל
[14] אִם תִּשְׁכְּבוּן בֵּין שְׁפַתָּיִם כַּנְפֵי יוֹנָה נֶחְפָּה בַכֶּסֶף וְאֶבְרוֹתֶיהָ בִּירַקְרַק חָרוּץ
[15] בְּפָרֵשׂ שַׁדַּי מְלָכִים בָּהּ תַּשְׁלֵג בְּצַלְמוֹן
[16] הַר אֱלֹהִים הַר בָּשָׁן הַר גַּבְנֻנִּים הַר בָּשָׁן
[17] לָמָּה תְּרַצְּדוּן הָרִים גַּבְנֻנִּים הָהָר חָמַד אֱלֹהִים לְשִׁבְתּוֹ אַף יְהוָֹהאהדונהי יִשְׁכֹּן לָנֶצַח
[18] רֶכֶב אֱלֹהִים רִבֹּתַיִם אַלְפֵי שִׁנְאָן אֲדֹנָי בָם סִינַי בַּקֹּדֶשׁ
[19] עָלִיתָ לַמָּרוֹם שָׁבִיתָ שֶּׁבִי לָקַחְתָּ מַתָּנוֹת בָּאָדָם וְאַף סוֹרְרִים לִשְׁכֹּן יָהּ אֱלֹהִים
[20] בָּרוּךְ אֲדֹנָי יוֹם יוֹם יַעֲמָס לָנוּ הָאֵל יְשׁוּעָתֵנוּ סֶלָה
[21] הָאֵל לָנוּ אֵל לְמוֹשָׁעוֹת וְלַיהוָֹהאהדונהי אֲדֹנָי לַמָּוֶת תּוֹצָאוֹת

[22] אך אלהים ימחץ ראש איביו קדקד שער מתהלך באשמיו
[23] אמר אדני מבשן אשיב אשיב ממצלות ים
[24] למען תמחץ רגלך בדם לשון כלביך מאיבים מנהו
[25] ראו הליכותיך אלהים הליכות אלי מלכי בקדש
[26] קדמו שרים אחר נגנים בתוך עלמות תופפות
[27] במקהלות ברכו אלהים אדני ממקור ישראל
[28] שם בנימן צעיר רדם שרי יהודה רגמתם שרי זבלון שרי נפתלי
[29] צוה אלהיך עזך עוזה אלהים זו פעלת לנו
[30] מהיכלך על ירושלם לך יובילו מלכים שי
[31] גער חית קנה עדת אבירים בעגלי עמים מתרפס ברצי כסף בזר עמים קרבות יחפצו
[32] יאתיו חשמנים מני מצרים כוש תריץ ידיו לאלהים
[33] ממלכות הארץ שירו לאלהים זמרו אדני סלה
[34] לרכב בשמי שמי קדם הן יתן בקולו קול עז
[35] תנו עז לאלהים על ישראל גאותו ועזו בשחקים
[36] נורא אלהים ממקדשיך אל ישראל הוא נתן עז ותעצמות לעם ברוך אלהים

Transliteration:
[1] lam'natzei'ach l'david miz'mor shir
[2] yakum elohim yafutzu oy'vav v'yanusu m'san'av mipanav
[3] k'hin'dof ashan tin'dof k'himeis donag mip'nei esh yov'du r'sha'im mip'nei elohim
[4] v'tzadikim yis'm'chu ya'al'tzu lif'nei elohim v'yasisu v'sim'chah
[5] shiru leilohim zam'ru sh'mo solu larocheiv ba'aravot b'yah sh'mo v'il'zu l'fanav
[6] avi y'tomim v'dayan al'manot elohim bim'on kod'sho
[7] elohim moshiv y'chidim baita motzi asirim bakosharot ach sor'rim shach'nu tz'chicha
[8] Elohim b'tzeit'cha lif'nei amecha b'tza'd'cha vishimon selah
[9] eretz ra'asha af shamayim nat'fu mip'nei elohim zeh sinai mip'nei elohim elohei yis'ra'eil

[10] *geshem n'davot tanif elohim nachalat'cha v'nil'ah atah chonan'tah*
[11] *chayat'cha yash'vu vah tachin b'tovat'cha le'ani elohim*
[12] *adonai yiten omer ham'vas'rot tzava rav*
[13] *mal'chei tz'va'ot yidodun yidodun un'vat bayit t'chaleik shalal*
[14] *im tish'k'vun bein sh'fatayim kan'fei yonah nech'pah vakesef v'ev'roteha birak'rak charutz*
[15] *b'fares shadai m'lachim ba tash'leg b'tzal'mon*
[16] *har elohim har bashan har gav'nunim har bashan*
[17] *lamah t'ratz'dun harim gav'nunim hahar chamad elohim l'shiv'to af YHVH yish'kon lanetzach*
[18] *rechev elohim ribotayim al'fei shin'an adonai vam sinai bakodesh*
[19] *alita lamarom shavita shevi lakach'ta matanot ba'adam v'af sor'rim lish'kon yah elohim*
[20] *baruch adonai yom yom ya'amos lanu ha'el y'shu'ateinu selah*
[21] *ha'el lanu el l'mosha'ot v'lei'YHVH Adonai lamavet totza'ot*
[22] *ach elohim yim'chatz rosh oy'vav kod'kod sei'ar mit'haleich ba'ashamav*
[23] *amar adonai mibashan ashiv ashiv mim'tzulot yam*
[24] *l'ma'an tim'chatz rag'l'cha b'dam l'shon k'lavecha mei'oy'vim minei'hu*
[25] *ra'u halichotecha elohim halichot eili mal'ki vakodesh*
[26] *kid'mu sharim achar nog'nim b'toch alamot tofeifot*
[27] *b'mak'heilot bar'chu elohim adonai mim'kor yis'ra'eil*
[28] *sham bin'yamin tza'ir rodeim sarei y'hudah rig'matam sarei z'vulun sarei naf'tali*
[29] *tzivah elohecha uzecha uzah elohim zu pa'al'ta lanu*
[30] *meiheichalecha al y'rushalam l'cha yovilu m'lachim shai*
[31] *g'ar chayat kaneh adat abirim b'eg'lei amim mit'rapeis b'ratzei chasef bizar amim k'ravot yech'patzu*
[32] *ye'etayu chash'manim mini mitz'rayim kush taritz yadav leilohim*

[33] *mam'l'chot ha'aretz shiru leilohim zam'ru adonai selah*
[34] *larocheiv bish'mei sh'mei kedem hein yitein b'kolo kol oz*
[35] *t'nu oz leilohim al yis'ra'eil ga'avato v'uzo bash'chakim*
[36] *nora elohim mimik'dashecha el yis'ra'eil hu noten oz v'ta'atzumot la'am baruch elohim*

Translation:

[1] For the Leader. A Psalm of David, a Song.

[2] Let *Elohim* arise, let His enemies be scattered; and let them that hate Him flee before Him.

[3] As smoke is driven away, so drive them away; as wax melteth before the fire, so let the wicked perish at the presence of *Elohim*.

[4] But let the righteous be glad, let them exult before *Elohim*; yea, let them rejoice with gladness.

[5] Sing unto *Elohim*, sing praises to His name; extol Him that rideth upon the skies, whose name is *Yah*; and exult ye before Him.

[6] A father of the fatherless, and a judge of the widows, is *Elohim* in His holy habitation.

[7] *Elohim* maketh the solitary to dwell in a house; He bringeth out the prisoners into prosperity; the rebellious dwell but in a parched land.

[8] O *Elohim*, when Thou wentest forth before Thy people, when Thou didst march through the wilderness; *Selah*

[9] The earth trembled, the heavens also dropped at the presence of *Elohim*; even yon Sinai trembled at the presence of *Elohim*, the God of Israel.

[10] A bounteous rain didst Thou pour down, *Elohim*; when Thine inheritance was weary, Thou didst confirm it.

[11] Thy flock settled therein; Thou didst prepare in Thy goodness for the poor, *Elohim*.

[12] *Adonai* giveth the word; the women that proclaim the tidings are a great host.

[13] Kings of armies flee, they flee; and she that tarrieth at home divideth the spoil.

[14] When ye lie among the sheepfolds, the wings of the dove are covered with silver, and her pinions with the shimmer of gold.

[15] When the Almighty scattereth kings therein, it snoweth in Zalmon.

[16] A mountain of *Elohim* is the mountain of Bashan; a mountain of peaks is the mountain of Bashan.

[17] Why look ye askance, ye mountains of peaks, at theah mountain which *Elohim* hath desired for His abode? Yea, *YHVH* will dwell therein for ever.

[18] The chariots of *Elohim* are myriads, even thousands upon thousands; *Adonai* is among them, as in Sinai, in holiness.

[19] Thou hast ascended on high, Thou hast led captivity captive; Thou hast received gifts among men, yea, among the rebellious also, that *Yah Elohim* might dwell there.

[20] Blessed be *Adonai*, day by day He beareth our burden, even the God who is our salvation. *Selah*

[21] God is unto us a God of deliverances; and unto *YHVH Adonai* belong the issues of death.

[22] Surely *Elohim* will smite through the head of His enemies, the hairy scalp of him that goeth about in his guiltiness.

[23] *Adonai* said: 'I will bring back from Bashan, I will bring them back from the depths of the sea;

[24] That thy foot may wade through blood, that the tongue of thy dogs may have its portion from thine enemies.'

[25] They see Thy goings *Elohim*, even the goings of my God, my King, in holiness.

[26] The singers go before, the minstrels follow after, in the midst of damsels playing upon timbrels.

[27] 'Bless ye *Elohim* in full assemblies, even *Adonai*, ye that are from the fountain of Israel.'

[28] There is Benjamin, the youngest, ruling them, the princes of Judah their council, the princes of Zebulun, the princes of Naphtali.

[29] Thy God hath commanded thy strength; be strong *Elohim*, Thou that hast wrought for us

[30] Out of Thy temple at Jerusalem, whither kings shall bring presents unto Thee.

[31] Rebuke the wild beast of the reeds, the multitude of the bulls, with the calves of the peoples, every one submitting himself with pieces of silver; He hath scattered the peoples that delight in war!
[32] Nobles shall come out of Egypt; Ethiopia shall hasten to stretch out her hands *Elohim*.
[33] Sing unto *Elohim*, ye kingdoms of the earth; O sing praises unto *Adonai*; *Selah*
[34] To Him that rideth upon the heavens of heavens, which are of old; lo, He uttereth His voice, a mighty voice.
[35] Ascribe ye strength unto *Elohim*; His majesty is over Israel, and His strength is in the skies;
[36] awful is *Elohim* out of thy holy places; the God of Israel, He giveth strength and power unto the people; blessed be *Elohim*.

Psalm 68 is listed amongst the psalms which are recited to express gratitude.[1] It is enunciated in the Sefardic liturgy prior to *Arvit* (Evening Prayer Service) on *Shavu'ot*, i.e. the "Festival of Weeks," at the conclusion of the seven weeks of "Counting of the *Omer*." We are informed that "the selection of this particular psalm is due to its description of the events that occurred on the day the Torah was given."[2] In Ashkenazi liturgy *Psalm 68:35* features in two poems enunciated during *Shacharit* (Morning Prayer Service) on *Yom Kippur* ("Day of Atonement"). In this regard, this verse inspired the hymn על ישראל אמונתו (*Al Yis'ra'eil Emunato*—"On Israel is His Faith") which is recited both during the morning service on *Yom Kippur*, as well as during the circumambulations (הקפות—*Hakafot*) of שמחת תורה (*Sim'chat Torah*—"Rejoicing with the Torah").[3] The poem אפסי ארץ (*Af'say Eretz*—"The Ends of the Earth") delineating the strength of the Divine One, as well as "the strength and might He shows the people of Israel,"[4] is equally recited in the Ashkenazic rite at *Shacharit* on *Yom Kippur*, and commences with *Psalm 68:35*.[5]

The sixty-eighth Psalm is recommended in Jewish Magic as a protection against evil spirits.[6] This psalm does not feature in every published version of the *Shimmush Tehillim*, but in those in which it is referenced, we are informed that an evil spirit can be countered by taking a "measure," i.e. a vessel, filled with water which has not been exposed to the sun, and whispering the current psalm over it. This is enacted whilst focussing on the associated Divine Name יה (*Yah*): י (*Yod*) from יקום (*yakum*— "arise"): verse 2; and ה (*Heh*) from the letter נ (*Nun*) in נורא (*nora*—awful [awesome]): verse 36, the glyph having been transposed by means of the א‏י"ק בכ"ר (*Ayak Bachar*) cipher.[7] Since the said Divine Name is associated with both the current and the previous psalm, Godfrey Selig elected to reference these two psalms conjointly in his version of the *Shimmush Tehillim*,[8] doing so without any reference to any magical use of *Psalm 67*. This is particularly odd considering the enormous importance of the previous psalm both in Jewish liturgies and in "Practical Kabbalah," and equally in the magical applications listed in the various recensions of the *Shimmush Tehillim*. Regarding reciting *Psalm 68* against an evil spirit, Selig noted with his standard verbosity, that the psalm should be recited over the water "in a low voice, and in the name of the patient," and afterwards to "work his body with water" following which "the evil spirit will depart from him."[9]

In a different recension of the *Shimmush Tehillim* we find the current psalm recommended to individuals who are "trapped in chains in prison." In this regard, they are instructed to recite the psalm three times a day "in purity," whilst concentrating on the Divine Name combination יאיא הדיה ונאי הייה which we addressed earlier in terms of יאי, the Divine Name construct derived from the capitals of *Psalm 67:5–8*, the letters of which having been intertwined with the twelve glyphs comprising יהוה (*YHVH*), אדני (*Adonai*), and אהיה (*Eh'yeh*). The current psalm is recited for the said purpose, in conjunction with the following prayer-incantation:

אנא יהוה אלהי מכל שונאי ואויבי הצילני ותוציאני
מן המאסר הזה כמו שהוצאת את עמך ישראל ממצרים
ועשית עמהם נסים וגבורות כן עשה עמי והושיעני
והצילני מכל אויבי ומכל רודפי והיה בעזרתי ככתוב
יהוה כגבור יצא כאיש מלחמות יעיר קנאה יריע אף
יצריח על אויביו יתגבר (*Isaiah 42:13*) יהוה מתיר
אסורים (*Psalm 146:7*) אמן אמן סלה סלה סלה

Transliteration:
> *Ana YHVH Elohai mikol son'ai v'oy'vai hatzileini v'totzi'eini min hama'asar hazeh k'mo shehotzeita et am'cha yis'ra'eil mimitz'rayim v'asita imahem nisim ug'vurot kein aseih imi v'hoshi'eini v'hatzileini mikol oy'vai umikol rod'fai v'heiyei b'ez'rati kakatuv YHVH k'gibor yeitzei k'ish mil'chamot ya'ir kin'ah yari'a af yatz'ri'ach al oy'vav yit'gabar (Isaiah 42:13) YHVH matir asurim (Psalm 146:7) Omein Omein Selah Selah*

Translation:
> Please, Lord my God, save me from all my haters and enemies. You shall lead me out of this captivity, just as you led your people Israel out of Egypt and performed miracles and heroic deeds upon them. So deal (also) with me, deliver me and save me from all my enemies and from all my persecutors. And be to my aid, as it is written *YHVH will go forth as a mighty man, He will stir up jealousy like a man of war; He will cry, yea, He will shout aloud, He will prove Himself mighty against His enemies. (Isaiah 42:13) YHVH looseth the prisoners. (Psalm 146:7)* Omein Omein Selah Selah.[10]

As far as the application of individual verses are concerned, it should be noted that the initials of the first four words of *Psalm 68:2* is conjoined in the Divine Name construct יאא which is employed in conditions of great violence and war.[11] I once recommended this Divine Name to an individual who was caught in a most unfortunate and violent battle. Following suggestions which Moses Zacutto shared in his book *Shorshei ha-Shemot* ("The Roots of Names"),[12] I told the said individual that if he wishes to fight and win a battle, that he should carry the Divine Name construct as an amulet. Furthermore, he was to visualise the component four letters of the Divine Name construct whenever he found himself in grave danger, whilst at the same time reciting the listed opening phrase of the verse conjointly with a simple statement, reading:

יקום אלהים יפוצו אויביו (*Psalm 68:2*) וכחו משען לי ואתה נוצח

Transliteration:
> *yakum elohim yafutzu oy'vav* (*Psalm 68:2*) *v'chocho mish'an li v'atah nutzach.*

Translation:
> Let *Elohim* arise, let His enemies be scattered (*Psalm 68:2*), His power rests on me, and you are defeated.

It is worth mentioning that the capitals of all seven words comprising *Psalm 68:2*, are combined in the Divine Name יאיאומם. We are told this Divine Name construct pertains to גבורה (*Gevurah*—"might"), which is employed against subterfuge, sabotage and corruption.[13] This Divine Name construct is used in conjunction with אבגיתץ (*Avgitatz*), the first six letters of the "Forty-two Letter Name of God," which we are told pertains to the "face" of שור (*Shor*—"a bull").[14] The latter term is likely to be a direct reference to the "bull" countenance of the "Living Creatures," each of which the Prophet Ezekiel recounted to have "had four faces." (*Ezekiel 1:6*), and by extension to the astrological sign *Taurus*. Be that as it may, it is maintained that in adjurations this Divine Name construct should be employed conjointly with the names of the "Spirit Intelligences" (Angels) דליאל (*Deli'el*); דיאל (*Di'el*); ארפיאל (*Ar'pi'el*) or אחפיאל (*Achifi'el*); סמאל (*Sama'el*); עניאל (*Ani'el*); חזקיאל (*Chez'ki'el* [*Chazaki'el*]); אדוניאל (*Adoni'el*); זעיריואל (*Z'eiriyu'el*); and גבריאל (*Gavri'el*).[15] We are further informed that the following Divine Names are directly aligned with these angelic names, and should be likewise employed in conjunction with אבגיתץ (*Avgitatz*), which is termed the "root" Divine Name construct:

אהיה אשר אהיה
יזל מבה הרי הקם לאו לוו פהל נלך ייי מלה חהו

As indicated, this Divine Name combination comprises *Eh'yeh Asher Eh'yeh*, as well as the thirteenth to the twenty-fourth tri-letter combinations of the "Name of Seventy-two Names," i.e. *Yezel Mebah Hari Hakem Lav Lov Pahal Nelach Yeyay Melah*

The Psalms of David — Book II : 215

Chaho, excluding כלי (*Keli*), the sixteenth tri-letter combination.[16] No reason is given why this tri-letter combination is not included in the listed set.

In addition to the applications listed above, *Psalm 68* is also popularly recommended, as in the case of *Psalm 67*, for recitation against fever and despair. However, whereas the previous psalm is employed for diseases of the head, the current one is utilised to relieve pains in the throat, including the preservation of the voice. Both psalms are likewise enunciated to avoid shipwreck, and for protection against theft, thieves, and robbers. The sixty-eighth Psalm is further used against enemies, assassins, betrayal (treachery), unjust denunciations, for safety from persecution, and against all manner of injuries and damage. Conversely the current psalm is recited for financial prosperity, and equally by those who have an anxious concern about their livelihood, as well as to express gratitude for good fortune. However, if the personality of the practitioner includes qualities and behaviour patterns which would inevitably preclude the achievement of "good fortune," it is worth keeping in mind that *Psalm 68* is utilised against laziness and procrastination, and to support repentant alcoholics. The current psalm is also enunciated for the purpose of finding a soul mate, and is recommended to women who are recovering from a miscarriage. Lastly, this psalm is employed in dealing with spiritual troubles, and is utilised by religionists as a prayer for the arrival of the Messiah.

As far as Christian Magic is concerned, the current psalm is listed in the ninth-century "*Leechbook of Bald*" to be good in dealing with demon possession.[17] In this regard, we are informed that a drink should be prepared "for a fiend sick man, to be drunk out of a *church bell*; githrife, cynoglossum, yarrow, lupin, betony, attorlothe, cassock, flower de luce, fennel, church lichen, lichen of Christ's mark *or cross* lovage; work up the drink off clear ale, sing seven masses over the worts, add garlic and holy water, add the drink into every drink which he will subsequently drink, and let him sing the psalm, *Beati immaculati* (*Psalm 119*), and *Exurgat* (*Psalm 68*), and *Salvum me fac, deus* (*Psalm 69*), and then let him drink the drink out of a church bell, and let the mass priest after the drink sing this over him, *Domine, sancte pater omnipotens.*"[18] The latter prayer can be found in Roman Catholic missals. Whilst perusing the concoction of herbal substances the demoniac is expected to imbibe here, it occurs to me that the tormented individual would likely be more interested in getting to the nearest latrine rather than listening to the concluding prayer of the "mass priest," especially after having consumed what appears to be a most potent purgative.

Psalm 68 is recommended in the Christian Byzantine magical manuscripts for a variety of purposes. In this regard, it is suggested for recitation during childbirth.[19] The same source maintains the psalm should be recited by an individual who wants "to do business elsewhere," and is afraid of robbers. In this regard, the instruction is to enunciate the current psalm twenty times, and to a copy a set of magical signs which is afterwards suspended "on the chimney of a bath or oven," until the return of the said individual.[20] We are further informed that "*Psalm 68* is for an expedition," regarding which it is noted that an individual who "wish to go to another land," should "encircle" a set of magical signs "with the Psalm."[21] Elsewhere we are told that this psalm is "for mollifying one's enemy,"[22] and "*Le Livre d'Or*" maintains that those who wish to give an individual sleepless nights, should copy the sixty-eighth Psalm "and bury it in front of his door."[23] The same source maintains that if you "wish someone to stay," that you should "get close to him, look at him," and enunciate the opening phrase of *Psalm 68:2*. On the other hand, it instructs you to recite the concluding phrase of the said verse, if you wish the said individual to depart.[24] In terms of this verse, a similar application is referenced elsewhere in which it is maintained that the first phrase of the said verse should be recited in order "to prevent serpents from moving," and the second phrase "when you wish to make it go away."[25] The same source recommends *Psalm 68:23* "against dangers of the waters and of the Sea; and to be saved quickly from them."[26]

Psalm 68 is one of a set of seven psalms, i.e. *Psalms 15, 131, 137, 117, 67, 68,* and *127*, which is listed in the "*Key of Solomon*" for recitation whilst dressing in the ritual garments,[27] and is also the sixth of nineteen psalms, i.e. *Psalms 8, 15, 22, 46, 47, 49, 51, 53, 68, 72, 84, 102, 110, 113, 126, 130, 131, 133,* and *139*, which are recited over the wax from which ritual candles are constructed.[28] *Psalm 68:2*, a very popular verse in both Jewish and

Christian magic, is included in the "*Key of Solomon*" in the outer border of the "*Fifth Pentacle of Moon*," which is employed to find answers during sleep. It is further said that the angel *Yachadi'el*, who is one of the angels said to be associated with this pentacle, "serveth unto destruction and loss, as well as unto the destruction of enemies."[29]

PSALM 69

[1] למנצח על שושנים לדוד
[2] הושיעני אלהים כי באו מים עד נפש
[3] טבעתי ביון מצולה ואין מעמד באתי במעמקי מים ושבלת שטפתני
[4] יגעתי בקראי נחר גרוני כלו עיני מיחל לאלהי
[5] רבו משערות ראשי שנאי חנם עצמו מצמיתי איבי שקר אשר לא גזלתי אז אשיב
[6] אלהים אתה ידעת לאולתי ואשמותי ממך לא נכחדו
[7] אל יבשו בי קויך אדני יְהוָֹהֱ‏‏אֲ‏‏דֹנָ‏‏יֱ‏‏אֱ‏‏לֹהִ‏‏ים צבאות אל יכלמו בי מבקשיך אלהי ישראל
[8] כי עליך נשאתי חרפה כסתה כלמה פני
[9] מוזר הייתי לאחי ונכרי לבני אמי
[10] כי קנאת ביתך אכלתני וחרפות חורפיך נפלו עלי
[11] ואבכה בצום נפשי ותהי לחרפות לי
[12] ואתנה לבושי שק ואהי להם למשל
[13] ישיחו בי ישבי שער ונגינות שותי שכר
[14] ואני תפלתי לך יְהוָֹהֱ‏‏אֲ‏‏דֹנָ‏‏יֱ‏‏אֱ‏‏לֹהִ‏‏ים עת רצון אלהים ברב חסדך ענני באמת ישעך
[15] הצילני מטיט ואל אטבעה אנצלה משנאי וממעמקי מים
[16] אל תשטפני שבלת מים ואל תבלעני מצולה ואל תאטר עלי באר פיה
[17] עננני יְהוָֹהֱ‏‏אֲ‏‏דֹנָ‏‏יֱ‏‏אֱ‏‏לֹהִ‏‏ים כי טוב חסדך כרב רחמיך פנה אלי
[18] ואל תסתר פניך מעבדך כי צר לי מהר עננני
[19] קרבה אל נפשי גאלה למען איבי פדני
[20] אתה ידעת חרפתי ובשתי וכלמתי נגדך כל צוררי
[21] חרפה שברה לבי ואנושה ואקוה לנוד ואין ולמנחמים ולא מצאתי
[22] ויתנו בברותי ראש ולצמאי ישקוני חמץ

[23] יהי שלחנם לפניהם לפח ולשלומים למוקש
[24] תחשכנה עיניהם מראות ומתניהם תמיד המעד
[25] שפך עליהם זעמך וחרון אפך ישיגם
[26] תחי טירתם נשמה באהליהם אל יהי ישב
[27] כי אתה אשר הכית רדפו ואל מכאוב חלליך יספרו
[28] תנה עון על עונם ואל יבאו בצדקתך
[29] ימחו מספר חיים ועם צדיקים אל יכתבו
[30] ואני עני וכואב ישועתך אלהים תשגבני
[31] אהללה שם אלהים בשיר ואגדלנו בתודה
[32] ותיטב ליהוה‎אֲדֹנָי‎אהדונהי משור פר מקרן מפריס
[33] ראו ענוים ישמחו דרשי אלהים ויחי לבבכם
[34] כי שמע אל אביונים יהוה‎אֲדֹנָי‎אהדונהי ואת אסיריו לא בזה
[35] יהללוהו שמים וארץ ימים וכל רמש בם
[36] כי אלהים יושיע ציון ויבנה ערי יהודה וישבו שם וירשוה
[37] וזרע עבדיו ינחלוה ואהבי שמו ישכנו בה

Transliteration:

[1] *lam'natzei'ach al shoshanim l'david*
[2] *hoshi'eini elohim ki va'u mayim ad nafesh*
[3] *tava'ti bivein m'tzulah v'ein ma'omad bati v'ma'amakei mayim v'shibolet sh'tafat'ni*
[4] *yaga'ti v'kar'i nichar g'roni kalu einai m'yacheil leilohai*
[5] *rabu misa'arot roshi son'ai chinam atz'mu matz'mitai oy'vai sheker asher lo gazal'ti az ashiv*
[6] *elohim atah yada'ta l'ival'ti v'ash'motai mim'cha lo nich'chadu*
[7] *al yeivoshu vi kovecha adonai YHVH tz'va'ot al yikal'mu vi m'vak'shecha elohei yis'ra'eil*
[8] *ki alecha nasati cher'pah kis'tah ch'limah fanai*
[9] *muzar hayiti l'echai v'noch'ri liv'nei imi*
[10] *ki kin'at beit'cha achalat'ni v'cher'pot chor'fecha naf'lu alai*
[11] *va'ev'keh vatzom naf'shi vat'hi lacharafot li*

[12] va'et'nah l'vushi sak va'ehi lahem l'mashal
[13] yasichu vi yosh'vei sha'ar un'ginot shotei sheichar
[14] va'ani t'filati l'cha YHVH eit ratzon elohim b'rov chas'decha aneini be'emet yish'echa
[15] hatzileini mitit v'al et'ba'ah inatz'lah mison'ai umima'amakei mayim
[16] al tish't'feini shibolet mayim v'al tiv'la'eini m'tzulah v'al te'tar alai b'eir piha
[17] aneini YHVH ki tov chas'decha k'rov rachamecha p'neih eilai
[18] v'al tas'teir panecha mei'av'decha ki tzar li maheir aneini
[19] kar'vah el naf'shi g'alah l'ma'an oy'vai p'deini
[20] atah yada'ta cher'pati uvosh'ti uch'limati neg'd'cha kol tzor'rai
[21] cher'pah shav'rah libi va'anushah va'akaveh lanud va'ayin v'lam'nachamim v'lo matzati
[22] vayit'nu b'varuti rosh v'litz'ma'i yash'kuni chometz
[23] y'hi shul'chanam lif'neihem l'fach v'lish'lomim l'mokeish
[24] tech'shach'nah eineihem meir'ot umat'neihem tamid ham'ad
[25] sh'foch aleihem za'mecha vacharon ap'cha yasigeim
[26] t'hi tiratam n'shamah b'aholeihem al y'hi yosheiv
[27] ki atah asher hikita radafu v'el mach'ov chalalecha y'sapeiru
[28] t'nah avon al avonam v'al yavo'u b'tzid'katecha
[29] yimachu miseifer chayim v'im tzadikim al yikateivu
[30] va'ani ani v'cho'eiv y'shu'at'cha elohim t'sag'veini
[31] ahal'lah shem elohim b'shir va'agad'lenu v'todah
[32] v'titav la'YHVH mishor par mak'rin maf'ris
[33] ra'u anavim yis'machu dor'shei elohim vichi l'vav'chem
[34] ki shomei'a el ev'yonim YHVH v'et asirav lo vazah
[35] y'hal'luhu shamayim va'aretz yamim v'chol romeis bam
[36] ki elohim yoshi'a tziyon v'yiv'neh arei y'hudah v'yash'vu sham vireishuha
[37] v'zera avadav yin'chaluha v'ohavei sh'mo yish'k'nu vah

Translation:
[1] For the Leader; upon *Shoshannim*. A Psalm of David.
[2] Save me *Elohim*; for the waters are come in even unto the soul.
[3] I am sunk in deep mire, where there is no standing; I am come into deep waters, and the flood overwhelmeth me.
[4] I am weary of my crying; my throat is dried; mine eyes fail while I wait for my God.
[5] They that hate me without a cause are more than the hairs of my head; they that would cut me off, being mine enemies wrongfully, are many; should I restore that which I took not away?
[6] *Elohim*, Thou knowest my folly; and my trespasses are not hid from Thee.
[7] Let not them that wait for Thee be ashamed through me, *Adonai YHVH* of hosts; let not those that seek Thee be brought to confusion through me, O God of Israel.
[8] Because for Thy sake I have borne reproach; confusion hath covered my face.
[9] I am become a stranger unto my brethren, and an alien unto my mother's children.
[10] Because zeal for Thy house hath eaten me up, and the reproaches of them that reproach Thee are fallen upon me.
[11] And I wept with my soul fasting, and that became unto me a reproach.
[12] I made sackcloth also my garment, and I became a byword unto them.
[13] They that sit in the gate talk of me; and I am the song of the drunkards.
[14] But as for me, let my prayer be unto Thee *YHVH*, in an acceptable time; *Elohim*, in the abundance of Thy mercy, answer me with the truth of Thy salvation.
[15] Deliver me out of the mire, and let me not sink; let me be delivered from them that hate me, and out of the deep waters.
[16] Let not the waterflood overwhelm me, neither let the deep swallow me up; and let not the pit shut her mouth upon me.
[17] Answer me *YHVH*, for Thy mercy is good; according to the multitude of Thy compassions turn Thou unto me.

[18] And hide not Thy face from Thy servant; for I am in distress; answer me speedily.
[19] Draw nigh unto my soul, and redeem it; ransom me because of mine enemies.
[20] Thou knowest my reproach, and my shame, and my confusion; mine adversaries are all before Thee.
[21] Reproach hath broken my heart; and I am sore sick; and I looked for some to show compassion, but there was none; and for comforters, but I found none.
[22] Yea, they put poison into my food; and in my thirst they gave me vinegar to drink.
[23] Let their table before them become a snare; and when they are in peace, let it become a trap.
[24] Let their eyes be darkened, that they see not; and make their loins continually to totter.
[25] Pour out Thine indignation upon them, and let the fierceness of Thine anger overtake them.
[26] Let their encampment be desolate; let none dwell in their tents.
[27] For they persecute him whom Thou hast smitten; and they tell of the pain of those whom Thou hast wounded.
[28] Add iniquity unto their iniquity; and let them not come into Thy righteousness.
[29] Let them be blotted out of the book of the living, and not be written with the righteous.
[30] But I am afflicted and in pain; let Thy salvation *Elohim*, set me up on high.
[31] I will praise the name of *Elohim* with a song, and will magnify Him with thanksgiving.
[32] And it shall please *YHVH* better than a bullock that hath horns and hoofs.
[33] The humble shall see it, and be glad; ye that seek after *Elohim*, let your heart revive.
[34] For *YHVH* hearkeneth unto the needy, and despiseth not His prisoners.
[35] Let heaven and earth praise Him, the seas, and every thing that moveth therein.

[36] For *Elohim* will save Zion, and build the cities of Judah; and they shall abide there, and have it in possession. [37] The seed also of His servants shall inherit it; and they that love His name shall dwell therein.

A single verse from *Psalm 69* features particularly prominently in Jewish liturgies. In this regard, the prayer titled ואני תפלתי (*Va'ani T'filati* —"But as for me, let my prayer") is comprised of *Psalm 69:14* reading:

ואני תפלתי לך יהוה עת רצון אלהים ברב חסדך עננני באמת ישעך

Translation:
> va'ani t'filati l'cha YHVH et ratzon elohim b'rov chas'decha aneini be'emet yish'echa

Transliteration:
> But as for me, let my prayer be unto Thee *YHVH*, in an acceptable time; *Elohim*, in the abundance of Thy mercy, answer me with the truth of Thy salvation.

This verse is enunciated during *Min'chah* (Afternoon Prayer Service) prior to removing *Torah* scrolls from the ark; during *Shacharit* (Morning Prayer Service) on festivals; and also as part of מה טבו (*Mah Tovu*—"How goodly"), a prayer comprised of five biblical verses, i.e. *Numbers 24:5*, *Psalms 5:8*, *26:8*, *95: 6*, and *69:14*, which is recited when entering the synagogue before the morning service.[1] The *Va'ani Tefilati* prayer is further recited during Sabbath *Min'chah* (Afternoon Prayer Service), this being said to be due to the preceding verse, i.e *Psalm 69:13*, reading "They that sit in the gate talk of me; and I am the song of the drunkards"). We are told that King David is here saying to the Divine One, "Master of the world, even though we drink....my prayer is unto Thee."[2] In this regard, a reason offered for uttering *Va'ani Tefilati* "is that it was customary to recite the Sabbath *Min'chah* service after eating and drinking,"[3] i.e. early afternoon. Thus it is said "that every Sabbath *Va'ani T'filati* is said in praise of the people of Israel, who, though they eat and drink, read the

Torah and pray."[4] As far as the number of times the verse is spoken at each of the said occasions, customs do not only vary between Ashkenazim and Sefardim, but even within the various Sefardi communities.[5]

Considering the references to eating, drinking and drunkenness, and keeping in mind that it is recommended for protection against harm,[6] it should come as no surprise that *Psalm 69* is recommended in Jewish Magic to individuals who are debauched, greedy, covetous, lecherous, adulterous,[7] or against what has been termed "evil longing,"[8] or more commonly the "evil inclination." In this regard, the standard Hebrew recension of the *Shimmush Tehillim* succinctly suggests that an individual who is a lecher, fornicator, or a sinner, should recite the current psalm over water and consume the liquid.[9] With his standard verbosity Godfrey Selig greatly embellished this simple instruction in his ever-popular version of the *Shimmush Tehillim*, stating the sixty-ninth Psalm "should be uttered daily over water, by the libertine and sensualist, who is so confirmed in his evil habits, as to become a slave to them, and who, however much he may desire to escape these habits, is unable to do so. After having prayed this Psalm over the water he should drink of it."[10] Elsewhere, in a different recension of the *Shimmush Tehillim*, we are told that whoever wishes to find mercy for sins committed, should attend morning prayers in the synagogue for a period of thirty days. He/she should recite *Psalm 69* twice each day, and after every recitation enunciate the following prayer-incantation:

יהי רצון מלפניך יהוה אלהי ואלהי אבותי שתשוב
מחרונך ותרחם עלי ותסלח לעונותי אשר עשיתי
[....insert transgressions....] ותקבל עינוי נפשי ברצון
ויהיה לפניך כזבחים ועולות וכשלמים ותמחול
ותכפר לעוני בעבור שמך הנקי והטהור אה וה
מץ חי כפר נא וסלח לעונותי ולפשעי וזדוני
ולא יזכרו עוד כי עמך מקור חיים באורך נראה
אור (*Psalm 36:10*) כי עמך הסליחה למען תורא
(*Psalm 130:4*)

Transliteration:
> Y'hi ratzon mil'fanecha YHVH elohai veilohei avotai shetashuv mecharon'cha ut'racheim alai v'tis'lach l'avonotai asher asiti [....insert transgressions....] v't'kabel inui naf'shi b'ratzon v'yih'yeh l'fanecha k'z'vachim v'olot uk'sh'lamim v'tim'chol ut'chaper la'avoni ba'avur shim'cha hanaki v'hatahor Aha Vaha Matz Chai kaper na us'lach l'avonotai ul'p'sha'ai uz'donai v'lo yizach'ru od ki im'cha m'kor chayim b'or'cha nir'eh or (Psalm 36:10) ki im'cha has'lichah l'ma'an tivarei (Psalm 130:4)

Translation:
> May it be your will *YHVH* my God, and God of my fathers, that you turn from your wrath. You shall have mercy on me, and forgive my trespasses which I have committed [....insert transgressions....]. You shall accept the torment of my soul with favour. May it be before you like a sacrifice, a burnt offering, and a peace offering. You shall pardon my transgression, and atone for the sake of your refined and pure name *Aha Vaha Matz Chai*. Expiate, I pray, and forgive my misdemeanours, iniquities, and wickedness. Let them be remembered no more, for with you is the fountain of life, in your light we see the light. (*Psalm 36:10*) For with you is forgiveness, that you may be feared. (*Psalm 130:4*)[11]

The Divine Name construct might perhaps read *Ah Vah Matz Chai*, but in this, as in every instance where the enunciation of a Divine Name is uncertain, the practitioner would simply follow the custom of spelling the construct. In the current instance we are told that the מץ portion of the Divine Name combination was derived from י״ה (*Yah*), the glyphs having been transposed by means of the א״ת ב״ש (*Atbash*) cipher.[12] Whatever the case may be, the same Divine Name construct with the addition of יה (*Yah*), features in a different application of the current psalm shared in the same resource. In this instance it is for a woman who is having difficulties conceiving, and the instruction comprises copying the psalm conjointly with the following prayer-incantation, which is to be carried on the person of the said individual:

אנא השם שתפתח רחמה ולא תעצר עוד מלדת
ותפקדה כמו שפקדת לשרה ולרבקה ורחל וחנה
אשר פקדת ונתעברו וילדו בנים לאחר כמה שנים
כך תפקוד זאת האשה [....name of recipient....] ותזכור
אותה ותמנה עמך בשם אה וה מץ חי יה בעגלא
ובזמן קריב

Transliteration:
> *Ana hashem shetif'tach rach'mah v'lo te'atzer od miledet v'tif'k'dah k'mo shepakad'ta l'sarah v'l'riv'kah v'rachel v'chanah asher pakad'ta v'nit'ab'ru v'yal'du banim l'achar kamah shanim kach tif'kod zot ha'ishah [....name of recipient....] v'tiz'kor otah utim'neh ameich b'shem Aha Vaha Matz Chai Yah ba'agala uviz'man kariv*

Translation:
> Please *Hashem*, may you open her womb, and no longer restrain her from giving birth, and take care of her, as you took care of Sarah, Rebekah, Rachel and Hannah, whom you have taken care of, and they conceived, and gave birth to sons after a few years. So should you take care of the woman [....name of recipient....], remember her, and increase (count) your people. In the name *Aha Vaha Matz Chai Yah*, speedily and very soon.[13]

The women referenced in the incantation are of course the well-known biblical personalities who received Divine support in order to conceive. Be that as it may, the same recension of the *Shimmush Tehillim* equally lists the current psalm as useful for different purposes, amongst which is the recitation of the current psalm three times every day in order to be saved from every affliction, i.e. every tribulation or distress.[14] A special reference is also made to the sixty-ninth Psalm being employed to be saved from a flood or deluge, a river, and from a body of water. In this instance, each recitation of the current psalm is followed by the following prayer-incantation:

אלהי הרוחות לכל בשר אתה אליך באתי בבכי
ובתחנונים שתצילני מהיות נשחת במים ומהיות

טובע בהם ולא בשום מים בעולם הן ים הן נהר
או מקוה מים או בור מכולם הצילני ואל נא אכשל
בעונותי ואל נא תגמלני כמעשי הרעים ורחם עלי
ותקדים רחמים לרוגזיך בעבור שמך הגדול והקדוש
חי חי יהוה צבאות כן דברי אשר יצא פמי

Transliteration:
> *Elohei haruchot l'chol basar atah eilecha bati babechi ub'tachanonim sh'tatzileini mihiyot nish'chat b'mayim umihiyot tovei'a bahem v'lo b'shum mayim ba'olam hein yam hein nahar o mik'vah mayim o bor mikulam hatzileini v'al na ekashel b'avonotai v'al na tig'm'leini k'ma'asai hara'im v'racheim alai v'tak'dim rachamim l'rog'zecha ba'avur shim'cha hagadol v'hakadosh Chai Chai YHVH Tz'va'ot kein d'vari asher yeitzei mipi*

Translation:
> God of spirits, you are there for all flesh. I came to you with weeping and supplication, that you might save me from being decayed in water, and from sinking into it, and in no water in the world, be it a sea, river, pool of water, or a well, save me from all. Let me not stumble because of my transgressions. You shall not reward me in accordance with my wicked deeds. Have mercy on me. You shall forestall your wrath with compassion for the sake of your great and holy Name *Chai Chai YHVH Tz'va'ot* [Life Life *YHVH* of Hosts]. This is my word that comes out of my mouth.[15]

The same recension references *Psalm 69* being employed for a pregnant woman who suffers miscarriages, or whose children die. In this regard, the current psalm is copied with the following prayer, which is afterwards suspended around the neck of the woman in question:

אל נא רפא נא לה לאשה הזאת [....name of recipient....]
שמע קול תחנוניה שלא תפיל פרי בטנה בעבור שמך
הגדול והקדוש תשמור ילדיה והחיים וזכרה לטובה

Transliteration:
> *El na r'fa na lah l'ishah hazot* [....name of recipient....] *sh'ma kol tachanonei'ah shelo tapil p'ri bit'nah ba'avur shim'cha hagadol v'hakadosh tish'mor yelade'ah v'hach'yeim v'z'ch'rah l'tovah*

Translation:
> God please heal her, this woman [....name of recipient....]. Hear the voice of her supplication, so that she does not lose the fruit of her body. For the sake of your great and holy Name, you shall preserve her children, life, and her memory for the good.[16]

As far as the magical application of individual verses from the current psalm is concerned, it should be noted that the following Divine Name construct formulated from the capitals of the thirteen words comprising *Psalm 69:7*, is employed for healing purposes:

אֲיֵבְקֹא יֵצְאַי בִמְאֵי

Reading *Ayeiviko'a Yetz'ayi Vim'eyi*, the glyphs and vowel points comprising this Divine Name construct are written down, in order to be carried on the person of the sufferer. It is said that, with the help of the Divine One, this will succeed in facilitating healing.[17]

As applicable to every psalm addressed thus far, the current one is equally employed for purposes not listed in "official" sources, such applications having been passed along by word of mouth from one generation to the next. In this regard, the psalm is recited against illness and for healing in general. As readers will have deduced from what was said earlier, it is employed against excesses, slavery to sinful passions, and also against jealousy and resentment. Again, in terms of earlier statements, the sixty-ninth Psalm is applied against destruction by water, i.e. to be saved from drowning. In fact, this psalm is recommended to individuals who find themselves in all manner of perilous circumstances, and who need protection in times of trouble and distress. On the other hand, the current psalm is enunciated against, and to diminish poverty, as well as to have success in business.

In Christian Magic *Psalm 69* is recommended in the Byzantine manuscripts to a small child who cries incessantly. In this regard, the psalm is written and worn as an amulet by the infant.[18] The said manuscripts also recommend the sixty-ninth Psalm "for a multitude of thoughts," though it is not clear whether these "thoughts" are being encouraged or halted.[19] It is further maintained that the current psalm is "for rough seas,"[20] and in this regard the psalm is recited with a concluding phrase reading "let us stand in good order, let us stand with fear of God, amen amen."[21] We are also informed in the Christian "*Le Livre d'Or*" that when an individual should be "at sea in bad weather," the storm would be abated by reciting the current psalm, and thus reaching the intended destination is assured.[22] Otherwise, I am sure those involved in, as it were, covert actions, would find it interesting that *Psalm 13:24* is conjoined in the "*Key of Solomon*" with the concluding three words of *Psalm 135:16* in the outer border of the "*Sixth Pentacle of the Sun*." This item is said to be excellent "for the operation of invisibility, when correctly made."[23]

PSALM 70

[1] לַמְנַצֵּחַ לְדָוִד לְהַזְכִּיר
[2] אֱלֹהִים לְהַצִּילֵנִי יְהוָֹהאדושהי‏אהדונהי לְעֶזְרָתִי חוּשָׁה
[3] יֵבֹשׁוּ וְיַחְפְּרוּ מְבַקְשֵׁי נַפְשִׁי יִסֹּגוּ אָחוֹר וְיִכָּלְמוּ חֲפֵצֵי רָעָתִי
[4] יָשׁוּבוּ עַל עֵקֶב בָּשְׁתָּם הָאֹמְרִים הֶאָח הֶאָח
[5] יָשִׂישׂוּ וְיִשְׂמְחוּ בְּךָ כָּל מְבַקְשֶׁיךָ וְיֹאמְרוּ תָמִיד יִגְדַּל אֱלֹהִים אֹהֲבֵי יְשׁוּעָתֶךָ
[6] וַאֲנִי עָנִי וְאֶבְיוֹן אֱלֹהִים חוּשָׁה לִּי עֶזְרִי וּמְפַלְטִי אַתָּה יְהוָֹהאדושהי‏אהדונהי אַל תְּאַחַר

Transliteration:
    [1] *lam'natzei'ach l'david l'haz'kir*
    [2] *elohim l'hatzileini YHVH l'ez'rati chushah*
    [3] *y'voshu v'yach'p'ru m'vak'shei naf'shi yisogu achor v'yikal'mu chafeitzei ra'ati*
    [4] *yashuvu al eikev bosh'tam ha'om'rim he'ach he'ach*
    [5] *yasisu v'yis'm'chu b'cha kol m'vak'shecha v'yom'ru tamid yig'dal elohim ohavei y'shu'atecha*
    [6] *va'ani ani v'ev'yon elohim chushah li ez'ri um'fal'ti atah YHVH al t'achar*

Translation:
    [1] For the Leader. A Psalm of David; to make memorial.
    [2] *Elohim* to deliver me, *YHVH* to help me, make haste.
    [3] Let them be ashamed and abashed that seek after my soul; let them be turned backward and brought to confusion that delight in my hurt.
    [4] Let them be turned back by reason of their shame that say: 'Aha, aha.'
    [5] Let all those that seek Thee rejoice and be glad in Thee; and let such as love Thy salvation say continually: 'Let *Elohim* be magnified.'
    [6] But I am poor and needy; *Elohim* make haste unto me; Thou art my help and my deliverer; *YHVH* tarry not.

As in the case of the previous psalm, *Psalm 70* is recited for protection against harm,[1] and is especially employed in times of war.[2] One resource maintains it is recited prior to battles,[3] whilst another noted that it is enunciated "to appease an enemy,"[4] However, according to the *Shimmush Tehillim* it is recited in battles in order to confront and be victorious over enemies.[5] In a variant recension of the *Shimmush Tehillim* the current psalm is noted to be useful to those who are in distress, or suffering tribulation. In this regard, the instruction is to recite the current psalm with the following prayer-incantation:

צורי מלכי אלהי עולם הקשיבה שועי ושמע תפילתי
והושיעני והצילני מהצרה הגדולה הזאת והצילני
וחלצני ממנה ואל אנקש ברוב עונותי ופשעי
אבל בצל כנפיך תסתירני (Psalm 17:8) ותפלטני
ויעמדו לי בשעה הזאת רחמיך וחסדיך כי גדולים
ורבים המה בשם יהוה והו והו והו יה יה יה
חי יהוה צבאות מלך עולמים ככתוב כי אני
יהוה אלהיך מחזיק ימינך האומר לך אל תירא אני
עזרתיך (Isaiah 41:13)

Transliteration:
> *Tzuri mal'ki elohei olam hak'shivah shav'i ush'ma t'filati v'hoshi'eini v'hatzileini meihatz'rah hag'dolah hazot v'hatzileini v'chal'tzeini mimenah v'al anakeish b'rov avonotai up'sha'ai aval b'tzeil k'nafecha tas'tireini (Psalm 17:8) ut'fal'teini v'yei'am'du li b'sha'ah hazot rachamecha v'chasadecha ki g'dolim v'rabim heimah b'shem YHVH Vaho Vaho Vaho Yah Yah Yah Chai YHVH Tz'va'ot melech olamim kakatuv ki ani YHVH elohecha machazik y'minecha ha'omer l'cha al tira ani azar'ticha (Isaiah 41:13)*

Translation:
> My rock, my King, Eternal God, hear my cry and hear my prayer. Deliver me and save me from this great tribulation, redeem me and release me from it. Let me not be entangled in the multitude of my transgressions and my iniquities, but *hide me in the shadow of Thy wings (Psalm 17:8)*. You will save me, and may your mercies and your bounties stand by me in this hour, for they are great and numerous. In the

> name *YHVH Vaho Vaho Vaho Yah Yah Yah Chai YHVH Tz'va'ot*, King of the Worlds, as it is written: *For I YHVH thy God hold thy right hand, who say unto thee: 'Fear not, I help thee.'* (*Isaiah 41:13*)[6]

Despite all the "war" talk surrounding the seventieth Psalm, it is interesting that the current psalm as well as the following one, are recommended for recitation in order to find a mate.[7]

So much for the application of the current psalm listed in "official" literature on "Practical Kabbalah." Much more is to be found in the "oral sources" of common folk. In this regard, it is enunciated against pride, and is again one of the psalms recited against being enslaved by sinful passions. *Psalm 70* is further recommended to individuals who require Divine protection, especially those who are in need of Divine aid and support, with special reference to the elderly. However, this psalm is also spoken for the protection of children, as well as for the healing and strengthening of sensitive individuals. It is not only spoken for protection in circumstances of war, but equally against fierce persecution, and, it is said, against wrongful or unfavourable judgement. On a more positive note, the seventieth Psalm is recounted for a good marriage, as well as to express gratitude for good fortune.

Psalm 70 is listed in Christian Magic for the purpose of healing. In this regard, *"Le Livre d'Or"* recommends the current psalm to be copied "onto a new piece of card with the name of the illness."[8] This item is afterwards fumigated a number of times during the day and at night with incense, whilst at the same time the writing being read over a period of fifteen days, following which it is said the illness will be healed.[9] Elsewhere we are informed that *Psalm 70:2* was equally employed for healing purposes.[10] Interestingly enough, in the Byzantine Christian magical manuscripts this verse is said to pertain to getting "whatever you desire, without fear."[11]

PSALM 71

[1] בך יהוה‎אהדונהי חסיתי אל אבושה לעולם

[2] בצדקתך תצילני ותפלטני הטה אלי אזנך והושיעני

[3] היה לי לצור מעון לבוא תמיד צוית להושיעני כי סלעי ומצודתי אתה

[4] אלהי פלטני מיד רשע מכף מעול וחומץ

[5] כי אתה תקותי אדני יהוה‎אהדונהי מבטחי מנעורי

[6] עליך נסמכתי מבטן ממעי אמי אתה גוזי בך תהלתי תמיד

[7] כמופת הייתי לרבים ואתה מחסי עז

[8] ימלא פי תהלתך כל היום תפארתך

[9] אל תשליכני לעת זקנה ככלות כחי אל תעזבני

[10] כי אמרו אויבי לי ושמרי נפשי נועצו יחדו

[11] לאמר אלהים עזבו רדפו ותפשוהו כי אין מציל

[12] אלהים אל תרחק ממני אלהי לעזרתי חושה

[13] יבשו יכלו שטני נפשי יעטו חרפה וכלמה מבקשי רעתי

[14] ואני תמיד איחל והוספתי על כל תהלתך

[15] פי יספר צדקתך כל היום תשועתך כי לא ידעתי ספרות

[16] אבוא בגברות אדני יהוה‎אהדונהי אזכיר צדקתך לבדך

[17] אלהים למדתני מנעורי ועד הנה אגיד נפלאותיך

[18] וגם עד זקנה ושיבה אלהים אל תעזבני עד אגיד זרועך לדור לכל יבוא גבורתך

[19] וצדקתך אלהים עד מרום אשר עשית גדלות אלהים מי כמוך

[20] אשר הראיתני צרות רבות ורעות תשוב תחייני ומתהמות הארץ תשוב תעלני

[21] תרב גדלתי ותסב תנחמני
[22] גם אני אודך בכלי נבל אמתך אלהי אזמרה לך בכנור קדוש ישראל
[23] תרננה שפתי כי אזמרה לך ונפשי אשר פדית
[24] גם לשוני כל היום תהגה צדקתך כי בשו כי חפרו מבקשי רעתי

Transliteration:

[1] b'cha YHVH chasiti al eivoshah l'olam

[2] b'tzid'kat'cha tatzileini ut'fal'teini hateih eilai oz'n'cha v'hoshi'eini

[3] heyeih li l'tzur ma'on lavo tamid tzivita l'hoshi'eini ki sal'i um'tzudati atah

[4] elohai pal'teini miyad rasha mikaf m'aveil v'chomeitz

[5] ki atah tik'vati adonai YHVH miv'tachi min'urai

[6] aleicha nis'mach'ti mibeten mim'ei imi atah gozi b'cha t'hilati tamid

[7] k'mofeit hayiti l'rabim v'atah machasi oz

[8] yimalei fi t'hilatecha kol hayom tif'artecha

[9] al tash'licheini l'eit zik'nah kich'lot kochi al ta'az'veini

[10] ki am'ru oy'vai li v'shom'rei naf'shi no'atzu yach'dav

[11] leimor elohim azavo rid'fu v'tif'suhu ki ein matzil

[12] elohim al tir'chak mimeni elohai l'ez'rati chushah

[13] y'voshu yich'lu sot'nei naf'shi ya'atu cher'pah uch'limah m'vak'shei ra'ati

[14] va'ani tamid ayacheil v'hosaf'ti al kol t'hilatecha

[15] pi y'sapeir tzid'katecha kol hayom t'shu'atecha ki lo yada'ti s'forot

[16] avo big'vurot adonai YHVH az'kir tzid'kat'cha l'vadecha

[17] elohim limad'tani min'urai v'ad heinah agid nif'l'otecha

[18] v'gam ad zik'nah v'seivah elohim al ta'az'veini ad agid z'ro'acha l'dor l'chol yavo g'vuratecha

[19] v'tzid'kat'cha elohim ad marom asher asita g'dolot elohim mi chamocha

[20] asher hir'itani tzarot rabot v'ra'ot tashuv t'chayeini umit'homot ha'aretz tashuv ta'aleini

[21] terev g'dulati v'tisov t'nachameini

[22] *gam ani od'cha vich'li nevel amit'cha elohai azam'rah l'cha v'chinor k'dosh yis'ra'eil*
[23] *t'raneinah s'fatai ki azam'rah lach v'naf'shi asher padita*
[24] *gam l'shoni kol hayom teh'geh tzid'katecha ki voshu chi chaf'ru m'vak'shei ra'ati*

Translation:

[1] In Thee *YHVH*, have I taken refuge; let me never be ashamed.
[2] Deliver me in Thy righteousness, and rescue me; incline Thine ear unto me, and save me.
[3] Be Thou to me a sheltering rock, whereunto I may continually resort, which Thou hast appointed to save me; for Thou art my rock and my fortress.
[4] O my God, rescue me out of the hand of the wicked, out of the grasp of the unrighteous and ruthless man.
[5] For Thou art my hope; *Adonai YHVH*, my trust from my youth.
[6] Upon Thee have I stayed myself from birth; Thou art He that took me out of my mother's womb; my praise is continually of Thee.
[7] I am as a wonder unto many; but Thou art my strong refuge.
[8] My mouth shall be filled with Thy praise, and with Thy glory all the day.
[9] Cast me not off in the time of old age; when my strength faileth, forsake me not.
[10] For mine enemies speak concerning me, and they that watch for my soul take counsel together,
[11] Saying: '*Elohim* hath forsaken him; pursue and take him; for there is none to deliver.'
[12] *Elohim* be not far from me; O my God, make haste to help me.
[13] Let them be ashamed and consumed that are adversaries to my soul; let them be covered with reproach and confusion that seek my hurt.
[14] But as for me, I will hope continually, and will praise Thee yet more and more.

[15] My mouth shall tell of Thy righteousness, and of Thy salvation all the day; for I know not the numbers thereof.
[16] I will come with Thy mighty acts, *YHVH Adonai*; I will make mention of Thy righteousness, even of Thine only.
[17] *Elohim*, Thou hast taught me from my youth; and until now do I declare Thy wondrous works.
[18] And even unto old age and hoary hairs, *Elohim* forsake me not; until I have declared Thy strength unto the next generation, Thy might to every one that is to come.
[19] Thy righteousness also *Elohim*, which reacheth unto high heaven; Thou who hast done great things *Elohim*, who is like unto Thee?
[20] Thou, who hast made me to see many and sore troubles, wilt quicken me again, and bring me up again from the depths of the earth.
[21] Thou wilt increase my greatness, and turn and comfort me.
[22] I also will give thanks unto Thee with the psaltery, even unto Thy truth, O my God; I will sing praises unto Thee with the harp, O Thou Holy One of Israel.
[23] My lips shall greatly rejoice when I sing praises unto Thee; and my soul, which Thou hast redeemed.
[24] My tongue also shall tell of Thy righteousness all the day; for they are ashamed, for they are abashed, that seek my hurt.

A single verse from the current psalm is particularly important in Jewish worship. In this regard, *Psalm 71:19* is recited conjointly with *Psalms 36:7* and *119:42*, during Sabbath *Min'chah* (Afternoon Prayer Service).[1] All three verses commence with the word צִדְקָתְךָ (*Tzid'kat'cha*—"Thy righteousness"), and are recited consecutively in direct numerical order in the Sefardic and Lubavich rituals, and in reverse order in the Ashkenazic rite.[2] I have addressed this earlier in some detail in the magical application of *Psalm 36*.

As in the case of the previous psalm, *Psalm 71* is likewise recommended for recitation in order to find a mate,[3] and it is equally enunciated to express gratitude.[4] However, the current psalm is popularly recited in Jewish Magic for the purpose of finding favour (למצוא חן—*Lim'tzo chen*).[5] In this regard, we are informed that this psalm is employed to find grace in the eyes of the authorities,[6] for protection against harm in perilous situations,[7] to abolish the evil eye,[8] and also during imprisonment.[9] As far as the latter is concerned, the *Shimmush Tehillim* instructs anyone seeking to be saved from imprisonment, or avoid capture, to recite the current psalm seven times a day in the morning, noon and evening.[10]

In another recension of this text, the seventy-first Psalm is suggested for recitation by anyone who finds him or herself in any distressful situation, whether it be "an affliction by an enemy or lack of food," or be it "when he [she] "will be in old age at the end of his [her] days." We are told the psalm should be enunciated every day in the morning and evening, and that it should be recited "with the Name which is written above." This is the Divine Name referenced in the application of the previous psalm listed directly above *Psalm 71* in the same recension of the *Shimmush Tehillim*, i.e. יהוה והו והו יה יה יה חי יהוה צבאות (*YHVH Vaho Vaho Vaho Yah Yah Yah Chai YHVH Tz'va'ot*).[11] Interestingly enough, a similar use is made of *Psalm 71:9*. In this regard, the capitals of the eight words comprising this verse are combined into the Divine Name construct אהל זככאת, which is employed in amulets in order "to be saved from trouble."[12]

Once again we find *Psalm 71* put to much more varied magical use in the oral traditions of the common folk. In this regard the current psalm is recited for Divine justice, equality, true liberty, peace, and universal brotherhood. Whilst this condition of global well-being is still sadly absent amongst humanity, it is certainly something to aim for, and in this regard the seventy-first Psalm is a great start. Yet, whilst we still reside in a world of division and strife, it should be noted that the current psalm is enunciated against usurers (loan sharks), to minimise anxiety caused by enemies, to diminish poverty, against and to be saved from defamation, slander and gossip, as well as for individuals who are in detention. However, the primary sentiment behind this psalm is well-being, and in this regard this psalm is recited for rain, success in business, and to express gratitude for good fortune.

In Christian magic the seventy-first Psalm is listed in the Byzantine magical manuscripts "for contempt."[13] There might be some uncertainty as to whether this is "to halt" or "engender" contempt, but the application of the current psalm is certainly clear in "*Le Livre d'Or*," in which we are told that enunciating this psalm prior to appearing before a Judge will ensure victory in a legal case.[14]

PSALM 72

[1] לשלמה אלהים משפטיך למלך תן וצדקתך לבן מלך
[2] ידין עמך בצדק ועניייך במשפט
[3] ישאו הרים שלום לעם וגבעות בצדקה
[4] ישפט עניי עם יושיע לבני אביון וידכא עושק
[5] ייראיך עם שמש ולפני ירח דור דורים
[6] ירד כמטר על גז כרביבים זרזיף ארץ
[7] יפרח בימיו צדיק ורב שלום עד בלי ירח
[8] וירד מים עד ים ומגהר עד אפסי ארץ
[9] לפניו יכרעו ציים ואיביו עפר ילחכו
[10] מלכי תרשיש ואיים מנחה ישיבו מלכי שבא וסבא אשכר יקריבו
[11] וישתחוו לו כל מלכים כל גוים יעבדוהו
[12] כי יציל אביון משוע ועני ואין עזר לו
[13] יחס על דל ואביון ונפשות אביונים יושיע
[14] מתוך ומחמס יגאל נפשם וייקר דמם בעיניו
[15] ויחי ויתן לו מזהב שבא ויתפלל בעדו תמיד כל היום יברכנהו
[16] יהי פסת בר בארץ בראש הרים ירעש כלבנון פריו ויציצו מעיר כעשב הארץ
[17] יהי שמו לעולם לפני שמש ינון שמו ויתברכו בו כל גוים יאשרוהו
[18] ברוך יהוה‎אדוני אלהים אלהי ישראל עשה נפלאות לבדו
[19] וברוך שם כבודו לעולם וימלא כבודו את כל הארץ אמן ואמן
[20] כלו תפלות דוד בן ישי

Transliteration:
[1] *lish'lomoh elohim mish'patecha l'melech tein v'tzid'kat'cha l'ven melech*
[2] *yadin am'cha v'tzedek va'aniyecha v'mish'pat*
[3] *yis'u harim shalom la'am ug'va'ot bitz'dakah*

[4] *yish'pot aniyei am yoshi'a liv'nei ev'yon vidakei osheik*
[5] *yira'ucha im shamesh v'lif'nei yarei'ach dor dorim*
[6] *yeireid k'matar al geiz kir'vivim zar'zif aretz*
[7] *yif'rach b'yamav tzadik v'rov shalom ad b'li yarei'ach*
[8] *v'yeir'd miyam ad yam uminahar ad af'sei aretz*
[9] *l'fanav yich'r'u tziyim v'oy'vav afar y'lacheichu*
[10] *mal'chei tar'shish v'iyim min'chah yashivu mal'chei sh'va us'va esh'kar yak'rivu*
[11] *v'yish'tachavu lo chol m'lachim kol goyim ya'av'duhu*
[12] *ki yatzil ev'yon m'shavei'a v'ani v'ein ozeir lo*
[13] *yachos al dal v'ev'yon v'naf'shot ev'yonim yoshi'a*
[14] *mitoch umeichamas yig'al naf'sham v'yeikar damam b'einav*
[15] *vichi v'yiten lo miz'hav sh'va v'yit'paleil ba'ado tamid kol hayom y'varachen'hu*
[16] *y'hi fisat bar ba'aretz b'rosh harim yir'ash kal'vanon pir'yo v'yatzitzu mei'ir k'eisev ha'aretz*
[17] *y'hi sh'mo l'olam lif'nei shemesh yinon sh'mo v'yit'bar'chu vo kol goyim y'ash'ruhu*
[18] *baruch YHVH elohim elohei yisra'eil oseih nif'la'ot l'vado*
[19] *uvaruch shem k'vodo l'olam v'yimalei ch'vodo et kol ha'aretz omein v'omein*
[20] *kalu t'filot david ben yishai*

Translation:

[1] A Psalm of Solomon. Give the king Thy judgments *Elohim*, and Thy righteousness unto the king's son;

[2] That he may judge Thy people with righteousness, and Thy poor with justice.

[3] Let the mountains bear peace to the people, and the hills, through righteousness.

[4] May he judge the poor of the people, and save the children of the needy, and crush the oppressor.

[5] They shall fear Thee while the sun endureth, and so long as the moon, throughout all generations.

[6] May he come down like rain upon the mown grass, as showers that water the earth.

[7] In his days let the righteous flourish, and abundance of peace, till the moon be no more.

[8] May he have dominion also from sea to sea, and from the River unto the ends of the earth.
[9] Let them that dwell in the wilderness bow before him; and his enemies lick the dust.
[10] The kings of Tarshish and of the isles shall render tribute; the kings of Sheba and Seba shall offer gifts.
[11] Yea, all kings shall prostrate themselves before him; all nations shall serve him.
[12] For he will deliver the needy when he crieth; the poor also, and him that hath no helper.
[13] He will have pity on the poor and needy, and the souls of the needy he will save.
[14] He will redeem their soul from oppression and violence, and precious will their blood be in his sight;
[15] That they may live, and that he may give them of the gold of Sheba, that they may pray for him continually, yea, bless him all the day.
[16] May he be as a rich cornfield in the land upon the top of the mountains; may his fruit rustle like Lebanon; and may they blossom out of the city like grass of the earth.
[17] May his name endure for ever; may his name be continued as long as the sun; may men also bless themselves by him; may all nations call him happy.
[18] Blessed be *YHVH Elohim*, the God of Israel, who only doeth wondrous things;
[19] And blessed be His glorious name for ever; and let the whole earth be filled with His glory. Amen, and Amen.
[20] The prayers of David the son of Jesse are ended.

Psalm 72 is one of the psalms recommended for recitation at a cemetery,[1] and it is also one of the psalm recited to express gratitude.[2] As in the case of the previous psalm, only single verses from the current psalm feature in Jewish liturgies. In this regard, the opening phrase of *Psalm 72:5*, reading "They shall fear Thee while the sun endureth," is recited during החמה ברכת (*Bir'kat haChamah*—"Blessing of the Sun"). This blessing comprises various biblical verses recited every twenty-eight years during *Shacharit* (Morning Prayer Service), at the conclusion of the cycle of the sun when it returns to exactly the same position on the same day of the week, i.e. Wednesday.³ Furthermore, *Psalms 72:18* and *19* are included with *Psalms 89:53*, as well as *Psalm 135:21* in the short ברוך ה׳ לעולם (*Baruch Hashem l'Olam*) prayer-blessing. As indicated earlier, this prayer is recited daily during *Shacharit* (Morning Prayer Service), prior to the prayer termed ויברך דוד (*Vay'varech David*—"and David blessed"), the latter being itself a blessing.⁴

Psalm 72 is recommended in Jewish Magic for the purpose of finding grace, favour and loving-kindness.⁵ In this regard, we are informed in the *Shimmush Tehillim* that the current psalm should be written down and carried, i.e. as an amulet, in order to find grace, favour and mercy in the eyes of all people, and it is equally said to protect against the loss of personal assets.⁶ The associated Divine Name is indicated to be אה (perhaps enunciated "*Aha*"), which is said to have been derived: א (*Alef*) from אלהים (*Elohim*): verse 1; and ה (*Heh*) from יאשרוהו (*y'ash'ruhu*—"call him happy"): verse 17.⁷ Godfrey Selig expanded on the simple instruction in the standard version of the *Shimmush Tehillim*, saying "write this Psalm with the name *Aha*, in the usual manner, upon pure parchment, and suspend it around the neck, and you will become a universal favourite, and find favour and grace from all men; you may then live unconcerned, for you can never come to poverty."⁸

In a variant recension of the *Shimmush Tehillim* we are informed that those who wish to find grace, favour, and compassion before a king, or an authority for that matter, should recite the current psalm in conjunction with the following prayer-incantation:

אל אדון מלך עולמים מלא רחמים וחסדים אדון על
כל המעשים מבורך בפי כל הנשמות לך אודה ואשבח
ואתפלל לפניך שתענייני היום ובכל יום ויום שתחנייני
לחן לחסד ולרחמים בעיניך ובעיני כל רואי ובעיני
המלך או השר הזה [....insert name of king (authority)....]
על עסק זה שאני צריך בשם אה אה אה אהו אהו
אמן אמן אמן סלה סלה סלה

Transliteration:
> *El adon melech olamim malei rachamim v'chasadim adon al kol hama'asim m'vorach b'fi chol han'shamot l'cha odeh v'eshabei'ach v'et 'palel l'fanecha shet'aneini hayom ub'chol yom vayom sh'tit'neini l'chen l'chesed ul'rachamim b'eineicha uv'einei kol ro'ai ub'einei* [....insert name of king (authority)....] *hamelech o hasar hazeh al eisek zeh she'ani tzarich b'shem Aha Aha Aha Aho Aho Omein Omein Omein Selah Selah Selah*

Translation:
> God Lord King of the worlds, full of mercy and grace, Lord of all deeds, blessed in the mouth of all souls, I want to thank you, praise you and pray before you, that you may answer me today and every day, that you may entrust me to grace, favour, and mercy in your eyes, and in the eyes of all who see me, and in the eyes of [....insert name of king (authority)....], the king or this prince over this business that I need. In the name *Aha Aha Aha Aho Aho. Amen Amen Amen Selah Selah Selah*.[9]

Regarding the seventy-second Psalm, an interesting magical curiosity is the following Divine Name construct, which was formulated from the letters comprising the phrase in *Psalm 72:1* reading אלהים משפטיך למלך תן וצדקתך לבן מלך (*Elohim mish'patecha l'melech tein v'tzid'kat'cha l'ven melech*—"Give the king Thy judgments *Elohim*, and Thy righteousness unto the king's son"):[10]

אבק ללת המך ילל
מכב מתן שנם פול
טצך יד

The Divine Name construct was composed by intertwining the first ten glyphs of the phrase with the next nine in direct order, and concluding by adding the remaining letters to the ten letter combinations in reverse order. It is said that the *gematria* of this Divine Name construct aligns "with its source" which is indicated to be עלם (*Elem*), the fourth tri-letter portion of the "Name of Seventy-two Names, which I have addressed earlier in both the first and current part of this tome."[11] It should be noted that the *gematria* of this portion of the "*Shem Vayisa Vayet*" is 140 [ע = 70 + ל = 30 + ם = 40], which does not equate even remotely with the total numerical value of the Divine Name construct we are addressing here. Readers may well wonder what this is all about. The, as it were, "essence" of this Divine Name construct is the Divine Name *Elohim* conjoined with the person of the "King." In this regard, the initials of the first five tri-letter combinations of the Divine Name construct spells אלהים (*Elohim*), and the middle letters of the five sets reads כל מלך (*kol melech*—"every king." It is the *gematria* of the latter expression which totals 140 [כ = 20 + ל = 30 + מ = 40 + ל = 30 + כ = 20]. As mentioned elsewhere, a permutation of עלם (*Elem*) is לעם (*l'am* —"to the people"), which is said to reference "those who need to know 'the statutes of God, and His laws' (*Exodus 18:16*)."[12] I further noted that this permutation pertains to "the Name *Elem* commanding the power which can uproot the heavenly hosts above and the nations of the earth below."[13] In this regard it is written in *Isaiah 24:21*:

יפקוד יהוה על צבא המרום במרום ועל מלכי
האדמה על האדמה

Transliteration:
Yif'kod YHVH al tz'va hamarom bamarom v'al mal'chei ha'adamah al ha'adamah

Translation:
YHVH will punish the host of the high heaven on high, and the kings of the earth upon the earth.

Another point to keep in mind is the combination יד (*Yad*), meaning "hand," which concludes the Divine Name construct under discussion. As noted elsewhere, "by employing a procedure of reduction in which the concluding zero is discarded, the *gematria* of עלם would be 14."[14] It is said this number does not only equate with יד (*Yad*—"hand" [י = 10 + ד = 4 = 14]), this being a reference to the "hand" of the Almighty One, but that it pertains to כוזו במוכסז כוזו (*Kuzu B'mochsaz Kuzu*), i.e. the "Fourteen Letter Name of God," which is believed to command "highly protective powers."[15] Be that as it may, it is said the עלם (*Elem*) tri-letter portion of the "*Shem Vayisa Vayet*," "has the power to 'open the heart,' and to heal the soul of an embittered individual," and it is further employed "to stimulate memory.[16] However, getting back to the Divine Name construct formed from *Psalm 72:1*, we are informed that in adjurations it is employed with its associated spirit-messenger צדקיאל (*Tzad'ki'el*), and written on the palm of the right hand, before a practitioner express a petitionary prayer.[17]

Psalm 72 is once again employed for a great variety of purposes not generally listed in published sources. In this regard, it is recited for an array of physical disorders, i.e. for ailments and problems of the heart, chest, kidneys, for anaemia, diseases of the limbs, as well as for weakness and trembling generally or caused by illness. It is also enunciated for pain in the jaws. Aside from this, it is recited, as in the case of the previous psalm, against and to diminish poverty, and to offer gratitude for good fortune. It is said the current psalm is good for marriage, and is recommended for enunciation during childbirth. It is also prescribed to those who are seeking Divine justice and equality, and is equally expressed against shameful vices, as well as for the forgiveness of errors and transgressions. It is worth noting that this psalm is recommended to farmers for a good harvest.

In terms of Christian Magic the seventy-second Psalm is recommended in "*Le Livre d'Or*" to a man who desires a certain woman. In this regard, the current psalm is written down with the name of the mother of the lady in question, and is afterwards attached to the arm of the man. It is said he will "be loved and cherished by her."[18] Otherwise, the seventy-second Psalm appears to be of particular importance in "*Key of Solomon*," considering the number of times it is referenced in this text. It is listed as one of the psalms recited during the construction of "pentacles," the rest being *Psalms 8, 21, 27, 32, 29, 51,* and *134. Psalm 72* is further enunciated prior to the so-called "cutting the reed,"[19] and in this regard it is recited with Psalms *117* and *124* over an associated parchment to ensure its "efficacy and strength."[20] The current psalm is also the tenth of nineteen psalms, i.e. *Psalms 8, 15, 22, 46,*

47, 49, 51, 53, 68, 72, 84, 102, 110, 113, 126, 130, 131, 133 and *139*, which are enunciated over the wax from which ritual candles are constructed.[21] It is equally one of the four psalms, i.e. *Psalm 82, 72, 134,* and *64*, enunciated during the "perfuming" of the silk cloth in which "the instruments of art" are wrapped when not in use.[22] In conclusion, it should be noted that *Psalm 72:8* and *9* are respectively listed in the "*Key of Solomon*" in the "outer borders of the first and second "*Pentacles of Saturn*," i.e. verse 9 included in the "First Pentacle of Saturn," which is said can "strike terror into the spirits," and verse 8 in the "Second Pentacle of Saturn, which we are told "is of great value against adversaries; and of especial use in repressing the pride of the Spirits."[23]

. ...Even if the golem enters a blazing fire,' the Maharal added, 'he will not be burned, nor will he drown in a river or be killed by a sword.'... ... .

Chapter 5
Tzafon — North
The Psalms of David — Book III

PSALM 73

[1] מזמור לאסף אך טוב לישראל אלהים לברי לבב
[2] ואני כמעט נטיו רגלי כאין שפכו אשרי
[3] כי קנאתי בהוללים שלום רשעים אראה
[4] כי אין הרצבות למותם ובריא אולם
[5] בעמל אנוש אינמו ועם אדם לא ינגעו
[6] לכן ענקתמו גאוה יעטף שית חמס למו
[7] יצא מחלב עינמו עברו משכיות לבב
[8] ימיקו וידברו ברע עשק ממרום ידברו
[9] שתו בשמים פיהם ולשונם תהלך בארץ
[10] לכן ישוב עמו הלם ומי מלא ימצו למו
[11] ואמרו איכה ידע אל ויש דעה בעליון
[12] הנה אלה רשעים ושלוי עולם השגו חיל
[13] אך ריק זכיתי לבבי וארחץ בנקיון כפי
[14] ואהי נגוע כל היום ותוכחתי לבקרים
[15] אם אמרתי אספרה כמו הנה דור בניך בגדתי
[16] ואחשבה לדעת זאת עמל הוא בעיני
[17] עד אבוא אל מקדשי אל אבינה לאחריתם
[18] אך בחלקות תשית למו הפלתם למשואות
[19] איך היו לשמה כרגע ספו תמו מן בלהות
[20] כחלום מהקיץ אדני בעיר צלמם תבזה
[21] כי יתחמץ לבבו וכליותי אשתונן
[22] ואני בער ולא אדע בהמות הייתי עמך
[23] ואני תמיד עמך אחזת ביד ימיני
[24] בעצתך תנחני ואחר כבוד תקחני
[25] מי לי בשמים ועמך לא חפצתי בארץ

[26] כלה שארי ולבבי צור לבבי וחלקי אלהים לעולם
[27] כי הנה רחקיך יאבדו הצמתה כל זונה ממך
[28] ואני קרבת אלהים לי טוב שתי באדני יהוה{אדני}אהדונהי מחסי לספר כל מלאכותיך

Transliteration:
[1] miz'mor l'asaf ach tov l'yis'ra'eil elohim l'varei leivav
[2] va'ani kim'at natayu rag'lai k'ayin shup'chah shup'chu ashurai
[3] ki kineiti bahol'lim sh'lom r'sha'im er'eh
[4] ki ein char'tzubot l'motam uvari ulam
[5] ba'amal enosh eineimo v'im adam lo y'nuga'u
[6] lachein anakat'mo ga'avah ya'ataf shit chamas lamo
[7] yatza meicheilev eineimo av'ru mas'kiyot leivav
[8] yamiku vidab'ru v'ra oshek mimarom y'dabeiru
[9] shatu vashamayim pihem ul'shonam tihalach ba'aretz
[10] lachein yashiv yashuv amo halom umei malei yimatzu lamo
[11] v'am'ru eichah yada el v'yeish dei'ah v'el'yon
[12] hineih eileh r'sha'im v'shal'vei olam his'gu chayil
[13] ach rik zikiti l'vavi va'er'chatz b'nikayon kapai
[14] va'ehi nagu'a kol hayom v'tochach'ti lab'karim
[15] im amar'ti asap'rah ch'mo hineih dor banecha vagad'ti
[16] va'achash'vah lada'at zot amal hu v'einai
[17] ad avo el mik'd'shei el avinah l'acharitam
[18] ach bachalakot tashit lamo hipal'tam l'mashu'ot
[19] eich hayu l'shamah ch'raga safu tamu min balahot
[20] kachalom meihakitz adonai ba'ir tzal'mam tiv'zeh
[21] ki yit'chameitz l'vavi v'chil'yotai eshtonan
[22] va'ani va'ar v'lo eida beheimot hayiti imach
[23] va'ani tamid imach achaz'ta b'yad y'mini
[24] ba'atzat'cha tan'cheini v'achar kavod tikacheini
[25] mi li bashamayim v'im'cha lo chafatz'ti va'aretz
[26] kalah sh'eiri ul'vavi tzur l'vavi v'chel'ki elohim l'olam
[27] ki hineih r'cheikecha yoveidu hitz'matah kol zoneh mimeka
[28] va'ani kiravat elohim li tov shati badonai YHVH mach'si l'saper kol mal'achotecha

Translation:
> [1] A Psalm of Asaph. Surely *Elohim* is good to Israel, even to such as are pure in heart.
> [2] But as for me, my feet were almost gone; my steps had well nigh slipped.
> [3] For I was envious at the arrogant, when I saw the prosperity of the wicked.
> [4] For there are no pangs at their death, and their body is sound.
> [5] In the trouble of man they are not; neither are they plagued like men.
> [6] Therefore pride is as a chain about their neck; violence covereth them as a garment.
> [7] Their eyes stand forth from fatness; they are gone beyond the imaginations of their heart.
> [8] They scoff, and in wickedness utter oppression; they speak as if there were none on high.
> [9] They have set their mouth against the heavens, and their tongue walketh through the earth.
> [10] Therefore His people return hither; and waters of fullness are drained out by them.
> [11] And they say: 'How doth God know? And is there knowledge in the Most High?'
> [12] Behold, such are the wicked; and they that are always at ease increase riches.
> [13] Surely in vain have I cleansed my heart, and washed my hands in innocency;
> [14] For all the day have I been plagued, and my chastisement came every morning.
> [15] If I had said: 'I will speak thus', behold, I had been faithless to the generation of Thy children.
> [16] And when I pondered how I might know this, it was wearisome in mine eyes;
> [17] Until I entered into the sanctuary of God, and considered their end.
> [18] Surely Thou settest them in slippery places; Thou hurlest them down to utter ruin.
> [19] How are they become a desolation in a moment! They are wholly consumed by terrors.

[20] As a dream when one awaketh, so *Adonai*, when Thou arousest Thyself, Thou wilt despise their semblance.
[21] For my heart was in a ferment, and I was pricked in my reins.
[22] But I was brutish, and ignorant; I was as a beast before Thee.
[23] Nevertheless I am continually with Thee; Thou holdest my right hand.
[24] Thou wilt guide me with Thy counsel, and afterward receive me with glory.
[25] Whom have I in heaven but Thee? And beside Thee I desire none upon earth.
[26] My flesh and my heart faileth; but *Elohim* is the rock of my heart and my portion for ever.
[27] For, lo, they that go far from Thee shall perish; Thou dost destroy all them that go astray from Thee.
[28] But as for me, the nearness of *Elohim* is my good; I have made *YHVH* my refuge, that I may tell of all Thy works.

Psalm 73 is recommended in "Practical Kabbalah" (Jewish Magic) to ward off fear.[1] This psalm is listed in the *Shimmush Tehillim* for the purpose of protection against compulsory baptism, i.e. forced conversion.[2] In this regard, it is recited seven times every day.[3] Expanding on this theme, Godfrey Selig wrote in his German/English translations of the *Shimmush Tehillim*, that the current psalm "should be repeated reverently seven times daily by those who are compelled to sojourn in a heathen, idolatrous or infidel country, and by doing so, no one need feel afraid that he will be induced to deny his faith."[4] However, in a variant recension of this text, individuals who are accused by wicked people of injustice and violence, are advised to recite the current psalm conjointly with the following prayer-incantation:

דגול מרבבה (*Song of Songs 5:10*) לפניך באתי
בבכי ובתחנונים שתרחמני ותושיעני והצילני מן
האנשים האלה אשר הם מתגרים בי על לא חמס
בכפי (*Job 16:17*) על כן הצילני מהם והשב להם

גמולם בראשם והפר עצתם ומחשבותם בשמך
הקדוש דגול מרבבה אמן אמן אמן סלה סלה
סלה

Transliteration:
> *Dagul Meir'vavah (Song of Songs 5:10) l'fanecha bati babechi ub'tachanonim shet'rachameini v'toshi'eini v'hatzileini min ha'anashim ha'eileh asher hem mit'garim bi al lo chamas b'chapai (Job 16:17) al kein hatzileini meihem v'hasheiv lahem g'mulam b'rosham v'hafer atzatam umach'sh'votam b'shim'cha hakadosh Dagul Meirvavah Omein Omein Omein Selah Selah Selah*

Translation:
> *Dagul Meir'vavah* [pre-eminent above ten thousand] (*Song of Songs 5:10*), I came before you with weeping and supplication, that you may have mercy on me and redeem me. Save me from these people who accuse me of (something), even though there is no violence (is) on my hands (*Job 16:17*). Therefore, save me from them, return their actions back on their heads, and destroy their plans and their thoughts. In your holy name *Dagul Meir'vavah. Amen Amen Amen Selah Selah Selah.*[5]

Psalm 73 is again recommended for a variety of purposes in oral traditions. In this regard, it is recited against envy of the rich, also to deal with any confusion resulting from the success of the wicked, equally for criminals to repent, and for success in a lawsuit. It is further enunciated against any inducement to deny personal faith, to encourage humility, and it is one of the psalms recommended for enunciation in the synagogue, and is employed as a prayer to "end the exile." This psalm is also recited against any danger from the sea. In this regard, I am acquainted with an individual, who is a strong advocate of the magical use of the seventy-third Psalm, and who maintained that in 1992 he miraculously escaped death on the Indonesian island of Flores, by uttering this Psalm when a devastating tsunami struck the island. On a more personal note, the current psalm is recommended for the "discovery of sources," and I can personally testify that this psalm is serving me well in finding, as it were, "hidden sources" in writing these tomes on "Practical Kabbalah" (Jewish Magic).

In Christian Magic *Psalm 73* is employed to have wishes granted.[6] In this regard, we are informed in "*Le Livre d'Or*" that the seventy-third Psalm should be written down and attached to the arm, in order to ensure what is requested will be granted.[7]

PSALM 74

[1] משכיל לאסף למה אלהים זנחת לנצח יעשן אפך בצאן מרעיתך
[2] זכר עדתך קנית קדם גאלת שבט נחלתך הר ציון זה שכנת בו
[3] הרימה פעמיך למשאות נצח כל הרע אויב בקדש
[4] שאגו צרריך בקרב מועדך שמו אותתם אתות
[5] יודע כמביא למעלה בסבך עץ קרדמות
[6] ועתה פתוחיה יחד בכשיל וכילפות יהלמון
[7] שלחו באש מקדשך לארץ חללו משכן שמך
[8] אמרו בלבם נינם יחד שרפו כל מועדי אל בארץ
[9] אותתינו לא ראינו אין עוד נביא ולא אתנו ידע עד מה
[10] עד מתי אלהים יחרף צר ינאץ אויב שמך לנצח
[11] למה תשיב ידך וימינך מקרב חיקך כלה
[12] ואלהים מלכי מקדם פעל ישועות בקרב הארץ
[13] אתה פוררת בעזך ים שברת ראשי תנינים על המים
[14] אתה רצצת ראשי לויתן תתננו מאכל לעם לציים
[15] אתה בקעת מעין ונחל אתה הובשת נהרות איתן
[16] לך יום אף לך לילה אתה הכינות מאור ושמש
[17] אתה הצבת כל גבולות ארץ קיץ וחרף אתה יצרתם
[18] זכר זאת אויב חרף יהוֹאֲדֹנָיוָה ועם נבל נאצו שמך
[19] אל תתן לחית נפש תורך חית ענייך אל תשכח לנצח
[20] הבט לברית כי מלאו מחשכי ארץ נאות חמס
[21] אל ישב דך נכלם עני ואביון יהללו שמך
[22] קומה אלהים ריבה ריבך זכר חרפתך מני נבל כל היום
[23] אל תשכח קול צרריך שאון קמיך עלה תמיד

Transliteration:
[1] mas'kil l'asaf lamah elohim zanach'ta lanetzach ye'shan ap'cha b'tzon mar'itecha

[2] z'chor adat'cha kanita kedem ga'al'ta sheivet nachalatecha har tziyon zeh shachan'ta bo
[3] harimah f'amecha l'mashu'ot netzach kol heira oyeiv bakodesh
[4] sha'agu tzor'recha b'kerev mo'adecha samu ototam otot
[5] yivada kemeivi l'ma'lah bisavach etz kar'dumot
[6] v'atah pitucheha yachad b'chashil v'cheilapot yahalomun
[7] shil'chu va'esh mik'dashecha la'aretz chil'lu mish'kan sh'mecha
[8] am'ru v'libam ninam yachad sar'fu chol mo'adei el ba'aretz
[9] ototeinu lo ra'inu ein od navi v'la'itanu yode'a ad mah
[10] Ad matai elohim y'charef tzar y'na'eitz oivey shim'cha lanetzach
[11] lamah tashiv yad'cha viminecha mikerev cheik'cha chaleih
[12] veilohim mal'ki mikedem po'eil y'shu'ot b'kerev ha'aretz
[13] atah forar'ta v'oz'cha yam shibar'ta rashei taninim al hamayim
[14] atah ritzatz'ta rashei liv'yatan tit'nenu ma'achol l'am l'tziyim
[15] atah baka'ta ma'yan vanachal atah hovash'ta naharot eitan
[16] l'cha yom af l'cha lailah atah hachinota ma'or vashamesh
[17] Atah hitzav'ta kol g'vulot aretz kayitz vachoref atah y'tzar'tam
[18] z'char zot oyeiv cheireif YHVH v'am naval ni'atzu sh'mecha
[19] al titein l'chayot nefesh torecha chayat aniyecha al tish'kach lanetzach
[20] habeit lab'rit ki mal'u machashakei eretz n'ot chamas
[21] al yashov dach nich'lam ani v'ev'yon y'hal'lu sh'mecha
[22] kuma elohim riva rivecha z'chor cher'pat'cha minei naval kol hayom
[23] al tish'kach kol tzor'recha sh'on kamecha oleh tamid

Translation:
> [1] *Maschil* of Asaph. Why *Elohim* hast Thou cast us off for ever? Why doth Thine anger smoke against the flock of Thy pasture?
> [2] Remember Thy congregation, which Thou hast gotten of old, which Thou hast redeemed to be the tribe of Thine inheritance; and mount Zion, wherein Thou hast dwelt.
> [3] Lift up Thy steps because of the perpetual ruins, even all the evil that the enemy hath done in the sanctuary.
> [4] Thine adversaries have roared in the midst of Thy meeting-place; they have set up their own signs for signs.
> [5] It seemed as when men wield upwards axes in a thicket of trees.
> [6] And now all the carved work thereof together they strike down with hatchet and hammers.
> [7] They have set Thy sanctuary on fire; they have profaned the dwelling-place of Thy name even to the ground.
> [8] They said in their heart: 'Let us make havoc of them altogether'; they have burned up all the meeting-places of God in the land.
> [9] We see not our signs; there is no more any prophet; neither is there among us any that knoweth how long.
> [10] How long *Elohim*, shall the adversary reproach? Shall the enemy blaspheme Thy name for ever?
> [11] Why withdrawest Thou Thy hand, even Thy right hand? Draw it out of Thy bosom and consume them.
> [12] Yet *Elohim* is my King of old, working salvation in the midst of the earth.
> [13] Thou didst break the sea in pieces by Thy strength; Thou didst shatter the heads of the sea-monsters in the waters.
> [14] Thou didst crush the heads of leviathan, Thou gavest him to be food to the folk inhabiting the wilderness.
> [15] Thou didst cleave fountain and brook; Thou driedst up ever-flowing rivers.
> [16] Thine is the day, Thine also the night; Thou hast established luminary and sun.
> [17] Thou hast set all the borders of the earth; Thou hast made summer and winter.

[18] Remember this, how the enemy hath reproached *YHVH*, and how a base people have blasphemed Thy name.
[19] O deliver not the soul of Thy turtle-dove unto the wild beast; forget not the life of Thy poor for ever.
[20] Look upon the covenant; for the dark places of the land are full of the habitations of violence.
[21] O let not the oppressed turn back in confusion; let the poor and needy praise Thy name.
[22] Arise *Elohim*, plead Thine own cause; remember Thy reproach all the day at the hand of the base man.
[23] Forget not the voice of Thine adversaries, the tumult of those that rise up against Thee which ascendeth continually.

Readers probably noticed that several psalms do not feature in Jewish Liturgies, and that in certain instances only verses suitable to specific prayers are included. In a number of instances psalms and verses are referenced, as it were, indirectly. In this regard, the phrase from *Psalm 74:16* reading לך יום אף לך לילה (*l'cha yom af l'cha lailah*—"Thine is the day, Thine also the night"), is the basis of the beautiful acrostic hymn אדיר במלוכה (*Adir Bim'lucha*—"Mighty in Kingship") which is sung during the celebration of Passover.[1] Other than this, it should be noted that *Psalm 74* is one the psalms recited for the Land of Israel.[2]

This psalm is listed in Jewish Magic as an aid to those who have "haters,"[3] or if an individual fears enemies.[4] One source maintains this psalm is employed "against a mob, whether of men or spirits."[5] In this regard, we are informed in the *Shimmush Tehillim* that if a person has enemies or spirits that oppress him/her, the said individual should recite the current psalm, and he/she "will see many wonders."[6] In his personal dramatic and standard verbose style, Godfrey Selig noted in his German/English translations of the *Shimmush Tehillim*, that "the frequent and earnest prayer of the 74th Psalm is said to defeat the persecution embittered by enemies, and will frustrate the oppressions of the self-mighty, wealth-seeking, hard-hearted people, and will at the same time bring them to a terrible end."[7] Be that as it may, in a variant version of the *Shimmush Tehillim*, it is said that this psalm should be employed against enemies and oppressors who rise up to destroy the congregation, i.e. the Jewish community. The instruction is to recite the seventy-fourth Psalm with fasting in the morning and in the evening.[8]

Psalm 74 is one of the psalms recited for the Jewish people and Judaism. It is further enunciated for protection against enemies, against threats, abuse, oppression, to defeat bitter persecution from foes, and to protect the working population and common folk during an occupation of a country.

As far as individual verses from the current psalm are concerned, an interesting curiosity is the association of *Psalm 74:21*, reading אל ישב דך נכלם עני ואביון יהללו שמך (*al yashov dach nich'lam ani v'ev'yon y'hal'lu sh'mecha*—"O let not the oppressed turn back in confusion; let the poor and needy praise Thy name"), with יהו (*Yichu*), the thirty-third tri-letter portion of the *Shem Vayisa Vayet* ("Name of Seventy-two Names"). In this regard, we are informed that the *gematria* of the term דך (*dach*—"oppressed" [ד = 4 + כ = 20 = 24]) from the said verse, is equal to that of יהו [י = 10 + ה = 8 + ו = 6 = 24].[9] As I noted elsewhere, we are told the letter combination דך "indicates the union of the four letters of the Ineffable Name (ד = 4) with the letter כ of כתר (*Keter*—'Crown')."[10] We are further informed that the "Name of Twenty-four," i.e. אזבוגה (*Azbogah, Azbugah*, etc. [א = 1 + ז = 7 + ב = 2 + ו = 6 + ג = 3 + ה = 5 = 24] is associated here, and, as mentioned elsewhere, this Divine Name "is good for rescue or deliverance."[11] Aside from this verse, it should be noted that *Psalm 74:17* is recommended for recitation "when taking in rain, snow, climactic shifts."[12]

The seventy-fourth Psalm is recommended in the Byzantine Christian magical manuscripts for the destruction of enemies.[13] In Post-Byzantine Manuscripts we find an application of the current psalm which is similar to its use in Jewish Magic. In this regard, an individual who fears an enemy is advised to recite *Psalm 74*. However, in this instance certain magical characters are copied, and the procedure is completed with a prayer addressed to the archangels *Micha'el*, *Gavri'el*, *Uri'el*, and *Rafa'el*, who are exhorted to prevent, hold, pursue, and make the path of the enemy "dark and slippery."[14] In *"Le Livre d'Or"* the practitioner is advised to write the current psalm, the name of his/her enemy, as well as certain magical characters, which is afterwards placed in a fire.[15]

In a very different vein, the mentioned Byzantine magical manuscripts maintain the current psalm should be recited when laying the foundation of a house, as a prophylactic against any resident evil spirit which might be attached to that locale. The suggestion is that the *Psalm 74* should be recited seven times over water, and the locale sprinkled with the liquid prior to laying the foundation of the building.[16]

PSALM 75

[1] לַמְנַצֵּחַ אַל תַּשְׁחֵת מִזְמוֹר לְאָסָף שִׁיר

[2] הוֹדִינוּ לְךָ אֱלֹהִים הוֹדִינוּ וְקָרוֹב שְׁמֶךָ סִפְּרוּ נִפְלְאוֹתֶיךָ

[3] כִּי אֶקַּח מוֹעֵד אֲנִי מֵישָׁרִים אֶשְׁפֹּט

[4] נְמֹגִים אֶרֶץ וְכָל יֹשְׁבֶיהָ אָנֹכִי תִכַּנְתִּי עַמּוּדֶיהָ סֶּלָה

[5] אָמַרְתִּי לַהוֹלְלִים אַל תָּהֹלּוּ וְלָרְשָׁעִים אַל תָּרִימוּ קָרֶן

[6] אַל תָּרִימוּ לַמָּרוֹם קַרְנְכֶם תְּדַבְּרוּ בְצַוָּאר עָתָק

[7] כִּי לֹא מִמּוֹצָא וּמִמַּעֲרָב וְלֹא מִמִּדְבַּר הָרִים

[8] כִּי אֱלֹהִים שֹׁפֵט זֶה יַשְׁפִּיל וְזֶה יָרִים

[9] כִּי כוֹס בְּיַד יְהֹוָהאֲדֹנָי וְיַיִן חָמַר מָלֵא מֶסֶךְ וַיַּגֵּר מִזֶּה אַךְ שְׁמָרֶיהָ יִמְצוּ יִשְׁתּוּ כֹּל רִשְׁעֵי אָרֶץ

[10] וַאֲנִי אַגִּיד לְעֹלָם אֲזַמְּרָה לֵאלֹהֵי יַעֲקֹב

[11] וְכָל קַרְנֵי רְשָׁעִים אֲגַדֵּעַ תְּרוֹמַמְנָה קַרְנוֹת צַדִּיק

Transliteration:

[1] *lam'natze'ach al tash'cheit miz'mor l'asaf shir*
[2] *hodinu l'cha elohim hodinu v'karov sh'me'cha sip'ru nif'le'otecha*
[3] *ki ekach mo'eid ani meisharim esh'pot*
[4] *n'mogim eretz v'chol yhosh'veha anochi tikanti amudeha selah*
[5] *amar'ti lahol'lim al taholu v'lar'sha'im al tarimu karen*
[6] *al tarimu lamarom kar'n'chem t'dab'ru v'tzavar atak*
[7] *ki lo mimotza umima'arav v'lo mimid'bar harim*
[8] *ki elohim shofeit zeh yash'pil v'zeh yarim*
[9] *ki chos b'yad YHVH v'yayin chamar malei mesech vayageir mizeh ach sh'mareha yim"tzu yish'tu kol rish'ei aretz*
[10] *va'ani agid l'olam azam'rah leilohei ya'akov*
[11] *v'chol kar'nei r'sha'im agadei'a t'romam'nah kar'not tzadik*

Translation:

[1] For the Leader; *Al-tashheth*. A Psalm of *Asaf*, a Song.
[2] We give thanks unto Thee *Elohim*, we give thanks, and Thy name is near; men tell of Thy wondrous works.
[3] 'When I take the appointed time, I Myself will judge with equity.

[4] When the earth and all the inhabitants thereof are dissolved, I Myself establish the pillars of it.' *Selah*
[5] I say unto the arrogant: 'Deal not arrogantly'; and to the wicked: 'Lift not up the horn.'
[6] Lift not up your horn on high; speak not insolence with a haughty neck.
[7] For neither from the east, nor from the west, nor yet from the wilderness, cometh lifting up.
[8] For *Elohim* is judge; He putteth down one, and lifteth up another.
[9] For in the hand of *YHVH* there is a cup, with foaming wine, full of mixture, and He poureth out of the same; surely the dregs thereof, all the wicked of the earth shall drain them, and drink them.
[10] But as for me, I will declare for ever, I will sing praises to the God of Jacob.
[11] All the horns of the wicked also will I cut off; but the horns of the righteous shall be lifted up.

Psalm 75 is included with *Psalms 16, 144* and *67* in the selection of psalms which are recited on a Saturday night.[1] We are informed that this powerful psalm is enunciated to eliminate pride,[2] and to affect the atonement for transgressions.[3] In terms of saying the seventy-fifth Psalm in Jewish Magic for the forgiveness of offences, i.e. to pardon what is collectively termed "sin" in common parlance, we are informed in the *Shimmush Tehillim* that the associated Divine Name is הד, the letter ה (*Heh*) from ק (*Kof*) in צדיק (*tzadik*— "righteous"): verse 11, the letter having been transposed by means of the א"ל ב"ת (*Albat*) cipher; and ד from הודינו (*hodinu*—"we give thanks"): verse 2.[4] A variant recension of the *Shimmush Tehillim* informs us the current psalm should be recited "to subjugate and destroy the god-forsaken, wicked and traitors."[5]

The seventy-fifth Psalm has been recommended as a prayer for forgiveness, i.e. the pardoning of sins, and it is recited against tyranny, to halt war, to encourage employers to deal justly with employees, and also for universal brotherhood and peace.

Psalm 75 is enunciated in the Byzantine Christian magical manuscripts, when "you wish to teach someone,"[6] and "*Le Livre d'Or*" maintains that an individual who recites it for you every day, "will be blessed by God and delivered from bondage and from prison."[7] In this regard, we are informed the current psalm will benefit the profits of merchants, when it is copied on fox skin "with the character and name of the Intelligence," on the day and in the hour of Jupiter. It is further noted that the written text should be carried wrapped "in some taffeta material, bound with gold," and the psalm recited every day.[8]

PSALM 76

[1] למנצח בנגינת מזמור לאסף שיר
[2] נודע ביהודה אלהים בישראל גדול שמו
[3] ויהי בשלם סוכו ומעונתו בציון
[4] שמה שבר רשפי קשת מגן וחרב ומלחמה סלה
[5] נאור אתה אדיר מהררי טרף
[6] אשתוללו אבירי לב נמו שנתם ולא מצאו כל אנשי חיל ידיהם
[7] מגערתך אלהי יעקב נרדם ורכב וסוס
[8] אתה נורא אתה ומי יעמד לפניך מאז אפך
[9] משמים השמעת דין ארץ יראה ושקטה
[10] בקום למשפט אלהים להושיע כל ענוי ארץ סלה
[11] כי חמת אדם תודך שארית חמת תחגר
[12] נדרו ושלמו ליהוה‎ אהדונהי אלהיכם כל סביביו יבילו שי למורא
[13] יבצר רוח נגידים נורא למלכי ארץ

Transliteration:

[1] lam'natze'ach bin'ginot miz'mor l'asaf shir
[2] noda bihudah elohim b'yis'ra'eil gadol sh'mo
[3] vay'hi v'shaleim suko um'onato v'tziyon
[4] shamah shibar rish'fei kashet magein v'cherev umil'chamah selah
[5] na'or atah adir meihar'rei taref
[6] esh'tol'lu abirei leiv namu sh'natam v'lo matz'u chol an'shei chayil y'deihem
[7] miga'arat'cha elohei ya'akov nir'dam v'rechev vasus
[8] Atah nora atah umi ya'amod l'fanecha mei'az apecha
[9] mishamayim hish'ma'ta din eretz yar'ah v'shakatah
[10] b'kum lamish'pat elohim l'hoshi'a kol an'vei eretz selah
[11] ki chamat adam todeka sh'eirit cheimot tach'gor
[12] nidaru v'shal'mu la'YHVH eloheichem kol s'vivav yovilu shai lamora
[13] yiv'tzor ru'ach n'gidim nora l'mal'chei aretz

Translation:
>[1] For the Leader; with string-music. A Psalm of Asaph, a Song.
>[2] In Judah is *Elohim* known; His name is great in Israel.
>[3] In Salem also is set His tabernacle, and His dwelling-place in Zion.
>[4] There He broke the fiery shafts of the bow; the shield, and the sword, and the battle. *Selah*
>[5] Glorious art Thou and excellent, coming down from the mountains of prey.
>[6] The stout-hearted are bereft of sense, they sleep their sleep; and none of the men of might have found their hands.
>[7] At Thy rebuke, O God of Jacob, they are cast into a dead sleep, the riders also and the horses.
>[8] Thou, even Thou, art terrible; and who may stand in Thy sight when once Thou art angry?
>[9] Thou didst cause sentence to be heard from heaven; the earth feared, and was still,
>[10] When *Elohim* arose to judgment, to save all the humble of the earth. *Selah*
>[11] Surely the wrath of man shall praise Thee; the residue of wrath shalt Thou gird upon Thee.
>[12] Vow, and pay unto *YHVH* your God; let all that are round about Him bring presents unto Him that is to be feared;
>[13] He minisheth the spirit of princes; He is terrible to the kings of the earth.

Psalm 76 is recited in Jewish Magic in order to be rescued from water and fire.[1] One source states the psalm is employed "against flood and fire,"[2] and Godfrey Selig noted in his version of the *Shimmush Tehillim* that "the 76th Psalm is said to be the quickest and most effective defence against danger from fire and water."[3] A variant recension of the *Shimmush Tehillim* maintains that the current psalm is to aid a "little one," by casting out an evil spirit from the mother of the infant. In this regard, the psalm is written down and suspended on her person.[4] In yet another recension of this text, the seventy-sixth Psalm is recommended for recitation by a judge prior to entering a court. He/she is advised to enunciate the psalm with the following prayer-incantation:

בשם אדון עולם ויוצר הכל אני [....personal name....]
נכנס בדין יהי רצון מלפניך כשם שאני נכנס בדין
נקי כך אצא נקי מהדין שלא יעותוני בדין ושלא
יהיה העונש בי אך אשפט כדין וכשורה שלא אלך
דרך עקלקלות ולא יהיה עול תלוי בי בשם יוצר כל
אמן אמן אמן סלה סלה סלה

> Transliteration:
> B'shem Adon Olam v'Yotzer haKol ani [....personal name....] nich'nas b'din y'hi ratzon mil'fanecha k'shem she'ani nich'nas b'din naki kach eitzei naki meihadin shelo ya'av'tuni b'din v'shelo yih'yeh ha'onesh bi ach esh'fot k'din uk'shurah shelo aleich derech akal'kalot v'lo yih'yeh avel talui bi b'shem Yotzer Kol Omein Omein Omein Selah Selah Selah

> Translation:
> In the name *Adon Olam v'Yotzer haKol* ("Lord of the World and Maker of All"), I [....personal name....], enter into judgment. May it be your will, just as I enter into court pure, so should I emerge from judgment pure, so that they may not corrupt me in the court, and that there will be no offence against me. But I will judge in accordance with the law, and according to the right order, so that I do not tread a path of deviousness, and no injustice will cling to me. In the Name *Yotzer Kol* ("Maker of All") *Amen Amen Amen Selah Selah Selah*.[5]

As noted, the seventy-sixth Psalm is recited for protection against water, floods and fire. In this regard we are informed that it is enunciated against destruction by water, i.e. to be saved from drowning, for protection against thunderbolts, and storms in general. It is also employed to overcome spiritual troubles, to alleviate fear during childbirth, as well as for insomnia. I regularly employ the current psalm to aid me in falling asleep.

Psalm 76 is also utilised in Christian Magic to dispel "spirits," though not the kind who found residence inside pregnant women., bur rather the variety which invades residences. In this regard, we are informed in "*Le Livre d'Or*" that the current psalm should be written down during the waxing Moon, and afterwards suspended on the door of the haunted residence, and the spirits "will be dispelled."[6]

PSALM 77

[1] למנצח על ידותון לאסף מזמור
[2] קולי אל אלהים ואצעקה קולי אל אלהים והאזין אלי
[3] ביום צרתי אדני דרשתי ידי לילה נגרה ולא תפוג מאנה הנחם נפשי
[4] אזכרה אלהים ואהמיה אשיחה ותתעטף רוחי סלה
[5] אחזת שמרות עיני נפעמתי ולא אדבר
[6] חשבתי ימים מקדם שנות עולמים
[7] אזכרה נגינתי בלילה עם לבבי אשיחה ויחפש רוחי
[8] הלעולמים יזנח אדני ולא יסיף לרצות עוד
[9] האפס לנצח חסדו גמר אמר לדר ודר
[10] השכח חנות אל אם קפץ באף רחמיו סלה
[11] ואמר חלותי היא שנות ימין עליון
[12] אזכור מעללי יה כי אזכרה מקדם פלאך
[13] והגיתי בכל פעלך ובעלילותיך אשיחה
[14] אלהים בקדש דרכך מי אל גדול כאלהים
[15] אתה האל עשה פלא הודעת בעמים עזך
[16] גאלת בזרוע עמך בני יעקב ויוסף סלה
[17] ראוך מים אלהים ראוך מים יחילו אף ירגזו תהמות
[18] זרמו מים עבות קול נתנו שחקים אף חצציך יתהלכו
[19] קול רעמך בגלגל האירו ברקים תבל רגזה ותרעש הארץ
[20] בים דרכך ושבילך במים רבים ועקבותיך לא נדעו
[21] נחית כצאן עמך ביד משה ואהרן

Transliteration:
[1] *lam'na'tzei'ach al y'dutun l'asaf miz'mor*
[2] *koli el elohim v'etz'akah koli el elohim v'ha'azin eilai*

[3] *b'yom tzarati adonai darash'ti yadi lailah nig'rah v'lo tafug mei'anah hinachem naf'shi*
[4] *ez'k'rah elohim v'ehemayah asichah v'tit'ateif ruchi selah*
[5] *achaz'ta sh'murot einai nif'am'ti v'lo adabeir*
[6] *chishav'ti yamim mikedem sh'not olamim*
[7] *ez'k'rah n'ginati balailah im l'vavi asichah vay'chapeis ruchi*
[8] *hal'olamim yiz'nach adonai v'lo yosif lir'tzot od*
[9] *he'afeis lanetzach chas'do gamar omer l'dor vador*
[10] *hashachach chanot el im kafatz b'af rachamav selah*
[11] *va'omar chaloti hi sh'not y'min el'yon*
[12] *ez'kor ma'al'lei yah ki ez'k'rah mikedem pil'echa*
[13] *v'hagiti v'chol pa'olecha uva'alilotecha asichah*
[14] *elohim bakodesh dar'kecha mi el gadol keilohim*
[15] *atah ha'el oseih feleh hoda'ta va'amim uzecha*
[16] *ga'al'ta biz'ro'a amecha b'nei ya'akov v'yoseif selah*
[17] *ra'ucha mayim elohim ra'ucha mayim yachilu af yir'g'zu t'homot*
[18] *zor'mu mayim avot kol nat'nu sh'chakim af chatzatzecha yit'halachu*
[19] *kol ra'am'cha bagal'gal hei'iru v'rakim teiveil rag'zah vatir'ash ha'aretz*
[20] *bayam dar'kecha ush'vil'cha b'mayim rabim v'ik'voteicha lo noda'u*
[21] *nachita chatzon amecha b'yad mosheh v'aharon*

Translation:
[1] For the Leader; for Jeduthun. A Psalm of Asaph.
[2] I will lift up my voice unto *Elohim*, and cry; I will lift up my voice unto *Elohim*, that He may give ear unto me.
[3] In the day of my trouble I seek *Adonai*; with my hand uplifted, mine eye streameth in the night without ceasing; my soul refuseth to be comforted.
[4] When I think thereon *Elohim*, I must moan; when I muse thereon, my spirit fainteth. *Selah*
[5] Thou holdest fast the lids of mine eyes; I am troubled, and cannot speak.
[6] I have pondered the days of old, the years of ancient times.

[7] In the night I will call to remembrance my song; I will commune with mine own heart; and my spirit maketh diligent search:
[8] 'Will *Adonai* cast off for ever? and will He be favourable no more?
[9] Is His mercy clean gone for ever? Is His promise come to an end for evermore?
[10] Hath God forgotten to be gracious? Hath He in anger shut up his compassions?' *Selah*
[11] And I say: 'This is my weakness, that the right hand of the Most High could change.
[12] I will make mention of the deeds of *Yah*; yea, I will remember Thy wonders of old.
[13] I will meditate also upon all Thy work, and muse on Thy doings.'
[14] *Elohim*, Thy way is in holiness; who is a great god like unto *Elohim*?
[15] Thou art the God that doest wonders; Thou hast made known Thy strength among the peoples.
[16] Thou hast with Thine arm redeemed Thy people, the sons of Jacob and Joseph. *Selah*
[17] The waters saw Thee *Elohim*; the waters saw Thee, they were in pain; the depths also trembled.
[18] The clouds flooded forth waters; the skies sent out a sound; Thine arrows also went abroad.
[19] The voice of Thy thunder was in the whirlwind; the lightnings lighted up the world; the earth trembled and shook.
[20] Thy way was in the sea, and Thy path in the great waters, and Thy footsteps were not known.
[21] Thou didst lead Thy people like a flock, by the hand of Moses and Aaron.

Psalm 77 is employed to resist succumbing to misfortune in days of trouble.[1] Some sources maintain the current psalm is recited for "protection against any type of danger,"[2] and against "all manner of distress."[3] In this regard, it is said in the standard published version of the *Shimmush Tehillim*, that this psalm is to, as it were, accustom an individual not to get into any trouble.[4] Godfrey Selig maintains in his German/English translations of the *Shimmush Tehillim* that "whosoever prays the 77th Psalm daily will not be overtaken by want or danger."[5] Interestingly enough, the Divine Name construct אהעפ, derived from the capitals of the words comprising the phrase אתה האל עשה פלא (*Psalm 77:15*), is employed in amulets to "ward off trouble."[6]

In a variant recension of the *Shimmush Tehillim* we find the seventy-seventh Psalm recommended to those who would like to be heard by every listener. In this regard, the current psalm is recited in conjunction with the following prayer-incantation:

אליך אקרא יהוה שמעיני וענייני וחנייני ותן לי
חן בעיני כל הבריות שישמעו קולי ודברי יהיו
מקובלים ונשמעים באזני כל אדם בין גדול
בין קטן ולא אהיה נבזה ונמאס בעיני שום אדם
בשם יהוה שדי אמן אמן סלה סלה

Transliteration:

> Eilecha ek'ra YHVH sh'm'eini v'aneini v'chaneini v'tein li chen b'einei kol hab'riyot sheyish'm'u koli ud'varai yih'yu m'kubalim v'nish'ma'im b'oz'nei kol adam bein gadol bein katan v'lo eh'yeh niv'zeh v'nim'as b'einei shum adam b'shem YHVH Shadai Omein Omein Selah Selah.

Translation:

> To you I will call *YHVH*, hear me, answer me, and have mercy on me, and grant me grace in the eyes of all creatures, so that they will hear my voice, and my words should be received and heard in the ears of every person, whether big or whether small, and may I not be despised and loathed in the eyes of a single person. In the Name *YHVH Shadai Amen Amen Selah Selah*.[7]

As far as the application of individual verses are concerned, it should be noted that the capitals of the words comprising *Psalm 77:15* reading אתה האל עשה פלא הודעת בעמים עזך (*atah ha'el oseih feleh hoda'ta va'amim uzecha*—"Thou art the God that doest wonders; Thou hast made known Thy strength among the peoples"), are conjoined with the initials and concluding letters of the words לֹא תִגְנוֹב [*lo tig'nov*—"Thou shalt not steal"] (*Exodus 20:15*), in order to formulate the following Divine Name construct which is employed to disclose the identity of a thief:[8]

$$\text{אֲהָעְפּ הֹבָעֲ לֹת אב}$$

We are informed the Divine Name construct should be written in *Ashurit*, i.e. biblical script, with *Tagin* (crownlets), and the vowel points are those employed in the enunciation of the said glyphs in the verse. The application of this Divine Name construct necessitates it to be written in holiness and purity on hard cheese, the latter having been produced exclusively by a Jewish woman who was not menstruating at the time of its manufacture. Following this action, the cheese is given for consumption to all suspects, and, it is said, the guilty party will not be able to swallow the cheese until he/she owns up, and the crime corrected.[9]

From what has been said thus far it should be clear that the current psalm is employed to deal with all manner of troubles and distress, and equally to prevent difficulties. Other than that, the seventy-seventh Psalm has been recommended against excesses, to encourage mutual love among family members, to ensure a happy old age and retirement, and against pains generally. The current psalm is also employed for the fruits of the earth, vines and vineyards, against harmful pests and insects, and, believe it or not, for the wellbeing of silkworms.

Psalm 77 is utilised in Christian Magic for the healing of individuals who are "bound to enchantments." In this regard, the "*Le Livre d'Or*" instructs the psalm should be written on a sheet of glass, and the writing afterwards washed in clean water. Following this action, the infused water is consumed by the sufferer.[10] Other than this application, it is worth noting that the outer rim of the third "Pentacle of Mars" in the "*Key of Solomon*" comprises *Psalm 77:13*.[11]

PSALM 78

[1] מַשְׂכִּיל לְאָסָף הַאֲזִינָה עַמִּי תּוֹרָתִי הַטּוּ אָזְנְכֶם לְאִמְרֵי פִי

[2] אֶפְתְּחָה בְמָשָׁל פִּי אַבִּיעָה חִידוֹת מִנִּי קֶדֶם

[3] אֲשֶׁר שָׁמַעְנוּ וַנֵּדָעֵם וַאֲבוֹתֵינוּ סִפְּרוּ לָנוּ

[4] לֹא נְכַחֵד מִבְּנֵיהֶם לְדוֹר אַחֲרוֹן מְסַפְּרִים תְּהִלּוֹת יְהוָֹהאֲדֹנָהִי וֶעֱזוּזוֹ וְנִפְלְאֹתָיו אֲשֶׁר עָשָׂה

[5] וַיָּקֶם עֵדוּת בְּיַעֲקֹב וְתוֹרָה שָׂם בְּיִשְׂרָאֵל אֲשֶׁר צִוָּה אֶת אֲבוֹתֵינוּ לְהוֹדִיעָם לִבְנֵיהֶם

[6] לְמַעַן יֵדְעוּ דּוֹר אַחֲרוֹן בָּנִים יִוָּלֵדוּ יָקֻמוּ וִיסַפְּרוּ לִבְנֵיהֶם

[7] וְיָשִׂימוּ בֵאלֹהִים כִּסְלָם וְלֹא יִשְׁכְּחוּ מַעַלְלֵי אֵל וּמִצְוֹתָיו יִנְצֹרוּ

[8] וְלֹא יִהְיוּ כַּאֲבוֹתָם דּוֹר סוֹרֵר וּמֹרֶה דּוֹר לֹא הֵכִין לִבּוֹ וְלֹא נֶאֶמְנָה אֶת אֵל רוּחוֹ

[9] בְּנֵי אֶפְרַיִם נוֹשְׁקֵי רוֹמֵי קָשֶׁת הָפְכוּ בְּיוֹם קְרָב

[10] לֹא שָׁמְרוּ בְּרִית אֱלֹהִים וּבְתוֹרָתוֹ מֵאֲנוּ לָלֶכֶת

[11] וַיִּשְׁכְּחוּ עֲלִילוֹתָיו וְנִפְלְאוֹתָיו אֲשֶׁר הֶרְאָם

[12] נֶגֶד אֲבוֹתָם עָשָׂה פֶלֶא בְּאֶרֶץ מִצְרַיִם שְׂדֵה צֹעַן

[13] בָּקַע יָם וַיַּעֲבִירֵם וַיַּצֶּב מַיִם כְּמוֹ נֵד

[14] וַיַּנְחֵם בֶּעָנָן יוֹמָם וְכָל הַלַּיְלָה בְּאוֹר אֵשׁ

[15] יְבַקַּע צֻרִים בַּמִּדְבָּר וַיַּשְׁקְ כִּתְהֹמוֹת רַבָּה

[16] וַיּוֹצִא נוֹזְלִים מִסָּלַע וַיּוֹרֶד כַּנְּהָרוֹת מָיִם

[17] וַיּוֹסִיפוּ עוֹד לַחֲטֹא לוֹ לַמְרוֹת עֶלְיוֹן בַּצִּיָּה

[18] וַיְנַסּוּ אֵל בִּלְבָבָם לִשְׁאָל אֹכֶל לְנַפְשָׁם

[19] וַיְדַבְּרוּ בֵּאלֹהִים אָמְרוּ הֲיוּכַל אֵל לַעֲרֹךְ שֻׁלְחָן בַּמִּדְבָּר

[20] הֵן הִכָּה צוּר וַיָּזוּבוּ מַיִם וּנְחָלִים יִשְׁטֹפוּ הֲגַם לֶחֶם יוּכַל תֵּת אִם יָכִין שְׁאֵר לְעַמּוֹ

[21] לָכֵן שָׁמַע יְהוָֹהאֲדֹנָהִי וַיִּתְעַבָּר וְאֵשׁ נִשְּׂקָה בְיַעֲקֹב וְגַם אַף עָלָה בְיִשְׂרָאֵל

[22] כִּי לֹא הֶאֱמִינוּ בֵּאלֹהִים וְלֹא בָטְחוּ בִּישׁוּעָתוֹ

[23] ויצו שחקים ממעל ודלתי שמים פתח
[24] וימטר עליהם מן לאכל ודגן שמים נתן למו
[25] לחם אבירים אכל איש צידה שלח להם לשבע
[26] יסע קדים בשמים וינהג בעזו תימן
[27] וימטר עליהם כעפר שאר וכחול ימים עוף כנף
[28] ויפל בקרב מחנהו סביב למשכנתיו
[29] ויאכלו וישבעו מאד ותאותם יבא להם
[30] לא זרו מתאותם עוד אכלם בפיהם
[31] ו**אף אלהים** עלה בהם ויהרג במשמניהם ובחורי ישראל הכריע
[32] בכל זאת חטאו עוד ולא האמינו בנפלאותיו
[33] ויכל בהבל ימיהם ושנותם בבהלה
[34] אם הרגם ודרשוהו ושבו ושחרו אל
[35] ויזכרו כי אלהים צורם ואל עליון גאלם
[36] ויפתוהו בפיהם ובלשנם יכזבו לו
[37] ולבם לא נכון עמו ולא נאמנו בבריתו
[38] והוא רחום יכפר עון ולא ישחית והרבה להשיב **אפו** ולא יעיר כל חמתו
[39] ויזכר כי בשר המה רוח הולך ולא ישוב
[40] כמה ימרוהו במדבר יעציבוהו בישימון
[41] וישובו וינסו אל וקדוש ישראל התוו
[42] לא זכרו את ידו יום אשר פדם מני צר
[43] אשר שם במצרים אתותיו ומופתיו בשדה צען
[44] ויהפך לדם יאריהם ונזליהם בל ישתיון
[45] ישלח בהם ערב ויאכלם וצפרדע ותשחיתם
[46] ויתן לחסיל יבולם ויגיעם לארבה
[47] יהרג בברד גפנם ושקמותם בחנמל
[48] ויסגר לברד בעירם ומקניהם לרשפים
[49] ישלח בם חרון **אפו** עברה וזעם וצרה משלחת מלאכי רעים
[50] יפלס נתיב לאפו לא חשך ממות נפשם וחיתם לדבר הסגיר
[51] ויך כל בכור במצרים ראשית אונים באהכלי חם

[52] ויסע כצאן עמו וינהגם כעדר במדבר
[53] וינחם לבטח ולא פחדו ואת אויביהם כסה הים
[54] ויביאם אל גבול קדשו הר זה קנתה ימינו
[55] ויגרש מפניהם גוים ויפילם בחבל נחלה וישכן באהליהם שבטי ישראל
[56] וינסו וימרו את אלהים עליון ועדותיו לא שמרו
[57] ויסגו ויבגדו כאבותם נהפכו כקשת רמיה
[58] ויכעיסוהו בבמותם ובפסיליהם יקניאוהו
[59] שמע אלהים ויתעבר וימאס מאד בישראל
[60] ויטש משכן שלו אהל שכן באדם
[61] ויתן לשבי עזו ותפארתו ביד צר
[62] ויסגר לחרב עמו ובנחלתו התעבר
[63] בחוריו אכלה אש ובתולתיו לא הוללו
[64] כהניו בחרב נפלו ואלמנתיו לא תבכינה
[65] ויקץ כישן אדני כגבור מתרונן מיין
[66] ויך צריו אחור חרפת עולם נתן למו
[67] וימאס באהל יוסף ובשבט אפרים לא בחר
[68] ויבחר את שבט יהודה את הר ציון אשר אהב
[69] ויבן כמו רמים מקדשו כארץ יסדה לעולם
[70] ויבחר בדוד עבדו ויקחהו ממכלאת צאן
[71] מאחר עלות הביאו לרעות ביעקב עמו ובישראל נחלתו
[72] וירעם כתם לבבו ובתבונות כפיו ינחם

Transliteration:
    [1] *mas'kil le'asaf ha'azinah ami torati hatu az'n'chem l'im'rei fi*
    [2] *ef'techa v'mashal pi abi'ah chidot mini kedem*
    [3] *asher shama'nu vaneida'eim va'avoteinu sip'ru lanu*
    [4] *lo nechacheid mib'neihem l'dor acharon m'sap'rim t'hilot YHVH ve'ezuzo v'nif'l'otav asher asah*
    [5] *vayakem eidut b'ya'akov v'torah sam b'yis'ra'eil asher tzivah et avoteinu l'hodi'am liv'neihem*
    [6] *l'ma'an yeid'u dor acharon banim yivaleidu yakumu visap'ru liv'neihem*

[7] v'yasimu veilohim kis'lam v'lo yish'k'chu ma'al'lei el umitz'votav yin'tzoru

[8] v'lo yih'yu ka'avotam dor soreir umoreh dor lo heichin libo v'lo ne'em'nah et el rucho

[9] b'nei ef'rayim nosh'kei romei kashet haf'chu b'yom k'rav

[10] lo sham'ru b'rit elohim uv'torato mei'anu lalechet

[11] vayish'kechu alilotav v'nif'l'otav asher her'am

[12] neged avotam asah fele b'eretz mitz'rayim s'deih tzo'an

[13] baka yam va'ya'avireim vayatzev mayim k'mo neid

[14] vayancheim be'anan yomam v'chol halailah b'or esh

[15] y'vaka tzurim bamid'bar vayash'k' kit'homot rabah

[16] vayotzi noz'lim misala vayored kan'harot mayim

[17] vayosifu od lachato lo lam'rot el'yon batziya

[18] vay'nasu el bil'vavam lish'al ochel l'naf'sham

[19] vay'dab'ru beilohim am'ru hayuchal el la'aroch shul'chan bamid'bar

[20] hein hikah tzur vayazuvu mayim un'chalim yish'tofu hagam lechem y'chal teit im yachin sh'eir l'amo

[21] l'chen shama YHVH vayit'abar v'esh nis'kah v'ya'akov v'gam af alah v'yis'ra'eil

[22] ki lo he'eminu beilohim v'lo vat'chu bishu'ato

[23] vay'tzav sh'chakim mima'al v'dal'tei shamayim patach

[24] vayam'teir aleihem man le'echol ud'gan shamayim natan lamo

[25] lechem abirim achal ishn zeirah shalach lahem lasova

[26] yasa kadim bashamayim vay'naheig b'uzo teiman

[27] vayam'teir aleihem ke'afar sh'eir uch'chol yamim of kanaf

[28] vayapeil b'kerev machaneihu saviv l'mish'k'notav

[29] vayoch'lu vayis'b'u m'od v'ta'avatam yavi lahem

[30] lo zaru mita'avatam od ach'lam b'fihem

[31] v'af elohim alah vahem vayaharog b'mish'maneihem uvachurei yis'ra'eil hich'ri'a

[32] b'chol zot chat'u od v'lo he'eminu b'nif'l'otav

[33] vay'chal bahevel y'meihem ush'notam babehalah

[34] im haragam ud'rashuhu v'shavu v'shicharu el

[35] vayiz'k'ru ki elohim tzuram v'el el'yon go'alam

[36] vay'fatuhu b'fihem uvil'shonam y'chaz'vu lo
[37] v'libam lo nachon imo v'lo ne'em'nu biv'rito
[38] v'hu rachumn y'chapeir avon v'lo yash'chit v'hir'bah l'hashiv apo v'lo ya'ir kol chamato
[39] vayiz'kor ki vasar hemah ru'ach holeich v'lo yashuv
[40] kamah yam'ruhu vamid'bar ya'atzivuhu bishimon
[41] vayashuvu vay'nasu el uk'dosh yis'ra'eil hit'vu
[42] lo zach'ru et yado yom asher padam mini tzar
[43] asher sam b'mitz'rayim ototav umof'tav bis'dei tzo'an
[44] vayahafoch l'dam y'oreihem v'noz'leihem bal yish'tayun
[45] y'shalach bahem arov vayoch'leim utz'far'dei'a vatash'chiteim
[46] vayitein lechasil y'vulam vigi'am la'arbeh
[47] yaharog babarad gaf'nam v'shik'motam bachanamal
[48] vayas'geir labarad b'iram umik'neihem lar'shafim
[49] y'shalach bam charon apo ev'rah vaza'am v'tzarah mish'lachat mal'achei ra'im
[50] y'faleis nativ l'apo lo chasach mimavet naf'sham v'chayatam ladever his'gir
[51] vayach kol b'chor b'mitz'rayim reishit onim b'aholei cham
[52] vayasa katzon amo vay'nahageim ka'eider bamid'bar
[53] vayan'cheim lavetach v'lo fachadu v'et oy'veihem kisah hayam
[54] vay'vi'eim el g'vul kad'sho har zeh kan'tah y'mino
[55] vay'garesh mip'neihem goyim vayapileim b'chevel nachalah vayash'kein b'aholeihem shiv'tei yis'ra'eil
[56] vay'nasu vayam'ru et elohim el'yon v'eidotav lo shamaru
[57] vayisogu vayiv'g'du ka'avotam neh'p'chu k'keshet r'miyah
[58] vayach'isuhu b'vamotam uvif'sileihem yak'ni'u hu
[59] shama elohim vayit'abar vayim'as m'od b'yis'ra'eil
[60] vayitosh mish'kan shilo ohel shikein ba'adam
[61] vayitein lash'vi uzo v'tif'ar'to v'yad tzar
[62] vayas'geir lacherev amo uv'nachalato hit'abar
[63] bachurav ach'lah esh uv'tulotav lo hulalu
[64] kohanav bacherev nafalu v'al'm'notav lo tiv'kenah

[65] vayikatz k'yashein adonai k'gibor mit'ronein miyayin
[66] vayach tzarav achor cher'pat olam natan lamo
[67] vayim'as b'ohel yoseif uv'sheivet ef'rayim lo vachar
[68] vayiv'char et sheivet y'hudah et har tziyon asher aheiv
[69] vayiven k'mo ramim mik'dasho k'eretz y'sadah l'olam
[70] vayiv'char b'david av'do vayikacheihu mimich'l'ot tzon
[71] mei'achar alot hevi'u lir'ot b'ya'akov amo uv'yis'ra'eil nachal'to
[72] vayir'eim k'tom l'vavo uvit'vunot kapav yan'cheim

Translation:

[1] *Maschil* of Asaph. Give ear, O my people, to my teaching; incline your ears to the words of my mouth.

[2] I will open my mouth with a parable; I will utter dark sayings concerning days of old;

[3] That which we have heard and known, and our fathers have told us,

[4] We will not hide from their children, telling to the generation to come the praises of *YHVH*, and His strength, and His wondrous works that He hath done.

[5] For He established a testimony in Jacob, and appointed a law in Israel, which He commanded our fathers, that they should make them known to their children;

[6] That the generation to come might know them, even the children that should be born; who should arise and tell them to their children,

[7] That they might put their confidence in *Elohim*, and not forget the works of God, but keep His commandments;

[8] And might not be as their fathers, a stubborn and rebellious generation; a generation that set not their heart aright, and whose spirit was not stedfast with God.

[9] The children of Ephraim were as archers handling the bow, that turned back in the day of battle.

[10] They kept not the covenant of *Elohim*, and refused to walk in His law;

[11] And they forgot His doings, and His wondrous works that He had shown them.

[12] Marvellous things did He in the sight of their fathers, in the land of Egypt, in the field of Zoan.

[13] He cleaved the sea, and caused them to pass through; and He made the waters to stand as a heap.
[14] By day also He led them with a cloud, and all the night with a light of fire.
[15] He cleaved rocks in the wilderness, and gave them drink abundantly as out of the great deep.
[16] He brought streams also out of the rock, and caused waters to run down like rivers.
[17] Yet went they on still to sin against Him, to rebel against the Most High in the desert.
[18] And they tried God in their heart by asking food for their craving.
[19] Yea, they spoke against *Elohim*; they said: 'Can God prepare a table in the wilderness?
[20] Behold, He smote the rock, that waters gushed out, and streams overflowed; can He give bread also? or will He provide flesh for His people?'
[21] Therefore *YHVH* heard, and was wroth; and a fire was kindled against Jacob, and anger also went up against Israel;
[22] Because they believed not in *Elohim*, and trusted not in His salvation.
[23] And He commanded the skies above, and opened the doors of heaven;
[24] And He caused manna to rain upon them for food, and gave them of the corn of heaven.
[25] Man did eat the bread of the mighty; He sent them provisions to the full.
[26] He caused the east wind to set forth in heaven; and by His power He brought on the south wind.
[27] He caused flesh also to rain upon them as the dust, and winged fowl as the sand of the seas;
[28] And He let it fall in the midst of their camp, round about their dwellings.
[29] So they did eat, and were well filled; and He gave them that which they craved.
[30] They were not estranged from their craving, their food was yet in their mouths,

[31] When the anger of *Elohim* went up against them, and slew of the lustieth among them, and smote down the young men of Israel.
[32] For all this they sinned still, and believed not in His wondrous works.
[33] Therefore He ended their days as a breath, and their years in terror.
[34] When He slew them, then they would inquire after Him, and turn back and seek God earnestly.
[35] And they remembered that *Elohim* was their Rock, and the Most High God their redeemer.
[36] But they beguiled Him with their mouth, and lied unto Him with their tongue.
[37] For their heart was not stedfast with Him, neither were they faithful in His covenant.
[38] But He, being full of compassion, forgiveth iniquity, and destroyeth not; yea, many a time doth He turn His anger away, and doth not stir up all His wrath.
[39] So He remembered that they were but flesh, a wind that passeth away, and cometh not again.
[40] How oft did they rebel against Him in the wilderness, and grieve Him in the desert!
[41] And still again they tried God, and set bounds to the Holy One of Israel.
[42] They remembered not His hand, nor the day when He redeemed them from the adversary.
[43] How He set His signs in Egypt, and His wonders in the field of Zoan;
[44] And turned their rivers into blood, so that they could not drink their streams.
[45] He sent among them swarms of flies, which devoured them; and frogs, which destroyed them.
[46] He gave also their increase unto the caterpillar, and their labour unto the locust.
[47] He destroyed their vines with hail, and their sycamore-trees with frost.
[48] He gave over their cattle also to the hail, and their flocks to fiery bolts.

[49] He sent forth upon them the fierceness of His anger, wrath, and indignation, and trouble, a sending of messengers of evil.
[50] He levelled a path for His anger; He spared not their soul from death, but gave their life over to the pestilence;
[51] And smote all the first-born in Egypt, the first-fruits of their strength in the tents of Ham;
[52] But He made His own people to go forth like sheep, and guided them in the wilderness like a flock.
[53] And He led them safely, and they feared not; but the sea overwhelmed their enemies.
[54] And He brought them to His holy border, to the mountain, which His right hand had gotten.
[55] He drove out the nations also before them, and allotted them for an inheritance by line, and made the tribes of Israel to dwell in their tents.
[56] Yet they tried and provoked *Elohim*, the Most High, and kept not His testimonies;
[57] But turned back, and dealt treacherously like their fathers; they were turned aside like a deceitful bow.
[58] For they provoked Him with their high places, and moved Him to jealousy with their graven images.
[59] *Elohim* heard, and was wroth, and He greatly abhorred Israel;
[60] And He forsook the tabernacle of *Shiloh*, the tent which He had made to dwell among men;
[61] And delivered His strength into captivity, and His glory into the adversary's hand.
[62] He gave His people over also unto the sword; and was wroth with His inheritance.
[63] Fire devoured their young men; and their virgins had no marriage-song.
[64] Their priests fell by the sword; and their widows made no lamentation.
[65] Then *Adonai* awaked as one asleep, like a mighty man recovering from wine.
[66] And He smote His adversaries backward; He put upon them a perpetual reproach.
[67] Moreover He abhorred the tent of Joseph, and chose not the tribe of Ephraim;

[68] But chose the tribe of Judah, the mount Zion which He loved.
[69] And He built His sanctuary like the heights, like the earth which He hath founded for ever.
[70] He chose David also His servant, and took him from the sheepfolds;
[71] From following the ewes that give suck He brought him, to be shepherd over Jacob His people, and Israel His inheritance.
[72] So he shepherded them according to the integrity of his heart; and lead them by the skilfulness of his hands.

A single verse from *Psalm 78* holds an important position in Jewish worship. In this regard, the thirteen words of *Psalm 78:38* reading והוא רחום יכפר עון ולא ישחית והרבה להשיב אפו ולא יעיר כל חמתו (*v'hu rachumn y'chapeir avon v'lo yash'chit v'hir'bah l'hashiv apo v'lo ya'ir kol chamato*—"But He, being full of compassion, forgiveth iniquity, and destroyeth not; yea, many a time doth He turn His anger away, and doth not stir up all His wrath"), is recited during the מלקות (*Mal'kot*—"flogging") practice, an ancient ritual flagellation of male worshippers on *Erev Yom Kippur* (Eve of the Day of Atonement).[1] Readers probably recall this verse being mentioned earlier in a prayer-incantation which is recited with *Psalm 51* by individuals who wish to confess sins, transgressions, or, as said, who "indulged in fornication."

Delineated "farcical" by Solomon Maimon, the eighteenth century philosopher,[2] the *Mal'kot* procedure is not commonly practised in modern-day Judaism, even though it is still enacted in some ultra-orthodox Jewish communities prior to the High Days of Penitence, i.e. *Yom Kippur*, as an atonement for transgressions which the worshipper may or may not have committed throughout the year, and which are believed to be deserving of a flogging.[3] However, the lashing comprises thirty-nine symbolical stripes with a narrow leather strap, which can hardly be defined anything more than a light touching of the back of the kneeling worshipper, even though I have seen the *Mal'kot* being delivered in one instance with some intensity which must have stung the recipient somewhat. In this regard, the association of *Psalm 78:38* pertains to this verse being recited three times during the flogging procedure. As said, the verse comprises thirteen words, hence the recitation of it three times would ensure that exactly thirty-nine lashings are given without the necessity to count. In this regard, it appears that uttering one word per blow is customary in Moroccan tradition,[4] and it was reported that amongst the Bukhara Jews the *Mal'kot* procedure was enacted by tying worshippers to a lashing post in the synagogue. Following this action, they would purify themselves in a מקוה (*Mik'veh*—"ritual bath").[5]

We are informed that *Psalm 78* is employed in Jewish Magic to find grace and favour in the eyes of authorities,[6] or, according to one source, to find "favour at court."[7] In terms of the latter statement, Godfrey Selig noted in his German/English translations of the *Shimmush Tehillim* that "whosoever prays the 78th Psalm earnestly and often, will be beloved and respected by kings and princes and will receive favour from them."[8] However, in a variant recension of the *Shimmush Tehillim* the current psalm is recommended to individuals who are seeking to be saved from evil spells, as well as to experience miracles, and an overflow of abundance in their lives. In this regard, the practitioner is instructed to recite the current psalm twenty-four times, each time conjointly with the following prayer-incantation:

יהי רצון מלפניך יהוה אלהים חיים רחום
וחנון קרוב לכל קוראיו קראתיך ממצר העליני
והצילני מן הדבר הרע הזה ועשה לי נסים ונפלאות
כאשר עשית לישראל במצרים ולמרדכי ואסתר
בשושן הבירה פלא ונסים כן עשה עמי פלא
ונסים בעת הזה בשם יהוה אלהים חיים רחום
וחנון אמן אמן סלה

Transliteration:

Y'hi ratzon mil'fanecha YHVH Elohim Chayim Rachum v'Chanun karov l'chol kor'av kar'aticha mimeitzar ha'aleini v'hatzileini min hadavar hara hazeh v'aseih li nisim v'nifla'ot k'asher asita l'yis'ra'eil b'mitz'rayim ul'mor'd'chai v'es'ter b'shushan habirah pele v'nisim kein aseih imi pele

> v'nisim b'eit hazeh b'shem YHVH Elohim Chayim Rachum v'Chanun Omein Omein Selah

Translation:
> May it be your will, *YHVH Elohim Chayim Rachum v'Chanun* ["*YHVH* God of Life Merciful and Gracious"], who is near to all who call him. I called you out of distress. Bring me out, deliver me from this evil word, and prepare miracles and wonders for me. As you have prepared wonders and miracles for Israel in Egypt, and for Mordechai and Esther in Susa Castle, so prepare miracles and wonders for me at this time. In the name *YHVH Elohim Chayim Rachum v'Chanun Amen Amen Selah*.[9]

The "wonders and miracles for Israel in Egypt, and for Mordechai and Esther in Susa Castle," respectively pertain to the biblical sagas of the incidents which resulted in the exodus of the Israelites from Egypt, and the saving of queen Esther and the nation of Israel from the machinations of the evil Hamman.

Different magical applications are listed in other recensions of the *Shimmush Tehillim*, some of them addressing *Psalms 78, 79* and *80* conjointly. In this regard, the said text maintains that those who are being harassed on a journey, and are shoved around by "haters," should recite these three psalms, which will result in them seeing "great miracles."[10] In yet a different recension of the said text, the seventy-eighth Psalm is recommended to those who are in captivity. In this regard, the psalm is written down conjointly with the following prayer-incantation:

> יהי רצון מלפניך יהוה אלהי שתצילני מן
> התפיסה הזאת אשר אני נמסר בתוכה והוציאני
> חפשי ממנה לשלום וחיים כחפצי ורצוני בעגלא
> ובזמן קריב אמן אמן אמן סלה סלה סלה

Transliteration:
> Y'hi ratzon mil'fanecha YHVH elohai sh'tatzileini min hat'fisah hazot asher ani nim'sar b'tochah v'hotzi'eini chof'shi mimenah l'shalom v'chayim k'chef'tzi ur'tzoni b'agala uviz'man kariv omein omein omein selah selah selah.

Translation:

> May it be your will *YHVH* my God, that you save me from this captivity into which I have been delivered. Lead me out of it as a free person, to peace and life, as it is my desire and my will, very speedily and shortly. *Amen Amen Amen Selah Selah Selah.*[11]

The same recension also recommends *Psalm 78* "against a one-day fever," and for epileptics.[12] In this regard, the psalm is written conjointly with the following prayer-incantation, which is afterwards suspended around the neck of the sick individual:

אסותא משמיא תהוי ל'[....name of recipient....]
רפואה שלימה ותלך לו הרוח אשר נכנסה בו
ולא תוכל עוד לישאר עליו ולא להזיקו ולא
ליגע בו עוד ולא במאתיים וארבעים ושמונה
איבריו בשם יהו יהו יהו יְהוָה יהיה הדבר
הזה בעגלא ובזמן קריב

Transliteration:

> *Asuta mish'maya tahavei l'*[...name of recipient...] *r'fu'ah sh'leimah v'teilech lo haru'ach asher nich'nusah bo v'lo tuchal od lisha'er alav v'lo l'haziko v'lo liga bo od v'lo b'matayim v'ar'ba'im ush'monah eiverav b'shem Yaho Yaho Yaho Y'huvuh yih'yeh hadavar hazeh b'agala uviz'man kariv*

Translation:

> Remedy from heaven. There shall be complete healing for [....name of recipient....]. The spirit that has entered into him shall depart from him, and he shall no longer remain with him, unable to harm him, no longer able to strike him down, and not able to strike down his 248 limbs. In the name *Yahu Yahu Yahu Y'huvuh*, this shall be the word, speedily and shortly.

The same source includes the following prayer-incantation to be prepared as an amulet for an epileptic:

תרחיק ממנו כל שדין וכל רוחין בישין ולילין
וכל דברים רעים שמריעין לבני אדם וכל מיני
פורענות המתרגשות בעולם אש ומים ואיבה
ומגיפה ודבר וחרב ורעב וכל אויבים המבקשים
רעתי יהיו איבריהם גרועים ומקוטעים ונשברים
ונחתכים ונתכים ומושלכים ארצה וכל מלכי
צבאות מעלה יוציאו וידחפו הרוח אשר שרתה
עליו וינגפו אותו בענין שישאר חי ובריא כאשר
היה בראשונה בשם יהו יהו יהו יְהֹוָה אמן אמן
אמן סלה סלה סלה

Transliteration:

Tar'chik mimenu kol shedin v'chol ruchin bishin v'lilin v'chol d'varim ra'im shemar'in liv'nei adam v'chol minei pur'anut hamit'rag'shot ba'olam esh umayim v'eivah umageifah v'dever v'cherev v'ra'av v'chol oy'vim ham'vak'shim ra'ati yih'yu eivareihem g'ru'im um'kuta'im v'nish'barim v'nich'tachim v'nit'chim umush'lachim ar'tzah v'chol mal'chei tz'va'ot ma'alah yotzi'u v'yidach'fu haru'ach asher shar'tah alav v'yinag'fu oto b'in'yan sheyish'er chai ubari k'asher hayah barishonah b'shem Yahu Yahu Yahu Y'huvuh Omein Omein Omein Selah Selah Selah.

Translation:

You shall remove from him all Demons, all evil Spirits and Lilits, all evil Things that do evil to humankind, all kinds of disasters that shake the world, fire and water and hostility and pestilence and plague and drought and famine, and all enemies who desire my doom. Their limbs shall be stripped and fragmented and broken and cut and dissolved, and cast to the earth. All the Kings of the upper Hosts shall come forth, and cast away the Spirit that ministered over him. They should strike him in this matter, so that the person may remain alive and well, as he has been before. In the name *Yahu Yahu Yahu Y'huvuh Amen Amen Amen Selah Selah Selah.*[14]

Amongst the magical practices found in the Cairo Geniza is a procedure, said to be "of 'proven' effectiveness,"[15] in which *Psalm 78* is employed to ascertain the identity of a thief from a list of suspects. Similarly to the application of *Psalm 16* listed in the *Shimmush Tehillim* for the same purpose, the names of the suspects are written on slips of paper, each of which are located separately inside small balls of clay, the shape and size of the latter said to be like nuts.[16] Afterwards the balls are placed inside a vessel full of water, and the seventy-eighth Psalm recited over the container, following which it is claimed "you will see the ball that has the name of the thief written on it split into two or three and the writing will be floating on the surface of the water."[17] The thief can then be arrested, and this is delineated "a great wonder," since only the ball of clay comprising the real identity of the thief will split.[18]

Besides the listed applications, the seventy-eighth Psalm is employed in the oft-mentioned "unofficial" sources, to encourage compassion of lenders towards debtors, and to halt wars. In this regard, it is worth noting that the following Divine Name construct, which was created by simply writing *Psalm 78:9* in reverse, is said to have the power "to transform a hater into a lover":

בְּרַק מֹויב וּכְפָה
תְשֶׁק יֶמוּר יְקָשׁוֹנ
מִירְפָא יְנֵב

It has been indicated that the stated outcome can be achieved by writing this Divine Name construct on deerskin parchment, which is afterwards carried on the person of the one requiring the fulfilment of that magical intention.[19]

It would seem *Psalm 78* is not extensively employed in Christian Magic, and it appears to have been recited mainly against enemies. In this regard, *"Le Livre d'Or"* informs anyone who has an enemy to write this psalm with certain magical characters inside "a bronze drinking vessel." Considering that the seventy-eighth Psalm comprises seventy-two verses, the "drinking vessel" would need to be extraordinarily large. Be that as it may, the vessel is afterwards filled with clean water, and the psalm recited seven times over it. The procedure is completed by pouring out the water at the front door of the enemy.²⁰ There is no indication as to what this action is meant to achieve.

PSALM 79

[1] מזמור לאסף אלהים באו גוים בנחלתך טמאו את היכל קדשך שמו את ירושלם לעיים
[2] נתנו את נבלת עבדיך מאכל לעוף השמים בשר חסידיך לחיתו ארץ
[3] שפכו דמם כמים סביבות ירושלם ואין קובר
[4] היינו חרפה לשכנינו לעג וקלס לסביבותינו
[5] עד מה יְהוָֹהאֲדֹנָי תאנף לנצח תבער כמו אש קנאתך
[6] שפך חמתך על הגוים אשר לא ידעוך ועל ממלכות אשר בשמך לא קראו
[7] כי אכל את יעקב ואת נוהו השמו
[8] אל תזכר לנו עונת ראשנים מהר יקדמונו רחמיך כי דלונו מאד
[9] עזרנו אלהי ישענו על דבר כבוד שמך והצילנו וכפר על חטאתינו למען שמך
[10] למה יאמרו הגוים איה אלהיהם יודע בגוים לעינינו נקמת דם עבדיך השפוך
[11] תבוא לפניך אנקת אסיר כגדל זרועך הותר בני תמותה
[12] והשב לשכנינו שבעתים אל חיקם חרפתם אשר חרפוך אדני
[13] ואנחנו עמך וצאן מרעיתך נודה לך לעולם לדור ודר נספר תהלתך

Transliteration:

[1] *miz'mor l'asaf elohim ba'u goyim b'nachalatecha tim'u et heichal kad'shecha samu et y'rushalam l'iyim*
[2] *nat'nu et niv'lat avadecha ma'achol l'of hashamayim b'sar chasidecha l'chaito aretz*
[3] *shaf'chu damam kamayim s'vivot y'rushalam v'ein koveir*
[4] *hayinu cher'pah lish'cheineinu la'ag vakeles lis'vivoteinu*
[5] *ad mah YHVH te'enaf lanetzach tiv'ar k'mo esh kin'atecha*

[6] *sh'foch chamat'cha el hagoyim asher lo y'da'ucha v'al mam'lochot asher b'shim'cha lo kara'u*
[7] *ki achal et ya'akov v'et naveihu heishamu*
[8] *al tiz'kar lanu avonot rishonim maheir y'kad'munu rachamecha ki dalonu m'od*
[9] *az'reinu elohei yish'einu al d'var k'vod sh'mecha v'hatzileinu v'chapeir al chatoteinu l'ma'an sh'mecha*
[10] *lamah yom'ru hagoyim ayeih eloheihem yivada bagoyim l'eineinu nik'mat dam avadecha hashafuch*
[11] *tavo l'fanecha en'kat asir k'godel z'ro'acha hoteir b'nei t'mutah*
[12] *v'hasheiv lish'cheineinu shiv'atayim el cheikam cher'patam asher cheir'fucha adonai*
[13] *va'anach'nu am'cha v'tzon mar'itecha nodeh l'cha l'olam l'dor vador n'sapeir t'hilatecha*

Translation:

[1] A Psalm of *Asaf. Elohim*, the heathen are come into Thine inheritance; they have defiled Thy holy temple; they have made Jerusalem into heaps.

[2] They have given the dead bodies of Thy servants to be food unto the fowls of the heaven, the flesh of Thy saints unto the beasts of the earth.

[3] They have shed their blood like water round about Jerusalem, with none to bury them.

[4] We are become a taunt to our neighbours, a scorn and derision to them that are round about us.

[5] How long *YHVH*, wilt Thou be angry for ever? How long will Thy jealousy burn like fire?

[6] Pour out Thy wrath upon the nations that know Thee not, and upon the kingdoms that call not upon Thy name.

[7] For they have devoured Jacob, and laid waste his habitation.

[8] Remember not against us the iniquities of our forefathers; let Thy compassions speedily come to meet us; for we are brought very low.

[9] Help us, O God of our salvation, for the sake of the glory of Thy name; and deliver us, and forgive our sins, for Thy name's sake.

[10] Wherefore should the nations say: 'Where is their God?' Let the avenging of Thy servants' blood that is shed be made known among the nations in our sight.
[11] Let the groaning of the prisoner come before Thee; according to the greatness of Thy power set free those that are appointed to death;
[12] And render unto our neighbours sevenfold into their bosom their reproach, wherewith they have reproached Thee *Adonai*.
[13] So we that are Thy people and the flock of Thy pasture will give Thee thanks for ever; we will tell of Thy praise to all generations.

Psalm 79 is one of the psalms recited for the Land of Israel.[1] It is employed in Jewish Magic to defeat or subjugate "haters,"[2] or "to be rid of one's foes."[3] Whilst the magical use of this psalm is not listed in all the standard published versions of the *Shimmush Tehillim*, in those in which it does appear, this psalm is said to be good to enunciate to kill "haters" (enemies).[4] In this regard, Godfrey Selig noted in his German/English translations of this text, "the frequent prayer of the 79th Psalm, it is said, is fatal to enemies and opponents."[5] In my personal opinion the latter is a most abhorrent application of the current psalm, and I am loathe to even mention it in this tome. Since all of us are part of One Great Consciousness called "I Am," it is clear that whatever we do unto others, we are doing directly unto ourselves, and whatever we do unto the least living thing on this planet, we are doing directly unto the Divine One who is manifested through all life. In this regard, it is the cultivated sense of separateness which inspired the lack of respect humans have for life on this planet, and this is in my estimation the ultimate "sin against the Eternal Living Spirit." Keeping this in mind, it is understandable that in a variant recension of the *Shimmush Tehillim*, the current psalm is in fact recited with the following prayer-incantation, in order "to avoid becoming a sinner":

אל נא הושיעה נא סלח נא כפר נא שאנא
לעונותי ולאשמותי ולחטעתי והצילני מחטוא
אליך לא היום ולא לעולם ומה שחטאתי

לפניך מרוק ברחמיך הרבים אבל לא על
ידי יסורין יהיו לרצון אמרי פי והגיון לבי
לפניך יהוה צורי וגאלי (Ps 19:15)

Transliteration:

> El Na Hoshi'ah Na S'lach Na kaper na sa'na la'avonotai v'la'ash'motai v'lachatapai v'hatzileini meichato eilecha lo hayom v'lo l'olam omah shechatati l'fanecha m'rok b'rachamecha harabim aval lo al yadei y'surin yih'yu l'ratzon im'rei fi v'heg'yon libi l'fanecha YHVH tzuri v'go'ali. (Ps 19:15)

Translation:

> El Na Hoshi'ah Na SLH N' KPR N' ("God please redeem, please forgive, please atone, please"), forgive my transgressions, my guilt, and my sins. Save me from sinning against you, whether today or at some point. And that which I have sinned before you, wipe away with your great mercy, but not by torment. *Let the words of my mouth and the meditation of my heart be acceptable before Thee YHVH, my Rock, and my Redeemer. (Ps 19:15)*[6]

The same source maintains the seventy-ninth Psalm should be recited with the following prayer-incantation "for a woman whose pregnancy is lost," i.e. who suffered a miscarriage:

יהי רצון מלפניך יהוה אלהי ואלהי אבותי
אלהי אברהם אלהי יצחק ואלהי יעקב
שתרחם על האשה הזאת בהריונה ותפתח
רחמה ותהר ותלד בן ולא תפסוק מלדת
בשם **אל נא** אמן אמן אמן סלה סלה סלה

Transliteration:

> Y'hi ratzon mil'fanecha YHVH elohai veilohei avotai elohei Avraham elohei Yitz'chak v'elohei Ya'akov shet'rachem al ha'ishah hazot b'her'yonah v'tif'tach rachamah v'taher v'teiled ben v'lo tif'sok miledet b'shem El Na omein omein omein selah selah selah.

Translation:
> May it be your will, Lord my God and God of my fathers, God of Abraham, God of Isaac and God of Jacob, that you have mercy on this woman in her pregnancy. You should open her womb, and she shall become pregnant, bear a son, and not stop giving birth anymore. In the name *El Na* ("God Please"). *Amen Amen Amen. Selah Selah Selah.*[7]

It should be noted that the current psalm is not only employed against enemies, but also against oppressors, and to preclude armies from looting. It is also enunciated for the protection of vines and vineyards.

In Christian Magic *Psalm 79* is recommended for recitation when the practitioner is observing "someone swearing falsely."[8] Aside from this, we are informed in *"Le Livre d'Or"* that the current psalm is employed to "be received honourably." In this regard, the psalm is recited seven times over rose oil. Following this action, a new tablet comprising a set of magical characters is washed in, and the face of the practitioner anointed with this substance.[9]

PSALM 80

[1] לַמְנַצֵּחַ אֶל שֹׁשַׁנִּים עֵדוּת לְאָסָף מִזְמוֹר
[2] רֹעֵה יִשְׂרָאֵל הַאֲזִינָה נֹהֵג כַּצֹּאן יוֹסֵף יֹשֵׁב הַכְּרוּבִים הוֹפִיעָה
[3] לִפְנֵי אֶפְרַיִם וּבִנְיָמִן וּמְנַשֶּׁה עוֹרְרָה אֶת גְּבוּרָתֶךָ וּלְכָה לִישֻׁעָתָה לָּנוּ
[4] אֱלֹהִים הֲשִׁיבֵנוּ וְהָאֵר פָּנֶיךָ וְנִוָּשֵׁעָה
[5] יְהֹוָהאהדונהי אֱלֹהִים צְבָאוֹת עַד מָתַי עָשַׁנְתָּ בִּתְפִלַּת עַמֶּךָ
[6] הֶאֱכַלְתָּם לֶחֶם דִּמְעָה וַתַּשְׁקֵמוֹ בִּדְמָעוֹת שָׁלִישׁ
[7] תְּשִׂימֵנוּ מָדוֹן לִשְׁכֵנֵינוּ וְאֹיְבֵינוּ יִלְעֲגוּ לָמוֹ
[8] אֱלֹהִים צְבָאוֹת הֲשִׁיבֵנוּ וְהָאֵר פָּנֶיךָ וְנִוָּשֵׁעָה
[9] גֶּפֶן מִמִּצְרַיִם תַּסִּיעַ תְּגָרֵשׁ גּוֹיִם וַתִּטָּעֶהָ
[10] פִּנִּיתָ לְפָנֶיהָ וַתַּשְׁרֵשׁ שָׁרָשֶׁיהָ וַתְּמַלֵּא אָרֶץ
[11] כָּסּוּ הָרִים צִלָּהּ וַעֲנָפֶיהָ אַרְזֵי אֵל
[12] תְּשַׁלַּח קְצִירֶהָ עַד יָם וְאֶל נָהָר יוֹנְקוֹתֶיהָ
[13] לָמָּה פָּרַצְתָּ גְדֵרֶיהָ וְאָרוּהָ כָּל עֹבְרֵי דָרֶךְ
[14] יְכַרְסְמֶנָּה חֲזִיר מִיָּעַר וְזִיז שָׂדַי יִרְעֶנָּה
[15] אֱלֹהִים צְבָאוֹת שׁוּב נָא הַבֵּט מִשָּׁמַיִם וּרְאֵה וּפְקֹד גֶּפֶן זֹאת
[16] וְכַנָּה אֲשֶׁר נָטְעָה יְמִינֶךָ וְעַל בֵּן אִמַּצְתָּה לָּךְ
[17] שְׂרֻפָה בָאֵשׁ כְּסוּחָה מִגַּעֲרַת פָּנֶיךָ יֹאבֵדוּ
[18] תְּהִי יָדְךָ עַל אִישׁ יְמִינֶךָ עַל בֶּן אָדָם אִמַּצְתָּ לָּךְ
[19] וְלֹא נָסוֹג מִמֶּךָּ תְּחַיֵּנוּ וּבְשִׁמְךָ נִקְרָא
[20] יְהֹוָהאהדונהי אֱלֹהִים צְבָאוֹת הֲשִׁיבֵנוּ הָאֵר פָּנֶיךָ וְנִוָּשֵׁעָה

Transliteration:
[1] *lam'natzei'ach el shoshanim eidut l'asaf miz'mor*
[2] *ro'eih yis'ra'eil ha'azinah noheig katzon yoseif yosheiv hak'ruvim hofi'ah*
[3] *lif'nei ef'rayim uvin'yamin um'nasheh or'rah et gevuratecha ul'chah lishu'atah lanu*
[4] *elohim hashiveinu v'ha'eir panecha v'nivashei'ah*
[5] *YHVH elohim tz'va'ot ad matai ashan'ta bit'filat amecha*

[6] *he'echal'tam lechem dim'ah v'tash'keimo bid'ma'ot shalish*
[7] *tesimenu madon lish'cheneinu v'oiveinu yil'agulamo*
[8] *elohim tz'va'ot hashiveinu v'ha'eir panecha v'nivashei'ah*
[9] *gefen mimitz'rayim tasi'a t'garesih goyim vatita'eha*
[10] *pinita l'faneha vatash'reish sharashehah vat'malei aretz*
[11] *kasu harim tzilah va'anafeha ar'zei el*
[12] *t'shalach k'tzireha ad yam v'el nahar yon'koteha*
[13] *lamah paratz'ta g'deireha v'aruha kol ov'rei darech*
[14] *y'char's'menah chazir miya'ar v'ziz sadai yir'enah*
[15] *elohim tz'va'ot shuv na habeit mishamayim ur'eih uf'kod gefen zot*
[16] *v'chanah asher nat'ah y'minecha v'al bein imatz'tah lach*
[17] *serufah va'esh k'suchah miga'arat panecha yoveidu*
[18] *t'hi yad'cha al ish y'minecha al ben adam imatz'ta lach*
[19] *v'lo nasog mimeka t'chayeinu uv'shim'cha nik'ra*
[20] *YHVH elohim tz'va'ot hashiveinu ha'eir panecha v'nivashei'ah*

Translation:

[1] For the Leader; upon *Shoshannim*. A testimony. A Psalm of Asaph.

[2] Give ear, O Shepherd of Israel, Thou that leadest Joseph like a flock; Thou that art enthroned upon the cherubim, shine forth.

[3] Before Ephraim and Benjamin and Manasseh, stir up Thy might, and come to save us.

[4] *Elohim*, restore us; and cause Thy face to shine, and we shall be saved.

[5] *YHVH Elohim* of hosts, how long wilt Thou be angry against the prayer of Thy people?

[6] Thou hast fed them with the bread of tears, and given them tears to drink in large measure.

[7] Thou makest us a strife unto our neighbours; and our enemies mock as they please.

[8] *Elohim*, restore us; and cause Thy face to shine, and we shall be saved.

[9] Thou didst pluck up a vine out of Egypt; Thou didst drive out the nations, and didst plant it.
[10] Thou didst clear a place before it, and it took deep root, and filled the land.
[11] The mountains were covered with the shadow of it, and the mighty cedars with the boughs thereof.
[12] She sent out her branches unto the sea, and her shoots unto the River.
[13] Why hast Thou broken down her fences, so that all they that pass by the way do pluck her?
[14] The boar out of the wood doth ravage it, that which moveth in the field feedeth on it.
[15] *Elohim* of hosts, return, we beseech Thee; look from heaven, and behold, and be mindful of this vine,
[16] And of the stock which Thy right hand hath planted, and the branch that Thou madest strong for Thyself.
[17] It is burned with fire, it is cut down; they perish at the rebuke of Thy countenance.
[18] Let Thy hand be upon the man of Thy right hand, upon the son of man whom Thou madest strong for Thyself.
[19] So shall we not turn back from Thee; quicken Thou us, and we will call upon Thy name.
[20] *YHVH Elohim* of hosts, restore us; cause Thy face to shine, and we shall be saved.

Psalm 80 is, like the previous psalm, one of a group of psalms recited for the Land of Israel.[1] The current psalm as well as the following one, are recited in Jewish Magic for protection against engaging in עבודת אלילים (*Avodat Elilim*—"idolatry"),[2] and/or עבודה זרה (*Avodah Zarah*—"heresy").[3] In this regard, Godfrey Selig noted in his German/English translations of the *Shimmush Tehillim* that "the constant and industrious prayer of 80th and 81st Psalms is said to be a happy means of saving men from falling into unbelief and saves them also from other errors."[4]

In a variant recension of the *Shimmush Tehillim* we are informed that the current psalm is "for a person who is expelled from his land, from his house, from his inheritance, and from his wife, by a king, prince or judge who drove him out, and desiring that he should ask for clemency."⁵ In this regard, the individual is instructed to visit a synagogue early for morning prayers, doing this every day for thirty days, and that he should pray this psalm twice a day, each time adding a prayer-incantation reading:

יהי רצון מלפניך יהוה אלהי ואלהי אבותי
שתשוב מחמתך ותרחם עלי ותסלח לעוני
וחטאתי וקבל תשובתי כשם שקבלת תשובתו
של מנשה בן חזקיהו מלך יהודה וכשם
שהשיבותו למלכותו כבראשונה כן יהי רצון
מִלְפניך יהוה אלהי שתשיבני למקומי ולביתי
ולאשתי ובני ואשמח עמהם בהם ישמחו עמי
בשמך הנקי והטהור אה אה מץ חי חי
השיבנו יהוה אליך ונשובה חדש ימינו כקדם
(Lamentations 5:21) אמן אמן אמן סלה סלה
סלה

Transliteration:

Y'hi ratzon mil'fanecha YHVH elohai veilohei avotai shetashuv m'chamat'cha ut'racheim alai v'tis'lach la'avonai v'chatatai v'kabel t'shuvati k'sheim shekibal'ta t'shuvato shel m'nasheh ben chiz'kiyahu melech y'hudah uk'sheim shehishivuto l'mal'chuto k'barishonah kein y'hi ratzon mil'fanecha YHVH elohai shetashiveini lim'komi ul'beiti v'l'ish'ti ubanai v'es'mach imahem b'heim yish'm'chu imi b'shim'cha hanaki v'hatahor Aha Aha Matz Chai Chai hashiveinu YHVH eilecha v'nashuvah chadeish yameinu k'kedem (Lamentations 5:21) omein omein omein selah selah selah.

Translation:

May it be your will *YHVH*, my God and God of my fathers, that you turn from your anger. You shall have mercy on me, and forgive my offenses and sins. Accept my repentance as you accepted the penance of Manasseh ben Hezekiah king of Judah. And just as they let him return to his kingdom as before, so may it be your will, Lord my God, that you let me return to my place, to my house, my wife and my children. I will rejoice with them and they will rejoice with me. In your refined and pure Name *Aha Aha Matz Chai Chai, turn Thou us unto Thee YHVH, and we shall be turned; renew our days as of old.* (Lamentations 5:21) Amen Amen Amen Selah Selah Selah.[6]

Whilst considering this application of the eightieth Psalm, it is worth keeping in mind, that three verbatim verses of this psalm, pertain directly to the longing for the restoration of home and hearth expressed in this prayer-incantation. In this regard, the heartfelt sentiment articulated in *Psalm 80:4, 8, and 20* is "restore us; cause Thy face to shine, and we shall be saved." Interestingly enough, in "Practical Kabbalah" the eighty-eight Hebrew glyphs comprising these three verses, were combined with the two glyphs of the Divine Name יָהּ (*Yah*), in order to formulate the following Divine Name construct termed שֵׁם הַשָׂרָף (*Shem Ha-Saraf*—"Name of the Seraf"):[7]

אַפֿ צְפֿ לֹךְ	לֵנְ בֵנְ הֵא	הֵי אִי יר
יךָ וךָ מפָֿ	מְוְ תְןְ צֵנְ	הַנ הַנ בְי
שְׁוְ שְׁוְ אֹךְ	יֵשׁ יֵשׁ וְוְ	בְעָ בֵעָ תנ
נֵה נֵה הֵןְ	וְאָ וִי שֵׁשׁ	וְל וְהָ יֵעָ
הָה הָו בָה	אִי אָהָ נֵיְ	רמ רָא וֹה

This letter square was constructed by simply copying the eighty-eight letters comprising the said three verses in a single line, with the addition of the two glyphs of the Divine Name יָהּ (*Yah*) as a suffix, in order to arrive at the necessary ninety glyphs comprising the letter square. The glyphs are then divided into six groups of fifteen letters each. The first set of fifteen glyphs comprise the rightmost position in the fifteen blocks, i.e. reading right to left from the topmost right block to the one leftmost bottom. The second fifteen are located in exact order left, adjacent to the first fifteen, and the third group of fifteen letters in turn form the opening letters of the central fifteen bi-letter combinations, whilst the fourth group of fifteen are located adjacent to the third set. The same procedure is applied in the location of the entire set of ninety-glyphs, at the conclusion of which we arrive at the mentioned "Name of the *Saraf*." Each of the fifteen six-letter combinations is said to reference the "secret" of the six wings, as it were, trademark of the "spirit intelligences" within the angelic hierarchy of the *Serafim*.[8]

It should be noted that *Psalm 80:20* is directly related to מהש (*Mahash*), the fifth portion of the "*Shem Vayisa Vayet*,"[9] and we have earlier cited this tri-letter combination in the application of *Psalm 30* for healing purposes. In this regard, the statement accompanying this application of the psalm equally included a reference to the biblical Hezekiah king of Judah.[10] Whilst on the subject of the fifth tri-letter portion of the "Name of Seventy-two Names," I have stated elsewhere that מהש (*Mahash*) is employed in conjunction with the Divine Name אל שדי (*El Shadai*) "during times of trouble and danger."[11] I also noted that "since the Name *Mahash* has the power to safeguard, it is beneficial to mention it when leaving a city in times of great danger."[12]

Other than the magical applications listed thus far, the eightieth Psalm is recited for musicians, and orators should note that this psalm is also said to aid in acquiring the gift of language. As noted, it supports the return of home and hearth to those who suffer exile, and in this regard, the current psalm is enunciated to preclude individuals from being harrassed and manhandled on journeys, and is also recited as a prayer to the Divine One to aid His people. It is further enunciated against difficult people, and, whilst it is utilised to protect against indulging in idolatry, it is also said to save friends from errors. Lastly, we are informed that it is employed for meditations, i.e. to maintain the appropriate mindset, etc.

In Christian Magic *Psalm 80* is listed in the Byzantine magical manuscripts to be good "to make a demon flee from your speech."[13] In this regard, the current psalm is written down, and carried on the person of the one seeking this magical benefit,[14] and it is affirmed "the demons will be made to flee."[15] Other than this application, *"Le Livre d'Or"* maintains that a woman "will be chaste," if the psalm is written with certain magical characters on "a new cooking pot," which is afterwards filled with clean water, the psalm enunciated seven times over it, and the woman washed with the water.[16]

PSALM 81

[1] למנצח על הגתית לאסף
[2] הרנינו לאלהים עוזנו הריעו לאלהי יעקב
[3] שאו זמרה ותנו תף כנור נעים עם נבל
[4] תקעו בחדש שופר בכסה ליום חגנו
[5] כי חק לישראל הוא משפט לאלהי יעקב
[6] עדות ביהוסף שמו בצאתו על ארץ מצרים שפת לא ידעתי אשמע
[7] הסירותי מסבל שכמו כפיו מדוד תעברנה
[8] בצרה קראת ואחלצך אענך בסתר רעם אבחנך על מי מריבה סלה
[9] שמע עמי ואעידה בך ישראל אם תשמע לי
[10] לא יהיה בך אל זר ולא תשתחוה לאל נכר
[11] אנכי יְהוָֹה‎אֲדֹנָי אלהיך המעלך מארץ מצרים הרחב פיך ואמלאהו
[12] ולא שמע עמי לקולי וישראל לא אבה לי
[13] ואשלחהו בשרירות לבם ילכו במועצותיהם
[14] לו עמי שמע לי ישראל בדרכי יהלכו
[15] כמעט אויביהם אכניע ועל צריהם אשיב ידי
[16] משנאי יְהוָֹה‎אֲדֹנָי יכחשו לו ויהי עתם לעולם
[17] ויאכילהו מחלב חטה ומצור דבש אשביעך

Transliteration:
[1] *lam'natzei'ach al hagitit l'asaf*
[2] *har'ninu leilohim uzeinu hari'u leilohei ya'akov*
[3] *s'u zim'ra ut'nu tof kinor na'im im navel*
[4] *tik'u vachodesh shofar bakeiseh l'yom chageinu*
[5] *ki chok l'yis'ra'eil hu mish'pat leilohei ya'akov*
[6] *edut bihoseif samo b'tzeito al eretz mitz'rayim s'fat lo yada'ti esh'mah*
[7] *hasiroti miseivel shich'mo kapav midud ta'avo'rnah*
[8] *batzarah karata va'achal'tzeka e'en'cha b'seiter ra'am ev'chan'cha al mei m'rivah selah*
[9] *sh'ma ami v'a'idah bach yis'ra'eil im tish'ma li*
[10] *lo yih'yeh v'cha el zar v'lo tish'tachaveh l'el neichar*

[11] *anochi YHVH elohecha hama'al'cha mei'eretz mitz'rayim har'chev picha va'amal'eihu*
[12] *v'lo shama ami l'koli v'yis'ra'eil lo avah li*
[13] *va'ashal'cheihu bish'rirut libam yeil'chu b'mo'atzoteihem*
[14] *lu ami shomei'a li yis'ra'eil bid'rachai y'haleichu*
[15] *kim'at oy'veihem achni'a v'al tzareihem ashiv yadi*
[16] *m'san'ei YHVH y'chachashu lo vihi itam l'olam*
[17] *vaya'achileihu meicheilev chitah umitzur d'vash as'bi'echa*

Translation:

[1] For the Leader; upon the *Gitith*. A Psalm of Asaph.
[2] Sing aloud unto God our strength; shout unto the God of Jacob.
[3] Take up the melody, and sound the timbrel, the sweet harp with the psaltery.
[4] Blow the horn at the new moon, at the full moon for our feast-day.
[5] For it is a statute for Israel, an ordinance of the God of Jacob.
[6] He appointed it in Joseph for a testimony, when He went forth against the land of Egypt. The speech of one that I knew not did I hear:
[7] 'I removed his shoulder from the burden; His hands were freed from the basket.
[8] Thou didst call in trouble, and I rescued thee; I answered thee in the secret place of thunder; I proved thee at the waters of Meribah. *Selah*
[9] Hear, O My people, and I will admonish thee: O Israel, if thou wouldest hearken unto Me!
[10] There shall no strange god be in thee; neither shalt thou worship any foreign god.
[11] I am *YHVH* thy God, who brought thee up out of the land of Egypt; open thy mouth wide, and I will fill it.
[12] But My people hearkened not to My voice; and Israel would none of Me.
[13] So I let them go after the stubbornness of their heart, that they might walk in their own counsels.
[14] Oh that My people would hearken unto Me, that Israel would walk in My ways!

[15] I would soon subdue their enemies, and turn My hand against their adversaries.
[16] The haters of *YHVH* should dwindle away before Him; and their punishment should endure for ever.
[17] They should also be fed with the fat of wheat; and with honey out of the rock would I satisfy thee.'

Psalm 81 is the שיר של יום (*shir shel yom*— "Psalm of the Day") for the fifth day of the week, i.e. Thursday.[1] It is recited by *Sefardim* prior to *Arvit* (Evening Prayer Service) on *Rosh Hashanah*, which we are told is due to the verse reading "blow the horn (*Shofar*) at the new moon, at the full moon for our feastday." (*Psalm 81:4*)[2] Some communities enunciate this psalm also on *Sim'chat Torah* ("Rejoicing with the Torah"), the reason said to be "the verses in the psalm that express joy through song and instrumental music,"[3] i.e. "Sing aloud unto God our strength; shout unto the God of Jacob. Take up the melody, and sound the timbrel, the sweet harp with the psaltery." (*Psalm 81:4*)

We are informed this psalm is good to recite in times of trouble.[4] However, as in the case of the previous psalm, the current psalm is equally listed in the *Shimmush Tehillim* as good to prevent oneself from engaging in idolatry.[5] In a different recension of the *Shimmush Tehillim* we are told that anyone seeking to avoid practising idolatry, should recite the current psalm every day, each time adding the following lengthy prayer-incantation:

אנא יהוה צבאות שמעיני והצילני מרוח טומאה
ומעבודה זרה אשר אין בה כח ולא חיות ולא
שום ממשות כי הבל המה מעשה תעתועים
(*Jeremiah 10:15; 51:18*) כי תהו המה (*I Samuel 12.21*)
אשר לא יועילו ולא יצילו (*I Samuel 12.21*) על כן
אנא אל מלך נעמן הרחק ממני יצר הרע והצלילהו
במעמקי ים והרחיקהו ממאתיים וארבעים ושמונה
איברים שבי לבלתי יוכל להטות לבבי לעשות
הרעה הגדולה הזאת יהוה אלהי צבאות אל אמת
השפילהו והכניעהו הרחיקהו בטליהו מלפני שלא
יוכל להחיטאני על דבר מצוה ועל רצון בוראי

לא בדבר קטון ולא בדבר גדול גלוי וידוע
לפניך שעבירה קטנה גוררת עבירה גדולה
ומצוה קטנה גוררת מצוה גדולה כמו שאמרו
רבותינו זכרונם לברכה בכמה מקומות הוי
זהיר במצוה קלה כבחמורה (Pirkei Avot 2:1)
ואזכה ללמוד וללמד לשמור ולעשות ולקיים
את כל דברי תלמוד תורתך בפי וכל חוקי
רצונך בשם הנורא והקדוש הנקרא אל מלך
נאמן אמן אמן אמן סלה סלה סלה

Transliteration:

Ana YHVH tz'va'ot sh'ma'eini v'hatzileini m'ru'ach tumah umei'avodah zarah asher ein bah ko'ach v'lo chiyut v'lo shum mamashut ki hevel heimah ma'aseih ta'tu'im (Jeremiah 10:15; 51:18) ki tohu heimah (I Samuel 12.21) asher lo yo'ilu v'lo yatzilu (I Samuel 12.21) al kein ana El Melech Ne'eman har'cheik mimeni yetzer hara v'hatzililei'hu b'ma'amakei yam v'har'chikeihu meimatayim v'ar'ba'im ush'monah eivarim shebi l'bil'ti yuchal l'hatot l'vavi la'asot hara'ah hag'dolah hazot YHVH elohei tz'va'ot el emet hash'pileihu v'hach'ni'eihu har'chikeihu bat'leihu mil'fanai shelo yuchal l'hach'ti'eini al davar mitz'vah v'al ratzon bori lo b'davar katon v'lo b'davar gadol galui v'yadu'a l'fanecha she'aveirah k'tanah goreret aveirah g'dolah umitz'vah k'tanah goreret mitz'vah g'dolah k'mo she'am'ru raboteinu zich'ronam liv'rachah b'kamah m'komot havei zahir b'mitz'vah kalah k'vachamorah (Pirkei Avot 2:1) v'ez'keih lil'mod ul'lameid lish'mor v'la'asot ul'kayeim et kol div'rei talmud toratecha b'fi v'chol chukei r'tzonecha b'shem hanora v'hakadosh hanik'ra El Melech Ne'eman omein omein omein selah selah selah.

Translation:

Please *YHVH* of hosts, hear me and deliver me from the spirit of impurity, and from idolatry, in which there is no strength, and no vitality, and no reality at all, *for they are vanity, a work of delusion* (*Jeremiah 10:15; 51:18*), for they are vain (*I Samuel 12.21*), which cannot profit nor deliver (*I Samuel 12.21*). Therefore, please *El Melech Ne'eman* ("God Faithful King"), remove the evil inclination from me. Sink it into the depths of the sea, and remove it from the 248 limbs that are within me, without it being able to incline my heart to do this great evil. Lord, God of hosts, true God, humble, subjugate and remove it, and destroy it before me, so that it cannot lead me to sin in a *Mitz'vah* [sacred religious ordinance], or in the will of my Creator, neither in a small matter nor in a great matter. It is evident and well known to you that a small transgression leads to a major transgression, and a small *Mitz'vah* a great *Mitz'vah*, as our rabbis, of blessed memory, said in some places *Be as careful with a light Mitz'vah [commandment] as with a weighty one* (*Pirkei Avot 2:1*). And may I be authorized to learn, teach, preserve, fulfill and uphold all the words of your *Torah* study in my mouth, and all the laws of your will. In the awesome and Holy Name Name called *El Melech Ne'eman* ("God Faithful King"). *Amen Amen Amen Selah Selah Selah.*[6]

In yet another variant recension of the *Shimmush Tehillim* we are informed that anyone who enunciates the eighty-first Psalm with its associated Divine Name, will succeed.[7] There is no indication which Divine Name is referenced in this instance. Be that as it may, I noted that the current psalm is recited in times of trouble, and in this regard the most troublesome existence is one beset by destitution and ill health. In this regard, this psalm is recited to protect paupers and beggars, to relieve depression brought on by poverty, in support of orphans, and against illness as well as for healing in general. *Psalm 81* is further enunciated to find faith in fortifying oneself against temptation, and, as in the case of the previous psalm, it is equally recited to save friends from errors. In conclusion, we are told it is employed to have justice for just people.

In Christian Magic the eighty-first Psalm is said to be "for staunching blood flow."[8] In this regard, "*Le Livre d'Or*" further maintains a set of magical characters should be written on an olive leaf, which is afterwards fumigated with mastic, and the leaf affixed to the arm of the sufferer. This is succeeded by the recitation of the current psalm, following which it is said "the haemorrhage will cease."[9]

PSALM 82

[1] מזמור לאסף **אלהים** נצב בעדת אל בקרב אלהים ישפט
[2] עד מתי תשפטו עול ופני רשעים תשאו סלה
[3] שפטו דל ויתום עני ורש הצדיקו
[4] פלטו דל ואביון מיד רשעים הצילו
[5] לא ידעו ולא יבינו בחשכה יתהלכו ימוטו כל מוסדי ארץ
[6] אני אמרתי אלהים אתם ובני עליון כלכם
[7] אכן כאדם תמותון וכאחד השרים תפלו
[8] קומה אלהים שפטה הארץ כי אתה תנחל בכל הגוים

Transliteration:
[1] *miz'mor l'asaf elohim nitzav ba'adat el b'kerev elohim yis'pat*
[2] *ad matai tish'p'tu avel uf'nei r'sha'im tish'u selah*
[3] *shif'tu dal v'yatom oni varash hatz'diku*
[4] *pal'tu dal v'ev'yon miyad r'sha'im hatzilu*
[5] *lo yad'u v'lo yavinu bachasheichah yit'halachu yimotu kol mos'dei aretz*
[6] *ani amar'ti elohim atem uv'nei el'yon kul'chem*
[7] *achein k'adam t'mutun uch'achad hasarim tipolu*
[8] *kumah elohim shaf'tah ha'aretz ki atah tin'chal b'chol hagoyim*

Translation:
[1] A Psalm of Asaph. *Elohim* standeth in the congregation of *Elohim*; in the midst of the judges He judgeth:
[2] 'How long will ye judge unjustly, and respect the persons of the wicked? *Selah*
[3] Judge the poor and fatherless; do justice to the afflicted and destitute.
[4] Rescue the poor and needy; deliver them out of the hand of the wicked.
[5] They know not, neither do they understand; they go about in darkness; all the foundations of the earth are moved.

[6] I said: Ye are godlike beings, and all of you sons of the Most High.
[7] Nevertheless ye shall die like men, and fall like one of the princes.'
[8] Arise *Elohim*, judge the earth; for Thou shalt possess all nations.

Psalm 82 is the שיר של יום (*shir shel yom*— "Psalm of the Day") for the third day of the week, i.e. Tuesday.[1] In this regard, the selection of this psalm appears to be based on the phrase in the first verse reading "*Elohim* standeth in the congregation of *Elohim*," and it is taught that on this day the Divine One "revealed the earth in His wisdom, and established the world for his community."[2] In Jewish Magic ("Practical Kabbalah") this psalm is recommended to one who wish to succeed on a mission.[3] According to the *Shimmush Tehillim* the current psalm should be recited "on the way," to achieve success on a mission and for a speedy return.[4] Godfrey Selig gives the term "mission" a distinctly business slant in his German/English version of the said text, saying "the prayer of the 82nd Psalm will assist an envoy to transact his business to the satisfaction of his employers, and his business affairs will succeed and prosper."[5]

In a variant recension of the *Shimmush Tehillim* we find the eighty-second Psalm recommended to individuals who are having difficulty walking, i.e. who are having problems with their legs and feet. In this regard, it is recommended that the sufferer write the current psalm with its associated Divine Name on deerskin parchment, which is afterwards attached to the right foot of the said individual. This action is concluded by reciting the following prayer-incantation:

יהי רצון מלפניך יהוה אלהי ואלהי אבותי שתתן
כח וגבורה ל'[....name of recipient....] ככתוב נותן
ליעף כח ולאין אונים עצמה ירבה (*Isaiah 40:29*)
ותשים רגליו כאילות ותוליכהו מהרה ובקלות
לבל ידאג ברגליו ולא יחת מלכת ולא ימעד

The Psalms of David — Book III / 307

בשם צבא רם ונשא יהיה הדבר שילך ולא ידאג
ולא יחת וילך וידרוך וירכב על במתי עולם על
כל הר וגבעה ושפילה ובקעה ושדה ועיר ולא יפחד
ולא יחת ולא יקרה לו מקרה רע ולא פגע רע כתיב
יהוה אלהים חלי וישם רגלי כאילות ועל במתי
ידריכני למנצה בנגינותי (Habakkuk 3:19)

Transliteration:

> Y'hi ratzon mil'fanecha YHVH elohai veilohei avotai shetitein ko'ach v'g'vurah l'[....name of recipient....] kakatuv notein laya'eif ko'ach ul'ein onim otz'mah yar'beh (Isaiah 40:29) v'tasim rag'lav k'ayalot v'tolicheihu m'heirah uv'kalut l'bal yid'ag b'rag'lav v'lo yeichat milechet v'lo yim'ad b'shem Tz'va Ram v'Nisa yih'yeh hadavar sheyeilech v'lo yid'ag v'lo yeichat v'yeileich v'yid'roch v'yir'kav al bamatei olam al kol har v'giv'ah ush'feilah ubik'ah v'sadeh v'ir v'lo yif'chad v'lo yeichat v'lo yikareh lo mik'reh ra v'lo pega ra k'tiv YHVH Adonai cheili vayasem rag'lai ka'ayalot v'al bamotai yad'richeini lam'na'tzei'ach bin'ginotai (Habakkuk 3:19)

Translation:

> May it be your will YHVH, my God and God of my fathers, that you give strength and power to [....name of recipient....], as it is written *He giveth power to the faint; and to him that hath no might He increaseth strength.* (Isaiah 40:29) You shall make his feet like the hind's, and lead him swiftly and with ease, so that he will not be worried about his feet, and is not broken and stumble when walking. The Name *Tz'va Ram v'Nisa* ("Host Lofty and Exalted") shall be the magic word, that he may walk, not be worried, and not be broken [hampered]. And he shall walk and journey over the heights of the world, over every mountain, high and lowland, and valley and field and city. And he shall not fear, and shall not be broken. And no evil

> incident or evil calamity shall befall him, as it is written *YHVH Adonai is my strength, and He maketh my feet like hinds' feet, and He maketh me to walk upon my high places. For the Leader. With my string-music.* (*Habakkuk 3:19*)[6]

I presume it is the use of the eighty-second Psalm to ensure success in a mission, which led to it being recommended in unwritten sources for the purpose of attracting business, and to affect the sales of wares. These applications probably inspired Godfrey Selig's earlier mentioned statement that the current psalm is employed to "assist an envoy to transact his business to the satisfaction of his employers." Be that as it may, the current psalm is also employed against the dangers of fire.

Psalm 82 is recommended in Christian Magic for recitation to ensure a warm welcome.[7] In this regard, we are informed in "*Le Livre d'Or*" to enunciate the current psalm over a set of written magical characters, and to dissolve the writing in common or rose oil. It is claimed that anointing the face with this substance will ensure that an individual is "agreeably and honourably received."[8] Elsewhere we find *Psalm 82:1–2* recommended "for winning a lawsuit."[9]

In conclusion, it should be noted that the eighty-second Psalm is one of four, i.e. *Psalm 82, 72, 134,* and *64*, listed in the "Key of Solomon" for recitation during the "perfuming" of the silk cloth in which "the instruments of art" are wrapped when not in use.[10]

PSALM 83

[1] שיר מזמור לאסף
[2] אלהים אל דמי לך אל תחרש ואל תשקט אל
[3] כי הנה אויביך יהמיון ומשנאיך נשאו ראש
[4] על עמך יערימו סוד ויתיעצו על צפוניך
[5] אמרו לכו ונכחידם מגוי ולא יזכר שם ישראל עוד
[6] כי נועצו לב יחדו עליך ברית יכרתו
[7] אהלי אדום וישמעאלים מואב והגרים
[8] גבל ועמון ועמלק פלשת עם ישבי צור
[9] גם אשור נלוה עמם היו זרוע לבני לוט סלה
[10] עשה להם כמדין כסיסרא כיבין בנחל קישון
[11] נשמדו בעין דאר היו דמן לאדמה
[12] שיתמו נדיבימו כערב וכזאב וכזבח וכצלמנע כל נסיכימו
[13] אשר אמרו נירשה לנו את נאות אלהים
[14] אלהי שיתמו כגלגל כקש לפני רוח
[15] כאש תבער יער וכלהבה תלהט הרים
[16] כן תרדפם בסערך ובסופתך תבהלם
[17] מלא פניהם קלון ויבקשו שמך יהוֹאֲדֹנָיוָה
[18] יבשו ויבהלו עדי עד ויחפרו ויאבדו
[19] וידעו כי אתה שמך יהוֹאֲדֹנָיוָה לבדך עליון על כל הארץ

Transliteration:

[1] *shir miz'mor l'asaf*
[2] *Elohim al domi lach al techerash v'al tish'kot el*
[3] *ki hineih oivecha yehemayun um'san'echa nas'u rosh*
[4] *al am'cha ya'arimu sod v'yit'ya'atzu al tz'funecha*
[5] *am'ru l'chu v'nach'chideim migoi v'lo yizacheir shem yis'ra'eil od*
[6] *ki no'atzu leivi yach'dav alecha b'rit yich'rotu*
[7] *aholei edom v'yish'm'eilim mo'av v'hag'rim*
[8] *g'val v'amon va'amaleik p'leshet im yosh'vei tzor*
[9] *gam ashur nil'vah imam hayu z'ro'a liv'nei lot selah*

[10] *aseih lahem k'mid'yan k'sis'ra ch'yavin b'nachal kishon*
[11] *nish'm'du v'ein dor hayu domen la'adamah*
[12] *shiteimo n'diveimo k'oreiv v'chiz'eiv uch'zevach uch'tzl'muna kol n'sicheimo*
[13] *asher am'ru nirashah lanu et n'ot elohim*
[14] *elohai shiteimo chagalgal k'kash lif'nei ru'ach*
[15] *k'esh tiv'ar ya'ar uch'lehavah t'laheit harim*
[16] *kein tir'd'feim b'sa'arecha uv'sufat'cha t'vahaleim*
[17] *malei f'neihem kalon vivak'shu shim'cha YHVH*
[18] *yeivoshu v'yibahalu adei ad v'yach'p'ru v'yoveidu*
[19] *v'yeid'u ki atah shim'cha YHVH l'vadecha el'yon al kol ha'aretz*

Translation:

[1] A Song, a Psalm of Asaph.

[2] *Elohim* keep not Thou silence; hold not Thy peace, and be not still, O God.

[3] For, lo, Thine enemies are in an uproar; and they that hate Thee have lifted up the head.

[4] They hold crafty converse against Thy people, and take counsel against Thy treasured ones.

[5] They have said: 'Come, and let us cut them off from being a nation; that the name of Israel may be no more in remembrance.'

[6] For they have consulted together with one consent; against Thee do they make a covenant;

[7] The tents of Edom and the Ishmaelites; Moab, and the Hagrites;

[8] Gebal, and Ammon, and Amalek; Philistia with the inhabitants of Tyre;

[9] Assyria also is joined with them; they have been an arm to the children of Lot. *Selah*

[10] Do Thou unto them as unto Midian; as to Sisera, as to Jabin, at the brook Kishon;

[11] Who were destroyed at En-dor; they became as dung for the earth.

[12] Make their nobles like Oreb and Zeeb, and like Zebah and Zalmunna all their princes;

[13] Who said: 'Let us take to ourselves in possession the habitations of *Elohim*.'

[14] O my God, make them like the whirling dust; as stubble before the wind.
[15] As the fire that burneth the forest, and as the flame that setteth the mountains ablaze;
[16] So pursue them with Thy tempest, and affright them with Thy storm.
[17] Fill their faces with shame; that they may seek Thy name, *YHVH*.
[18] Let them be ashamed and affrighted for ever; yea, let them be abashed and perish;
[19] That they may know that it is Thou alone whose name is *YHVH*, the Most High over all the earth.

It is customary for some Jewish worshippers to recite *Psalm 83* after *Shacharit* (Morning Prayer Service),[1] and others recite it prior to *Arvit* (*Ma'ariv* or Evening Service).[2] In Jewish Magic the current psalm is enunciated in times of war,[3] and for "victory in battle."[4] In this regard, the standard version of the *Shimmush Tehillim* maintains the current psalm should be written and suspended on the person of the individual requiring protection in war. We are informed that following this action "they will not defeat you, and if they conquer you, they will not do you evil"[5] To ensure this outcome, Godfrey Selig is more meticulous in his German/English version of the *Shimmush Tehillim*, as to exactly what should be done with the current psalm. Thus he noted that "you should write the 83rd Psalm properly, upon pure parchment, and suspend it around your neck, and by so doing you will abide safely in war, avoiding defeat and captivity. If you should, however, be overcome, your captors will not harm you, for even in captivity no harm can befall you."[6] Interestingly enough, the initials of the words comprising *Psalm 83:14*, were arranged into the Divine Name construct אשב בכלר, which is likewise included in amulets for the purpose of protection in conditions of war.[7]

It is worth noting that the current psalm is one of the psalms selected for recitation for the Land of Israel.[8] In this regard, one recension of the *Shimmush Tehillim* recommends the employment of *Psalm 83* to eradicate "an evil enemy, a hater of Israel." Here the practitioner is instructed to copy the psalm, as well as the name of the said adversary, on a shard of pottery. This item is afterwards cast into the residence of the enemy, and the action completed by enunciating the following prayer-incantation:

אל נורא הוא ושמו נורא משרתיו אש ומלאכיו
אש לוהט וכל סביביו אש לוהט נהר דינור נגיד
ונפיק מן קדמוהי אלף אלפין ישמשוניה ורבו
רבוובן קדמוהי יקומון (Daniel 7:10) יהא רעוא מן
קדם כורסי יקריה שתהוי ל'[....name of recipient....]
האויב הרע השונא ישראל דבר וחרב ורעב ויגון
ונגף שינגף וירגיז [....name of recipient....] זה השונא
ויאבד מן העולם בשם אל קנוא ונוקם יהוה
יהיה יהיה אמן אמן אמן סלה סלה סלה

Transliteration:

El Nora Hu uSh'mo Nora m'shar'tav esh umal'achav esh loheit v'chol savivav esh loheit n'har dinur nageid v'nafeik min kodamohi elef al'fin y'sham'shuneih v'ribo riv'van kadamohi yikumun (Daniel 7:10) y'hei ra'ava min kadam kur'sei yikareih sh'tahavei l'[....name of recipient....] *ha'oyeiv hara hason'ei yis'ra'el dever v'cherev v'ra'av v'yagon v'negef sh'yin'gov v'yar'giz* [....name of recipient....] *zeh hason'ei v'ya'aveid min ha'olam b'shem El Kano v'Nokeim YHVH Yih'yeh Yih'yeh Omein Omein Omein Selah Selah Selah.*

Translation:

El Nora Hu uSh'mo Nora ("An Awesome God is He, and Awesome is His Name"). His servants are fire, and his angels are blazing fire, and all his surroundings are blazing fire. *A fiery stream issued and came forth from before him; thousand thousands ministered unto him, and ten thousand times ten thousand stood before him.* (*Daniel 7:10*) May it be pleasing before the throne of His glory that for [....name of recipient....], the evil enemy, the hater of Israel, there will be pestilence, drought, hunger, sorrow and agitation, [....name of recipient....], this hater, will be laid low, exterminated, and cut off from the world. In the Name *El Kano v'Nokeim YHVH Yih'yeh Yih'yeh* ("Jealous and Avenging God, *YHVH*, He Will Be, He Will Be"). *Amen Amen Amen Selah Selah Selah.*[9]

In yet a different recension of the *Shimmush Tehillim*, we find *Psalms 82* and *83* recited conjointly when "you want to go into a city."[10] It is clearly the fear of assault and an untimely demise, which inspire the enunciation of the current psalm prior to entering an extensive urban area. The propensity of humans to demonise and be hostile towards their own kind knows no bounds. In fact, mankind is often less inclined to let the sun shine over those they consider "the other." There will certainly be no peace in this world, until there is self-discipline, as well as acknowledgement and respect for even those considered the least amongst their own kind. We all know what we would like to see. A world organised so that all humans were cared for and supplied according to needs, not necessarily wants. A world with a minimum of sickness, starvation and all the ills human creatures inflict on each other. A "warless" world for certain. However, before any of this can happen, humans will have to alter from *within* to a drastic extent, and that can only be done by *spiritual* changes. Some of these changes are happening, but scarcely fast enough, or widely enough for that matter.

We noted that the eighty-third Psalm is recited for the Land of Israel. In this regard, it is enunciated for any crisis in Israel, as well as for the Jewish nation and Judaism. It is also employed against threats, abuse, oppression, murder, to avoid capture and captivity, and for protection and safety in conditions of war.

Psalm 83 is equally employed in Christian Magic for the destruction of an enemy. In this regard, it is said in *"Le Livre d'Or"* that an individual should write a set of magical characters inside "a new cooking pot," which is afterwards filled with the bathwater of a woman. The psalm is read over the water seven times, and this liquid emptied at the residence of the enemy. It is maintained this action will result in the destruction of the said foe.[11] Aside from this application, we are informed in the Byzantine Christian magical manuscripts that the phrase from *Psalm 83:15* reading "as the flame that setteth the mountains ablaze," is used when an individual is expecting a loan of money.[12]

In conclusion, it should be noted that in the "*Key of Solomon*," *Psalm 83* as well as *Psalm 67* are enunciated over a feather of a swallow or a crow, prior to it being fashioned into a writing pen.[13]

PSALM 84

[1] למנצח על הגתית לבני קרח מזמור
[2] מה ידידות משכנותיך יהוה‎אדוני‎אהדונהי צבאות
[3] נכספה וגם כלתה נפשי לחצרות יהוה‎אדוני‎אהדונהי לבי ובשרי ירננו אל אל חי
[4] גם צפור מצאה בית ודרור קן לה אשר שתה אפרחיה את מזבחותיך יהוה‎אדוני‎אהדונהי צבאות מלכי ואלהי
[5] אשרי יושבי ביתך עוד יהללוך סלה
[6] אשרי אדם עוז לו בך מסלות בלבבם
[7] עברי בעמק הבכא מעין ישיתוהו גם ברכות יעטה מורה
[8] ילכו מחיל אל חיל יראה אל אלהים בציון
[9] יהוה‎אדוני‎אהדונהי אלהים צבאות שמעה תפלתי האזינה אלהי יעקב סלה
[10] מגננו ראה אלהים והבט פני משיחך
[11] כי טוב יום בחצריך מאלף בחרתי הסתופף בבית אלהי מדור באהלי רשע
[12] כי שמש ומגן יהוה‎אדוני‎אהדונהי אלהים חן וכבוד יתן יהוה‎אדוני‎אהדונהי לא ימנע טוב להלכים בתמים
[13] יהוה‎אדוני‎אהדונהי צבאות אשרי אדם בטח בך

Transliteration:

[1] *lam'natzei'ach al hagitit liv'nei korach miz'mor*
[2] *mah y'didot mish'k'notecha YHVH tz'va'ot*
[3] *nich's'fah v'gam kal'tah naf'shi l'chatz'rot YHVH libi uv'sari y'ran'nu el el chai*
[4] *gam tzipor matz'ah vayit ud'ror kein lah asher shatah ef'rochehah et miz'b'chotecha YHVH tz'va'ot mal'ki veilohai.*
[5] *ash'rei yosh'vei veitecha od y'hal'lucha selah*
[6] *ash'rei adam oz lo vach m'silot bil'vavam*
[7] *ov'rei b'eimek habacha ma'yan y'shituhu gam b'rachot ya'teh moreh*
[8] *yeil'chu meichayil el chayil yeira'eh el elohim b'tziyon*

[9] *YHVH elohim tz'va'ot shim'ah t'filati ha'azinah elohei ya'akov selah*
[10] *magineinu r'eih elohim v'habeit p'nei m'shichecha*
[11] *ki tov yom bachatzeirecha mei'alef bachar'ti his'tofeif b'veit elohai midur b'aholei resha*
[12] *ki shemesh umagein YHVH Elohim chein v'chavod yitein YHVH lo yim'na tov lahol'chim b'tamim*
[13] *YHVH tz'va'ot ash'rei adam botei'ach bach*

Translation:

[1] For the Leader; upon the *Gitith*. A Psalm of the sons of Korah.
[2] How lovely are Thy tabernacles *YHVH* of hosts!
[3] My soul yearneth, yea, even pineth for the courts of *YHVH*; my heart and my flesh sing for joy unto the living God.
[4] Yea, the sparrow hath found a house, and the swallow a nest for herself, where she may lay her young; Thine altars *YHVH* of hosts, my King, and my God—.
[5] Happy are they that dwell in Thy house, they are ever praising Thee. *Selah*
[6] Happy is the man whose strength is in Thee; in whose heart are the highways.
[7] Passing through the valley of Baca they make it a place of springs; yea, the early rain clotheth it with blessings.
[8] They go from strength to strength, every one of them appeareth before *Elohim* in Zion.
[9] *YHVH Elohim* of hosts, hear my prayer; give ear, O God of Jacob. *Selah*
[10] Behold *Elohim* our shield, and look upon the face of Thine anointed.
[11] For a day in Thy courts is better than a thousand; I had rather stand at the threshold of the house of my God, than to dwell in the tents of wickedness.
[12] For the *YHVH Elohim* is a sun and a shield; *YHVH* giveth grace and glory; no good thing will He withhold from them that walk uprightly.
[13] *YHVH* of hosts, happy is the man that trusteth in Thee.

Psalm 84 is a joyous psalm expressing great well-being, and is a particular favourite at Jewish weddings.¹ In Jewish Magic it is employed against sickness,² with particular reference to patients who are losing weight due to illness.³ In this regard, we are informed in the *Shimmush Tehillim*, that for someone whose body is emaciated from severe illnesses, the current psalm should be recited over a new pot filled with water drawn from a water source which has not seen the sun. The water is poured over the sick individual, which is said will benefit him/her with the help of the Divine One.⁴ We are informed that in the current instance the associated Divine Name is אב (*Av*—"Father"). א (*Alef*) from צבאות (*tz'va'ot*—"hosts"): verse 2; ב *Bet* from בך (*bakh*—"in thee"): verse 13.⁵ A variant recension of the *Shimmush Tehillim* maintains the associated Divine Name to be אל (*El*—"God"), the א (*Alef*) said to have been derived from ת (*Tav*) in צבאות (*tz'va'ot*): verse 2, the letter having been transposed by means of the א"ת ב"ש (*Atbash*) cipher; and ל (*Lamed*) from ב (*Bet*) in בך (*bakh*): verse 13, the Hebrew glyph having been converted by means of the most obscure א"מ ב"ל (*Ambal*[?]) cipher.⁶

It should be noted that, whilst Godfrey Selig equally references "*Av*" to be the Divine Name associated with the current psalm, his rendition of the origins of the said Name is corrupted.⁷ That is however not the worst of it. Selig revisioned weight loss to malodour, which is probably due to the psalm being also employed for this purpose, though this is not listed in any of the primary recensions of the *Shimmush Tehillim* which I have seen. Be that as it may, Selig informs us in his German/English version of the *Shimmush Tehillim*, "when a man, through a severe and protracted illness, has acquired a repulsive, disgusting and bad odour, he should pronounce this Psalm with the prescribed holy name of *Af*, which means Father, over a pot of water upon which the sun never shone, and then pour the water all over himself, and then the bad smell will leave him."⁸

I have seen the current psalm employed against bad odours generally, and whilst we noted the current psalm is recited to benefit those who are suffering excessive weight loss due to severe illness, it is equally recommended to alleviate weakness and trembling generally. Other than these applications, *Psalm 84* is prescribed to farmers, with special reference to the protection of fields and gardens, as well to the preservation of goods and livestock. On the other hand, the current psalm is employed for purposes of the non-material kind. In this regard, it is one of the psalms suggested for recitation in the synagogue, and to increase trust in the Divine One.

We also find the eighty-fourth Psalm recommended in one recension of the *Shimmush Tehillim*, to an individual who wishes to commit him or herself to an intense study of the *Torah*. In this regard, the said individual is instructed to recite the current psalm in conjunction with the following brief prayer-incantation:

מעם יהוה בקשתי ושאלתי שיתן לי כח וגבורה
ויכולת ללמוד תורה הרבה והגדות ולא אתבטל
לעולם מללמוד תורה ומצוה בשם אהו חהו החו
חהו יהוה צבאות אמן נצח סלה

>Transliteration:
>>*Mei'im YHVH bakashati v'she'eilati sheyitein li ko'ach v'g'vurah v'yochelet lil'mod torah har'beih v'hagadot v'lo et'batel l'olam milil'mod torah umitz'vah b'shem Aho Chaho Hacho Chaho YHVH Tz'va'ot Omein Netzach Selah.*

>Translation:
>>From *YHVH* I prayed and asked that you may give me power, and strength, and ability to study *Torah* and *Haggadot* [traditional Jewish narratives] intensely, and I will never stop learning the *Torah* and a *Mitz'vah* (sacred ordinance).In the name *Aho Chaho Hacho Chaho YHVH Tz'va'ot, Amen Eternal Selah*.[9]

As far as individual verses are concerned, it has been noted that *Psalm 84:2* reading מה ידידות משכנותיך יהוה צבאות (*mah y'didot mish'k'notecha YHVH tz'va'ot*—"How lovely are Thy tabernacles *YHVH* of hosts!"), was formulated into the Divine

Name construct מַהִידְמִשְׁיִהָאֵל (*Mah'y'dimish'yiha'la*). The Divine Name is comprised of the initial two letters of each of the first four words of the verse conjoined in exact order, with the addition of the אֵל suffix.[10] However, there are other variants of this Name, i.e. מַיְדִמְשִׁיהָאֵל (*May'dimish'yuha'eil*), and מַירוֹמִשְׁיהָאֵל (*Mair'omish'yuha'eil*).[11] We are informed that the ten letters of this Divine Name construct pertains to the ten *Sefirot*, and that the חשמלים (*Chashmalim*—"Shining Ones"), the angelic order aligned with חסד (*Chesed*—"Lovingkindness") on the Sefirotic Tree, "receives" from (are empowered by) this Divine Name construct.[12]

The letters comprising *Psalm 84:12* were arranged in the following Divine Name construct, which is said to have the power to bring success:[13]

כיתם ידני שוים מבהת
שכוב ווהם מנלי גהאב
נמיל יימה ההנל ולעב
האטו

This Divine Name construct was formulated by means of a fairly common procedure, in which the fifty-four glyphs comprising this verse is divided into four groups of thirteen letters each. These are intertwined in, as it were, a zigzag manner. The first set of thirteen glyphs are written in the standard Hebrew manner from right to left, whilst the second thirteen are respectively located in reverse to the left, alongside the first set. In turn the third set is positioned left, adjacent to the second group of letters in the direct order, and the concluding set located similarly in reverse, thus arriving at the thirteen four-letter combinations comprising this Divine Name construct. Be that as it may, to achieve the mentioned success, the bearer of the amulet is instructed to locate the item together with any relevant magical seals, as well as a little incense, inside a bag, wrapper, or envelope. The item is afterwards tied to the right arm of the one requiring this magical support.[14]

In Christian Magic *Psalm 84* is recited to acquire good luck.[15] However, in the Byzantine magical manuscripts it is employed against "an enemy, whom you fear."[15] In this instance, it is pronounced speedily, written down, and carried.[16] The said manuscripts lists the same method elsewhere to implore "the anger of God."[17] Elsewhere still we find the eighty-fourth Psalm being enlisted with *Psalms 49*, and *142* (or *143*) for the purpose of finding stolen objects. In this regard, the psalms are first recited, then written with certain magical symbols on a sheet of virgin parchment, "using a new pen and new ink, which have not yet been used."[18] When retiring to bed the said parchment is located under the head, and it is said the identity of the thief, as well as the locale where the stolen objects are held, will be revealed.[19] All of these application are somewhat odd considering the jubilant contents of the current psalm.

A more positive application of the current psalm is shared in "*Le Livre d'Or*," in which we are informed that an individual seeking access to a Prince, should write the psalm, and bind it to his/her arm. It is said this will ensure that the said individual "will be honourably received."[20] In conclusion, as noted earlier, *Psalm 84* is one of nineteen psalms in the "*Key of Solomon*," i.e. *Psalms 8, 15, 22, 46, 47, 49, 51, 53, 68, 72, 84, 102, 110, 113, 126, 130, 131, 133*, and *139*, which are recited over the wax from which ritual candles are constructed.[21]

PSALM 85

[1] למנצח לבני קרח מזמור
[2] רצית יהוה‎אהדונהי ארצך שבת שבית יעקב
[3] נשאת עון עמך כסית כל חטאתם סלה
[4] אספת כל עברתך השיבות מחרון אפך
[5] שובנו אלהי ישענו והפר כעסך עמנו
[6] הלעולם תאנף בנו תמשך אפך לדר ודר
[7] הלא אתה תשוב תחינו ועמך ישמחו בך
[8] הראנו יהוה‎אהדונהי חסדך וישעך תתן לנו
[9] אשמעה מה ידבר האל יהוה‎אהדונהי כי ידבר שלום אל עמו ואל חסידיו ואל ישובו לכסלה
[10] אך קרוב ליראיו ישעו לשכן כבוד בארצנו
[11] חסד ואמת נפגשו צדק ושלום נשקו
[12] אמת מארץ תצמח וצדק משמים נשקף
[13] גם יהוה‎אהדונהי יתן הטוב וארצנו תתן יבולה
[14] צדק לפניו יהלך וישם לדרך פעמיו

Transliteration:
   [1] *lam'natzei'ach liv'nei korach miz'mor*
   [2] *ratzita YHVH ar'tzecha shav'ta sh'vit ya'akov*
   [3] *nasata avon amecha kisita chol chatatam selah*
   [4] *asafta chol ev'ratecha heshivota meicharon apecha*
   [5] *shuvenu Elohei yish'enu v'hafer ka'as'cha imanu*
   [6] *hal'olam t'enaf banu tim'shoch ap'cha l'dor vador*
   [7] *halo atah tashuv t'chayeinu v'am'cha yis'm'chu vach*
   [8] *har'einu YHVH chas'decha v'yesh'acha titen lanu*
   [9] *esh'm'ah mah y'dabeir ha'el YHVH ki y'dabeir shalom el amo v'el chasidav v'al yashuvu l'chis'lah*
   [10] *ach karov lirei'av yish'o lish'kon kavod b'ar'tzeinu*
   [11] *chesed v'emet nif'gashu tzedek v'shalom nashaku*
   [12] *emet mei'eretz titz'mach v'tzedek mishamayim nish'kaf*
   [13] *gam YHVH yitein hatov v'ar'tzeinu titein y'vulah*
   [14] *tzedek l'fanav y'haleich v'yashem l'derech p'amav*

Translation:
   [1] For the Leader. A Psalm of the sons of Korah.

[2] *YHVH*, Thou hast been favourable unto Thy land, Thou hast turned the captivity of Jacob.
[3] Thou hast forgiven the iniquity of Thy people, Thou hast pardoned all their sin. *Selah*
[4] Thou hast withdrawn all Thy wrath; Thou hast turned from the fierceness of Thine anger.
[5] Restore us, O God of our salvation, and cause Thine indignation toward us to cease.
[6] Wilt Thou be angry with us for ever? Wilt Thou draw out Thine anger to all generations?
[7] Wilt Thou not quicken us again, that Thy people may rejoice in Thee?
[8] Show us Thy mercy *YHVH*, and grant us Thy salvation.
[9] I will hear what God *YHVH* will speak; for He will speak peace unto His people, and to His saints; but let them not turn back to folly
[10] Surely His salvation is nigh them that fear Him; that glory may dwell in our land.
[11] Mercy and truth are met together; righteousness and peace have kissed each other.
[12] Truth springeth out of the earth; and righteousness hath looked down from heaven.
[13] Yea *YHVH* will give that which is good; and our land shall yield her produce.
[14] Righteousness shall go before Him, and shall make His footsteps a way.

Psalm 85 is delineated "a prayer of returned exiles."[1] Inspired by the third verse reading "Thou hast forgiven the iniquity of Thy people, Thou hast pardoned all their sin. *Selah*," the current psalm is enunciated during *Min'chah* (Afternoon Prayer Service) on *Erev Yom Kippur* (Eve of the Day of Atonement) in the Israeli, Syrian, Turkish Jewish liturgies,[2] and likewise in certain Spanish and Portuguese communities.[3] Whilst recommended for recitation in times of trouble,[4] the magical use of *Psalm 85* is more about winning favour,[5] or more commonly, to please or pacify a friend.[6] In terms of the latter application, we are told in the *Shimmush Tehillim* that, to appease a companion, or, according to a different recension, "when a man is angry with you," you should go out into the open, turn your face to the sky southward, and recite the current psalm seven times[7] (five times in another recension).[8]

Following this recitation one version instructs "then go to him,"[9] and it is said this action will ensure a favourable reception.[10] The Divine Name associated with *Psalm 85* is said to be וֹה (*Voh*), ו from וישעך תתן לנו (*v'yesh'acha titen lanu*— "and grant us Thy salvation"): verse 8; and ה (*Heh*) from הראנו יהוה חסדך (*har'einu YHVH chas'decha*—"Show us Thy mercy *YHVH*") verse 8.[11] Godfrey Selig, with the standard verbosity which we have come to recognise in his German/English versions of the *Shimmush Tehillim*, queried "do you wish that your former friend, but who now lives at enmity with you, should again be reconciled to you, if you can discover no disposition on his part to make it up with you, then go out into an open field, turn your face toward the South, and pronounce this Psalm, with its prescribed holy name *Vah*, Show us Thy mercy *YHVH* seven times in succession, and he will approach and receive you in great friendship."[12]

As readers might expect by now, we find the current psalm employed for quite a different purpose in a variant recension of the *Shimmush Tehillim*, i.e. "for the 'opening of the heart'."[13] To affect this outcome, the practitioner is instructed to place honey, flour and goat's milk in a clean vessel, and to recite the eighty-fifth Psalm over the vessel. The said food substances are afterwards mixed and knead together into a cake, and the Divine Name combination אל רחום שמך (*El Rachum Sh'mach*—"Merciful God is your Name") written with olive oil on the dough. The cake is then baked and consumed by the practitioner, and the procedure concluded with the following prayer incantation:

(*Psalms 31:2*) בנו נקרא בך יהוה חסיתי אל איבושה
כי אני מבקש שתפתח לבי ללמוד תורתיך
ותסיר ממני כל טפשות וסכלות והולילות
ושכחה ואבין ואשכיל ואחכם במאור תורתך
הקדושה בספרא ובספרי ובכל חכמה ומדע
בשם פתחיאל רפאל ענאל יה יהו טרפיאל
זכריאל נצחיאל מלכיאל אמן נצח סלה

Transliteration:
> *Banu nik'ra b'cha YHVH chasiti al eivoshah (Psalms 31:2) ki ani m'vakeish shetif'tach libi lil'mod tor'teicha v'tasir mimeni kol tip'shut v'sich'lut v'holilut v'shik'chah v'avin v'as'kil v'ech'kam bim'or torateicha hak'doshah b'sif'ra ub'sif'ri uv'chol choch'mah umada b'shem Pat'chi'el Rafa'el An'el Yah Yaho Tar'pi'el Zach'ri'el N'tzachi'el Mal'chi'el Omein Netzach Selah.*

Translation:
> We are told *In thee YHVH have I taken refuge; let me never be ashamed* (*Psalms 31:2; 71:1*), for I ask that you open my heart to learn your *Torah*, and you shall remove all stupidity, and nonsense, and folly, and forgetfulness from me. And I will understand, comprehend, and become wise in the glow of your holy *Torah*, in the book and in the writings, as well as in every wisdom and science. In the name *Pat'chi'el Rafa'el An'el Yah Yaho Tar'pi'el Zach'ri'el N'tzachi'el Mal'chi'el Amen* Eternal *Selah*.[14]

Once again we find the eighty-fifth Psalm employed for a variety of purposes not listed in "official sources." In this regard, we noted that it is recited to appease a friend, and we are told that it is employed for the purpose of reconciling with a long-standing friend, as well as to find favour in the eyes of friends. It is also utilised against enemies, threats, in perilous situations, and to alleviate psychological damage resulting from trauma, i.e. what is termed "post-traumatic stress disorder." Aside from that, it is enunciated for illness and healing in general, and further to acquire the "loyalty of Good Spirits."

In Christian magic *Psalm 85* is employed in "*Le Livre d'Or*" for the purpose of ensuring luck and good fortune. In this regard, it was written on laurel leaves, perfumed "with mastic and incense, mixed with rose oil." This substance is used to anoint the face of the one seeking the sanction of lady luck.[15] Elsewhere *Psalm 85:12* and *13*, reading "truth springeth out of the earth; and righteousness hath looked down from heaven; yea *YHVH* will give that which is good; and our land shall yield her produce," is likewise recited "to be lucky in all things."[16]

PSALM 86

[1] תפלה לדוד הטה יהוה‎אדני‎אהדונהי אזנך ענני כי ענו ואביון אני

[2] שמרה נפשי כי חסיד אני הושע עבדך אתה אלהי הבוטח אליך

[3] חנני אדני כי אליך אקרא כל היום

[4] שמח נפש עבדך כי אליך אדני נפשי אשא

[5] כי אתה אדני טוב וסלח ורב חסד לכל קראיך

[6] האזינה יהוה‎אדני‎אהדונהי תפלתי והקשיבה בקול תחנונותי

[7] ביום צרתי אקראך כי תענני

[8] אין כמוך באלהים אדני ואין כמעשיך

[9] כל גוים אשר עשות יבואו וישתחוו לפניך אדני ויכבדו לשמך

[10] כי גדול אתה ועשה נפלאות אתה אלהים לבדך

[11] הורני יהוה‎אדני‎אהדונהי דרכך אהלך באמתך יחד לבבי ליראה שמך

[12] אודך אדני אלהי בכל לבבי ואכבדה שמך לעולם

[13] כי חסדך גדול עלי והצלת נפשי משאול תחתיה

[14] אלהים זדים קמו עלי ועדת עריצים בקשו נפשי ולא שמוך לנגדם

[15] ואתה אדני אל רחום וחנון ארך אפים ורב חסד ואמת

[16] פנה אלי וחנני תנה עזך לעבדך והושיעה לבן אמתך

[17] עשה עמי אות לטובה ויראו שנאי ויבשו כי אתה יהוה‎אדני‎אהדונהי עזרתני ונחמתני

Transliteration:
[1] *t'filah l'david hateih YHVH az'n'cha aneini ki ani v'ev'yon ani*
[2] *sham'rah naf'shi ki chasid ani hosha av'd'cha atah elohai habotei'ach eilecha*
[3] *chaneini adonai ki eilecha ek'ra kol hayom*
[4] *samei'ach nefesh av'decha ki eilecha adonai naf'shi esa*

[5] *ki atah adonai tov v'salach v'rav chesed l'chol kor'echa*
[6] *ha'azinah YHVH t'filati v'hak'shivah b'kol tachanunotai*
[7] *b'yom tzarati ek'ra'eka ki ta'aneini*
[8] *ein kamocha va'elohim adonai v'ein k'ma'asecha*
[9] *kol goyim asher asita yavo'u v'yish'tachavu l'fanecha adonai vichab'du lish'mecha*
[10] *ki gadol atah v'oseih nif'la'ot atah elohim l'vadecha*
[11] *horeini YHVH dar'kecha ahaleich ba'amitecha yacheid l'vavi l'yir'ah sh'mecha*
[12] *od'cha adonai elohai b'chol l'vavi va'achab'dah shim'cha l'olam*
[13] *ki chas'd'cha gadol alai v'hitzal'ta naf'shi mish'ol tach'tiyah*
[14] *elohim zeidim kamu alai va'adat aritzim bik'zhu naf'shi v'lo sh'mucha l'neg'dam*
[15] *v'atah adonai el rachum v'chanun erech apayim v'rav chesed v'emet*
[16] *p'neih eilai v'chaneini tinah uz'cha l'av'decha v'hoshi'ah l'ven amatecha*
[17] *aseih imi ot l'tovah v'yir'u shon'ai v'yeivoshu ki atah YHVH azar'tani v'nicham'tani*

Translation:

[1] A Prayer of David. Incline Thine ear *YHVH*, and answer me; for I am poor and needy.

[2] Keep my soul, for I am godly; O Thou my God, save Thy servant that trusteth in Thee.

[3] Be gracious unto me *Adonai*; for unto Thee do I cry all the day.

[4] Rejoice the soul of Thy servant; for unto Thee *Adonai*, do I lift up my soul.

[5] For Thou *Adonai*, art good, and ready to pardon, and plenteous in mercy unto all them that call upon Thee.

[6] Give ear *YHVH* unto my prayer; and attend unto the voice of my supplications.

[7] In the day of my trouble I call upon Thee; for Thou wilt answer me.

[8] There is none like unto Thee among the gods *Adonai*, and there are no works like Thine.

[9] All nations whom Thou hast made shall come and prostrate themselves before Thee *Adonai*; and they shall glorify Thy name.
[10] For Thou art great, and doest wondrous things; Thou art God alone.
[11] Teach me *YHVH* Thy way, that I may walk in Thy truth; make one my heart to fear Thy name.
[12] I will thank Thee *Adonai* my God, with my whole heart; and I will glorify Thy name for evermore.
[13] For great is Thy mercy toward me; and Thou hast delivered my soul from the lowest nether-world.
[14] *Elohim*, the proud are risen up against me, and the company of violent men have sought after my soul, and have not set Thee before them.
[15] But Thou *Adonai*, art a God full of compassion and gracious, slow to anger, and plenteous in mercy and truth.
[16] O turn unto me, and be gracious unto me; give Thy strength unto Thy servant, and save the son of Thy handmaid.
[17] Work in my behalf a sign for good; that they that hate me may see it, and be put to shame, because Thou *YHVH*, hast helped me, and comforted me.

Psalms 85 and *86* are amongst the additional psalms recited in the Sefardic rite during *Yom Kippur* (Day of Atonement). Furthermore, as in the instance of the previous psalm, and equally applying to the following one, *Psalm 86* is enunciated in times of trouble.[1] Aside from this, *Psalm 86:11* has been recommended for recitation whilst walking, i.e. turning the act of strolling into a fully focussed walking meditation.[2] As it is, this verse references walking, and the rhythm of the words can be quite easily adjusted to align with the marching rhythm of your footsteps, as shown below:

הורני יהוה דרכך
אהלך באמתך
יחד לבבי ליראה שמך

Transliteration:
> *Horeini Adonai darkecha*
> *Ahalech ba'amitecha*
> *Yaheid l'vavi l'yirah sh'mecha.*

Translation:
> Teach me *YHVH* Thy way,
> I that I may walk in Thy truth;
> make one my heart to fear Thy name.

Whilst not listed in every published edition of the *Shimmush Tehillim*, the current psalm is employed in Jewish Magic for the purpose of escaping "a bad spell,"[3] and especially to rescue a possessed individual from an evil spirit.[4] In a variant recension of the *Shimmush Tehillim* we are informed that individuals who are seeking mercy, in order to be saved from every affliction and every evil spirit, should enunciate the current psalm with the following associated prayer-incantation:

יהי רצון מלפניך שתצילני מרוח רעה ומצרה
ומיצר הרע ומצר ושונא שלא יוכלו להרע לי
ולא לעשות לי שום נזק בעולם ולא יפחדוני
ולא יגעו במאתיים וארבעים ושמונה איברים
שבי בשם הקדוש אל ארך אפים אמן אמן אמן
אמן סלה סלה

Transliteration:
> *Y'hi ratzon mil'fanecha sh'tatzileini miru'ach ra'ah umitzarah um'yeitzer hara umitzar v'sonei shelo yuch'lu l'hara li v'lo la'asot li shum nezek ba'olam v'lo yaf'chiduni v'lo yig'u b'matayim v'ar'ba'im ush'monah eiverim shebi b'shem hakadosh El Erech Apayim Omein Omein Omein Selah Selah*

Translation:
> May it be your will to deliver from an evil spirit, from an affliction, from an evil impulse, from an adversary and hater, that they may do me no evil, and never cause me any harm. They shall not frighten me, nor strike down the 248 members that

are in me. In the holy Name *El Erech Apayim* ("Long-suffering God"), *Amen Amen Amen Selah Selah*.[5]

In his German/English versions of the *Shimmush Tehillim*, Godfrey Selig maintained that *Psalms 86* to *88* "are left without a holy name, and there is nothing further said about them, than that a person should accustom himself to pray them often, because by so doing much good can be done and much evil avoided."[6]

As far as the use of individual verses for magical purposes are concerned, it should be noted that the initials of the first five words of *Psalm 86:3* reading חנני אדני כי אליך אקרא (*chaneini adonai ki eilecha ek'ra*—"be gracious unto me *Adonai*; for unto Thee do I cry"), were conjoined in the Divine Name construct האבאא, which is employed in amulets as "a call for help."[7] This verse is also directly related to ללה (*Lelah*), the sixth portion of the "*Shem Vayisa Vayet*,"[8] which I noted elsewhere "is said to combine the opposing principles of דין (*Din*—'Judgment' [also *Gevurah*—'Severity']) and רחמים (*Rachamim*—'Compassion' [also *Chesed*—'Mercy']) on the sefirotic Tree."[9]

Be that as it may, we are informed the Divine Name construct יולו was formulated from the phrase in *Psalm 86:9* reading יבואו וישתחוו לפניך אדני (*yavo'u v'yish'tachavu l'fanecha adonai*—"[they] shall come and prostrate themselves before Thee *Adonai*").[10] This Divine Name construct is employed in prayer during times of need.[11] Whilst functioning perfectly well on its own, it was reported in the name of the great Rabbi Isaac Luria, that this Divine Name construct should be applied in conjunction with the set of Divine Names formed from *Psalm 8:2*.[12] I have addressed the latter in some detail in the first part of this tome.[13] Thinking of magical actions in "times of need," it should be noted, that in ancient days travelling away from home was fraught with danger. That being said, many readers would remind me correctly that it is no less dangerous travelling in modern-day vehicles at great speed on congested roads. Thus the magical use of biblical verses for safety and protection on the road, are as relevant today as it was in days of yore. In this regard, a Jewish traveller is instructed to place his/her hand on the מזוזה

(*Mezuzah*) at the front door, and, prior to leaving the residence, to recite *Psalm 86:17* ten times with great intent (*kavvanah g'dulah*). We are informed that this action will ensure the said individual is well protected.[14]

The eighty-sixth Psalm is recommended in the oral traditions shared amongst the common folk, for enunciation against plagues and epidemics, as well as against illness and for healing in general. It is recommended to individuals who find themselves in difficulty, and it is equally employed against threats, trouble and distress. It is further said to be good for protection in perilous situations and in times of trouble. In this regard, it is worth noting that childbirth is certainly a most stressful and perilous situation for many women. Hence the current psalm is recited during confinement. On the other hand, this psalm is recited for תשובה —*teshuvah* (spiritual return), i.e. atonement or repentance.

In Christian Magic *Psalm 86* is employed "to ensure that the wine is good."[15] In this regard, "*Le Livre d'Or*" instructs the practitioner to "read this Psalm twenty times over a wine press," followed by copying a set of magical characters to be located inside the wine press, and it is said "there will be blessings upon the wine."[16]

PSALM 87

[1] לבני קרח מזמור שיר יסודתו בהררי קדש
[2] אהב יהוה‎אדני‎אהדונהי שערי ציון מכל משכנות יעקב
[3] נכבדות מדבר בך עיר האלהים סלה
[4] אזכיר רהב ובבל לידעי הנה פלשת וצר עם כוש זה ילד שם
[5] ולציון יאמר איש ואיש ילד בה והוא יכוננה עליון
[6] יהוה‎אדני‎אהדונהי יספר בכתוב עמים זה ילד שם סלה
[7] ושרים כחללים כל מעיני בך

Transliteration:
[1] *liv'nei korach miz'mor shir yesudato b'har'rei kodesh*
[2] *oheiv YHVH sha'arei tziyon mikol mish'k'not ya'akov*
[3] *nich'badot m'dubar bach ir ha'elohim selah.*
[4] *az'kir rahav uvavel l'yod'ai hineih f'leshet v'tzor im kush zeh yulad sham.*
[5] *ulatziyon yei'amar ish v'ish yulad bah v'hu y'chon'neha el'yon*
[6] *YHVH yis'por bich'tov amim zeh yulad sham selah*
[7] *v'sharim k'chol'lim kol ma'yanai bach*

Translation:
[1] A Psalm of the sons of Korah; a Song. His foundation is in the holy mountains.
[2] *YHVH* loveth the gates of Zion more than all the dwellings of Jacob.
[3] Glorious things are spoken of Thee, O city of *Elohim*. *Selah*
[4] 'I will make mention of Rahab and Babylon as among them that know Me; behold Philistia, and Tyre, with Ethiopia; this one was born there.'
[5] But of Zion it shall be said: 'This man and that was born in her; and the Most High Himself doth establish her.'
[6] *YHVH* shall count in the register of the peoples: 'This one was born there.' *Selah*
[7] And whether they sing or dance, all my thoughts are in Thee.

Psalm 87 is one of the psalms enunciated in times of trouble,[1] and it is likewise said for the well-being of Jerusalem.[2] In Jewish Magic the current psalm is in fact noted to be good for saving any city.[3] In this regard, the eighty-seventh Psalm as well as *Psalm 88* are listed conjointly in the *Shimmush Tehillim* for recitation to liberate a city or a community.[4] I suspect it is due to *Psalms 86* to *88* not featuring in every publication of the *Shimmush Tehillim*, which led to Godfrey Selig's statement that "there is nothing further said about them."[5] However, there is a lot said in a variant recension of the *Shimmush Tehillim* about the current psalm being employed to deliver a city and/or a community besieged by enemies. In this instance, to redeem a city from the enemies who set upon it to take it captive, the practitioner is instructed to recite this psalm twenty-three times, each time enunciating the following prayer-incantation:

אנא אלהי עולם יושב הכרובים לפניך באתי
להפיל תחנתי ואל תתעלם מתחנתי ותפילתי
ותושיע ותמלט זאת העיר הטובה והאנשים
הטובים אשר בה אנשי חסד ומשפט ונותנין
צדקה לעניים ומתנות לאביונים ושומרים
מצוות בכל יכולתם ולא הולכים אחר תאות
לבם על כן יהוה אלהי תרחם עליהם ותפלטם
מיד אויביהם הצרים עליהם לאבדם מן העולם
ותשיב גמולם בראשם וימותו בעונם אנא יהוה
יה חי שדי שתשמרני ותצילני מכל רע אמן
אמן אמן סלה סלה סלה

Transliteration:
> *Ana elohei olam yosheiv hak'ruvim l'fanecha bati l'hapil t'chinati v'al tit'alem mit'chinati v't'filati v'toshi'a ut'maleit zot ha'ir hatovah v'ha'anashim hatovim asher bah an'shei chesed umish'pat v'not'nin tz'dakah la'aniyim umatanot l'ev'yonim v'shom'rim mitz'vot b'chol y'chol'tam v'lo hol'chim achar ta'avat libam al kein YHVH elohai t'racheim aleihem v't'fal'teim miyad oy'veihem hatzarim aleihem l'ov'dam min ha'olam v'tashiv*

> g'mulam barosham v'yamutu b'avonam ana YHVH Yah Chai Shadai shetish'm'reini v'tatzileini m'chol ra.

Translation:
> Please, Eternal God, who is enthroned (above) the Keruvim, I have come to cast my supplication before you. And you shall not hide yourself from my supplication and my prayer. And you shall redeem and save this good city and the good people who are in it, and are people of grace and justice, and give alms to the poor, and a camp to the needy, and keep the *Mitz'vot* (sacred ordinances) to the best of their ability. And they do not follow the desires of their heart. Therefore, *YHVH* my God, you should have mercy on them, and deliver them out of the hand of their enemies, who oppress them in order to exterminate them from the world. And you shall return their deeds back on their heads, and they shall perish because of their iniquity. Please *YHVH Yah Chai Shadai*, guard me and save me from all evil. *Amen Amen Amen Selah Selah Selah.*[6]

Considering what has been said regarding the magical application of *Psalm 87* in the *Shimmush Tehillim*, it should come as no surprise that this psalm is enunciated "to deliver one from prison."[7]

As far as individual verses are concerned, it should be noted that *Psalm 87:2* is directly affiliated with מנק (*Menak*), the sixty-sixth tri-letter portion of the "*Shem Vayisa Vayet*,"[8] and אי"ע (*Iya*), the sixty-seventh tri-letter portion of the "Name of Seventy-two Names." The latter tri-letter combination is said to be an acronym of the phrase reading אלהים יכוננה עליון (*Elohim Y'chon'neha Elyon*—"*Elohim* the most High will establish her"), this being a reference to *Psalm 87:5*.[9] Besides these associations, we find the phrase in *Psalm 87:6* reading זה ילד שם (*zeh yulad sham*—"this one was born there"), was employed in the formulation of a unique Divine Name construct. In this regard, the two letters comprising the word שם (*sham*—"there"), were transformed by means of the א"ת ב"ש (*Atbash*) cipher into the Divine Name יְבֻ (*Yevu*).[10] The vowels employed in the vocalisation of this Divine Name were derived from the two words זה ילד (*zeh yulad*—"this one was born"), i.e. the initial two words of the mentioned phrase from *Psalm 87:6*. We are informed that the *gematria* of the Name יב [י = 10 + ב = 2 = 12] references the twelve letters comprising the Divine Names אהיה יהוה אדני (*Eh'yeh YHVH Adonai*),[11] the three Divine Names respectively aligned with כתר (*Keter*—"Crown"), תפארת (*Tif'eret*—"beauty"), and מלכות (*Mal'chut*—"Kingship") on the sefirotic Tree.[12] These three *Sefirot* are in turn aligned with the "three Selves," i.e. נשמה (*Neshamah*—Divine Self), רוח (*Ru'ach*—Conscious Self), and נפש (*Nefesh*— Instinctual Self).[13] Be that as it may, it is said the Divine Names אהיה יהוה אדני (*Eh'yeh YHVH Adonai*) "sweetens" the, as it were, "fivefold power" of אלהים (*Elohim*) deriving from the expression שם סלה (*sham selah*—"there *Selah*"), the latter being the concluding two words of the said verse.[14]

To understand the meaning of this, it should be noted that the conjoined *gematria* of the words שם סלה (*sham selah* [ש = 300 + מ = 40 + ס = 60 + ל = 30 + ה = 5 = 435]) are around five times that of the Divine Name אלהים (*Elohim* [א = 1 + ל = 30 + ה = 5 + י = 10 + מ = 40 = 85]). Furthermore, as mentioned elsewhere, this five-letter Divine Name "is traditionally associated in Jewish esotericism with the qualities of 'severity,' 'judgment,' and 'fear',"[15] and it has been said that "this Name judges all who traverse the world with the appropriate judgments, whether they be positive or adverse, for life or for death."[16] Thus it is believed the malevolent impact of אלהים is "sweetened" by the daily recitation of a set unique Divine Name invocations. These comprise the twelve permutations of יהוה (*YHVH*) and אהיה (*Eh'yeh*), pertaining to the daylight hours, twelve months, and twelve zodiacal periods, which are enunciated in the morning after *Shacharit* (Morning Prayer Service), and the vocalisation of the twenty-four permutations of אדני (*Adonai*), traditionally affiliated with the hours of the "night cycle."[17] In this regard, I noted that "those who invoke these 'Divine Names' at their proper times, are able to interrupt and neutralise the negative impact of the 'Spiritual Forces' of the twenty-eight Lunar Mansions, and also to completely neutralise whatever malevolence might be in store for the invocants."[18] I have addressed the relevant procedure in great detail in previous volumes of this series of texts on "Practical Kabbalah."[19]

Once again we are informed in unofficial sources that, besides being utilised to deliver cities and communities besieged by enemies, and free those who are imprisoned, *Psalm 78* is equally employed against treachery (betrayal). The current psalm is further enunciated for the protection of paupers and beggars, and to extend the lives of familial breadwinners.

In Christian Magic the eighty-seventh Psalm is listed in the Byzantine magical manuscripts for recitation "against a hostile ruler."[20] Elsewhere, in "*Le Livre d'Or*" the current psalm is written with a set of magical characters, this being done "with the blood of a dove," fumigated with mastic and aloe wood, and attached to the arm. In this regard, the practitioner is told that "all your affairs will be soon fulfilled."[21]

PSALM 88

[1] שיר מזמור לבני קרח למנצח על מחלת לענות משכיל להימן האזרחי
[2] יְהוָֹהאֲדֹנָיאהדונהי אלהי ישועתי יום צעקתי בלילה נגדך
[3] תבוא לפניך תפלתי הטה אזנך לרנתי
[4] כי שבעה ברעות נפשי וחיי לשאול הגיעו
[5] נחשבתי עם יורדי בור הייתי כגבר אין איל
[6] במתים חפשי כמו חללים שכבי קבר אשר לא זכרתם עוד והמה מידך נגזרו
[7] שתני בבור תחתיות במחשכים במצלות
[8] עלי סמכה חמתך וכל משבריך ענית סלה
[9] הרחקת מידעי ממני שתני תועבות למו כלא ולא אצא
[10] עיני דאבה מני עני קראתיך יְהוָֹהאֲדֹנָיאהדונהי בכל יום שטחתי אליך כפי
[11] הלמתים תעשה פלא אם רפאים יקומו יודוך סלה
[12] היספר בקבר חסדך אמונתך באבדון
[13] היודע בחשך פלאך וצדקתך בארץ נשיה
[14] ואני אליך יְהוָֹהאֲדֹנָיאהדונהי שועתי ובבקר תפלתי תקדמך
[15] למה יְהוָֹהאֲדֹנָיאהדונהי תזנח נפשי תסתיר פניך ממני
[16] עני אני וגוע מנער נשאתי אמיך אפונה
[17] עלי עברו חרוניך בעותיך צמתותני
[18] סבוני כמים כל היום הקיפו עלי יחד
[19] הרחקת ממני אהב ורע מידעי מחשך

Transliteration:

[1] *shir miz'mor liv'nei korach lam'natzei'ach al machalat l'anot mas'kil l'heiman ha'ez'rachi*
[2] *YHVH Elohei y'shu'ati yom tza'ak'ti valaila neg'decha*
[3] *tavo l'faneicha t'filati hateih az'necha l'rinati*
[4] *ki sav'ah v'ra'ot naf'shi v'chayai lish'ol higi'u*

[5] nech'shav'ti im yor'dei vor hayiti k'gever ein eyal
[6] bameitim chaf'shi k'mo chalalim shoch'vei kever asher lo z'char'tam od v'heimah mi yad'cha nig'zaru
[7] shatani b'vor tach'tiyot b'machashakim bim'tzolot
[8] alai sam'chah chamatecha v'chol mish'barecha inita Selah
[9] hir'chak'ta m'yuda'ai mimeni shatani to'eivot lamo kalu v'lo eitzei
[10] eini da'avah mini oni k'raticha YHVH b'chol yom shitach'ti eilecha chapai
[11] halameitim ta'aseh pele im r'fa'im yakumu yoducha Selah
[12] ha'y'supar bakever chas'decha emunat'cha ba'avadon
[13] hayivada bachoshech pil'echa v'tzid'kat'cha b'eretz n'shiyah
[14] va'ani eilecha YHVH shiva'ti uvaboker t'filati t'kad'mecha
[15] lama YHVH tiz'nach naf'shi tas'tir panecha mimeni
[16] ani ani v'govei'a mino'ar nasati eimecha ufanah
[17] alai av'ru charonecha bi'utecha tzim'tutuni
[18] sabuni chamayim kol hayom hikifu alai yachad
[19] hir'chak'ta mimeni oheiv varei'a m'yuda'ai mach'shach

Translation:

[1] A Song, a Psalm of the sons of Korah; for the Leader; upon *Mahalath Leannoth. Maschil* of Heman the Ezrahite.
[2] YHVH, God of my salvation, what time I cry in the night before Thee,
[3] Let my prayer come before Thee, incline Thine ear unto my cry.
[4] For my soul is sated with troubles, and my life draweth nigh unto the grave.
[5] I am counted with them that go down into the pit; I am become as a man that hath no help;
[6] Set apart among the dead, like the slain that lie in the grave, whom Thou rememberest no more; and they are cut off from Thy hand.
[7] Thou hast laid me in the nethermost pit, in dark places, in the deeps.

[8] Thy wrath lieth hard upon me, and all Thy waves Thou pressest down. *Selah*

[9] Thou hast put mine acquaintance far from me; Thou hast made me an abomination unto them; I am shut up, and I cannot come forth.

[10] Mine eye languisheth by reason of affliction; I have called upon Thee *YHVH*, every day, I have spread forth my hands unto Thee.

[11] Wilt Thou work wonders for the dead? Or shall the shades arise and give Thee thanks? *Selah*.

[12] Shall Thy mercy be declared in the grave? or Thy faithfulness in destruction?

[13] Shall Thy wonders be known in the dark? and Thy righteousness in the land of forgetfulness?

[14] But as for me, unto Thee *YHVH*, do I cry, and in the morning doth my prayer come to meet Thee.

[15] *YHVH*, why castest Thou off my soul? Why hidest Thou Thy face from me?

[16] I am afflicted and at the point of death from my youth up; I have borne Thy terrors, I am distracted.

[17] Thy fierce wrath is gone over me; Thy terrors have cut me off.

[18] They came round about me like water all the day; they compassed me about together.

[19] Friend and companion hast Thou put far from me, and mine acquaintance into darkness.

As noted earlier *Psalm 88* is enunciated in Jewish Magic conjointly with the previous psalm to rescue a city or a community.[1] However, it should be noted that the current psalm is also recommended for recitation during illness.[2] In this regard, we are told in one recension of the *Shimmush Tehillim*, that the current psalm is good for those who are afflicted with serious diseases. Here the practitioner is instructed to recite the eighty-eighth Psalm eighteen times conjointly with the phrase from *Exodus 34:6* reading ויעבר יהוה על פניו (*vaya'avor YHVH al panav*—"And YHVH passed by before him"). This is followed by reciting the following prayer-incantation:

רפאיני יהוה וארפא הושיעני ואושעה כי תהלתי
אתה (Jeremiah 17:14) יהוה אלהי רפאיני מחלי זה
כמו שרפאתה חזקיה מלך יהודה ומרים הנביאה
ונעמן מצרעתו כן יהי רצון מלפניך שתרפאני
ותחזקני בבריאות שלימה ואמצני וצדקני וכפר
עונותי והשיבני בתשובה שלימה לעבדך בלבב
שלם באמת ברוך אתה יהוה רופא חולים

Transliteration:

> R'fa'eini YHVH v'eirafei hoshi'eini v'ivashei'ah ki t'hilati atah (Jeremiah 17:14) YHVH elohai r'fa'eini meicholi zeh k'mo sherafatah chiz'kiya melech y'hudah umir'yam han'vi'ah v'na'aman mitzarato ken y'hi ratzon mil'fanecha sh'tir'pa'eini v't'chaz'keini b'bri'ut sh'leimah v'am'tzeini v'tzad'keini v'kaper avonotai v'hashiveini b't'shuvah sh'leimah l'av'd'cha b'leivav shaleim b'emet baruch atah YHVH rofei cholim

Translation:

> Heal me, YHVH, and I shall be healed; save me. and I shall be saved; for Thou art my praise. (Jeremiah 17:14) YHVH my God, heal me from this disease, as you healed Hezekiah the king of Judah, Miriam the prophetess, and Na'aman of his leprosy. So may it be your will that you heal me and strengthen me in complete health. Make me strong, vindicate me, and atone for my transgressions. Let me, your servant, with all my heart return in truth, in complete repentance. Blessed are you, Lord, healer of the sick.[3]

Hezekiah, King of Judah; *Miriam*, the sister of Moses; and *Na'aman*, are biblical personalities who were cured from serious medical conditions. There is no certainty as to what King Hezekiah suffered from, but Miriam and Na'aman were both afflicted with leprosy, and, as said, all three experienced miraculous recovery, hence the reference to these specific personalities in the prayer-incantation.

The current psalm is amongst several listed against all kinds of trouble and distress. It is employed for protection against heartless individuals, tyranny, abandonment and feeling forsaken, to find safety from fear, as well as for Divine Justice and equality. It is further enunciated against pride, and to encourage humility. It is also recited against storms in general.

As far as individual verses from the current psalm are concerned, it should be noted that *Psalm 88:2* is directly affliated with אלד (*Elad*), the tenth portion, *Psalm 88:14* with כוק (*K'vek*), the thirty-fifth portion, and *Psalm 88:15* with הזי (*Hezi*), the ninth portion of the "*Shem Vayisa Vayet.*"[4]

In terms of the use of the eighty-eighth Psalm in Christian Magic, it is said in "*Le Livre d'Or*" that an individual who has been harmed by an enemy in any way, should write the current psalm inside "a new cooking pot, filled with water from a well or a spring" which has not been exposed to the sun or moonlight. Following this action, a set of magical characters are copied onto a plate of glass, which is then cleaned in the water. It appears a woman is washed with this liquid, and the resulting substance disposed of "at the door of the enemy."[5]

PSALM 89

[1] משכיל לאיתן האזרחי
[2] חסדי יהו‎ה‎אדני‎אהדונהי עולם אשירה לדר ודר אודיע אמונתך בפי
[3] כי אמרתי עולם חסד יבנה שמים תכן אמונתך בהם
[4] כרתי ברית לבחירי נשבעתי לדוד עבדי
[5] עד עולם אכין זרעך ובניתי לדר ודור כסאך סלה
[6] ויודו שמים פלאך יהו‎ה‎אדני‎אהדונהי אף אמונתך בקהל קדשים
[7] כי מי בשחק יערך ליהו‎ה‎אדני‎אהדונהי ידמה ליהו‎ה‎אדני‎אהדונהי בבני אלים
[8] אל נערץ בסוד קדשים רבה ונורא על כל סביביו
[9] יהו‎ה‎אדני‎אהדונהי אלהי צבאות מי כמוך חסין יה ואמונתך סבובותיך
[10] אתה מושל בגאות הים בשוא גליו אתה תשבחם
[11] אתה דכאת כחלל רהב בזרוע עזך פזרת אויביך
[12] לך שמים אף לך ארץ תבל ומלאה אתה יסדתם
[13] צפון וימין אתה בראתם תבור וחרמון בשמך ירננו
[14] לך זרוע עם גבורה תעז ידך תרום ימינך
[15] צדק ומשפט מכון כסאך חסד ואמת יקדמו פניך
[16] אשרי העם יודעי תרועה יהו‎ה‎אדני‎אהדונהי באור פניך יהלכון
[17] בשמך יגילון כל היום ובצדקתך ירומו
[18] כי תפארת עזמו אתה וברצונך תרום קרנינו
[19] כי ליהו‎ה‎אדני‎אהדונהי מגננו ולקדוש ישראל מלכנו
[20] אז דברת בחזון לחסידיך ותאמר שויתי עזר על גבור הרימותי בחור מעם
[21] מצאתי דוד עבדי בשמן קדשי משחתיו

[22] אֲשֶׁר יָדִי תִּכּוֹן עִמּוֹ אַף זְרוֹעִי תְאַמְּצֶנּוּ

[23] לֹא יַשִּׁא אוֹיֵב בּוֹ וּבֶן עַוְלָה לֹא יְעַנֶּנּוּ

[24] וְכַתּוֹתִי מִפָּנָיו צָרָיו וּמְשַׂנְאָיו אֶגּוֹף

[25] וֶאֱמוּנָתִי וְחַסְדִּי עִמּוֹ וּבִשְׁמִי תָּרוּם קַרְנוֹ

[26] וְשַׂמְתִּי בַיָּם יָדוֹ וּבַנְּהָרוֹת יְמִינוֹ

[27] הוּא יִקְרָאֵנִי אָבִי אָתָּה אֵלִי וְצוּר יְשׁוּעָתִי

[28] אַף אָנִי בְּכוֹר אֶתְּנֵהוּ עֶלְיוֹן לְמַלְכֵי אָרֶץ

[29] לְעוֹלָם אֶשְׁמָר לוֹ חַסְדִּי וּבְרִיתִי נֶאֱמֶנֶת לוֹ

[30] וְשַׂמְתִּי לָעַד זַרְעוֹ וְכִסְאוֹ כִּימֵי שָׁמָיִם

[31] אִם יַעַזְבוּ בָנָיו תּוֹרָתִי וּבְמִשְׁפָּטַי לֹא יֵלֵכוּן

[32] אִם חֻקֹּתַי יְחַלֵּלוּ וּמִצְו‍ֹתַי לֹא יִשְׁמֹרוּ

[33] וּפָקַדְתִּי בְשֵׁבֶט פִּשְׁעָם וּבִנְגָעִים עֲו‍ֹנָם

[34] וְחַסְדִּי לֹא אָפִיר מֵעִמּוֹ וְלֹא אֲשַׁקֵּר בֶּאֱמוּנָתִי

[35] לֹא אֲחַלֵּל בְּרִיתִי וּמוֹצָא שְׂפָתַי לֹא אֲשַׁנֶּה

[36] אַחַת נִשְׁבַּעְתִּי בְקָדְשִׁי אִם לְדָוִד אֲכַזֵּב

[37] זַרְעוֹ לְעוֹלָם יִהְיֶה וְכִסְאוֹ כַשֶּׁמֶשׁ נֶגְדִּי

[38] כְּיָרֵחַ יִכּוֹן עוֹלָם וְעֵד בַּשַּׁחַק נֶאֱמָן סֶלָה

[39] וְאַתָּה זָנַחְתָּ וַתִּמְאָס הִתְעַבַּרְתָּ עִם מְשִׁיחֶךָ

[40] נֵאַרְתָּה בְּרִית עַבְדֶּךָ חִלַּלְתָּ לָאָרֶץ נִזְרוֹ

[41] פָּרַצְתָּ כָל גְּדֵרֹתָיו שַׂמְתָּ מִבְצָרָיו מְחִתָּה

[42] שַׁסֻּהוּ כָּל עֹבְרֵי דָרֶךְ הָיָה חֶרְפָּה לִשְׁכֵנָיו

[43] הֲרִימוֹתָ יְמִין צָרָיו הִשְׂמַחְתָּ כָּל אוֹיְבָיו

[44] אַף תָּשִׁיב צוּר חַרְבּוֹ וְלֹא הֲקֵימֹתוֹ בַּמִּלְחָמָה

[45] הִשְׁבַּתָּ מִטְּהָרוֹ וְכִסְאוֹ לָאָרֶץ מִגַּרְתָּה

[46] הִקְצַרְתָּ יְמֵי עֲלוּמָיו הֶעֱטִיתָ עָלָיו בּוּשָׁה סֶלָה

[47] עַד מָה יְהֹוָהאֲדֹנָי תִּסָּתֵר לָנֶצַח תִּבְעַר כְּמוֹ אֵשׁ חֲמָתֶךָ

[48] זְכָר אֲנִי מֶה חָלֶד עַל מַה שָּׁוְא בָּרָאתָ כָל בְּנֵי אָדָם

[49] מִי גֶבֶר יִחְיֶה וְלֹא יִרְאֶה מָּוֶת יְמַלֵּט נַפְשׁוֹ מִיַּד שְׁאוֹל סֶלָה

[50] אַיֵּה חֲסָדֶיךָ הָרִאשֹׁנִים אֲדֹנָי נִשְׁבַּעְתָּ לְדָוִד בֶּאֱמוּנָתֶךָ

[51] זכר אדני חרפת עבדיך שאתי בחיקי כל רבים עמים

[52] אשר חרפו אויביך יהוה‎ אשר חרפו עקבות משיחך

[53] ברוך יהוה‎ לעולם אמן ואמן

Transliteration:

[1] *mas'kil l'eitan ha'ez'rachi*

[2] *chas'dei YHVH olam ashirah l'dor vador odi'a emunat'cha b'fi*

[3] *ki amarti olam chesed yibaneh shamayim tachin emunat'cha vahem*

[4] *karati v'rit liv'chiri nish'ba'ti l'david av'di*

[5] *ad olam achin zar'echa uvaniti l'dor vador kis'acha Selah*

[6] *v'yodu shamayim pil'acha YHVH af emunatecha bik'hal k'dshim*

[7] *ki mi vashachak ya'aroch la'YHVH yid'meh la'YHVH biv'nei eilim*

[8] *el na aratz b'sod k'dshim rabah v'nora al kol s'vivav*

[9] *YHVH elohei tz'va'ot mi chamocha chasin Yah v'emunat'cha s'vivoteicha*

[10] *atah moshel b'gei'ut hayam b'sho'o galav atah t'shab'cheim*

[11] *atah dikita chechalal rahav biz'ro'a uz'cha pizar'ta oy'veicha*

[12] *l'cha shamayim af l'cha aretz teiveil um'lo'ah atah y'sad'tam*

[13] *tzafon v'yamin atah v'ratam tavor v'cher'mon b'shim'cha y'raneinu*

[14] *l'cha z'ro'a im gevurah ta'oz yad'cha tarum y'minecha*

[15] *tzedek umish'pat m'chon kis'echa chesed v'emet y'kad'mu fanecha*

[16] *ash'rei ha'am yod'ei t'ru'ah YHVH b'or panecha y'haleichun*

[17] *b'shim'cha y'dilun kol hayom uv'tzid'kat'cha yarumu*

[18] *ki tif'eret uzamo atah uvir'tzon'cha tarum kar'neinu*

[19] ki la'YHVH magineinu v'lik'dosh yis'ra'eil mal'keinu
[20] az dibar'ta v'chazon lachasidecha vatomer shiviti eizer al gibor harimoti vachur mei'am
[21] matzati david av'di b'shemen kad'shi m'shach'tiv
[22] asher yadi tikon imo af z'ro'i t'am'tzenu
[23] lo yashi oyeiv bo uvein av'lah lo y'anenu
[24] v'chatoti mipanav um'san'av egof
[25] ve'emunati v'chas'di imo uvish'mi tarum kar'no
[26] v'sam'ti vayam yado uvan'harot y'mino
[27] hu yik'ra'eini avi atah eili v'tzur y'shu'ati
[28] af ani b'chor et'neihu el'yon l'mal'chei aretz
[29] l'olam esh'mor lo chas'di uv'riti ne'emenet lo
[30] v'sam'ti la'ad zar'o v'chis'o shamayim
[31] im ya'az'vu vanav torati uv'mish'patai lo yeileichun
[32] im chuklotai y'chaleilu umitz'votai lo yish'moru
[33] ufakad'ti v'sheivet pish'am uvin'ga'im avonam
[34] v'chas'di lo afir mei'imo v'lo ashakeir be'emunati
[35] lo achaleil b'riti umotza s'fatai lo ashaneh
[36] achat nish'bati v'kad'shi im l'david achazeiv
[37] zar'o l'olam yih'yeh v'chis'o chashemesh neg'di
[38] k'yarei'ach yikon olam v'eid bashachak ne'eman selah
[39] v'atah zanachta vatim'as hit'abarta im m'shichecha
[40] nei'artah b'rit av'decha chilal'ta la'aretz niz'ro
[41] paratz'ta chol g'deirotav sam'ta miv'tzarav m'chitah
[42] shasuhu kol ov'rei darech hayah cher'pah lish'cheinav
[43] harimota y'min tzarav his'mach'tah kol oy'vav
[44] af tashiv tzur har'bo v'lo hakeimoto bamil'chamah
[45] hish'bata mit'haro v'chis'o la'aretz migar'tah
[46] hik'tzr'ta y'mei alomav he'etita alav bushah selah
[47] ad mah YHVH tisateir lanetzach tib'ar k'mo esh chamatecha
[48] z'char ani meh chaled al mah shav barata chol b'nei adam
[49] mi geber yich'yeh v'lo yir'eh mavet y'maleit naf'sho miyad sh'ol selah

[50] *ayeih chasadecha harishonim adonai nish'ba'ta l'david be'emunatecha*
[51] *z'chor adonai cher'pat avadecha sh'eiti v'cheiki kol rabim amim*
[52] *asher cheir'po oy'vecha YHVH asher cheir'po ik'vot mish'checha*
[53] *baruch YHVH l'olam omein v'omein*

Translation:

[1] *Maschil* of Ethan the Ezrahite.

[2] I will sing of the mercies of *YHVH* for ever; to all generations will I make known Thy faithfulness with my mouth.

[3] For I have said: 'For ever is mercy built; in the very heavens Thou dost establish Thy faithfulness.

[4] I have made a covenant with My chosen, I have sworn unto David My servant:

[5] For ever will I establish thy seed, and build up thy throne to all generations.' *Selah*

[6] So shall the heavens praise Thy wonders *YHVH*, Thy faithfulness also in the assembly of the holy ones.

[7] For who in the skies can be compared unto the *YHVH*, who among the sons of might can be likened unto *YHVH*,

[8] A God dreaded in the great council of the holy ones, and feared of all them that are about Him?

[9] *YHVH* God of hosts, who is a mighty one, like unto Thee *Yah*? And Thy faithfulness is round about Thee.

[10] Thou rulest the proud swelling of the sea; when the waves thereof arise, Thou stillest them.

[11] Thou didst crush Rahab, as one that is slain; Thou didst scatter Thine enemies with the arm of Thy strength.

[12] Thine are the heavens, Thine also the earth; the world and the fulness thereof, Thou hast founded them.

[13] The north and the south, Thou hast created them; Tabor and Hermon rejoice in Thy name.

[14] Thine is an arm with might; strong is Thy hand, and exalted is Thy right hand.

[15] Righteousness and justice are the foundation of Thy throne; mercy and truth go before Thee.

[16] Happy is the people that know the joyful shout; they walk *YHVH*, in the light of Thy countenance.
[17] In Thy name do they rejoice all the day; and through Thy righteousness are they exalted.
[18] For Thou art the glory of their strength; and in Thy favour our horn is exalted.
[19] For of *YHVH* is our shield; and the Holy One of Israel is our king.
[20] Then Thou spokest in vision to Thy godly ones, and saidst: 'I have laid help upon one that is mighty; I have exalted one chosen out of the people.
[21] I have found David My servant; with My holy oil have I anointed him;
[22] With whom My hand shall be established; Mine arm also shall strengthen him.
[23] The enemy shall not exact from him; nor the son of wickedness afflict him.
[24] And I will beat to pieces his adversaries before him, and smite them that hate him.
[25] But My faithfulness and My mercy shall be with him; and through My name shall his horn be exalted.
[26] I will set his hand also on the sea, and his right hand on the rivers.
[27] He shall call unto Me: Thou art my Father, my God, and the rock of my salvation.
[28] I also will appoint him first-born, the highest of the kings of the earth.
[29] For ever will I keep for him My mercy, and My covenant shall stand fast with him.
[30] His seed also will I make to endure for ever, and his throne as the days of heaven.
[31] If his children forsake My law, and walk not in Mine ordinances;
[32] If they profane My statutes, and keep not My commandments;
[33] Then will I visit their transgression with the rod, and their iniquity with strokes.

[34] But My mercy will I not break off from him, nor will I be false to My faithfulness.
[35] My covenant will I not profane, nor alter that which is gone out of My lips.
[36] Once have I sworn by My holiness: Surely I will not be false unto David;
[37] His seed shall endure for ever, and his throne as the sun before Me.
[38] It shall be established for ever as the moon; and be steadfast as the witness in sky.' *Selah*
[39] But Thou hast cast off and rejected, Thou hast been wroth with Thine anointed.
[40] Thou hast abhorred the covenant of Thy servant; Thou hast profaned his crown even to the ground.
[41] Thou hast broken down all his fences; Thou hast brought his strongholds to ruin.
[42] All that pass by the way spoil him; he is become a taunt to his neighbours.
[43] Thou hast exalted the right hand of his adversaries; Thou hast made all his enemies to rejoice.
[44] Yea, Thou turnest back the edge of his sword, and hast not made him to stand in the battle.
[45] Thou hast made his brightness to cease, and cast his throne down to the ground.
[46] The days of his youth hast Thou shortened; Thou hast covered him with shame. *Selah*
[47] How long *YHVH*, wilt Thou hide Thyself for ever? How long shall Thy wrath burn like fire?
[48] O remember how short my time is; for what vanity hast Thou created all the children of men!
[49] What man is he that liveth and shall not see death, that shall deliver his soul from the power of the grave? *Selah*
[50] Where are Thy former mercies *Adonai*, which Thou didst swear unto David in Thy faithfulness?
[51] Remember *Adonai*, the taunt of Thy servants; how I do bear in my bosom the taunt of so many peoples;

[52] Wherewith Thine enemies have taunted *YHVH*, wherewith they have taunted the footsteps of Thine anointed.

[53] Blessed be *YHVH* for evermore. Amen, and Amen.

Psalm 89 is recommended to individuals who are seeking mercy from heaven.[1] However, in Jewish Magic the current psalm is mainly employed "against the effects of sickness,"[2] i.e. it should be recited by those who are losing limbs,[3] or whose organs are disintegrating as a result of severe illness.[4] In this regard, we are informed in the popular editions of the *Shimmush Tehillim* that an individual whose limbs and bones are broken from disease, should recite the eighty-ninth Psalm olive oil. "Wool from a shorn ram" is afterwards soaked with the oil, then lit, and the smoke passed over the sufferer.[5] According to other recensions the oil-soaked wool is from "a sheep," which is prepared as a bandage to be tied around the sufferer.[6] Be that as it may, the said standard version of the *Shimmush Tehillim* further recommends the enunciation of the current psalm to free a captive. To affect this purpose the practitioner is instructed to go outside into the open air, and to recite the psalm with eyes turned skywards.[7]

As readers may expect by now, Godfrey Selig's German/English versions of the eighty-ninth Psalm expands the brief instructions to be found in the *Shimmush Tehillim*, saying "Should one of your own family or dear friends waste away so rapidly, in consequence of a severe illness, so that they are already nearly helpless and useless, speak this Psalm over olive oil and pour the oil over the wool that has been shorn from a ram (or buck sheep), and with it anoint the body and limbs of the patient, and he will speedily recover." They likewise include the second application, noting that "if your friend is under arrest, and you desire his liberation, go into an open field, raise your eyes toward heaven and repeat this Psalm, with a prayer suited to the circumstances, which should be uttered in full confidence in God."[8]

In a variant recension of the *Shimmush Tehillim* the current psalm is recommended to those who wish to give alms or perform charitable deeds. In this regard, the practitioner is instructed to enunciate the psalm every day in conjunction with the following prayer-incantation:[9]

אֵל אֱלֹהֵי עוֹלָם שָׁמְרֵנִי וְחַזְּקֵנִי וְאַמְּצֵנִי וְצַדְּקֵנִי
וְזָכְרֵנִי וְתֵן לִי יְכוֹלֶת לָתֵת צְדָקָה לָעֲנִיִּים בְּשֵׁם
הַגָּדוֹל וְהַקָּדוֹשׁ מֶלֶךְ **פֶּלֶא גִּבּוֹר** אָמֵן אָמֵן אָמֵן
סֶלָה סֶלָה סֶלָה

Transliteration:
> *El Elohei olam sham'reini v'chaz'keini v'am'tzeini v'tzad'keini v'zach'reini v'tein li y'cholet lateit tz'dakah la'aniyim b'shem hagadol v'hakadosh Melech Pele Gibor Omein Omein Omein Selah Selah Selah*

Translation:
> God, Eternal God, keep me, empower me, make me strong, vindicate me, remember me, and grant me the capacity to give alms to the poor. In the great and holy name *Melech Pele Gibor* ("Mighty Wondrous King"). *Amen Amen Amen Selah Selah Selah.*[10]

Whilst *Psalm 89* is recommended to those who suffer the crippling after effects of sickness, this psalm is also recited against being plagued with illness generally, as well as for the recovery of patients. It is equally enunciated to allow the sickly to perform their daily tasks without fatigue. Aside from this, the current psalm is employed against all manner of trouble and tribulations, as well as against despair. As noted, it is recited prior to performing charitable acts. In this regard, it is uttered for gifts received or to be given, and equally to maintain the dignity of those who are on the receiving end, and to ensure that they are not "eating bread of shame." Aside from these applications, the current psalm is recounted against spiritual troubles, and for old age and a happy retirement,

In Christian Magic the eighty-ninth Psalm is listed in the Byzantine magical manuscripts for use in conditions of war. In this regard, it is spoken, written, and bound to the right hand.[11] On the other hand, it is recommended elsewhere for headaches. In this instance we are informed in *"Le Livre d'Or"* that this psalm should be written on the head of the sufferer, enunciated over holy water, and sprinkled in the residence, following which it is said "God's blessing will be upon it."[12] In this instance the main issue is exactly how the fifty-three verses comprising *Psalm 89* are to be written on the relatively small space afforded by the human skull! A much simpler application is the employment of *Psalm 89:18* against headaches.[13]

. ...And because the golem always sat in a corner of the courtroom at the edge of a table resting his head on his hands, looking indeed like an unfinished vessel, lacking wisdom and understanding nothing, and not worrying about a thing under the sun, the people called him Yossele the golem, while some name him Yossele the mute... ... .

Index of Magical Applications

1. General

Affliction & the Afflicted: **[Part 1]** 38;

Bad Incidents [to be rescued from]: **[Part 2]** 46:8
Bad Things & Circumstances [against]: **[Part 1]** 26; 30; **[Part 2]** 67

Danger [protection against any type of]: **[Part 2]** 49:6; 77
Disaster [generally against]: **[Part 2]** 48; 57
Disasters [public]: **[Part 1]** 16; **[Part 2]** 45
Disasters [unforseen]: **[Part 1]** 40

Everything [for]: **[Part 1]** 9; 25; 32:7; 39

Grievous Circumstances [a call for help in]: **[Part 2]** 67

Help [a call for]: **[Part 1]** 16:8; 19:15; 20:2; 20:10; 27:7; 30:11; 34:8; 41:4; **[Part 2]** 46:8; 46:12; 67; 67:1–2; 86:3

Injuries & Damage [of every kind]: **[Part 1]** 14; 17:8; **[Part 2]** 68
Injury [against suffering]: **[Part 2]** 67
Invisibility [to see & not be seen]: **[Part 1]** 31:21

Liberty [for true]: **[Part 2]** 71
Life & Rescue: **[Part 1]** 31
Lost Keys [finding]: **[Part 1]** 16

Need [to be saved from every]: **[Part 2]** 42; 86:9

Odours [against bad]: **[Part 2]** 84
Open Doors [in spite of a lost key]: **[Part 1]** 24

Praise: **[Part 1]** 8; 19; 33; **[Part 2]** 65
Protection [general]: **[Part 1]** 32:7; **[Part 2]** 48; 67
Prosperity [general]: **[Part 2]** 67
Purpose & Need [for any]: **[Part 1]** 4

Redstring [preparation]: **[Part 1]** 33
Respect [general]: **[Part 2]** 78

Safety [general]: **[Part 2]** 67
Secret Things [revelation & certitude of]: **[Part 1]** 16; 31
Suffering: **[Part 1]** 38; 39

Temporal affairs & Trouble [of every kind]: **[Part 1]** 22; 25
Troublesome Situations [for protection in]: **[Part 2]** 67

2. Health, Healing & General Physical Well-being
Anaemia: **[Part 1]** 21; 37; **[Part 2]** 72
Asthma: **[Part 1]** 3:9

Backache: **[Part 1]** 3
Bites: **[Part 1]** 21; 31
Blood [diseases]: **[Part 1]** 6
Body [emaciated from severe illnesses]: **[Part 2]** 84
Bones [diseases]: **[Part 1]** 6:3-4; 21; 31:11; 33; 34:21; 38:11
Bones [broken or disintegrating due to severe illness]: **Part 2]** 89
Broken limbs: **[Part 1]** 37

Cancer: **[Part 1]** 37
Chest [diseases of]: **[Part 1]** 21; **[Part 2]** 72
Constipation [to alleviate]: **[Part 1]** 31:10
Convalescence: **[Part 2]** 65

Deafness [loss of hearing]: **[Part 1]** 37
Diarrhea [to alleviate]: **[Part 1]** 31:10
Digestive Tract [ailments of]: **[Part 1]** 31:10
Diseases [general]: **[Part 1]** 29; **[Part 2]** 87
Diseases [serious or incurable]: **[Part 1]** 9; 21   **[Part 2]** 88
Dumb [for the]: **[Part 1]** 38

Energy [for]: **[Part 2]** 43
Epidemics [against]: **[Part 2]** 43; 51
Epilepsy: **[Part 1]** 16; 37; 78
Eyes [diseases of & pain in the]: **[Part 1]** 6; 10; 12; 13; 37

Fatigue (languor/lethargy): **[Part 1]** 31
Fever [against]: **[Part 1]** 8:2; 13; 15; 16; 17; 18; 19; 34; 37; **[Part 2]** 49; 67; 68; 78
Feet [problems with]: **[Part 2]** 82
Fever [against chronic or incurable]: **[Part 2]** 49; 50; 67
Food Poisoning [to alleviate]: **[Part 1]** 31:10

Gangrene: **[Part 1]** 37

Haemorrhage & Loss of Blood [to halt]: **[Part 1]** 1:1–3; **[Part 2]** 51:3
Head [against diseases of the]: **[Part 2]** 67
Headaches [brought on by stress]: **[Part 2]** 57
Headaches & Pains in the Head [Against]: **[Part 1]** 2; 3; 7
Healing [to facilitate]: **[Part 2]** 67; 69:7
Heart [ailments & problems]: **[Part 1]** 13; 21; 31:11; 34:19; 38:11; **[Part 2]** 44; 45; 51:12; 62:9; 72

Illness [against being plagued with]: **[Part 2]** 89
Illness [against the effects of]: **[Part 2]** 89
Illness & Healing [in general]: **[Part 1]** 4; 6; 6:1–4; 7; 9; 10; 13; 16; 18; 20; 23; 25; 27; 29; 30; 30:3; 31; 32; 33; 34:18; 37; 38; 39; 41; **[Part 2]** 42; 49; 51; 55; 69; 81; 84; 85; 86; 88
Indigestion [to alleviate]: **[Part 1]** 31:10
Infections [protection against]: **[Part 2]** 49:6
Infirmity: **[Part 1]** 6; 15

Jaws [pain in]: **[Part 1]** 38; **[Part 2]** 45; 72

Kedachat [to counteract (a type of fever)]: **[Part 2]** 49; 67
Kidneys [diseases of]: **[Part 1]** 15; 19; **[Part 2]** 45; 72

Legs [problems with]: **[Part 2]** 82
Limbs [diseases of]: **[Part 1]** 16; **[Part 2]** 72
Limbs & Bodily Organs [losing or disintegrating due to severe illness]: **Part 2]** 89
Liver Problems: **[Part 1]** 13

Malaria: **[Part 2]** 49; 67
Muscles [ailments of]: **[Part 1]** 38:4; **[Part 2]**
Mutes [when unable to speak]: **[Part 2]** 59

Pains [general]: **[Part 2]** 77
Paralysis: **[Part 2]** 50
Plagues (Epidemics/Pandemics) [to be saved & protected from]:
[Part 1] 33; **[Part 2]** 86

Recovery [of patients]: **[Part 2]** 89
Rheumatism: **[Part 1]** 15; 31

Shoulders [pain]: **[Part 1]** 3
Skin [ailments of]: **[Part 1]** 38:4
Sportsmen: **[Part 1]** 17
Stomach [diseases of]: **[Part 1]** 13; 21

Toothache [pains in teeth & gums]: **[Part 1]** 3
Throat [pains in]: **[Part 1]** 2; **[Part 2]** 68
Tuberculosis: **[Part 1]** 3:9

Voice [preservation of]: **[Part 1]** 32; **[Part 2]** 68

Walking [difficulties with]: **[Part 2]** 82
Weakness & Trembling [generally & due to illness]: **[Part 1]** 12; 31:11; 37; **[Part 2]** 72; 84
Weight Loss [due to illness]: 84
Wounds [healing of]: **[Part 1]** 37

3. Mental & Emotional Well-being

Adultery [against]: **[Part 2]** 69
Alcoholics [repentant]: **[Part 2]** 68
Anxiety: **[Part 1]** 4; 22; 23; **[Part 2]** 56
Anxiety [caused by enemies]: **[Part 1]** 3; 5; 6; 7; 9; 17; 22; 25; 31; 35; 38; **[Part 2]** 43; 54; 55; 56; 57; 59; 71
Apathy [indifference/disinterest]: **[Part 1]** 38; **[Part 2]** 48
Avarice [against]: **[Part 2]** 69

Character [for self improvement & a good]: **[Part 1]** 13; 15; 20; 21; **[Part 2]**
Chastity [to maintain]: **[Part 1]** 11
Choice [in life]: **[Part 1]** 24;
Comfort [in need of]: **[Part 1]** 23
Confusion [resulting from the success of the wicked]: **[Part 1]** 1; 37; **[Part 2]** 49; 73

Debauchery [against]: **[Part 2]** 51; 69
Depression (brought on by poverty) [to relieve]: **[Part 2]** 81
Depression (brought on by unemployment) [to relieve]: **[Part 1]** 39
Depression [to counteract]: **[Part 1]** 30; **[Part 2]** 42; 43; 66;
Despair [against]: **[Part 1]** 3; 15; 24; 41; **[Part 2]** 42; 54; 56; 67; 68; 89
Difficulties [for prevention of]: **[Part 2]** 77
Difficulties & Sorrow [to be saved from]: **[Part 1]** 30; 33
Difficulty [for a person in]: **[Part 1]** 25; 26; **[Part 2]** 86
Disruptive Changes [in life]: **[Part 2]** 48; 57
Distress [for all manner of]: **[Part 2]** 71; 77
Drunkeness [against & for loss of reason due to]: **[Part 1]** 37; **[Part 2]** 68
Drunkards [to cure]: **[Part 1]** 37

Evil Counsel (bad advice) [protection against]: **[Part 1]** 12; 38
Evil Inclination/Desire to Receive [(יצר הרע—*yetzer hara*) against]: **[Part 1]** 15; **[Part 2]** 56; 59; 69
Excesses [against]: **[Part 2]** 69; 77

Fear (Paranoia) [against]: **[Part 1]** 11; 14; 20:3 **[Part 2]** 49:6
Fear [safety from]: **[Part 1]** 4; 11; 12; 20:3; 22; 23; 26; **[Part 2]** 49:6; 54; 56; 73; 88
Forgiveness: **[Part 1]** 25
Fornication [(זנות—*z'nut*) against]: **[Part 2]** 51; 69
Forsaken [feeling]: **[Part 1]** 27; **[Part 2]** 88
Frightening Experiences & being Fearful: **[Part 2]** 53
Frustration [with wickedness of others]: **[Part 1]** 36; **[Part 2]** 52; 53; 58

Gratitude [to express]: **[Part 1]** 9; 17; 18; 21; 23; 33; **[Part 2]** 42; 57; 63; 68; 71; 72
Greed [against]: **[Part 2]** 69
Guilt [when suffering from]: **[Part 2]** 51

Honesty & Honest People: **[Part 2]** 50
Humility [to encourage]: **[Part 2]** 73; 88

Incredulity [disbelief]: **[Part 1]** 13; **[Part 2]** 52
Injustice [perplexed by]: **[Part 1]** 10
Injustice [when incited to commit]: **[Part 2]** 62
Injustice & Violence [against being falsely accused of]: **[Part 2]** 73
Internal desolation: **[Part 1]** 29
Insanity [against]: **[Part 1]** 15

Laziness & Procrastination [against]: **[Part 1]** 5; **[Part 2]** 68
Lechery [against]: **[Part 2]** 69
Loss of Reason [due to alcohol]: **[Part 1]** 37

Melancholy [against]: **[Part 1]** 15
Mental Ailments [against]: **[Part 1]** 6:2–3; 6:5; 19:8; 34:19
Mentally Ill [dangerously insane]: **[Part 1]** 12
Mercy [for sins committed]: **[Part 2]** 69
Mood (*Ruach Ra/Evil Spirit*) [against a bad/dark]: **[Part 1]** 5; 29; 40; **[Part 2]** 66
Morality [to counter diminishing of]: **[Part 2]** 67

Nervous Disorders [to be healed from]: **[Part 1]** 12; 28; 37
Nocturnal Emissions [Against]: **[Part 2]** 44

Obsession [against]: **[Part 1]** 15

Peace of Mind: **[Part 1]** 20
Peace of Soul: **[Part 1]** 6; 31; 37; **[Part 2]** 50
Perverted Activities [against all kinds of]: **[Part 1]** 11; **[Part 2]**
Post-traumatic Stress Disorder [psychological damage resulting from trauma]: **[Part 1]** 7; **[Part 2]** 85
Pride [against]: **[Part 1]** 11; 17; 28; **[Part 2]** 70; 75; 88
Purification [against all that is unclean]: **[Part 1]** 22
Purification [psychologically & spiritually]: **[Part 2]** 51

Ruin [danger of]: **[Part 1]** 11; 24

Sadness: **[Part 1]** 30; **[Part 2]** 42; 43; 56
Sensitive Individuals [for depression brought on by heartless persons]: **[Part 1]** 4
Sensitive Individuals [to heal & strengthen]: **[Part 2]** 56; 70
Shameful Vices: **[Part 2]** 72
Sinful Passions [against slavery to]: **[Part 1]** 9–10; **[Part 2]** 56; 59; 69; 70
Sins [forgiveness of]: **[Part 2]** 69
Sorrow [protection against all]: **[Part 2]** 50
Sorrow to Joy [turning]: **[Part 1]** 16

Temptation [against & for relief from]: **[Part 1]** 12; 13; 25; **[Part 2]** 50
Tragedy & Calamaties [protection against]: **[Part 1]** 13
Trouble [to ward of]: **[Part 2]** 67; 77:15
Trouble [to become accustomed to stay out of]: **[Part 2]** 77
Trouble & Tribulations [against all manner of]: **[Part 1]** 4; 16; 22; 25; 29; **[Part 2]** 45; 61; 65; 70; 89
Troubles & Distress: **[Part 1]** 6; 9:10; 20; 25; 31; 34; 34:18; **[Part 2]** 55; 69; 70; 77; 86; 88

Uplifted [to be]: **[Part 1]** 8; 19; 24; **[Part 2]** 47; 48

Vanity [against]: **[Part 1]** 11; 30

4. Sleep & Dreams
Dream Question (*She'elat Chalom*) [receiving answers in]: **[Part 1]** 4:2; 12; 13; 23; 39; **[Part 2]** 42
Dreams [for problems with]: **[Part 2]** 51:13
Dreams [interpretation of & help in understanding]: **[Part 2]** 42

Insomnia [inability to sleep]: **[Part 1]** 4; **[Part 2]** 62; 76

Nightmares: **[Part 1]** 30:3

Waking [(magical alarm clock) to wake at specific times: **[Part 2]** 57:9

5. Intelligence, Study, Memory, Speech & Secret Sciences

Ignorance [against]: **[Part 1]** 17
Intelligence [to awaken]: **[Part 1]** 16; 19; 19:8–10
Intelligence [to sharpen & increase]: **[Part 1]** 16; 19; 19:8–10; 22; **[Part 2]** 54
Intuition: **[Part 1]** 16

Language [gift of]: **[Part 2]** 80

Memory [for a good]: **[Part 1]** 12; 19; 19:8–10

Occult Intrigues: **[Part 1]** 25
Occult Sciences [to comprehend the]: **[Part 2]** 50

Preaching (sermons/lectures): **[Part 1]** 34

Sciences [human]: **[Part 1]** 18
Sources [discovery of]: **[Part 2]** 73
Speech [to acquire the gift of]: **[Part 2]** 50
Speakers [to be heard by every listener]: **[Part 2]** 77
Study [love of]: **[Part 1]** 30; 31
Success [in studying & learning]: **[Part 1]** 25

Thought & Contemplation [for]: **[Part 2]** 51:12

Will [force of]: **[Part 1]** 30; **[Part 2]** 50
Wisdom [to encourage]: **[Part 1]** 19

6. Journeys & Travel

Accidents [protection against & during chariot & motor-vehicle]: **[Part 1]** 36:7

Detours: **[Part 1]** 11

Journeys [to stop being harrassed & manhandled on]: **[Part 2]** 78–80
Journeys [external to cities to be successful]: **[Part 1]** 4
Journeys [when undertaking]: **[Part 1]** 17; 34; **[Part 2]** 67

Index of Magical Applications / 361

Lost when Traveling [to find your way]: **[Part 1]** 32

Protection [against enemies on the road]: **[Part 1]** 17

River [to ford/cross]: **[Part 1]** 22; **[Part 2]** 64

Safety [against danger at sea & on land]: **[Part 1]** 22; 26; 29
Sea [against storms at]: **[Part 1]** 2; 21; 23:1; 24; 29; **[Part 2]** 43
Sea [danger from the]: **[Part 1]** 17; **[Part 2]** 73
Sea/Lake [before crossing]: **[Part 1]** 21
Sea-sickness [against]: **[Part 1]** 29
Shipwreck [to avoid]: **[Part 2]** 67; 68

Travel [alone at night]: **[Part 2]** 49
Travel [for success on the road]: **[Part 1]** 17:8; 34
Travel [in safety]: **[Part 2]** 76; 86:17
Travel [to say on the road]: **[Part 1]** 17; 20

Voyage [to complete in good health]: **[Part 2]** 64

Walking [for contemplation whilst]: **[Part 2]** 86:11

7. Success

Desires [successfully granted]: **[Part 1]** 4

Good Fortune [in all undertakings]: **[Part 2]** 57; 65
Governmental Officials [before meeting with]: **[Part 1]** 34

Influence [to exert]: **[Part 2]** 65

Need [for every purpose/requirement]: **[Part 1]** 4

Requests [granted]: **[Part 1]** 4; 8:2; 8:10; 15; 16:1–5; 16:5; 34; **[Part 2]** 65; 67 [conjointly with *Psalm 61*]
Requests [from higher authorities fulfilled]: **[Part 1]** 4; 21:2; 34

Success [in a mission]: **[Part 2]** 82
Success [in dealings with authorities]: **[Part 1]** 5

Success [in general & in all endeavours]: **[Part 1]** 1; 1:1–3; 1:3; 4; 24; 33:6; **[Part 2]** 57; 65; 81; 84

Wish [fulfilled]: **[Part 2]** 65:3

8. Career, Trade, Transactions, Financial Success Livelihood, Good Fortune & Charity

Alms & Charity [recited prior to giving]: **[Part 2]** 89
Assets [protection against loss of personal]: **[Part 2]** 72

Business [attracting]: **[Part 2]** 82
Business [goodwill & love of others in]: **[Part 1]** 8; **[Part 2]**
Business [success in]: **[Part 1]** 19; 20; 33; 36; **[Part 2]** 57; 63; 69; 71
Business Negotiations [(deals) to encourage good]: **[Part 2]** 55:23; 57
Business Partners [against unfair]: **[Part 2]** 63
Business Transactions [to conclude]: **[Part 1]** 4

Charity & Good Deeds: **[Part 1]** 14; 21; 25; 32
Commerce [for success in all manner of]: **[Part 2]** 63
Commodities [for success in acquiring]:
Councils & Meetings [business]: **[Part 1]** 2

Dangerous work: **[Part 2]** 49
Debtors: **[Part 1]** 36; 39
Debtors [compassion of lenders toward]: **[Part 2]** 78
Dignity [to maintain of the poor]: **[Part 2]** 89
Diligent Workers [protection from perverse actions & crooked people]: **[Part 2]** 58
Dismissed [when laid off]: **[Part 1]** 39; 41; **[Part 2]** 42; 43
Donations: **[Part 1]** 18

Employment Position [handed to another individual]: **[Part 2]** 42
Employer & Employee [to prevent discord after disagreements]: **[Part 1]** 40
Employers [against hard-hearted]: **[Part 2]** 52
Employers [against torment by]: **[Part 2]** 52; 65

Employers [to deal justly with employees]: **[Part 2]** 75
Enemies [who cause loss]: **[Part 1]** 41; **[Part 2]** 42; 43

Familial Breadwinners [extending lives of]: **[Part 2]** 87
Financial Success: **[Part 1]** 4:7; 24; **[Part 2]** 45:5
Food [lack of]: **[Part 2]** 71
Fortune [in business]: **[Part 1]** 5

Gifts [received or to be given]: **[Part 2]** 89
Good Fortune: **[Part 1]** 4
Good Fortune [gratitude for]: **[Part 1]** 17; 18; 23; 33; **[Part 2]** 42; 57; 63; 65; 68; 70; 71; 72

Idleness in a Profession [against]: **[Part 1]** 41;

Livelihood [anxious concern about]: **[Part 1]** 23; **[Part 2]** 62; 68
Livelihood (*Dikir'nosa*) [name of]: **[Part 1]** 4:7
Livelihood [for a good]: **[Part 1]** 8:2; 23; 24; 33:18; **[Part 2]** 55:23

Merchants [against dishonest]: **[Part 2]** 65
Misdeeds [to repent of]: **[Part 1]** 21
Misfortune [against bad luck]: **[Part 1]** 5; 22; 25; 26
Misfortune [against succumbing to in times of trouble]: **[Part 2]** 77
Misfortune [to banish]: **[Part 2]** 67
Musicians [for]: **[Part 2]** 80

Partnership [for a good portion when dissolving a business]: **[Part 2]** 63
Partnership [when seeking with associates a]: **[Part 2]** 63
Paupers & Beggars [protection of]: **[Part 2]** 81; 87
Poverty [against & for diminishing of]: **[Part 1]** 9; 30; 34; 39; **[Part 2]** 67; 69; 71; 72; 101
Poverty [to encourage alms to the poor]: **[Part 1]** 21
Prosperity [financial]: **[Part 1]** 23; **[Part 2]** 45:5; 62; 68

Rich [against envy of the]: **[Part 1]** 1; 37; **[Part 2]** 49; 73

Sale of Wares [to affect the]: **[Part 2]** 82
Share Profits [to ensure a better portion]: **[Part 2]** 63

Sickly [to allow to work without fatigue]: **[Part 2]** 89
Superiors [against torment by]: **[Part 2]** 52

Trade [good fortune in]: **[Part 2]** 63
Treasures: **[Part 1]** 32
Trip [success on a business]: **[Part 1]** 17; 17:8

Unemployment [against]: **[Part 1]** 39; 41
Usurers [against loan sharks]: **[Part 1]** 14; **[Part 2]** 54; 71

Work [to find]: **[Part 1]** 39; **[Part 2]** 47

9. Food, Agriculture, Plant Growth, Fisheries, Animal Husbandry & Nature

Animals [protection against noxious]: **[Part 2]** 50
Animals [protection of]: **[Part 1]** 35
Animals [protection of domestic]: **[Part 1]** 35

Beasts [protection against wild, dangerous & savage]: **[Part 1]** 22; 27; 36; **[Part 2]** 57; 90; 123
Birds: **[Part 2]** 49
Bites: **[Part 1]** 21; 31

Cattle & Livestock [to control stubborn]: **[Part 1]** 27; **[Part 2]**
Cattle & Livestock [raising]: **[Part 2]** 49
Crops: **[Part 1]** 4; 36; **[Part 2]** 62

Deluge [to be saved from a]: **[Part 2]** 69
Dogs & Dog Attack [against ferocious]: **[Part 2]** 58
Drowning [to be saved from]: **[Part 2]** 69; 76

Earthquakes: **[Part 2]** 54

Famine [relief from a]: **[Part 1]** 33; 36
Farmers: **[Part 2]** 84
Fertility of Fields [in water scarcity]: **[Part 2]** 63
Fertility of Vines & Trees: **[Part 1]** 1; 1:3
Fields [protection of]: **[Part 1]** 36; **[Part 2]** 49; 84
Fire [against]: **[Part 2]** 76

Index of Magical Applications / 365

Fire [*dangers of*]: **[Part 1]** 10; 16; 17; **[Part 2]** 82
Fire [to contain & halt]: **[Part 1]** 22
Firestorm [at sea or on land]: 42:5
Fishermen [for filling the nets of]: **[Part 2]** 53
Flocks [sheep]: **[Part 2]** 67
Floods [protection against]: **[Part 1]** 17; 24; 25; 31; **[Part 2]** 76
Floods [to be rescued from]: **[Part 1]** 24; **[Part 2]** 69
Fruits of the Earth: **[Part 2]** 77
Fruit Trees: **[Part 1]** 1; **[Part 2]**

Gardens [protection of]: **[Part 1]** 36; **[Part 2]** 49; 84
Good Weather: **[Part 1]** 10; **[Part 2]** 73

Harvest [for a good]: **[Part 2]** 72
Henhouses: **[Part 2]** 67
Horses [health of]: **[Part 2]** 49

Land or Water [for need or danger on]: **[Part 1]** 6; 26; 29
Lightning/Thunderbolts [protection against]: **[Part 1]** 17; 28; **[Part 2]** 76

Natural Disaster: **[Part 1]** 18; **[Part 2]**
Nature [when in]: **[Part 1]** 19; **[Part 2]**

Pests & Insects [harmful]: **[Part 1]** 17; **[Part 2]** 77
Places [for the safety & well-being of]: **[Part 2]** 61
Planting Seeds, Vines & Trees: **[Part 1]** 1; 1:3
Plants [nurturing]: **[Part 1]** 1; 1:3
Preservation [of goods & livestock]: **[Part 2]** 84

Rabies [when bitten]: **[Part 2]** 64
Rain [to get]: **[Part 2]** 62; 71
River [to be saved from a]: **[Part 2]** 69

Serpents [protection against]: **[Part 1]** 13; 22; 37
Silkworms: **[Part 2]** 77
Storms [in general]: **[Part 1]** 10; 17; 28; **[Part 2]** 49; 67; 76; 88
Sustenance: **[Part 1]** 4; 24; 41
Sustenance [during unsuitable weather for agriculture]: **[Part 1]** 31

Trees [against shedding fruit]: **[Part 1]** 1; 1:3; **[Part 2]**

Vines & Vineyards [protection of]: **[Part 1]** 1; 1:3; **[Part 2]** 49; 77; 79
Volcanoes: **[Part 1]** 16; 17

Water [against life-threatening danger from]: **[Part 1]** 2; 26
Water [against destruction by]: **[Part 2]** 69; 76
Water or Fire [to be saved from]: **[Part 2]** 76

10. Human Interaction, Friendship, Brotherhood, & Reconciliation

City [when entering a]: **[Part 2]** 82–83
City (New Environment) [to conquer a strange & to be kindly received in a]: **[Part 1]** 27; **[Part 2]** 82–83
Companion [to appease a]: **[Part 2]** 85
Crowds & Passersby [when gazing at]: **[Part 1]** 35:18

Difficult People [again]: **[Part 2]** 80

Enemies [reconciliation with]: **[Part 1]** 9; 28
Enemies [turning into friends]: **[Part 1]** 9; 16
Errors [saving friends from]: **[Part 2]** 80, 81
Exploitation [against being taken advantage of]: **[Part 1]** 35

Favour & Grace [of princes, magistrates & authorities]: **[Part 1]** 5; 20:6; 34; **[Part 2]** 71; 72; 78
Favour [to find]: **[Part 1]** 1:3; 4; 5; 8; **[Part 2]** 42; 47; 67; 71; 72; 85
Favour [with all men]: **[Part 1]** 14; 15; **[Part 2]** 47; 67
Fellow Humans [to be loved & respected by]: **[Part 2]** 47
Friend [to reconcile with an long standing]: **[Part 2]** 85
Friends [to be received favourably]: **[Part 1]** 34
Friends [to find favour in the eyes of]: **[Part 2]** 85
Friendships [against false]: **[Part 2]** 54

Grace, Favour & Loving-kindness: **[Part 2]** 72
Grace & Favour [in the eyes of God & Man]: **[Part 2]** 67

Grace, Favour & Mercy [in the eyes of all people]: **[Part 2]** 51:14; 72

Grace & Mercy [to receive]: **[Part 1]** 20:5; 20:6; 32; **[Part 2]** 72

Harm [protection from]: **[Part 1]** 3; 5; 7; 14; 20; 23; 27; 31; 35; 40; **[Part 2]** 48; 55; 59; 69; 70

Heartless Individuals [protection against]: **[Part 2]** 88

Humiliation [against]: **[Part 1]** 22

Hurt [against being]: **[Part 1]** 35; 41; **[Part 2]** 55

Hurt [by perverted individuals]: **[Part 1]** 8

Kings [to be rescued from evil]: **[Part 1]** 18; 38; 39

Kings, Judges & Ruling Authorities [to be saved from]: **[Part 1]** 40;

Maintaining Self [before a spiritual/temporal authority]: **[Part 1]** 21; 21:2;

Mercy/Compassion [to request]: **[Part 1]** 12; 32

Perseverance [for]: **[Part 2]** 61

Rulers [when appearing before]: **[Part 1]** 21; 40

Truth [when veracity is doubted]: **[Part 1]** 14

Universal Brotherhood: **[Part 1]** 32; **[Part 2]** 45; 71; 75

Well Received [to be]: **[Part 1]** 15

Words [fearing not being heard]: **[Part 1]** 14

11. Relationships, Love, Marriage, Family & Homes

Abandonment: **[Part 1]** 27; **[Part 2]** 88

Adultery [against]: **[Part 2]** 69

Ancestors [invoking the beneficial powers of]: **[Part 1]** 16

Dissolution of Relationships [against resulting sorrow]: **[Part 1]** 42

Domestic Obstacles [against sorrow resulting from]: **[Part 2]** 66

Domestic Torment & Violence [against]: **[Part 1]** 11

Family Honour [to restore after an unjust accusation]: **[Part 2]** 55
Finding a Mate: **[Part 1]** 32; 38; **[Part 2]** 70;

Heritage [to recover]: **[Part 1]** 24; **[Part 2]** 60
Home [on entering a]: **[Part 2]** 61
Home [upon entering with apprehension]: **[Part 2]** 61
Husband [for one who hates his wife]: **[Part 2]** 46
Husband [for one who tires of his wife]: **[Part 2]** 46
Husband [union with]: **[Part 1]** 30
Husband/Wife [to reestablish peace between]: **[Part 2]** 45; 46
Husband/Wife [to revitalise love & companionship between]: **[Part 2]** 46

Infertile Couples [to prevent divorce of]: **[Part 1]** 20
Infidelity [personal or national]: **[Part 2]** 59

Loneliness: **[Part 1]** 25; **[Part 2]**
Love [for wrong/upsetting]: **[Part 1]** 40
Love [honest]: **[Part 2]** 43;
Love [mutual among family members]: **[Part 2]** 77
Love [to find enduring: **[Part 2]** 45:11
Love [to receive, engender & increase]: **[Part 1]** 32; 38
Loved Ones: **[Part 1]** 20

Marital Love: **[Part 2]** 44;
Marriage: **[Part 1]** 19; [for men] 31; 32; **[Part 2]** 70; 72
Married [when getting]: **[Part 2]** 46
Mate [finding a]: **[Part 1]** 32; 38; **[Part 2]** 68; 70; 71
Misunderstanding between a Couple [to heal]: **[Part 2]** 44

Residence [prior to building]: **[Part 2]** 42
Residence or Apartment [being fearful staying in a]: **[Part 2]** 61
Residence or Apartment [for success in a new]: **[Part 2]** 61
Residence or Apartment [occupying a new]: **[Part 1]** 41:14
Residence or Apartment [to live unafraid in a: **[Part 2]** 61
Relative or Friend [in difficulty]: **[Part 1]** 20

Sorrow [resulting from the dissolution of a relationship]: **[Part 2]** 42

Soul Mate [finding a]: **[Part 2]** 68
Spouse [against harshness of a]: **[Part 1]** 10; 11

Wedding [on day of]: **[Part 1]** 19
Wife [for one who hates her husband]: **[Part 2]** 46
Wife/Husband [against an evil & abusive spouse]: **[Part 2]** 45
Wife/Husband [against an evil & abusive spouse]: **[Part 2]** 46
Woman [against an angry]: **[Part 2]** 45

12. Pregnancy, Childbirth & Children
Barren Women [for]: **[Part 1]** 36

Childbirth [difficult confinement or dangerous delivery]: **[Part 1]** 1; 1:1–3; 19; 19:6; 26; **[Part 2]** 46:8
Childbirth [during confinement]: **[Part 1]** 1–4; 20; 21–24; 22; 32:7; 33; **[Part 2]** 47; 72; 86
Children [for crying]: **[Part 1]** 8; 9; 34:8–9; 41:5
Children [for retarded]: **[Part 1]** 15
Children [for sick]: **[Part 1]** 8; 9
Children [protection of]: **[Part 1]** 35; **[Part 2]** 70
Children [restoring health of]: **[Part 1]** 9
Circumcision [on the day]: **[Part 1]** 12
Conception [to ensure]: **[Part 1]** 36

Delivery of a Child [successful]: **[Part 1]** 19; 20
Delivery of a Premature Child [successful]: **[Part 1]** 41

Evil Eye [protection of women during childbirth against the]: **[Part 2]** 67

Fear [during labour]: **[Part 2]** 76

Lilit [protection of women during childbirth against the demoness]: **[Part 2]** 67

Miscarriage [against]: **[Part 1]** 1; 1:1–3; 32; 33; 33:1; **[Part 2]** 67:5–8; 69
Miscarriage [for a woman to fall pregnant again following a]: **[Part 2]** 79
Miscarriage [to recover from a]: **[Part 2]** 55:9; 68

Pregnancy [to cause]: **[Part 1]** 5; 33; **[Part 2]** 69
Pregnancy [to ensure a safe]: **[Part 1]** 1; 4; 8; 20; 33; 35; **[Part 2]** 57; 93
Pregnant Woman [to cast out an evil spirit from a]: **[Part 2]** 76
Premature Delivery [against]: **[Part 1]** 1; 1:1–3

Rebellious Children [to instill obedience in]: **[Part 1]** 23

Unborn [against possible afflictions of the]: **[Part 2]** 67:5–8

Woman in labour [support for]: **[Part 1]** 20

13. Dying, Death, Orphans, Old Age & Life Extension

Cemetry [for recitation at a]: **[Part 2]** 72
Children [for a woman whose offspring died]: **[Part 1]** 33
Children [against the loss of]: **[Part 1]** 20; **[Part 2]** 69

Death [against an unnatural & strange]: **[Part 1]** 13 (good for one day); 32:7
Death [fear of]: **[Part 1]** 38; **[Part 2]** 48; 54
Death [for a good]: **[Part 1]** 17; 38
Death [protecting infants & children from]: **[Part 1]** 33

Elderly [to support the]: **[Part 2]** 70; 71

Funeral [on the day]: **[Part 1]** 23

Life [for a long]: **[Part 1]** 23; **[Part 2]** 61
Longevity: **[Part 1]** 23; **[Part 2]** 61

Mourning [during time of]: **[Part 1]** 23; 27; **[Part 2]** 49

Old Age [beset by]: **[Part 2]** 70; 71;
Old Age & Retirement [happy]: **[Part 1]** 29; 30; **[Part 2]** 70; 71; 77; 89
Orphans: **[Part 1]** 26; 34; **[Part 2]** 67; 81

Parents [loss of]: **[Part 1]** 20

Visiting the Graves [of loved ones]: **[Part 1]** 25; 34

Widows/Widowers: **[Part 1]** 34; **[Part 2]** 67

14. Religion & Spirituality
Accounting of the Soul [*Chesh'bon Hanefesh*]: 15
Atonement/Repentance [תשובה—*teshuvah* (spiritual return)]: **[Part 1]** 6; 15; 20; 25; 32; 38; **[Part 2]** 47; 51; 62; 86

Baptism [against compulsory]: **[Part 2]** 73
Beit Hamikdash (the Holy Temple) [to build]: **[Part 2]** 42; 43
Blasphemy [against]: **[Part 1]** 14; 23

Candle-lighting [with]: **[Part 1]** 18:29
Celestial Accusers [to be recited from *Rosh Hashanah* (New Year) onwards to strip]: **[Part 1]** 27
Confused Religiously: **[Part 1]** 25
Controlled Daydream [(*She'elah b'Hakitz*) divinatory answers to queries whilst fully awake]: **[Part 2]** 51
Conversion [against forced]: **[Part 2]** 73

Divine Aid & Support [in need of]: **[Part 2]** 70
Divine Justice & Equality: **[Part 2]** 57; 60; 71; 72; 88
Divine One [awesomeness of the]: **[Part 1]** 29
Divine One [calling on the Eternal Presence of the]: **[Part 1]** 41
Divine One [desire to speak to the]: **[Part 2]** 51
Divine One [perplexed by distance of the]: **[Part 1]** 10
Divine Protection [in need of]: **[Part 2]** 70

Ending Sorrows [of the Jewish people]: **[Part 2]** 43
Exile [for one who seeks restoration of home & hearth]: **[Part 2]** 80:4, 8 & 20
Exile (to end the exile of the Jewish People): **[Part 2]** 42; 67; 73; 80

Faith [against inducement to deny]: **[Part 2]** 73
Faith [for doubts about]: **[Part 1]** 1; 2; 19; 37
Faith [to strengthen]: **[Part 1]** 11; **[Part 2]** 46
Fasting [for one who is]: **[Part 1]** 39; **[Part 2]**

Fidelity [to religion, justice & righteousness]: **[Part 1]** 26; **[Part 2]** 59

Good spirits [loyalty of]: **[Part 1]** 26; **[Part 2]** 85
Good Year [to be recited from *Rosh Hashanah* (New Year) onwards to ensure a]: **[Part 1]** 27
Gratitude [to the Divine One]: **[Part 1]** 9; 18; **[Part 2]** 65; 68
Gratitude [for success & prosperity]: **[Part 2]** 65

Hands [after washing]: **[Part 1]** 23; **[Part 2]**
Hands [with washing]: **[Part 1]** 26:6; **[Part 2]**
Heresy (עבודה זרה—*Avodah Zarah*) [for protection against engaging in]: **[Part 2]** 80

Idolatry (עבודת אלילים—*Avodat Elilim*): **[Part 2]** 80; 81
Israel [for crisis in]: **[Part 1]** 20; **[Part 2]** 83

Jerusalem [for the well-being of]: **[Part 2]** 87
Jewish Nation [for the]: **[Part 2]** 53; 74; 83
Judaism: **[Part 2]** 53; 74; 83

Land of Israel [for the well-being of the]: **[Part 2]** 74; 79; 83

Meal [reciting before the blessing of a]: **[Part 1]** 23
Meditation [whilst walking]: **[Part 2]** 86:11
Meditations: **[Part 1]** 16:8; **[Part 2]** 80
Mercy [request for Divine]: **[Part 1]** 32; **[Part 2]** 89
Mercy [from heaven]: **[Part 1]** 32; **[Part 2]** 89

Non-Jews [gentiles] [for Jews who are captured by]: **[Part 2]** 53

Opening the Heart [greater comprehension of spiritual studies]: **[Part 1]** 16; 22; **[Part 2]** 85

Penance [for successful prayer during]: **[Part 2]** 56
Penitence: **[Part 1]** 6; 31; 37; **[Part 2]** 50
Pendulum [divinatory answers by means of a]: **[Part 2]** 51
Persecution [against religious persecution in foreign lands]: **[Part 1]** 30

Praise [of the Divine One]: **[Part 2]** 65; 66
Pray [desire to]: **[Part 2]** 51
Prayer [for forgiveness]: **[Part 2]** 51; 62; 75
Prayer [for the answering of]: **[Part 2]** 42
Prayer [for the arrival of the Messiah]: **[Part 2]** 45; 68
Prayer [prior to petitionary]: **[Part 2]** 72:1
Prayer to the Divine One [to aid His people]: **[Part 2]** 80
Prayers [to voice, empower, or ensure being heard]: **[Part 1]** 4:4; 28; 30:12
Psalms [desire to recite]: **[Part 2]** 51

Religious Commandments [for success in performing a *Mitzvah*]: **[Part 1]** 25

Salvation: **[Part 1]** 34:18
She'elah b'Hakitz [divinatory answers to queries whilst fully awake]: **[Part 2]** 51
Spiritual Cleansing: **[Part 1]** 15
Spiritual Awakening [to achieve a spirit of holiness]: **[Part 1]** 15
Spiritual Matters [success in]: **[Part 1]** 39
Spiritual Science: **[Part 2]** 48
Spiritual Troubles: **[Part 1]** 20; 29; 38; 41; **[Part 2]** 59; 68; 76; 89
Statement of Faith: **[Part 1]** 23; 33
Statement of Faith & Appreciation of the Divine One: **[Part 1]** 40
Synagogue [in the]: **[Part 1]** 5; 26; 27; **[Part 2]** 63; 65; 73; 84

Temptation [faith to fortify self & resist]: **[Part 2]** 81
Torah Principles [to maintain]: **[Part 1]** 37
Torah study [commitment to intense]: **[Part 2]** 84
Torah study (Opening the Heart) [prior to]: **[Part 1]** 1; 16; 19
Trust in the Divine One [increasing]: **[Part 1]** 23; **[Part 2]** 56; 62; 84

15. Malevolent Spirit Forces, Ghosts & Evil Spells

Angels [for protection against possible injury during exorcism]: **[Part 1]** 31:19

Demons [to slay]: **[Part 1]** 15
Demonic Attack [against]: **[Part 1]** 3; 3:2–9

Demonic Forces [to defeat]: **[Part 1]** 32:7
Demonic Obsession [against]: **[Part 1]** 10; 21
Demonic Possession [against]: **[Part 2]** 66

Evil [protection against & freedom from all]: **[Part 1]** 30; 36; **[Part 2]** 55
Evil [security from]: **[Part 1]** 17
Evil [to be saved from all]: **[Part 2]** 46:8
Evil [to fear no]: **[Part 1]** 12
Evil Powers [causing fever]: **[Part 1]** 8:2
Evil Spells [to counteract & be saved from]: **[Part 2]** 59; 67; 78
Evil Spirits [protection against & to avert attacks from]: **[Part 1]** 5; 5:8; 10:17; 11; 15; 19; 24; 29; 39:2; 40; **[Part 2]** 67; 68;
Evil Spirits [to cast out]: **[Part 1]** 5:8; 10; 15; 29; 30:12; **[Part 2]** 50:21; 66; 86
Evil Spirits [freedom from]: **[Part 1]** 24; 40

Ghosts [protection against all]: **[Part 2]** 50

Harmful Spirits [protection against all]: **[Part 2]** 50
Haunted houses: **[Part 2]** 47

Pregnant Woman [to cast out an evil spirit from a]: **[Part 2]** 76

Spells [to escape bad]: **[Part 1]** 6; **[Part 2]** 59; 86
Spirit Forces [to control]: **[Part 1]** 18:46
Spirit Forces [protection against being oppressed by]: **[Part 2]** 74
Spiritual Protection: **[Part 1]** 3

Unclean Spirits [protection against]: **[Part 1]** 10

Visions [demonic]: **[Part 1]** 21

Water [before consuming water when demons are active]: **[Part 1]** 29.3–10
Witchcraft & Bewitchment [against]: **[Part 1]** 27; 31; 34; 37; **[Part 2]** 51; 57

16. Hatred, Jealousy, Evil Eye, Enemies, Adversity & Animosity

Adversaries [when risen against you]: **[Part 1]** 35
Adversity: **[Part 1]** 33
Anger [when being faced with]: **[Part 2]** 85
Animosity after Arguments [to remove]: **[Part 1]** 36

Betrayal (treachery) [against]: **[Part 1]** 21; 26; 30; 34; 35; 41; **[Part 2]** 55; 68; 87

Corruption [against]: **[Part 2]** 68:2

Danger [freedom from]: **[Part 1]** 20; 25; **[Part 2]**
Danger [protection against]: **[Part 1]** 11; 19:8–10; 24; 25; 26; **[Part 2]** 50

Enemies [against]: **[Part 1]** 3; 7; 24; 26; 28; 30; **[Part 2]** 55; 68; 79; 85
Enemies [before confronting]: **[Part 1]** 22
Enemies [defeating bitter persecution from]: **[Part 2]** 74
Enemies [Divine retribution against]: **[Part 2]** 55
Enemies [enticing an individual into transgressions]: **[Part 2]** 64
Enemies [for one who fears]: **[Part 2]** 74
Enemies [protection against]: **[Part 1]** 7; 9; 10; 22:20; 35; **[Part 2]** 44; 50; 54; 74
Enemies [protection against the oppression of]: **[Part 2]** 74
Enemies [protection against persistent]: **[Part 1]** 18:1
Enemies [protective shield against]: **[Part 1]** 3:4
Enemies [safety from]: **[Part 2]** 44
Enemies [to appease]: **[Part 2]** 70
Enemies [to be rid of enemies]: **[Part 2]** 79
Enemies [to conquer]: **[Part 1]** 7:7–18
Enemies [to defeat]: **[Part 2]** 79
Enemies [to escape]: **[Part 2]** 50
Enemies [to get rid of]: **[Part 1]** 11; 79
Enemies [to kill]: **[Part 2]** 79
Enemies [to preclude harm being inflicted by]: **[Part 1]** 14; **[Part 2]** 48
Enemies [to put fear in the hearts of]: **[Part 2]** 48; 53

Enemies [to scare]: **[Part 2]** 53
Enemies [to subdue known or secret]: **[Part 2]** 53; 54; 54:6; 55; 55:9
Enemies [to subjugate]: **[Part 2]** 79
Enemies/Robbers [when hiding in fear of being discovered by]: **[Part 2]** 54
Enemy [against an affliction by an]: **[Part 2]** 71
Evil Decrees & Evil Tidings [against]: **[Part 1]** 36
Evil Eye (Ayin Hara) [against & to avert the]: **[Part 1]** 5; 5:8; 20; 20:3; 31; 32; **[Part 2]** 71
Evil People [not to envy]: **[Part 1]** 37
Evil People [protection against]: **[Part 1]** 11; 38

Fugitive [when fleeing from enemies]: **[Part 2]** 57

Hate [for haters to depart]: **[Part 1]** 7
Haters [for those who have]: **[Part 2]** 74
Haters [to frighten]: **[Part 2]** 48; 53
Haters [to defeat]: **[Part 2]** 79
Haters [to kill]: **[Part 2]** 79
Haters [to subjugate]: **[Part 2]** 79
Haters [to transform into lovers]: **[Part 2]** 78:9
Hatred [against]: **[Part 1]** 10; 25:19; 30; 35
Hostilility [against inimicality/quarreling]: **[Part 2]** 54

Intimidation [against]: **[Part 1]** 7

Jealousy & Resentment [against]: **[Part 1]** 20; **[Part 2]** 51; 69

Malice [against]: **[Part 1]** 5; 30; 34; **[Part 2]** 52; 53; 54; 62
Malediction [against unmerited]: **[Part 2]** 61
Peace [to establish with enemies]: **[Part 1]** 16; 28
Plots [protection against wicked]: **[Part 2]** 46:8

Sabotage [against]: **[Part 2]** 68:2
Subterfuge [against]: **[Part 2]** 68:2

Temptation [against lies from enemies leading an individual into]: **[Part 1]** 64

Traitors [to subjugate & destroy]: **[Part 2]** 75
Trouble [to be saved/rescued from]: **[Part 2]** 54:9; 71:9
Trouble & Danger [against]: **[Part 1]** 20; 25; 26; 26:8

Wicked [to subjugate & destroy the]: **[Part 2]** 75

17. Slander, Falsehood & Wrongdoing

Accused Unjustly [to clear a group of people]: **[Part 2]** 60

Bad Language: **[Part 1]** 5; **[Part 2]** 63
Busybodies [against mischievous]: **[Part 1]** 35

Confession [of sins & transgressions]: **[Part 2]** 51

Defamation, Slander & Gossip [against & to be saved from]: **[Part 1]** 4; 14; 31; 37; 38, 39; **[Part 2]** 51; 52; 56; 62; 64; 71

Evil & Slanderous Libel [against]: **[Part 1]** 36
Evil Doers [for the annihilation of]: **[Part 1]** 36

Falsehoods [against spreading]: **[Part 2]** 52
Forgiveness [of errors & transgressions]: **[Part 1]** 16; 31; 37; **[Part 2]** 50; 72; 75

Lies [against]: **[Part 1]** 11; 33; **[Part 2]** 52; 57

Meddling [against (in the affairs of others)]: **[Part 2]** 52

Sin [after committing & being burdened with]: **[Part 1]** 25; 32; **[Part 2]** 51
Sins [atonement for]: **[Part 2]** 75
Sins [forgiveness of]: **[Part 2]** 62; 75
Sin [to discourage transgression]: **[Part 1]** 12
Sinner [to avoid becoming a]: **[Part 2]** 79
Sinners [for]: **[Part 2]** 44

Tongue [binding an evil]: **[Part 1]** 31; 31:19
Transgressions [atonement for]: **[Part 2]** 75

Unjust Accusations [against]: **[Part 1]** 7; 17; 25
Unjust Denunciations [against]: **[Part 2]** 68

Wicked Men [against]: **[Part 1]** 11
Wrongdoing [victim of]: **[Part 1]** 39; **[Part 2]** 64

18. Robbery, Theft & Common Criminality
Criminals [to halt gangs of]: **[Part 2]** 48
Criminals [to locate]: **[Part 1]** 35
Criminals [to repent]: **[Part 2]** 73

Robbers & Bandits [to flee]: **[Part 1]** 18:1
Robbers & Brigands [to escape]: **[Part 2]** 50

Theft, Thieves & Robbers [protection against]: **[Part 1]** 5; 7; 11; 18:1; 26; 36; **[Part 2]** 50; 54; 61; 67; 68
Thiefs [to discover identity of]: **[Part 1]** 16; 29; 77:15; 78
Thiefs [to halt burglars before harm & to cause repentance of]: **[Part 1]** 15

19. Justice, Legal Matters, Law Suits & Judgment
Court of Law [in a]: **[Part 1]** 20; **[Part 2]**
Court of Law [against enemies in a]: **[Part 1]** 7; 38:14–15

Judge [appearing before a]: **[Part 1]** 5; **[Part 2]** 43
Judge [to be recited before sitting in judgement]: **[Part 2]** 76
Judgement [for good]: **[Part 1]** 20
Judgement [for wrongful or unfavourable]: **[Part 1]** 7; 12; 25; 38; **[Part 2]** 51; 70
Judicial Matters [general]: **[Part 1]** 20
Justice [for just people]: **[Part 2]** 81

Lawsuit [success in a]: **[Part 1]** 7; 35; 38:14–15; **[Part 2]** 73
Lawsuit [winning against the unrighteous, quarrelsome & vengeful]: **[Part 1]** 35; 38:14–15

Perjury: **[Part 2]** 62

Trials & Sentencing: **[Part 1]** 12
Tribunals [when having to appear before]: **[Part 1]** 7

Verdicts [against opponents conspiring in law courts to pass personal]: **[Part 2]** 55

20. Punishment, Vengeance & Imprisonment
Captive [to free a]: **[Part 2]** 89

Detention [for individuals in]: **[Part 2]** 71

Imprisonment: **[Part 1]** 31; **[Part 2]** 56; 67; 71
Imprisonment [against unjust & to be freed from]: **[Part 1]** 31; 33
Imprisonment [in chains, handcuffs, etc.]: **[Part 2]** 56; 67; 68
Imprisonment [liberation from]: **[Part 1]** 31; **[Part 2]** 67; 71; 87
Imprisonment [protection against]: **[Part 2]** 67

Prisoners [for release of]: **[Part 1]** 31; 26; **[Part 2]** 67
Punishment [against suffering]: **[Part 1]** 13

Retaliation [on enemies]: **[Part 2]** 54; 55
Revenge [to seek]: **[Part 1]** 2:5; 7:7; 18:49' **[Part 2]** 54; 55

Vengeance [in secret]: **[Part 2]** 51

21. Anger, Rage, Belligerence, Violence, War & Peace
Abuse [against]: **[Part 2]** 53; 74; 83
Abuse [against verbal]: **[Part 1]** 39; **[Part 2]** 64
Anger [against]: **[Part 1]** 4; 36; 37
Armies [against looting]: **[Part 2]** 79
Armies [protection against invading]: **[Part 1]** 27; 34
Assassins [against]: **[Part 1]** 5; 11; 26; 36; **[Part 2]** 54; 61; 68
Attack of a City [for Divine Intervention during an]: **[Part 2]** 47
Attack/Plunder of a City [against]: **[Part 2]** 60
Attackers [who intend to kill]: **[Part 1]** 7

Bandits [to be saved from]: **[Part 2]** 50
Battle [to be victorious in a]: **[Part 2]** 60; 83
Battles [prior to]: **[Part 2]** 70

Captivity [avoiding]: **[Part 2]** 71; 83

Capture [to avoid]: **[Part 2]** 71; 83
Cities or Communities [for protection of]: **[Part 2]** 87–88
City [against enemy troops attacking & plundering a]: **[Part 2]** 60
City and/or Community (besieged by enemies) [to liberate]: **[Part 2]** 87; 87–88

Enemy at War [defence against]: **[Part 1]** 11:2
Exiles & Refugees [to support]: **[Part 1]** 38; 41; **[Part 2]** 60

Fatherland [protection of the]: **[Part 1]** 32; 41; **[Part 2]** 43; 61

Land of Israel [to eradicate the "haters" (enemies) of]: **[Part 2]** 83

Mob [against a (whether of men or spirits)]: **[Part 2]** 74
Murder [against]: **[Part 2]** 83
Murderer [to ascertain the location of a]: **[Part 2]** 46:8
Murderers [killing individuals at their residence]: **[Part 2]** 59

Naval Ships [against attacks from]: **[Part 1]** 5:9

Occupation [protection of working population/peasants enduring an]: **[Part 2]** 74
Oppression [against]: **[Part 1]** 35; **[Part 2]** 53; 74; 83
Oppressed [for those who are]: **[Part 1]** 9; 35
Oppressors [against]: **[Part 1]** 35; 37; **[Part 2]** 58; 79

Peace: **[Part 1]** 36; **[Part 2]** 45; 46; 71; 75
Perilous Situations & Times of Trouble [protection in]: **[Part 1]** 4; 6; 7; 9; 13; 16; 18; 20; 20:3; 23; 25; 26; 27; 29; 30; 31; 32; 33; 37; 38; 39; 41; **[Part 2]** 42; 49; 51; 54; 55; 56; 67; 69; 71; 81; 85; 86; 87
Perils [against all]: **[Part 1]** 11
Persecution [against fierce]: **[Part 1]** 7; 34; 36; **[Part 2]** 54; 67; 70
Persecution [safety from]: **[Part 1]** 11; 12; **[Part 2]** 68
Prisoners of War [to free]: **[Part 2]** 43

Rage [alleviate personal]: **[Part 1]** 31

Siege [for Divine Intervention during a]: **[Part 2]** 47

Slaves [to free]: **[Part 2]** 54
Soldiers [safety for]: **[Part 2]** 60

Threats [against]: **[Part 1]** 30; 38; **[Part 2]** 53; 74; 83; 85; 86
Torment [against]: **[Part 1]** 3
Troop Commander [protection of a]: **[Part 2]** 47
Troops [to strengthen]: **[Part 2]** 47
Tyranny [against]: **[Part 1]** 2; **[Part 2]** 57; 58; 75; 88

Violence [for protection in conditions of great]: **[Part 2]** 68:2
Violence [when incited to commit]: **[Part 2]** 62

War [before going to]: **[Part 2]** 60
War [for protection & safety in conditions of]: **[Part 2]** 68:2; 83; 83:14
War [for victory in a]: **[Part 2]** 60; 83
War [in times of]: **[Part 2]** 70; 83; 83:14
War [to halt]: **[Part 1]** 2; **[Part 2]** 43; 46–47; 75; 78; 88
Wounded [when seriously by criminals]: **[Part 1]** 37

"Suddenly, the Golem sprang up on his feet. Then we dressed him in the clothes we had brought with us.... We also put shoes on him. In short, he looked like the rest of us: he saw, heard, and understood, but he did not have the capacity for speech.

At six in the morning, before the break of dawn, four men returned home. As we walked back, the Maharal told the golem: 'Know that we created you out of the dust of the earth to guard the Jews from all harm and from all the ills and troubles they suffer at the hands of their enemies and oppressors. Your name will be Yosef. You will live with me, sleep in a room in my court, and serve as the shamesh of the court. No matter where I send you, you will obey each one of my commands....'

'I called the golem Yosef,' the Maharal told us, 'because I drew into him the spirit of Yosef Sheyda who is mentioned in the Talmud, a creature half man and half demon, who also served the sages of the Talmud and saved them a number of times from great calamities....Even if the golem enters a blazing fire,' the Maharal added, 'he will not be burned, nor will he drown in a river or be killed by a sword.'

And because the golem always sat in a corner of the courtroom at the edge of a table resting his head on his hands, looking indeed like an unfinished vessel, lacking wisdom and understanding nothing, and not worrying about a thing under the sun, the people called him Yossele the golem, while some name him Yossele the mute... ... ."

— Yudl Rosenberg
(The Golem and the Wondrous Deeds of the Maharal of Prague)

REFERENCES & BIBLIOGRAPHY

INTRODUCTION

1. **Lancaster, B.L.:** *The Essence of Kabbalah*, Arcturus Publishing Limited, London 2005.
2. **Swart, J.G.:** *The Book of Self Creation*, The Sangreal Sodality Press, Johannesburg 2021.
   —*The Book of Sacred Names*, The Sangreal Sodality Press, Johannesburg 2011.
3. **Unterman, A.:** *The Kabbalah Tradition*, Penguin Books Ltd., London & New York 2008.
4. *Ibid.*
5. **Lancaster, B.L.:** *The Essence of Kabbalah, Op. Cit.*
6. *Ibid.*
7. **Aharon of Apta:** *Or ha-Ganuz* quoted in **Idel, M.:** *Hasidism: Between Ecstasy and Magic*, SUNY Press, Albany 1995.
8. **Idel, M.:** *Hasidism: Between Ecstasy and Magic*, SUNY Press, Albany 1995.
   Cordovero, M.: *Pardes Rimmonim*, Yarid ha-Sefarim, Jerusalem 2000.
9. **Swart, J.G.:** *The Book of Immediate Magic* (Part 1), The Sangreal Sodality Press, Johannesburg 2015.
10. *Ibid.*

CHAPTER 3

1. **Hirsch, E.G.:** *The Aim, Scope and Method of the Jewish Religious School*, published in **Hyamson, A.M.; Mocatta Library and Museum; & Independent Order of B'nai B'rith:** *The Menorah: A Monthly Magazine for the Jewish Home*, Vol. 34 No.3, The Menorah Company, New York 1903.
2. **Swart, J.G.:** *The Book of Self Creation, Op. Cit.*
   —*The Book of Sacred Names, Op. Cit.*
   —*The Book of Seals & Amulets, Op. Cit.*
   —*The Book of Immediate Magic* (Part 1), *Op. Cit.*
   —*The Book of Immediate Magic* (Part 2), The Sangreal Sodality Press, Johannesburg 2018.
3. *Zohar Part 3 ("Mish'patim")*, 101a.
4. **Gruber, M.I.:** *Rashi's Commentary on Psalms*, Jewish Publication Society, Philadelphia 2008.
   Harrán, D.: *Three Early Modern Hebrew Scholars on the Mysteries of Song*, Koninklijke Brill NV, Leiden 2015.
5. **Meyerhoff Hieronimus, J.Z.:** *Sanctuary of the Divine Presence: Hebraic Teachings on Initiation and Illumination*, Inner Traditions, Rochester 2012.
6. *Ibid.*
7. *Ibid.*
8. *Ibid.*
9. *Ibid.*
10. **Kaplan, A.:** *The Seven Beggars & Other Kabbalistic Tales of Rebbe Nachman of Breslov*, Jewish Lights Publishing Woodstock 2012.
11. *Ibid.*
12. *Ibid.*
13. *Ibid.*
    Kaplan, A. & Sutton, A.: *Innerspace: Introduction to Kabbalah, Meditation and Prophecy*, Moznaim Publishing Corporation, Jerusalem 1990.
14. **Swart, J.G.:** *The Book of Self Creation, Op. Cit.*
15. **Kaplan, A.:** *The Seven Beggars & Other Kabbalistic Tales of Rebbe Nachman of Breslov, Op. Cit.*
16. **Sternhartz, N.:** *Likutei Halachot*, Keren Had'pasa d'Chasidei Breslav, Jerusalem 1985.
17. *Ibid.*
    Kaplan, A.: *The Seven Beggars & Other Kabbalistic Tales of Rebbe Nachman of Breslov, Op. Cit.*

18. **Kaplan, A.:** *Ibid.*
19. *Ibid.*
20. **Liebes, Y.:** *Studies in Jewish Myth and Messianism*, transl. Stein, B., State University of New York Press, Albany 1993.
21. **Swart, J.G.:** *The Book of Seals & Amulets*, Op. Cit.
22. *Ibid.*
    Neusner, J.: *A History of the Jews in Babylonia: Later Sasanian Times*, E.J. Brill, Leiden 1970.
    Klein, M.: *A Time to Be Born: Customs and Folklore of Jewish Birth*, The Jewish Publication Society, Philadelphia 1998.
    Isaacs, R.H.: *Ascending Jacob's Ladder: Jewish Views of Angels, Demons, and Evil Spirits*, Jason Aronson, Northvale 1998.
    Hurwitz, S.: *Lilith-The First Eve: Historical and Psychological Aspects of the Dark Feminine*, Daimon Verlag, Einsiedeln 1999.
    Schwartz, H., Loebel-Fried, Ginsburg, E.K.: *Tree of Souls: The Mythology of Judaism*, Oxford University Press Inc., New York 2004.
    Silverman, E.K.: *From Abraham to America: A History of Jewish Circumcision*, Rowman & Littlefield Publishers Inc., Lanham 2006.
23. **Thompson, R.C.:** *Semitic Magic: Its Origins and Development*, Luzac & Co., London 1909.
    Montgomery, J.A.: *Aramaic Incantation Texts from Nippur*, University Museum, Philadelphia 1913.
    Hurwitz, S.: *Lilith-The First Eve: Historical and Psychological Aspects of the Dark Feminine*, Daimon Verlag, Einsiedeln 1999.
    Khanam, R.: *Demonology: Socio-religious Belief of Witchcraft*, Global Vision Publishing House, Delhi 2003.
    Scurlock, J. & Andersen, B.R.: *Diagnoses in Assyrian and Babylonian Medicine*, University of Illinois Press, Urbana 2005.
24. **Swart, J.G.:** *The Book of Seals & Amulets*, Op. Cit.
25. *Ibid.*
26. *Ibid.*
27. **Liebes, Y.:** *Studies in Jewish Myth and Messianism*, Op. Cit.
28. *Ibid.*
29. *Ibid.*
30. **Swart, J.G.:** *The Book of Self Creation*, Op. Cit.
31. **Wolfson, E.R.:** *Through a Speculum that Shines: Vision and Imagination in Medieval Jewish Mysticism*, Princeton University Press, Princeton 1994.
    —*Circle in the Square: Studies in the Use of Gender in Kabbalistic Symbolism*, State University of New York Press, Albany 1995.

Leet, L: *Renewing the Covenant: A Kabbalistic Guide to Jewish Spirituality*, Inner Traditions International, Rochester 1999.
Gafni, M.: *The Mystery of Love*, Atria Books, New York 2003.
Green, A.: *A Guide to the Zohar*, Stanford University Press, Stanford 2004.
Idel, M.: *Kabbalah and Eros*, Yale University Press, New Haven & London 2005.
Hoffman, E. & Schachter-Shalomi, Z.M.: *The Way of Splendor: Jewish Mysticism and Modern Psychology*, Rowman & Littlefield Publishers Inc., Lanham 2006.
Rosler, I.B.: *Eros Revisited: Love for the Indeterminate Other*, Lexington Books, 2007.
Segol, M.: *Kabbalah and Sex Magic: A Mythical-Ritual Genealogy*, Penn State University Press, Pennsylvania 2021.

32. **Schleicher, M.:** *Intertextuality in the Tales of Rabbi Nahman of Bratslav: A Close Reading of Sippurey Ma'asiyot*, Koninklijke Brill NV, Leiden 2007.

33. **Caputi, J.:** *The Age of Sex Crime*, Bowling Green State University Popular Press, Bowling Green 1987.
    Letherby, G.; Williams, K.; Birch, P. & Cain, M.: *Sex as Crime*, Routledge, London & New York 2011.
    Hayes, S.; Carpenter, B. & Dwyer, A.: *Sex, Crime and Morality*, Routledge, London & New York 2012.
    Gartner, R. & McCarthy, B.: *The Oxford Handbook of Gender, Sex, and Crime*, Oxford University Press, Oxford & New York 2014.
    Sanders, T.: *The Oxford Handbook of Sex Offences and Sex Offenders*, Oxford University Press, Oxford & New York 2017.
    Fanghanel, A.; Milne, E.; Zampini, G.; Banwell, S. & Fiddler, M.: *Sex & Crime*, Sage Publications Ltd., Los Angeles & London 2021.

34. **Weintraub, S.Y.:** *Healing of Soul, Healing of Body: Spiritual Leaders Unfold the Strength & Solace in Psalms*, Jewish Light Publishing, Woodstock 2002.

35. *Ibid.*
36. *Ibid.*
37. *Ibid.*
    Nachman of Bratslav & Greenbaum, A.: *Rebbe Nachman's Tikkun: The Comprehensive Remedy*, Breslov Research Institute, Jerusalem ; New York 1984.

38. **Liebes, Y.:** *Studies in Jewish Myth and Messianism, Op. Cit.*
39. *Ibid.*

40. *Ibid.*
41. **Mark, Z.:** *The Revealed and Hidden Writings of Rabbi Nachman of Bratslav: His Worlds of Revelation and Rectification*, transl. Shulman, Y.D., Hebrew University Magnes Press, Jerusalem 2011.
42. *Ibid.*
43. **Weintraub, S.Y.:** *Healing of Soul, Healing of Body, Op. Cit.*
44. *Ibid.*
45. **Liebes, Y.:** *Studies in Jewish Myth and Messianism, Op. Cit.*
46. **Friedmann, J.L.:** *Music in the Hebrew Bible: Understanding References in the Torah, Nevi'im and Ketuvim*, McFarland & Company Inc. Publishers, Jefferson 2014.
47. *Ibid.*
    Schleicher, M.: *Intertextuality in the Tales of Rabbi Nahman of Bratslav, Op. Cit.*
48. **Swart, J.G.:** *The Book of Self Creation, Op. Cit.*
    —*The Book of Sacred Names, Op. Cit.*
49. **Liebes, Y.:** *Studies in Jewish Myth and Messianism, Op. Cit.*
    Nachman of Bratslav & Greenbaum, A.: *Rebbe Nachman's Tikkun, Op. Cit.*
    Westheimer, R.K. & Mark, J.: *Heavenly Sex: Sexuality and the Jewish Tradition*, New York University Press, New York 1995.
    Weintraub, S.Y.: *Healing of Soul, Healing of Body, Op. Cit.*
    Mark, Z.: *The Revealed and Hidden Writings of Rabbi Nachman of Bratslav, Op. Cit.*
    Gillingham, S.: *Psalms Through the Centuries, Volume 1*, John Wiley & Sons Ltd., Chichester & Hoboken 2012.
    Friedmann, J.L.: *Music in the Hebrew Bible, Op. Cit.*
50. **Gillingham, S.:** *Ibid.*
51. **Weintraub, S.Y.:** *Healing of Soul, Healing of Body, Op. Cit.*
52. *Ibid.*
53. **Friedmann, J.L.:** *Music in the Hebrew Bible, Op. Cit.*
54. **Nachman of Bratzlav:** *Likutei Moharan*, Mechon Nachalat Tzvi, Jerusalem 2004.
    Unterman, A.: *The Kabbalah Tradition*, Penguin Books Ltd., London & New York 2008.
55. *Ibid.*
56. **Mark, Z.:** *The Revealed and Hidden Writings of Rabbi Nachman of Bratslav, Op. Cit.*
57. **Curtis, D.A.L.:** *Tikun Haklali: The General Correction*, Kabbalah4All.com.
58. **Kaplan, A. & Sutton, A.:** *Innerspace, Op. Cit.*

59. *Ibid.*
60. *Ibid.*
61. **Kaplan, A.:** *Sefer Yetzirah: The Book of Creation In Theory and Practice*, Samuel Weiser Inc., York Beach 1990 (Revised edition with index 1997).
62. **Swart, J.G.:** *The Book of Immediate Magic (Part 2), Op. Cit.*
63. *Ibid.*
64. **Gillingham, S.:** *Psalms Through the Centuries, Volume 2*, John Wiley & Sons Ltd., Hoboken & Chichester.
65. **Baruch, S.Z. ben & Mangel, N.:** *Siddur Tehillat Hashem al pi Nusach ha-Ari Zal with English Translation, Annotated Edition*, Merkoz L'inyonei Chinuch Inc., Brooklyn 2003.
    Churba, A.: *Siddur Keter Shelomo: Complete Weekday and Shabbat Siddur with linear English translation according to the customs of Aram Soba*, Congregation Shaare Rachamim, Brooklyn 2011.
    Scherman, N. & Zlotowitz, G.: *Siddur Kol Sim'chah: The Artscroll Sephardic Siddur*, The Schottenstein Edition, Mesorah Publications, Brooklyn 2019.
    Nulman, M.: *The Encyclopedia of Jewish Prayer*, Jason Aronson, Northvale 1993.
    Welcz, I.; Reinman, Y.Y. & Sonnenfeld, J.H. ben A.S.: *When Erev Pesach falls on Shabbos: A Compendium of Laws and Customs pertaining to Preparations and Conduct when erev Pesach falls on a Shabbos*, Shmuel Mordechi Wolner and Nesivos Bais Yakov, Brooklyn 2008.
    Swart, J.G.: *The Book of Immediate Magic (Part 2), Op. Cit.*
66. **Fine, L.:** *Safed Spirituality: Rules of Mystical Piety, The Beginning of Wisdom*, Paulist Press, Mahwah 1984.
67. **Scherman, N. & Zlotowitz, G.:** *Siddur Kol Sim'chah, Op. Cit.*
    Nulman, M.: *The Encyclopedia of Jewish Prayer, Op. Cit.*
68. **Swart, J.G.:** *The Book of Seals & Amulets, Op. Cit.*
    —*The Book of Magical Psalms - Part 1*, The Sangreal Sodality Press, Johannesburg 2014.
69. *Ibid.*
70. **Gillingham, S.:** *Psalms Through the Centuries, Volume 2, Op. Cit.*
71. *Ibid.*
72. *Ibid.*
    Scholem, G.: *Kabbalah*, Keter Publishing House, Jerusalem 1974.
    Klein, M.: *Not to Worry: Jewish Wisdom & Folklore*, The Jewish Publication Society, Philadelphia 2003.
    Swart, J.G.: *The Book of Seals & Amulets, Op. Cit.*

73. **Klein, M.:** *Ibid.*
74. **Zion, N. & Spectre, B.:** *A Different Light: The Big Book of Hanukkah*, Devora Publishing, New York 2000.
75. **Sears, D.:** *Seven Branches of the Menorah: Kabbalistic Meditation on Psalm 67*, undated electronic publication.
76. *Ibid.*
77. **Swart, J.G.:** *The Book of Sacred Names, Op. Cit.*
78. **Sears, D.:** *Seven Branches of the Menorah, Op. Cit.*
79. *Ibid.*
80. *Ibid.*
81. *Ibid.*
82. *Ibid.*
83. *Ibid.*
84. *Ibid.*
85. **Palvanov, E.:** *Garments of Light: 70 Illuminating Essays on the Weekly Torah Portion and Holidays*, Efraim Palvanov, Toronto 2017.
86. *Ibid.*
87. **Sears, D.:** *Seven Branches of the Menorah, Op. Cit.*
88. *Ibid.*
89. *Ibid.*
90. *Ibid.*
91. *Ibid.*
92. *Ibid.*
93. *Ibid.*
94. **Swart, J.G.:** *The Book of Immediate Magic (Part 1 & 2), Op. Cit.*
95. **Sears, D.:** *Seven Branches of the Menorah, Op. Cit.*
96. **Swart, J.G.:** *The Book of Magical Psalms - Part 1, Op. Cit.*
97. *Ibid.*
   Nulman, M.: *The Encyclopedia of Jewish Prayer, Op. Cit.*
98. **Swart, J.G.:** *The Book of Self Creation, Op. Cit.*
   —*The Book of Magical Psalms - Part 1, Op. Cit.*
99. **Swart, J.G.:** *The Book of Magical Psalms - Part 1, Op. Cit.*
100. **Swart, J.G.:** *The Book of Sacred Names, Op. Cit.*
   —*The Book of Seals & Amulets, Op. Cit.*
   —*The Book of Immediate Magic (2 Parts), Op. Cit.*
101. **Swart, J.G.:** *The Book of Magical Psalms - Part 1, Op. Cit.*
102. **Tzadok, A. bar:** *Segulot (Spiritual Remedies) for Daily Use: Segulah #1 for Blessing from the RaMBaN*, http://www.koshertorah.com/segulot.html
103. *Ibid.*
104. **Swart, J.G.:** *The Book of Sacred Names, Op. Cit.*
   —*The Book of Seals & Amulets, Op. Cit.*

105. *Ibid.*
106. *Ibid.*
107. *Ibid.*
108. **Tzadok, A. bar:** *Segulot (Spiritual Remedies) for Daily Use*, Op. Cit
109. *Ibid.*
110. *Ibid.*
111. *Ibid.*
112. **Nulman, M.:** *The Encyclopedia of Jewish Prayer*, Op. Cit.
    Swart, J.G.: *The Book of Magical Psalms - Part 1*, Op. Cit.
113. *Ibid.*
114. *Ibid.*
115. *Ibid.*
116. **Hoffman, L.A.:** *My People's Prayer Book: Traditional Prayers, Modern Commentaries, Vol. 8— Kabbalat Shabbat (Welcoming Shabbat in the Synagogue)*, Jewish Lights Publishing, Woodstock 2005.
117. *Ibid.*
118. *Ibid.*
119. **Swart, J.G.:** *The Book of Magical Psalms - Part 1*, Op. Cit.
120. **Bortz, A.:** *The Voice of Silence: A Rabbi's Journey into a Trappist Monastery and Other Contemplations*, WestBow Press, Bloomington 2017.
121. *Ibid.*
122. **Hoffman, L.A.:** *My People's Prayer Book, Vol. 8*, Op. Cit.
123. *Ibid.*
    Ginsburg, E.K.: *Sod ha-Shabbat (The Mystery of the Sabbath)* from the *Tola'at Ya'aqov of R. Meir ibn Gabbai*, State University of New York Press, Albany 1989.
124. **Freedman, H. & Maurice Simon, M.:** *Midrash Rabbah*, Vol. 3, transl. Cohen, A., Soncino Press, London 1961.
    Chernus, I.: *Mysticism in Rabbinic Judaism: Studies in the History of Midrash*, Walter de Gruyter & Co., Berlin & New York 1982.
    Ben-Menahem, H.; Hecht, N. & Wosner, S.: *Controversy and Dialogue in the Jewish Tradition: A Reader*, Routledge, Abingdon & New York 2005.
    Fluegel, M.: *Exodus, Moses and the Decalogue Legislation: The Central Doctrine and Regulative Organum of Mosaism*, M. Fleugel Co., Baltimore 1910.
    Neudecker, R.: *The Voice of God on Mount Sinai: Rabbinic Commentaries on Exodus 20:1 in the Light of Sufi and Zen-Buddhist Texts*, Gregorian & Biblical Press, Rome 2012.

125. **Kaplan, A.:** *The Bahir, Op. Cit.*
     Wolfson, E.R.: *Through a Speculum that Shines, Op. Cit.*
126. **Swart, J.G.:** *The Book of Magical Psalms - Part 1, Op. Cit.*
     Jacobs, L.: *The Jewish Mystics*, Schocken Books, New York 1977
     Cohn-Sherbok, D.: *Kabbalah and Jewish Mysticism: An Introductory Anthology*, Oneworld Publications, London 2006.
     —**with Cohn-Sherbok, L.:** *Jewish & Christian Mysticism: An Introduction*, The Continuum Publishing Company, New York 1994.
127. *Ibid.*
128. **Hoffman, L.A.:** *My People's Prayer Book, Vol. 8, Op. Cit.*
129. *Ibid.*
130. *Ibid.*
131. *Ibid.*
132. **Swart, J.G.:** *The Book of Sacred Names, Op. Cit.*
     —*The Book of Seals & Amulets, Op. Cit.*
     —*The Book of Immediate Magic* (2 Parts), *Op. Cit.*
133. **Ginsburg, E.K.:** *Sod ha-Shabbat, Op. Cit.*
134. **Swart, J.G.:** *The Book of Magical Psalms - Part 1, Op. Cit.*
135. **Hoffman, L.A.:** *My People's Prayer Book, Vol. 8, Op. Cit.*
136. *Ibid.*
137. **Summit, J.A.:** *The Lord's Song in a Strange Land: Music and Identity in Contemporary Jewish Worship*, Oxford University Press, Oxford & New York 2000.
138. **Kaplan, A.:** *The Seven Beggars & Other Kabbalistic Tales of Rebbe Nachman of Breslov, Op. Cit.*
139. *Ibid.*
140. **Schwartz, H.:** *Tree of Souls: The Mythology of Judaism*, Oxford University Press, Oxford & New York 2004.
141. **Bortz, A.:** *The Voice of Silence, Op. Cit.*
142. **Jacobs, L.:** *The Jewish Mystics, Op. Cit.*
     Cohn-Sherbok, D.: *Kabbalah and Jewish Mysticism, Op. Cit.*
     —**with Cohn-Sherbok, L.:** *Jewish & Christian Mysticism, Op. Cit.*
143. *Ibid.*
144. **Swart, J.G.:** *The Book of Magical Psalms - Part 1, Op. Cit.*
145. **Bortz, A.:** *The Voice of Silence, Op. Cit.*
146. **Halamish, M.:** *An Introduction to the Kabbalah*, transl. Bar-Ilan, R. & Wiskind-Elper, O., State University of New York Press, Albany 1999.

147. **Weintraub, S.Y.:** *Healing of Soul, Healing of Body, Op. Cit.*
148. **Scholem, G.:** *Origins of the Kabbalah*, Princeton University Press, Princeton 1990.
   Nulman, M.: *The Encyclopedia of Jewish Prayer, Op. Cit.*
149. **Ginsburg, E.K.:** *The Sabbath in the Classical Kabbalah*, State University of New York Press, Albany 1989,
150. *Ibid.*
151. *Ibid.*
152. *Ibid.*
153. **Rebiger, B.:** *Sefer Shimmush Tehillim: Buch vom magischen Gebrauch der Psalmen, Edition, Übersetzung und Kommentar*, TSAJ 137 (Tübingen: Mohr Siebeck, 2010.
154. **Glazerson, M.:** *Music and Kabbalah*, Jason Aronson, Northvale 1997.
155. *Ibid.*
156. *Ibid.*
157. *Ibid.*
158. **Lifshitz, B.:** *The Jewish Law Annual Volume 19*, Routledge, Abingdon 2011.
159. *Ibid.*
160. **Weintraub, S.Y.:** *Healing of Soul, Healing of Body, Op. Cit.*
161. **Luzzatto, M.:** *Derech Etz Chayim*, A.D. Goldberg, Wickliffe 2001.
   Buxbaum, Y.: *Jewish Spiritual Practices*, Jason Aronson, Northvale 1990.
   Etkes, I.: *The Gaon of Vilna: The Man and His Image*, University of California Press, Berkeley, Los Angeles & London 2002.
   Rubin, Y.D.: *Talelei Oros: The Prayer Anthology: Tefillah Vol. 1*, Feldheim Publishers, Jerusalem 2005.
   Garb, J.: Shamanic Trance in Modern Kabbalah, The University of Chicago Press, Chicago & London 2011.
   Kaplan, L. & Koltun-Fromm, K.: *Imagining the Jewish God*, Lexington Books, Lanham & London 2016.
162. **Lifshitz, B.:** *The Jewish Law Annual Volume 19, Op. Cit.*
163. **Baumol, A.:** *The Poetry of Prayer: Tehillim in Tefillah*, Gefen Publishing House, Jerusalem & New York 2009.
164. **Weintraub, S.Y.:** *Healing of Soul, Healing of Body, Op. Cit.*
165. **Baumol, A.:** *The Poetry of Prayer, Op. Cit.*
166. **Swart, J.G.:** *The Book of Self Creation, Op. Cit.*
167. *Ibid.*
168. *Ibid.*

169. **Baumol, A.:** *The Poetry of Prayer*, Op. Cit.
170. *Ibid.*
171. *Ibid.*
172. *Ibid.*
173. **Buxbaum, Y.:** *Jewish Spiritual Practices*, Op. Cit.
174. **Weintraub, S.Y.:** *Healing of Soul, Healing of Body*, Op. Cit.
175. **Kepnes, S.:** *Jewish Liturgical Reasoning*, Oxford University Press, Oxford & New York 2007.
176. *Ibid.*
177. **Swart, J.G.:** *The Book of Immediate Magic* (Part 1), Op. Cit.
178. **Min Haketoret/Eyal Golan:** *Hallelujah (Psalm 150)*, https://www.youtube.com/watch?v=e_bcVshggeE

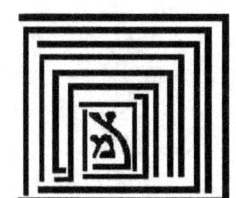

CHAPTER 4
Psalm 42

1. **Feldman, Y.Y.**: *Tehillim Eis Ratzon: A Time of Favor*, Feldheim Publishers, Jerusalem & New York 2004.
2. **Nulman, M.**: *The Encyclopedia of Jewish Prayer*, Op. Cit.
3. **Swart, J.G.**: *The Book of Self Creation*, Op. Cit.
   —*The Book of Sacred Names*, Op. Cit.
   —*The Book of Seals & Amulets*, Op. Cit.
   —*The Book of Immediate Magic* (2 Parts), Op. Cit.
   —*The Book of Magical Psalms - Part 1*, Op. Cit.
4. *Le Livre des Psaumes Hébreu-Français et Phonétique: Traduction Français et Transcription Phonétique du Livre des Psaumes. Prières pour les malades, la subsistance. Prières prononcées sur la tombe des tsadikim, hachkavot, différents kaddich, allumage des bougies. Message du Ramban et autre prières*, Nouvelle Edition, Editions Sinai, Tel Aviv 2006.
   Ronen, D.: *Tehilim Kavvanot ha-Lev*, Machon Shirah Chadashah, Petah Tikva 2013.
5. **Azulai, H.Y.D.**: *Sefer Tehillim Sha'arei Rachamim: im Segulot v'Tefilot ha'Chida*, Agudat Zichron Rachamim, Jerusalem 1997.
6. **Kimchi, D. ben Y.**: *Sefer Tehillim: im Perush Rabbi David Kimchi*, Amsterdam 1731.
   Sefer Shimmush Tehillim, Éliás Békéscsaba Klein, Budapest.
   Seder Tefilot Tikun Ezra: kolel tefilot kol hashanah, Taubstummen Instituts Druckerei, Wien 1815.
   Grünwald, M.: *Ueber den Einfluss der Psalmen auf die Katholische Liturgie, mit steter Rücksichtnahme auf die Talmudisch-Midraschische Literatur*, Commissions-Verlag von J. Kauffmann, Frankfurt am Main 1891.
   Refuah v'Chayim m'Yerushalayim im Shimush Tehilim, Defus Yehudah vi-Yerushalayim, Jerusalem 1931.
   Landsberg, M.: *Sefer Tehillim im Peirush Rashi Metzudat David Metzudat Tziyon v'alav sovev Peirush Divrei Mosheh*, S.D. Friedman, Brooklyn 2015.
   Rebiger, B.: *Sefer Shimmush Tehillim*, Op. Cit.
   Brauner, R.: *Synopsis of Sefer Shimush Tehillim, containing protections against numerous calamities: attributed to Rav Hai Gaon*, Reuven Brauner sixth edition, Raanana 2012.

	Hai ben Sherira Gaon & Varady, A.N.: *Shimush Tehillim (the Theurgical Use of Psalms)*, document shared on Creative Commons Attribution-ShareAlike (CC BY-SA) 4.0 International, May 4th 2015.]
7.	*Ibid.*
8.	**Singer, I. & Adler, C.:** *The Jewish Encyclopedia: A Descriptive Record of the History, Religion, Literature and Customs of the Jewish People from the Earliest Times to the Present Day*, Funk & Wagnalls Company, New York & London 1901–1906.
9.	**Brauner, R.:** *Synopsis of Sefer Shimush Tehillim, Op. Cit.*
	Hai ben Sherira Gaon & Varady, A.N.: *Shimush Tehillim, Op. Cit.*
10.	*Ibid.*
	Kimchi, D. ben Y.: *Sefer Tehillim, Op. Cit.*
	Sefer Shimmush Tehillim, Op. Cit.
	Seder Tefilot Tikun Ezra, Op. Cit.
	Grünwald, M.: *Ueber den Einfluss der Psalmen auf die Katholische Liturgie, Op. Cit.*
	Refuah v'Chayim m'Yerushalayim im Shimush Tehilim, Op. Cit.
	Trachtenberg, J.: *Jewish Magic and Superstition: A Study in Folk Religion*, Behrman's Jewish Book House Publishers, New York 1939.
	Landsberg, M.: *Sefer Tehillim im Peirush Rashi, Op. Cit.*
	Rebiger, B.: *Sefer Shimmush Tehillim, Op. Cit.*
11.	**Rebiger, B.:** *Ibid.*
12.	*Ibid.*
13.	**Selig, G.:** *Sepher Schimmusch Tehillim. Oder: Gebrauch der Psalme zum leiblichen Wohl der Menschen*, Johann Andreas Kunze, Berlin 1788/ Verlag E. Schubert, Bilfingen 1972.
	—*Secrets of the Psalms: A Fragment of the Practical Kabala, with Extracts from other Kabalistic writings, as translated by the author*, Dorene, Arlington 1929.
	The Sixth and Seventh Books of Moses or, Moses' Magical Spirit-art, known as the Wonderful Arts of the Old Wise Hebrews, taken from the Mosaic books of the Cabala and the Talmud, for the good of mankind. Translated from the German, word for word, according to Old Writings, with Numerous Engravings, The Arthur Westbrook Co., 1870.
	Peterson, J.H.: *The Sixth and Seventh Books of Moses or Moses' Magical Spirit-Art: Known as the Wonderful Arts of the Old Wise Hebrews, Taken from the Mosaic Books of the Kabbalah and the Talmud, for the Good of Mankind*, Ibis Press, Newburyport 2008.

14. **Kimchi, D. ben Y.:** *Sefer Tehillim, Op. Cit.*
    Sefer Shimmush Tehillim, Op. Cit.
    Seder Tefilot Tikun Ezra, Op. Cit.
    Grünwald, M.: *Ueber den Einfluss der Psalmen auf die Katholische Liturgie, Op. Cit.*
    Refuah v'Chayim m'Yerushalayim im Shimush Tehilim, Op. Cit.
    Landsberg, M.: *Sefer Tehillim im Peirush Rashi, Op. Cit.*
    Rebiger, B.: *Sefer Shimmush Tehillim, Op. Cit.*
15. **Rebiger, B.:** *Ibid.*
16. *Ibid.*
17. **Zacutto, M.:** *Shorshei ha-Shemot*, Hotzaat Nezer Shraga, Jerusalem 1999.
18. **Avraham Rimon of Granada:** *Brit Menuchah*, Machon Ramchal, Jerusalem 1998.
19. **Zacutto, M.:** *Shorshei ha-Shemot, Op. Cit.*
20. **Rebiger, B.:** *Sefer Shimmush Tehillim, Op. Cit.*
21. **Zacutto, M.:** *Shorshei ha-Shemot, Op. Cit.*
22. *Ibid.*
23. *Ibid.*
24. **Zellmann-Rohrer, M.:** *"Psalms Useful for Everything:" Byzantine and Post-Byzantine Manuals for the Amuletic Use of the Psalter*, Dumbarton Oaks Research Library and Collection, Washington 2019.
25. *Ibid.*
26. **Kieckhefer, R.:** *Forbidden Rites: A Necromancer's Manual of the Fifteenth Century*, The Pennsylvania State University Press, Pennsylvania 1997.
27. **Lecouteux, C.:** *Dictionary of Ancient Magic Words and Spells from Abraxas to Zoar*, transl. Graham, J.E., Inner Traditions, Rochester & Toronto 2014.
28. **Zellmann-Rohrer, M.:** *Psalms Useful for Everything, Op. Cit.*
29. **Rankine, D. & Barron, P.H.:** *The Book of Gold: A 17th Century Magical Grimoire of Amulets, Charms, Prayers, Sigils and Spells using the Biblical Psalms of King David*, Avalonia, London 2010.
    Marty, J. & MacParthy, F.: *Usage Mago-Théurgiques des Psaumes: Selon la Kabbala Judaique et Chrétienne: Sefer Shimoush Théhilim & Le Livre d'Or*, Sesheta Publications, Brestot 2018.
30. **Mathers, S.L. Macgregor:** *Key of Solomon the King: Clavicula Salomonis*, Routledge & Kegan Paul, London 1974.

Psalm 43

1. **Nulman, M.:** *The Encyclopedia of Jewish Prayer*, Op. Cit.
2. *Ibid.*
3. *Le Livre des Psaumes Hébreu-Français*, Op. Cit.
   Ronen, D.: *Tehilim Kavvanot ha-Lev*, Op. Cit.
4. **Azulai, H.Y.D.:** *Sefer Tehillim Sha'arei Rachamim*, Op. Cit.
5. **Kimchi, D. ben Y.:** *Sefer Tehillim*, Op. Cit.
   Sefer Shimmush Tehillim, Op. Cit.
   Seder Tefilot Tikun Ezra, Op. Cit.
   Le Livre des Psaumes Hébreu-Français et Phonétique, Op. Cit.
   Refuah v'Chayim m'Yerushalayim im Shimush Tehilim, Op. Cit.
   Landsberg, M.: *Sefer Tehillim im Peirush Rashi*, Op. Cit.
   Selig, G.: *Sepher Schimmusch Tehillim*, Op. Cit.
   The Sixth and Seventh Books of Moses, Op. Cit.
   Peterson, J.H.: *The Sixth and Seventh Books of Moses*, Op. Cit.
   Rebiger, B.: *Sefer Shimmush Tehillim*, Op. Cit.
   Brauner, R.: *Synopsis of Sefer Shimush Tehillim.* Op. Cit.
   Hai ben Sherira Gaon & Varady, A.N.: *Shimush Tehillim (the Theurgical Use of Psalms)*, Op. Cit.
6. **Selig, G.:** *Sepher Schimmusch Tehillim*, Op. Cit.
   The Sixth and Seventh Books of Moses, Op. Cit.
   Peterson, J.H.: *The Sixth and Seventh Books of Moses*, Op. Cit.
7. **Singer, I. & Adler, C.:** *The Jewish Encyclopedia*, Op. Cit.
8. **Rebiger, B.:** *Sefer Shimmush Tehillim*, Op. Cit.
9. **Zellmann-Rohrer, M.:** *Psalms Useful for Everything*, Op. Cit.
10. **Skemer, D.C.:** *Binding Words: Textual Amulets in the Middle Ages*, The Pennsylvania State University Press, Pennsylvania 2006.
11. **Zellmann-Rohrer, M.:** *Psalms Useful for Everything*, Op. Cit.
12. **Rankine, D. & Barron, P.H.:** The Book of *Gold*, Op. Cit.
    Marty, J. & MacParthy, F.: *Usage Mago-Théurgiques des Psaumes*, Op. Cit.

Psalm 44

1. **Singer, I. & Adler, C.:** *The Jewish Encyclopedia*, Op. Cit.
   Le Livre des Psaumes Hébreu-Français et Phonétique, Op. Cit.
   Azulai, H.Y.D.: *Sefer Tehillim Sha'arei Rachamim*, Op. Cit.
   Ronen, D.: *Tehilim Kavvanot ha-Lev*, Op. Cit.
   Rebiger, B.: *Sefer Shimmush Tehillim*, Op. Cit.
   Brauner, R.: *Synopsis of Sefer Shimush Tehillim.* Op. Cit.
2. **Selig, G.:** *Sepher Schimmusch Tehillim*, Op. Cit.
   The Sixth and Seventh Books of Moses, Op. Cit.
   Peterson, J.H.: *The Sixth and Seventh Books of Moses*, Op. Cit.

3. **Kimchi, D. ben Y.**: *Sefer Tehillim, Op. Cit.*
   Refuah v'Chayim m'Yerushalayim im Shimush Tehilim, Op. Cit.
   Landsberg, M.: *Sefer Tehillim im Peirush Rashi, Op. Cit.*
4. **Brauner, R.**: *Synopsis of Sefer Shimush Tehillim. Op. Cit.*
5. **Rebiger, B.**: *Sefer Shimmush Tehillim, Op. Cit.*
6. *Ibid.*
7. *Ibid.*
8. *Ibid.*
9. **Zacutto, M.**: *Shorshei ha-Shemot, Op. Cit.*
   Swart, J.G.: *The Book of Sacred Names, Op. Cit.*
10. *Ibid.*
11. **Schiffman, L.H. & Swartz, M.D.**: *Hebrew and Aramaic Incantation Texts from the Cairo Genizah: Selected Texts from Taylor-Schechter Box K1*, Sheffield Academic Press, Sheffield 1992.
12. **Rankine, D. & Barron, P.H.**: The Book of *Gold, Op. Cit.*
    Marty, J. & MacParthy, F.: *Usage Mago-Théurgiques des Psaumes, Op. Cit.*

Psalm 45

1. **Singer, I. & Adler, C.**: *The Jewish Encyclopedia, Op. Cit.*
   Le Livre des Psaumes Hébreu-Français et Phonétique, Op. Cit.
   Azulai, H.Y.D.: *Sefer Tehillim Sha'arei Rachamim, Op. Cit.*
   Ronen, D.: *Tehilim Kavvanot ha-Lev, Op. Cit.*
   Brauner, R.: *Synopsis of Sefer Shimush Tehillim. Op. Cit.*
2. **Kimchi, D. ben Y.**: *Sefer Tehillim, Op. Cit.*
   Sefer Shimmush Tehillim, Op. Cit.
   Seder Tefilot Tikun Ezra, Op. Cit.
   Refuah v'Chayim m'Yerushalayim im Shimush Tehilim, Op. Cit.
   Landsberg, M.: *Sefer Tehillim im Peirush Rashi, Op. Cit.*
   Rebiger, B.: *Sefer Shimmush Tehillim, Op. Cit.*
3. **Rebiger, B.**: *Ibid.*
4. **Selig, G.**: *Sepher Schimmusch Tehillim, Op. Cit.*
   The Sixth and Seventh Books of Moses, Op. Cit.
   Peterson, J.H.: *The Sixth and Seventh Books of Moses, Op. Cit.*
5. **Rebiger, B.**: *Sefer Shimmush Tehillim, Op. Cit.*
6. *Ibid.*
7. **Zacutto, M.**: *Shorshei ha-Shemot, Op. Cit.*
   Swart, J.G.: *The Book of Seals & Amulets, Op. Cit.*
8. *Sefer Raziel ha-Malach*, Yarid ha-Sefarim, Jerusalem 2003.
9. **Singer, I. & Adler, C.**: *The Jewish Encyclopedia, Op. Cit.*
10. **Swart, J.G.**: *The Book of Seals & Amulets, Op. Cit.*
11. *Ibid.*

12. *Ibid.*
13. *Sefer Raziel ha-Malach, Op. Cit.*
14. **Zacutto, M.:** *Shorshei ha-Shemot, Op. Cit.*
    Swart, J.G.: *The Book of Seals & Amulets, Op. Cit.*
15. **Swart, J.G.:** *Ibid.*
16. *Ibid.*
    Sefer Raziel ha-Malach, Op. Cit.
    Zacutto, M.: *Shorshei ha-Shemot, Op. Cit.*
    Singer, I. & Adler, C.: *The Jewish Encyclopedia, Op. Cit.*
17. **Zacutto, M.:** *Shorshei ha-Shemot, Op. Cit.*
    Swart, J.G.: *The Book of Seals & Amulets, Op. Cit.*
18. **Swart, J.G.:** *Ibid.*
19. **Zacutto, M.:** *Shorshei ha-Shemot, Op. Cit.*
20. **Zellmann-Rohrer, M.:** *Psalms Useful for Everything, Op. Cit.*
21. *Ibid.*
22. **Rankine, D. & Barron, P.H.:** The Book of *Gold, Op. Cit.*
    Marty, J. & MacParthy, F.: *Usage Mago-Théurgiques des Psaumes, Op. Cit.*
23. *Ibid.*

Psalm 46

1. **Kimchi, D. ben Y.:** *Sefer Tehillim, Op. Cit.*
   Sefer Shimmush Tehillim, Op. Cit.
   Seder Tefilot Tikun Ezra, Op. Cit.
   Refuah v'Chayim m'Yerushalayim im Shimush Tehilim, Op. Cit.
   Le Livre des Psaumes Hébreu-Français et Phonétique, Op. Cit.
   Azulai, H.Y.D.: *Sefer Tehillim Sha'arei Rachamim, Op. Cit.*
   Grünwald, M.: *Ueber den Einfluss der Psalmen auf die Katholische Liturgie, Op. Cit.*
   Rebiger, B.: *Sefer Shimmush Tehillim, Op. Cit.*
   Ronen, D.: *Tehilim Kavvanot ha-Lev, Op. Cit.*
   Landsberg, M.: *Sefer Tehillim im Peirush Rashi, Op. Cit.*
   Brauner, R.: *Synopsis of Sefer Shimush Tehillim. Op. Cit.*
   Hai ben Sherira Gaon & Varady, A.N.: *Shimush Tehillim (the Theurgical Use of Psalms), Op. Cit.*
2. **Singer, I. & Adler, C.:** *The Jewish Encyclopedia, Op. Cit.*
3. **Brauner, R.:** *Synopsis of Sefer Shimush Tehillim. Op. Cit.*
   Hai ben Sherira Gaon & Varady, A.N.: *Shimush Tehillim (the Theurgical Use of Psalms), Op. Cit.*
4. **Selig, G.:** *Sepher Schimmusch Tehillim, Op. Cit.*
   The Sixth and Seventh Books of Moses, Op. Cit.
   Peterson, J.H.: *The Sixth and Seventh Books of Moses, Op. Cit.*

5. **Kimchi, D. ben Y.**: *Sefer Tehillim, Op. Cit.*
   Sefer Shimmush Tehillim, Op. Cit.
   Seder Tefilot Tikun Ezra, Op. Cit.
   Grünwald, M.: *Ueber den Einfluss der Psalmen auf die Katholische Liturgie, Op. Cit.*
   Refuah v'Chayim m'Yerushalayim im Shimush Tehilim, Op. Cit.
   Rebiger, B.: *Sefer Shimmush Tehillim, Op. Cit.*
   Landsberg, M.: *Sefer Tehillim im Peirush Rashi, Op. Cit.*
   Brauner, R.: *Synopsis of Sefer Shimmush Tehillim. Op. Cit.*
   Hai ben Sherira Gaon & Varady, A.N.: *Shimush Tehillim (the Theurgical Use of Psalms), Op. Cit.*
6. *Ibid.*
7. *Ibid.*
8. **Rebiger, B.**: *Ibid.*
9. *Ibid.*
10. **Kimchi, D. ben Y.**: *Sefer Tehillim, Op. Cit.*
    Sefer Shimmush Tehillim, Op. Cit.
    Seder Tefilot Tikun Ezra, Op. Cit.
    Grünwald, M.: *Ueber den Einfluss der Psalmen auf die Katholische Liturgie, Op. Cit.*
    Refuah v'Chayim m'Yerushalayim im Shimush Tehilim, Op. Cit.
    Rebiger, B.: *Sefer Shimmush Tehillim, Op. Cit.*
    Landsberg, M.: *Sefer Tehillim im Peirush Rashi, Op. Cit.*
    Brauner, R.: *Synopsis of Sefer Shimmush Tehillim. Op. Cit.*
    Hai ben Sherira Gaon & Varady, A.N.: *Shimush Tehillim (the Theurgical Use of Psalms), Op. Cit.*
11. **Rebiger, B.**: *Ibid.*
12. **Kimchi, D. ben Y.**: *Sefer Tehillim, Op. Cit.*
    Sefer Shimmush Tehillim, Op. Cit.
    Seder Tefilot Tikun Ezra, Op. Cit.
    Grünwald, M.: *Ueber den Einfluss der Psalmen auf die Katholische Liturgie, Op. Cit.*
    Refuah v'Chayim m'Yerushalayim im Shimush Tehilim, Op. Cit.
    Rebiger, B.: *Sefer Shimmush Tehillim, Op. Cit.*
    Landsberg, M.: *Sefer Tehillim im Peirush Rashi, Op. Cit.*
    Brauner, R.: *Synopsis of Sefer Shimmush Tehillim. Op. Cit.*
    Hai ben Sherira Gaon & Varady, A.N.: *Shimush Tehillim (the Theurgical Use of Psalms), Op. Cit.*
13. **Rebiger, B.**: *Sefer Shimmush Tehillim, Op. Cit.*
14. **Selig, G.**: *Sepher Schimmusch Tehillim, Op. Cit.*
    The Sixth and Seventh Books of Moses, Op. Cit.
    Peterson, J.H.: *The Sixth and Seventh Books of Moses, Op. Cit.*

15. **Rebiger, B.**: *Sefer Shimmush Tehillim, Op. Cit.*
16. *Kabbalah Ma'asit uS'gulot*, Jerusalem - The National Library of Israel Ms. Heb. 4°601
17. **Rebiger, B.**: *Sefer Shimmush Tehillim, Op. Cit.*
18. *Ibid.*
19. **Feldman, Y.Y.**: *Tehillim Eis Ratzon, Op. Cit.*
20. **Zacutto, M.**: *Shorshei ha-Shemot, Op. Cit.*
    Swart, J.G.: *The Book of Sacred Names, Op. Cit.*
21. **Davis, E. & Frenkel, D.A.**: *Ha-Kami'a ha-Ivri: Mikra'i Refu'i Kelali im Tatzlumim v'Iyurim Rabim*, Machon l'Mada'e ha-Yahadut, Jerusalem 1995.
    Rosenberg, Y.Y.: *Rafael ha-Malach*, Asher Klein, Jerusalem 2000.
    Green, A.: *Judaic Artifacts: Unlocking the Secrets of Judaic Charms and Amulets*, Astrolog Publishing House, Hod Hasharon 2004.
22. **Zacutto, M.**: *Shorshei ha-Shemot, Op. cit.*
23. **Tirshom, J. ben E.**: *Shoshan Yesod Olam* in *Collectanea of Kabbalistic and Magical Texts*, Bibliothèque de Genève: Comites Latentes 145, Genève.
    Ms. Günzburg #775, Russian National Library, Moscow.
    Ba'al Shem, E.; Ba'al-Shem, J. & Hillel, M.: *Sefer Toldot Adam*, Machon Bnei Yishaschar, Jerusalem 1994.
    Zacutto, M.: *Shorshei ha-Shemot, Op. cit.*
    Kaplan, A.: *Meditation and Kabbalah*, Samuel Weiser Inc., York Beach 1988.
    —*Sefer Yetzirah: The Book of Creation In Theory and Practice*, Samuel Weiser Inc., York Beach 1990 (Revised edition with index 1997).
    Samuel, G.: *The Kabbalah Handbook: A Concise Encyclopedia of Terms and Concepts in Jewish Mysticism*, Jeremy P. Tarcher/Penguin, New York 2007.
    Graham, L.D.: *The Seven Seals of Judeo-Islamic Magic: Possible Origins of the Symbols*, https://www.academia.edu/1509428/The_Seven_Seals_of_Judeo-Islamic_Magic_Possible_Origins_of_the_Symbols (2012).
    —*Margin of Error: A Search for Words Lost Before 1784 CE by Excessive Trimming of Folio 37 in the Kabbalah Manuscript Moscow-Günzburg 775 (14-15th century CE)*, Giluy Milta B'alma (article gmb042) (2013).
    —*A Comparison of the Seven Seals in Islamic Esotericism and Jewish Kabbalah*, https://www.academia.edu/5998229/A_comparison_of_the_Seven_Seals_in_Islamic_esotericism_and_Jewish_Kabbalah (2014).

24. **Ba'al Shem, E.; Ba'al-Shem, J. & Hillel, M.:** *Ibid.*
25. **Kaplan, A.:** *Meditation and Kabbalah, Op. cit.*
    —*Sefer Yetzirah: The Book of Creation, Op. cit.*
    Samuel, G.: *The Kabbalah Handbook, Op. cit.*
    Graham, L.D.: *The Seven Seals of Judeo-Islamic Magic, Op. cit.*
    —*Margin of Error, Op. cit.*
    —*A Comparison of the Seven Seals in Islamic Esotericism and Jewish Kabbalah, Op. cit.*
26. **Tirshom, J. ben E.:** *Shoshan Yesod Olam, Op. cit.*
    Ms. Günzburg #775, *Op. cit.*
    Zacutto, M.: *Shorshei ha-Shemot, Op. cit.*
    Graham, L.D.: *Margin of Error, Op. cit.*
27. **Tirshom, J. ben E.:** *Ibid.*
28. *Ibid.*
29. **Ba'al Shem, E. & Ba'al-Shem, J.:** *Sefer Toldot Adam*, First Edition, Zolkiev 1720.
30. **Kaplan, A.:** *Meditation and Kabbalah, Op. cit.*
31. **Kaplan, A.:** *Sefer Yetzirah: The Book of Creation, Op. cit.*
32. **Ba'al Shem, E.; Ba'al-Shem, J. & Hillel, M.:** *Sefer Toldot Adam, Op. cit.*
33. *Ibid.*
34. **Tirshom, J. ben E.:** *Shoshan Yesod Olam, Op. cit.*
    Ms. Günzburg #775, *Op. cit.*
    Zacutto, M.: *Shorshei ha-Shemot, Op. cit.*
    Graham, L.D.: *Margin of Error, Op. cit.*
35. **Kaplan, A.:** *Sefer Yetzirah: The Book of Creation, Op. cit.*
36. **Tirshom, J. ben E.:** *Shoshan Yesod Olam, Op. cit.*
37. **Samuel, G.:** *The Kabbalah Handbook, Op. cit.*
38. **Ba'al Shem, E.; Ba'al-Shem, J. & Hillel, M.:** *Sefer Toldot Adam, Op. cit.*
39. *Ibid.*
40. *Ibid.*
41. *Ibid.*
42. *Ibid.*
43. *Ibid.*
44. *Ibid.*
45. *Ibid.*
46. *Ibid.*
47. *Ibid.*
48. *Ibid.*
49. *Ibid.*
50. *Ibid.*

51. *Ibid.*
52. **Rankine, D. & Barron, P.H.:** The Book of *Gold, Op. Cit.*
    Marty, J. & MacParthy, F.: *Usage Mago-Théurgiques des Psaumes, Op. Cit.*
53. **Mathers, S.L. Macgregor:** *Key of Solomon the King, Op. cit.*

Psalm 47

1. **Scherman, N.; Goldwurm, H. & Gold, A.:** *Rosh Hashanah: Its Significance, Laws & Prayers: A Presentation Anthologized from Talmudic and Traditional Sources*, Meshorah Publications Ltd, Brooklyn 1983.
2. **Greenberg, I.:** *The Jewish Way: Living the Holidays*, Touchstone, New York 1988.
3. *Ibid.*
4. **Shiloah, A.:** *Jewish Musical Traditions*, Wayne State University Press, Detroit 1992.
5. **Greenberg, I.:** *The Jewish Way, Op. Cit.*
6. *Ibid.*
7. **Scherman, N.; Goldwurm, H. & Gold, A.:** *Rosh Hashanah, Op. Cit.*
8. **Nulman, M.:** *The Encyclopedia of Jewish Prayer, Op. Cit.*
9. **Kaplan, M.M.:** *The Meaning of God in Modern Jewish Religion*, Wayne State University Press, Detroit 1994.
10. **Scherman, N.; Goldwurm, H. & Gold, A.:** *Rosh Hashanah, Op. Cit.*
11. *Ibid.*
12. **Swart, J.G.:** *The Book of Self Creation, Op. Cit.*
    —*The Book of Magical Psalms - Part 1, Op. Cit.*
13. *Ibid.*
14. **Kaplan, M.M.:** *The Meaning of God in Modern Jewish Religion, Op. Cit.*
15. *Ibid.*
16. **Klein, I.:** *A Guide to Jewish Religious Practice*, The Jewish Theological Seminary of America, New York & Jerusalem 1979.
17. *Ibid.*
18. **Dan, J.:** *Jewish Mysticism: The Middle Ages*, Vol. II, Jason Aronson Inc., Northvale 1998.
19. *Ibid.*
20. *Ibid.*
21. **Scherman, N.; Goldwurm, H. & Gold, A.:** *Rosh Hashanah, Op. Cit.*
22. **Klein, I.:** *A Guide to Jewish Religious Practice, Op. Cit.*
    Nulman, M.: *The Encyclopedia of Jewish Prayer, Op. Cit.*

23. **Garr, J.D.:** *Living Emblems: Ancient Symbols of Faith*, Golden Key Press, Atlanta 2007.
24. *Ibid.*
25. **Scherman, N.; Goldwurm, H. & Gold, A.:** *Rosh Hashanah, Op. Cit.*
26. **Cohen, J.M.:** *Prayer and Penitence: A Commentary on the High Holy Day Machzor*, Jason Aronson Inc., Northvale 1994.
27. **Azulai, H.Y.D.:** *Sefer Tehillim Sha'arei Rachamim, Op. Cit.*
    Ronen, D.: *Tehilim Kavvanot ha-Lev, Op. Cit.*
    Feldman, Y.Y.: *Tehillim Eis Ratzon, Op. Cit.*
28. *Le Livre des Psaumes Hébreu-Français et Phonétique, Op. Cit.*
29. **Singer, I. & Adler, C.:** *The Jewish Encyclopedia, Op. Cit.*
30. **Kimchi, D. ben Y.:** *Sefer Tehillim, Op. Cit.*
    Sefer Shimmush Tehillim, Op. Cit.
    Seder Tefilot Tikun Ezra, Op. Cit.
    Grünwald, M.: *Ueber den Einfluss der Psalmen auf die Katholische Liturgie, Op. Cit.*
    Refuah v'Chayim m'Yerushalayim im Shimush Tehilim, Op. Cit.
    Rebiger, B.: *Sefer Shimmush Tehillim, Op. Cit.*
    Landsberg, M.: *Sefer Tehillim im Peirush Rashi, Op. Cit.*
    Brauner, R.: *Synopsis of Sefer Shimmush Tehillim. Op. Cit.*
    Hai ben Sherira Gaon & Varady, A.N.: *Shimush Tehillim (the Theurgical Use of Psalms), Op. Cit.*
31. **Selig, G.:** *Sepher Schimmusch Tehillim, Op. Cit.*
    The Sixth and Seventh Books of Moses, Op. Cit.
    Peterson, J.H.: *The Sixth and Seventh Books of Moses, Op. Cit.*
32. **Rebiger, B.:** *Sefer Shimmush Tehillim, Op. Cit.*
33. **Zellmann-Rohrer, M.:** *Psalms Useful for Everything, Op. Cit.*
34. *Ibid.*
35. **Rankine, D. & Barron, P.H.:** The Book of *Gold, Op. Cit.*
    Marty, J. & MacParthy, F.: *Usage Mago-Théurgiques des Psaumes, Op. Cit.*
36. **Skinner, S. & Rankine, D.:** *A Collection of Magical Secrets: taken from Peter de Abano, Cornelius Agrippa and from other famous Occult Philosophers, and a Treatise of Mixed Cabalah which comprises the Angelic Art taken from Hebrew Sages*, Avalonia, London 2009.
37. **Skinner, S. & Rankine, D.:** *The Veritable Key of Solomon*, Golden Hoard Press Pty. Ltd., Singapore 2015.
38. **Kieckhefer, R.:** *Forbidden Rites: A Necromancer's Manual of the Fifteenth Century*, The Pennsylvania State University Press, Pennsylvania 1998.
39. **Mathers, S.L. Macgregor:** *Key of Solomon the King, Op. cit.*
40. *Ibid.*

Psalm 48

1. **Nulman, M.:** *The Encyclopedia of Jewish Prayer, Op. Cit.*
   Magonet, J.: *A Rabbi Reads the Psalms, Op. Cit.*
   Berlin, A. & Brettler, M.Z.: *The Jewish Study Bible: Jewish Publication Society Tanakh Translation*, Oxford University Press Inc., Oxford & New York 2004.
2. **Feldman, Y.Y.:** *Tehillim Eis Ratzon, Op. Cit.*
3. **Singer, I. & Adler, C.:** *The Jewish Encyclopedia, Op. Cit.*
   Le Livre des Psaumes Hébreu-Français et Phonétique, Op. Cit.
   Azulai, H.Y.D.: *Sefer Tehillim Sha'arei Rachamim, Op. Cit.*
   Ronen, D.: *Tehilim Kavvanot ha-Lev, Op. Cit.*
   Rebiger, B.: *Sefer Shimmush Tehillim, Op. Cit.*
   Brauner, R.: *Synopsis of Sefer Shimush Tehillim. Op. Cit.*
4. **Kimchi, D. ben Y.:** *Sefer Tehillim, Op. Cit.*
   Sefer Shimmush Tehillim, Op. Cit.
   Seder Tefilot Tikun Ezra, Op. Cit.
   Grünwald, M.: *Ueber den Einfluss der Psalmen auf die Katholische Liturgie, Op. Cit.*
   Refuah v'Chayim m'Yerushalayim im Shimush Tehilim, Op. Cit.
   Rebiger, B.: *Sefer Shimmush Tehillim, Op. Cit.*
   Landsberg, M.: *Sefer Tehillim im Peirush Rashi, Op. Cit.*
   Hai ben Sherira Gaon & Varady, A.N.: *Shimush Tehillim (the Theurgical Use of Psalms), Op. Cit.*
5. **Selig, G.:** *Sepher Schimmusch Tehillim, Op. Cit.*
   The Sixth and Seventh Books of Moses, Op. Cit.
   Peterson, J.H.: *The Sixth and Seventh Books of Moses, Op. Cit.*
6. **Rebiger, B.:** *Sefer Shimmush Tehillim, Op. Cit.*
7. **Zellmann-Rohrer, M.:** *Psalms Useful for Everything, Op. Cit.*
8. *Ibid.*
9. *Ibid.*
10. **Rankine, D. & Barron, P.H.:** The Book of *Gold, Op. Cit.*
    Marty, J. & MacParthy, F.: *Usage Mago-Théurgiques des Psaumes, Op. Cit.*
11. **Zellmann-Rohrer, M.:** *Psalms Useful for Everything, Op. Cit.*

Psalm 49

1. **Klein, I.:** *A Guide to Jewish Religious Practice, Op. Cit.*
   Nulman, M.: *The Encyclopedia of Jewish Prayer, Op. Cit.*
   Feldman, Y.Y.: *Tehillim Eis Ratzon, Op. Cit.*
2. **Singer, I. & Adler, C.:** *The Jewish Encyclopedia, Op. Cit.*
   Le Livre des Psaumes Hébreu-Français et Phonétique, Op. Cit.
   Azulai, H.Y.D.: *Sefer Tehillim Sha'arei Rachamim, Op. Cit.*

         Dennis, G.W.: *The Encyclopedia of Jewish Myth, Magic and Mysticism*, Llewellyn Publications, Woodbury 2007.
         Ronen, D.: *Tehilim Kavvanot ha-Lev*, Op. Cit.
3.   **Brauner, R.:** *Synopsis of Sefer Shimush Tehillim.* Op. Cit.
4.   **Kimchi, D. ben Y.:** *Sefer Tehillim*, Op. Cit.
      Sefer Shimmush Tehillim, Op. Cit.
      Seder Tefilot Tikun Ezra, Op. Cit.
      Grünwald, M.: *Ueber den Einfluss der Psalmen auf die Katholische Liturgie*, Op. Cit.
      Refuah v'Chayim m'Yerushalayim im Shimush Tehilim, Op. Cit.
      Rebiger, B.: *Sefer Shimmush Tehillim*, Op. Cit.
      Landsberg, M.: *Sefer Tehillim im Peirush Rashi*, Op. Cit.
      Hai ben Sherira Gaon & Varady, A.N.: *Shimush Tehillim (the Theurgical Use of Psalms)*, Op. Cit.
5.   *Ibid.*
6.   **Rebiger, B.:** *Sefer Shimmush Tehillim*, Op. Cit.
7.   **Selig, G.:** *Sepher Schimmusch Tehillim*, Op. Cit.
      The Sixth and Seventh Books of Moses, Op. Cit.
      Peterson, J.H.: *The Sixth and Seventh Books of Moses*, Op. Cit.
8.   *Ibid.*
9.   **Rebiger, B.:** *Sefer Shimmush Tehillim*, Op. Cit.
10. **Schrire, T.:** *Hebrew Amulets*, Routledge & Kegan Paul, London 1966.
      Davis, E. & Frenkel, D.A.: *Ha-Kami'a ha-Ivri*, Op. Cit.
      Green, A.: *Judaic Artifacts*, Op. Cit.
11. **Rankine, D. & Barron, P.H.:** The Book of *Gold*, Op. Cit.
      Marty, J. & MacParthy, F.: *Usage Mago-Théurgiques des Psaumes*, Op. Cit.
12. **Skinner, S. & Rankine, D.:** *A Collection of Magical Secrets*, Op. Cit.
13. **Mathers, S.L. Macgregor:** *Key of Solomon the King*, Op. Cit.

Psalm 50

1.   **Singer, I. & Adler, C.:** *The Jewish Encyclopedia*, Op. Cit.
      Le Livre des Psaumes Hébreu-Français et Phonétique, Op. Cit.
      Azulai, H.Y.D.: *Sefer Tehillim Sha'arei Rachamim*, Op. Cit.
      Ronen, D.: *Tehilim Kavvanot ha-Lev*, Op. Cit.
      Brauner, R.: *Synopsis of Sefer Shimush Tehillim.* Op. Cit.
2.   **Kimchi, D. ben Y.:** *Sefer Tehillim*, Op. Cit.
      Sefer Shimmush Tehillim, Op. Cit.
      Seder Tefilot Tikun Ezra, Op. Cit.
      Refuah v'Chayim m'Yerushalayim im Shimush Tehilim, Op. Cit.

	Rebiger, B.: *Sefer Shimmush Tehillim, Op. Cit.*
	Landsberg, M.: *Sefer Tehillim im Peirush Rashi, Op. Cit.*
	Hai ben Sherira Gaon & Varady, A.N.: *Shimush Tehillim (the Theurgical Use of Psalms), Op. Cit.*
3.	*Ibid.*
4.	**Selig, G.:** *Sepher Schimmusch Tehillim, Op. Cit.*
	The Sixth and Seventh Books of Moses, Op. Cit.
	Peterson, J.H.: *The Sixth and Seventh Books of Moses, Op. Cit.*
5.	*Ibid.*
6.	**Rebiger, B.:** *Sefer Shimmush Tehillim, Op. Cit.*
7.	*Ibid.*
8.	**Singer, I. & Adler, C.:** *The Jewish Encyclopedia, Op. Cit.*
9.	**Zacutto, M.:** *Shorshei ha-Shemot, Op. cit.*
10.	**Rankine, D. & Barron, P.H.:** The Book of *Gold, Op. Cit.*
	Marty, J. & MacParthy, F.: *Usage Mago-Théurgiques des Psaumes, Op. Cit.*

Psalm 51

1.	**Nulman, M.:** *The Encyclopedia of Jewish Prayer, Op. Cit.*
	Feldman, Y.Y.: *Tehillim Eis Ratzon, Op. Cit.*
2.	*Le Livre des Psaumes Hébreu-Français et Phonétique, Op. Cit.*
	Azulai, H.Y.D.: *Sefer Tehillim Sha'arei Rachamim, Op. Cit.*
	Ronen, D.: *Tehilim Kavvanot ha-Lev, Op. Cit.*
	Brauner, R.: *Synopsis of Sefer Shimush Tehillim. Op. Cit.*
3.	**Singer, I. & Adler, C.:** *The Jewish Encyclopedia, Op. Cit.*
4.	**Brauner, R.:** *Synopsis of Sefer Shimush Tehillim. Op. Cit.*
5.	**Kimchi, D. ben Y.:** *Sefer Tehillim, Op. Cit.*
	Sefer Shimmush Tehillim, Op. Cit.
	Seder Tefilot Tikun Ezra, Op. Cit.
	Refuah v'Chayim m'Yerushalayim im Shimush Tehilim, Op. Cit.
	Rebiger, B.: *Sefer Shimmush Tehillim, Op. Cit.*
	Landsberg, M.: *Sefer Tehillim im Peirush Rashi, Op. Cit.*
	Hai ben Sherira Gaon & Varady, A.N.: *Shimush Tehillim (the Theurgical Use of Psalms), Op. Cit.*
6.	**Rebiger, B.:** *Sefer Shimmush Tehillim, Op. Cit.*
7.	*Ibid.*
	Kimchi, D. ben Y.: *Sefer Tehillim, Op. Cit.*
	Sefer Shimmush Tehillim, Op. Cit.
	Seder Tefilot Tikun Ezra, Op. Cit.
	Refuah v'Chayim m'Yerushalayim im Shimush Tehilim, Op. Cit.
	Landsberg, M.: *Sefer Tehillim im Peirush Rashi, Op. Cit.*
	Hai ben Sherira Gaon & Varady, A.N.: *Shimush Tehillim (the Theurgical Use of Psalms), Op. Cit.*

8. **Selig, G.:** *Sepher Schimmusch Tehillim, Op. Cit.*
   The Sixth and Seventh Books of Moses, Op. Cit.
   Peterson, J.H.: *The Sixth and Seventh Books of Moses, Op. Cit.*
9. **Rebiger, B.:** *Sefer Shimmush Tehillim, Op. Cit.*
10. **Schrire, T.:** *Hebrew Amulets, Op. Cit.*
    Green, A.: *Judaic Artifacts, Op. Cit.*
11. **Davis, E. & Frenkel, D.A.:** *Ha-Kami'a ha-Ivri, Op. Cit.*
    Green, A.: *Judaic Artifacts, Op. Cit.*
12. **Zacutto, M.:** *Shorshei ha-Shemot, Op. cit.*
13. **Davis, E. & Frenkel, D.A.:** *Ha-Kami'a ha-Ivri, Op. Cit.*
    Green, A.: *Judaic Artifacts, Op. Cit.*
14. **Eliram (Amslam), S.:** *Sefer Segulot, Terufot u'Mazalot,* Eliram–Sifre Kodesh, Jerusalem 2002.
15. **Zacutto, M.:** *Shorshei ha-Shemot, Op. Cit.*
16. *Ibid.*
17. *Ibid.*
18. *Ibid.*
19. **Zellmann-Rohrer, M.:** *Psalms Useful for Everything, Op. Cit.*
20. **Lecouteux, C.:** *Dictionary of Ancient Magic Words and Spells from Abraxas to Zoar, Op. Cit.*
21. **Kieckhefer, R.:** *Forbidden Rites, Op. Cit.*
22. *Ibid.*
23. **Skinner, S. & Rankine, D.:** *A Collection of Magical Secrets, Op. Cit.*
24. *Ibid.*
25. **Zellmann-Rohrer, M.:** *Psalms Useful for Everything, Op. Cit.*
26. **Heim, R.:** *Incantamenta Magica Graeca Latina: Collegit, disposuit, edidit R. Heim,* B.G. Teubneri, Lipsiae 1892.
27. **Lecouteux, C.:** *Dictionary of Ancient Magic Words and Spells from Abraxas to Zoar, Op. Cit.*
    Braekman, W.L.: *Middeleeuwse Witte en Zwart Magie in het Nederlands Taalgebied. Gecommentarieerd Compendium van Incantamenta tot einde 16de Eeuw,* Royal Academy, Ghent 1997.
28. *Ibid.*
29. **Rankine, D. & Barron, P.H.:** *The Book of Gold, Op. Cit.*
    Marty, J. & MacParthy, F.: *Usage Mago-Théurgiques des Psaumes, Op. Cit.*
30. **Lecouteux, C.:** *Dictionary of Ancient Magic Words and Spells from Abraxas to Zoar, Op. Cit.*
31. **Mathers, S.L. Macgregor:** *Key of Solomon the King, Op. cit.*

Psalm 52

1. **Azulai, H.Y.D.:** *Sefer Tehillim Sha'arei Rachamim, Op. Cit.*
   Ronen, D.: *Tehilim Kavvanot ha-Lev, Op. Cit.*
2. **Singer, I. & Adler, C.:** *The Jewish Encyclopedia, Op. Cit.*
3. *Le Livre des Psaumes Hébreu-Français et Phonétique, Op. Cit.*
4. **Kimchi, D. ben Y.:** *Sefer Tehillim, Op. Cit.*
   Refuah v'Chayim m'Yerushalayim im Shimush Tehilim, Op. Cit.
   Rebiger, B.: *Sefer Shimmush Tehillim, Op. Cit.*
   Landsberg, M.: *Sefer Tehillim im Peirush Rashi, Op. Cit.*
   Brauner, R.: *Synopsis of Sefer Shimush Tehillim. Op. Cit.*
5. **Selig, G.:** *Sepher Schimmusch Tehillim, Op. Cit.*
   The Sixth and Seventh Books of Moses, Op. Cit.
   Peterson, J.H.: *The Sixth and Seventh Books of Moses, Op. Cit.*
6. **Rebiger, B.:** *Sefer Shimmush Tehillim, Op. Cit.*
7. *Ibid.*
8. **Lecouteux, C.:** *Dictionary of Ancient Magic Words and Spells from Abraxas to Zoar, Op. Cit.*
9. **Rankine, D. & Barron, P.H.:** The Book of *Gold, Op. Cit.*
   Marty, J. & MacParthy, F.: *Usage Mago-Théurgiques des Psaumes, Op. Cit.*

Psalm 53

1. **Singer, I. & Adler, C.:** *The Jewish Encyclopedia, Op. Cit.*
   Le Livre des Psaumes Hébreu-Français et Phonétique, Op. Cit.
   Azulai, H.Y.D.: *Sefer Tehillim Sha'arei Rachamim, Op. Cit.*
   Ronen, D.: *Tehilim Kavvanot ha-Lev, Op. Cit.*
   Brauner, R.: *Synopsis of Sefer Shimush Tehillim. Op. Cit.*
2. *Sefer Shimmush Tehillim, Op. Cit.*
   Seder Tefilot Tikun Ezra, Op. Cit.
   Hai ben Sherira Gaon & Varady, A.N.: *Shimush Tehillim (the Theurgical Use of Psalms), Op. Cit.*
3. **Kimchi, D. ben Y.:** *Sefer Tehillim, Op. Cit.*
   Grünwald, M.: *Ueber den Einfluss der Psalmen auf die Katholische Liturgie, Op. Cit.*
   Refuah v'Chayim m'Yerushalayim im Shimush Tehilim, Op. Cit.
   Rebiger, B.: *Sefer Shimmush Tehillim, Op. Cit.*
   Landsberg, M.: *Sefer Tehillim im Peirush Rashi, Op. Cit.*
4. **Selig, G.:** *Sepher Schimmusch Tehillim, Op. Cit.*
   The Sixth and Seventh Books of Moses, Op. Cit.
   Peterson, J.H.: *The Sixth and Seventh Books of Moses, Op. Cit.*
5. *Ibid.*
6. **Rebiger, B.:** *Sefer Shimmush Tehillim, Op. Cit.*
7. *Ibid.*

8. **Rankine, D. & Barron, P.H.:** The Book of *Gold, Op. Cit.*
   Marty, J. & MacParthy, F.: *Usage Mago-Théurgiques des Psaumes, Op. Cit.*
9. **Mathers, S.L. Macgregor:** *Key of Solomon the King, Op. cit.*
10. *Ibid.*

Psalm 54

1. **Feldman, Y.Y.:** *Tehillim Eis Ratzon, Op. Cit.*
2. **Brauner, R.:** *Synopsis of Sefer Shimush Tehillim. Op. Cit.*
3. **Singer, I. & Adler, C.:** *The Jewish Encyclopedia, Op. Cit.*
   Le Livre des Psaumes Hébreu-Français et Phonétique, Op. Cit.
   Azulai, H.Y.D.: *Sefer Tehillim Sha'arei Rachamim, Op. Cit.*
   Ronen, D.: *Tehilim Kavvanot ha-Lev, Op. Cit.*
4. **Kimchi, D. ben Y.:** *Sefer Tehillim, Op. Cit.*
   Refuah v'Chayim m'Yerushalayim im Shimush Tehilim, Op. Cit.
   Landsberg, M.: *Sefer Tehillim im Peirush Rashi, Op. Cit.*
   Selig, G.: *Sepher Schimmusch Tehillim, Op. Cit.*
   The Sixth and Seventh Books of Moses, Op. Cit.
   Peterson, J.H.: *The Sixth and Seventh Books of Moses, Op. Cit.*
5. **Rebiger, B.:** *Sefer Shimmush Tehillim, Op. Cit.*
6. *Ibid.*
7. **Swart, J.G.:** *The Book of Magical Psalms - Part 1, Op. Cit.*
8. *Ibid.*
   Zacutto, M.: *Shorshei ha-Shemot, Op. Cit.*
9. *Ibid.*
10. **Davis, E. & Frenkel, D.A.:** *Ha-Kami'a ha-Ivri, Op. Cit.*
    Rosenberg, Y.Y.: *Rafael ha-Malach, Op. Cit.*
    Green, A.: *Judaic Artifacts, Op. Cit.*
11. *Ibid.*
12. **Swart, J.G.:** *The Book of Seals & Amulets, Op. Cit.*
13. **Rankine, D. & Barron, P.H.:** *The Book of Gold, Op. Cit.*
    Marty, J. & MacParthy, F.: *Usage Mago-Théurgiques des Psaumes, Op. Cit.*
14. **Zellmann-Rohrer, M.:** *Psalms Useful for Everything, Op. Cit.*
15. **Lecouteux, C.:** *Dictionary of Ancient Magic Words and Spells from Abraxas to Zoar, Op. Cit.*
16. **Mathers, S.L. Macgregor:** *Key of Solomon the King, Op. cit.*
17. *Ibid.*

Psalm 55

1. **Feldman, Y.Y.:** *Tehillim Eis Ratzon, Op. Cit.*
2. *Le Livre des Psaumes Hébreu-Français et Phonétique, Op. Cit.*
   Azulai, H.Y.D.: *Sefer Tehillim Sha'arei Rachamim, Op. Cit.*
   Ronen, D.: *Tehilim Kavvanot ha-Lev, Op. Cit.*

3. **Singer, I. & Adler, C.:** *The Jewish Encyclopedia, Op. Cit.*
   Brauner, R.: *Synopsis of Sefer Shimush Tehillim. Op. Cit.*
4. **Kimchi, D. ben Y.:** *Sefer Tehillim, Op. Cit.*
   Refuah v'Chayim m'Yerushalayim im Shimush Tehilim, Op. Cit.
   Rebiger, B.: *Sefer Shimmush Tehillim, Op. Cit.*
   Landsberg, M.: *Sefer Tehillim im Peirush Rashi, Op. Cit.*
5. **Selig, G.:** *Sepher Schimmusch Tehillim, Op. Cit.*
   The Sixth and Seventh Books of Moses, Op. Cit.
   Peterson, J.H.: *The Sixth and Seventh Books of Moses, Op. Cit.*
6. **Rebiger, B.:** *Sefer Shimmush Tehillim, Op. Cit.*
7. *Ibid.*
8. **Davis, E. & Frenkel, D.A.:** *Ha-Kami'a ha-Ivri, Op. Cit.*
   Rosenberg, Y.Y.: *Rafael ha-Malach, Op. Cit.*
   Green, A.: *Judaic Artifacts, Op. Cit.*
9. **Zacutto, M.:** *Shorshei ha-Shemot, Op. Cit.*
   Swart, J.G.: *The Book of Seals & Amulets, Op. Cit.*
10. *Ibid.*
11. **Zacutto, M.:** *Shorshei ha-Shemot, Op. Cit.*
12. *Ibid.*
13. *Ibid.*
14. **Rubinstein, Y.Y.:** *Sefer Zichron Ya'akov Yosef,* Defus Yehudah v'Yerushalayim, Yerushalayim 1930.
    Eliram (Amslam), S.: *Sefer Segulot, Terufot u'Mazalot, Op. Cit.*
15. *Ibid.*
16. *Ibid.*
17. *Ibid.*
18. **Zellmann-Rohrer, M.:** *Psalms Useful for Everything, Op. Cit.*
19. *Ibid.*
20. *Ibid.*
21. **Rankine, D. & Barron, P.H.:** *The Book of Gold, Op. Cit.*
    Marty, J. & MacParthy, F.: *Usage Mago-Théurgiques des Psaumes, Op. Cit.*
22. **Zellmann-Rohrer, M.:** *Psalms Useful for Everything, Op. Cit.*

Psalm 56

1. *Le Livre des Psaumes Hébreu-Français et Phonétique, Op. Cit.*
   Azulai, H.Y.D.: *Sefer Tehillim Sha'arei Rachamim, Op. Cit.*
   Ronen, D.: *Tehilim Kavvanot ha-Lev, Op. Cit.*
2. **Kimchi, D. ben Y.:** *Sefer Tehillim, Op. Cit.*
   Singer, I. & Adler, C.: *The Jewish Encyclopedia, Op. Cit.*
   Refuah v'Chayim m'Yerushalayim im Shimush Tehilim, Op. Cit.
   Rebiger, B.: *Sefer Shimmush Tehillim, Op. Cit.*

	Brauner, R.: *Synopsis of Sefer Shimush Tehillim. Op. Cit.*
	Landsberg, M.: *Sefer Tehillim im Peirush Rashi, Op. Cit.*
3.	**Selig, G.:** *Sepher Schimmusch Tehillim, Op. Cit.*
	The Sixth and Seventh Books of Moses, Op. Cit.
	Peterson, J.H.: *The Sixth and Seventh Books of Moses, Op. Cit.*
4.	**Rebiger, B.:** *Sefer Shimmush Tehillim, Op. Cit.*
5.	**Zellmann-Rohrer, M.:** *Psalms Useful for Everything, Op. Cit.*
6.	*Ibid.*
7.	*Ibid.*
8.	*Ibid.*
9.	*Ibid.*
10.	**Rankine, D. & Barron, P.H.:** *The Book of Gold, Op. Cit.*
	Marty, J. & MacParthy, F.: *Usage Mago-Théurgiques des Psaumes, Op. Cit.*
11.	**Skinner, S. & Rankine, D.:** *A Collection of Magical Secrets, Op. Cit.*
12.	**Mathers, S.L. Macgregor:** *Key of Solomon the King, Op. cit.*

Psalm 57

1.	**Singer, I. & Adler, C.:** *The Jewish Encyclopedia, Op. Cit.*
	Le Livre des Psaumes Hébreu-Français et Phonétique, Op. Cit.
	Azulai, H.Y.D.: *Sefer Tehillim Sha'arei Rachamim, Op. Cit.*
	Rosenberg, Y.Y.: *Rafael ha-Malach, Op. Cit.*
	Ronen, D.: *Tehilim Kavvanot ha-Lev, Op. Cit.*
	Rebiger, B.: *Sefer Shimmush Tehillim, Op. Cit.*
	Brauner, R.: *Synopsis of Sefer Shimush Tehillim. Op. Cit.*
2.	**Feldman, Y.Y.:** *Tehillim Eis Ratzon, Op. Cit.*
3.	**Kimchi, D. ben Y.:** *Sefer Tehillim, Op. Cit.*
	Sefer Shimmush Tehillim, Op. Cit.
	Seder Tefilot Tikun Ezra, Op. Cit.
	Grünwald, M.: *Ueber den Einfluss der Psalmen auf die Katholische Liturgie, Op. Cit.*
	Refuah v'Chayim m'Yerushalayim im Shimush Tehilim, Op. Cit.
	Rebiger, B.: *Sefer Shimmush Tehillim, Op. Cit.*
	Landsberg, M.: *Sefer Tehillim im Peirush Rashi, Op. Cit.*
	Hai ben Sherira Gaon & Varady, A.N.: *Shimush Tehillim (the Theurgical Use of Psalms), Op. Cit.*
4.	**Rebiger, B.:** *Sefer Shimmush Tehillim, Op. Cit.*
5.	**Selig, G.:** *Sepher Schimmusch Tehillim, Op. Cit.*
	The Sixth and Seventh Books of Moses, Op. Cit.
	Peterson, J.H.: *The Sixth and Seventh Books of Moses, Op. Cit.*
6.	**Kimchi, D. ben Y.:** *Sefer Tehillim, Op. Cit.*
	Sefer Shimmush Tehillim, Op. Cit.

        Seder Tefilot Tikun Ezra, Op. Cit.
        Grünwald, M.: *Ueber den Einfluss der Psalmen auf die Katholische Liturgie, Op. Cit.*
        Refuah v'Chayim m'Yerushalayim im Shimush Tehilim, Op. Cit.
        Rebiger, B.: *Sefer Shimmush Tehillim, Op. Cit.*
        Landsberg, M.: *Sefer Tehillim im Peirush Rashi, Op. Cit.*
        Hai ben Sherira Gaon & Varady, A.N.: *Shimush Tehillim (the Theurgical Use of Psalms), Op. Cit.*

7. **Rebiger, B.:** *Sefer Shimmush Tehillim, Op. Cit.*
8. *Ibid.*
9. *Ibid.*
10. **Selig, G.:** *Sepher Schimmusch Tehillim, Op. Cit.*
    The Sixth and Seventh Books of Moses, Op. Cit.
    Peterson, J.H.: *The Sixth and Seventh Books of Moses, Op. Cit.*
11. **Rebiger, B.:** *Sefer Shimmush Tehillim, Op. Cit.*
12. **Zacutto, M.:** *Shorshei ha-Shemot, Op. Cit.*
13. *Ibid.*
14. *Ibid.*
15. *Refuah v'Chayim m'Yerushalayim im Shimush Tehilim, Op. Cit.*
    Eliram (Amslam), S.: *Sefer Segulot, Terufot u'Mazalot, Op. Cit.*
16. **Zellmann-Rohrer, M.:** *Psalms Useful for Everything, Op. Cit.*
17. *Ibid.*
18. *Ibid.*
19. **Zellmann-Rohrer, M.:** *Psalms Useful for Everything, Op. Cit.*
20. **Lecouteux, C.:** *Dictionary of Ancient Magic Words and Spells from Abraxas to Zoar, Op. Cit.*
21. **Rankine, D. & Barron, P.H.:** *The Book of Gold, Op. Cit.*
    Marty, J. & MacParthy, F.: *Usage Mago-Théurgiques des Psaumes, Op. Cit.*

Psalm 58

1. **Kimchi, D. ben Y.:** *Sefer Tehillim, Op. Cit.*
    Singer, I. & Adler, C.: *The Jewish Encyclopedia, Op. Cit.*
    Le Livre des Psaumes Hébreu-Français et Phonétique, Op. Cit.
    Azulai, H.Y.D.: *Sefer Tehillim Sha'arei Rachamim, Op. Cit.*
    Refuah v'Chayim m'Yerushalayim im Shimush Tehilim, Op. Cit.
    Rebiger, B.: *Sefer Shimmush Tehillim, Op. Cit.*
    Brauner, R.: *Synopsis of Sefer Shimush Tehillim. Op. Cit.*
    Landsberg, M.: *Sefer Tehillim im Peirush Rashi, Op. Cit.*
    Ronen, D.: *Tehilim Kavvanot ha-Lev, Op. Cit.*

	Selig, G.: *Sepher Schimmusch Tehillim*, Op. Cit.
	The Sixth and Seventh Books of Moses, Op. Cit.
	Peterson, J.H.: *The Sixth and Seventh Books of Moses*, Op. Cit.
2.	**Rebiger, B.:** *Sefer Shimmush Tehillim*, Op. Cit.
3.	*Ibid.*
4.	**Zellmann-Rohrer, M.:** *Psalms Useful for Everything*, Op. Cit.
5.	*Ibid.*
6.	**Lecouteux, C.:** *Dictionary of Ancient Magic Words and Spells from Abraxas to Zoar*, Op. Cit.
7.	**Rankine, D. & Barron, P.H.:** *The Book of Gold*, Op. Cit.
	Marty, J. & MacParthy, F.: *Usage Mago-Théurgiques des Psaumes*, Op. Cit.
8.	**Skinner, S. & Rankine, D.:** *A Collection of Magical Secrets*, Op. Cit.

Psalm 59

1.	**Feldman, Y.Y.:** *Tehillim Eis Ratzon*, Op. Cit.
2.	**Singer, I. & Adler, C.:** *The Jewish Encyclopedia*, Op. Cit.
	Le Livre des Psaumes Hébreu-Français et Phonétique, Op. Cit.
	Azulai, H.Y.D.: *Sefer Tehillim Sha'arei Rachamim*, Op. Cit.
	Ronen, D.: *Tehilim Kavvanot ha-Lev*, Op. Cit.
3.	**Campbell, W.K. & Miller, J.D.:** *The Handbook of Narcissism and Narcissistic Personality Disorder: Theoretical Approaches, Empirical Findings, and Treatments*, John Wiley & Sons Inc., Hoboken 2011.
4.	**Kimchi, D. ben Y.:** *Sefer Tehillim*, Op. Cit.
	Sefer Shimmush Tehillim, Op. Cit.
	Seder Tefilot Tikun Ezra, Op. Cit.
	Grünwald, M.: *Ueber den Einfluss der Psalmen auf die Katholische Liturgie*, Op. Cit.
	Refuah v'Chayim m'Yerushalayim im Shimush Tehilim, Op. Cit.
	Rebiger, B.: *Sefer Shimmush Tehillim*, Op. Cit.
	Brauner, R.: *Synopsis of Sefer Shimush Tehillim*. Op. Cit.
	Landsberg, M.: *Sefer Tehillim im Peirush Rashi*, Op. Cit.
	Hai ben Sherira Gaon & Varady, A.N.: *Shimush Tehillim (the Theurgical Use of Psalms)*, Op. Cit.
5.	**Rebiger, B.:** *Sefer Shimmush Tehillim*, Op. Cit.
6.	*Ibid.*
	Kimchi, D. ben Y.: *Sefer Tehillim*, Op. Cit.
	Sefer Shimmush Tehillim, Op. Cit.
	Seder Tefilot Tikun Ezra, Op. Cit.
	Grünwald, M.: *Ueber den Einfluss der Psalmen auf die Katholische Liturgie*, Op. Cit.

Refuah v'Chayim m'Yerushalayim im Shimush Tehilim, Op. Cit.
Landsberg, M.: *Sefer Tehillim im Peirush Rashi, Op. Cit.*
Hai ben Sherira Gaon & Varady, A.N.: *Shimush Tehillim (the Theurgical Use of Psalms), Op. Cit.*

7. **Selig, G.:** *Sepher Schimmusch Tehillim, Op. Cit.*
The Sixth and Seventh Books of Moses, Op. Cit.
Peterson, J.H.: *The Sixth and Seventh Books of Moses, Op. Cit.*
8. *Ibid.*
9. *Ibid.*
10. **Rebiger, B.:** *Sefer Shimmush Tehillim, Op. Cit.*
11. *Ibid.*
12. **Zellmann-Rohrer, M.:** *Psalms Useful for Everything, Op. Cit.*
13. **Lecouteux, C.:** *Dictionary of Ancient Magic Words and Spells from Abraxas to Zoar, Op. Cit.*
14. **Zellmann-Rohrer, M.:** *Psalms Useful for Everything, Op. Cit.*
15. **Rankine, D. & Barron, P.H.:** *The Book of Gold, Op. Cit.*
Marty, J. & MacParthy, F.: *Usage Mago-Théurgiques des Psaumes, Op. Cit.*
16. **Skemer, D.C.:** *Binding Words, Op. Cit.*

Psalm 60

1. **Singer, I. & Adler, C.:** *The Jewish Encyclopedia, Op. Cit.*
Le Livre des Psaumes Hébreu-Français et Phonétique, Op. Cit.
Azulai, H.Y.D.: *Sefer Tehillim Sha'arei Rachamim, Op. Cit.*
Ronen, D.: *Tehilim Kavvanot ha-Lev, Op. Cit.*
2. **Kimchi, D. ben Y.:** *Sefer Tehillim, Op. Cit.*
Sefer Shimmush Tehillim, Op. Cit.
Seder Tefilot Tikun Ezra, Op. Cit.
Grünwald, M.: *Ueber den Einfluss der Psalmen auf die Katholische Liturgie, Op. Cit.*
Refuah v'Chayim m'Yerushalayim im Shimush Tehilim, Op. Cit.
Rebiger, B.: *Sefer Shimmush Tehillim, Op. Cit.*
Brauner, R.: *Synopsis of Sefer Shimmush Tehillim. Op. Cit.*
Landsberg, M.: *Sefer Tehillim im Peirush Rashi, Op. Cit.*
Hai ben Sherira Gaon & Varady, A.N.: *Shimush Tehillim (the Theurgical Use of Psalms), Op. Cit.*
3. *Ibid.*
Selig, G.: *Sepher Schimmusch Tehillim, Op. Cit.*
The Sixth and Seventh Books of Moses, Op. Cit.
Peterson, J.H.: *The Sixth and Seventh Books of Moses, Op. Cit.*
4. **Rebiger, B.:** *Sefer Shimmush Tehillim, Op. Cit.*
5. **Selig, G.:** *Sepher Schimmusch Tehillim, Op. Cit.*
The Sixth and Seventh Books of Moses, Op. Cit.
Peterson, J.H.: *The Sixth and Seventh Books of Moses, Op. Cit.*

6. **Rebiger, B.:** *Sefer Shimmush Tehillim, Op. Cit.*
7. *Ibid.*
8. **Swart, J.G.:** *The Book of Self Creation, Op. Cit.*
9. *Ibid.*
10. *Ibid.*
    Swart, J.G.: *The Book of Sacred Names, Op. Cit.*
    —*The Book of Immediate Magic* (Part 1), *Op. Cit.*
11. *Ibid.*
12. *Ibid.*
13. **Zellmann-Rohrer, M.:** *Psalms Useful for Everything, Op. Cit.*
14. *Ibid.*
15. *Ibid.*
16. **Rankine, D. & Barron, P.H.:** *The Book of Gold, Op. Cit.*
    Marty, J. & MacParthy, F.: *Usage Mago-Théurgiques des Psaumes, Op. Cit.*
17. **Mathers, S.L. Macgregor:** *Key of Solomon the King, Op. cit.*

Psalm 61

1. *Le Livre des Psaumes Hébreu-Français et Phonétique, Op. Cit.*
   Azulai, H.Y.D.: *Sefer Tehillim Sha'arei Rachamim, Op. Cit.*
   Ronen, D.: *Tehilim Kavvanot ha-Lev, Op. Cit.*
2. **Singer, I. & Adler, C.:** *The Jewish Encyclopedia, Op. Cit.*
3. **Brauner, R.:** *Synopsis of Sefer Shimush Tehillim. Op. Cit.*
4. **Kimchi, D. ben Y.:** *Sefer Tehillim, Op. Cit.*
   Refuah v'Chayim m'Yerushalayim im Shimush Tehilim, Op. Cit.
   Rebiger, B.: *Sefer Shimmush Tehillim, Op. Cit.*
   Landsberg, M.: *Sefer Tehillim im Peirush Rashi, Op. Cit.*
5. **Rebiger, B.:** *Sefer Shimmush Tehillim, Op. Cit.*
6. **Selig, G.:** *Sepher Schimmusch Tehillim, Op. Cit.*
   The Sixth and Seventh Books of Moses, Op. Cit.
   Peterson, J.H.: *The Sixth and Seventh Books of Moses, Op. Cit.*
7. **Swart, J.G.:** *The Book of Sacred Names, Op. Cit.*
8. **Rosenberg, Y.Y.:** *Rafael ha-Malach, Op. Cit.*
9. **Selig, G.:** *Sepher Schimmusch Tehillim, Op. Cit.*
   The Sixth and Seventh Books of Moses, Op. Cit.
   Peterson, J.H.: *The Sixth and Seventh Books of Moses, Op. Cit.*
10. **Rebiger, B.:** *Sefer Shimmush Tehillim, Op. Cit.*
11. *Ibid.*
12. **Lecouteux, C.:** *Dictionary of Ancient Magic Words and Spells from Abraxas to Zoar, Op. Cit.*
13. **Zellmann-Rohrer, M.:** *Psalms Useful for Everything, Op. Cit.*
14. *Ibid.*

15.	**Rankine, D. & Barron, P.H.:** *The Book of Gold, Op. Cit.*
	Marty, J. & MacParthy, F.: *Usage Mago-Théurgiques des Psaumes, Op. Cit.*

Psalm 62

1.	*Le Livre des Psaumes Hébreu-Français et Phonétique, Op. Cit.*
	Azulai, H.Y.D.: *Sefer Tehillim Sha'arei Rachamim, Op. Cit.*
	Ronen, D.: *Tehilim Kavvanot ha-Lev, Op. Cit.*
2.	**Singer, I. & Adler, C.:** *The Jewish Encyclopedia, Op. Cit.*
	Brauner, R.: *Synopsis of Sefer Shimush Tehillim. Op. Cit.*
3.	**Kimchi, D. ben Y.:** *Sefer Tehillim, Op. Cit.*
	Sefer Shimmush Tehillim, Op. Cit.
	Seder Tefilot Tikun Ezra, Op. Cit.
	Grünwald, M.: *Ueber den Einfluss der Psalmen auf die Katholische Liturgie, Op. Cit.*
	Refuah v'Chayim m'Yerushalayim im Shimush Tehilim, Op. Cit.
	Rebiger, B.: *Sefer Shimmush Tehillim, Op. Cit.*
	Landsberg, M.: *Sefer Tehillim im Peirush Rashi, Op. Cit.*
	Hai ben Sherira Gaon & Varady, A.N.: *Shimush Tehillim (the Theurgical Use of Psalms), Op. Cit.*
4.	**Rebiger, B.:** *Sefer Shimmush Tehillim, Op. Cit.*
5.	**Selig, G.:** *Sepher Schimmusch Tehillim, Op. Cit.*
	The Sixth and Seventh Books of Moses, Op. Cit.
	Peterson, J.H.: *The Sixth and Seventh Books of Moses, Op. Cit.*
6.	**Kimchi, D. ben Y.:** *Sefer Tehillim, Op. Cit.*
	Sefer Shimmush Tehillim, Op. Cit.
	Seder Tefilot Tikun Ezra, Op. Cit.
	Grünwald, M.: *Ueber den Einfluss der Psalmen auf die Katholische Liturgie, Op. Cit.*
	Refuah v'Chayim m'Yerushalayim im Shimush Tehilim, Op. Cit.
	Landsberg, M.: *Sefer Tehillim im Peirush Rashi, Op. Cit.*
	Hai ben Sherira Gaon & Varady, A.N.: *Shimush Tehillim (the Theurgical Use of Psalms), Op. Cit.*
7.	**Rebiger, B.:** *Sefer Shimmush Tehillim, Op. Cit.*
8.	*Ibid.*
	Kimchi, D. ben Y.: *Sefer Tehillim, Op. Cit.*
	Sefer Shimmush Tehillim, Op. Cit.
	Seder Tefilot Tikun Ezra, Op. Cit.
	Grünwald, M.: *Ueber den Einfluss der Psalmen auf die Katholische Liturgie, Op. Cit.*
	Refuah v'Chayim m'Yerushalayim im Shimush Tehilim, Op. Cit.
	Landsberg, M.: *Sefer Tehillim im Peirush Rashi, Op. Cit.*
	Hai ben Sherira Gaon & Varady, A.N.: *Shimush Tehillim (the Theurgical Use of Psalms), Op. Cit.*

9. **Selig, G.:** *Sepher Schimmusch Tehillim, Op. Cit.*
   The Sixth and Seventh Books of Moses, Op. Cit.
   Peterson, J.H.: *The Sixth and Seventh Books of Moses, Op. Cit.*
10. **Rebiger, B.:** *Sefer Shimmush Tehillim, Op. Cit.*
11. *Ibid.*
12. **Davis, E. & Frenkel, D.A.:** *Ha-Kami'a ha-Ivri, Op. Cit.*
    Green, A.: *Judaic Artifacts, Op. Cit.*
13. **Zellmann-Rohrer, M.:** *Psalms Useful for Everything, Op. Cit.*
14. **Lecouteux, C.:** *Dictionary of Ancient Magic Words and Spells from Abraxas to Zoar, Op. Cit.*
15. **Rankine, D. & Barron, P.H.:** *The Book of Gold, Op. Cit.*
    Marty, J. & MacParthy, F.: *Usage Mago-Théurgiques des Psaumes, Op. Cit.*
16. **Skinner, S. & Rankine, D.:** *A Collection of Magical Secrets, Op. Cit.*

Psalm 63

1. **Feldman, Y.Y.:** *Tehillim Eis Ratzon, Op. Cit.*
2. *Le Livre des Psaumes Hébreu-Français et Phonétique, Op. Cit.*
   Brauner, R.: *Synopsis of Sefer Shimush Tehillim. Op. Cit.*
   Ronen, D.: *Tehilim Kavvanot ha-Lev, Op. Cit.*
3. **Singer, I. & Adler, C.:** *The Jewish Encyclopedia, Op. Cit.*
   Azulai, H.Y.D.: *Sefer Tehillim Sha'arei Rachamim, Op. Cit.*
4. **Rosenberg, Y.Y.:** *Rafael ha-Malach, Op. Cit.*
5. **Brauner, R.:** *Synopsis of Sefer Shimush Tehillim. Op. Cit.*
6. **Kimchi, D. ben Y.:** *Sefer Tehillim, Op. Cit.*
   Sefer Shimmush Tehillim, Op. Cit.
   Seder Tefilot Tikun Ezra, Op. Cit.
   Grünwald, M.: *Ueber den Einfluss der Psalmen auf die Katholische Liturgie, Op. Cit.*
   Refuah v'Chayim m'Yerushalayim im Shimush Tehilim, Op. Cit.
   Rebiger, B.: *Sefer Shimmush Tehillim, Op. Cit.*
   Landsberg, M.: *Sefer Tehillim im Peirush Rashi, Op. Cit.*
   Hai ben Sherira Gaon & Varady, A.N.: *Shimush Tehillim (the Theurgical Use of Psalms), Op. Cit.*
7. **Selig, G.:** *Sepher Schimmusch Tehillim, Op. Cit.*
   The Sixth and Seventh Books of Moses, Op. Cit.
   Peterson, J.H.: *The Sixth and Seventh Books of Moses, Op. Cit.*
8. **Kimchi, D. ben Y.:** *Sefer Tehillim, Op. Cit.*
   Sefer Shimmush Tehillim, Op. Cit.
   Seder Tefilot Tikun Ezra, Op. Cit.
   Grünwald, M.: *Ueber den Einfluss der Psalmen auf die Katholische Liturgie, Op. Cit.*

	Refuah v'Chayim m'Yerushalayim im Shimush Tehilim, Op. Cit. **Landsberg, M.:** *Sefer Tehillim im Peirush Rashi, Op. Cit.* **Hai ben Sherira Gaon & Varady, A.N.:** *Shimush Tehillim (the Theurgical Use of Psalms), Op. Cit.*
9.	**Selig, G.:** *Sepher Schimmusch Tehillim, Op. Cit.* *The Sixth and Seventh Books of Moses, Op. Cit.* **Peterson, J.H.:** *The Sixth and Seventh Books of Moses, Op. Cit.*
10.	**Rebiger, B.:** *Sefer Shimmush Tehillim, Op. Cit.*
11.	*Ibid.*
12.	*Ibid.*
13.	**Zellmann-Rohrer, M.:** *Psalms Useful for Everything, Op. Cit.*
14.	*Ibid.*
15.	*Ibid.*
16.	**Rankine, D. & Barron, P.H.:** *The Book of Gold, Op. Cit.* **Marty, J. & MacParthy, F.:** *Usage Mago-Théurgiques des Psaumes, Op. Cit.*
17.	**Skinner, S. & Rankine, D.:** *A Collection of Magical Secrets, Op. Cit.*

Psalm 64

1.	**Kimchi, D. ben Y.:** *Sefer Tehillim, Op. Cit.* *Sefer Shimmush Tehillim, Op. Cit.* *Seder Tefilot Tikun Ezra, Op. Cit.* **Grünwald, M.:** *Ueber den Einfluss der Psalmen auf die Katholische Liturgie, Op. Cit.* **Singer, I. & Adler, C.:** *The Jewish Encyclopedia, Op. Cit.* **Azulai, H.Y.D.:** *Sefer Tehillim Sha'arei Rachamim, Op. Cit.* *Refuah v'Chayim m'Yerushalayim im Shimush Tehilim, Op. Cit.* *Le Livre des Psaumes Hébreu-Français et Phonétique, Op. Cit.* **Ronen, D.:** *Tehilim Kavvanot ha-Lev, Op. Cit.* **Rebiger, B.:** *Sefer Shimmush Tehillim, Op. Cit.* **Landsberg, M.:** *Sefer Tehillim im Peirush Rashi, Op. Cit.* **Brauner, R.:** *Synopsis of Sefer Shimush Tehillim. Op. Cit.* **Hai ben Sherira Gaon & Varady, A.N.:** *Shimush Tehillim (the Theurgical Use of Psalms), Op. Cit.*
2.	**Selig, G.:** *Sepher Schimmusch Tehillim, Op. Cit.* *The Sixth and Seventh Books of Moses, Op. Cit.* **Peterson, J.H.:** *The Sixth and Seventh Books of Moses, Op. Cit.*
3.	**Rebiger, B.:** *Sefer Shimmush Tehillim, Op. Cit.*
4.	*Ibid.*
5.	**Lecouteux, C.:** *Dictionary of Ancient Magic Words and Spells from Abraxas to Zoar, Op. Cit.*

6. **Rankine, D. & Barron, P.H.:** *The Book of Gold, Op. Cit.*
   Marty, J. & MacParthy, F.: *Usage Mago-Théurgiques des Psaumes, Op. Cit.*
7. **Mathers, S.L. Macgregor:** *Key of Solomon the King, Op. cit.*

Psalm 65

1. **Nulman, M.:** *The Encyclopedia of Jewish Prayer, Op. Cit.*
2. **Feldman, Y.Y.:** *Tehillim Eis Ratzon, Op. Cit.*
3. **Singer, I. & Adler, C.:** *The Jewish Encyclopedia, Op. Cit.*
   Brauner, R.: *Synopsis of Sefer Shimush Tehillim. Op. Cit.*
4. *Le Livre des Psaumes Hébreu-Français et Phonétique, Op. Cit.*
   Azulai, H.Y.D.: *Sefer Tehillim Sha'arei Rachamim, Op. Cit.*
   Rosenberg, Y.Y.: *Rafael ha-Malach, Op. Cit.*
   Ronen, D.: *Tehilim Kavvanot ha-Lev, Op. Cit.*
5. **Kimchi, D. ben Y.:** *Sefer Tehillim, Op. Cit.*
   Sefer Shimmush Tehillim, Op. Cit.
   Seder Tefilot Tikun Ezra, Op. Cit.
   Refuah v'Chayim m'Yerushalayim im Shimush Tehilim, Op. Cit.
   Rebiger, B.: *Sefer Shimmush Tehillim, Op. Cit.*
   Landsberg, M.: *Sefer Tehillim im Peirush Rashi, Op. Cit.*
   Brauner, R.: *Synopsis of Sefer Shimush Tehillim. Op. Cit.*
   Hai ben Sherira Gaon & Varady, A.N.: *Shimush Tehillim (the Theurgical Use of Psalms), Op. Cit.*
6. **Davis, E. & Frenkel, D.A.:** *Ha-Kami'a ha-Ivri, Op. Cit.*
   Green, A.: *Judaic Artifacts, Op. Cit.*
7. **Kimchi, D. ben Y.:** *Sefer Tehillim, Op. Cit.*
   Sefer Shimmush Tehillim, Op. Cit.
   Seder Tefilot Tikun Ezra, Op. Cit.
   Singer, I. & Adler, C.: *The Jewish Encyclopedia, Op. Cit.*
   Refuah v'Chayim m'Yerushalayim im Shimush Tehilim, Op. Cit.
   Rebiger, B.: *Sefer Shimmush Tehillim, Op. Cit.*
   Landsberg, M.: *Sefer Tehillim im Peirush Rashi, Op. Cit.*
   Brauner, R.: *Synopsis of Sefer Shimush Tehillim. Op. Cit.*
   Hai ben Sherira Gaon & Varady, A.N.: *Shimush Tehillim (the Theurgical Use of Psalms), Op. Cit.*
8. **Selig, G.:** *Sepher Schimmusch Tehillim, Op. Cit.*
   The Sixth and Seventh Books of Moses, Op. Cit.
   Peterson, J.H.: *The Sixth and Seventh Books of Moses, Op. Cit.*
9. **Rebiger, B.:** *Sefer Shimmush Tehillim, Op. Cit.*
10. *Ibid.*
11. **Zellmann-Rohrer, M.:** *Psalms Useful for Everything, Op. Cit.*

12. **Rankine, D. & Barron, P.H.:** *The Book of Gold, Op. Cit.*
    Marty, J. & MacParthy, F.: *Usage Mago-Théurgiques des Psaumes, Op. Cit.*
13. **Skinner, S. & Rankine, D.:** *A Collection of Magical Secrets, Op. Cit.*
14. *Ibid.*
15. **Zellmann-Rohrer, M.:** *Psalms Useful for Everything, Op. Cit.*
16. *Ibid.*
17. *Ibid.*

Psalm 66

1. **Singer, I. & Adler, C.:** *The Jewish Encyclopedia, Op. Cit.*
2. *Le Livre des Psaumes Hébreu-Français et Phonétique, Op. Cit.*
   Azulai, H.Y.D.: *Sefer Tehillim Sha'arei Rachamim, Op. Cit.*
   Ronen, D.: *Tehilim Kavvanot ha-Lev, Op. Cit.*
   Brauner, R.: *Synopsis of Sefer Shimush Tehillim. Op. Cit.*
3. **Kimchi, D. ben Y.:** *Sefer Tehillim, Op. Cit.*
   Refuah v'Chayim m'Yerushalayim im Shimush Tehilim, Op. Cit.
   Rebiger, B.: *Sefer Shimmush Tehillim, Op. Cit.*
   Landsberg, M.: *Sefer Tehillim im Peirush Rashi, Op. Cit.*
4. *Ibid.*
5. **Selig, G.:** *Sepher Schimmusch Tehillim, Op. Cit.*
   The Sixth and Seventh Books of Moses, Op. Cit.
   Peterson, J.H.: *The Sixth and Seventh Books of Moses, Op. Cit.*
6. **Rebiger, B.:** *Sefer Shimmush Tehillim, Op. Cit.*
7. *Ibid.*
8. **Zellmann-Rohrer, M.:** *Psalms Useful for Everything, Op. Cit.*
9. **Rankine, D. & Barron, P.H.:** *The Book of Gold, Op. Cit.*
   Marty, J. & MacParthy, F.: *Usage Mago-Théurgiques des Psaumes, Op. Cit.*
10. *Ibid.*
11. **Skinner, S. & Rankine, D.:** *A Collection of Magical Secrets, Op. Cit.*

Psalm 67

1. **Nulman, M.:** *The Encyclopedia of Jewish Prayer, Op. Cit.*
   Zalman, S. & Mangel, N.: *Siddur Tehillat Hashem, Op. Cit.*
   Churba, A.: *Siddur Keter Shelomo, Op. Cit.*
   Scherman, N. & Zlotowitz, G.: *Siddur Kol Sim'chah, Op. Cit.*
2. *Ibid.*

3. **Nulman, M.:** *The Encyclopedia of Jewish Prayer, Op. Cit.*
   Pool, D. de S.: *Book of Prayer*, Union of Sefardic Congregations, New York 1974.
4. **Nulman, M.:** *The Encyclopedia of Jewish Prayer, Op. Cit.*
5. *Ibid.*
6. *Ibid.*
7. *Ibid.*
8. *Ibid.*
   Ibn Gabbai, M. ben. E. & Ginsburg, E.K.: *Sod ha-Shabbat: The Mystery of the Sabbath*, State University of New York Press, Albany 1989,
   Garter, E.: *Service of the Heart: A Guide to the Jewish Prayer Book*, Rowman & Littlefield, Lanham 2005.
   Welcz, I.; Reinman, Y.Y. & Sonnenfeld, J.H. ben A.S.: *When Erev Pesach falls on Shabbos, Op. Cit.*
9. **Gillingham, S.:** *Psalms Through the Centuries, Volume 2, Op. Cit.*
10. *Ibid.*
11. **Zalman, S. & Mangel, N.:** *Siddur Tehillat Hashem, Op. Cit.*
    Churba, A.: *Siddur Keter Shelomo, Op. Cit.*
    Scherman, N. & Zlotowitz, G.: *Siddur Kol Sim'chah, Op. Cit.*
    Nulman, M.: *The Encyclopedia of Jewish Prayer, Op. Cit.*
    Welcz, I.; Reinman, Y.Y. & Sonnenfeld, J.H. ben A.S.: *When Erev Pesach falls on Shabbos, Op. Cit.*
    Swart, J.G.: *The Book of Immediate Magic* (Part 2), *Op. Cit.*
12. **Singer, I. & Adler, C.:** *The Jewish Encyclopedia, Op. Cit.*
    Le Livre des Psaumes Hébreu-Français et Phonétique, Op. Cit.
    Azulai, H.Y.D.: *Sefer Tehillim Sha'arei Rachamim, Op. Cit.*
    Ronen, D.: *Tehilim Kavvanot ha-Lev, Op. Cit.*
    Brauner, R.: *Synopsis of Sefer Shimush Tehillim. Op. Cit.*
13. **Singer, I. & Adler, C.:** *Ibid.*
    Brauner, R.: *Ibid.*
14. **Fine, L.:** *Safed Spirituality*, Paulist Press, *Op. Cit.*
    Dennis, G.W.: *The Encyclopedia of Jewish Myth, Magic and Mysticism, Op. Cit.*
15. **Kimchi, D. ben Y.:** *Sefer Tehillim, Op. Cit.*
    Sefer Shimmush Tehillim, Op. Cit.
    Seder Tefilot Tikun Ezra, Op. Cit.
    Refuah v'Chayim m'Yerushalayim im Shimush Tehilim, Op. Cit.
    Rebiger, B.: *Sefer Shimmush Tehillim, Op. Cit.*
    Landsberg, M.: *Sefer Tehillim im Peirush Rashi, Op. Cit.*
    Brauner, R.: *Synopsis of Sefer Shimush Tehillim. Op. Cit.*

	Hai ben Sherira Gaon & Varady, A.N.: *Shimush Tehillim* (*the Theurgical Use of Psalms*), *Op. Cit.*
	Selig, G.: *Sepher Schimmusch Tehillim, Op. Cit.*
	The Sixth and Seventh Books of Moses, Op. Cit.
	Peterson, J.H.: *The Sixth and Seventh Books of Moses, Op. Cit.*
16.	*Ibid.*
17.	**Rosenberg, Y.Y.:** *Rafael ha-Malach, Op. Cit.*
18.	**Lipshitz, S. ben Y.Y.:** *Segulot Yisrael*, Kahn & Fried, Munkatch 1905.
	Eliram (Amslam), S.: *Sefer Segulot, Terufot u'Mazalot, Op. Cit.*
19.	**Swart, J.G.:** *The Book of Seals & Amulets, Op. Cit.*
	—*The Book of Immediate Magic* (Part 2), *Op. Cit.*
20.	**Lipshitz, S. ben Y.Y.:** *Segulot Yisrael*, Kahn & Fried, Munkatch 1905.
	Eliram (Amslam), S.: *Sefer Segulot, Terufot u'Mazalot, Op. Cit.*
21.	**Rebiger, B.:** *Sefer Shimmush Tehillim, Op. Cit.*
22.	*Ibid.*
23.	*Ibid.*
24.	**Swart, J.G.:** *The Book of Seals & Amulets, Op. Cit.*
25.	*Ibid.*
	Schrire, T.: *Hebrew Amulets, Op. cit.*
	Shachar, I.: *Jewish Tradition in Art, Op. cit.*
	Davis, E. & Frenkel, D.A.: *Ha-Kami'a ha-Ivri, Op. cit.*
	Green, A.: *Judaic Artifacts, Op. cit.*
26.	**Swart, J.G.:** *The Book of Seals & Amulets, Op. Cit.*
27.	*Ibid.*
	Zacutto, M.: *Shorshei ha-Shemot, Op. cit.*
	Davis, E. & Frenkel, D.A.: *Ha-Kami'a ha-Ivri, Op. cit.*
	Green, A.: *Judaic Artifacts, Op. cit.*
28.	**Rosenberg, Y.:** *Rafael ha-Malach, Op. cit.*
29.	**Swart, J.G.:** *The Book of Seals & Amulets, Op. Cit.*
	Davis, E. & Frenkel, D.A.: *Ha-Kami'a ha-Ivri, Op. cit.*
	Green, A.: *Judaic Artifacts, Op. cit.*
30.	*Ibid.*
31.	*Ibid.*
32.	**Zacutto, M.:** *Shorshei ha-Shemot, Op. cit.*
	Swart, J.G.: *The Book of Seals & Amulets, Op. Cit.*
33.	*Ibid.*
34.	*Ibid.*

35. *Ibid.*
    Swart, J.G.: *The Book of Sacred Names, Op. Cit.*
    —*The Book of Immediate Magic* (Part 1), *Op. Cit.*
36. **Zacutto, M.:** *Shorshei ha-Shemot, Op. cit.*
    Swart, J.G.: *The Book of Seals & Amulets, Op. Cit.*
37. *Ibid.*
38. **Wardlaw Jr., T.R.:** *Elohim within the Psalms: Petitioning the Creator to Order Chaos in Oral-derived Literature*, Bloomsbury T&T Clark, London & New York 2016.
39. **Zacutto, M.:** *Shorshei ha-Shemot, Op. cit.*
    Swart, J.G.: *The Book of Sacred Names, Op. Cit.*
40. **Gillingham, S.:** *Psalms Through the Centuries, Volume 2, Op. Cit.*
41. **Zellmann-Rohrer, M.:** *Psalms Useful for Everything, Op. Cit.*
42. *Ibid.*
43. *Ibid.*
44. *Ibid.*
45. **Rankine, D. & Barron, P.H.:** *The Book of Gold, Op. Cit.*
    Marty, J. & MacParthy, F.: *Usage Mago-Théurgiques des Psaumes, Op. Cit.*
46. **Skinner, S. & Rankine, D.:** *A Collection of Magical Secrets, Op. Cit.*
47. **Mathers, S.L. Macgregor:** *Key of Solomon the King, Op. cit.*
48. *Ibid.*
49. *Ibid.*
50. *Ibid.*

Psalm 68

1. **Feldman, Y.Y.:** *Tehillim Eis Ratzon, Op. Cit.*
2. **Nulman, M.:** *The Encyclopedia of Jewish Prayer, Op. Cit.*
3. *Ibid.*
   Scherman, N.; Zlotowitz, M. & Gold, A.: *The Complete ArtScroll Machzor: Yom Kippur*, Mesorah Publications, Brooklyn 2019.
4. *Ibid.*
5. *Ibid.*
6. **Singer, I. & Adler, C.:** *The Jewish Encyclopedia, Op. Cit.*
   Le Livre des Psaumes Hébreu-Français et Phonétique, Op. Cit.
   Azulai, H.Y.D.: *Sefer Tehillim Sha'arei Rachamim, Op. Cit.*
   Ronen, D.: *Tehilim Kavvanot ha-Lev, Op. Cit.*
   Brauner, R.: *Synopsis of Sefer Shimush Tehillim. Op. Cit.*
7. **Kimchi, D. ben Y.:** *Sefer Tehillim, Op. Cit.*
   Refuah v'Chayim m'Yerushalayim im Shimush Tehilim, Op. Cit.

	Rebiger, B.: *Sefer Shimmush Tehillim, Op. Cit.*
	Landsberg, M.: *Sefer Tehillim im Peirush Rashi, Op. Cit.*
8.	**Selig, G.:** *Sepher Schimmusch Tehillim, Op. Cit.*
	The Sixth and Seventh Books of Moses, Op. Cit.
	Peterson, J.H.: *The Sixth and Seventh Books of Moses, Op. Cit.*
9.	*Ibid.*
10.	**Rebiger, B.:** *Sefer Shimmush Tehillim, Op. Cit.*
11.	**Zacutto, M.:** *Shorshei ha-Shemot, Op. cit.*
12.	*Ibid.*
13.	*Ibid.*
14.	*Ibid.*
15.	*Ibid.*
16.	*Ibid.*
17.	**Cockayne, O.:** *Leechdoms, Wortcunning, and Starcraft of Early England*, Vol. II, Longman Roberts & Green London 1865.
	Wellcome, S.H. & British Medical Association Liverpool: *Anglo-Saxon Leechcraft: An Historical Sketch of Early English Medicine: Lecture Memoranda*, Burroughs Wellcome & Co., London & New York 1912.
	Huguelet, P. & Koenig, H.G.: *Religion and Spirituality in Psychiatry*, Cambridge University Press, Cambridge 2009.
18.	*Ibid.*
19.	**Zellmann-Rohrer, M.:** *Psalms Useful for Everything, Op. Cit.*
20.	*Ibid.*
21.	*Ibid.*
22.	**Lecouteux, C.:** *Dictionary of Ancient Magic Words and Spells from Abraxas to Zoar, Op. Cit.*
23.	**Rankine, D. & Barron, P.H.:** *The Book of Gold, Op. Cit.*
	Marty, J. & MacParthy, F.: *Usage Mago-Théurgiques des Psaumes, Op. Cit.*
24.	*Ibid.*
25.	**Skinner, S. & Rankine, D.:** *A Collection of Magical Secrets, Op. Cit.*
26.	*Ibid.*
27.	**Mathers, S.L. Macgregor:** *Key of Solomon the King, Op. cit.*
28.	*Ibid.*
29.	*Ibid.*

Psalm 69

1.	**Nulman, M.:** *The Encyclopedia of Jewish Prayer, Op. Cit.*
2.	*Ibid.*
3.	*Ibid.*
4.	*Ibid.*

5. *Ibid.*
6. **Feldman, Y.Y.:** *Tehillim Eis Ratzon, Op. Cit.*
7. *Le Livre des Psaumes Hébreu-Français et Phonétique, Op. Cit.*
   Azulai, H.Y.D.: *Sefer Tehillim Sha'arei Rachamim, Op. Cit.*
   Ronen, D.: *Tehilim Kavvanot ha-Lev, Op. Cit.*
   Brauner, R.: *Synopsis of Sefer Shimush Tehillim. Op. Cit.*
8. **Singer, I. & Adler, C.:** *The Jewish Encyclopedia, Op. Cit.*
9. **Kimchi, D. ben Y.:** *Sefer Tehillim, Op. Cit.*
   Sefer Shimmush Tehillim, Op. Cit.
   Seder Tefilot Tikun Ezra, Op. Cit.
   Refuah v'Chayim m'Yerushalayim im Shimush Tehilim, Op. Cit.
   Rebiger, B.: *Sefer Shimmush Tehillim, Op. Cit.*
   Landsberg, M.: *Sefer Tehillim im Peirush Rashi, Op. Cit.*
   Hai ben Sherira Gaon & Varady, A.N.: *Shimush Tehillim (the Theurgical Use of Psalms), Op. Cit.*
10. **Selig, G.:** *Sepher Schimmusch Tehillim, Op. Cit.*
    The Sixth and Seventh Books of Moses, Op. Cit.
    Peterson, J.H.: *The Sixth and Seventh Books of Moses, Op. Cit.*
11. **Rebiger, B.:** *Sefer Shimmush Tehillim, Op. Cit.*
12. *Ibid.*
13. *Ibid.*
14. *Ibid.*
15. *Ibid.*
16. *Ibid.*
17. **Zacutto, M.:** *Shorshei ha-Shemot, Op. cit.*
    Davis, E. & Frenkel, D.A.: *Ha-Kami'a ha-Ivri, Op. cit.*
    Green, A.: *Judaic Artifacts, Op. cit.*
18. **Zellmann-Rohrer, M.:** *Psalms Useful for Everything, Op. Cit.*
19. *Ibid.*
20. *Ibid.*
21. *Ibid.*
22. **Rankine, D. & Barron, P.H.:** *The Book of Gold, Op. Cit.*
    Marty, J. & MacParthy, F.: *Usage Mago-Théurgiques des Psaumes, Op. Cit.*
23. **Mathers, S.L. Macgregor:** *Key of Solomon the King, Op. cit.*

Psalm 70

1. **Feldman, Y.Y.:** *Tehillim Eis Ratzon, Op. Cit.*
2. *Le Livre des Psaumes Hébreu-Français et Phonétique, Op. Cit.*
   Azulai, H.Y.D.: *Sefer Tehillim Sha'arei Rachamim, Op. Cit.*
   Ronen, D.: *Tehilim Kavvanot ha-Lev, Op. Cit.*
3. **Singer, I. & Adler, C.:** *The Jewish Encyclopedia, Op. Cit.*
4. *Ibid.*

5.	**Kimchi, D. ben Y.:** *Sefer Tehillim, Op. Cit.*
	Sefer Shimmush Tehillim, Op. Cit.
	Seder Tefilot Tikun Ezra, Op. Cit.
	Grünwald, M.: *Ueber den Einfluss der Psalmen auf die Katholische Liturgie, Op. Cit.*
	Refuah v'Chayim m'Yerushalayim im Shimush Tehilim, Op. Cit.
	Rebiger, B.: *Sefer Shimmush Tehillim, Op. Cit.*
	Landsberg, M.: *Sefer Tehillim im Peirush Rashi, Op. Cit.*
	Brauner, R.: *Synopsis of Sefer Shimush Tehillim. Op. Cit.*
	Hai ben Sherira Gaon & Varady, A.N.: *Shimush Tehillim (the Theurgical Use of Psalms), Op. Cit.*
	Selig, G.: *Sepher Schimmusch Tehillim, Op. Cit.*
	The Sixth and Seventh Books of Moses, Op. Cit.
	Peterson, J.H.: *The Sixth and Seventh Books of Moses, Op. Cit.*
6.	**Rebiger, B.:** *Sefer Shimmush Tehillim, Op. Cit.*
7.	**Feldman, Y.Y.:** *Tehillim Eis Ratzon, Op. Cit.*
8.	**Rankine, D. & Barron, P.H.:** *The Book of Gold, Op. Cit.*
9.	*Ibid.*
	Marty, J. & MacParthy, F.: *Usage Mago-Théurgiques des Psaumes, Op. Cit.*
10.	**Meyer, M. & Smith, R:** *Ancient Christian Magic: Coptic Texts of Ritual Power*, Princeton University Press, Princeton 1999.
11.	**Zellmann-Rohrer, M.:** *Psalms Useful for Everything, Op. Cit.*

Psalm 71

1.	**Nulman, M.:** *The Encyclopedia of Jewish Prayer, Op. Cit.*
2.	*Ibid.*
3.	**Feldman, Y.Y.:** *Tehillim Eis Ratzon, Op. Cit.*
4.	*Ibid.*
5.	*Le Livre des Psaumes Hébreu-Français et Phonétique, Op. Cit.*
	Azulai, H.Y.D.: *Sefer Tehillim Sha'arei Rachamim, Op. Cit.*
	Ronen, D.: *Tehilim Kavvanot ha-Lev, Op. Cit.*
6.	**Rosenberg, Y.:** *Rafael ha-Malach, Op. cit.*
7.	*Ibid.*
8.	**Eliram (Amslam), S.:** *Sefer Segulot, Terufot u'Mazalot, Op. Cit.*
9.	**Singer, I. & Adler, C.:** *The Jewish Encyclopedia, Op. Cit.*
10.	**Kimchi, D. ben Y.:** *Sefer Tehillim, Op. Cit.*
	Sefer Shimmush Tehillim, Op. Cit.
	Seder Tefilot Tikun Ezra, Op. Cit.
	Grünwald, M.: *Ueber den Einfluss der Psalmen auf die Katholische Liturgie, Op. Cit.*

Refuah v'Chayim m'Yerushalayim im Shimush Tehilim, Op. Cit.
Rebiger, B.: *Sefer Shimmush Tehillim*, Op. Cit.
Landsberg, M.: *Sefer Tehillim im Peirush Rashi*, Op. Cit.
Brauner, R.: *Synopsis of Sefer Shimush Tehillim*. Op. Cit.
Hai ben Sherira Gaon & Varady, A.N.: *Shimush Tehillim* (*the Theurgical Use of Psalms*), Op. Cit.
Selig, G.: *Sepher Schimmusch Tehillim*, Op. Cit.
The Sixth and Seventh Books of Moses, Op. Cit.
Peterson, J.H.: *The Sixth and Seventh Books of Moses*, Op. Cit.

11. **Rebiger, B.:** *Sefer Shimmush Tehillim*, Op. Cit.
12. **Rosenberg, Y.:** *Rafael ha-Malach*, Op. cit.
    Davis, E. & Frenkel, D.A.: *Ha-Kami'a ha-Ivri*, Op. cit.
    Green, A.: *Judaic Artifacts*, Op. cit.
13. **Zellmann-Rohrer, M.:** *Psalms Useful for Everything*, Op. Cit.
14. **Rankine, D. & Barron, P.H.:** *The Book of Gold*, Op. Cit.
    Marty, J. & MacParthy, F.: *Usage Mago-Théurgiques des Psaumes*, Op. Cit.

Psalm 72

1. **Feldman, Y.Y.:** *Tehillim Eis Ratzon*, Op. Cit.
2. *Ibid.*
3. **Nulman, M.:** *The Encyclopedia of Jewish Prayer*, Op. Cit.
   Koppelman Ross, L.: *Celebate! The Complete Jewish Holidays Handbook*, Rowan & Littlefield Publishers Inc., Lanham 2004.
   Brown, J.: New Heavens and a New Earth: The Jewish Reception of Copernican Thought, Oxford University Press, Oxford & New York 2013.
4. **Nulman, M.:** *Ibid.*
5. **Singer, I. & Adler, C.:** *The Jewish Encyclopedia*, Op. Cit.
   Le Livre des Psaumes Hébreu-Français et Phonétique, Op. Cit.
   Azulai, H.Y.D.: *Sefer Tehillim Sha'arei Rachamim*, Op. Cit.
   Ronen, D.: *Tehilim Kavvanot ha-Lev*, Op. Cit.
6. **Kimchi, D. ben Y.:** *Sefer Tehillim*, Op. Cit.
   Sefer Shimmush Tehillim, Op. Cit.
   Seder Tefilot Tikun Ezra, Op. Cit.
   Grünwald, M.: *Ueber den Einfluss der Psalmen auf die Katholische Liturgie*, Op. Cit.
   Rebiger, B.: *Sefer Shimmush Tehillim*, Op. Cit.
   Landsberg, M.: *Sefer Tehillim im Peirush Rashi*, Op. Cit.
   Brauner, R.: *Synopsis of Sefer Shimush Tehillim*. Op. Cit.
   Hai ben Sherira Gaon & Varady, A.N.: *Shimush Tehillim* (*the Theurgical Use of Psalms*), Op. Cit.
7. *Ibid.*

8. **Selig, G.:** *Sepher Schimmusch Tehillim, Op. Cit.*
The Sixth and Seventh Books of Moses, Op. Cit.
Peterson, J.H.: *The Sixth and Seventh Books of Moses, Op. Cit.*
9. **Rebiger, B.:** *Sefer Shimmush Tehillim, Op. Cit.*
10. **Zacutto, M.:** *Shorshei ha-Shemot, Op. cit.*
11. *Ibid.*
12. *Ibid.*
Swart, J.G.: *The Book of Sacred Names, Op. Cit.*
13. *Ibid.*
14. *Ibid.*
15. *Ibid.*
16. *Ibid.*
17. **Zacutto, M.:** *Shorshei ha-Shemot, Op. cit.*
18. **Rankine, D. & Barron, P.H.:** *The Book of Gold, Op. Cit.*
Marty, J. & MacParthy, F.: *Usage Mago-Théurgiques des Psaumes, Op. Cit.*
19. **Mathers, S.L. Macgregor:** *Key of Solomon the King, Op. cit.*
20. *Ibid.*
21. *Ibid.*
22. *Ibid.*
23. *Ibid.*

CHAPTER 5

Psalm 73

1. *Le Livre des Psaumes Hébreu-Français et Phonétique, Op. Cit.*
   Azulai, H.Y.D.: *Sefer Tehillim Sha'arei Rachamim, Op. Cit.*
   Ronen, D.: *Tehilim Kavvanot ha-Lev, Op. Cit.*
2. **Singer, I. & Adler, C.:** *The Jewish Encyclopedia, Op. Cit.*
3. **Kimchi, D. ben Y.:** *Sefer Tehillim, Op. Cit.*
   Sefer Shimmush Tehillim, Op. Cit.
   Seder Tefilot Tikun Ezra, Op. Cit.
   Grünwald, M.: *Ueber den Einfluss der Psalmen auf die Katholische Liturgie, Op. Cit.*
   Refuah v'Chayim m'Yerushalayim im Shimush Tehilim, Op. Cit.
   Rebiger, B.: *Sefer Shimmush Tehillim, Op. Cit.*
   Landsberg, M.: *Sefer Tehillim im Peirush Rashi, Op. Cit.*
   Brauner, R.: *Synopsis of Sefer Shimush Tehillim. Op. Cit.*
   Hai ben Sherira Gaon & Varady, A.N.: *Shimush Tehillim (the Theurgical Use of Psalms), Op. Cit.*
4. **Selig, G.:** *Sepher Schimmusch Tehillim, Op. Cit.*
   The Sixth and Seventh Books of Moses, Op. Cit.
   Peterson, J.H.: *The Sixth and Seventh Books of Moses, Op. Cit.*
5. **Rebiger, B.:** *Sefer Shimmush Tehillim, Op. Cit.*
6. **Lecouteux, C.:** *Dictionary of Ancient Magic Words and Spells from Abraxas to Zoar, Op. Cit.*
7. **Rankine, D. & Barron, P.H.:** *The Book of Gold, Op. Cit.*
   Marty, J. & MacParthy, F.: *Usage Mago-Théurgiques des Psaumes, Op. Cit.*

Psalm 74

1. **Nulman, M.:** *The Encyclopedia of Jewish Prayer, Op. Cit.*
2. **Feldman, Y.Y.:** *Tehillim Eis Ratzon, Op. Cit.*
3. **Azulai, H.Y.D.:** *Sefer Tehillim Sha'arei Rachamim, Op. Cit.*
   Ronen, D.: *Tehilim Kavvanot ha-Lev, Op. Cit.*
4. *Le Livre des Psaumes Hébreu-Français et Phonétique, Op. Cit.*
5. **Singer, I. & Adler, C.:** *The Jewish Encyclopedia, Op. Cit.*
6. **Kimchi, D. ben Y.:** *Sefer Tehillim, Op. Cit.*
   Sefer Shimmush Tehillim, Op. Cit.
   Seder Tefilot Tikun Ezra, Op. Cit.
   Grünwald, M.: *Ueber den Einfluss der Psalmen auf die Katholische Liturgie, Op. Cit.*
   Refuah v'Chayim m'Yerushalayim im Shimush Tehilim, Op. Cit.
   Rebiger, B.: *Sefer Shimmush Tehillim, Op. Cit.*

Landsberg, M.: *Sefer Tehillim im Peirush Rashi, Op. Cit.*
Brauner, R.: *Synopsis of Sefer Shimush Tehillim. Op. Cit.*
Hai ben Sherira Gaon & Varady, A.N.: *Shimush Tehillim (the Theurgical Use of Psalms), Op. Cit.*
7. Selig, G.: *Sepher Schimmusch Tehillim, Op. Cit.*
The Sixth and Seventh Books of Moses, Op. Cit.
Peterson, J.H.: *The Sixth and Seventh Books of Moses, Op. Cit.*
8. Rebiger, B.: *Sefer Shimmush Tehillim, Op. Cit.*
9. Zacutto, M.: *Shorshei ha-Shemot, Op. cit.*
Swart, J.G.: *The Book of Sacred Names, Op. Cit.*
10. *Ibid.*
11. *Ibid.*
12. Weintraub, S.Y.: *Healing Activities and P'sukim from Tehillim: Words of Psalms in/as Jewish Meditations for Healing*, essay published by UJA Federation of New York, 2000.
13. Zellmann-Rohrer, M.: *Psalms Useful for Everything, Op. Cit.*
14. Tselikas, A.: *Spells and Exorcisms in Three Post-Byzantine Manuscripts*, in Petropoulos, J.: *Greek Magic, Ancient, Medieval, and Modern*, Routledge, London 2008.
Lecouteux, C.: *Dictionary of Ancient Magic Words and Spells from Abraxas to Zoar, Op. Cit.*
15. Rankine, D. & Barron, P.H.: *The Book of Gold, Op. Cit.*
Marty, J. & MacParthy, F.: *Usage Mago-Théurgiques des Psaumes, Op. Cit.*
16. Zellmann-Rohrer, M.: *Psalms Useful for Everything, Op. Cit.*

Psalm 75

1. Jacobson, B.S.: *The Sabbath Service: An Exposition and Analysis of Its Structure, Contents, Language and Ideas*, Sinai Publishing, Tel Aviv 1981.
Nulman, M.: *The Encyclopedia of Jewish Prayer, Op. Cit.*
2. *Le Livre des Psaumes Hébreu-Français et Phonétique, Op. Cit.*
Azulai, H.Y.D.: *Sefer Tehillim Sha'arei Rachamim, Op. Cit.*
Ronen, D.: *Tehilim Kavvanot ha-Lev, Op. Cit.*
3. Singer, I. & Adler, C.: *The Jewish Encyclopedia, Op. Cit.*
Brauner, R.: *Synopsis of Sefer Shimush Tehillim. Op. Cit.*
4. Kimchi, D. ben Y.: *Sefer Tehillim, Op. Cit.*
Sefer Shimmush Tehillim, Op. Cit.
Seder Tefilot Tikun Ezra, Op. Cit.
Grünwald, M.: *Ueber den Einfluss der Psalmen auf die Katholische Liturgie, Op. Cit.*
Refuah v'Chayim m'Yerushalayim im Shimush Tehilim, Op. Cit.
Rebiger, B.: *Sefer Shimmush Tehillim, Op. Cit.*

      Landsberg, M.: *Sefer Tehillim im Peirush Rashi, Op. Cit.*
      Brauner, R.: *Synopsis of Sefer Shimush Tehillim. Op. Cit.*
      Hai ben Sherira Gaon & Varady, A.N.: *Shimush Tehillim (the Theurgical Use of Psalms), Op. Cit.*
      Selig, G.: *Sepher Schimmusch Tehillim, Op. Cit.*
      The Sixth and Seventh Books of Moses, Op. Cit.
      Peterson, J.H.: *The Sixth and Seventh Books of Moses, Op. Cit.*
5. Rebiger, B.: *Sefer Shimmush Tehillim, Op. Cit.*
6. Zellmann-Rohrer, M.: *Psalms Useful for Everything, Op. Cit.*
7. Rankine, D. & Barron, P.H.: *The Book of Gold, Op. Cit.*
   Marty, J. & MacParthy, F.: *Usage Mago-Théurgiques des Psaumes, Op. Cit.*
8. *Ibid.*

Psalm 76

1. *Le Livre des Psaumes Hébreu-Français et Phonétique, Op. Cit.*
   Azulai, H.Y.D.: *Sefer Tehillim Sha'arei Rachamim, Op. Cit.*
   Ronen, D.: *Tehilim Kavvanot ha-Lev, Op. Cit.*
   Kimchi, D. ben Y.: *Sefer Tehillim, Op. Cit.*
   Sefer Shimmush Tehillim, Op. Cit.
   Seder Tefilot Tikun Ezra, Op. Cit.
   Grünwald, M.: *Ueber den Einfluss der Psalmen auf die Katholische Liturgie, Op. Cit.*
   Refuah v'Chayim m'Yerushalayim im Shimush Tehillim, Op. Cit.
   Rebiger, B.: *Sefer Shimmush Tehillim, Op. Cit.*
   Landsberg, M.: *Sefer Tehillim im Peirush Rashi, Op. Cit.*
   Brauner, R.: *Synopsis of Sefer Shimush Tehillim. Op. Cit.*
   Hai ben Sherira Gaon & Varady, A.N.: *Shimush Tehillim (the Theurgical Use of Psalms), Op. Cit.*
2. Singer, I. & Adler, C.: *The Jewish Encyclopedia, Op. Cit.*
3. Selig, G.: *Sepher Schimmusch Tehillim, Op. Cit.*
   The Sixth and Seventh Books of Moses, Op. Cit.
   Peterson, J.H.: *The Sixth and Seventh Books of Moses, Op. Cit.*
4. Rebiger, B.: *Sefer Shimmush Tehillim, Op. Cit.*
5. *Ibid.*
6. Rankine, D. & Barron, P.H.: *The Book of Gold, Op. Cit.*
   Marty, J. & MacParthy, F.: *Usage Mago-Théurgiques des Psaumes, Op. Cit.*

Psalm 77

1. *Le Livre des Psaumes Hébreu-Français et Phonétique, Op. Cit.*
   Azulai, H.Y.D.: *Sefer Tehillim Sha'arei Rachamim, Op. Cit.*
   Ronen, D.: *Tehilim Kavvanot ha-Lev, Op. Cit.*

2. **Brauner, R.:** *Synopsis of Sefer Shimush Tehillim. Op. Cit.*
   Hai ben Sherira Gaon & Varady, A.N.: *Shimush Tehillim (the Theurgical Use of Psalms), Op. Cit.*
3. **Singer, I. & Adler, C.:** *The Jewish Encyclopedia, Op. Cit.*
4. **Kimchi, D. ben Y.:** *Sefer Tehillim, Op. Cit.*
   Sefer Shimmush Tehillim, Op. Cit.
   Seder Tefilot Tikun Ezra, Op. Cit.
   Grünwald, M.: *Ueber den Einfluss der Psalmen auf die Katholische Liturgie, Op. Cit.*
   Refuah v'Chayim m'Yerushalayim im Shimush Tehilim, Op. Cit.
   Rebiger, B.: *Sefer Shimmush Tehillim, Op. Cit.*
   Landsberg, M.: *Sefer Tehillim im Peirush Rashi, Op. Cit.*
5. **Selig, G.:** *Sepher Schimmusch Tehillim, Op. Cit.*
   The Sixth and Seventh Books of Moses, Op. Cit.
   Peterson, J.H.: *The Sixth and Seventh Books of Moses, Op. Cit.*
6. **Rosenberg, Y.:** *Rafael ha-Malach, Op. cit.*
   Davis, E. & Frenkel, D.A.: *Ha-Kami'a ha-Ivri, Op. cit.*
   Green, A.: *Judaic Artifacts, Op. cit.*
7. **Rebiger, B.:** *Sefer Shimmush Tehillim, Op. Cit.*
8. **Zacutto, M.:** *Shorshei ha-Shemot, Op. cit.*
9. *Ibid.*
10. **Rankine, D. & Barron, P.H.:** *The Book of Gold, Op. Cit.*
    Marty, J. & MacParthy, F.: *Usage Mago-Théurgiques des Psaumes, Op. Cit.*
11. **Mathers, S.L. Macgregor:** *Key of Solomon the King, Op. cit.*

Psalm 78

1. **Nulman, M.:** *The Encyclopedia of Jewish Prayer, Op. Cit.*
2. **Maimon, S.:** *The Autobiography of Solomon Maimon: The Complete Translation*, transl. Reiter, P., Princeton University Press, Princeton & Oxford 2018.
3. **Steinsaltz, A. & Even-Israel, A.:** *A Guide to Jewish Prayer*, Schocken Books, New York 2000.
   Koppelman Ross, L.: *Celebrate! The Complete Jewish Holidays Handbook*, Rowman & Littlefield Publishers Inc., Oxford 2004.
4. **Nulman, M.:** *The Encyclopedia of Jewish Prayer, Op. Cit.*
5. **Shkalim, E.:** *A Mosaic of Israel's Traditions: Holidays, Feasts, Fasts*, Devora Publishing Company, Jerusalem 2006.
6. *Le Livre des Psaumes Hébreu-Français et Phonétique, Op. Cit.*
   Azulai, H.Y.D.: *Sefer Tehillim Sha'arei Rachamim, Op. Cit.*
   Ronen, D.: *Tehilim Kavvanot ha-Lev, Op. Cit.*

   Kimchi, D. ben Y.: *Sefer Tehillim, Op. Cit.*
   Refuah v'Chayim m'Yerushalayim im Shimush Tehilim, Op. Cit.
   Rebiger, B.: *Sefer Shimmush Tehillim, Op. Cit.*
   Landsberg, M.: *Sefer Tehillim im Peirush Rashi, Op. Cit.*
   Brauner, R.: *Synopsis of Sefer Shimmush Tehillim. Op. Cit.*
7. **Singer, I. & Adler, C.**: *The Jewish Encyclopedia, Op. Cit.*
8. **Selig, G.**: *Sepher Schimmusch Tehillim, Op. Cit.*
   The Sixth and Seventh Books of Moses, Op. Cit.
   Peterson, J.H.: *The Sixth and Seventh Books of Moses, Op. Cit.*
9. **Rebiger, B.**: *Sefer Shimmush Tehillim, Op. Cit.*
10. *Ibid.*
11. *Ibid.*
12. *Ibid.*
13. *Ibid.*
14. *Ibid.*
15. **Schäfer, P. & Shaked, S.**: *Magische texte aus der Kairoer Geniza*, Band I, J.C.B. Mohr (Paul Siebeck), Tübingen 1994.
   Harari, Y.: *Jewish Magic before the Rise of Kabbalah*, Wayne State University Press, Detroit 2017.
   Swartz, M.D.: *The Mechanics of Providence: The Workings of Ancient Jewish Magic and Mysticism*, Mohr Siebeck, Tübingen 2018.
16. *Ibid.*
17. **Swartz, M.D.**: *The Mechanics of Providence: The Workings of Ancient Jewish Magic and Mysticism*, Mohr Siebeck, Tübingen 2018.
18. *Ibid.*
   Schäfer, P. & Shaked, S.: *Magische texte aus der Kairoer Geniza*, Band I, J.C.B. Mohr (Paul Siebeck), Tübingen 1994.
   Harari, Y.: *Jewish Magic before the Rise of Kabbalah*, Wayne State University Press, Detroit 2017.
19. **Zacutto, M.**: *Shorshei ha-Shemot, Op. cit.*
20. **Rankine, D. & Barron, P.H.**: *The Book of Gold, Op. Cit.*
   Marty, J. & MacParthy, F.: *Usage Mago-Théurgiques des Psaumes, Op. Cit.*

Psalm 79

1. **Feldman, Y.Y.**: *Tehillim Eis Ratzon, Op. Cit.*
2. *Le Livre des Psaumes Hébreu-Français et Phonétique, Op. Cit.*
   Azulai, H.Y.D.: *Sefer Tehillim Sha'arei Rachamim, Op. Cit.*
   Ronen, D.: *Tehilim Kavvanot ha-Lev, Op. Cit.*
3. **Singer, I. & Adler, C.**: *The Jewish Encyclopedia, Op. Cit.*

4. **Kimchi, D. ben Y.**: *Sefer Tehillim, Op. Cit.*
Refuah v'Chayim m'Yerushalayim im Shimush Tehilim, Op. Cit.
Rebiger, B.: *Sefer Shimmush Tehillim, Op. Cit.*
Landsberg, M.: *Sefer Tehillim im Peirush Rashi, Op. Cit.*
Brauner, R.: *Synopsis of Sefer Shimush Tehillim. Op. Cit.*
5. **Selig, G.**: *Sepher Schimmusch Tehillim, Op. Cit.*
The Sixth and Seventh Books of Moses, Op. Cit.
Peterson, J.H.: *The Sixth and Seventh Books of Moses, Op. Cit.*
6. **Rebiger, B.**: *Sefer Shimmush Tehillim, Op. Cit.*
7. *Ibid.*
8. **Zellmann-Rohrer, M.**: *Psalms Useful for Everything, Op. Cit.*
9. **Rankine, D. & Barron, P.H.**: *The Book of Gold, Op. Cit.*
Marty, J. & MacParthy, F.: *Usage Mago-Théurgiques des Psaumes, Op. Cit.*

Psalm 80

1. **Feldman, Y.Y.**: *Tehillim Eis Ratzon, Op. Cit.*
2. **Singer, I. & Adler, C.**: *The Jewish Encyclopedia, Op. Cit.*
Le Livre des Psaumes Hébreu-Français et Phonétique, Op. Cit.
Azulai, H.Y.D.: *Sefer Tehillim Sha'arei Rachamim, Op. Cit.*
Kimchi, D. ben Y.: *Sefer Tehillim, Op. Cit.*
Sefer Shimmush Tehillim, Op. Cit.
Seder Tefilot Tikun Ezra, Op. Cit.
Landsberg, M.: *Sefer Tehillim im Peirush Rashi, Op. Cit.*
Brauner, R.: *Synopsis of Sefer Shimush Tehillim. Op. Cit.*
Hai ben Sherira Gaon & Varady, A.N.: *Shimush Tehillim (the Theurgical Use of Psalms), Op. Cit.*
3. **Ronen, D.**: *Tehilim Kavvanot ha-Lev, Op. Cit.*
Rebiger, B.: *Sefer Shimmush Tehillim, Op. Cit.*
4. **Selig, G.**: *Sepher Schimmusch Tehillim, Op. Cit.*
The Sixth and Seventh Books of Moses, Op. Cit.
Peterson, J.H.: *The Sixth and Seventh Books of Moses, Op. Cit.*
5. **Rebiger, B.**: *Sefer Shimmush Tehillim, Op. Cit.*
6. *Ibid.*
7. **Zacutto, M.**: *Shorshei ha-Shemot, Op. cit*
8. *Ibid.*
9. *Ibid.*
Swart, J.G.: *The Book of Sacred Names, Op. Cit.*
10. **Swart, J.G.**: *The Book of Magical Psalms - Part 1, Op. Cit.*
11. **Zacutto, M.**: *Shorshei ha-Shemot, Op. cit*
Swart, J.G.: *The Book of Sacred Names, Op. Cit.*
12. *Ibid.*

13. **Zellmann-Rohrer, M.:** *Psalms Useful for Everything, Op. Cit.*
14. *Ibid.*
15. *Ibid.*
16. **Rankine, D. & Barron, P.H.:** *The Book of Gold, Op. Cit.*
    Marty, J. & MacParthy, F.: *Usage Mago-Théurgiques des Psaumes, Op. Cit.*

Psalm 81

1. **Nulman, M.:** *The Encyclopedia of Jewish Prayer, Op. Cit.*
   Berlin, A. & Brettler, M.Z.: *The Jewish Study Bible, Op. Cit.*
2. **Nulman, M.:** *Ibid.*
3. *Ibid.*
4. **Feldman, Y.Y.:** *Tehillim Eis Ratzon, Op. Cit.*
5. **Singer, I. & Adler, C.:** *The Jewish Encyclopedia, Op. Cit.*
   Le Livre des Psaumes Hébreu-Français et Phonétique, Op. Cit.
   Azulai, H.Y.D.: *Sefer Tehillim Sha'arei Rachamim, Op. Cit.*
   Ronen, D.: *Tehilim Kavvanot ha-Lev, Op. Cit.*
   Kimchi, D. ben Y.: *Sefer Tehillim, Op. Cit.*
   Sefer Shimmush Tehillim, Op. Cit.
   Seder Tefilot Tikun Ezra, Op. Cit.
   Refuah v'Chayim m'Yerushalayim im Shimush Tehilim, Op. Cit.
   Rebiger, B.: *Sefer Shimmush Tehillim, Op. Cit.*
   Landsberg, M.: *Sefer Tehillim im Peirush Rashi, Op. Cit.*
   Brauner, R.: *Synopsis of Sefer Shimmush Tehillim. Op. Cit.*
   Hai ben Sherira Gaon & Varady, A.N.: *Shimush Tehillim* (the Theurgical Use of Psalms), *Op. Cit.*
   Selig, G.: *Sepher Schimmusch Tehillim, Op. Cit.*
   The Sixth and Seventh Books of Moses, Op. Cit.
   Peterson, J.H.: *The Sixth and Seventh Books of Moses, Op. Cit.*
6. **Rebiger, B.:** *Ibid.*
7. *Ibid.*
8. **Lecouteux, C.:** *Dictionary of Ancient Magic Words and Spells from Abraxas to Zoar, Op. Cit.*
9. **Rankine, D. & Barron, P.H.:** *The Book of Gold, Op. Cit.*
   Marty, J. & MacParthy, F.: *Usage Mago-Théurgiques des Psaumes, Op. Cit.*

Psalm 82

1. **Nulman, M.:** *The Encyclopedia of Jewish Prayer, Op. Cit.*
   Berlin, A. & Brettler, M.Z.: *The Jewish Study Bible, Op. Cit.*
2. **Nulman, M.:** *Ibid.*

3. **Singer, I. & Adler, C.:** *The Jewish Encyclopedia, Op. Cit.*
   Le Livre des Psaumes Hébreu-Français et Phonétique, Op. Cit.
   Azulai, H.Y.D.: *Sefer Tehillim Sha'arei Rachamim, Op. Cit.*
   Ronen, D.: *Tehilim Kavvanot ha-Lev, Op. Cit.*
4. **Kimchi, D. ben Y.:** *Sefer Tehillim, Op. Cit.*
   Sefer Shimmush Tehillim, Op. Cit.
   Seder Tefilot Tikun Ezra, Op. Cit.
   Grünwald, M.: *Ueber den Einfluss der Psalmen auf die Katholische Liturgie, Op. Cit.*
   Refuah v'Chayim m'Yerushalayim im Shimush Tehilim, Op. Cit.
   Rebiger, B.: *Sefer Shimmush Tehillim, Op. Cit.*
   Landsberg, M.: *Sefer Tehillim im Peirush Rashi, Op. Cit.*
   Brauner, R.: *Synopsis of Sefer Shimush Tehillim. Op. Cit.*
   Hai ben Sherira Gaon & Varady, A.N.: *Shimush Tehillim (the Theurgical Use of Psalms), Op. Cit.*
5. **Selig, G.:** *Sepher Schimmusch Tehillim, Op. Cit.*
   The Sixth and Seventh Books of Moses, Op. Cit.
   Peterson, J.H.: *The Sixth and Seventh Books of Moses, Op. Cit.*
6. **Rebiger, B.:** *Sefer Shimmush Tehillim, Op. Cit.*
7. **Lecouteux, C.:** *Dictionary of Ancient Magic Words and Spells from Abraxas to Zoar, Op. Cit.*
8. **Rankine, D. & Barron, P.H.:** *The Book of Gold, Op. Cit.*
   Marty, J. & MacParthy, F.: *Usage Mago-Théurgiques des Psaumes, Op. Cit.*
9. **Skinner, S. & Rankine, D.:** *A Collection of Magical Secrets, Op. Cit.*
10. **Mathers, S.L. Macgregor:** *Key of Solomon the King, Op. cit.*

Psalm 83

1. **Berlin, A. & Brettler, M.Z.:** *The Jewish Study Bible, Op. Cit.*
2. **Heidenheim, M.W. ben S.:** *Siddur Shafah Berurah*, M. Lehrberger & Co., Rödelheim 1839.
   —*Siddur Shefat Emet: Daily prayers with English Instructions*, Joseph L. Werblowsky, New York.
3. **Singer, I. & Adler, C.:** *The Jewish Encyclopedia, Op. Cit.*
   Le Livre des Psaumes Hébreu-Français et Phonétique, Op. Cit.
   Azulai, H.Y.D.: *Sefer Tehillim Sha'arei Rachamim, Op. Cit.*
   Ronen, D.: *Tehilim Kavvanot ha-Lev, Op. Cit.*
4. **Brauner, R.:** *Synopsis of Sefer Shimush Tehillim. Op. Cit.*
5. **Kimchi, D. ben Y.:** *Sefer Tehillim, Op. Cit.*
   Sefer Shimmush Tehillim, Op. Cit.
   Seder Tefilot Tikun Ezra, Op. Cit.

        Grünwald, M.: *Ueber den Einfluss der Psalmen auf die Katholische Liturgie, Op. Cit.*
        Refuah v'Chayim m'Yerushalayim im Shimush Tehilim, Op. Cit.
        Rebiger, B.: *Sefer Shimmush Tehillim, Op. Cit.*
        Landsberg, M.: *Sefer Tehillim im Peirush Rashi, Op. Cit.*
        Brauner, R.: *Synopsis of Sefer Shimush Tehillim. Op. Cit.*
        Hai ben Sherira Gaon & Varady, A.N.: *Shimush Tehillim (the Theurgical Use of Psalms), Op. Cit.*
6.   **Selig, G.:** *Sepher Schimmusch Tehillim, Op. Cit.*
        The Sixth and Seventh Books of Moses, Op. Cit.
        Peterson, J.H.: *The Sixth and Seventh Books of Moses, Op. Cit.*
7.   **Schrire, T.:** *Hebrew Amulets, Op. cit.*
        Davis, E. & Frenkel, D.A.: *Ha-Kami'a ha-Ivri, Op. cit.*
        Green, A.: *Judaic Artifacts, Op. cit.*
8.   **Feldman, Y.Y.:** *Tehillim Eis Ratzon, Op. Cit.*
9.   **Rebiger, B.:** *Sefer Shimmush Tehillim, Op. Cit.*
10. *Ibid.*
11. **Rankine, D. & Barron, P.H.:** *The Book of Gold, Op. Cit.*
        Marty, J. & MacParthy, F.: *Usage Mago-Théurgiques des Psaumes, Op. Cit.*
12. **Zellmann-Rohrer, M.:** *Psalms Useful for Everything, Op. Cit.*
13. **Mathers, S.L. Macgregor:** *Key of Solomon the King, Op. cit.*

Psalm 84

1.   **Magonet, J.:** *A Rabbi Reads the Psalms, Op. Cit.*
2.   *Ibid.*
        Singer, I. & Adler, C.: *The Jewish Encyclopedia, Op. Cit.*
3.   *Le Livre des Psaumes Hébreu-Français et Phonétique, Op. Cit.*
        Azulai, H.Y.D.: *Sefer Tehillim Sha'arei Rachamim, Op. Cit.*
        Ronen, D.: *Tehilim Kavvanot ha-Lev, Op. Cit.*
        Brauner, R.: *Synopsis of Sefer Shimush Tehillim. Op. Cit.*
4.   **Kimchi, D. ben Y.:** *Sefer Tehillim, Op. Cit.*
        Sefer Shimmush Tehillim, Op. Cit.
        Seder Tefilot Tikun Ezra, Op. Cit.
        Grünwald, M.: *Ueber den Einfluss der Psalmen auf die Katholische Liturgie, Op. Cit.*
        Refuah v'Chayim m'Yerushalayim im Shimush Tehillim, Op. Cit.
        Rebiger, B.: *Sefer Shimmush Tehillim, Op. Cit.*
        Landsberg, M.: *Sefer Tehillim im Peirush Rashi, Op. Cit.*
        Brauner, R.: *Synopsis of Sefer Shimush Tehillim. Op. Cit.*
        Hai ben Sherira Gaon & Varady, A.N.: *Shimush Tehillim (the Theurgical Use of Psalms), Op. Cit.*
5.   *Ibid.*

6. **Rebiger, B.:** *Sefer Shimmush Tehillim, Op. Cit.*
7. **Selig, G.:** *Sepher Schimmusch Tehillim, Op. Cit.*
   The Sixth and Seventh Books of Moses, Op. Cit.
   Peterson, J.H.: *The Sixth and Seventh Books of Moses, Op. Cit.*
8. *Ibid.*
9. **Rebiger, B.:** *Sefer Shimmush Tehillim, Op. Cit.*
10. **Avraham Rimon of Granada:** *Brit Menuchah, Op. Cit.* .
    Zacutto, M.: *Shorshei ha-Shemot, Op. Cit*
11. *Ibid.*
12. *Ibid.*
13. **Zacutto, M.:** *Ibid.*
14. *Ibid.*
15. **Lecouteux, C.:** *Dictionary of Ancient Magic Words and Spells from Abraxas to Zoar, Op. Cit.*
16. **Zellmann-Rohrer, M.:** *Psalms Useful for Everything, Op. Cit.*
17. *Ibid.*
18. **Skinner, S. & Rankine, D.:** *A Collection of Magical Secrets, Op. Cit.*
19. *Ibid.*
20. **Rankine, D. & Barron, P.H.:** *The Book of Gold, Op. Cit.*
    Marty, J. & MacParthy, F.: *Usage Mago-Théurgiques des Psaumes, Op. Cit.*
21. **Mathers, S.L. Macgregor:** *Key of Solomon the King, Op. cit.*

Psalm 85

1. **Nulman, M.:** *The Encyclopedia of Jewish Prayer, Op. Cit.*
2. *Ibid.*
3. *Ibid.*
   Pool, D. de Sola: *Prayers for the Day of Atonement According to the Custom of the Spanish and Portuguese Jews,* Union of Sephardic Congregations, New York 1939.
4. **Feldman, Y.Y.:** *Tehillim Eis Ratzon, Op. Cit.*
5. **Singer, I. & Adler, C.:** *The Jewish Encyclopedia, Op. Cit.*
6. *Le Livre des Psaumes Hébreu-Français et Phonétique, Op. Cit.*
   Azulai, H.Y.D.: *Sefer Tehillim Sha'arei Rachamim, Op. Cit.*
   Ronen, D.: *Tehilim Kavvanot ha-Lev, Op. Cit.*
   Brauner, R.: *Synopsis of Sefer Shimush Tehillim. Op. Cit.*
7. **Kimchi, D. ben Y.:** *Sefer Tehillim, Op. Cit.*
   Sefer Shimmush Tehillim, Op. Cit.
   Seder Tefilot Tikun Ezra, Op. Cit.
   Grünwald, M.: *Ueber den Einfluss der Psalmen auf die Katholische Liturgie, Op. Cit.*
   Refuah v'Chayim m'Yerushalayim im Shimush Tehilim, Op. Cit.

	Rebiger, B.: *Sefer Shimmush Tehillim, Op. Cit.*
	Landsberg, M.: *Sefer Tehillim im Peirush Rashi, Op. Cit.*
	Hai ben Sherira Gaon & Varady, A.N.: *Shimush Tehillim (the Theurgical Use of Psalms), Op. Cit.*
8.	**Rebiger, B.:** *Ibid.*
9.	*Ibid.*
10.	*Ibid.*
	Kimchi, D. ben Y.: *Sefer Tehillim, Op. Cit.*
	Sefer Shimmush Tehillim, Op. Cit.
	Seder Tefilot Tikun Ezra, Op. Cit.
	Grünwald, M.: *Ueber den Einfluss der Psalmen auf die Katholische Liturgie, Op. Cit.*
	Refuah v'Chayim m'Yerushalayim im Shimush Tehilim, Op. Cit.
	Landsberg, M.: *Sefer Tehillim im Peirush Rashi, Op. Cit.*
	Hai ben Sherira Gaon & Varady, A.N.: *Shimush Tehillim (the Theurgical Use of Psalms), Op. Cit.*
11.	*Ibid.*
12.	**Selig, G.:** *Sepher Schimmusch Tehillim, Op. Cit.*
	The Sixth and Seventh Books of Moses, Op. Cit.
	Peterson, J.H.: *The Sixth and Seventh Books of Moses, Op. Cit.*
13.	**Rebiger, B.:** *Sefer Shimmush Tehillim, Op. Cit.*
14.	*Ibid.*
15.	**Rankine, D. & Barron, P.H.:** *The Book of Gold, Op. Cit.*
	Marty, J. & MacParthy, F.: *Usage Mago-Théurgiques des Psaumes, Op. Cit.*
16.	**Skinner, S. & Rankine, D.:** *A Collection of Magical Secrets, Op. Cit.*

Psalm 86

1.	**Feldman, Y.Y.:** *Tehillim Eis Ratzon, Op. Cit.*
2.	**Weintraub, S.Y.:** *Healing Activities and P'sukim from Tehillim, Op. Cit.*
3.	*Le Livre des Psaumes Hébreu-Français et Phonétique, Op. Cit.*
4.	**Singer, I. & Adler, C.:** *The Jewish Encyclopedia, Op. Cit.*
	Azulai, H.Y.D.: *Sefer Tehillim Sha'arei Rachamim, Op. Cit.*
	Ronen, D.: *Tehilim Kavvanot ha-Lev, Op. Cit.*
	Kimchi, D. ben Y.: *Sefer Tehillim, Op. Cit.*
	Refuah v'Chayim m'Yerushalayim im Shimush Tehillim, Op. Cit.
	Rebiger, B.: *Sefer Shimmush Tehillim, Op. Cit.*
	Landsberg, M.: *Sefer Tehillim im Peirush Rashi, Op. Cit.*
	Brauner, R.: *Synopsis of Sefer Shimush Tehillim. Op. Cit.*
5.	**Rebiger, B.:** *Ibid.*

6. **Selig, G.:** *Sepher Schimmusch Tehillim, Op. Cit.*
   The Sixth and Seventh Books of Moses, Op. Cit.
   Peterson, J.H.: *The Sixth and Seventh Books of Moses, Op. Cit.*
7. **Davis, E. & Frenkel, D.A.:** *Ha-Kami'a ha-Ivri, Op. cit.*
   Green, A.: *Judaic Artifacts, Op. cit.*
8. **Zacutto, M.:** *Shorshei ha-Shemot, Op. cit.*
   Swart, J.G.: *The Book of Sacred Names, Op. Cit.*
9. *Ibid.*
10. **Zacutto, M.:** *Shorshei ha-Shemot, Op. cit.*
11. *Ibid.*
12. *Ibid.*
13. **Swart, J.G.:** *The Book of Magical Psalms - Part 1, Op. Cit.*
14. **Eliram (Amslam), S.:** *Sefer Segulot, Terufot u'Mazalot, Op. Cit.*
15. **Lecouteux, C.:** *Dictionary of Ancient Magic Words and Spells from Abraxas to Zoar, Op. Cit.*
16. **Rankine, D. & Barron, P.H.:** *The Book of Gold, Op. Cit.*
    Marty, J. & MacParthy, F.: *Usage Mago-Théurgiques des Psaumes, Op. Cit.*

Psalm 87

1. **Feldman, Y.Y.:** *Tehillim Eis Ratzon, Op. Cit.*
2. *Ibid.*
3. *Le Livre des Psaumes Hébreu-Français et Phonétique, Op. Cit.*
   Azulai, H.Y.D.: *Sefer Tehillim Sha'arei Rachamim, Op. Cit.*
   Ronen, D.: *Tehilim Kavvanot ha-Lev, Op. Cit.*
4. **Kimchi, D. ben Y.:** *Sefer Tehillim, Op. Cit.*
   Refuah v'Chayim m'Yerushalayim im Shimush Tehilim, Op. Cit.
   Rebiger, B.: *Sefer Shimmush Tehillim, Op. Cit.*
   Landsberg, M.: *Sefer Tehillim im Peirush Rashi, Op. Cit.*
   Brauner, R.: *Synopsis of Sefer Shimush Tehillim. Op. Cit.*
5. **Selig, G.:** *Sepher Schimmusch Tehillim, Op. Cit.*
   The Sixth and Seventh Books of Moses, Op. Cit.
   Peterson, J.H.: *The Sixth and Seventh Books of Moses, Op. Cit.*
6. **Rebiger, B.:** *Sefer Shimmush Tehillim, Op. Cit.*
7. **Singer, I. & Adler, C.:** *The Jewish Encyclopedia, Op. Cit.*
8. **Zacutto, M.:** *Shorshei ha-Shemot, Op. cit.*
   Swart, J.G.: *The Book of Sacred Names, Op. Cit.*
9. *Ibid.*
10. **Zacutto, M.:** *Shorshei ha-Shemot, Op. cit.*
11. *Ibid.*

12. **Swart, J.G.:** *The Book of Self Creation, Op. Cit.*
    —*The Book of Sacred Names, Op. Cit.*
    —*The Book of Seals & Amulets, Op. Cit.*
    —*The Book of Immediate Magic* (Part 1 & 2), *Op. Cit.*
13. *Ibid.*
14. **Zacutto, M.:** *Shorshei ha-Shemot, Op. cit.*
15. **Swart, J.G.:** *The Book of Sacred Names, Op. Cit.*
16. **Gikatilla, J.:** *Gates of Light: Sha'are Orah,* transl. Avi Weinstein, Alta Mira Press, Walnut Creek 1998.
17. **Swart, J.G.:** *The Book of Sacred Names, Op. Cit.*
    —*The Book of Immediate Magic* (Part 1 & 2), *Op. Cit.*
18. *Ibid.*
19. *Ibid.*
20. **Zellmann-Rohrer, M.:** *Psalms Useful for Everything, Op. Cit.*
21. **Rankine, D. & Barron, P.H.:** *The Book of Gold, Op. Cit.*
    Marty, J. & MacParthy, F.: *Usage Mago-Théurgiques des Psaumes, Op. Cit.*

Psalm 88

1. **Singer, I. & Adler, C.:** *The Jewish Encyclopedia, Op. Cit.*
   Le Livre des Psaumes Hébreu-Français et Phonétique, Op. Cit.
   Azulai, H.Y.D.: *Sefer Tehillim Sha'arei Rachamim, Op. Cit.*
   Ronen, D.: *Tehilim Kavvanot ha-Lev, Op. Cit.*
   Kimchi, D. ben Y.: *Sefer Tehillim, Op. Cit.*
   Refuah v'Chayim m'Yerushalayim im Shimush Tehilim, Op. Cit.
   Rebiger, B.: *Sefer Shimmush Tehillim, Op. Cit.*
   Landsberg, M.: *Sefer Tehillim im Peirush Rashi, Op. Cit.*
   Brauner, R.: *Synopsis of Sefer Shimush Tehillim. Op. Cit.*
2. **Feldman, Y.Y.:** *Tehillim Eis Ratzon, Op. Cit.*
3. **Rebiger, B.:** *Sefer Shimmush Tehillim, Op. Cit.*
4. **Zacutto, M.:** *Shorshei ha-Shemot, Op. cit.*
   Swart, J.G.: *The Book of Sacred Names, Op. Cit.*
   —*The Book of Immediate Magic* (Part 1), *Op. Cit.*
5. **Rankine, D. & Barron, P.H.:** *The Book of Gold, Op. Cit.*
   Marty, J. & MacParthy, F.: *Usage Mago-Théurgiques des Psaumes, Op. Cit.*

Psalm 89

1. **Feldman, Y.Y.:** *Tehillim Eis Ratzon, Op. Cit.*
2. **Singer, I. & Adler, C.:** *The Jewish Encyclopedia, Op. Cit.*

3. *Le Livre des Psaumes Hébreu-Français et Phonétique, Op. Cit.*
Azulai, H.Y.D.: *Sefer Tehillim Sha'arei Rachamim, Op. Cit.*
Ronen, D.: *Tehilim Kavvanot ha-Lev, Op. Cit.*
4. **Brauner, R.:** *Synopsis of Sefer Shimush Tehillim. Op. Cit.*
5. **Kimchi, D. ben Y.:** *Sefer Tehillim, Op. Cit.*
Sefer Shimmush Tehillim, Op. Cit.
Seder Tefilot Tikun Ezra, Op. Cit.
Grünwald, M.: *Ueber den Einfluss der Psalmen auf die Katholische Liturgie, Op. Cit.*
Rebiger, B.: *Sefer Shimmush Tehillim, Op. Cit.*
Landsberg, M.: *Sefer Tehillim im Peirush Rashi, Op. Cit.*
Hai ben Sherira Gaon & Varady, A.N.: *Shimush Tehillim* (*the Theurgical Use of Psalms*), *Op. Cit.*
6. **Rebiger, B.:** *Sefer Shimmush Tehillim, Op. Cit.*
7. **Kimchi, D. ben Y.:** *Sefer Tehillim, Op. Cit.*
Sefer Shimmush Tehillim, Op. Cit.
Seder Tefilot Tikun Ezra, Op. Cit.
Grünwald, M.: *Ueber den Einfluss der Psalmen auf die Katholische Liturgie, Op. Cit.*
Rebiger, B.: *Sefer Shimmush Tehillim, Op. Cit.*
Landsberg, M.: *Sefer Tehillim im Peirush Rashi, Op. Cit.*
Hai ben Sherira Gaon & Varady, A.N.: *Shimush Tehillim* (*the Theurgical Use of Psalms*), *Op. Cit.*
8. **Selig, G.:** *Sepher Schimmusch Tehillim, Op. Cit.*
The Sixth and Seventh Books of Moses, Op. Cit.
Peterson, J.H.: *The Sixth and Seventh Books of Moses, Op. Cit.*
9. **Rebiger, B.:** *Sefer Shimmush Tehillim, Op. Cit.*
10. *Ibid.*
11. **Zellmann-Rohrer, M.:** *Psalms Useful for Everything, Op. Cit.*
12. **Rankine, D. & Barron, P.H.:** *The Book of Gold, Op. Cit.*
Marty, J. & MacParthy, F.: *Usage Mago-Théurgiques des Psaumes, Op. Cit.*
13. **Skinner, S. & Rankine, D.:** *A Collection of Magical Secrets, Op. Cit.*

also published by The Sangreal Sodality Press

Shadow Tree Series
Volume 1

THE BOOK OF SELF CREATION

Jacobus G. Swart

'The Book of Self Creation' is a study guide for all who seek Divinity within, and who prefer to steer the courses of their lives in a personal manner. The doctrines and techniques addressed in this book will aid practitioners in the expansion of their personal consciousness and spiritual evolution. Combining the principles and teachings of Practical Kabbalah and the Western Mystery Tradition, this book offers step by step instructions on the conscious creation of physical life circumstances, such being always in harmony with the mind-set of the practitioner.

The 'Shadow Tree Series' comprises a unique collection of Western Esoteric studies and practices which Jacobus G. Swart, spiritual successor to William G. Gray and co-founder of the Sangreal Sodality, actuated and taught over a period of forty years. He commenced his journey into the domain of Jewish Mysticism in the early 1970's investigating mainstream Kabbalah, later diversifying into the magical mysteries of Practical Kabbalah. He equally expanded his personal perspectives of the Western Magical Tradition under the careful tutelage of the celebrated English Kabbalist William G. Gray.

ISBN 978-0-620-65589-7   *Paperback*

also published by The Sangreal Sodality Press

Shadow Tree Series
Volume 2

THE BOOK OF SACRED NAMES

Jacobus G. Swart

'The Book of Sacred Names' is a practical guide into the meditational and magical applications of ancient Hebrew Divine Names. Perpetuating the tenets of traditional Kabbalists who recognised the fundamental bond between 'Kabbalah' and 'Magic,' Jacobus Swart offers step by step instructions on the deliberate and conscious control of personal life circumstances, by means of the most cardinal components of Kabbalistic doctrines and techniques—Divine Names!

The material addressed in this tome derives from the extensive primary literature of '"Practical Kabbalah",' much of which is appearing in print for the first time in English translation.

The 'Shadow Tree Series' comprises a unique collection of Western Esoteric studies and practices which Jacobus Swart, spiritual successor to William G. Gray and co-founder of the Sangreal Sodality, has actuated and taught over a period of forty years. Having commenced his Kabbalah studies in Safed in the early 1970's, he later broadened his 'kabbalistic horizons' under the careful guidance of the famed English Kabbalist William G. Gray.

ISBN 978-0-620-50702-8   *Paperback*

also published by The Sangreal Sodality Press

Shadow Tree Series
Volume 3

THE BOOK OF SEALS & AMULETS

Jacobus G. Swart

Having introduced a 'nuts and bolts' insight into the inner workings of Ceremonial Magic and "Practical Kabbalah" in 'The Book of Self Creation' and 'The Book of Sacred Names,' Jacobus Swart unfolds further magical resources in "The Book of Seals & Amulets." This tome comprises a comprehensive investigation into the meaning and relevance of Celestial Alphabets, Magical Seals, Magic Squares, Divine and Angelic Names, etc., as well as their employment in Hebrew Amulets in order to benefit personal well-being in a most significant manner.

Continuing the standards set in the earlier volumes of this series, Jacobus Swart offers detailed instruction on the contents and construction of Hebrew Amulets. He again consulted the enormous array of relevant primary Hebrew literature, large sections of which are available to an English readership for the first time.

The 'Shadow Tree Series' comprises a unique collection of Western Esoteric studies and practices which Jacobus G. Swart, spiritual successor to William G. Gray and co-founder of the Sangreal Sodality, actuated and taught over a period of forty years. He commenced his Kabbalah odyssey in Safed in the early 1970's studying the doctrines of Lurianic Kabbalah. He also incorporated the teachings of his late mentor, the celebrated English Kabbalist William G. Gray, in his personal Kabbalistic worldview.

ISBN 978-0-620-59698-5   *Paperback*

also published by The Sangreal Sodality Press

Shadow Tree Series
Volume 4

THE BOOK OF IMMEDIATE MAGIC - PART 1

Jacobus G. Swart

'The Book of Immediate Magic - Part One' perpetuates the fundamental tenets of "Self Creation" in which it is maintained that the 'Centre' establishes the 'Circumference,' and that personal reality is emanated in harmony with personal 'Will.' Hence this tome comprises an enhancement and expansion of the magical doctrines of Kabbalah Ma'asit ("Practical Kabbalah") addressed in the first three volumes of this "Shadow Tree Series" of Jewish Magical texts. Jacobus Swart claims that working "Immediate Magic" is neither impossible when we fully understand that consciousness is just one vast ocean, and that thoughts are the waves we make in it. It is all a matter of coordinating consciousness.

The 'Shadow Tree Series' comprises a unique collection of Western Esoteric studies and practices which Jacobus G. Swart, spiritual successor to William G. Gray and co-founder of the Sangreal Sodality, has actuated and taught over a period of forty years. He commenced his journey into the domain of Jewish Mysticism in the early 1970's investigating mainstream Kabbalah, later diversifying into the magical mysteries of Practical Kabbalah. He equally expanded his personal perspectives of the Western Magical Tradition under the careful tutelage of the celebrated English Kabbalist William G. Gray.

ISBN 978-0-620-69313-4   *Paperback*

also published by The Sangreal Sodality Press

Shadow Tree Series
Volume 4

THE BOOK OF
IMMEDIATE MAGIC - PART 2

Jacobus G. Swart

'The Book of Immediate Magic - Part One' perpetuates the fundamental tenets of "Self Creation" in which it is maintained that the 'Centre' establishes the 'Circumference,' and that personal reality is emanated in harmony with personal 'Will.' Hence this tome comprises an enhancement and expansion of the magical doctrines of *Kabbalah Ma'asit* ("*Practical Kabbalah*") addressed in the first three volumes of this "Shadow Tree Series" of Jewish Magical texts. Jacobus Swart claims that working "Immediate Magic" is neither impossible when we fully understand that consciousness is just one vast ocean, and that thoughts are the waves we make in it. It is all a matter of coordinating consciousness.

As in the case of all the previous volumes, the current text is dealing with the topic of the 'magical' in this Tradition. In this regard, Jacobus Swart again consulted an array of primary Hebrew literature, major portions of which are being made accessible in translation to an English readership.

The 'Shadow Tree Series' comprises a unique collection of Western Esoteric studies and practices which Jacobus G. Swart, spiritual successor to William G. Gray and co-founder of the Sangreal Sodality, has actuated and taught over a period of forty years. He commenced his journey into the domain of Jewish Mysticism in the early 1970's investigating mainstream Kabbalah, later diversifying into the magical mysteries of Practical Kabbalah. He equally expanded his personal perspectives of the Western Magical Tradition under the careful tutelage of the celebrated English Kabbalist William G. Gray.

ISBN 978-0-620-69313-4 *Paperback*

also published by The Sangreal Sodality Press

Shadow Tree Series
Volume 5

THE BOOK OF MAGICAL PSALMS - PART 1

Jacobus G. Swart

Countless individuals all over the world are chanting the *'Psalms of David'* every hour of every day, which makes the *'Book of Psalms'* the most practically applied text in the Hebrew Bible. In this regard this biblical text is reckoned amongst the greatest and most popular works of 'Jewish Magic,' its popularity being due to the Psalms addressing the loftiest "realms of spirit," the lowliest aspects of human existence, and everything in between. They offer ready-made prayers, supplications, and incantations for all to express what is in their hearts and minds. Furthermore, considered to be Divinely inspired, the Psalms comprise a direct link between a 'human mouth' and a 'Divine Ear'!

The material addressed in *'The Book of Magical Psalms – Part 1'* derives from the extensive primary literature of 'Practical Kabbalah,' much of which is shared in this tome for the first time in English translation. This definitive study includes the magical use of the biblical *'Book of Psalms'* for every conceivable purpose in prayers, incantations, adjurations, and Hebrew amulets.

The 'Shadow Tree Series' comprises a unique collection of Western Esoteric studies and practices which Jacobus G. Swart, spiritual successor to William G. Gray and co-founder of the Sangreal Sodality, has actuated and taught over a period of forty years. He commenced his journey into the domain of Jewish Mysticism in the early 1970's investigating mainstream Kabbalah, later diversifying into the magical mysteries of Practical Kabbalah. He equally expanded his personal perspectives of the Western Magical Tradition under the careful tutelage of the celebrated English Kabbalist William G. Gray.

ISBN 978-0-620-93176-2   *Paperback*

also published by The Sangreal Sodality Press

THE LADDER OF LIGHTS (OR QABALAH RENOVATA)

William G. Gray

The Tree of Life works in relation to consciousness somewhat like a computer. Data is fed in, stored in associative banks, and then fed out on demand. The difference between the Tree and a computer, however, is that a computer can only produce various combinations of the information that has been programmed into it. The Tree, operating through the intelligent consciousness of living beings, whether embodied in this world or not, acts as a sort of Universal Exchange throughout the entire chain of consciousness sharing its scheme, and the extent of this is infinite and incalculable.

The Tree of Life is a means and not an end. It is not in itself an object for worship or some idol for superstitious reverence. It is a means, a method, a map and a mechanism for assisting the attainment of the single objective common to all creeds, systems, mysteries and religions—namely, the mystical union of humanity and divinity. With this end in view, this book is an aid to whoever desires to climb the Tree of Life.

'.....the most original commentary on basic Kabbalistic knowledge that I have read for God knows how many years.'
Israel Regardie

'.....beautifully presented and set in excellent marching order.....For one new to the subject, this is a fine text and an exceptionally lucid introduction to a veiled and meditative lore which is still being enlarged from year to year.'
Max Freedom Long (*Huna Vistas*)

ISBN 978-0-620-40303-0   *Paperback*

also published by The Sangreal Sodality Press

AN OUTLOOK ON OUR INNER WESTERN WAY

William G. Gray

'*An Outlook on Our Inner Western Way*' is a unique book. This is no dusty, quaint grimoire — it is a sane and simple method of true attainment for those who seek communion with their higher selves.

In this book, William Gray shows simply and lucidly, how to *live* the Western Inner Tradition. Tracing the cosmology of Western magic, he substantiates its vitality and urgency for our future.

William G. Gray is rated one of the most prolific — and controversial — occultists today. Blending keen insight, modern psychological models and an overall sense of practicality, his books have torn at the mouldy veils of so-called occult secrets, laying out a no-non sense foundation by which modern Western humanity may once again regain its precious magical soul.

ISBN 978-0-620-40306-1   *Paperback*

also published by The Sangreal Sodality Press

Sangreal Sodality Series
Volume 1

WESTERN INNER WORKINGS

William G. Gray

The '*Sangreal Sodality Series*' is a home study course comprising the fundamental text books of the Sangreal Sodality, that revives the instrumentality inherent in our western Tradition. The series makes available to us, in our own cultural symbolism, a way to enlightenment that we can practice on a daily basis.

'*Western Inner Workings*' provides a practical framework for the western student's psycho-spiritual development. Each day includes a morning meditation, a mid-day invocation, evening exercises, and a sleep subject. Incorporating symbols that are 'close to home,' these rituals increase consciousness in comfortable increments.

ISBN 978-0-620-40304-7   *Paperback*

also published by The Sangreal Sodality Press

A Beginners Guide to Living Kabbalah

William G. Gray

This compendium comprises six Kabbalistic works by William G. Gray, some of which are appearing here in print for the first time. The texts included in this compilation are ranging from the simplest introduction to the Spheres and Paths of the Kabbalistic Tree of Life system, to related meditation techniques and associated ritual magical procedures, to an advanced system of what could be termed 'inter-dimensional spiritual communication.'

The title 'A Beginners Guide to Living Kabbalah' is perhaps somewhat misleading, as this compilation equally contains works of an advanced nature, and the ritual and meditation techniques addressed in this tome, pertain to both beginners as well as advanced practitioners of 'Practical Kabbalah.'

ISBN 978-0-620-42887-3   *Paperback*

also published by The Sangreal Sodality Press

LESSONS LEARNED FROM OCCULT LETTERS

William G. Gray

In this book William G. Gray, the renowned English Kabbalist and Ceremonial Magician, delineated some of the lessons he learned from the letters which passed between himself and Emil Napoleon Hauenstein, his Austrian mentor and friend, whom he affectionately called "E.N.H." Contrary to opinions expressed regarding Emil Napoleon Hauenstein's status as a "Magus," it should be noted that he was nothing of the kind. He classified himself a "mystic," and was a Martinist. Whilst he was an "Initiate" of the well-known French Occultist Papus (Gerard Encausse), he had a particularly poor opinion of ritual magic and never shared a single magical practice with William Gray.

On the other hand, E.N.H. addressed important psycho-spiritual occult principles and doctrines in his letters, and encouraged his young friend to acquire a greater understanding of what it means to be an "Occultist." William Gray gained a clear comprehension that "Goodness, Love, Truth, Kindness, and such Spiritual qualities in us that come direct from God must come *first*. Cleverness, intellectuality, and mental attributes can then be safely developed in the course of time." Since "Occultism is the study and practice of subjects and laws which are beyond the bounds and limitations of ordinary physical or even mental experience," Emil Napoleon Hauenstein directed his young protegé in unfolding a well-regulated "Self," who is in full control of all his personal faculties, whether these be physical, mental, emotional or spiritual. This is of particular importance in understanding, as William Gray noted, that "Occultism is *not* a pastime, it is a Power, a Purpose, a Progress, and a Path"—*a Way of Life!*

ISBN 978-0-620-79024-6   *Paperback*

www.ingramcontent.com/pod-product-compliance
Lightning Source LLC
Chambersburg PA
CBHW071233300426
44116CB00008B/1018